Time Out

Edinburgh

Glasgow, Lothian & Fife

Penguin Books

PENGUIN BOOKS

Published by the Penguin Group
Penguin Books Ltd, 27 Wrights Lane, London W8 5TZ, England
Penguin Books USA Inc., 375 Hudson Street, New York, New York 10014, USA
Penguin Books Australia Ltd, Ringwood, Victoria, Australia
Penguin Books Canada Ltd, 10 Alcorn Avenue, Toronto, Ontario, Canada M4V 3B2
Penguin Books (NZ) Ltd, 182-190 Wairau Road, Auckland 10, New Zealand

Penguin Books Ltd, Registered Offices: Harmondsworth, Middlesex, England

First published 1998
Second edition 2000
10 9 8 7 6 5 4 3 2 1

Copyright © Time Out Group Ltd, 1998, 2000
All rights reserved

Colour reprographics by Westside Digital Media, 9 Bridle Lane, London W1
and Precise Litho, 34-35 Great Sutton Street, London EC1
Printed and bound by Cayfosa-Quebecor, Ctra. de Caldes, Km 3 08 130 Sta, Perpètua de Mogoda, Barcelona, Spain

Edited and designed by
Time Out Guides Limited
Universal House
251 Tottenham Court Road
London W1P OAB
Tel + 44 (0) 20 7813 3000
Fax + 44 (0) 20 7813 6001
Email guides@timeout.com
www.timeout.com

Editorial

Editor Thom Dibdin
Deputy Editor Lesley McCave
Listings Editor Clare Simpson
Proofreader Ros Sales
Indexer Cathy Heath

Editorial Director Peter Fiennes
Series Editors Ruth Jarvis, Caro Taverne
Deputy Series Editor Jonathan Cox

Design

Art Director John Oakey
Art Editor Mandy Martin
Senior Designer Scott Moore
Designers Benjamin de Lotz, Lucy Grant,
Picture Editor Kerri Miles
Deputy Picture Editor Olivia Duncan-Jones
Picture Admin Kit Burnet
Scanning & Imaging Dan Conway, Chris Quinn
Ad make-up Glen Impey

Advertising

Group Advertisement Director Lesley Gill
Sales Director Mark Phillips
International Sales Manager Mary L Rega
Advertisement Sales (Edinburgh) Christie Dessy

Administration

Publisher Tony Elliott
Managing Director Mike Hardwick
Financial Director Kevin Ellis
Marketing Director Gillian Auld
General Manager Nichola Coulthard
Production Manager Mark Lamond
Production Controller Samantha Furniss
Accountant Catherine Bowen

Features in this guide were written and researched by: Introduction Thom Dibdin; **History** Barry Didcock; **Edinburgh Today** Thom Dibdin, Alastair Mabbott; **Edinburgh by Numbers** Thom Dibdin; **Scottish Icons** Keith Davidson; **Sightseeing** *Introduction, Calton Hill & Broughton, Edinburgh by Season* Thom Dibdin; *Royal Mile, Arthur's Seat & Duddingston, Leith* Alastair Mabbott; *New Town, Stockbridge* Susanna Beaumont, Thom Dibdin; *South Edinburgh, West Edinburgh* Keith Davidson, Thom Dibdin; **Accommodation** Jason Hall; **Restaurants** Jonathan Trew; **Cafés & Bistros** Jonathan Trew; **Bars & Pubs** Jonathan Trew; **Shops & Services** Katrina Dixon; **Art Galleries** Susanna Beaumont; **Children** Jane Ellis; **Film** Alastair Mabbott, Thom Dibdin; **Gay & Lesbian** Nancy Riach, Bob Orr; **Music: Classical & Opera** Alastair Mabbott, Carol Main; **Music: Rock, Folk & Jazz** Alastair Mabbott, Sue Wilson, Kenny Mathieson; **Nightlife** Thom Dibdin, Alastair Mabbott; **Sport & Fitness** Mike Wilson; **Theatre & Dance** Thom Dibdin; **Trips Out Of Town** *Introduction* Thom Dibdin; *Glasgow* Caroline Ednie; *Day Trips* Susanna Beaumont, Kirsty Walker, Thom Dibdin; *Further Afield* Susanna Beaumont; **Directory** Clare Simpson, Sarah Sharma.

The Editor would like to thank the following: Ruth Anderson, John and Pauline Pinder, The staff of the Edinburgh Room at Edinburgh Central Library, Laura Bolton, Caroline Ednie, Lesley McCave, Dan Dibdin, Humph, Jane, Josh Simpson, Ros Sales, Ruth Jarvis, Nu Tran, Peter Fiennes, Caro Taverne, Sophie Blacksell, Cathy Heath, John Scott, James Mitchell, Paget Scott-McCarthy.

Maps by JS Graphics, 17 Beadles Lane, Old Oxted, Surrey RH8 9JG.

Photography by Marius Alexander except: page 8 **Scottish National Portrait Gallery**; pages 12-13 **Courtesy of Edinburgh City Libraries.**

The following pictures were supplied by the featured establishments: pages **186, 187, 188, 221 and 222.**

Contents

Introduction

You can see the sky in Edinburgh. Not the insipid, smog-laden sky that you might glimpse from the sky-scraper vaulted canyons of so many modern cities, but a full-on, edge-to-edge expanse, which would do any prairie proud. Seen from the Mound as the summer evening sun sets over the Caledonian Hotel, or on a crisp winter morning, when the frost glistens on Arthur's Seat and the sharp stench of brewery yeast tangs the nostrils, it is a beautiful expanse.

It is skies like these that set off the city's natural peaks and man-made monuments to their best advantage. But when the clouds dip down, low, grey and brooding, then the city's neo-classical architecture comes into its own. Here are buildings that were made to keep the weather out, but that can also absorb a population bent on cultural improvement. Because, behind the façades and the grey imperiousness, inside the places of entertainment – whether the most genteel, highbrow palace or the most raucous, populist dive – there is an audience that is willing to be educated and, more importantly, one that has an opinion.

The city's residents have a reputation for tight-lipped indifference – just as Glasgow's have a reputation for vivacious chat and comment. Yet the truth about Edinburgh is that, just as the grey architecture houses a beating social heart, so the tight faces of its people hide a cosmopolitan outlook that has embraced and absorbed a multitude of opinions and ideas from across the world. And is more than willing to keep on doing so.

Edinburgh is, after all, a capital. Even in the long centuries without a parliament, it was the sort of cultural melting pot any fully functional capital should be. This was often in spite of, rather than because of, the city's institutions. But even they have begun to realise that diversity in opinion and style is a good thing. And it was, after all, the institutions that allowed the Edinburgh International Festival to set up in the first place – although the founders would no doubt wince at what what the Fringe has become.

Allowing the city's different festivals to keep on growing and expanding and diversifying is a way to keep that pot bubbling away. Over-regulation and control will only reduce the festival's appeal and set the city on a course for hidebound insularity. So long as new ideas are allowed to flourish, then Edinburgh will continue to be a place to relish as its social life changes and mutates as fast as its ever-changing sky-scape.

ABOUT THE TIME OUT CITY GUIDES

The *Time Out Edinburgh Guide* is one of an expanding series of *Time Out* City Guides produced by the people behind London and New York's successful listings magazines. Our guides are all written and updated by resident experts who have striven to provide you with all the most up-to-date information you'll need to explore the city, whether you're a local or first-time visitor.

THE LOWDOWN ON THE LISTINGS

Above all, we've tried to make this book as useful as possible. Addresses, telephone numbers, transport information, opening times, admission prices and credit card details are all included in our listings. And, as far as possible, we've given details of facilities, services and events, all checked and correct at the time the guide went to press. However, owners and managers can change their arrangements at any time. Before you go out of your way, we'd strongly advise you to telephone and check opening times, dates of exhibitions and other particulars. While every effort has been made to ensure the accuracy of the information contained in this guide, the publishers cannot accept responsibility for any errors it may contain.

PRICES & PAYMENT

We have noted whether venues such as shops, hotels and restaurants accept credit cards or not but have only listed the major cards – American Express (**AmEx**), Diners Club (**DC**), MasterCard (**MC**) and Visa (**V**). Many businesses will also accept other cards, including Switch or Delta, JCB, Discover or Carte Blanche. Many shops, restaurants and attractions also accept travellers' cheques issued by a major financial institution.

The prices we've supplied should be treated as guidelines, not gospel. Fluctuating exchange rates and inflation can cause prices, in shops and restaurants particularly, to change rapidly.

There is an online version of this guide, as well as weekly events listings for more than 30 international cities, at http://www.timeout.com

If prices vary wildly from those we've quoted, ask whether there's a good reason. If not, go elsewhere. Please write and let us know. Our aim is to give the best and most up-to-date advice, so we always want to know if you've been badly treated or overcharged.

THE LIE OF THE LAND

In order to make this book as easy to use as possible, we have arranged the sightseeing chapters in areas that are convenient to walk around. These are the areas that we have used throughout. The Royal Mile, the backbone of the Old Town, is the first place most people head for, followed by the New Town. Other parts of the city follow in their order, leaving the large swathes of land that lie to the south and west of the city to last – they might not be so easy to amble around but they are all too often overlooked and do contain some hidden surprises.

Edinburgh's bus system is extensive and surprisingly efficient. Almost too much so in some areas like Princes Street, Tollcross and North Bridge, which are served by as many as 20 different routes. To simplify things we have kept the listings down to a manageable and useful level, choosing bus routes for their frequency of service and geographical spread.

We've included postcodes for any venue you might want to write to (namely hotels), as well as email and website addresses where possible. And there's a series of fully-indexed **colour street maps** of both Edinburgh and Glasgow, and a map of the surrounding countryside at the back of the guide, starting on *page 299*.

TELEPHONE NUMBERS

The area code for Edinburgh is 0131. All telephone numbers printed in this guide take this code, unless otherwise stated (Glasgow phone numbers, for example, are listed in full with their 0141 prefix). Numbers preceded by 0800 can be called free of charge from within the UK, and some of them can be dialled (though not all free of charge) from the US.

ESSENTIAL INFORMATION

For all the practical information you might need for visiting the city – including visa and customs information, disabled access, emergency telephone numbers, a list of useful websites and the lowdown on the local transport network – turn to the **Directory** chapter at the back of this guide. It starts on *page 271*.

MAPS

We have include a series of fully indexed colour maps to the city at the back of this guide – they start on page 299 – and, where possible, we've printed a page number of the map and a grid reference against all the venues that appear on the maps. When a venue is covered by more than one map, we have given the handy Princes Street map on page 314 preference.

LET US KNOW WHAT YOU THINK

We hope you enjoy the *Time Out Edinburgh Guide*, and we'd like to know what you think of it. We welcome tips for places that you consider we should include in future editions of the guide and take notice of your critical comments of our choices. There's a reader's reply card at the back of this book. You can also email your comments to: edinburghguide@timeout.com

In Context

Scottish National Portrait Gallery.

History

From Dunedin to devolution: Edinburgh, once defined by its physical attributes, now looks to the promises and aspirations of its politicians for its identity.

With its sprawling fortress perched high on a rocky outcrop, there can be few cities in the world that have as dominant or as historically important a focus as Edinburgh. That this castle in the air is joined to a palace on the ground by an ancient road, along whose route history has been made a hundred times over, only adds drama to the story.

But strip away the clutter of the Old Town in your mind's eye, ignore the grandeur of the Georgian New Town, the rigid Victorian tenements and the bleak 20th-century architecture; put back the man-made loch that skirted the Castle Rock's northern edge for centuries and the open moorland which stretched both north and south from this ancient volcanic plug since before history was even written, and you have a sense of the breathtaking physical geography that has drawn people to this place – and kept them living here – for thousands of years.

Early history

There is no evidence that the Romans occupied the Castle Rock, although from their fort at Inveresk, five miles (eight kilometres) away, they would have had a fine view of its imposing bulk. But it is known to have been a stronghold for Celtic tribes such as the Gododdin. King Mynyddog ruled from the Castle Rock around the start of the seventh century, and it was the Gododdin who named it Dunedin, meaning 'hill fort'.

In AD 638, southern Scotland was conquered by the Northumbrians, who built on the rock and Anglicised its name to Edinburgh. Popular belief has it that the etymology of the name is therefore 'Edwin's burgh', though this is incorrect. Later the Castle became known as Castrum Puellarum, or Maidens' Castle. In the mid-tenth century, the MacAlpin kings repelled the Northumbrians southwards again and, in

1018, Malcolm II (1005-34) defeated them at Carham. The Castle Rock and the surrounding area became Scottish.

Malcolm III (1058-93) built a hunting lodge on the Rock. It is Malcolm, also known as Malcolm Canmore ('big head'), who is commemorated in Shakespeare's *Macbeth*. But in Edinburgh, Malcolm is best remembered as the husband of Margaret, the Saxon princess he married in about 1070. The union produced three daughters and six sons, three of whom ruled as King of Scotland.

> **'The monks also brewed beer, and others in the area followed suit: the site of the Parliament is a brewery.'**

Margaret built a chapel on the rock, St Margaret's Chapel, now the oldest building in Edinburgh. She died there after her husband was killed in an ambush near Alnwick in 1093. A power struggle ensued and Malcolm's brother Donald Bane (also featured in *Macbeth*) laid siege to the Castle. Margaret's sons took her body and escaped down the western side of the Rock, enveloped in a cloaking fog according to the historian John of Fordun, writing in the late 14th century.

David I (1124-53) was the last of Margaret's sons to assume the throne of Scotland. He ruled for nearly 30 years and was the first Scottish king to strike his own coinage. In 1128 he founded the Augustinian abbey at Holyrood – Edinburgh folklore has it that he was hunting one day when he was knocked from his horse and attacked by a stag, only to be saved when a cross (or 'rood') appeared in his hand. To show his thanks to God he founded the abbey.

In truth, Holyrood Abbey was only one of several founded by David I at established royal centres throughout his reign, part of the 'Davidian Revolution'. This also saw 15 or so Scottish towns granted the status of royal burgh. Edinburgh was not the most important of these – Berwick, Scotland's largest town, and Roxburgh were described as burghs even before 1124, and Perth had a long-standing importance. But by 1153 Edinburgh had its own mint and could be said to be one of Scotland's major towns.

GETTING RELIGION

Holyrood Abbey was completed in 1141 and Augustinian monks were brought from St Andrews to fill it. The presence of the canons led to the lower half of what is now the Royal Mile being named the Canongate. It was cut off from Edinburgh by the defensive gate at the

Netherbow and remained a separate burgh until 1856. The monks also brewed beer, and others in the area followed suit: the site of the Scottish Parliament is a former brewery.

The Palace of Holyroodhouse wasn't built until 1498, but with the abbey in place, Edinburgh began to creep down the spine of the volcanic ridge that leads from the Castle Rock. The Cowgate, running parallel to the Canongate, began to develop as the entrance through which cattle were herded to market. In 1230, the Black Friars (Dominicans) arrived in Edinburgh and established a friary in the east end of the Cowgate. With the Abbey already in place and a succession of religious orders arriving in the town (the Dominicans were followed by the Franciscans, or Grey Friars, in 1429), Edinburgh became an ecclesiastical centre.

The other main religious building in the town was the Church of St Giles (today's St Giles' Cathedral). Historians have found mention of a church in Edinburgh as early as 845, but whatever was on the site of St Giles was replaced by Alexander I in 1120 and the church was formally dedicated by Bishop David de Bernham of St Andrews in 1243.

The Middle Ages

Although always associated with its Castle, Edinburgh and its environs had at this point seen relatively few battles. It was only during the 15th and 16th centuries that the town came to be associated with royalty, thus assuming a

The window of **St Margaret's Chapel**.

certain psychological significance for invaders. Its strategic importance in the earlier period was limited because it was easy to bypass (unlike Stirling Castle, where many of the defining battles of the late 13th and early 14th centuries were fought). The English king, Edward I, did take up residence in the Abbey during his siege of Edinburgh in 1296, and by 1311 it was in English hands. But even its defensive capabilities were questioned: Robert the Bruce was so appalled at the ease with which his nephew, Sir Thomas Randolph, recaptured it in 1314 that he had it rebuilt.

> **'Despite the turbulence, during James III's reign the Cowgate began to be the fashionable place to live.'**

In 1328 the Treaty of Edinburgh was signed, ending the wars of independence with England (in Scotland's favour). The following year Robert the Bruce granted Edinburgh the status of royal burgh, thus giving it an important degree of fiscal independence. Bruce died the same year. His heir, David II, was only five in 1329, so Edward III once again tried to conquer Scotland. In 1337, the Countess of March – known as Black Agnes – led the defence of the Castle for five months before Edward took it. The English king rebuilt it in parts, but a mere four years later Sir William Douglas recaptured it for the Scots. The Canongate was less lucky in this period: it was burned by Richard II's troops in 1380.

David II died in 1371 with no heir and Robert the Steward, who had already been Guardian of Scotland twice, became Robert II. The Stewart succession had begun. This was a period of lawlessness that saw successive kings murdered or killed in battle, to be succeeded by children who were too young to rule in their own right. It was also the period in which Edinburgh came to be recognised as a royal city.

The need for strong regents was vital and the people of Edinburgh witnessed some bloody power plays as the various court factions slugged it out in a succession of reigns. James I (1406-37) tried to curb the power of the nobles, but was murdered in Perth in 1437 for his troubles. His son, James II (1437-60), was only six at the time and he was crowned hastily in Holyrood Abbey by his mother. Three years later, in 1440, James himself witnessed a political assassination in Edinburgh Castle when the young Earl of Douglas was murdered by Sir William Crichton and Sir Alexander Livingstone, the acting regents.

ALL MAPPED OUT

The Old Town began to take shape during this period; the Grassmarket and the Cowgate started to form more fully, though development to the south and north was made difficult by physical features such as the Craig Burn, which was dammed in the mid-15th century for defensive purposes and became the Nor' Loch. At the same time the town's first defensive wall was built: called the King's Wall, it ran eastwards from half way down the south side of the Castle Rock, above the Grassmarket and the Cowgate, to the Netherbow, and then dipped down to the Nor' Loch. As the town crept along the spine of the ridge, the familiar herringbone pattern of closes and wynds began to emerge. This is still visible today in parts, but in medieval times the closes and wynds would have been muddy, steep, slippery and, as like as not, covered in ordure from humans as well as animals. Soap was not manufactured in Edinburgh until 1554.

The principal landmarks in the medieval city were the Castle, the Lawnmarket immediately east of it, the High Kirk (church) of St Giles, the Mercat Cross and the Tolbooth, on the south side of the High Street. The Tolbooth was, literally, the booth where tolls were paid and the buildings on the site were regularly destroyed, rebuilt and upgraded. A bell in the Tolbooth sounded when goods were to be sold and to mark the start of the curfew; later a prison was added and by the 15th century both Parliament and the Court of Session would meet there.

The reign of James III (1460-88), like that of his father, was turbulent. He was nine when he came to the throne and struggles over the regency soon broke out. His mother, Mary of Gueldres, demanded that Parliament (sitting in the Castle) name her regent. Meanwhile, the young king was at the bottom of the hill in Holyrood Abbey, with the Bishop of St Andrews. The precarious situation caused the Edinburgh mob to riot. It was the first recorded glimpse of the volatile and well-organised body that would regularly cause havoc over the next few hundred years.

Despite the turbulence, it was during James III's reign that the Cowgate began to be seen as the fashionable place to live. Dwellings were also built in the Canongate, beginning in 1485.

Hemmed in by its defensive walls, Edinburgh was becoming overcrowded; the Canongate houses were notable for their spacious rooms and back gardens. But the lack of a defensive wall left the area open to attack: the Abbey it had grown up around was sacked and looted by a host of interlopers over the centuries.

The area round about the town was sprinkled with small villages. Restalrig, for instance, whose church dates back to the 12th century, is

Key events

c638 Southern Scotland under the control of Northumbria.
c950 The MacAlpin kings repel the Northumbrians.
1018 Malcolm II defeats the Northumbrians at Carham and Edinburgh Castle becomes Scottish.
1093 Malcolm III killed. Civil war follows.
1128 Augustinian Abbey of Holyrood founded by David I.
1314 Robert the Bruce's nephew, Thomas Randolph, retakes the castle from the English.
1329 Edinburgh receives royal charter from Robert the Bruce.
1333 Berwick lost to the English.
1349 The Black Death arrives, returning in 1362 and 1379: a third of the Scottish population is estimated to have died from the plague.
1477 James III charters markets to be held in the Grassmarket.
1482 James III grants the Blue Blanket to the town.
1489 Mons Meg used at the siege of Dumbarton.
1498 Holyroodhouse built by James IV.
1513 Citizens muster under the Blue Blanket at the Mercat Cross to march to Flodden.

James IV is killed in the battle. Following the defeat, the Flodden Wall is built to defend the city. It is completed in 1560.
1544 English army attacks from the sea, sacks Holyroodhouse and its Abbey, but fails to gain entrance to the city.
1566 David Rizzio murdered in Holyroodhouse.
1582 James VI (*pictured*) issues a charter for the Townis College, later Edinburgh University.
1603 James VI accedes to the English throne and removes the Court to London.
1633 Edinburgh becomes capital of Scotland.
1639 Parliament House finished. Used by Scottish Parliament until 1707. It is now used in connection with the Court of Session.
1673 The city's first coffeehouse opens, in Parliament Close.
1675 Physic Garden founded by the Nor' Loch.
1681 Tea tasted in the city for the first time; James Dalrymple, known as the father of Scots law, publishes his *Institutions of the Law of Scotland*.
1685 Duckings cease in the Nor' Loch.
1695 The Bank of Scotland chartered.

now part of Edinburgh. Tower houses were built at Liberton, Cramond, Craiglockhart and Merchiston – where the inventor of logarithms, John Napier, was born in 1550.

COMMERCIAL BREAKS

Commerce flourished under James III. Between 1320 and 1450 Edinburgh's share of wool exports rose from 21 per cent to 71 per cent – as the only major town with a port between the Tweed and the Forth, it was ideally placed to capitalise on foreign trade opportunities. In 1469 the town ceased to be ruled by the merchant burgesses and became a self-electing corporation. In 1477 James III chartered markets to be held in the Grassmarket, partly because of the congestion on the High Street, where the cloth sellers,

beggars and fishwives plied their trade from stalls and booths around St Giles. When these became permanent and could be locked they were called luckenbooths.

> **'The Duke of Albany escaped the Castle by drugging his jailers, and fled to France.'**

In 1482, James granted the Blue Blanket to the citizens of Edinburgh. This was a symbol of the independence of the municipality, of its right to levy customs at the port of Leith and of the exclusive rights of the town's craftsmen. These included the candlemakers, who are known to have been organised by 1488 and who worked in the area around Candlemaker Row.

1698 A run of seven disastrous harvests begins, increasing discontent and rioting in the city.
1702-7 Scottish Parliament sits in Edinburgh discussing the Act of Union. It is eventually ratified in 1707.
1726 Last burning of a witch in Edinburgh.
1727 Royal Bank of Scotland founded.
1736 Porteous Riots.
1749 William Younger founds his brewery.
1767 James Craig's plans for the New Town adopted. Theatre Royal, Edinburgh's first licensed theatre, opens.
1770 Queen Street begun.
1771 *Encyclopedia Britannica* published by William Smellie in Anchor Close; Sir Walter Scott born in College Wynd.
1784 Last execution in the Grassmarket.
1787 The Edinburgh edition of Robert Burns's poems published. The opening lines of his *Address to Edinburgh* are: 'Edina, Scotia's darling seat'.
1788 Deacon Brodie hanged at the Tolbooth.
1792 Riots in George Square.
1802 *Edinburgh Review* founded.
1817 *Blackwood's Magazine* founded; the *Scotsman* founded and published from 347 High Street.
1821 Edinburgh School of Arts formed.
1822 Work is begun on the National Monument.
1824 The Great Fire destroys much of the High Street, lasts three days and results in the formation of the world's first municipal fire service; Botanic Garden moves to Inverleith.
1832 Dean Bridge built; New Town extended across it in 1850.
1836 Waverley Station begun.
1843 The Disruption splits the Church.

1847 Alexander Graham Bell, the inventor of the telephone, born in South Charlotte Street.
1864 Last public hanging in Edinburgh.
1886 Edinburgh International Exhibition held on the Meadows.
1890 Forth Rail Bridge opened.
1895 Electric street lighting introduced.
1903 First private car registered in Edinburgh.
1904 The *Scotsman* moves to North Bridge.
1908 Scottish National Exhibition held in Saughton Park.
1912-14 Suffragette attacks in the city.
1916 A German zeppelin bombs Edinburgh.
1947 The first Edinburgh International Festival takes place.
1956 Last tram runs. National Library opened by Elizabeth II.
1960 Elizabeth II attends the General Assembly to celebrate the 400th anniversary of the Reformation.
1964 Heriot-Watt University founded.
1970 Commonwealth Games held in the city; Meadowbank Stadium opened.
1980 *Blackwood's Magazine* folds. Sir Compton Mackenzie had stated in 1967 that 'as long as *Blackwood's Magazine* continued to appear I had no fears for Edinburgh's supremacy as a city'.
1993 Irvine Welsh's novel *Trainspotting* is published.
1997 Scotland votes 'Yes' for the return of a Scottish parliament with tax-varying powers. Edinburgh International Festival celebrates 50 years.
1998 Holyrood announced as site of Scottish Parliament.
1999 The Queen opens the Scottish Parliament.
2000 The *Scotsman* moves to Holyrood Park.

There was a reason for James's kindness to Edinburgh. Three years earlier, in 1479, he had imprisoned his two brothers at the behest of his Flemish astrologer. One, the Earl of Mar, had died in the Canongate Tolbooth; the other, the Duke of Albany, had escaped from the Castle by drugging his jailers and fled to France. The English then attempted to put Albany on the throne. James mustered an army to face them, but a group of disgruntled nobles took the opportunity to hang his favourites and imprison him in the Castle. The English, under the command of the future Richard III, then entered the Tolbooth and demanded that James be released into Richard's hands. Once more the Edinburgh mob rioted, causing Albany to realise that his brother still had popular support. James kept the throne.

His son, James IV (1480-1513), repaid their support in bricks and mortar when he founded the Palace of Holyroodhouse in 1498, though the monks of the Abbey were less pleased at being displaced by the building work.

CAPITAL IN WAITING
With the Scottish kings increasingly treating the town as their royal residence, the idea that Edinburgh should become Scotland's capital began to gain currency.

James IV's reign coincided with the end of the medieval age and he was eager to seem modern and forward-looking. In keeping with this spirit of the new age, the king allowed the barbers and surgeons of Edinburgh – both already allowed to practise medicine – to form a guild. He gave them the sole right to sell whisky (which was regarded as a medicine) and decreed that once a year they should be given the body of a hanged criminal from which to learn more about human anatomy. James also founded the Scottish navy.

The arts benefited as well. The first Scottish printing press opened in 1507, at the foot of Blackfriars Wynd, the narrow street that led from the High Street to the Dominican Friary. Founded by Walter Chapman and Andro Myllar, it published books on government and law, and works by two of Scotland's greatest poets, William Dunbar and Robert Henryson.

The first of Dunbar's work to be published was in 1508 and his words offer a snapshot of life in the town. In one vitriolic passage he attacks the city fathers for their tight-fisted attitudes and in another voices a concept that has currency to this day: Edinburgh is a city of two contrasting faces, one rich and one poor. Among Edinburghers the distillation of that idea can be found in the phrase 'fur coat and nae knickers', and writers from James Hogg to Robert Louis Stevenson have found mileage in the idea that behind the elegant façade lurks something demonic.

The 16th century

Holyrood saw an event of some splendour on 8 August 1503, when James married Henry VII's 12-year-old daughter, Margaret Tudor. Less splendid were the events that followed. As part of the marriage settlement, James had signed the Treaty of Perpetual Peace with England. The grand title failed to live up to political reality, however, and only a decade later the countries went to war again when the French persuaded James to attack England. In early autumn 1513, the citizens of Edinburgh mustered at the Mercat Cross on the High Street to join an army that, when it took its fateful position on Branxton Hill in Northumberland, was 20,000 strong. The Battle of Flodden was a disaster for the Scots. The army was routed and 10,000 Scots were killed, James among them.

In Edinburgh, the shock of the defeat was palpable. Disbelief turned to panic when the townspeople realised the English might press north and attack Edinburgh. Work on the Flodden Wall began, though the attack never materialised. Still visible in parts today, it had six entry points and, once completed in 1560, formed the town's boundary for a further two centuries.

The death of James V, in 1542, continued the dynastic turmoil and added a religious element. It was thought that stability could be ensured by marrying off his infant daughter, the future Mary, Queen of Scots. But to whom? The Scots were split between those who wanted a French

alliance (Cardinal Beaton and Mary's mother, Mary of Guise) and those who wanted an English one. Henry VIII of England sent the Earl of Hertford's army to Scotland to 'persuade' the Scots that a marriage to his son, Edward, was preferable. Hertford landed at Leith in the early summer of 1544 and looted both Abbey and Palace in an episode that has come to be known as the 'rough wooing'. Hertford's force of 10,000 men then stormed the Netherbow but were repulsed; instead they seized £50,000-worth of grain and two ships.

'Knox believed James ruled Scotland for God, whereas James believed in the divine right of kings.'

Three years later, the English returned with an army commanded by the Duke of Somerset. They set up a base at Haddington, 18 miles East of Edinburgh, and, in September 1547, the Battle of Pinkie Cleuch was fought at Musselburgh, just outside the town. The Scots lost and were chased back to the gates, but the Castle was held. The harassment only stopped in 1548, when a force of French and Dutch troops landed at Leith. Mary was sent to live in France and, in 1549, the port was fortified against further attack. She eventually married her cousin, Lord Darnley, in 1565. By that time the religious turmoil had begun.

REFORMING ZEAL

In 1560, the Reformation Parliament declared Protestantism Scotland's official religion. The faction that had previously been pro-French and pro-Mary now also became pro-Catholic, while the Protestant forces rallied against them.

John Knox, a legendary figure in Edinburgh history and the architect of the Reformation in Scotland, became the leader of the Reformed Church. He hated Mary, and the period between her arrival at Leith from France in August 1561 and her abdication in 1567 saw much friction between the Catholic monarchy and the Protestant Church.

Mary remains one of Scotland's most romantic figures. Much of the myth-making turns on the events of 1566, when her favourite, the Savoyard David Rizzio, was murdered by a group of noblemen in Holyroodhouse – a group led by her husband, Lord Darnley. Not long afterwards, Darnley was killed in an explosion at his house and Mary married Lord Bothwell. But the marriage was opposed and a rising of the nobles caused Mary to flee to England after relinquishing the throne to the son she had borne Darnley, the future James VI (1567-1625).

John Knox, architect of the Reformation.

James was born in a tiny room in the Castle, which can still be seen today. He proved to be a man of great learning and wrote the first anti-tobacco tract, *Counterblast Against Tobacco*, in 1604. But if he was forward-looking in that respect, he was less so in others: Knox believed James ruled Scotland for God, whereas James believed in the divine right of kings.

James later forced through the Five Articles of Perth, which tempered the power of the Kirk as a Protestant vehicle. He hankered after the throne of England. On 26 March 1603 the King was woken by a banging on the outer gate of Holyroodhouse. It was Sir Robert Carey, who had ridden for 36 hours with news from London: Queen Elizabeth was dead. James VI was to be crowned James I, King of England.

The 17th century

Three years into the 17th century, Scotland lost its king to London when James VI (or 'Jamie Saxt' as he was known) succeeded to the throne of England. History remembers him as James VI (of Scotland) and I (of England). A century later Scotland was to lose its Parliament, too, when the Act of Union was signed and the Scottish Parliament dissolved.

The years between 1603 and 1707 were ones of social unrest and religious turmoil as Scotland came to terms with absentee rule. James said he would return every three years,

but it was 14 years before he set foot on Scottish soil again. The country suffered a loss of national identity and a feeling of uncertainty. One aspect of this 'crisis of the intellect' was the witch hunts. These were initiated in James VI's reign but took place regularly until 1670. They resulted in hundreds of (mainly) women being burned at the stake in Edinburgh, after first being half-drowned in the Nor' Loch.

But the first years of the 17th century were not unprofitable for Edinburgh. Merchants such as George Heriot (known in the town as 'Jinglin' Geordie') were thriving, as was the University of Edinburgh, founded in 1582 as the Townis College. Other building work in the early 17th century bears testament to the town's prosperity: the east wing of the Castle was rebuilt by Sir James Mason, Parliament House was begun in 1632 (the Scottish Parliament was by then resident in the city) and a year later Holyroodhouse was extended. Gladstone's Land, one of many merchant houses erected in this period, was built in the early decades of the century.

Goldsmiths, watchmakers and bookbinders flourished in Parliament Square and with Edinburgh now the legal centre of Scotland, the town's lawyers amassed great wealth. In 1609, James ordered that the magistrates should wear robes like those of the aldermen of London and gave the royal assent for a sword to be carried in front of the provost on official occasions.

THE NATIONAL COVENANT

But in 1637 something happened to reignite a religious passion not seen in Scotland since the days of the Reformation, 90 years earlier. And Edinburgh and its mob played a significant role. James died in 1625 and was succeeded by his son, Charles I. He was crowned King of Scotland in 1633 at Holyroodhouse.

In an effort to impose religious uniformity on both countries of his domain, Charles introduced a new prayer book to Scotland. Called the *Book of Common Prayer*, it followed the pattern of the Episcopalian church service, unpopular with the Presbyterians.

The new prayer book proved so unpopular with the people that on the occasion of its first use in St Giles, on 23 July 1637, a certain old cabbage seller by the name of Jenny Geddes threw her stool at Dean Hanna shouting: 'Dost thou say Mass at my lug?' The Bishop of Edinburgh mounted the pulpit to calm the crowd but was mobbed. The riot spread outside and into the streets. This 'spontaneous' uprising is another great Edinburgh folk story – but in truth, trouble had been brewing for some time and it is likely that the riot was carefully planned beforehand.

John Slezer's 1693 view of Edinburgh from the north-east, before the New Town brought

Either way, Charles was furious. But the *Book of Common Prayer* and the heavy taxes the King had levied on Edinburgh still irked the Scots. A document called the National Covenant was drawn up, signed in blood by some, asserting the Scots' rights to both spiritual and civil liberty. On the last day of February 1638, it was read from the pulpit of Greyfriars Church. Over the next two days a host of lairds and burgesses came to sign it.

> ### 'The young men of the town were apt to use their pistols to shoot fowl from their windows.'

The Castle was held by forces loyal to the King, but in the town the rule of the Covenant held sway. Meanwhile, Charles was distracted in England when civil war broke out. By 1649, Oliver Cromwell had assumed power in England and on 30 January, Charles I was executed in London. The Scots were outraged that their Parliament had not been consulted – after all, Charles had been King of Scotland as

well as England – and six days later the Scots proclaimed Charles II king if he would accept the Covenanters' demands. Instead, Charles asked the Marquis of Montrose, who had been loyal to his father, to conquer Scotland for him. But Montrose was defeated and captured. Brought to Edinburgh, he was paraded up the High Street and, on 21 May 1650, executed in front of a crowd that was not entirely unsympathetic towards him. Nevertheless, Charles came to Scotland, landing at Leith later that year. No other monarch would visit Edinburgh until George IV in 1822.

Cromwell's response was to invade. He defeated the Scots under General Leslie at the Battle of Dunbar on 3 September 1650. While Charles escaped to be crowned King of Scotland, in January 1651 Cromwell's troops burned Holyroodhouse and he imposed crippling taxes for the maintenance of his army.

PESTILENCE & PLAGUE
Those 13 years of rebellion and religious turmoil hit Edinburgh hard: trade dropped off dramatically and plague ravaged the city in 1644, killing 20 per cent of the population. Nevertheless, it remained a lively place

fresh air to the city's cramped surrounds.   *Picture courtesy of Edinburgh City Libraries.*

throughout the 17th century. Golf was played in virtually any open space, archery was practised and the young men of the town were apt to use their pistols to shoot fowl from their windows. The Kirk, meanwhile, was forever berating the townspeople for spending Sundays in ale houses.

Sanitation got no better, though: plague visited the city again in 1645 and it wasn't until 1687 that Parliament decreed that the council provide 20 carts to remove refuse. Water was still being taken around in barrels by the water caddies, or drawn from private wells.

Meanwhile, tea was tasted for the first time in the city in 1681, the same year James Dalrymple published his *Institutions of the Law of Scotland*. He is remembered as the 'Father of Scottish Law', an important sobriquet as it was Scotland's independent legal system (along with its separate religious and educational set-ups) that came to be seen as proof of nationhood after 1707.

A map drawn in 1647 shows a bewildering number of closes running off the High Street and down through the Cowgate, with St Giles and the old burying ground behind. Edinburgh spread a little beyond the Flodden Wall in 1617

when High Riggs was bought by the town; further areas were added in 1639, notably the Pleasance and Calton Hill.

MURDER MOST FOUL

When Charles II was returned to the throne in 1660 after Cromwell's death – the period known as the Restoration – he reneged on acts made in favour of Covenanters and discontent simmered once again. Revolt broke out in Galloway in 1666 and, in 1679, the Covenanters won a victory at the Battle of Drumclog. Charles sent the Duke of Monmouth to crush the Covenanters, which he did at the Battle of Bothwell Brig later that year. In a period of history that has become known as 'the killing time', the survivors were marched to Greyfriars Kirkyard in Edinburgh and imprisoned there for five months. They had little food, shelter or water and many died or were executed. Several hundred others were sent as slaves to Barbados.

James VII (II) ascended the throne in 1685 on the death of his brother Charles, but his Catholicism made him unpopular. The Dukes of Argyll and Monmouth tried to unseat him and failed; James's reign stuttered on. In 1688, when he fathered an heir, English noblemen sought to replace him with a Protestant, William of Orange, and his wife Mary, who was James's daughter. James fled to France and the protection of Louis XIV.

> **'The city was still medieval in its geography: it was one cramped, towering, organic whole, clinging grimly on to the hillside.'**

William and Mary came to the throne in 1688. Many in Edinburgh and in the Scottish Parliament favoured William – they burned effigies of the Pope on news of his landing – but Scotland as a whole was largely pro-James, especially in the Highlands. This lobby became known as the Jacobites, after 'Jacobus', the Latin word for James. The Duke of Gordon held Edinburgh Castle for James, but only until 1689.

The 1690s were bad for Edinburgh. A series of terrible harvests affected food supplies, an English war with France was bad for trade, Catholic and Protestant factions were once more circling each other warily and, in 1698, the failure of the Darien Scheme virtually bankrupted the nation.

Funded partly by the Edinburgh financiers and merchants who had helped set up the Bank of Scotland in 1695, the Darien Scheme involved sending an expedition from Leith to the Caribbean to establish a trading link between east and west. Through a combination of misfortune and English hostility, it was a disaster.

When news of the failure reached Edinburgh there was rioting on a massive scale: the Tolbooth was stormed and all the prisoners released, while much of the Cowgate and the Royal Exchange were torched.

The collapse of the scheme strengthened the hand of those south of the border who sought to bully Scotland into a union with England.

END OF AN AULD SANG

On 3 October 1706 a crowd gathered on the High Street to watch, for the last time, the 'Riding', the ceremony that preceded the opening of Parliament. The Act of Union became law in January 1707, and the dissolution of Parliament followed in April. When the Lord High Chancellor of Scotland, Lord Seafield, was presented with the Act for royal assent, he is said to have touched it with his sceptre and said the words: 'There's an end of an auld sang'. It would be nearly 300 years before the Scottish Parliament sat again.

The Age of Improvement

The 18th century is known in Edinburgh as the 'Age of Improvement'. The phrase refers to the massive building programme started in the 1760s and to the spirit of intellectual inquiry that flourished among the town's lawyers, academics and churchmen (known as 'the Enlightenment'). Edinburgh was buzzing with the words of men like the philosopher David Hume and Adam Smith, author of *The Wealth of Nations*.

By 1720, the city had two newspapers, and the formation of a school of design, in 1760, pre-dated London's Royal Academy by eight years. The Honourable Company of Edinburgh Golfers was founded in 1744 and, in 1777, the Royal High School moved to grand new premises in High School Yards, at the foot of Infirmary Street. The number of students at the university doubled between 1763 and 1783 (the year the Royal Society of Edinburgh was founded); it had quadrupled by 1821. Lawyers were everywhere – there were 65 wig-makers in the city by 1700 – and the Faculty of Advocates became pivotal in the city's social and intellectual life.

In 1725, the Lord Provost, George Drummond, drew up plans for a new medical school and, in 1729, the first infirmary opened at Robertson's Close. In 1731 the Medical Society was founded and, in 1736, the infirmary was granted a Royal Charter. A second hospital opened in College Wynd in the same year. But at the start of the century, the city was still medieval in its geography. Edinburgh gave the appearance of being one cramped, towering, organic whole, clinging grimly on to the hillside with an enormous channel – the High Street – running down the middle.

The old city walls still formed the town boundaries, by and large, so as the population grew to well over 50,000 during the 18th century, the only way to build was up. This practice resulted in the 'lands'; six, seven, eight storeys tall and prone to collapse with great loss of life.

Nobles and lairds lived almost side by side with the common people, and visitors regularly commented on the well-established Edinburgh tradition of emptying chamber pots out of the top windows. 'Gardey loo', was the famous warning shout, often matched by a hasty 'Haud yer haun!' (Hold your hand!) from the pedestrians getting showered beneath.

BIRTH OF THE NEW TOWN

So it was with a lungful of fresh air that Edinburgh finally burst out across the valley to the north, creating one of the finest architectural enclaves in the world – the New

Town. Progress, harmony, rationalisation – and claret – were the order of the day as far as the Enlightenment was concerned. And three of those four principles were brought to bear on the competition, announced in 1766, for the best plan to extend Edinburgh to the north and from which the New Town grew.

The competition was won by a 21-year-old architect called James Craig. The prize-winning plan has not been saved, but a later plan, from 1767, shows three main streets – South, North and Principal – crossed by smaller streets and positioned between two Grand Squares. These streets eventually became Princes Street, George Street and Queen Street. Princes Street was originally meant to be called St Giles' Street after the city's saint, but George III objected.

As part of the overall scheme, the Nor' Loch was drained and the North Bridge, which spanned the valley, was started in 1763. In 1781, the Mound was begun, using the earth from the work going on to the north. By the time the Mound was completed, in 1830, an estimated two million cartloads of earth had been dumped on it. The city also pushed south up to the old Kirk O'Fields, where a new college for the university was built in 1789; in 1768, the Theatre Royal had gone up in what was known as Shakespeare Square. It was the first licensed stage in Scotland and stood on the site of the old post office at the east end of Princes Street.

Overspill from the Old Town to the New Town was considerable and by 1791 there were 7,200 people living there. The city had also pushed southwards and George Square was laid out in 1766 but, with its panoramic views over the Forth, it was the New Town that became a haven for lawyers and merchants. David Hume was one of the first people to move to the New Town: he built a house at the corner of St Andrew Square. The result of this movement of the wealthier classes northwards was that a type of social apartheid formed. Once more, the notion of the city with two faces surfaced.

> **'He was marched down to the Grassmarket, lynched and left dangling from a dyer's pole.'**

The late 18th century also provided Edinburgh with one of its most fascinating characters: Deacon William Brodie, town councillor by day, burglar by night. Hanged in 1788, it is his double life that Stevenson is said to have used as the model for his novel *The Strange Case of Dr Jekyll and Mr Hyde*.

With the easing of congestion in the Old Town, tempers seemed to cool a little – the mob saw relatively little action in the 18th century. The Porteous Riots of 1736, however, were a notable and violent exception. Irritated by the decision to hang two smugglers and incensed by the shooting of several townspeople by soldiers at the hanging, the mob stormed the Tolbooth and 'arrested' the unpopular captain of the guard, Captain Porteous. He was marched down to the Grassmarket, lynched and left dangling from a dyer's pole.

Neither was Edinburgh much affected by the two significant Jacobite rebellions of 1715 and 1745, though Prince Charles Edward Stuart – aka Bonnie Prince Charlie – did spend six weeks in Edinburgh in 1745 after his victory over Sir John Cope at Prestonpans. Charlie's dream of reclaiming Scotland for the Stuarts died at Culloden a year later. After the defeat, 14 of the standards carried by the clan chiefs at Culloden were taken into the town by chimney sweeps and burned.

But violence came knocking again at the end of the century, when revolution broke out in France and many in Great Britain feared an invasion. The Edinburgh Volunteers were formed to defend the city. With the violence came political discourse, and parliamentary reform was discussed. In 1802, the *Edinburgh Review* was founded and it became a forum for anti-government opinions; other publications followed as Edinburgh became pre-eminent in the world of publishing and bookselling.

GREAT SCOTT

Edinburgh-born Sir Walter Scott was a titan of the later years of this era. He was internationally respected and, in early-19th-century terms, a blockbusting novelist. It was pressure from him that led to the 'Honours of Scotland' – the crown, sceptre and sword of state – being searched for and uncovered in the Castle in 1818. They had been lost since 1603. Meanwhile, Scott was able to entice George IV to Edinburgh, in 1822, for what was the first official visit of a monarch to Scotland since Charles I in 1641. If he could have seen beyond the pomp of this curious occasion, George would have discovered a city on the slide. In 1818, work began on the Union Canal to join Edinburgh with the Forth and Clyde Canal, but the National Monument to the dead of the Napoleonic Wars, which was begun in 1822 on Calton Hill, was never finished. The Parthenon-like structure stands there still, long ago dubbed 'Scotland's Disgrace', but now also a reminder that Scotland was once more losing its way. Power was in London and the intellectual activity of the Enlightenment was declining – Edinburgh's glory days were behind it.

The Victorian era

Edinburgh underwent a third period of expansion during the Victorian era, when suburbs such as Marchmont, Morningside and Bruntsfield were built. The city that had become two when the New Town was built found itself with a third face. Each 'city' had its own characteristics and type of inhabitants: the solid Victorian suburbs were peopled by the growing middle class, the grand New Town remained the area of choice for lawyers and judges, while the teeming Old Town became a slum.

'The dissenting churchmen marched down Hanover Street to Canonmills.'

Edinburgh also witnessed one of the most significant moments in 19th-century Scottish history in 1843, when the Church was split in two and a breakaway group, the Free Kirk, was formed. But unlike the religious turbulence of previous centuries, this 'revolution' was peaceful. Meanwhile, the city retained its reputation as a place of law and learning, while Glasgow to the west became the country's industrial powerhouse. It is a distinction that remains to this day.

URBAN BLIGHT

At the start of the 19th century, the population of Edinburgh and Leith was 102,987. By 1881, the population of Greater Edinburgh was 320,549. One of the reasons for the dramatic increase was the influx of people from other parts of Scotland and from Ireland. Indeed, Burke and Hare, two of Edinburgh's most infamous criminals, were both Irish immigrants.

With the population rise came unemployment. The riots of 1812 and 1818 both had economic causes at their root and by the 1830s outbreaks of cholera and typhoid had decimated the Old Town. That was compounded in 1824, by a fire that destroyed much of the High Street with great loss of life and resulted in the formation of the world's first municipal fire service.

Meanwhile, a study conducted by Dr George Bell in the 1850s found that 159 of the Old Town's closes lacked drainage and fresh water and concluded that Blackfriars Wynd was home to 1,000 people sharing just 142 houses. Cholera returned to the city in 1848. Bell also bemoaned the alcoholism endemic in the Old Town's inhabitants. A separate study undertaken in 1842 by a young Edinburgh doctor, William Tait, found that of Edinburgh's 200 brothels, most were in the Old Town. Attempts were made to restore the Old Town, particularly by William Chambers (Lord Provost from 1865-69), but the area was on a downward spiral that continued into the 20th century.

In contrast to the decrepitude of the Old Town were the public buildings thrown up during the 19th century: schools, churches, galleries, railway stations, hospitals, banks and bridges – the Victorians had a zeal for them all.

It was matched, after the 'Disruption' of 1843, by the missionary zeal of the Free Kirk, which came into being in May 1843 when 474 ministers seceded from the Church to form a breakaway organisation. The occasion was the General Assembly, the grievance was the right of congregations to choose their own minister, and the scene of the split was the Church of St Andrew and St George on George Street. Led by Dr David Welsh, Dr Thomas Chalmers and Dr Thomas Guthrie, the dissenting churchmen marched down Hanover Street to Tanfield Hall in Canonmills. 'No spectacle since the Revolution,' noted Lord Cockburn in his journal, 'reminded one so forcibly of the Covenanters.' The split wasn't resolved until 1929.

MAKING PROGRESS

In 1847, Guthrie helped set up three charity schools after meeting some boys in Holyrood Park who said they had never been to school. Guthrie also became active in the temperance movement, which sought to curb the kind of drinking that Dr George Bell had identified as a social ill some years earlier. This movement had some success, in 1853, when a bill was passed that shut the inns on Sundays. Meanwhile, public hangings were stopped, in 1864, and moved to within the walls of Calton jail, which had opened in 1817. George Bryce was the last criminal to suffer the indignity of a public execution and it is said that 20,000 people turned up to watch him die.

Fewer turned up to the early meetings of those engaged in the struggle for women's suffrage. Nevertheless, one of the first three women's suffrage societies was formed in Edinburgh, in 1867. The same year saw the Improvement Act, which stripped the old wooden fronts from the lands (a terrible fire hazard) and opened up some of the most crowded areas. The move was initiated by Lord Provost Chambers, who lent his name to Chambers Street, which was built in 1871.

This moral and ideological progress was matched by technological advances, particularly in the fields of transport and medicine. In the early 17th century London was 13 days away by coach; towards the end of the century the journey could be done in four. But, with the age of steam, transport became far easier – 1850 saw the first public train from London to Edinburgh and, in 1862, the famous Flying Scotsman did the run in just ten-and-a-half hours. In 1890, the Forth Railway Bridge, an imposing structure spanning the Forth at South Queensferry, was built. Unusually for a nation that has made understatement an art form, it has long been hailed by Scots as the 'Eighth Wonder of the World'.

Between 1845 and 1846, rail tunnels were built between Haymarket and Waverley Stations, through the south flank of Calton Hill and under the Mound. These brought tourists and travellers straight into the heart of the city, where they would emerge to face the Castle, the Gothic bulk of the Scott Monument (begun in 1840), the galleries at the foot of the Mound and the splendour of Princes Street Gardens. A century and a half later, this is still the best way to arrive in the city. Meanwhile, in the world of medicine, men such as James Young Simpson and Joseph Lister were gaining international renown for their work in the fields of anaesthetics and antiseptics.

'The suffragettes' more adventurous exploits included attempts to blow up the Royal Observatory and Rosslyn Chapel.'

Towards the end of the Victorian era, Glasgow had begun to assume increasing importance in Scotland, to the detriment of Edinburgh. The two international festivals that Glasgow held – in 1888 and 1901 – far outshone the one that took place on the Meadows in Edinburgh in 1886, and men such as the designer Charles Rennie Mackintosh were creating an artistic and architectural legacy that is still revered today. The appearance of Gladstone in Edinburgh, in 1880 and 1881, to fight campaigns in Midlothian, gave the city some political kudos, but as the historian and journalist Allan Massie has pointed out, Edinburgh at the end of the 19th century was just the biggest small town in Scotland.

The modern age

Look around Edinburgh today and the most obvious legacy of the 20th century is the dappling of hideous, grey edifices thrown up in the 1960s. During this time, very little was added architecturally to the city. The suburbs continued to creep outwards, but buildings were more likely to be pulled down than put up, as the city fathers (and private contractors)

finally got to grips with the decaying Old Town and moved the population outwards to areas such as Niddrie and Craigmillar. In fact, the greatest construct of 20th-century Edinburgh was the arts festival.

This period wasn't totally without significant feats of construction, however. The two great station hotels at either end of Princes Street were opened in the early 1900s, though Princes Street Station – served by the Caledonian Hotel – is long gone. Meanwhile, the King's Theatre opened in 1906, and the Usher Hall followed in 1913. And then, in 1939, St Andrew's House opened to house the Scottish Office and later became the headquarters of the Secretary of State for Scotland. The building resembles a Stalinist blockhouse, though it compares favourably with many that came after. The worst of these are the St James Centre and New St Andrew's House, built at the east end of Princes Street in 1971. Leith Street was flattened to make way for these buildings and, in the process, Edinburgh lost the house in Picardy Place in which Sherlock Holmes creator Arthur Conan Doyle was born, in 1859.

The author was Catholic and his 19th-century childhood was plagued by sectarian taunts. However, the civil unrest that broke out in Ireland in the second decade of the 20th century caused even greater religious intolerance in the city. This exploded in the 1930s, when Edinburgh-born John Cormack, who had served in Ireland with the British Army, founded the Protestant Action League, though as an organisation it was short-lived and little-remembered.

Longer lasting were the effects of the women's suffrage movement. Between 1912 and 1914 supporters in Edinburgh regularly damaged post boxes, though their more adventurous exploits included attempts to blow up the Royal Observatory and Rosslyn Chapel, and the setting of a fire at Fettes College. Post boxes came under attack again in Edinburgh in the 1950s, when they were defaced by Scottish Nationalists after the coronation of Queen Elizabeth II.

Meanwhile, Edinburgh's infrastructure was being upgraded. New reservoirs were built to bring more water into the city, the telephone service was expanded and, in 1924, a radio station opened. Fashions changed, fewer women were employed in domestic service, nursery schools opened and, in 1912, the World Council of Churches was formed as a result of a meeting in the Assembly Hall.

Edinburgh's lack of heavy industry saved the city twice during the 20th century's middle years. It allowed it to avoid the ravages of the

Depression and, a decade or so later, the bombs of the Luftwaffe. Leith was one of the few areas that was badly affected.

LEISURE CENTRE

Sport became woven into the fabric of Edinburgh life in the 1900s, although most of the city's sporting institutions were born in the previous century. The city's two football teams were founded within a year of each other – Heart of Midlothian in 1874 and Hibernian in 1875. Both have enjoyed (occasional) periods of success over the years. Support is divided partly according to religion – Hearts are Protestant, Hibs are Catholic – and partly according to geography: Hearts to the west, Hibs to the east.

> **'Edinburgh's population has greeted the Parliament's arrival with a certain amount of cynicism.'**

Rugby union has been played in the city since the 19th century, with international matches being held on the pitches at Raeburn Place. In 1922 the Scottish Football Union (as it was then called) bought a plot of land at Murrayfield and built a stadium. It was inaugurated on 21 March 1925, when Scotland played England for the Grand Slam.

The oldest of all these sports, however, is curling. Its origins are lost in time, but the Royal Caledonian Curling Club was formed in Edinburgh in 1838 and is now regarded as the sport's 'mother club'. The World Curling Federation is also based in Edinburgh.

But if sport didn't appeal there were other leisure pursuits to follow. In 1913 the Zoological Gardens were established and, 20 years later, a huge Olympic-size open-air swimming pool opened on the coast at Portobello. City folk could now catch a tram to the seaside (the system was city-wide by 1922), spend their days in the sun and enjoy a view over the Forth.

But Edinburgh being Edinburgh, life wasn't always thoroughly modern: the privilege of sanctuary for debtors in Holyrood Abbey, established back in 1128, was still in existence as late as 1904.

EDINBURGH TODAY

Many of Edinburgh's traditional industries, such as publishing, declined during the 20th century. The addition of two universities (Heriot-Watt and Napier) helped to strengthen the city's already-strong academic reputation, however, and Edinburgh is one of Europe's top financial centres, specialising in fund management and insurance.

The International Festival has kept the city on the artistic map since 1947. Previously, in the inter-war years, the 'Scottish Renaissance' saw a flowering of literary and artistic talent. It centred around writers and artists such as Hugh MacDiarmid, James Bridie, Edwin Muir, Naomi Mitchison, Lewis Grassic Gibbon and Neil Gunn. Milnes Bar on Hanover Street was a regular meeting place and many of the writers are pictured around the walls.

Something of that feel has returned in recent years thanks to the success of a few vibrant publishing houses and the international success of Irvine Welsh's novel *Trainspotting*. It has also brought some realism to the image of Edinburgh by helping to throw the spotlight on the city's ills, such as the heroin epidemic that swept through the city in the 1980s, and thus undermining the tartan-and-shortbread image, willfully fostered by the shops that today throng the Lawnmarket.

The Commonwealth Games have come twice to Edinburgh (1970 and 1986), though with a burgeoning number of conference facilities in the city it is delegates rather than athletes who congregate in Edinburgh today. It is all part of a tourist industry that now brings £2.4 billion to Scotland annually, and on which Edinburgh's economy largely depends.

But the event that history might possibly come to regard as the century's most significant came right at its close, with the partial devolution of Scotland and the establishment of a Scottish Parliament in the capital once again. While this has brought grand plans in its wake, Edinburgh's population has greeted its arrival with a certain amount of cynicism. It is now up to the MSPs and the demands of their constituents to make the parliament work for Scotland as a whole. Now, more than ever before, it is the people of Scotland – and not just the residents of Edinburgh – who have the future of the nation's capital in their hands.

The modern Edinburgh – now spread wide over seven hills – would be unrecognisable to the earliest settlers of the Castle Rock. The population is approaching half a million people and many of them are unable to see either the castle in the air or the palace on the ground from where they live in their high-rise flats or low-lying tenements. But the ghosts of Scott, Stevenson, St Margaret, Queen Mary, Hume and the rest – as well as the buildings, books, ideas and memories they left – will remind both populace and visitors that the city's history is a living thing that continues to grow with them. Edinburgh may be a place in love with its own past, but with a new millennium and a new Parliament in place, it can do no harm to stop dreaming and start flirting with the future.

Edinburgh Today

A city in awe of its future and in denial about its past,
Edinburgh is still shaping up for its role as Scottish capital.

The nature of Edinburgh's soul, its identity as a city, has always been closely linked to its buildings. How could the city not be so inclined, given such a strong physical presence at its head as Edinburgh Castle?

The relationship between psyche and architecture is bound up in that old cliché about the city with fur coat and nae knickers. In the New Town the grim, grey exteriors of the townhouses hide all manner of sins. The people are withdrawn, douce even, hiding behind a formality in their social and business lives as well in their homes – yet lift a bit of that old drab surface and all manner of colourful lives are revealed. By contrast, out in the modern suburbs, where the housing is of a rather less solid design, and in the tenements, where everyone lives cheek-by-jowl, people are a lot more friendly. Not up to Glasgow's standards perhaps, but it is in these places that Edinburgh's heart beats rather closer to the surface. It may not always be a pretty sight, but what you get is a reality, not some stiff projection.

This is as it ever was. But in 1997, Edinburgh's relationship with its architecture took a new and dynamic turn, with the decision to construct the new Scottish Parliament opposite Palace of Holyroodhouse. At one stroke, Edinburgh went from being a city whose psyche could be read by anyone who cared to wander around the streets, to one whose whole being could be encapsulated in a single building. No matter that it was not even built yet – nor that it remains that way – because the building goes way beyond its purpose as the new home for Scottish democracy. To the citizens of Edinburgh it is a touchpaper that will ignite all the various arguments that have beset Edinburgh society for centuries, and allow them to be played out.

When it looked as if the ancient Queensferry House on the parliamentary site would have to be demolished, then those who are against any form of devolution were secretly delighted. Here was the Parliament building symbolically destroying everything that is good and old and solid about Scotland. Their rather more open-minded opponents believed that the old building could be incorporated into the new. But the real scandal is that while both sides were re-visiting a battle that had long been won, no one was bothering to ensure that the best job possible was made of marrying the old and the new into a fruitful union.

This failure to bring traditional and modern together in the most forward-thinking manner is often echoed across Edinburgh and epitomised in the way the parliamentary site was chosen. The position, down by the Queen's Edinburgh pad, is certainly appropriate in symbolic terms. It is down here that John Knox went to have a few words with his queen, and is where the ultimate corporal authority in Scotland resides. Besides, it fills in a gap that even in Robert Louis Stevenson's day was a mess of breweries and gas works. But the decision was hard fought, with two other sites vying for supremacy. The Royal High School on Calton Hill had been earmarked since the 1970s but was thought to be too hard to upgrade. A new-build site in Leith did not have such difficulties, but was too far away from the centre of the city. Either could have worked, although neither was as good as Holyrood. The problem is that the final decision was not arrived at by simply choosing the best site – far too easy an option for this city where Machiavellian intrigue fits as easily as a Masonic emblem – or, indeed, that the best site was chosen at all, but that the decision came about through an impressively overt bout of political manoeuvring and horse-trading.

One decision that reflects a more positive element of Edinburgh's makeup is the appointment the Catalan architect Enric Miralles as the head of the project. Insular and guarded against its neighbours though Edinburgh may be, when it comes to foreign liaisons it has a far better record. An English architect would have been anathema to most Scots and, although Edinburgh has rather closer links with England than other parts of the country do, that goes for the citizens of the capital too. But continental Europe does not bring that same sense of dread to the people of Edinburgh that it does to those from south of the border (indeed, the city is famed for its internationalism).

The really big issue surrounding the new Parliament, the one that concerns every man, woman and child on the Bruntsfield to Leith omnibus, is money. In order to bring the building to the Holyrood site, its champion, the First Minister Donald Dewar, was forced to promise that it was the cheapest option. Fifty million pounds is the figure he said it would cost; in March 2000 that had risen to £230 million; only to be capped at £195 million when the MSPs (Members of the Scottish Parliament), finally gave their blessing to the project, by a majority of just nine, in April 2000.

The Queen at the **State Opening of Parliament**, a momentous occasion in Scotland's history.

While the rise and rise of the cost of the building has been seized upon by everybody and anybody who has a bone to pick, this soar-away inflation of the budget has done untold damage to confidence in the Executive of the new Parliament itself. It is one thing to spend a very large sum of money on a new building, but quite another to go over-budget by 300 per cent. This does not smack of mere incompetence, but of a far greater sin in any true resident of Edinburgh's book: financial incompetence. The difference between the first quoted price and the final cost – whatever figure that may turn out to be – is seen as waste: money that could have been better spent on health, housing or any of the social ills that the people of Scotland and Edinburgh believe their Parliament was set up to solve.

'Modern Scotland is still not an independent nation, merely one that has had certain powers devolved to it.'

This whole stushie, all this debate and argument, points to one very important fact: there is, at this birth of the new Scotland, a belief in the Parliament. Healthy cynicism exists, but most people see the Parliament as their Parliament. Their involvement is not limited to the dutiful election of MSPs every few years, but stretches to the right to partake in its daily debates.

Scotland's Parliament has, after all, been a long time coming. And, by dint of living in the place where it is based, Edinburgh's residents have an even greater sense of ownership than most – at least for now while there is plenty of debate to be had about its siting.

THE OLD SONG

An understanding of both the Parliament and its political history goes a long way to understanding Edinburgh today. When the Queen, the Duke of Edinburgh and the Prince of Wales processed up the Royal Mile on 1 July 1999 to open the first Scottish Parliament for 300 years, they were watched by many who had been working towards that day for decades, but still doubted they would see it in their lifetime.

Scotland's parliamentary origins can be traced back to the 12th century, but it was entirely subordinate to the monarch until 1560, when the exiled Mary, Queen of Scots allowed it to meet in her absence. Her son, James VI, however, reasserted the royal authority and neither he nor his successor, Charles I, felt any need for a Parliament to help them rule. In 1638, the National Covenant called for free assemblies which were independent of the monarch and

there followed 12 years of unprecedented freedom of speech until Cromwell banned any Parliaments other than the Palace of Westminster (although the Scots were allowed to send 30 MPs there). In 1661, the Parliament was revived again, but worsening economic conditions brought about 1707's Act of Union with England and it was disbanded.

Modern Scotland is still not an independent nation, merely one that has had certain powers devolved to it in matters such as housing, law and order, social work services, health services and the arts. The Scottish Parliament also has the right to vary income tax by up to three pence in the pound. But Westminster is still the sovereign power in the United Kingdom, retaining control over such matters as defence, foreign policy, the civil service, social security, broadcasting and immigration. Seventy-two Scottish seats remain there, with some MSPs still doubling as MPs in the House of Commons.

It was no surprise to anyone but the most optimistic SNP activist that Labour should dominate the first Parliament. The Scottish Labour Party, founded by Keir Hardie in 1888, has the firmest hold on both the Scottish psyche and Scotland's political institutions, particularly in the urban and industrial areas of the central belt. Indeed, its unchallenged strength in the west has rebounded on the party in recent years, with accusations of cronyism and 'jobs for the boys' carrying over into its first term in the Parliament.

With considerations like these in mind, the Conservatives are starting to claw back some of the ground lost in the 1997 general election. At their highest strength in 1955, the Tories scored 50.1 per cent of the vote in Scotland, a figure that was gradually eaten away, until 1997 left them with no Scottish MPs at Westminster at all. The party's traditional heartlands are the well-heeled farming areas of the Lowlands and Perthshire and the more affluent districts of the major cities. Unable to mimic their southern colleagues' increasingly 'little Englander' stance without looking ridiculous to the Scottish electorate, they are having to forge a new and distinctly Scottish identity and may in fact recover faster than their English counterparts.

The north and the Highlands and Islands tend to vote SNP or Liberal Democrat, though rogue patches of this or that political hue crop up all over the country. The Liberal Democrats, for instance, have strong support in the Borders, although they too have fallen from mighty heights. In 1908, 58 per cent of the Scottish electorate voted for the Liberals, their predecessors. Now they are only the fourth-largest party and rely on their coalition with Labour for what influence they have.

The Scottish Nationalist Party (SNP) is currently the second most powerful force in Scotland. It was founded in 1928 as a response to the failure of both Labour and the Liberal Party to support home rule bills, and its popularity was dented in the 1930s by association in people's minds with the growing fascist nationalist parties in Europe. The SNP won its first seat at Motherwell in 1945, but lost it in the general election a few months later. From then until the 1970s, when the discovery of North Sea oil pushed the independence question further up the political agenda, the party fell into a pattern of winning seats in spectacular victories only to have them snatched back a few years later.

A referendum was finally held in 1979, with 52 per cent of those who voted favouring devolution. Labour Prime Minister James Callaghan, however, decided that, since this represented only 33 per cent of the electorate, there was no mandate to carry it out. Being seen to shift the goalposts in this way earned Callaghan little but scorn and within months his government was swept away after a vote of no confidence and a Conservative landslide.

Despite being passionately opposed to devolution, Callaghan's successor, Margaret Thatcher, probably did more than any other single individual to bring it about. Through policies that were felt to be anti-Scottish – foremost among them her testing of the hated Community Charge (Poll Tax) in Scotland a year before the rest of the United Kingdom – she created a climate hostile to rule from London. Even after she had been deposed, the bond of trust between Scotland and Westminster remained broken. The Conservative presence in Scotland was annihilated in the 1997 general election and on 11 September, in a referendum pledged by Tony Blair while he was still in opposition, Scots voted themselves a Parliament. The knotty decision of where to put it was not an issue; having one at all was enough.

IN TRUTH AS IN FICTION

Now the Parliament is here and work on the site has started, it has begun to make its mark in the literature set in Edinburgh. Most tellingly the building, or rather the building site, plays a pivotal role in *Set in Darkness*, the 12th of Ian Rankin's best-selling novels featuring Inspector John Rebus. Rankin creates an almost palpable sense of place in his writing and, with all but one of the Rhebus novels set in Edinburgh, the books have provided a fascinating reflection of the city over the last ten or more years. Rankin was probably not the first modern writer to

Rallying round... the **SNP** go out in force.

recognise the value in using Edinburgh as a setting. The two faces of the city are perfect for detective fiction. Quentin Jardine's series of Skinner novels have also been successful, although they have a greater level of wish-fulfilment to them and kowtow to authority to a degree that Rankin and his fellow travellers would never countenance.

Plenty of writers through the ages, from James Hogg in his *Confessions of a Justified Sinner* to Muriel Spark in *The Prime of Miss Jean Brodie*, have recognised and used the two-facedness of Edinburgh in their writing. They have utilised the city's sinister side to explore issues relevant to those who do not have to go there. But it is the modern writers of the early 21st century who are daring to use the contrast in the reverse direction. While even Rankin is still dependent on Rhebus's forays into the dark side for his success, writers like Laura Hird, with her splendid *Born Free*, and the young bloods of the Rebel Inc crew, whose literary spoutings have yet to make the mark on a mass market, are following in Irvine Welsh's footsteps and creating bold and daring fiction that tells life as it is for those who live in Edinburgh's underbelly.

The themes of conflict between old and new, between upper and lower classes and the haves and have-nots is taken to its furthest extreme by Paul Johnson's series of future detective thrillers, which started with *Body Politic*. Set in 2025, his vision is of an Edinburgh that has become a city state and is governed by bureaucrats who have turned it into a living tartan theme park and museum. Fortunately, the arrival of the Parliament and the furore over its construction have taken the wind out of Johnson's sails. Chillingly possible though his predictions may have been, they have become highly improbable, thanks to the vociferous debate and argument from Edinburgh's citizens – and no, there is no collective name for them. Edinburgh today, beneath that grey exterior, is building itself its own new future.

Architecture

Solid, commanding and rather stern, Edinburgh's architecture was built with class, to last.

Edinburgh is justifiably classed as one of Europe's finest cities, so it's not surprising that the city has a knowingly handsome air. A 'dream of a great genius', wrote one 1820s visitor, while Mary Shelley had the narrator of her Gothic classic *Frankenstein* comment on 'the beauty and regularity of the New Town of Edinburgh, its romantic castle and its environs, the most delightful in the world…'.

Topographically, Edinburgh has been dealt a spectacular hand. The Pentland Hills lie to the south and a coastal plain stretches north and east to the Firth of Forth; while Arthur's Seat and Castle Rock, impressive remnants of volcanic action, along with Calton Hill and the Salisbury Crags, lend geographical drama to the city. This setting has helped shape a city of two distinct characters. Crowned by Edinburgh Castle, hugging tightly to Castle Rock, the Old Town looks across to the New Town, a triumph of classical formality played out in a gridiron of well-disciplined streets. In 1995 UNESCO designated the Old Town and

New Town a World Heritage Site and this remarkably well-preserved city has a knack for seducing the visitor.

Edinburgh is a place that demands to be walked. Calf muscles can take a battering on its many slopes, but the city's architecture, a glorious embodiment of its history and character, more than compensates for any muscle ache.

PREHISTORIC TO MEDIEVAL

Bronze Age settlers first colonised the natural citadel of the Castle Rock in around 900 BC. In the first century AD, after centuries of relative inactivity, the rocky outcrop became home to a succession of settlements.

Under the ambitious rule of the House of Canmore, the Castle Rock emerged as a fortified stronghold (today's Edinburgh Castle). The small but squatly Romanesque **St Margaret's Chapel** (c1110), with its characteristic rounded, chevron-decorated chancel arch, is the earliest architectural survivor.

In 1125, the expanding settlement was declared a royal burgh and, in 1128, the **Abbey of Holyrood** was founded. Linear development gradually linked Holyrood to the Castle Rock along the rocky spine of the Old Town, defining the route of today's Royal Mile.

Architecturally, little remains from Edinburgh's infant years. Instability and limited funds meant that few structures were built of stone. Most of the houses were crudely made from wattle and post, covered in clay for insulation and thatched with straw, rushes or heather. Their lifespan was no more than a couple of decades, even assuming they escaped the fires that were a common occurrence during the frequent sacks by the English.

Of the handful of stone structures, St Giles (today's **St Giles' Cathedral** on the Royal Mile), the only parish church in the burgh, dates from 1120, but little remains of the original building. It was extensively remodelled in the late 14th century, when Gothic transepts and a series of chapels were added. **Holyrood Abbey** was also virtually rebuilt, between 1195 and 1230, the addition of arcades of pointed arches emphasising the vertical.

The **Castle** fell twice to the English during this period, prompting a huge rebuilding programme in 1356.

St Giles' **crown spire** was an inspiration.

SCOTTISH RENAISSANCE

As its national stature grew during the reign of James III (1460-88), Edinburgh witnessed a surge in confidence and building activity. Holyrood Abbey became a royal residence and was expanded, leading to the 1498 addition of the **Palace of Holyroodhouse**, and Edinburgh Castle was augmented by **Crown Square** and its baronial **Great Hall**, topped with a hammerbeam roof.

Money was pumped into churches, most notably the now-demolished Trinity College Church and, in around 1500, a **crown spire** was added to the central tower of St Giles. An array of flying buttresses bedecked with gilded pinnacles, it became a template for the numerous crown spires dotted across Scotland.

Further invasion attempts by the English in the 1540s prompted Scotland to improve relations with France and open up trade with Europe, heralding the Old Town's mercantile boom years. The city's growing internationalism was mirrored in a fusion of local and continental building patterns.

THE RISE OF THE TENEMENT

As the population of the city increased, more housing was required. But the rocky and uneven terrain of the Old Town, combined with the ancient 'feu' system of land tenure, which granted leases in perpetuity, made horizontal development problematic. Thus expansion was forced upwards, leading to the birth of the tenement. Originally denoting a holding of land, the word came to mean separate dwellings stacked in storeys, linked by a common stairwell.

Wynds and closes developed rib-like from the Royal Mile. Houses already standing had extra storeys tacked on, often haphazardly, in addition to jutting windows and a confusion of roof levels. **John Knox's House** (c1490), with its protruding upper windows and storeys, is one of the few remaining examples, but it's a relatively restrained one – some timber-framed storeys protruded as far as two metres (seven feet) into the street.

Building regulations, however, reined in the quick-buck property speculators, stipulating, from the 1620s, tile or slate roofs and, in 1674, stone façades as fire precautions.

Daringly exploiting the ridge of the Old Town, tenements frequently bridged different levels, making them some of the tallest domestic buildings in Europe. Those that stood cheek-by-jowl along the Royal Mile had more in common with the architecture of northern continental Europe than that of England.

By the late 17th century, tenements built in sandstone or harling (a mix of rubble and plaster) and characterised by flat frontages

The **North Bridge** opened the gates to the New Town and expansion.

and a verticality accentuated by gables and dormer windows soared up along the Royal Mile. The Lawnmarket, below the Castle, was home to the grander examples. The five-storey **Gladstone's Land** (c1620-30) retains the once-commonplace street arcade and an oak-panelled interior. With the upper Royal Mile awash with merchants, its lower reaches had become the choice location of the nobility, and mansions flanked the approach to the Palace of Holyroodhouse. **Moray House** (c1628), with its pyramid-topped gate-piers, and the vast **Queensberry House** (c1634), currently redundant but to be converted into offices for the new Scottish Parliament, are the grandest survivors. The Palace itself was rebuilt in the 1670s. In a triumphant blend of Scottish and European influences, a thick-set façade with turreted towers fronted an inner courtyard with classical arcades.

> **'Edinburgh, not given to extended periods of mourning, soon came to see architecture as pivotal to asserting its own character.'**

With the city becoming increasingly wealthy, a new **Parliament House** was built next to St Giles in 1637, adding weight to Edinburgh's role as Scotland's capital. The building was given a classical overhaul in the early 19th century.

Elsewhere the city flaunted its internationalism, as with the easy handling of Renaissance style in the grandly ornamented **George Heriot School** (1628), south of the Royal Mile. Along the Royal Mile, churches were built, namely John Mylne's handsome **Tron Kirk** (1663, today the Old Town Information Centre) and the aristocratic and slightly Dutch-looking **Canongate Kirk** (1688), with its delicate, curving gables.

GETTING DOLLED UP
The 1707 Act of Union with England provoked an identity crisis for Edinburgh, and some dubbed the city 'a widowed metropolis'. But Edinburgh, not given to extended periods of mourning, soon came to see architecture as pivotal to asserting its own character.

The collapse in 1751 of a Royal Mile tenement highlighted the antiquity and the run-down state of the Old Town and the need for 'modern' living quarters. In 1752, the city's Lord Provost, George Drummond, drew up proposals to expand Edinburgh, creating the grandiose Exchange (now the **City Chambers**) on the Royal Mile and, in 1765, the **North Bridge**. The Bridge, which was the first to cross Nor' Loch, gave easy access to Leith and, importantly, a swathe of redundant land to the north of the Old Town. This was to become the site of the 'new towns' that are collectively known as today's New Town.

Conceived as Edinburgh's 'civilised' face, the first new town, designed in 1766 by James Craig, was built to a regimented layout, comprising **George Street**, flanked by **Princes Street** and **Queen Street**. The architectural style was predominately classicism. Influenced by the growing Europe-wide fascination with the ancient Greek and Roman civilisations and the increasingly popular fashion for neoclassicism, Edinburgh's new architecture adopted proportion, grandeur and classical trimmings as its hallmarks.

A leading practitioner, Robert Adam, designed **Charlotte Square** (from 1792). A residential enclave acting as a grand full stop to the west end of George Street, its buildings boasted rooftop sphinxes, balustrades and fanlights (semicircular windows above the front door) and, importantly after the cramped conditions of the Old Town, the space of the square itself. **Register House** (c1788), on the axis of North Bridge, is another example of Adam's well-mannered classicism. Its cupolas and pedimented portico are a gracious retort to the haphazard gables of the Old Town.

It's a wynd up the **Royal Mile**. *See page 24.*

CLASSICAL REINVENTION

By the early 1800s, architecture had an increasingly crucial role in expressing the city's newly cultivated identity. As early as 1762, Edinburgh was dubbed the 'Athens of the North'. The city's topography made the analogy plausible and, besides, Edinburgh liked the idea of being the intellectual 'Athenian' metropolis compared to the imperial 'Roman' capital, London.

As the Scottish Enlightenment held sway, the architect William Playfair gave stone and mortar representation to Calton Hill's status as Edinburgh's 'acropolis'. His **City Observatory** (1818), a mini-cruciform temple capped by a dome, stands next to his Parthenon-esque **National Monument**. Begun in 1826 to commemorate the Napoleonic Wars, its 12 huge columns, set on a vast stepped plinth, were an attempt to provide the classical illusion to end all classical illusions. But it remained unfinished due to a funding crisis – earning it the nickname 'Edinburgh's Disgrace'. Later it formed a visual link to Thomas Hamilton's **Royal High School** (1829), on the lower slopes of Calton Hill. Described as the 'noblest monument of the Scottish Greek revival', it was neoclassicism at its most authoritarian, with a central 'temple' flanked by grand antechambers.

On the Mound, meanwhile, the prolific Playfair delivered further classical rhetoric with the **Royal Scottish Academy** (1823) and the **National Gallery of Scotland** (1850), a monumental, temple-inspired duo parading an army of columns and classical trimmings.

On the residential front, a succession of upmarket new towns clustered around Craig's original. The ostentatiously wide **Great King Street** and the columned residences of **Moray Place** contributed to what was, by the 1840s, one of the most extensive and well-ordered neo-classical suburbs in Europe.

Punctuated by private 'pleasure gardens', the New Town gave urban living a picturesque rural charm and trumpeted Edinburgh as an ambitious and architecturally inspired city.

SCOTTISH BARONIAL STYLE & ECLECTICISM

In 1822, George IV visited Edinburgh dressed in pink stockings and a kilt. His sartorial advisor was Sir Walter Scott, author and campaigner for the 'tartanisation' of Scotland.

With its internationalism established in the determinedly classical New Town, Edinburgh turned its attention to the home-grown architecture of the Old Town. The city's commercial, political and legal centre needed upgrading. The 1827 Improvement Act advised that new buildings and those in need of a facelift should adopt the 'Old Scot' style. Turrets, crenellations and crows feet, à la Scots baronial, elbowed a return into the architectural style; **Cockburn Street**, the first vehicular link between the Royal Mile and what is today Waverley Station, is a determined example.

Elsewhere, new public buildings masqueraded as rural piles airlifted from the Scottish Highlands. The **Royal Infirmary** (1870), to the south of the Royal Mile, sported a central clock tower and an array of turrets. **Fettes College** (1865-70), north of the New Town, was an exuberant intermarriage of local baronial and French chateau. The 'tartan touch' also hit the expanding tenement suburbs – Marchmont, to the south of the city, sports numerous turrets and gables.

This growing adventurousness gave way to architectural promiscuity. The city's well-off institutions showed confident but sometimes florid excess, with a 'pick and mix' approach to building style. The headquarters of the **Bank of Scotland**, grandly posed on the precipice of the Mound, adopted full-on baroque; the British Linen Bank (now a **Bank of Scotland** branch) on St Andrew's Square opted for the Renaissance palazzo look, its Corinthian columns topped by six colossal statues.

Gothic revival also made its mark courtesy of Augustus Pugin. The master of the decorated pinnacle and soaring spire designed the **Tolbooth Church** (1844), below Castle Esplanade. Today it is The Hub, a café and ticket centre run by the Edinburgh International Festival. But the finest line in romantic Gothic came in George Meikle Kemp's **Scott Monument** (1840) on Princes Street – an elaborate, filigreed, spire-like affair enshrining a statue of Sir Walter Scott.

MUSCULAR POST-MODERNISM

Little disturbed by industrialisation, late 19th-century Edinburgh saw no huge bursts of construction. The impetus to build was further anaesthetised by two world wars. The Euro-wide, clean-cut, 1930s modernism made little impression, save in the robustly authoritarian **St Andrew's House** (1937-39), on the lower reaches of Calton Hill. Designed by Thomas Tait and today home to the Scottish Executive, it is a true architectural heavyweight, with an imposing, symmetrical façade.

In the suburbs a few avant-garde adventurers experimented. Architect **William Kininmonth's house** in Dick Place (1933), with its cool play of curves and verticals, is one of the finest examples of the international style in Scotland.

The redevelopment of the Old Town was the major planning and social issue during the first half of the 20th century. With the upwardly mobile residents siphoned off to the New Town, a large part of the Old Town had, by the Victorian era, developed into an overcrowded slum. As early as 1892 the influential urban planner Sir Patrick Geddes (who inspired the revamp of Ramsey Gardens, just below Castle Esplanade) had proposed seeding the area with members of the university as a means of adding to its intellectual weight. But his plan was not adopted.

> **'The sacrifice of George Square sent a rallying call to the preservation troops, with the effect that much of the Old Town was saved.'**

Instead, by the inter-war years, residents were being encouraged to decamp to a series of council-built satellite townships on the periphery of the city, first among them the Craigmillar Estate. This social engineering, achieved through town planning, was a crude mirror of the earlier and socially exclusive New Town. The fate of the increasingly depopulated Old Town however, remained in the balance.

In 1949, the Abercrombie Plan saw slum tenements demolished, along with the grander George Square, to create space for a new university campus. The sacrifice of George Square, particularly, to make way for the unpopular 1960s architectural style that replaced it, sent a rallying call to the preservation troops, with the effect that much of the Old Town was saved – but thereafter resolutely contemporary architecture has dared make only rare appearances in the Old Town. Even outside the Old Town there are few notable exceptions save the low-slung, glass-panelled **Royal Commonwealth Pool** (1967) and Basil Spence's **University Library** (1965) to the south. The city instead suffered explosions of 1960s brutalism, as seen in the ugly, blockish **St James Centre**, just off Princes Street. The subsequent backlash sent the city planners into cautious mode, inviting accusations of architectural timidity. These reached their height in 1989 when a redundant site on the Royal Mile was filled by the Scandic Crown Hotel (now the **Crowne Plaza**), which was built in the Old Town-imitation style.

The competition's intense, but this dome's dynamic – the **Our Dynamic Earth** attraction.

A flirtation with late-20th-century architecture is shown in the Exchange, the city's new financial quarter on Lothian Road, just outside the confines of the Old and New Towns. Terry Farrell's **Edinburgh International Conference Centre** forms the nucleus, with big-name companies inhabiting the surrounding office blocks (Edinburgh is the fourth largest financial services centre in Europe). Built in the 1990s but in 1980s style, the Exchange's **Festival Square** and the **Standard Life Building** are one-liners in overly muscular commercial architecture and sad examples of modernism at its most mediocre.

DEVOLUTION & BEYOND

Debate over the location of the new Scottish Parliament highlighted Edinburgh's ongoing architectural sensitivity. Calton Hill, long seen as the symbolic heart of Scotland's nationhood (the Royal High School was converted in 1979 to house the proposed Scottish Assembly), had the historical upper hand.

The decision in 1998 by the Scottish Office to site the Parliament in Canongate, near the Palace of Holyroodhouse – the British monarch's official residence in Scotland – was viewed in some quarters as a sign of political complaisance. Work on the site, formerly William Younger's brewery, is currently under way. The Spanish architect, Enric Miralles, was selected in 1998, in conjunction with the Scottish practice RMJM, as the architect for the new Parliament, which is due to open in 2003. Canongate as a whole is also witnessing an extensive programme of new building. Its central location, to the east of the Old Town, and the stunning backdrop of Arthur's Seat made it a prime target for redevelopment. Michael Hopkin's **Our Dynamic Earth**, a vast tent-like structure, opened in 1999. Further up Holyrood Road, meanwhile, is the new, yet architecturally uninspired, offices of the **Scotsman** newspaper. Helping to ensure that commercial concerns are balanced with the need to maintain the Old Town's residential population, the swathe of land sandwiched between Canongate and Holyrood Road is a fast being developed with a mix of housing and public buildings.

Perhaps the biggest architectural hit of the last few years is, however, the **Museum of Scotland**. Situated next to the Royal Museum of Scotland on the fringes of the Old Town, it was designed by architects Benson and Forsyth and opened in 1998. Built in sandstone, it is warmly monumental and topped by a vast turret. And, importantly, it is seen as successfully bringing together the resolutely contemporary with a sensitivity to Edinburgh's architectural past.

Having been accused of suffering from the 'post-New Town siesta' syndrome by some critics, it is hoped that Edinburgh is now more conscious of the need to protect its architectural heritage, wake up to the future and ensure that the 'dream of a great genius' is kept an architectural reality.

> ▶ For more information on the sights mentioned in bold in this chapter, *see* chapter **Sightseeing**.

Edinburgh by Numbers

20,000 The estimated number of people who attended the last public hanging in Edinburgh – of George Bruce of Ratho on 21 June 1864.

25,000 The number of people who marched through Edinburgh in 1992 to campaign for democracy for Scotland.

8 The number of groups taking part in the first Edinburgh Fringe in 1948.

605 The number of groups taking part in the Fringe in 1987 – the largest in its history.

169 The number of Fringe shows seen by Nigel Tantrum in 1994.

£20,000 The amount of money pledged in 1945 by Sir John Falconer, Edinburgh's Lord Provost, for the purpose of an international arts festival.

180,000 The number of tickets sold for shows during the first Edinburgh International Festival in 1947.

400,000 The approximate number of people who saw one or more performance during the 53rd Edinburgh International Festival in 1999.

37,500 The total number of seats in venues with a public entertainments licence in Edinburgh during August.

65 The number of wig-makers in Edinburgh in 1700.

71 The number of mills powered by the Water of Leith along the ten-mile stretch between Balerno and Leith in 1828.

257 The number of Covenanters shipped as slaves to Barbados in 1679.

2,000,000 The estimated number of cartloads of soil removed from the foundations of the New Town and deposited on the Mound between 1781 and its completion in 1830.

6,000,000 The number of oysters harvested a year from their beds in the Forth at the height of the trade.

0 The number of oysters in the Forth today.

35,000 Population of Edinburgh in 1678.

40,420 Population of Edinburgh in 1722.

64,479 Population of Edinburgh in 1755.

175,407 Population of Edinburgh in 1831.

320,549 Population of Edinburgh in 1881.

439,101 Population of Edinburgh in 1931.

467,000 Population of Edinburgh in 1951.

447,550 Population of Edinburgh in 1995.

1,000,000 The estimated population of Edinburgh during August in 1999.

2,700 The number of plants in the Edinburgh Physic Garden when it was at its one-acre site at Trinity Hospital (now Waverley Station) in 1689.

4,000 The approximate number of species in the Royal Botanic Garden at the Leith Walk site in 1812.

14,000 the number of species in the Royal Botanic Garden and its three outstations at Benmore, Dawyck and Logan 1994.

13 days Edinburgh-London stagecoach journey time in 1712 (the fare was £4/10/- or £4.50).

4 days Edinburgh-London post-coach journey time in 1773 (the fare was £4/14/6 or £4.73).

14 hours Edinburgh-London service on North British Railways in 1847.

10 and a half hours Edinburgh-London run of the Flying Scotsman (the oldest named train in the world) in 1862.

5 hours, 22 minutes Edinburgh-London run by British Rail in 1977.

3 hours, 59 minutes Edinburgh-London run by GNER's Scottish Pullman service, summer 1988.

£21,000 The amount of money raised by public subscription towards the building of the National Monument on Calton Hill, which started in 1822. £42,000 was needed and the half-completed monument was dubbed 'Scotland's Disgrace'.

1,984 The number of yards in a Scots mile.

914 miles The total length of the streets of Edinburgh.

22 miles The length of the Water of Leith.

12 The average number of days a year when snow was lying at 9am at Edinburgh Airport (1961-90).

106mm The greatest rainfall recorded in a single day in Edinburgh (1787).

238mm The greatest rainfall recorded in a single month in Edinburgh – August 1948.

65mm The average rainfall at Edinburgh Airport during August (1961-90).

4.67 hours The average sunlight per day in August at Edinburgh Airport (1961-90).

3% The percentage of vehicles that are buses on the streets of Edinburgh.

50% The percentage of journeys in Edinburgh taken by bus.

83% The percentage of vehicles that are cars on the streets of Edinburgh.

259 hectares (640 acres) The size of Queen's Park (Arthur's Seat).

1,415 hectares (3,500 acres) The total area of Edinburgh public parks owned by the City Council.

141 The number of police boxes built throughout the city in 1933.

129 The number of Members of Scottish Parliament (MSPs).

£50 million The anticipated cost of the new Parliament in January 1998. By March 2000, it had grown to £230 million, but the following month was capped at £195 million.

Scottish Icons

Never mind the quality of the historical accuracy,
just feel the width of that international appeal.

Over the the last decade or two there has been a growing self-consciousness in Scotland about the myths perpetuated in the name of national identity. The result has been a peculiar, post-modern embracing of cultural icons – despite revelations about their lack of authenticity. It's as if Scots have cottoned on to the fact that some of these kitsch artefacts are quite good after all, whatever their provenance. The country might still have a frightening capacity for lapsing into a cartoon version of itself, but there are hints of a New Caledonia if you only know where to look.

Take tartan. Any claims that Highlanders of old traipsed through the heather in distinctive kilts with everyone of the same clan sporting the same design is arrant nonsense.

Up until the late 18th century, Scotland was split in two. Lowlanders saw themselves as cultured, forward-looking and fond of trousers, while they regarded the Highlanders as Gaelic-speaking hoodlums in barbaric attire. Highland costume included a great length of material wrapped around the upper body and thighs, fastened at the waist so the lower part formed a skirt – the belted plaid. Those who had money wore a plaid of ostentatious design; those who did not wore brown. Tartan-style designs, even for the rich, didn't reach Scotland until the 16th century and probably came from Flanders.

It wasn't until the 1720s that the kilt as we know it today was invented. An English businessman struck a deal with a clan chief near Inverness to smelt iron ore on his land.

Local men were employed and their belted plaid proved such a hindrance when it came to felling trees or working a furnace that the inventive Englishman came up with a sawn-off plaid that dispensed with the upper portion and left just the skirt. The kilt was born, but still there was no relation between tartan and clan identity.

Use of the kilt spread and, by the time of the Battle of Culloden in 1746 (when Bonnie Prince Charlie was defeated), it was seen as part of traditional Highland dress – so it was subsequently banned by a London-based government intent on wiping out all traces of a culture that could lend armed support to Catholic rebellion against the British crown. In a generation, the Highland way of life – not to mention its fashion sense – was destroyed. But once the clan structure had been broken, the people 'pacified', and the men directed into Highland regiments of the British Army, public opinion in the Lowlands and England started to feel more comfortable with the now harmless 'noble savage' from the north. The Highlands became hip…

The crucial turning point, when Highland imagery became the basis of a national identity for all Scots, came in 1822 with George IV's visit to Edinburgh. A reigning British monarch hadn't set foot over the border in two centuries so a visit of some note was required, in an Edinburgh that was re-inventing itself with the building of the monumental public works of the New Town. Novelist and arch-romantic Sir Walter Scott was entrusted with the organisation of the visit.

> **'Frankly, you're better off wearing a kilt at a wedding than looking like a geek in a top hat and tails.'**

The result was a sick joke. The king, a preposterous, ailing blimp with a taste for cherry brandy and opium, arrived in Edinburgh to take part in a caricature of a Highland pageant entirely invented by the novelist. The Scottish aristocracy and bourgeoisie, clad in a comical pastiche of Highland costume (as directed by Scott, with an arbitrary choice of garish tartans), fell over themselves to fawn before the king, quite happy to forget that his great uncle (Butcher Cumberland) had bloodied the glens 76 years before.

From George IV's visit on, manufacturers created and provided tartans for all. Any linkage to clan names was, in effect, one giant 19th-century marketing scam.

So what about modern Scots – have they dropped tartan? Not on your nelly. They've come to realise that, despite its chequered history, it's fun. And, frankly, you're better off wearing a kilt at a wedding than looking like a geek in a top hat and tails – whether you're in Edinburgh or the Home Counties. Tartan features on the international fashion scene and even football clubs have been getting in on the act by commissioning their own special designs.

In fact, this change of heart could be said to apply to many of Scotland's national symbols as the country rises up to become a nation again. The people have realised that when intelligence and style are applied to the icons of their culture, no matter how falsely conceived or immodestly constructed these icons may be, then they can actually become worthwhile.

Bagpipes – national squeeze

Bagpipes are indeed the traditional sound of the Highlands, although go further back and the Irish harp was once the instrument of choice. The

international reputation of Highland pipes was probably fixed by their association with British imperialism in the 19th century – when the army came to town it was often to a pipe accompaniment. Bagpipe-style instruments from India, North Africa and the rest of Europe never enjoyed such prominent advertising. Musically primitive, a massed band of pipers can be irritating or downright scary. But there's no denying that a lone piper playing a lament is one of the most haunting sounds in world music. A set of pipes can cost anything from £475 to £2,775; for details, *see p168* **Sounds good**.

The Ceilidh – national rave

It used to mean 'gathering', but now means lots of people hopping around to traditional dance tunes played by everyone from muscular rock 'n' reel bands to a dextrous auld mannie with an accordion. Ceilidhs are in vogue and several venues host nights. **St Bride's Centre**, 10 Orwell Terrace, EH11 (346 1405) has fundraising ceilidhs on a frequent basis while the **Caledonian Brewery** (*see p96*) has regular bashes on a Saturday.

Haggis – national dish

Haggis is minced lung, heart and liver from a sheep, mixed with oatmeal and pepper and cooked in a sheep's stomach. The world regards haggis as Scottish, but all kinds of peoples from ancient times

have eaten animal bits in a wrap of skin, stomach or intestine. Haggis was on the menu from at least the 13th century in Scotland, but it took a Robert Burns poem, *Address to a Haggis*, to fix it as a national comestible. Eaten occasionally throughout the year, sales rocket for 25 January, when the country celebrates Burns' birthday. Be sure to try one made by **Macsweens of Edinburgh** (*see p179*). A vegetarian version is also available.

Highland Games – national sport

The first recorded instances of the games as we know them today date from the second decade of the 19th century and many gatherings overseas are as long-lived and authentic as anything in Scotland. The actual events do have a longer pedigree in that people have danced, played music and thrown things around in the Highlands for centuries, but modern games are no more authentic than the average tartan. Any gathering will have its own local flavour, but visitors should find caber tossing, weight putting, dancing and piping competitions at all of them. In the last few years, a games has been run at Stewart's-Melville playing fields on Ferry Road (319 2005), held in July and August with an eye to tourists. Glasgow hosts the world pipe band championships, which also incorporates a games on Glasgow Green. It's normally held every August; phone 0141 287 5190 for further details.

The Kilt – national dress

There are several outfitters on the Royal Mile that cater to passing tourists, but if you want to get away from the hustle and bustle, head for Leith. A made-to-measure kilt from **Kinloch Anderson** (*see p176*) will cost around £300, but should last longer than you will. The shop also has a small area set aside for an exhibition on the history of tartan with a couple of items dating from the time of George IV's visit.

Shortbread – national biscuit

Many of the mass-produced brands taste like tinder-dry bits of Scots pine, so go for the best. Shortbread House of Edinburgh keeps winning awards. It's neither widely available nor cheap, but you can usually find some in the food hall at **Jenners** department store or **John Lewis** (for both, *see p171*).

Whisky – national drug

Irish is good, American is more rock 'n' roll, but Scotch whisky, with its unequalled variety and character, blows the opposition away. Single malts have a complexity that rewards careful drinking, but whiskies that have been bottled direct from the cask without any adulteration are something else again. For these, try **Royal Mile Whiskies** or join the **Scotch Malt Whisky Society** (for both, *see p177*). Expect to pay at least £30-£35 for a bottle of cask-strength malt and often much, much more.

Sightseeing

Introduction

A round-up of the museums and galleries to look out for.

Edinburgh is certainly the elegant city that Scotland needs as its capital but, well-preserved though it may be, it has avoided becoming a living museum. Instead, its history is faithfully presented in modern exhibitions that both portray its past in a credible manner and enhance the pleasures of a subsequent walk around the city. This is despite the best efforts of the operators of the sort of tourist traps that bedeck their guides in tartan and expect their customers to believe the romantic myths put about by Sir Walter Scott. A certain amount of Disneyfication might seem to be going on at the likes of the **Scotch Whisky Heritage Centre** (*see page 43*) or **Shaping a Nation** (*see page 87*), but Edinburgh has repelled invaders who are far more stout and even more insidious than the would-be tartanisers.

It is safe to say that both **Edinburgh Castle** (*see page 41*) and the **Palace of Holyroodhouse** (*see page 54*) will continue to provide the solid backbone to most Edinburgh sightseeing itineraries for many years to come. It is worth remembering that the Palace of Holyroodhouse is the Queen's residence in Edinburgh and is closed to the public when she is there. As this guide went to press, six new galleries in the **National War Museum of Scotland** were due to open inside the Castle. They will explore the influence of the military in the last 400 years of Scottish history and present the experience of the individual Scot in war and peace.

The two big museums to see are the double whammy of the **Royal Museum** and the **Museum of Scotland** (for both, *see page 81*), situated together on Chambers Street. Both are good museums, but it is perhaps the latter that has the most to offer the visitor to Scotland. The thematically arranged journey from pre-history in the basement to icons chosen by modern Scots on the top floor also provides a strong basis for understanding the history of the city that can be seen from its roof.

For insight into the local events and people who made Edinburgh the city it is today, the various museums and attractions down the length of the Royal Mile and around the Old and New Towns together create a complex and fascinating picture. The **Huntly House Museum** (*see page 53*) on the Canongate might show the worst tendencies of the civic museum

to cram everything into glass cases, but its wide range of exhibits adds an extra level of understanding to the more modern, naturalistic displays in **The People's Story** (*see page 55*) opposite, **Gladstone's Land** (*see page 44*) on the Lawnmarket, or the **Georgian House** (*see page 63*) on Charlotte Square. Then there are the smaller, specialist museums that add their own peculiar twist to Edinburgh's story. the **Sir Jules Thorn Exhibition of the History of Surgery** (*see page 81*) in which, by reading between the lines, much can be learned about social attitudes in the city is one such; the **Newhaven Heritage Museum** (*see page 93*) is another.

All museums are reviewed in the relevant sightseeing chapters. The website www.ebs.hw.ac.uk/EDC/MAG/ has details of City of Edinburgh-run museums. As this guide went to press, the Scottish Executive announced a commitment to make entry to all National Museum of Scotland museums free by April 2001 – in Edinburgh this will apply to the Royal Museum and the Museum of Scotland.

SIGHTSEEING TOURS

If walking round Edinburgh gets too much – and there are enough hills for that to be sooner rather than later – make use of one of the three operators that run open-top bus tours around the Old and New Towns. All start from Waverley Bridge and while each offers a slightly different route, there is not a lot to choose between them. All tours take about an hour, if traffic is not too heavy, and leave every 10 to 20 minutes from about 9am to 7pm in the summer, 9am to 5pm in the spring and autumn, and 10am to 4pm in the winter. All go past most of the major sights and offer a one-day, 'hop on, hop off' ticket, which allows passengers to stop off at any point along the way.

The white and blue buses of the **Edinburgh Classic Tour** are run by LRT (554 4494; tickets £7, concessions £5.50). The driver provides a commentary but each passenger has their own headphones with a choice of pre-recorded commentaries in English, Japanese, German, French, Spanish, Italian or Dutch. **Guide Friday** (556 2244; tickets £7, concessions £5.50) has a guide on its green and cream buses who gives a running commentary and can answer questions along the route. The red and cream buses of the **Mac Vintage**

Art galleries

Edinburgh's art scene has undergone something of a makeover during the last few years. Although the city boasts a superb collection of art through the ages in the august **National Gallery**, its contemporary art front was once far from lively.

Glasgow had eclipsed the capital with its robust reputation as a hotbed of young talent, while Edinburgh seemed to be resting on overtly conservative laurels. The Glasgow School of Art continues to produce a vibrant band of young artists who have included Turner Prize-winner Douglas Gordon and shortlisted Christine Borland, along with Ross Sinclair, Simon Starling and Smith and Stewart. Meanwhile, doubtless empowered by devolution, Edinburgh's galleries have entered a new era of greater internationalism. Artists based around Scotland who are already recognised on the international circuit are now receiving more coverage in the capital's galleries and there is a move away from lingering parochialism.

The part of the Old Town above Market Street has been dubbed the 'gallery quarter', with art spaces such as the **Collective**, the **Fruitmarket** and **Stills** injecting a buzz into the scene. The likes of Nathan Coley, Roderick Buchanan, Dalziel and Scullion and Martin Boyce are part of a wave of innovative Scotland-based artists whose work is now being championed in Edinburgh. Adding further impetus to Edinburgh's art scene is the fact that the British Art Show, the touring vehicle for Britain's hottest artists, kicked off its country-wide tour in Edinburgh in April 2000.

The National Galleries of Scotland group has five galleries within the city. The latest addition, the **Dean Gallery**, opened in 1999 and is located just over the road from the **Scottish National Gallery of Modern Art**. Currently the grounds of both galleries are being re-landscaped to make way for a sculpture park. Each gallery has a print room, and the Dean Gallery also has an archive room, which can be visited by appointment. And if that much-admired work of art is not on current display but in gallery storage, it is possible to request a viewing (in theory at least; phone 624 6200 for details).

The National Galleries produces a useful bi-monthly gallery guide with details of current exhibitions, its regular programme of lunchtime lectures and other events. A handy guide to the contemporary art spaces of Edinburgh – and Scotland as a whole – is the Collective's bi-monthly guide, which can be picked up at galleries and tourist offices.

The following non-commercial galleries are reviewed in the guide. Commercial galleries are reviewed on *pages 186-8*.

City Art Centre (*see page 49*); **Collective Gallery** (*see page 49*); **Dean Gallery** (*see page 69*); **Edinburgh College of Art** (*see page 79*); **Fruitmarket Gallery** (*see page 49*); **Inverleith House** (*see page 66; pictured*); **National Gallery of Scotland** (*see page 57*); **Portfolio Gallery** (*see page 79*); **Royal Scottish Academy** (*see page 58*); **Scottish National Gallery of Modern Art** (*see page 69*); **Scottish National Portrait Gallery** (*see page 60*); **Stills Gallery** (*see page 49*).

Tours (220 0770; tickets £7.50, concessions £5) are all over 30 years old and come with a conductor as well as a guide. This locally run company aims to emphasise the contrast between the Old and New Towns; it is also in the process of setting up evening bus tours.

A rather different bus tour of the city can be taken by catching LRT's number 32 or 52 service, from the foot of Leith Walk or Cameron Toll. The buses go in opposite directions around the city and while you won't have a guide to tell you all about the historic richness of all you pass, over the two hours it takes to circle the city you will get to see the real Edinburgh, from the Pentland Hills to the waterfront at Leith.

Royal Mile

Edinburgh's inner-city area might be desirable property today, but in years past it was both a slum and then a ghetto as the rich moved out.

The Royal Mile, the oldest part of the city, is built on the ridge that slopes from Edinburgh Castle down to the Palace of Holyroodhouse. Protected by the Castle Rock on the west and the now-drained Nor' Loch on the site of Princes Street Gardens, the Old Town was hemmed within city walls in the Middle Ages. As population growth forced housing to be built higher and higher, the long gardens that once ran either side of the ridges were also built over, making this a densely housed area. The dramatic descents on either side mean that buildings that look only a few floors high from the High Street can tower many storeys on the other side.

All these tenements, known as 'lands', were packed so tightly together inside the city walls that different parts of society shared the same houses, usually with the prosperous and noble on the upper floors. After the North Bridge was opened in 1772, the gentry moved to the New Town and although the tenements started to fall into disrepair, their decay was checked and they still predominate on the Royal Mile, interspersed with the remaining 60 or so 'closes' (alleys) of the hundreds that once riddled the area.

The Royal Mile is still infused with the intrigue and drama that comes from a capital city that has been through turbulent times and has seen more than its fair share of historical figures and events. The lack of sanitation facilities, which gave rise to the famous Old Town cry of 'gardey loo' (a corruption of the French 'gardez l'eau') when flinging household waste out the window, led to a third of the population being wiped out by bubonic plague.

The chaotic, crowded, smelly, noisy Edinburgh of the 17th and 18th centuries still seems to lurk just under the surface. With such an atmosphere, the area lends itself to ghost tours (*see page 52* **Witches & wynds**). Inevitably, the vast majority of the shops are aimed at the tourist market: woollen mills, craft shops, tartan outfitters – they're all here.

Castlehill

Unlike so many castles that lie in ruins, the grey and imposing fortress that is **Edinburgh Castle** (*see page 41*) has been in constant use for 1,000 years. It is extraordinarily well

The **Royal Mile** on a quiet day.

preserved and kept scrupulously tidy. The military presence gives it an atmosphere that's brisk (although that could just be the wind) and devoid of the tackiness found at other historic sites. The Castle was a royal residence until the Lang Siege of 1571-3 when Mary, Queen of Scots' supporters in the Castle were bombarded by the regent governing on the behalf of her son, the infant King James VI of Scotland and I of England. The ensuing refurbishment was intended to turn the Castle into an impregnable military fortress and the royal residence was changed to Holyroodhouse.

The Castle is entered from the Esplanade, where the world-famous and nearly always sold-out **Edinburgh Military Tattoo** has been held every Festival since 1950. When the Esplanade is not covered by the seats set up for

the Tattoo, the most impressive visible feature of the Castle is the curve of the massive artillery emplacement, the Half Moon Battery, built to protect the Castle's vulnerable eastern side after the Lang Siege. Behind it on the left is the Palace, now one of the **Castle Museums** (*see below*). The Gatehouse – with the bronze statues of Robert the Bruce and William Wallace on either side of the gate – was added in 1886-8 as a conscious attempt to make the Castle look more picturesque. Behind the Half Moon Battery, the Old Palace buildings drop sheer down to Johnston Terrace. The Mills Mount Battery, from where the one o'clock gun is fired, is not visible from here – it's behind the trees to the right, facing out over Princes Street. Cliché though it is, you can always tell Edinburgh natives because, instead of flinching when the gun goes off, they automatically check their watches.

The view from the southern parapet of the Esplanade looks out over the suburbs of Edinburgh, which were once open heath, up to the Pentland Hills. The northern aspect is over the New Town to Fife and there is a small gate at the eastern end, which leads down to Princes Street Gardens. The military memorials on the Esplanade are self-explanatory. But on the left of the gate on the way out on to the Royal Mile is a most poignant memorial, in the shape of a small bronze well, which marks the place where over 300 women were burned as witches between 1479 and 1722.

Also visible from the Esplanade – on the extreme left as you face away from the Castle – is Ramsay Gardens, an irregular complex of romantic baronial buildings bristling with spiral staircases and overhangs. Constructed around the poet Alan Ramsay's octagonal 'goose-pie' house, the buildings were mostly erected in the late 19th century to lure the upper classes back into the Old Town. The low, flat building beside them was once the Castlehill reservoir, built in 1851, which supplied water to Princes Street. Nowadays, it houses the **Edinburgh Old Town Weaving Company** (*see page 42*), an exhibition and working weaving mill for tartan cloth. The **Camera Obscura** (*see below*) is in the black-and-white tower on the roof of the next building down. It contains a system of lenses and mirrors that project images of the surrounding area on to a disc inside. The building on the right of Castlehill is **Cannonball House**, so called because of the two cannon balls lodged in the west gable end wall, about halfway up. They are said to have been placed there to mark the level of the Comiston Springs, which used to feed the Castlehill reservoir.

Opposite Ramsay Lane, the narrow cobbled road down to the Mound, is the **Scotch Whisky Heritage Centre** (*see page 43*). There are guided tours through a three-floor exhibition, which culminates in the Tasting Bar. The Tolbooth St John's Kirk stands where Castlehill meets the top of Johnston Terrace. Designed by Augustus Pugin in 1844, its Gothic spire is the tallest in Edinburgh at 73 metres (240 feet). The church was bought by the Edinburgh International Festival in 1998 and beautifully refurbished as its headquarters: **The Hub** (*see page 43*), which also houses a year-round café, shop and ticket centre, where tickets for all official festival events (including the Science Festival and Edinburgh's Hogmanay) are sold.

Camera Obscura

Castlehill, EH1 (226 3709). Bus 35, 35A. **Open** *Nov-Mar* 10am-5pm daily; *Apr-Oct* 9.30am-6pm Mon-Fri; 10am-6pm Sat, Sun. **Admission** £4.25; £2.10 concessions; £12 family. **Credit** MC, V. **Map** p44 A1.

It's all done with mirrors in this attraction at the top of the Royal Mile, which was created by optician Maria Short in the 1850s. The main event is a 20-minute show in the domed hut on the roof. Images of the surrounding area – and from this high up that's pretty extensive – are reflected and refracted onto a white disc in the middle of the small, darkened room. As the lenses turn the circle, the guide will invite kids to 'pick up' people and buses on pieces of paper, which is quite amusing but ultimately a bit twee. The hologram exhibition on the way up is thorough and well presented. It's worth leaving time to go out on the roof afterwards as the binoculars there give excellent views over the New Town and Calton Hill. It is not, however, worth visiting on a cloudy day as the camera is dependent on natural light for the strength of the image.

Edinburgh Castle

Castlehill, EH1 (enquiries 668 8800/ticket office 225 9846). Bus 35, 35A. **Open** *Apr-Sept* 9.30am-6pm daily; *Oct-Mar* 9.30am-5pm daily. **Admission** £7; £2-£5 concessions. **Credit** AmEx, DC, MC, V. **Map** p314 B2.

Edinburgh Castle is a fascinating hotchpotch of buildings built between the 12th century and the present day. A visit can easily last anything from a couple of hours to a whole afternoon. Since there's a lot of walking and cobbled pathways, you're advised to wear sensible shoes. A guided tour and a taped audio guide – available in six languages – is included in the entry price. The tour guides are very friendly and happy to answer questions or have their photo taken with visitors. The audio guide is recommended and its soundtrack, including gunfire and spooky music, helps the imagination along, although it is advisable to ask how to use it as it can be confusing.

Edinburgh Castle at twilight. There's nowt quite like it. *See page 41.*

Close to the summit of the castle is **St Margaret's Chapel**, a tiny, simple and contemplative space that is also the oldest building in Edinburgh. Further along, **Crown Square** was created in the reign of King James III (1460-88) as the focal point of the Castle and contains the main sights. On the immediate right of the entrance to the square is the **Scottish National War Memorial**, a grandly sober building that was formerly a barracks and transformed into a shrine to the war dead in 1927. It's worth standing well back get the full impact of it. The **Great Hall**, opposite, is a breathtaking room, with its original timbered roof, Victorian wood-panelling and elaborate displays of medieval weaponry. On the left side of the Square as you face the Great Hall is the **Palace**, which was inhabited by the later Stewart monarchs and also contains the apartment where Mary, Queen of Scots gave birth to James VI in a tiny wood-lined room known as the **Cabinet**. The exhibition on the Palace's first floor, built around the Honours of Scotland (the Scottish crown jewels, along with the recent addition of the Stone of Scone, which was finally brought here from

Westminster Abbey in 1996) is of the standard befitting a national treasure. The Castle is paradise for anyone interested in military history. Various regimental museums house displays of weapons, uniforms and medals. There's also a dog cemetery and dungeons housing **Mons Meg** – a giant 500-year-old cannon. Weather permitting, you can wander along the battlements and admire the views. To round things off, there is a beautifully designed but overpriced café and lots of gift shops crammed with tartan kitsch.

Edinburgh Old Town Weaving Company

555 Castlehill, EH1 (226 1555/www.scotweb.co.uk/ edinburgh/weaving). Bus 35, 325A. **Open** *exhibition* 9am-5.30pm Mon-Sat; 10am-5pm Sun; *shop* 9am-6pm Mon-Sat; 10am-5.30pm Sun; extended hours in summer. **Admission** *tour* £4; £2-£3 concessions; £8 family. **Credit** AmEx, MC, V. **Map** p44 A1.

Though the workers on the looms of this noisy attraction wear earmuffs, it's not quite loud enough for visitors to need them. It is possible to wander round some of the tartan looms as they work, before buying their output in the shop. There is also a guided tour through an exhibition about the production of tartan – 'from sheep to shop', the chance to have a go at weaving tartan yourself, and an exhibition of tartan through the ages.

The Hub

348 Castlehill, EH1 (Edinburgh's Festival Centre 473 2002/Edinburgh International Festival 473 2099/ Hub tickets 473 2000/hub@eif.co.uk). Bus 35, 35A. **Open** *The Hub & shop 9.30am-5.30pm daily; ticket line Apr-July 9.30am-5.30pm Mon-Sat; Aug, Sept 9.30am-8pm Mon-Sat; 10am-8pm Sun; Festival extended hours (phone for details).* **Admission** free. **Credit** *tickets* AmEx, DC, MC, V. **Map** p44 A1.
The Tolbooth St John's Church was built as the Victoria Hall for the Established Church General Assembly in 1844, following the 'Disruption' of the previous year. Having fallen out of use as a church in the 1960s, in 1999 it was lovingly refurbished using the highest-quality craftsmanship for the Edinburgh International Festival, which has its offices in the roof. The bold colour scheme of the Assembly Hall upstairs – said to adhere to Pugin's original palette but audacious nonetheless – is worth seeing all by itself. The rich, red stairwell is decorated with some 200 plaster statues by Jill Watson of people who have performed in the International Festival over the years.

Scotch Whisky Heritage Centre

354 Castlehill, EH1 (220 0441/ www.whisky-heritage.co.uk). Bus 35, 35A. **Open** *Apr-Sept 9.30am-6.30pm daily (last tour 4.30pm); Oct-Mar 10am-5.30pm daily (last tour 4.30pm).* **Admission** £5.50; £2.75-£3.85 concessions; £13.50 family. **Credit** AmEx, DC, MC, V. **Map** p44 A1.
A blatantly tourist-oriented attraction with guides who take the visitor through rooms illustrating the processes by which the Scottish national drink is made, followed by a ghost-train-like tour through various tableaux on the history of distilling and ending up with a free dram in the tasting bar. Overall, it's well thought-out, if a bit too long. The shop has some good blends but is distinctly lacking in single malts – best to buy them further down the High Street. If you're in a group, ask about discounts.

Lawnmarket

The **Lawnmarket** is the part of the Royal Mile between the Hub and the traffic lights. It is named after the cloth that was sold here, known as 'lawn', and boasts a fine example of an Edinburgh townhouse. **Gladstone's Land** (*see page 44*), a property dating from 1550, was extensively rebuilt by an ancestor of Prime Minister William Gladstone 70 years later and is now owned by the National Trust for Scotland. The 16th-century interior, with its oriel-shaped balcony and segmental arch, are all well preserved, but the house is only open between April and October.

There are numerous closes and wynds to investigate on the Lawnmarket. On the north side they run through to the Mound and include Mylne's Court, which leads to the public access to the Scottish Parliament Debating Chamber (*see page 46* **Order! Order!**) and James's Court, where James Boswell lived and was visited by Dr Johnson. While in the restored 18th-century courtyard at the bottom of the latter, one might feel the tug of **The Jolly Judge** (*see page 148*), a cosy pub with an open fire and a wooden ceiling painted with flowers and fruit. Robert Burns stayed in a house on Lady Stair's Close on his first visit to Edinburgh, so it is appropriate that Lady Stair's House, built in 1622, has been turned into the **Writers' Museum** (*see page 44*), which displays relics of Burns, Sir Walter Scott and Robert Louis Stevenson.

The entrances to the wynds on the south side of the Lawnmarket lead through to the raised pavement above Victoria Street. **Riddles Close** leads into two courtyards; it was here that David Hume first lived in Edinburgh, and from here that he published his *Political Discourses*. Brodie's Close was the home of the notorious Deacon Brodie, a respected member of Edinburgh society who led a double life as a burglar. He was put to death outside St Giles' Cathedral, ironically on a gibbet he had designed himself. The ugly block of the Scottish Parliament offices on the corner of George IV Bridge is the only modern architectural carbuncle on the Royal Mile.

At this point the Royal Mile is intersected by George IV Bridge on the right and the Mound, winding down to Princes Street, on the left. The Mound was constructed at the end of the 19th century, using the excavated spoil created by the building of the New Town. It is dominated by the head office of the Bank of Scotland, which was initially of clear classical design, but the baroque flourishes added in the 1860s make it look more like a palace as it gazes imperiously over the New Town. It is especially striking when floodlit at night. The Bank has a collection of maps, notes and banking paraphernalia, which is on view at the **Museum on the Mound** (*see page 44*) during banking hours in the summer. A relaxed coffee house, **Common Grounds** is a convenient watering hole on the Mound and has a daunting but delicious range of coffees. Past here and to the left is the Gatehouse of the Church of Scotland New College and Assembly Hall, which has been pressed into service as the temporary premises of the Scottish Parliament until its custom-built home at Holyrood is completed in 2003. From the entrance, the view back up towards the Castle is a classic Edinburgh image, immortalised in countless photographs.

George IV Bridge leads south towards **Greyfriars Bobby** and the **Southside**. On the left is the monumental block of the National Library, facing the Central Library, which contains the Edinburgh, Scottish and reference rooms.

Gladstone's Land

477B Lawnmarket, EH1 (226 5856/www.nts.org.uk). Bus 35, 35A. **Open** *Apr-Oct* 10am-5pm Mon-Sat; 2-5pm Sun (last entry 4.30pm). **Admission** £3.20; £2.20 concessions; £8.60 family. **Map** p44 A1.

This National Trust for Scotland property is kept in the style that the former owner, Thomas Gledstanes, would have had it in the 17th century. Gledstanes bought the six-storey property in 1617 and extended it forward into the street to create room for an arcade and booths at the front. The NTS style of display is not really suited to such confined rooms, but the guides are helpful and help make this an essential stop in any tour of the Royal Mile that hopes to get under the un-soaped skin of historic Edinburgh.

Museum on the Mound

Bank of Scotland Head Office, the Mound, EH1 (529 1288). Bus 23, 29, 45. **Open** *early June-early Sept* 10am-4.45pm Mon-Fri; closed Sat, Sun & mid-Sept to early June. **Admission** free. **Map** p44 B1.

This small museum displays some of the Bank of Scotland's collection of old documents, banking

Writers' Museum – a museum about writers.

artefacts and old notes and coins. The bank was founded by the Parliament of Scotland in 1695 and is one of the few institutions created by that parliament to have survived.

Writers' Museum

Lady Stair's House, Makars' Court, Lawnmarket, EH1 (529 4901). Bus 35, 35A. **Open** 10am-5pm Mon-Sat; *Festival also* noon-5pm Sun. **Admission** free. **Map** p44 A1.

Lady Stair's House, built in 1622, provides a suitable Old Town environment to contemplate the combined literary might of Robert Burns, Sir Walter Scott and Robert Louis Stevenson. The exhibits are skewed towards memorabilia – Scott's chess set, Burns' snuff box and the like – but the museum provides a suitable atmosphere to contemplate the greats of Scottish literature. Other Scottish writers,

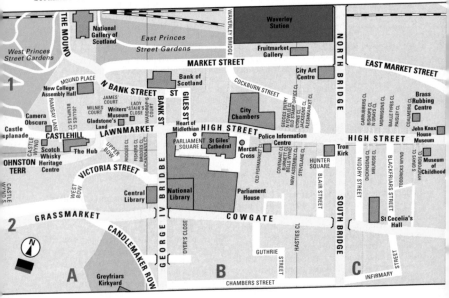

including contemporary authors, are featured in the museum's programme of temporary exhibitions. The courtyard immediately outside the museum has been designated Makars' Court, after the old Scots word for poet, and contains inscriptions commemorating famous Scottish writers, from the 14th century to the present.

High Street above the Bridges

Daniel Defoe called the High Street 'the largest, longest and finest street for buildings and number of inhabitants, not in Britain only, but in the world'. The section above the Bridges is undeniably impressive and was used in the film version of Thomas Hardy's *Jude the Obscure* as a stand-in for Oxford. The High Court of Justiciary, the supreme criminal court in Scotland, stands at the crossroads, newly graced with a bronze statue of David Hume, absurdly (for a 1997 statue of an 18th-century philosopher) garbed in classical dress. Round the back of the Court, in Giles Street, **Pâtisserie Florentin** (*see page 139*) is a fashionable place to down coffee and cake. It is worth remembering its extended opening hours if you're partial to a cup of joe in the late evening.

The three brass bricks laid into the pavement opposite Hume mark the place where the last public hanging in Edinburgh took place: of George Bruce on 21 June 1864; it was watched by 20,000 people. Next to the bricks is the building where Scottish Parliamentary committees meet, with the **Parliament Visitor Centre** taking up the ground floor. Built in 1818 to a design based on the Acropolis in Athens, this block forms one wall of Parliament Square. Parliament House runs along the back of the square. The great hall inside is used by lawyers from the adjoining District Court, Court of Session and High Court.

The Heart of Midlothian, laid out in cobblestones by the roadside near the entrance of **St Giles' Cathedral** (*see page 46*), marks the spot of the old Tolbooth Prison, where executions took place, the victims' heads frequently being displayed afterwards. It is a local custom to spit on this spot. St Giles' is where John Knox preached the Reformation. For the pedantic, the fabric of the building itself is referred to as St Giles', while the church is known as the High Kirk of Edinburgh. The **Lower Aisle Restaurant**, entered round the corner on the south side, is good for a reasonably priced lunchtime bite among lawyers over from the courts.

Although it is an open square now, Parliament Square used to be crowded by many shops and 'lucken booths' – the lockable shops or booths built in the 15th century to offset the cost of building St Giles'. In the shadow of the Mercat Cross, east of the cathedral, traders struck deals in a

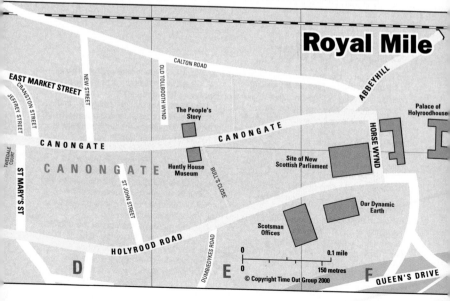

Royal Mile

thriving commercial climate. Executions were carried out here, too, and it is where royal proclamations are read out.

The City Chambers face St Giles' and the Mercat Cross from the other side of the road. Completed in 1761, and thus one of the first truly Georgian buildings in Edinburgh, it was originally the Royal Exchange but failed because traders still preferred to do their business in the open air at the Mercat Cross. The building was also an attempt to bury Mary King's Close, both literally and in people's memories. During the plague in 1645, Mary King's Close was subjected to a brutal form of quarantine that involved the whole close being blocked up and all its inhabitants left to die. Butchers were sent in later to dismember the corpses. Large sections of the buildings are still intact amid the City Chambers' foundations. The close is reputed to be one of the most haunted places in Scotland and even sceptics can find it eerie. In one room the ghost of a little girl has been placated with gifts – dolls, sweets and coins – left by visitors.

Further down the High Street, just past the **Police Information Centre** (*see below*), is the Fringe Office, the epicentre of Edinburgh Festival Fringe activity. During August the pavements are close to impassable due to snaking queues for tickets, performers in weird costumes pressing flyers on passers-by and the crowds who throng around the street performers.

Police Information Centre

188 High Street, EH1 (226 6966). Bus 35, 35A. **Open** *May-Aug* 10am-10pm daily; *Sept, Oct, Mar, Apr* 10am-8pm daily; *Nov-Feb* 10am-6pm daily. **Admission** free. **Map** p44 B1.

Even the police in Edinburgh have a museum of sorts, having turned their fully functional information centre into the Police Information Centre. Not that there's much to see: a bit of history of policing in Edinburgh and a couple of cases with memorabilia. But that does include one artefact covered in the cured skin of executed serial killer William Burke. Yummy.

St Giles' Cathedral

High Street, EH1 (225 4363/visitors' centre 225 9442). Bus 35, 35A. **Open** *Easter to mid-Sept* 9am-7pm Mon-Fri; 9am-5pm Sat; 1-5pm Sun; *mid-Sept to Easter* 9am-5pm Mon-Sat; 1-5pm Sun. **Services** 8am (holy communion), noon (daily service) weekdays; 8am, 10am, 11.30am, 6pm (recital of music), 8pm (evening service) Sun. **Admission** free; donations welcome. **Map** p44 B1.

There has been a church on the site of St Giles' Cathedral since 854. The oldest remnants are the four pillars surrounding the Holy Table in the centre, which date from around 1120. The ornate crown spire they support was completed in 1495. St Giles' suffered the usual destruction wrought by the English armies and the Reformation. After the dust had settled John Knox (1505-72) spent 12 years as its parish minister. Charles I made it a cathedral in 1633, and it retained its status as a Presbyterian cathedral even after bishops were banished in the Glorious Revolution of 1688.

Order! Order!

The decision of the referendum in the autumn of 1997 to create a Scottish Parliament carried one weighty problem: where to put the thing. Edinburgh already had one Parliament building, the L-shaped Parliament Hall and High Court of the Justiciary, built in 1639 on Parliament Square next door to St Giles' Cathedral on the High Street. The large Hall, 37m (122 feet) long with a 12-metre (42-feet) wide hammer-beam roof, however, had been used by the Scottish Law Courts since the last Scottish Parliament was dissolved in 1707.

Prior to the failed referendum for a Scottish Assembly in 1979, the main hall of the Royal High School on Regent Terrace had been converted into a debating chamber. So the pavement outside the school, opposite St Andrew's House, seemed

an auspicious site for the permanent vigil for a Scottish Parliament that was kept there between 1992 and 1997.

The government thought otherwise, and it was decided to create a modern purpose-built building. Leith, where the Scottish Office is sited next to Victoria Docks, had its advocates. So, indeed, did Glasgow. But in the event the site of an old brewery at the bottom of the Royal Mile, opposite the Palace of Holyroodhouse, was chosen. In the meantime, the democratic process of the devolved Scottish Parliament takes place at the top of the Royal Mile.

The main debating chamber of the Church of Scotland General Assembly Hall, off the Lawnmarket, is where the actual Parliament meets. Access to the public viewing gallery is via Mylne's Court, either

Inside, a great vaulted ceiling shelters a medieval interior dominated by the banners and plaques of many Scottish regiments. The main entrance takes visitors past the West Porch screen, which was originally designed as a royal pew for Queen Victoria. The dazzling West Window is by Icelandic stained-glass artist Leifur Breidfjord and was dedicated to Robert Burns' memory in 1984.

The organ is an even more recent addition, from 1992, with a glass back revealing the workings. The Knights of the Thistle have their own chapel, an intimate panelled room with intricate wooden carvings of thistles, roses and shamrocks, divided into Knights' stalls.

Cockburn Street & the Bridges

The atmosphere of Cockburn Street, on the left, tends to fluctuate with the vitality of youth culture, but it has been looking tired in that regard for a few years now. A range of identikit clothing stores notwithstanding, it veers towards the biker end of hippie, with New Age influences starting to nose their way in. The arrival of shops selling upmarket craft items, and two modern art spaces, the **Collective Gallery** and **Stills Gallery** (for both, *see page 49*), hasn't completely shaken off the scent of patchouli. The Scotsman Steps are a convenient but steep route down to the **City Art Centre** and the **Fruitmarket Gallery** (for both, *see page 49*).

The area around the **Tron Kirk**, on the corner with South Bridge, was the traditional gathering place for revellers bringing in the

New Year until Edinburgh's official Hogmanay celebrations began in 1993 and the focus moved down to Princes Street. The Kirk is now used as the **Old Town Information Centre** (*see page 49*) from March to September. **Hunter Square**, beside it, was given an overhaul a few years ago to make it a pleasant place to sit and watch the world go by. The **City Café** may have been superseded as one of the capital's hippest bar and café joints since it opened in the late 1980s, but it's still an attractive, well-designed, cosmopolitan place to enjoy a drink or a meal.

At the traffic lights here, the High Street is cut in two by North Bridge and South Bridge, known together as 'the Bridges' and built to open up the New Town in the late 18th century. Although South Bridge looks like a continuous street, it is in fact supported by 19 massive arches, only one of which is visible. The last building on the left of North Bridge, looking towards the New Town, is the rugged, iconic building that housed Scotsman Publications (publishers of the *Scotsman*, *Scotland on Sunday* and the *Evening News*) for the past century. Purpose-built for the company, it was vacated in 1999 for new premises at Holyrood and transformed into a luxury hotel. At the front of the building, there's an enclosed spiral staircase that provides a short cut down to Market Street and Waverley Station, but don't use it unless you have to or actually enjoy the stench of stale urine.

from the Lawnmarket or Mound Place. Wednesdays and Thursdays are the best times to catch the Parliament in session.

Down the road on George IV Bridge is the Committee Chambers building with the Scottish Parliament Visitor Centre, a shop and information desk. With only a few screens setting out, in simple terms, the Parliament's powers and objectives there isn't a lot in the main room of the Visitor Centre that couldn't be condensed into a pamphlet. But there are also detailed architects' models and plans of the permanent Parliament building being constructed at Holyrood, and facsimiles of a few interesting historical documents, such as the Roll of the first Parliament in 1293, an act from 1457 banning the playing of football and golf and the record of proceedings of the final day of the last Parliament.

The **General Assembly Hall** – temporary home to the Scottish Parliament.

Scottish Parliament Visitor Centre & Shop

George IV Bridge, EH1 (348 5000/ www.scottish-parliament.com). Bus 23, 28, 45 **Open** 10am-5pm Mon-Fri (from 9am Tue-Thur when parliament is sitting); some Saturdays in summer; closed Sun. **Admission** free. **Map** p44 B1.

Tron Kirk – how inspiring. *See page 49.*

It is the entirely believable setting for foul murders in several Edinburgh-set detective thrillers.

City Art Centre

2 Market Street, EH1 (529 3993/www.cac.org.uk). Bus 3, 12, 16, 17, 24. **Open** 10am-5pm Mon-Sat; closed Sun; *Festival* phone for opening times. **Admission** free; charge for occasional exhibitions. **Credit** MC, V. **Map** p44 C1.

Built as offices for the *Scotsman* newspaper towards the end of the 19th century, this six-storey building was converted into the City Art Centre in 1979. It is funded by the City of Edinburgh Council and has been described as the 'Ford Cortina of art galleries', in as much as it puts on exhibitions for all the family. Past successes have included such block-buster exhibitions as Star Trek as well as shows of Chinese artefacts and contemporary photography. It frequently hosts temporary exhibitions drawn from the city's collection of 19th- and 20th-century Scottish art, although sadly the bulk of this is in semi-permanent storage. Cultural consumerism is encouraged in the gallery's shop, and relaxation in the ground-floor licensed café.

Collective Gallery

22-28 Cockburn Street, EH1 (220 1260). Bus 35, 35A. **Open** phone for opening times. **Admission** free. **Credit** *shop* AmEx, MC, V. **Map** p44 B1.

Recently reopened after a Lottery-funded refit, the Collective is one of the city's most vibrant exhibition spaces and now boasts a resource centre, the so-called 'Lounge', with an appropriate line-up of comfy chairs for use both by the casual browser and the keen researcher. There is also what is intriguingly called the 'Mind Bar', with bar stools, an array of art mags to flick through and glasses of water – no liquor, sadly – for the thirsty. Established in 1984, the Collective is known for showcasing work by the most dynamic artists on Scotland's art scene. Besides trumpeting local talent, the artist-run gallery has a track record for guest-curated shows that bring together established artists from further afield. The shows in the three-roomed space are not consistently strong but there is always a sense of adventure on entering the gallery to confront a video work or a sculptural agglomeration. The small Project Room has likewise carved itself a niche as a space to be reckoned with. Hosting a programme of often debut, solo shows, it gives a glimpse of who might be who in contemporary Scottish art.

Fruitmarket Gallery

45 Market Street, EH1 (225 2383/ info@fruitmarket.co.uk/www.fruitmarket.co.uk). Bus 3, 12, 16, 17, 24. **Open** 11am-6pm Mon-Sat; noon-5pm Sun; *Festival* extended hours (phone for details). **Admission** free. **Credit** *shop* AmEx, MC, V. **Map** p44 B1.

Next door to Waverley Station, this one-time fruit market was given a major overhaul in 1992 by the high-profile Edinburgh architect Richard Murphy.

A two-level rectangular, glass-fronted space, it is billed as Scotland's top contemporary art gallery, through receiving the highest gallery grant from the Scottish Arts Council. As well as hosting touring shows – frequently from Oxford's Museum of Modern Art – which have included exhibitions by Marina Abramovic, Yoko Ono and Kiki Smith, the Fruitmarket curates its own programme of exhibitions. Scotland-based artists with international reputations, such as Martin Boyce and Ross Sinclair and the collaborating duo Stephanie Smith and Edward Stewart, have shown in the space, along with a diverse range of artists from further afield. Over the years the Fruitmarket has also established a tradition of bringing to Britain, often for the first time, work by artists from beyond the Western world, including a hugely popular show of paintings by artists from China. The gallery also operates a strong programme of artist talks and events. The lower floor is partly given over to a stylish café and a well-stocked bookshop selling everything from exhibition catalogues to philosophical treatises.

Stills Gallery

23 Cockburn Street, EH1 (622 6200/ info@stills.demon.co.uk). Bus 35, 35A. **Open** 10am-5pm Tue-Sat; closed Mon, Sun. **Admission** free. **Credit** MC, V. **Map** p44 B1.

Since opening in the late 1970s, Stills has evolved from a primarily photographic space into one of the city's most dynamic contemporary art venues. Revamped and enlarged in 1997 by Edinburgh architects Reiach and Hall in collaboration with Glasgow artist Nathan Coley, the gallery is today a clean-cut, concrete-floored rectangular space. Within the Stills complex there are a mezzanine café, which frequently puts on small exhibitions, digital imagery labs, which can be used if booked in advance, and a small bookshop. The widening of the exhibitions policy has enabled Stills to bring some exciting artists – such as Tomoko Takehashi, Joel-Peter Witkin and Tracey Emin – to Scotland, as well as show work by artists based here, and hence present some of the sharpest contemporary art shows in Edinburgh.

Tron Kirk & Old Town Information Centre

High Street, EH1 (225 1637). Bus 7, 8, 31, 35, 35A. **Open** *Easter-May* 10am-5pm Mon, Thur-Sun; closed Tue, Wed; *June-Sept* 10am-7pm daily; closed Oct-Easter. **Admission** free; donations welcome. **No credit cards. Map** p44 C2.

The Tron Kirk was completed in 1648 and reduced in size to accommodate the South Bridge in 1785. The current steeple was built after the original was destroyed in the fire known as the 'great conflagra-tion' of 1824. The building is now owned by the City Council and houses an informative exhibit about the development of the Old Town, which includes excavated remains of Marlin's Wynd – an early 1600s alley, which was demolished to make way for the Kirk.

Sightseeing

High Street below the Bridges

Over the traffic lights, just behind the upmarket but welcoming Bank Hotel (*see page 111*), **Niddry Street** dips steeply down towards the Cowgate. Its shabby walls have been done up to represent 19th-century Edinburgh in at least one BBC drama, and behind them is a rabbit warren of cellars built into the arches of South Bridge and forgotten. It's an atmospheric place, open to guided tours, but still in the early stages of commercial exploitation. In the 1990s, the financial potential of these subterranean expanses for clubs and art spaces was noted, though there are still areas yet to be opened up. The **Vaults**, just up Niddry Street from the cellars, is a popular night spot. For contrast, the **Medieval Torture Museum** is here too, displaying instruments of torture that were once used on suspected witches in Germany in the Middle Ages. Its range of devices is steadily expanding, and it hopes to be able to lay claim to the dubious honour of being the largest of its kind in the world but at the moment it is only accessible on the Mercat tour of the Vaults (*see page 54*).

The **Crowne Plaza Edinburgh** (also still referred to as the Scandic Crown, its former name) has been maligned for its individual interpretation of Scottish baronial style. Actually it is a valiant and largely successful attempt to blend into its surroundings. On the right is Blackfriars Street, a street well known to backpackers and hostellers, which also boasts **Black Bo's** (*see page 148*), a pub well on its way to becoming a fully fledged Edinburgh institution.

A tasteful and well-designed glass façade fronts the **Museum of Childhood** (*see below*), opened in 1955 as the first museum in the world to examine the history of childhood. Its founder used to make sure that visitors understood the difference between a museum of childhood and a museum for children, but the multitude of toys, games and displays are good enough to fascinate both kids and adults. The **Brass Rubbing Centre** (*see below*), which is also popular with kids, is on Chalmers Close, just about opposite the museum.

All that saved the awkwardly positioned house that is now the **John Knox House Museum** (*see below*) from demolition in 1830 was reverence for its illustrious former occupant. Now it is widely believed that the leader of the Reformation, who turned Scotland from a Catholic to a Protestant country, never lived there at all, but it is a good job that someone sought to preserve it. It sports many features of fine Old Town houses: timber galleries and gables, overhanging beams and religious quotations and carvings around the outside walls. The house was built by goldsmith James Mossman and inside, as well as exhibits associated with Knox, is a reconstruction of Mossman's workbench. The house is connected to the adjacent **Netherbow Arts Centre**, which contains a 75-seat theatre, storytelling centre and café.

This end of the High Street is the point where the east gate of the city, the Netherbow, used to stand. Down Tweeddale Court, you can see a surviving length of the city wall and sheds that were once used to store sedan chairs. Back out on the High Street, there's a reference to the city boundary in the name of the pub on the corner: **The World's End** (*see page 151*).

Brass Rubbing Centre

Trinity Apse, Chalmers Close, High Street, EH1 (556 4364). Bus 35, 35A. **Open** 10am-5pm Mon-Sat; *Festival also* 10am-5pm Sun. **Admission** free. **Map** p44 C1.

Just up from John Knox House Museum (*see below*), the Brass Rubbing Centre is housed in an airy church, the only surviving fragment of the Gothic Trinity College Church, which was founded in 1460. The centre demonstrates that, although brass rubbing might be a good kid's activity, it has an artistic side, too, particularly when Celtic knots are concerned. Cheery, friendly staff and good schematic guides show how to do it. Rubbings cost from 90p according to size.

John Knox House Museum

43 High Street, EH1 (556 9579). Bus 35, 35A. **Open** 10am-4.30pm Mon-Sat; closed Sun. **Admission** £2.25; 75p-£1.75 concessions. **Credit** MC, V. **Map** p44 C1.

Although it is only probable that the religious reformer John Knox died here in 1572, the belief that he did has been enough to stop one of Edinburgh's oldest residences, built in 1450, from being razed. The house now holds a detailed exhibition on the Scottish Reformation, complete with an audio re-enactment of Knox's debate with the Catholic Mary, Queen of Scots. With such a complex topic,

Knox here: the **John Knox House Museum**.

Museum of Childhood – not just for the littl'uns.

the displays are by necessity very wordy and the house itself is not shown to its best advantage. But the trick of contrasting Knox with royalist James Mossman (who certainly did live here and who made the Scottish Crown on view in the Castle) works well.

Museum of Childhood

42 High Street, EH1 (529 4142). Bus 35, 35A. **Open** 10am-5pm Mon-Sat; *Festival also* 1-5pm Sun. **Admission** free. **Credit** *shop* MC, V. **Map** p44 C2. Don't think yourself too old for this one. This museum, founded by local councillor Patrick Murray in 1955, is about childhood and not a venue for children. Its small rooms and winding staircases are packed with centuries of toys, schoolbooks and kids' paraphernalia. There's so much here that you need to take it slowly to appreciate the masses of tiny objects in dolls' houses, toy circuses and train sets. Some of it is quite recent and frequently evokes a heartfelt 'I had one of those!' from misty-eyed visitors. There are occasional temporary exhibitions and a good shop.

Canongate

The next section of the Royal Mile, the **Canongate**, takes its name from the route taken by the Augustinian canons to the gates of Edinburgh after their arrival at Holyrood in 1128. Outside the city wall, Canongate was an independent burgh from Edinburgh until as recently as 1856.

Recognisable from its clock, bell tower and outside stair, the Canongate Tolbooth was built in 1592 to collect tolls from people entering the city, but it also served as council chamber, police court and prison for the burgh of Canongate. It now houses **The People's Story** (*see page 55*), an absorbing museum of Edinburgh's social history so dedicated to getting the feel right that you can actually smell woodsmoke as you enter. Beneath it lies the Tolbooth Tavern, a classic Edinburgh watering hole. **Huntly House**, opposite, is three timber-framed houses joined into one in 1570 and surmounted by three overhanging white-painted gables of a kind that were once common in the Old Town. It is also a **museum** (*see page 53*), exhibiting artefacts from the earliest-known inhabitation of the area right through the ages.

Few know of **Dunbar's Close Garden**, a secret little park at the end of an unassuming close on the north side of the Canongate, laid out in the manner of a 17th-century garden with ornamental flowerbeds and manicured hedges. It is a beautiful refuge from the summer crowds, with a view of the old Royal High School, which was for many years intended as the site for the Scottish Parliament.

The bell-shaped Dutch design of **Canongate Church** marks it out strongly from the rest of the buildings on the Royal Mile and makes it one of Edinburgh's most individual and attractive churches. It was built for the displaced congregation of Holyrood Abbey, which was destroyed in 1688. It is Edinburgh's military church, but also buried in the churchyard are David Rizzio, murdered secretary of Mary, Queen of Scots, economist Adam Smith and Robert Burns' beloved 'Clarinda' (Mrs Agnes McLehose), for whom he wrote *Ae Fond Kiss*.

Burns' muse is also commemorated by a tea-room, **Clarinda's** (*see page 138*), a little further down. Just on the right side of twee, with patterned plates on the wall and flowers on the tables, it provides the best chance of a light meal at this end of the Canongate. Rather more modern poets are marked at the **Scottish Poetry Library** (*see page 55*), which is down Crichton's Close, on the opposite side of the Canongate to Clarinda's.

There are some attractive houses near the gates of Holyrood, most obviously two well-kept, gleaming white ones, Canongate Manse and Whiteford House, now a Scottish war veterans' residence. White Horse Close is pretty, too. The gabled building at the end was once the inn from where the stage coach to London left. In 1745 it was called into service as the officers' quarters of Prince Charles Edward Stuart's army.

At the bottom of the Royal Mile stands the **Palace of Holyroodhouse** (*see page 54*), originally built by James IV to be near the Abbey, with various additions and refurbishments being made by subsequent monarchs. Despite being burned and looted by Henry VIII's army in 1544, and further damaged in 1650 when Cromwell's army used it as a barracks and accidentally burned down the south wing, its finished form radiates a combination of solidity and elegance. The purpose of the strange, squat building just inside the fence by the main road is unknown. It might have been a bathhouse, or perhaps a doocot (where 'doos' or pigeons nest).

Holyrood Abbey, now an irreparable ruin, was founded by David I in 1128. It was sacked by Edward II in 1322, damaged in 1544 and 1570 with the loss of the choir and transepts and violated further by a Presbyterian mob in 1688.

Opposite the gates of Holyroodhouse is the site of the new **Scottish Parliament**, now scheduled for completion in autumn 2003.

Witches & wynds

Descending from either side of the Royal Mile are 61 closes and wynds: narrow, steeply sloping passageways with houses towering six or even ten storeys above. The word 'close' refers to an alley that is open only at one end and could be closed at night and is still used today to refer to the central stairwell in tenements; a 'wynd' is an alley that is open at both ends. During the Middle Ages, Edinburgh was one of the most overcrowded cities in Europe and these alleys were the most densely populated and sordid areas of all. Walking tours through and under these medieval closes combine stories of historical brutality with tales of ghosts and the supernatural.

Not all guided tours as as fanciful as the ghosts and ghoulie tours, however. During the Fringe, there are free tours of the Royal Mile, lead by the **Edinburgh Festival Voluntary Guides Association**. The tours last about two hours and leave every ten minutes for an hour in the morning and the afternoon. All year, the **McEwan's 80/- Edinburgh Literary Pub Tour** makes the most of the fact that many of Edinburgh's more prominent writers were partial to a drop or two. Lead by a pair of arguing Edinburgh

residents – Clart and McBrain – the tour visits pubs from the Grassmarket to the New Town and concentrates on past, not contemporary, writers.

Mary King's Close, the historically most terrifying and supernaturally most potent of Edinburgh's closes, is now buried under the City Chambers, inaccessible except via the trip operated by **Mercat Walking Tours**. The story of the close is horrific. All the street's residents were killed during an epidemic of the Black Death. What is most shocking is that the City Fathers walled off the close in a failed attempt to quarantine the plague, denying everyone who lived there both food and water. It is difficult for the guide's stories to compete with the unimaginable terror of the past.

Less weighed down by such a single tragedy, other tours highlight the routine tortures, murders and witch hunts of medieval Edinburgh. The walks operated by Mercat Walking Tours and **Robin's Ghost & History Tour** mix tales of the supernatural with local history and offer the opportunity to descend into the buried vaults and streets that run beneath the city. The Mercat tour of the vaults doesn't take itself, or the ghost

Designed by Spanish architect Enric Miralles, it was criticised from the start by a lobby which sees it as an 'unedifying collection of upturned boats'. It is, however, the cornerstone of one of the most radically transformed areas of Edinburgh. The whole lower half of Holyrood Road, which runs parallel to the Canongate, has been refurbished in anticipation of the Parliament with fashionable new apartment blocks, hotels, upmarket shops and the businesslike but attractive new premises of Scotsman Publications.

The first element of the new development to be completed was the multimedia tourist attraction **Our Dynamic Earth** (*see page 54*). With the crags of Arthur's Seat as its backdrop, it stands on the site where James Hutton, 'the father of geology', lived and worked, and uses varied means to tell the story of the planet from the Big Bang to the present day.

Up Holyrood Road, past the plain but striking Queensberry House Hospital, Moray House Teacher Training College and the more mundane surroundings further up, lies the junction with the Pleasance. To the left can be seen parts of the old Flodden Wall. Straight ahead runs the Cowgate, with St Cecilia's Hall, which houses the **Russell Collection of Early Keyboard Instruments** (*see page 55*), past Blackfriars Street on the right-hand side. Turning right up St Mary's Street leads back up to the Netherbow. If you need refreshment before going on, the woody and homely **Holyrood Tavern** is a typical Old Town pub.

Huntly House Museum

142-146 Canongate, EH8 (529 4143). Bus 24, 25, 35, 35A. **Open** *10am-5pm Mon-Sat; Festival also 2-5pm Sun.* **Admission** *free.* **Map** *p45 E2.*

This is a packed, old-fashioned museum in three original tenements opposite the Canongate Tolbooth. There's too much to see for many of the displays to be more than crammed glass cases, but with the guidebook they help form a rounded picture of Edinburgh as it developed from Roman times, through the building of the New Town, to the 19th century. However, it is the tenements themselves, united into a single block in 1570, that are the real museum here. Corners that would once have been whole rooms have been furbished and laid out

stories, too seriously and provides a good insight into the history of the area. Robin's tour is more detached from the history of the Middle Ages and is not as interesting or scary. **Auld Reekie Tours**, on the other hand, being run from the Medieval Torture Museum, do like to dwell on the gruesome, though their Witchcraft & Persecution Tour is apparently led by genuine white witches.

The **Witchery Murder & Mystery Tour**, with your guide Adam Lyal (deceased), doesn't go underground and is more in the tradition of pantomime than a history lecture. But the guide works the crowd effectively, drawing shrieks and giggles if not real fright. An overemployed extra ambushes the tour at various points, dressed as a mad monk or medieval harridan, which is a bit naff although this trip down the Cowgate after dark does suggest that the shady world of Burke and Hare could still exist in contemporary Edinburgh.

Auld Reekie Tours

Medieval Torture Museum, 45 Niddry Street, EH1 (557 4700). Bus 35, 35A. **Open** *phone 10am-10pm daily.* **Tours** *Underground City Tour Sept-June 12.30-3.30pm daily on the half-hour; July, Aug 10.30am-5.30pm daily on the half-hour; Ultimate Ghost & Torture Tour Sept-June 7-10pm on the hour; July, Aug*

One of the city's back alleys.

6-10pm; Witchcraft & Persecution Tour 10pm Fri, Sat; Royal Mile Tour, VIP Tour (Old and New Town), Georgian New Town Tour all by appointment. **Meeting point** *(all tours): Tron Kirk, High Street.* **Tickets** *Underground City Tour £5; Ultimate Ghost & Torture Tour £6; £5 concessions; Witchcraft & Persecution Tour £8; £7 concessions; Royal Mile Tour, VIP Tour, Georgian New Town Tour phone for details.* **Credit** *AmEx, MC, V.* **Map** *p44 C2.*

as they would have been in the past. The building's structure is also fascinatingly visible and there are some real oddities in the collections – the eclectic nature of which is indicated by the inclusion of the National Covenant and Greyfriars Bobby's collar and feeding bowl.

Our Dynamic Earth

Holyrood Road, EH8 (550 7800/ enquiries@dynamicearth.co.uk/ www.dynamicearth.co.uk). Bus 24, 25, 35, 35A. **Open** *Apr-Oct* 10am-6pm daily; *Nov-Mar* 10am-5pm Wed-Sun; closed Mon, Tue. **Admission** £5.95; concessions vary (phone for details); £16.50 family. **Credit** MC, V. **Map** p45 F2.

The gleaming, tent-like entrance hall of this ultra-modern attraction is the tip of a subterranean playground, with simulated earth tremors, a dizzying 'helicopter ride' across glaciers and well-planned displays depicting the different zones of Earth, its weather, flora and fauna. The experience is largely successful, and the acclaim it drew from the public meant that comparisons with the underachieving Dome in London were inevitable. Unfortunately, passage through the experience is one way, meaning that there is no coming back to bits that you find particularly interesting.

Palace of Holyroodhouse

Holyrood Road, EH8 (556 1096). Bus 24, 25, 35, 35A. **Open** *Apr-Oct* 9.30am-6pm daily (last entry 5.15pm); *Nov-Mar* 9.30am-4.45pm daily (last entry 3.45pm). **Admission** £6; £3-£4.50 concessions; £13.50 family. **Credit** AmEx, MC, V. **Map** p45 F1.

Originally built by James IV with refurbishments made by subsequent monarchs, the Palace was frequently used by Queen Victoria when travelling to or from Balmoral, a tradition kept up by the present Queen, who frequently stays here. When she is in residence, the Palace is closed to the public, but when it is open, the furniture, tapestries, paintings and objets d'art from several centuries are on display, as are the private apartments and lavishly decked-out bed of Mary, Queen of Scots. The memory of Mary is indelibly associated with the Palace. In 1576, six months pregnant, she watched as four Scottish noblemen murdered her secretary David Rizzio with the consent of her husband, Lord Darnley, who wanted to kill the baby she was carrying. She fled to Edinburgh Castle and there gave birth to her child, James VI. The Great Gallery alone would make a visit worthwhile. It is 45m (150ft) long and is decked out with over 100 bizarre portraits by Dutch artist Jacob de Wit, who was under contract

---

▶ ## Witches & wynds (continued)

Edinburgh Festival Voluntary Guides

Cannonball House, Castlehill, EH1 (no phone). Bus 1, 6, 34, 35. **Tours** Aug only 10-11am Mon-Sat, 2-3pm daily, every 10mins. **Admission** free.

McEwan's 80/- Edinburgh Literary Pub Tour

Suite 2, 97b West Bow, EH1 (226 6665/ www.scot-lit-tour.co.uk). Bus 2. **Tours** Apr, May, Oct, Nov 7.30pm Thur-Sun; *June-Sept* 7.30pm daily; *Dec-Mar* 7.30pm Fri. **Meeting point** (all tours): the Beehive Inn, Grassmarket. **Tickets** £7; £5 concessions. Phone for details of private tours and literary lunches and suppers.

Mercat Walking Tours

Mercat House, Niddry Street South, EH1 (557 6464/www.mercat-tours.co.uk). Bus 35, 35A. **Open** phone Apr-Sept 9.30am-9pm daily; Oct-Mar 9.30am-5.30pm daily. **Tours** *Mary King's Close Tour* (advance booking essential) Apr-Sept 8 tours daily; Oct-Mar 2 tours daily; *Royal Mile Walk* Apr-Sept 11am, 2pm daily; Oct-Mar 11.15am daily; *Vaults Tour* Apr-Sept 11am-4pm on the hour daily; Oct-Mar noon, 4pm daily. **Meeting point** (all

tours): the Mercat Cross, St Giles' Cathedral, High Street. **Tickets** *Mary King's Close Tour* £5; £3-£4 concessions; *Royal Mile Walk* £6; £3-£5 concessions; *Vaults Tour* £5; £3-£4 concessions. **Credit** MC, V. **Map** p44 B1.

Robin's Ghost & History Tour

12 Niddry Street South, EH1 (557 9933). Bus 35, 35A. **Open** phone Apr-Sept 9.30am-9pm daily; Oct-Mar 9.30am-5.30pm daily. **Tours** *Ghosts & Witches Tour* Apr-Sept 7pm, 9pm daily; Oct-Mar 7pm daily; *Grand Tour* 10am daily; *Vaults Tour* 2.30pm daily. **Meeting point** (all tours): Tourist Information Centre, Princes Street. **Tickets** *Ghosts & Witches Tour* £5; £4 concessions; *Grand Tour* £5; £4 concessions; *Vaults Tour* £5; £4 concessions. **Credit** MC, V. **Map** p314 D2.

Witchery Tours

352 Castlehill, Royal Mile, EH1 (225 6745/lyal@witcherytours.demon.co.uk/ www.witcherytours.com). Bus 35, 35A. **Open** phone 10am-6pm daily. **Tours** (advance bookings only; phone for times) *Ghost & Gore Tour* May-Sept twice in evening; *Murder & Mystery Tour* all year twice in evening. **Meeting point** (all tours): outside Witchery Restaurant, Castlehill. **Tickets** *Ghost & Gore Tour* £7; £4 concessions; *Murder & Mystery Tour* £7. **Credit** AmEx, MC, V. **Map** p44 A1.

Palace of Holyroodhouse – it could almost be Hollywood. *See page 54.*

to Charles II. The King wanted 2,000 years' worth of his ancestors painted and de Wit complied, creating a host of imaginary monarchs and giving every single one, real or fabled, Charles II's protuberant nose. In this room, for a month in 1745, Prince Charles Edward Stuart held dances that captivated Edinburgh society.

The People's Story

163 Canongate, EH8 (529 4057). Bus 24, 25, 35, 35A. **Open** 10am-5pm Mon-Sat; *Festival also* 2-5pm Sun. **Admission** free. **Map** p45 E1.

This intelligently organised museum focuses on the lives of the people of Edinburgh from the late 18th century to the present day. Many of the artefacts and documents stem from the organisation of labour, while the tableaux illustrate the common people's living and working conditions. Use of authentic smells and tape loops enhance the experience. The Tolbooth, which was built in 1591, was used as the Canongate's jail, so the law and disorder section seems particularly appropriate. The video show in the top room puts the whole museum into perspective, while the guidebook contains some fascinating living history anecdotes.

Russell Collection of Early Keyboard Instruments

St Cecilia's Hall, Cowgate, EH1 (museum 650 2805/2806/faculty 650 2427/ www.music.ed.ac.uk/russell). Bus 7, 8, 31, 35, 35A. **Open** 2-5pm Wed, Sat (except public & university holidays); closed Mon, Tue, Thur, Fri, Sun; *Festival* 10.30am- 12.30pm Mon-Sat; closed Sun. **Admission** £3; £2 concessions. **No credit cards**. **Map** p44 C2.

This important collection of 51 harpsichords, spinets and virginals (which produce a note by plucking the strings) and clavichords and early pianos (in which the strings are struck) forms a living museum for restoration, the study of keyboard organology and performance practice. The instruments date from the mid-16th century and many are beautifully painted works of artistic as well as technical merit. The elliptical and serenely decorated St Cecilia's Hall (1763, Robert Mylne) is Scotland's oldest purpose-built concert hall and is still in use – once a year for concerts using the Russell Collection.

Scottish Poetry Library

5 Crichton's Close, Canongate, EH8 (557 2876). Bus 24, 25, 35, 35A. **Open** noon-6pm Mon-Fri; noon-4pm Sat; closed Sun. **Admission** free; donations welcome. **Membership** *annual* £15, £10 concessions. **No credit cards**. **Map** p45 E1.

The emphasis of the library's extensive collection is on 20th-century poetry, written in Scotland in Scots, Gaelic or English. It also has a good collection of older Scottish poetry and contemporary work from around the world. Everyone is welcome to peruse the library and it has a computer for generating specialist lists and bibliographies.

New Town

Epic town planning and grand visions from over 200 years ago have left a spacious inner city, where Georgian splendour is at its grandest.

The New Town originally referred to the development of Princes, George and Queen Streets under a plan by James Craig of 1766. Today the name is used loosely to describe the succession of new town developments running north from Princes Street that were built in the late 18th and early 19th centuries. As a gracious, upmarket residential alternative to the cramped Old Town, the New Town was consciously out to impress. If its wide streets, grassy squares and classical style of architecture contrast sharply with the mood and look of the Old Town today, the difference was even greater when it was built. Shops and offices now occupy the original New Town but further north the quiet, residential streets have changed little over the centuries. Regarded as one of the best examples of romantic classical architecture in the world, the New Town's well-ordered streets and circuses are a delight to wander round.

Princes Street

Princes Street is where the people of Edinburgh shop. It provides a grand dividing line between the Old and New Towns,

combining glimpses of everyday Edinburgh life with some spectacular views. Shops and department stores look south across Princes Street Gardens, with the drama of Edinburgh Castle, the jagged skyline of the Old Town and the brooding presence of Salisbury Crags, Arthur's Seat and Calton Hill delivering a stunning vista. **Princes Street Gardens** occupy the ravine that runs below the Castle, the ridge of the Old Town and Princes Street. They were originally the site of Nor' Loch, and Craig's plans had them as gardens with a central canal. But as early as 1769, private builders were planning to start constructing on the south side of Princes Street, at the east end next to North Bridge. Fortunately for posterity, 14 owners of buildings along Princes Street – including David Hume – presented an interdict to the council to halt all work on the south side, citing Craig's plan and the 'free air, and an agreeable prospect', which had enticed them from the Old Town in the first place. The council wanted to allow building no higher than the level of Princes Street, as exists today at Waverley Market. The battle raged in the courts and went as far as the House of Lords, until being finally

Life's a circus, and a square or two: North West Circus Place.

Looking east along **Princes Street**.

settled by an Act of Parliament in 1816, preserving the gardens as a pleasure ground, in perpetuity.

Today the Princes Street Gardens are well-clipped, rolling swathes of grass, crossed with bench-lined paths. In clement weather, they are an ideal place to rest or stroll. Crossing the bridges in the west garden leads to an interesting walk around the base of Castle Rock and a path that runs from behind the bandstand up to the Castle Esplanade.

Statues of numerous famous city residents edge the gardens. At the west end is Sir James Young Simpson, the Victorian pioneer of the use of chloroform in childbirth who was frequently found self-anaesthetised on the floor of his lab. Allegedly. He stands opposite the coolly classical 1930s building that houses **Fraser's** department store, the first of Princes Street's architecturally inconsistent parade of shops. The broadcaster Moray McLaren famously lambasted the street as 'one of the most chaotically tasteless streets in the United Kingdom'. Originally laid out in the 1780s to form a cohesive face to the Old Town, it is now an endearing mishmash of overdressed Victoriana department stores and more minimalist 20th-century additions. Many of the shops have second- or third-storey cafés or restaurants that offer excellent views up to the Castle and Old Town. Waterstone's (*see page 167*), Boots (*see page 183*) and Jenners (*see page 171*) are all good places to take the weight off shopping-weary legs.

Until recently, town planners and style purists viewed Princes Street as Edinburgh's architectural Achilles' heel. There have been many proposals to implement stylish homogeneity. In 1938 the idea was to rebuild in glass and steel and, in 1958, a series of high-level pedestrian walkways linking each building was proposed. Today's mutterings concerning a shopping mall below street level, with entries from the Gardens, have reached the public enquiry stage of the planning process. Plans to cut back traffic have, however, already come to positive fruition with private cars banned from travelling east along the street.

The Mound

On the corner of Princes Street and the Mound, the statue of the wig-maker turned poet, Allan Ramsay, stands over a floral clock dating from 1903. Although it is usually fairly quiet, the flat, cobbled expanse known simply as the 'bottom of the Mound' is transformed into a hive of activity come the Festival. Clothes stalls, performance artists and musicians jostle for space and attract huge crowds against the grand backdrop of the twin Doric temples of the **National Gallery of Scotland** and the **Royal Scottish Academy** (*see page 58*). These were designed by William Playfair, the 19th-century architect behind many of Edinburgh's classical revival buildings. The plainer and more refined National Gallery was built 20 years after the rather more embellished Royal Scottish Academy, which is topped by sphinxes and an incongruous statue of the young Queen Victoria. Originally the statue was displayed at street level, but it is said that Victoria was displeased by her chubby appearance, and demanded its roof-top elevation to avoid close scrutiny by her subjects.

National Gallery of Scotland

The Mound, EH2 (624 6200/nginfo@natgalscot.ac.uk/ www.natgalscot.ac.uk). Bus 3, 3A, 12, 16, 17. **Open** 10am-5pm Mon-Sat; noon-5pm Sun; *Festival* extended hours (phone for details). **Admission** free except for special loan exhibitions. **Credit** *shop* AmEx, MC, V. **Map** p314 C2.

One of the city's landmark classical revival buildings, the National Gallery was built in 1848 by the prolific Edinburgh architect William Playfair. Originally housing both the **Royal Scottish Academy** (*see p58*) and the National Gallery, it became the latter's exclusive home in 1911. Sumptuously decorated in 'stately home' style, the succession of galleries are bedecked with a rich collection of paintings, sculpture and furniture. From early Florentine and Northern and Italian Renaissance art – including Raphael's *Bridgewater Madonna*, Hugo van der Goes' *Trinity Panel* and the recently acquired *Madonna and Child* by Botticelli – the collection courses through the centuries.

Horsing around outside the **Balmoral Hotel**. *See page 59.*

Poussin's *Seven Sacraments* is a high point, as are Rubens' *The Feast of Herod* and Joshua Reynolds' *The Ladies Waldegrave*. French art is well represented by Watteau, Chardin and those key players of Impressionism, Monet and Pissarro. A lower gallery, built in the 1970s, is given over to Scottish art and luminaries such as Wilkie and Raeburn, painter of the so-called 'Skating Minister' (otherwise known as the *Rev Walker Skating on Duddingston Loch*). The vicar is one of the gallery's big cultural exports and is found on everything from fridge magnets to chocolates (both of which are conveniently on sale in the gallery shop).

Royal Scottish Academy

The Mound, EH2 (225 6671). Bus 3, 3A, 12, 16, 17. **Open** 10am-5pm Mon-Sat; 2-5pm Sun. Closed from early 2001 (*see below*). **Admission** *annual exhibition* £2; free to most other exhibitions. **Credit** *shop* MC, V. **Map** p314 C2.

The Royal Scottish Academy grandly lords it over Princes Street. Built originally to house the Society of Antiquaries and the Royal Society, the robustly neo-classical building was designed by William Playfair in the 1830s. Converted in 1911 into the headquarters of the Royal Scottish Academy, the building today also fills the role of a large-scale temporary exhibitions space. The year is mapped out by annual shows of work by members of the Royal Scottish Society of Watercolourists, the Society of Scottish Artists and the Royal Scottish Academy itself. More gutsy shows are delivered by annual exhibitions of student art. In summer, the RSA's neighbour, the National Gallery, frequently fills the gallery with one of its big Festival exhibitions. Note that the RSA is scheduled to close in early 2001 for a £22-million upgrade and will reopen in mid-2003. The renovation is to include an underground walkway to the National Gallery, due to open in 2005.

East end of Princes Street

Jenners, the world's oldest privately owned department store, commands a corner position on Princes Street and St Andrew Street. Founded in 1838 by two Leith drapers, it was extravagantly rebuilt in 1893 after a fire destroyed the original building. An estimated 25,000 people crowded the streets for the unveiling of its elaborately carved, statue-encrusted frontage, which was inspired by the façade of Oxford's Bodleian Library. Across St Andrew Street stands Scotland's first steel-framed store, built in 1906, and today housing Burton's. It is ornately topped by a group of gilded figures perched on a small belvedere and wrestling with an open-work sphere.

Gothic excess reaches great heights in the **Scott Monument** (*see page 59*), a 61-metre (200-foot) high memorial to Sir Walter Scott, the prolific 19th-century author and promoter of Scotland's romantic past. Dubbed the city's 'medieval space rocket', it stands on the corner of Waverley Bridge (named after Scott's

Waverley novels) and Princes Street. Dominating the skyline – John Ruskin, the 19th-century art critic known for his cutting ripostes, likened it to a misplaced church spire – it was originally to have been sited in the less public residential enclave of Charlotte Square. An advocate of Scottish national dress, Scott is appropriately shown wearing a rustic shepherd's plaid. His dog, Maida, sits at his feet. To the left of the Scott Monument, somewhat overshadowed by its extravagance, is a diminutive statue of the Scots-born Victorian missionary and explorer, David Livingstone.

Princes Street ends with the **Balmoral Hotel** (*see page 105*), a huge late-Victorian edifice. Its clock usually runs three minutes fast to hurry passengers to Waverley Station just down the steps beneath it – except over Hogmanay when it announces the new year to the thousands who throng Princes Street below. Facing the hotel and North Bridge is the regal **General Register House**, which was built in 1774 by Robert Adam, the key member of the famous Adam dynasty of architects. The best impression of what is, perhaps, the most perfect example of classical restraint in Edinburgh is gained from across the road in front of the GPO building. In front of Register House, the statue of the Duke of Wellington, hero of the Battle of Waterloo, gallops towards North Bridge. Looking east along Waterloo Place is a fine view of Calton Hill crowned by the National Monument and the Nelson Monument. Round the corner, on Leith Street, there is a small explosion of 1960s architectural brutalism in the form of the St James Shopping Centre, built on the site of an 18th-century square. On the other side of Register House, West Register Street leads through to St Andrew's Square and George Street and, conveniently, passes the **Café Royal** (*see page 151*). This is not just a good pub to stop off at for a spot of refreshment, but is also an extravagantly dressed, late 19th-century building with murals of, among others, the inventors Michael Faraday and James Watt.

Scott Monument

East Princes Street Gardens, EH2 (529 4068). Bus 3, 3A, 12, 16, 17, 80. **Open** *June-Sept* 9am-8pm Mon-Sat; 10am-8pm Sun; *Oct, Mar-May* 9am-6pm Mon-Sat; 10am-6pm Sun; *Nov-Feb* 9am-4pm Mon-Sat; 10am-4pm Sun. **Admission** £2.50. **No credit cards. Map** p314 C2.
This over-elaborate and ornate counterpoint to the austerity of most of Edinburgh's architecture is a fitting memorial to Sir Walter Scott, who orches-trated George IV's celebrated tartanising visit to Edinburgh in 1822. It was designed by the self-taught architect George Meikle Kemp, and was completed in 1840, 14 years after Scott's death. At 61m (200ft) it is a city-centre landmark.

George Street

The wide and grand **George Street** forms the backbone of the first New Town. In the first half of the 18th century, it was realised that Edinburgh was getting too cramped and, in 1752, a long, wordy pamphlet was published setting out proposals to enlarge the town to the north and south. The proposals were largely down to the work of George Drummond, the Lord Provost at the time, and are remarkable in that they were, for the most part, carried out over the next 80 years. The first stage was the building of North Bridge, which started in 1765. The following year, an architectural competition was held to find a plan for the New Town. It was won by 21-year old James Craig's simple and sensible solution. The layout of three parallel roads – Princes, George and Queen Streets – ended by two squares, replaced Craig's earlier design of radial roads, which was inspired by the Union Jack – a symbol that was a bit too highly charged for the Scots after the 1707 Act of Union. Craig, however, was obviously keen for royal approval. He dedicated his final plan to George III, who in turn had an influence on the names of the streets. George Street is named after the monarch and Princes Street after his sons. The story goes that the original name of St Giles was dropped as it reminded the King of a sleazy quarter of London. The architectural plans are on view in **Huntly House Museum** (*see page 53*) on the Canongate in the Old Town.

St Andrew Square

Today, George Street is home to smart shops and businesses. At its eastern end is St Andrew Square, named after Scotland's patron saint. At its centre stands the Melville Monument. A 40-metre (135-foot) Doric column inspired by Rome's Trajan Column, it is topped by a statue of Henry Dundas, first Earl of Melville, a notorious 18th-century political wheeler dealer. The square has long been the financial heart of Edinburgh. The **Royal Bank of Scotland** has its headquarters in a former mansion on its east side. The mansion was built in 1772 for Sir Laurence Dundas on the site that, in Craig's plan, was reserved for St Andrew's Church. It is set back from the square, and its private lawn is a rare sight in the New Town and a mark of Sir Laurence's political muscle in overruling the council's planning orders. The bank is still a working branch and the sumptuously decorated iron dome of the Telling Room (1860) is open during banking hours. Next door, the **Bank of Scotland** is housed in an outlandishly loud pseudo palazzo with rooftop statues. The banking hall is once again very fine and is also open during banking hours.

To the north of the Square, an explosion of Gothic-cum-medieval architecture is delivered by the **Scottish National Portrait Gallery** (*see below*), at the east end of Queen Street. A confident, late-19th-century building dotted with pinnacles and sculptures of intellectual heroes from down the ages, its red sandstone façade is best seen in the late evening summer sun. It does not, however, fit in with the classical constraint of the rest of the New Town. The huge entrance foyer, decorated with murals recounting Scotland's history, is definitely worth a look. Appropriately, Sir Henry Raeburn lived over the way at 32 York Place. Besides being a portrait artist to Edinburgh's Enlightenment luminaries, Raeburn owned large parts of what is now Stockbridge and was responsible for the building there.

The east end of George Street starts off with the 1940s green and black former Guardian Royal Exchange office. It is Scandinavian in tone, with a vast front door elaborately carved and flanked by columns and bronze figures. Just past it is the **Dome** (*see page 152*), which was once a bank but, like the many other former financial institutions that once lined George Street, it has been transformed into a vast drinking den. Epitomising the grandiose excess of Edinburgh's 19th-century banks, its richly decorated domed interior is also worth taking a look at. It may even have prompted John Ruskin's 1853 critical onslaught. Commenting on the city's liberal use of classical columns, Ruskin declared: 'Your decorations are just as monotonous as your simplicities'. Opposite the Dome is **St Andrew's Church**, built in 1787, which had been intended for the plot of land captured by Dundas. Although the exterior is dwarfed by its surrounding buildings, the interior is no minor achievement in classical grace. It was here that the Assembly of the Church of Scotland was held in May 1843, during which 472 ministers marched out of the church, down Dundas Street to the Tanfield Hall to establish the Free Church of Scotland.

Scottish National Portrait Gallery

1 Queen Street, EH2 (624 6200/ pginfo@natgalscot.ac.uk/www.natgalscot.ac.uk). Bus 8, 12, 16, 17, 25, 25A. **Open** 10am-5pm Mon-Sat; noon-5pm Sun; *Festival* extended hours (phone for details). **Admission** free except for loan exhibitions. **Credit** *shop* AmEx, MC, V. **Map** p306 F4.

Housed in an elaborately pinnacled, Gothic revival edifice, the Portrait Gallery is a must for those wanting to get to grips with Scotland's history or check out its more contemporary heroes and heroines. The foyer is decorated with stunning murals detailing

Going back to your roots

General Register House and West Register House are not only architecturally splendid, they are both working buildings and, together with New Register House and the Edinburgh Room of the Central Library, hold a large number of documents that are useful for anyone wanting to find out more about their Scottish antecedents. The organisational system of the three Register Houses also offers an implausibly Orwellian mix of nomenclanture, which is an object lesson for anyone relying on names to trace their way back through history. The library holds local records and newspapers as well as a wealth of research material on local events such as the Edinburgh International Festival.

Public records in Scotland are held by two departments: the **National Archives of Scotland** (NAS) and the **General Register Office** (GRO). The National Archives are home to a veritable cornucopia of documents: wills, sasines (property records), taxation records, church records and burgh records. The book,

Tracing Scottish Local History (HMSO), is a detailed guide to all these records and how to use them to best effect. The Register Office is, unsurprisingly, where all the parish registers (pre-1855), statutory registers of births, marriages and deaths (from 1855) and census returns (1851-91) are kept, as well as all the later census returns that are not yet available for public access. The registers of births, marriages and deaths, as well as some census records, are indexed on a computer database.

All of which is reasonably obvious. It gets complicated when you try to work out where all these archives and registers are kept: the National Archives are in **General Register House**, at the east end of Princes Street, with an overflow building in **West Register House** on Charlotte Square. Its West Search Room contains maps and plans, records of government departments and microfilm records. It also has a small exhibition of documents illustrating 800 years of Scottish

Don't fancy yours much. Inside the **Scottish National Portrait Gallery**. *See page 60.*

important moments in Scottish history, while paintings of kings and queens, including the tragic figure of Mary, Queen of Scots and Bonny Prince Charlie, give a brilliant visual guide to the rise and fall of the Scottish monarchy. The upper galleries are filled with portraits of statuesque, tartan-dressed lairds and ladies. A further gallery is devoted to 20th-century achievers including designer Jean Muir, dancer

Moira Shearer and writer Irvine Welsh. A downstairs gallery hosts small temporary shows of work by contemporary artists, while one upstairs gallery is becoming increasingly strong on contemporary photography shows by Scotland-based artists and international names – Magnum photographers and the Kobal Photographic Portrait Award have featured in the past.

history and an exhibition devoted to maps and plans. The General Register Office is not in General Register House, it is next door, in **New Register House**, which, just to keep someone amused, is on West Register Street.

Searching the records is an absorbing process, but it is not quick – go armed with as much information from relatives as possible. And if you need to consult the National Archives, it is best to write or email first (but only with specific inquiries) to find where the required documents are kept. The NAS, GRO and the Central Library have leaflets that will help and there are staff who will give advice at the front desks of the various offices. The Scottish Room of the Central Library (downstairs from the Edinburgh Room) also has books on different families and on how to start the search.

Edinburgh Room

Central Library, George IV Bridge, EH1 (242 8030). Bus 23, 28, 45. **Open** *10am-*

8pm Mon-Thur; 10am-5pm Fri; 9am-1pm Sat; closed Sun.* **Admission** *free.* **Map** *p314 C3.*

General Register Office

New Register House, West Register Street, EH1 (334 0380/wood.ccta.gov.uk/grosweb/ grosweb.nsf/pages/home). Bus 3, 3A, 12, 16, 17, 80. **Open** *9am-4.30pm Mon-Fri; closed Sat, Sun.* **Admission** *free.* **Map** *p314 D1.*

National Archives of Scotland

General Register House, 2 Princes Street, EH1 (535 1314/research@nas.gov.uk). Bus 3, 3A, 12, 16, 17, 80. **Open** *9am-4.45pm Mon-Fri; closed Sat, Sun.* **Admission** *free.* **Map** *p314 D1.*

West Search Room

West Register House, Charlotte Square, EH2 (535 1314). **Open** *9am-4.30pm Mon-Fri; closed Sat, Sun.* **Admission** *free.* **Map** *p314 A1.*

The middle of George Street

A flamboyant-looking statue of George IV, erected to mark his visit to Edinburgh in 1822, stands at George Street's junction with Hanover Street. This is a good spot to take in the view. To the north, down Hanover Street past the Royal Botanic Garden and over the Firth of Forth, lies Fife. To the south, you get a full sense of the neo-classical vigour of the Royal Scottish Academy and, beyond, crowning the Mound, the Assembly Hall and New College. The Assembly Hall and New College were built on a direct axis with Tolbooth Church (now **The Hub**, the information centre for Edinburgh International Festival; *see page 43*), which stands behind at the top of the Lawnmarket. From George Street, it appears that the Assembly Hall and New College borrow the church's imposing spire. This architectural pun was no accident on the part of its designer, William Playfair, and would have been well understood by his contemporaries: Tolbooth Church was started in 1842 as the Assembly Hall for the Church of Scotland but, following the Disruption of 1843, the Church split. In designing the Assembly Hall and New College for the newly formed Free Church he obviously felt a little ecclesiastical humour would not go amiss.

Tolbooth Church spire could almost belong to the **Assembly Hall** and **New College**.

Further along George Street are **The Assembly Rooms** (*see page 208*). Built by public subscription in 1787, they became a favoured haunt of Edinburgh's Regency partying set. During the Festival, the building is transformed into one of the Fringe's largest venues. This stretch of George Street was once a popular quarter for literary types. The poet Shelley and his first wife Harriet Westbrook honeymooned at 84 George Street, above today's Victoria Wine shop, and Sir Walter Scott lived around the corner at 39 North Castle Street. No.45 George Street (today Justerini & Brooks) was the headquarters of the influential literary journal, *Blackwood's Magazine*, which counted Henry James and Oscar Wilde among its contributors. More recently, **Milne's Bar** (*see page 152*), on the corner of Hanover and Rose Streets, was a popular 1960s hangout for a generation of Scots writers such as Norman McCraig and Sorley McLean. Their photographs and words still hang on the wall.

Charlotte Square

Concluding George Street is **Charlotte Square**. Named after George III's wife, Queen Charlotte, it was designed by Robert Adam in 1791, just before his death. It is one of Edinburgh's classiest residential enclaves. Adam conceived and designed the frontages as a whole, but each individual house was built separately, with only the façades – discreetly ornamented with sphinxes and pediments – down to him. The **National Trust for Scotland Head Office** (*see page 63*) is at Nos.26-31, on the south side of the square and is open to the public, with a small art gallery, a shop and a handy café. The north side of the square is the best-preserved façade, with the Trust's **Georgian House**, at No.7 (*see page 63*), offering the chance to look at how the interior of a domestic house would have been when the square was built. No.6 is the official residence of Scotland's first minister. A monument to Prince Albert, husband of Queen Victoria, sits in the central grass square overlooked by **West Register House**, a grandly domed and porticoed affair originally built as St George's Church. The square has been home to numerous illustrious residents over the centuries, the most notable being Alexander Graham Bell, the inventor of the telephone, who was born in 1847 at 16 South Charlotte Street.

Just off Charlotte Square is **Young Street**. One of an ordered network of narrow streets that run along either side of George Street, it gives a fuller picture of Craig's New Town plan. Tucked away from the grander streets, this is where the less financially fortunate lived. It is

Passers-by on **Charlotte Square** are blissfully unaware of its grandeur.

also a favoured haunt of one Inspector John Rebus, who drinks at the **Oxford Bar** (3 Young Street; 539 7119) in Ian Rankin's best-selling detective novels.

To the north of Young Street, parallel to George Street, are **Queen Street** and **Queen Street Gardens**. These gardens, like the many others that punctuate the New Town, were created as stretches of disciplined ruralness for the residents of the grand squares and terraces. They remain accessible only to residents. Further along Queen Street, at No.8, is a townhouse built by Robert Adam, and next to it Thomas Hamilton's Royal College of Physicians.

Georgian House

7 Charlotte Square, EH2 (226 3318/www.nts.org.uk). Bus 13, 19, 55, 82. **Open** *Apr-Oct* 10am-5pm Mon-Sat; 2-5pm Sun; closed Nov-Mar. **Admission** £5; £3.50 concessions; free children; group discounts on request. **Credit** *shop* MC, V. **Map** p314 A1.
The National Trust for Scotland has refurbished this prestigious, Robert Adam-designed New Town res-

idence to the sumptuous glory it would have shown when rich businessman John Lamont lived here in the early 19th century. The rooms, from drawing room to kitchen, contain period furnishings, right down to the newspapers. There's a guide in each room to relate all the anecdotes about lifestyle and furnishings, and everything can be looked at right up close – so long as you don't touch.

National Trust for Scotland Head Office

26-31 Charlotte Square, EH2 (243 9300/restaurant reservations 243 9399/www.nts.org.uk). Bus 13, 19, 55, 82. **Open** *Gallery* 10am-5pm Mon-Sat; noon-5pm Sun (last entry 4.30pm). *Shop* 10am-5.30pm Mon-Sat; closed Sun. *Coffee House* 10am-6pm daily. *Restaurant* 6-11pm daily. **Admission** free. **Credit** *shop* MC, V. **Map** p314 A1.
The National Trust for Scotland has spent £13.6 million restoring these four townhouses to their original state and making them suitable as modern offices. The public rooms, which are entered at No.28, allow visitors to see many of the original elements, such as plasterwork and wallpaper. Three

galleries upstairs give the NTS the opportunity to show off some of its art collection, including important works by 20th-century Scottish artists, which are on loan to the Trust and are displayed in the grand drawing room, featuring some impressive Regency furnishings. There are pointers to the Trust's other properties and considerable land-holdings around Scotland as well as information on the conversion itself. The ground-floor coffee house is a stylish place to pause during the day, while the restaurant at No.27 is proving popular at night.

Dundas Street & environs

A gridiron of grandly ordered streets continues north from Queen Street down the hill to the Water of Leith. The streets are lined with solid, well-proportioned sandstone residences turned slate grey with age. The area around **Dundas Street** is considered to be the heart of today's New Town, although it was constructed after the first 18th-century new town. It is one of six further developments built in the early 19th century as speculative ventures on the part of the landowners cashing in on Edinburgh's need for upmarket dwellings. Scottish property laws allowed landowners to stipulate architectural style, so the New Town's cohesive classical formality is played out with little interruption. Resolutely residential and exclusive, these new areas did not wish to attract outsiders or the Old Town hoi polloi. Apart from churches, there were originally no public buildings, squares or markets: only in recent decades have shops and restaurants opened along the main roads. There is still a classy air to the area, but it is now home to a wider social mix. The best approach to exploring this part of the New Town is simply to follow your feet as it is nearly impossible to get completely lost.

The New Town has been home to many well-known people, who are often remembered on stone-carved inscriptions on the front of their former residences. Robert Louis Stevenson lived just below Queen Street Gardens at 17 Heriot Row. It is said that as a sickly child he looked onto these gardens and found inspiration for his novel *Treasure Island*. Later, as a young bohemian in his signature black velvet jacket, he bypassed the elegance of the New Town and headed uphill to the Old Town and its more rough-and-ready drinking haunts. Dundas Street contains a number of private art galleries and, at No.13, the **Edinburgh World Heritage Trust** (557 5222). Its small library is open to the public (phone for opening times) and is packed with information on the city and its architecture. Cutting across Dundas Street is **Great King Street**. Built in 1804, it is a

Just your average New Town pad.

brilliant declaration of the classical New Town look. Fanlights, windows and even chimney stacks are symmetrically arranged to give maximum impact to the architectural grandeur. Another famous New Town resident, JM Barrie, author of *Peter Pan*, lodged as a student at No.3.

Just beyond lies Drummond Place, named after George Drummond, six-times Lord Provost and driving force behind the building of the first New Town. Built in the shape of a horseshoe with a central garden and cobbled roads, it sums up the New Town's ethos for urban living: smart tenement buildings which were consciously designed to look like upmarket houses with ample front doors and high ceilings overlook a spacious oasis of greenery. Doubtless finding pleasure in all this was Compton Mackenzie, the author of *Whisky Galore,* who lived at 31 Drummond Place.

The Moray Estate is one of the grandest of the New Town's residential quarters. It lies to the west of Howe Street and is best approached from Heriot Row. Built on land belonging to the Earl of Moray in 1822, this development is formed by a succession of linked crescents. The architectural climax comes in Moray Place. An overbearing, 12-sided circus, punctuated by sturdy columns set into the façade, this is New Town classical formality at its proudest.

Stockbridge

More than a village, Stockbridge provides a link to Edinburgh's spectacular Royal Botanic Garden and the Water of Leith walkway.

At first glance Stockbridge appears unremarkable. The area joins seamlessly to the city, but it started life as an outlying village clustered round the old wooden Stock Bridge over the Water of Leith, to the north-west of the New Town. Less architecturally conformist than many of Edinburgh's suburbs, Stockbridge retains the air of a self-contained township with its turn-of-the-century tenemented streets, genteel terraces and occasional villas. Historically, it was a centre of small-scale industry when mills and tanneries began to line the banks of the Water of Leith back in the early 18th century. Later came breweries and filth. Downhill from the New Town, the river soon became an open sewer and general rubbish tip. Today, however, the river has been cleaned up and the Water of Leith walkway is one of Edinburgh's quiet and scenic secrets.

Pop into the **Bailie** for a bevvy.

St Stephen Street & environs

In the late 1960s and early 1970s cheap rented accommodation turned Stockbridge into a bohemian and student heartland. Recent gentrification has blunted the groovy edge but second-hand shops still line Stockbridge's main shopping area of **Deanhaugh Street** and **Raeburn Place**. **St Stephen Street**, just south of the bridge, was once home to Nico (of Velvet Underground fame) and a wealth of junk-cum-antique shops, only a few of which remain. On the corner is the **Bailie**, a cosy drinking hole that has several photographs showing Stockbridge in its earlier days. Further along are Regency-style shops and a marooned old gateway that is the last vestige of Stockbridge's meat and vegetable market. It was built in 1826 after a public campaign led by one Captain Carnegie, and was a coup for local shoppers. Town officials had hoped that Stockbridge, like neighbouring New Town, would aspire to residential classiness and strive to be a market-free zone.

A good sense of the formidable construction work that went into the making of the New Town is given where the end of India Street looms over North West Circus Place, just up the hill from the Bailie bar. A proper junction would have made too much of a gradient and the raised end of India Street, reached by the steps to the left of the post office, shows just how much the roads were raised above ground level to give the houses basements and to flatten out the land. Along India Place, on the corner with Gloucester Street, is Duncan's Land, one of the area's oldest buildings. Now a restaurant, the sturdy stone and rubble house dates from the late 1790s. It was the birthplace, in 1796, of David Roberts, the painter of Middle Eastern souks and Pharaonic temples, known for his penchant for dressing up as a sheik. The carved lintel, inscribed 'Fear Only God 1650', is in fact 'borrowed' from an earlier building. Opposite Duncan's Land, a mass of modern flats stands on the site of a series of streets demolished in the name of slum tenement clearance in the 1960s and 1970s.

The present **Stock Bridge** was built in 1900. Just to the right, off Kerr Street, is **Hamilton Place**. Along it, past the Theatre Workshop and Saxe-Coburg Street, is the low-slung, neo-classical **Edinburgh Academy** on Henderson Row. Built in 1824, it was the fittingly austere location for the filming of *The Prime of Miss Jean Brodie*. Down Saxe-Coburg Street itself lies the quaint 1820s square, Saxe-Coburg Place.

Not all building in 19th century Edinburgh was as classically regimented as the New Town. **The Colonies**, which lie on the north side of Glenogle road, between Saxe-Coburg Place and the Water of Leith, are the first of a series of artisan dwellings that were built by the Edinburgh Co-operative Building Company from the 1860s onwards. They defy Edinburgh's usual preference for tenements. Eleven narrow streets (named after members and supporters of the co-operative) are lined with two-storey stone terraces. What makes them unusual is their 'double sidedness'. The entrance to the upper level dwelling is from external steps that run from one street, with access to the ground floor dwelling from the opposite side.

The **Royal Botanic Garden** (*see page 68* **Green fingers & glasshouses**), **Inverleith Park** and **Inverleith House** (*see below*) are across Bridge Place, at the west end of Glenogle Road and right, along Arboretum Place.

Inverleith House

Royal Botanic Garden, Inverleith Row, EH3 (552 7171/www.rbge.org.uk/inverleith-house). Bus 8, 23, 27. **Open** (phone to check first) 10am-5pm Wed-Sun; closed Mon, Tue. **Admission** free. **No credit cards. Map** p305 C1.

A sturdy but stately stone mansion with brilliant views of Edinburgh's skyline, Inverleith House dates back to the late 18th century. It was converted to a

In the leaves in **Inverleith Park**.

gallery in 1960 and until 1984 was home to the **Scottish National Gallery of Modern Art** (*see page 69*). Situated slap bang in the middle of the **Royal Botanic Garden** (*see page 68* **Green fingers & glasshouses**), Inverleith House enjoys a degree of splendid isolation from the city-centre art scene. Yet it is well worth venturing past the herbaceous borders, as this is one of Edinburgh's finest gallery spaces, with a strong and zappy exhibitions programme. The House is now run by the Botanic Gardens, which is why the shows make frequent reference to the natural world, though they are not confined to exhibitions of botanical paintings and displays from the Botanics' extensive archives. Callum Innes has shown here, along with Myron Stout, Agnes Martin and famed bricklayer Carl Andre. As well as showing work by international artists, Inverleith House keeps a sharp eye on local, up-and-coming artists, by curating group shows of home-grown talent and hosting the Absolut Scotland Open art competition.

The Raeburn Estate

Back in Stockbridge, just off Deanhaugh Street at the top of Leslie Place, lies the **Raeburn Estate**. An early-19th-century speculative

Visitors get to see the hole picture in **Inverleith House**.

property development by the artist Sir Henry Raeburn, it seduced the moneyed classes to move down the hill. Although the whole is less triumphal in scale than the New Town, **St Bernard's Crescent** is an architectural heavyweight, with thick Grecian columns and vast front doors. Over the way is the rather more delicate **Danube Street**, with wrought-iron balconies and rooftop balustrades. Behind this show of architectural propriety, Dora Noyce ran a brothel up until the 1980s. Known for serving liquid refreshment from a silver teapot, the infamous Mrs Noyce described her establishment as 'more of a YMCA with extras'.

Overlooking the Water of Leith is Dean Terrace, which rises up to **Ann Street**. Unassuming and bijou, Ann Street is today one of Edinburgh's most exclusive addresses. Named after Raeburn's wife, it has dolls' house-like proportions compared with the lofty heights of the New Town. There is a cottage-garden ambience to the street, with each terraced house fronted by a small garden. Many famous residents have found refuge here, including Thomas de Quincey, the 19th-century author of *The Confessions of an English Opium Eater*.

The Dean

To the west and up the hill from Ann Street is the one-time Dean estate. John Learmonth bought the estate with an eye to financial gain in 1825. As Edinburgh's Lord Provost, Learmonth negotiated the building of Dean Bridge to cross the Water of Leith and link the estate to the city. Not entirely successful on the money-making front, thanks to a saturated mid-19th-century property market, Learmonth's development fell short of his aspirations. Later, rows of tenements with bay windows were added. They continue to stand proud along the east of Queensferry Road.

What looks like a castle imported from a Disneyesque landscape can been seen from further along Queensferry Road, by looking north down Learmonth Avenue. This is **Fettes College**, a private school for boys built in the 1860s. A flamboyant coupling of the French chateau and Scots Baronial styles, it is topped by a soaring clock tower. Tony Blair was educated here, as was James Bond. According to espionage fiction, Bond was sent to Fettes after an 'incident' with a maid at his former school, Eton College. Back on Queensferry Road is Stewart's **Melville College**. Another architectural flight of fancy, this is an 1848 hybrid of Renaissance and Jacobean styles marched out in a sea of leaded domes. It was built as one of Edinburgh's many so-called 'pauper palaces', funded by wealthy benefactors to school and house poor, often orphaned,

children. Just around the corner, off Dean Path, is **Dean Cemetery**. It was laid out in 1845, and among its famous dead are architect William Playfair, pioneering photographer David Octavius Hill and the man who inspired Conan Doyle's Sherlock Holmes, Dr Joseph Bell. The tombs are among the most magnificent and bombastic in Edinburgh, built for wealthy and powerful men who knew exactly how they wanted to be remembered. A stroll through the graveyard can also provide a practical demonstration of the development of the art of the Celtic knot from the graveyard's opening in 1845.

The Water of Leith

From its source in the Pentland Hills, which lie south-west of Edinburgh, the **Water of Leith** travels 21 miles (33 kilometres) before flowing into the Firth of Forth at Leith. It once provided power for the many mills that lined its banks. Now, it is a tranquil escape route from the city, thanks to the Water of Leith Walkway Trust, which has built well-signposted pedestrian routes along the banks from Balerno, on the outskirts of Edinburgh, right down to Leith. A guidebook is available at the **Water of Leith Visitors Centre** (24 Lanark Road; 455 7367).

Although there are plenty of places to join the walkway, the Stock Bridge is as good as any. From the stairway on the north-east end of the bridge, the path leads downriver towards the Royal Botanic Garden. Going upriver along Saunders Street, the path goes through Dean Village to the **National Gallery of Modern Art** and the **Dean Gallery** (for both, *see page 69*) and, beyond that, to Roseburn.

The path is at its most dramatic at the end of Saunders Street, where it enters a ravine between the New Town and the private Dean Gardens to the north. Along the walkway is a neo-classical circular temple, **St Bernard's Well**. The story goes that three schoolboys discovered a mineral water spring there in 1760. Cashing in on the craze for 'taking the waters', in 1788 Lord Gardenstone commissioned architect Alexander Nasmyth to build a temple to replace an earlier well-house. The pump room (only occasionally opened to the public) is richly decorated in mosaics. Above, standing beneath the temple's dome, is a statue of Hygeia, the goddess of health. Further along the walkway, there are epic views of Dean Bridge, which was built in the 1820s by engineer Thomas Telford. To the north of the bridge stands **Holy Trinity Church**, built as an 1830s reproduction of the English Perpendicular style.

As the walkway passes under Dean Bridge and rises along Miller Row to Old Dean Bridge, it

Sightseeing

It's all water under the mill at **Dean Village**.

enters **Dean Village**, originally called the Village of the Water of Leith. Mills first clustered here in the 15th century; the Incorporation of Baxters (bakers) ran 11 watermills, supplying milled meal to the whole of Edinburgh. Today, Dean Village is faintly reminiscent of a Bavarian village with gabled houses staggered along a deep gorge. It is a surprisingly quiet and secluded spot considering its proximity to the city centre. **Bell's Brae** (brae is Gaelic for 'upper part') runs steeply up to Dean Bridge. Formerly the main road running north out of Edinburgh, the Brae is still lined with a rich agglomeration of 17th-century stone buildings. Opposite Old Dean Bridge is **Baxter's Tolbooth**, which was given

an unappealing makeover in the 1970s. Still visible, however, is a stone carved with wheat sheaves and bakers' shovels with the inscription 'God's Providence Is Our Inheritance', dating from 1675. Just beyond the bridge is **West Mill**, now converted into flats, and **Well Court** (1884), which was built as artisan housing in an act of Victorian philanthropy by John Ritchie Findlay, proprietor of the *Scotsman* newspaper, whose own home overlooked the village.

The Water of Leith walkway continues just above Well Court, following the river through shady nooks and past weirs to pass under Belford Bridge. Here, steps lead up to Belford Road; it's a five-minute walk to the National Gallery of Modern Art and the Dean Gallery. Alternatively, about a quarter of mile beyond, a steep path winds up to the rear of the Gallery of Modern Art. Looking back across the river there is a splendid view of **Donaldson's School for the Deaf**. It was designed by William Playfair in the 1840s, and its turrets and ornate grandeur appealed to Queen Victoria, who is said to have suggested taking up residence here rather than at the Palace of Holyroodhouse. The Gallery of Modern Art is another of Edinburgh's one-time grand educational institutions, this time in neo-classical style. It looks out across Belford Road, on to a former orphanage, which is now the Dean Gallery, built by Thomas Hamilton in

Green fingers & glasshouses

When it comes to green spaces, Edinburgh offers up the full gamut. There are the neatly manicured lawns of Princes Street Gardens, the more rugged and rolling Holyrood Park topped by Arthur's Seat and the **Royal Botanic Garden**. Here a gentle stroll along the herbaceous borders will revive any traveller weary of notching up the city's sights. What's more, the garden, which lies just to the north of the New Town, commands some of the best views of Edinburgh. With the Pentland Hills lying beyond, the city's full topographical glory – St Giles Cathedral, Salisbury Crags, the National Monument – is marched out on the skyline.

One of only two Royal Botanic Gardens in Britain (the other is London's Kew), Edinburgh's Royal Botanic Garden traces its history back to the 17th century. It was in 1670, when botany and medicine were closely linked, that Andrew Balfour and Robert Sibbald, two doctors somewhat disgruntled with the lot of the Scottish medical profession, decided to found a garden.

Originally sited next to the Palace Of Holyroodhouse, it moved to its present site (by way of two other locations) in 1823. Today, its 28 hectares (72 acres) are home to over 2,000 specimens of trees, a rock garden, a world-famous collection of rhododendrons, a peat garden and the recently landscaped **Pringle Chinese Collection**, modelled on the mountainous environment of south-west China, where you can wander through four vegetation zones by way of a pagoda and a small mountain stream with its obligatory Chinese-style wooden bridge. The Pringle is the largest collection of Chinese plants outside China and represents a special interest taken by Scottish scientific explorers over the last 150 years.

The **Glasshouse Experience**, a series of ten glasshouses, offers the chance to view at close quarters everything from a cocoa tree through to giant ferns. The Temperate Palm House is particularly impressive. Constructed in 1858, the 21-m (70-ft) high structure is the tallest glasshouse in Britain.

1833. Usually one for the severe classical repertoire, here Hamilton loosened his architectural style and opted for showy roof-top pavilions.

Dean Gallery

Belford Road (624 6200/deaninfo@natgalscot.ac.uk/ www.natgalscot.ac.uk). Bus 13. **Open** 10am-5pm Mon-Sat; noon-5pm Sun; *Festival* extended hours (phone for details). **Admission** free; £1-£2 charge for occasional exhibitions. **Credit** *shop* AmEx, MC, V. **Map** p308 A5.

Opened in 1999 as part of the National Galleries of Scotland's empire, the Dean Gallery neighbours the National Gallery of Modern Art (*see below*). You can easily combine a visit to both in a day. Criticised in some quarters for the upmarket-shopping-mall feel of its ground floor and the large amount of space given over to work by Sir Eduardo Paolozzi (there is a mock-up of the sculptor's studio), the Dean does, nevertheless, hold one of Britain's strongest collections of surrealist and Dada artworks. Drawn from the collections of Roland Penrose and the celebrated collector and marmalade heiress Gabrielle Keiller, it includes work by the big boys of surrealism: Dalí, Giacometti, Miró and Picasso. The Study Collection room contains a fascinating array of text and 'surreal artefacts' and makes for a highly interesting browse. Keen researchers can request access to the library. The upstairs galleries are given over to temporary shows by 20th-century artists and have included exhibitions by Gary Hume, Magritte and Giorgio Morandi.

Scottish National Gallery of Modern Art

Belford Road, EH4 (624 6200/ gmainfo@natgalscot.ac.uk/www.natgalscot.ac.uk). Bus 13. **Open** 10am-5pm Mon-Sat; noon-5pm Sun. **Admission** free except for special loan exhibitions. **Credit** *shop* AmEx, MC, V. **Map** p308 A5.

Since 1984, Scotland's national collection of modern art has been housed in what was once John Watson's School. A 19th-century, neo-classical edifice set in parkland, dotted with sculptures by Paolozzi, Henry Moore and Dan Graham, the gallery makes an ideal day-trip destination, particularly as its sister gallery, the Dean Gallery (*see above*), lies just over the way.

Any external hints at austerity are kicked aside by the bright, airy galleries. Works from a permanent collection of 20th-century Scottish art are rotated around the downstairs galleries. Although not so strong on the work of the most contemporary of bright young things in the Scottish scene, the collection is hot on the older generation of artists, particularly the so-called 1980s Glasgow Boys – Peter Howson, Steven Campbell, Adrian Wiszniewski and Ken Currie. The upstairs galleries are given over to international art. Big names from fauvism, surrealism and abstract expressionism such as Matisse, Magritte, Picasso and Pollock feature along with British greats like Francis Bacon, Helen Chadwick and Damien Hirst. The permanent collection is augmented by temporary exhibitions such as the Bürgi Collection of works by Paul Klee (until October 2000).

Enjoying the **Royal Botanic Garden**.

In the middle of the garden is **Inverleith House** (*see page 66*), which is now an art gallery, and the **Terrace Café**, where you can eat both inside and outside. There is a gift shop next to the West Gate that has an interesting selection of plants for sale, and some fascinating publications about the Garden, the work carried out there and Scottish wild plants.

The RBGE is more than a visitor attraction. As a working scientific institution for research on the systematics and biology of plants, it maintains one of the world's largest collections of living plants. At Inverleith and the three specialist gardens at **Younger, Logan** and **Dawyck**, there are nearly 17,000 species (about 6 per cent of the world's flowering plants) from across the globe. There is also a **Herbarium** at Inverleith, which houses some two million preserved plant specimens covering the whole of the plant kingdom, and an extensive library.

Royal Botanic Garden

Inverleith Row, EH3 (552 7171/ www.rbge.org.uk). Bus 8, 23, 27. **Open** *Feb* 9.30am-5pm daily; *Mar* 9.30am-6pm daily; *Apr-Aug* 9.30am-7pm daily; *Sept* 9.30am-6pm daily; *Oct* 9.30am-5pm daily; *Nov-Jan* 9.30am-4pm daily. **Admission** free, but suggested donation of £2.50 to Glasshouse Experience. **Credit** *shop* V. **Map** p306 D2.

Calton Hill & Broughton

There are fine views across Edinburgh and a whiff of fresh air to be had on the hill that gives the city its Doric crown.

Sightseeing

Looking down to **Calton Hill** from Edinburgh Castle.

Calton Hill contends with Arthur's Seat and Castle Rock as the best place from which to view Edinburgh. The top of the Nelson Monument gives the viewer a sense of the bulk and anarchy of the Old Town to the south; the formality of the New Town to the north-west; and the modern chaos of Granton's gas towers and Leith's docks to the north. Almost all of Scotland's capital is in view as it sweeps down from the Pentland hills to the Firth of Forth. On a clear day, the views over the Forth to Fife and east towards North Berwick are also splendid.

The hill is a favoured and atmospheric spot. When a sunny summer afternoon turns chilly and a sea mist, known locally as a 'haar', sweeps up from the Forth, the view of mist-torn chimneys and tenements creates an impression of what Edinburgh was like when it was called 'Auld Reekie' – although the smoking chimneys are long gone with the advent of Clean Air Acts. This is a hill on the edge of old Edinburgh, the site of the City Observatory, from which science regimented

time. And also the site of the modern **Beltane** celebrations (*see page 94*), when pagan ritual still marks time's passage.

Waterloo Place

Most visitors approach the hill from the west: along Princes Street or across North Bridge. Looking up, it is easy to understand why Edinburgh retains the accolade of the 'Athens of the North'. What is rather more strange is that the name came before the Greek-inspired architecture was built – from the city's position on the grand tours of the late 18th century and its relationship with imperial, 'Roman' London. The classical-styled architecture followed to justify and immortalise the phrase.

Turning the corner into **Waterloo Place** brings exposure to the full impact of the 19th century neo-classical architectural regime. Some call it balanced and perfectly proportioned. Others find it stultifying in its grey formality – small wonder that, until recently, Edinburgh had a reputation for dour rectitude. A glimpse of what has replaced the rectitude, or rather what lies underneath its upright moral fibre, is visible down to the left from Regent Bridge. Just by the **Pivo Caffé** (*see page 156*) is where Renton ran into a car in the opening scenes of *Trainspotting*. The bridge is an impressive structure built over a 15-metre (50-foot) deep ravine.

A few yards further along, Waterloo Place bisects the **Old Calton Burying Ground**. The steps to the right lead up to the largest part of the graveyard, the last resting place of many of the main figures of the Enlightenment. The two most imposing memorials are Robert Adam's tower for the philosopher and historian David Hume and the obelisk to the political reformers of 1793-4 who were transported for having the audacity to demand the vote for the Scots. A plaque at the entrance lists some further inhabitants of note. The cemetery is worth a wander if you have time. The back of the tombs at the far, left-hand end of the cemetery give a fine and rather less obvious – but nonetheless photogenic – view of Edinburgh Castle than the one from the top of Calton Hill, as well as the **Venue** nightclub (*see page 211*) immediately below. The rather Gothic building backing onto that corner of the graveyard is the old **Governor's House** of the Calton Gaol: designed by Archibald Elliot, it is the first piece of turreted architecture visible from the East Coast trains into Waverley Station; it is often, quite vocally and amusingly to those in the know, mistaken for the Castle itself.

The Burying Ground was divided in 1815, when Princes Street was extended and the North Bridge built. Before then, access to the hill had been up the steep road, which is itself known, slightly confusingly, as Calton Hill and which now runs from the end of Waterloo Place down to Leith Street. **Rock House**, set back above the road on the north side, is one of the only houses in Edinburgh to have good views both north and south and, not surprisingly, was home to a succession of photographers from the 1830s until 1945. It is said to be the place where modern art photography was born and is being bought for the nation by the Museums of Scotland who plan to open it as a museum of photography.

The most direct route up Calton Hill from here is via the steps at the end of Waterloo Place. Once up the first set of steps, either go straight ahead and meander up the side of the hill or, if you have more energy, take the steep steps to the right.

Regent Road

Before the final assault on the hill, **Regent Road**, leading straight on from Waterloo Place, has a few sights to offer. The big building on

the right is **St Andrew's House**, which was built on the site of **Calton Gaol**. A sturdy example of modernist, 1930s architecture, its formality and presence make it a suitable home to the civil service. The first part of the gaol was built in 1791-5. A new prison building and the Governor's House were added in 1815. Even back then the Governor's House was considered in bad taste. Not so, at least at the time, the public executions that used to take place on the prison roof, in full view of the crowds on Calton Hill, until 1864.

On the left of Regent road, just before the turning that is the vehicular access to Calton Hill, was the site of the permanent **Vigil for a Scottish Parliament**. The tarmac of the pavement, since replaced, was scorched and burned by the braziers that kept those keeping the vigil warm during the long cold nights between 1992 and 1997. It seemed an auspicious site for the vigil, next door to the Royal High School, which everyone thought would house the new Scottish Parliament as it had been converted into a debating chamber before the failed referendum for a Scottish Assembly in 1976. However, after the 'yes-yes' vote of autumn 1997, the government said 'no-no' to the Royal High School and chose the Holyrood site.

The **Royal High School**, designed by Thomas Hamilton and modelled on the Temple of Theseus in Athens, was completed in 1829. It is the most extensive of the neo-classical buildings of that time, with a massive Doric central block and pillared wings. Because of its monumental size, it is difficult to get a proper perspective, even when walking past on the other side of Regent Road, so it's best to notice the detail here and contemplate its grandeur from one of the closes at the lower end of the Royal Mile. The view down to Holyrood, the dome of **Our Dynamic Earth** (*see page 54*) and the **Canongate Churchyard** (*see page 51*), and up to the **Castle** (*see page 41*) are worth straying this far for. While the Royal High School's architecture is appropriate for its function, Hamilton's **Robert Burns Memorial**, just across the road, is completely out of tune with its purpose. The large collection of Burns relics that were once displayed there can be seen in the **Writers' Museum** (*see page 44*). The paths on the right lead down to Calton Road and provide a suitable shortcut to Holyrood if you're not going back up the hill. A few steps past the Burns Memorial is the entrance to the New Calton graveyard, which is large but not overly fascinating.

Calton Hill

Arriving, slightly puffed, at the top of the steps up the hill, you're confronted by a large cannon. This rather magnificent beast is Portuguese in origin and provides a suitably phallic accompaniment to many a wedding photograph, with the **Nelson Monument** (*see page 73*) thrusting boldly in the background. Nearby, the set of 12 Doric columns that form the National Monument to those who lost their lives in the Napoleonic Wars was erected in the 1820s. Although it is generally regarded with affection nowadays, it was dubbed 'Edinburgh's Disgrace' when the original plans to build a replica of the Parthenon were thwarted because only half the £42,000 required was raised by public donation.

The building in the walled grounds is the **City Observatory** (*see below*) by William Playfair, which is based on the Temple of the Winds in Athens. The original City Observatory (James Craig, 1792) is the three-storey Gothic tower on the south-western corner of the walls – although it was never put to the use for which it was designed. In the opposite corner to this is a disused astronomical dome that has housed several attempts at visitor attractions. Incorporated into the south-eastern wall of the observatory is Playfair's monument to his uncle, Professor John Playfair.

The circular building to the south-west of the observatory is another Playfair copy. It is a monument to the philosopher Dugald Steward and based on the monument to Lysicrates on the Acropolis at Athens. Looking west from this monument, the modern monstrosity in the foreground is the **St James Centre**, which is, at least, grey.

Although Calton Hill has plenty of open space to wander round, rest upon and enjoy the views from, the Regent Gardens to the east are private and belong to the residents of the **Regent**, **Carlton** and **Royal Terraces**. These New Town terraces are unique in that they follow the contours of the hill and not a grid pattern. They are regarded as being particularly fine examples of the New Town architectural style.

City Observatory

Calton Hill, EH7 (556 4365/www.roe.ac.uk/asewww). **Bus** *1, 11, 22, 24.* **Open** Fri evenings, phone for times, and by arrangement only. **Map** p307 G4.

The City Observatory has played an important role in Edinburgh's naval history. It was founded in 1776, and in 1812 it began work as a time service for merchant ships docked at Leith. The ships relied on an accurate chronometer to fix their position by the stars. Inside the observatory is the Politician's Clock – so called because it has two faces. The first, facing into the observatory, was used to set the time at night

The **National Monument**, aka Edinburgh's Disgrace.

View from Calton Hill, past the **Dugald Steward Monument** to the Old Town and the Castle.

according to the stars. The second faced out so that ships' captains could set their timepieces, which they had carried all the way up from Leith Docks.

There have been several attempts to open the observatory as an attraction, but at present access is only through the The Astronomical Society of Edinburgh on most Friday evenings. Group visits can be arranged at any time throughout the year.

Nelson Monument
Calton Hill, EH7 (556 2716). Bus 1, 11, 22, 24. **Open** *Apr-Sept* 1-6pm Mon; 10am-6pm Tue-Sat; closed Sun; *Oct-Mar* 10am-3pm Mon-Sat; closed Sun. **Admission** £2. **No credit cards.** **Map** p307 G4.

The view from the top of this monument, which was designed in the shape of Nelson's telescope by Robert Burn in 1807, is worth the entry price. Also, invest in the photocopied brochure to help work out what you're looking at. In 1852, another timepiece was placed on top of the Nelson Monument. This is a large white ball, which is raised to the cross on the white mast from where it still drops at 1pm each day, except when it is too misty or the wind is too high. This meant that chronometers no longer had to be hauled all the way up from Leith. In 1861, a steel wire over 1,220m (4,000ft) long was attached between the monument and the Castle to facilitate the firing of the 1pm gun that still shocks the unwary to this day. Be warned that, with 143 steps, it's quite a climb to the top, the door up there is only 42cm (17in) wide and the parapet is sturdy but not very high.

Broughton

Although not part of Calton Hill, **Broughton** is an easy walk from here. There is a gate at the north side of the hill on Royal Terrace by the **Greenside Church** – referred to imaginatively by Robert Louis Stevenson as 'the church on the hill'.

Picardy Place, the huge roundabout at the top of Leith Walk, was once home to a colony of Protestant French silk weavers who fled to Edinburgh from Picardy in 1685. Today it is home to a statue of Sherlock Holmes, whose creator, Sir Arthur Conan Doyle, was born at 11 Picardy Place and, for a bit of light relief, two outsize sculptures of a foot and a grasshopper by the Leith-born artist Sir Eduardo Paolozzi, which lie in front of the Roman Catholic cathedral of St Mary's.

Broughton Street is a bustling and lively community with plenty of good bars, cafés and restaurants for the weary. It is the centre of Edinburgh's gay community and wears its name of the Pink Triangle with pride. At the bottom of Broughton Street, across the roundabout, is **Mansfield Church**, with walls covered in murals by Phoebe Traquair. The church has been bought by the Mansfield Traquair Trust and while the whole building is being turned into offices, the murals are being restored for public display.

Arthur's Seat & Duddingston

Edinburgh's mountain in its midst makes a pleasant walk, but it is packed with history too – if you know where to look.

Arthur's Seat

No other European city has such a mass of splendidly rugged landscape at its heart as Edinburgh has in the extinct volcano, **Arthur's Seat**. Looming sternly out of Holyrood Park, it might not have erupted for more than 350 million years, but the lava flows that shaped the local geology are still clearly visible. Conan Doyle thought the hill so distinctive and recognisable that he referred to it in his dinosaur epic *The Lost World* to conjure up an appropriate primordial image in his readers' minds.

Although people tend to think its name refers to King Arthur, the name is more likely to be a corruption of 'Archer's Seat'. The 260-hectare (650-acre) **Holyrood Park** surrounding it, now a public park, was first used around 9,000 years ago for hunting. Terraces, known in Scotland as run-rigs, were developed by farmers on the lower slopes and can still be seen on the eastern ones. From the 12th century onwards it was used as a hunting ground by Scottish kings, becoming a royal park in the 16th century.

The 250-metre (823-foot) peak and the neighbouring **Whinney Hill**, lower by 75 metres (250 feet), are encircled by Queen's Drive, which has entrances off Holyrood Road, London Road and the top of Dalkeith Road. It can also be approached from the other side via Duddingston Road West.

The face Arthur's Seat presents to the Old Town is the dark, forbidding curve of **Salisbury Crags**. A path, the **Radical Road**, runs directly below the rock face. Like so much else in Edinburgh, the road was Sir Walter Scott's idea, a scheme to keep former soldiers occupied after they had finished their military service. Along the Radical Road, some of the features that nudged James Hutton towards his invention of the modern discipline of geology are visible in the rocks. Hutton's memory and discoveries are honoured in the multimedia visitor attraction **Our Dynamic Earth** (*see page 54*), aptly sited a stone's throw from Salisbury Crags.

Turning left at the Holyrood Palace entrance to the park, Queen's Drive passes **St Margaret's Loch**, with the ruined **St Anthony's Chapel** perched above it. Just before the loch, there is a grille set into the wall on the right. This is **St Margaret's Well**, the surround of which originally stood near Restalrig Church where, during the plague years, a spring was relied upon as a source of clean water. The surround was removed in 1860 to make way for a railway depot and put here, where there was already a natural spring.

Past St Margaret's Well is the starting point for a path that divides at the beginning of the valley known as **Hunter's Bog**. Going to the right leads up to the top of Salisbury Crags, straight ahead the valley rises to a twisting and steep path (with steps) to the summit, while the paths to the left go up through the Dasses, also to the peak of Arthur's Seat. All the paths can give the feeling of being in the heart of the countryside, but the approaches to the peak are steep in places. The peak is most easily approached from the car park beside Dunsapie Loch on the east side, past Whinney Hill. It's at a fairly easy gradient and not too strenuous a walk.

Once on the summit, the views are easily worth the effort. The panorama encompasses the outer suburbs of Edinburgh in the west, Bass Rock protruding from the waves in the east, the hills of Fife in the north and the Pentland Hills in the south.

Duddingston

From the north-east end of Dunsapie Loch a steep path leads down into **Duddingston**. Alternatively, continue along Queen's Drive to the foot of the hill, where it joins Holyrood Park Road, and turn left down towards Duddingston, passing beneath the rock formations named Lion's Haunch and Samson's Ribs.

The name Duddingston is said to have come from a Gaelic word meaning 'the house on the sunny side of the hill'. The area has been settled since the 12th century, but artefacts from the

The impressive
volcanic bulk of
Arthur's Seat.

All that remains of **St Anthony's Chapel** in Holyrood Park. *See page 74.*

late Bronze Age have also been found there.
The chief occupations of the parishioners of
Duddingston were farming (the soil is very
fertile) and weaving (they produced a coarse
flaxen material known as 'Duddingston
hardings'). Salt was another mainstay.

Duddingston Village is tiny, consisting
mainly of the Causeway and Old Church Road,
set back off the main road of Duddingston Road
West. The village and its surrounding green
belt were declared a conservation area in
1975, and it remains a little slice of countryside
in the midst of a big city.

Duddingston Loch has provided modern
Edinburgh with one of its favourite symbols, and
one that is practically an unofficial logo for the
city: the wry painting of *Reverend Robert Walker
Skating on Duddingston Loch* by Sir Henry
Raeburn (1756-1823), now in the National Gallery
of Scotland (*see page 57*). Accounts from the 19th
century describe the loch as swarming with
multitudes of skaters whenever it froze. The loch
is also virtually synonymous with the sport of
curling. Edinburgh devotees of 'the roaring
game' migrated to Duddingston in 1795 when
their traditional ground of the Nor' Loch below
Edinburgh Castle was drained and its
replacement at Canonmills met with indifference.
The club attracted many eminent citizens, and
every frosty day the magistrates led a procession
to the loch 'with great pomp and circumstance'.
Rules formulated at Duddingston were adopted
by curlers all over the country.

Even without its capacity to freeze over, the
loch has always been a popular spot for its
sheer natural beauty. It is just over 500 metres
(1,640 feet) long and less than 250 metres (820
feet) at its widest point. The waterside outside
Duddingston Village is usually crowded with
ducks, geese and swans padding around on the
lookout for bread. It is a bird sanctuary too:
there is a heronry in the trees at the western
end and bitterns have been spotted in the
reedbeds there. The best views of the loch,
for ornithological purposes, are from the
slopes above Queen's Drive.

The small octagonal building at the edge of
the loch is **Thomson's Tower**, named after
Reverend John Thomson (1778-1840), the most
famous of the parish's ministers. It was
Thomson who gave rise to the enduring Scots
phrase 'we're a Jock Tamson's bairns'–
meaning that everyone shares the same
humanity and none is innately better than any
other. Sir Walter Scott was a friend of
Thomson's and frequently visited. He wrote
part of *The Heart of Midlothian* in this stunted,
turret-like construction at the foot of the
Manse's garden. The well-connected Reverend
Thomson, a landscape painter, also played host
to JMW Turner at the Manse.

Duddingston Kirk dates from 1124 and has
a Norman arch separating the chancel and the
nave. The north aisle was added in 1631, and
many alterations have been made to the
building, such as the enlarging of the windows,

which destroyed many of the original features. The carvings around the church, especially the south doorway, are rough and ready but fascinating, and the image of a fully dressed Christ on the cross suggested to some scholars that the original church was actually the work of Saxons.

The little tower, on the left of the church gates and now called **Session House**, was originally a watchtower. At the height of 'resurrectionist' activity, the graveyard had to be guarded to prevent the bodies of the freshly buried dead being stolen and sold to anatomists for dissection.

On the right-hand side of the gates is the 'loupin-on stone', a stepped platform to help horsemen mount. A punishment appliance called 'the jougs' (from the word 'yoke') – an iron collar in which wrongdoers were clamped – is attached to the wall behind. Common to most parishes at one time, the Duddingston jougs are now almost unique in having survived in their original place.

Across the road is the west entrance to the Causeway, Duddingston Village's main street. The Causeway is a narrow road, with Arthur's Seat looming above the roofs of the big houses set back from the road.

Weary travellers would often stop in Duddingston to dismount and seek rest and refreshment. **The Sheep Heid Inn** (*see page 156*) on the Causeway is one of the oldest public houses in Scotland and was a favourite of James VI and I. In 1580 he presented the landlord with a ram's head, which was later stolen. The inn has retained all its charm. Shelves abound

with books, trophies and knick-knacks and the walls are adorned with a mass of pictures. There's also a beer garden outside, overlooked by an indoor terrace.

Duddingston is proud of the fact that Bonnie Prince Charlie slept here on 19 September 1745, when he held a Council of War before the Battle of Prestonpans and stayed close to his forces rather than head back to Holyrood Palace for the night. Where he actually slept has been the subject of much conjecture – it was finally decided the white pebble-dashed cottage at the end of the Causeway was the most likely place.

Through the village away from Arthur's Seat, Duddingston Road is the location of the main attraction of the area for some: **Duddingston Golf Course**, which celebrated its centenary in 1995. It's in the grounds of the neo-classical **Mansion House**, with a Corinthian portico, which was built in 1768 by Sir William Chambers as a bachelor pad. The Mansion House is currently occupied by a firm of architects and signposted by some rather unwelcoming 'private road' signs, but it's worth a glimpse through the trees, as is the folly known as the **Temple**, at the 16th tee, which gave the club its logo.

Over the main road from the entrance leading to the clubhouse is the **Innocent Railway** walkway and cycle track. The path sadly doesn't afford any views of the Bawsinch Nature Reserve over the wall, or Prestonfield Golf Course on the other side, but leads back to the Salisbury Crags end of Holyrood Park.

Sightseeing

What better double whammy than **Duddingston Kirk** and **Loch**? *See page 76.*

South Edinburgh

With its meadows and hills, there are plenty of places to walk the dog.

Edinburgh's south side is the great swathe of land that stretches from the Cowgate south to Blackford Hill and between Newington, to the east, and Morningside, to the west. It contains beautiful green spaces, academic institutions, and streets and buildings where the narrative of Scottish history is apparent to even the most casual passer-by. At times it seems as if the visitor is spoiled for choice when it comes to recreational and cultural nourishment. Odd, then, how the most popular attraction in the whole area is a dead dog.

Greyfriars

The real mystery of **Greyfriars Kirk** (*see below*), opposite Chambers Street at the south end of George IV Bridge, has nothing to do with ghostly grey friars, poltergeists assaulting tourists or how an estimated 80,000 corpses have been squeezed into the kirkyard. The central conundrum is the unparalleled interest in a certain shaggy hound who turned up his toes in 1872.

Bobby was the loyal mutt who lived by his late master's grave for 14 years and was an object of affection for many. His **statue** is outside the entrance to the churchyard. But when he died, the minister at the time waited until cover of darkness to plant the pooch in the only unconsecrated plot left available. After all, a dumb animal could not be left lying in sacred soil. The misleading notice in the kirkyard says Bobby 'was buried nearby' his master. The minister had a better handle on the great scheme of things than many visitors since.

Greyfriars Kirkyard has played a pivotal role in the history of Scotland. It is where the National Covenant was signed in 1638 and where the bodies of executed Covenanters were buried alongside common criminals. They, and the survivors of the Battle of Bothwell Brig (1679), were kept in the Covenanters' Prison in the south-west of the yard under desperate conditions for five months. Martyrs' Monument, with its chilling inscription 'Halt passenger, take heed of what you do see, This tomb doth shew for what some men did die', is their memorial and can be found in the north-east part of the yard, just by the steps down to Candlemaker Row. Wandering around the kirkyard when there's a haar (sea mist) provides a palpable time-slip effect, but even on a sunny day there

Confused? The signwriters certainly were.

are hardly any modern buildings in sight to break the historical spell. George Heriot's School (*see page 80*) adds to the atmosphere, as does a portion of the Flodden Wall. This was the defence structure built around Edinburgh in 1513 after the Battle of Flodden, in anticipation of the arrival of the English armies.

Down Candlemaker Row, past the **Portfolio Gallery** (*see page 79*), then right along the Cowgate, one of the first buildings on the right is the **Magdalen Chapel** (*see page 79*). Dwarfed by the surrounding tenements, it is now the headquarters of the Scottish Reformation Society. It is said that the chapel is where the first General Assembly of the Church of Scotland was held in 1578. In the bloody days of the late 17th century, it served as a mortuary for those executed Covenanters whose bodies were buried at Greyfriars.

Greyfriars Kirk

2 Greyfriars Place, Candlemaker Row, EH1 (visitors centre 226 5429/www.greyfriarskirk.com). Bus 23, 28, 40, 45. **Open** *Sun services 11.30am (morning), 12.30pm (Gaelic); Easter-Oct also 10.30am-4.30pm Mon-Fri; 10.30am-2.30pm Sat; Nov-Mar also 1.30-3.30pm Thur; closed Mon-Wed, Fri, Sat.* **Admission** *free.* **Map** *p309 F6.*

Greyfriars Kirk pulls off the trick of being simple but not austere. Formerly the site of a Franciscan friary, it dates from 1620 but was severely damaged, then rebuilt, after a fire in 1845. The small visitors' exhibition on the church's 400-year history contains a display about the National Covenant, but most people go for the original portrait of *Greyfriars Bobby* (John MacLeod, 1887).

Magdalen Chapel

41 Cowgate, EH1 (tel/fax 220 1450). Bus 23, 28, 40, 45. **Open** *9.30am-4pm Mon-Fri; closed Sat, Sun.* **Admission** free. **Map** p309 F6.

Built between 1541 and 1547, with the steeple added in 1626, the Chapel is now in the hands of the Scottish Reformation Society, but still open to casual visitors. One point of interest is the only surviving pre-Reformation stained glass in Scotland. Sadly, the glass in question – four fading rounds that were inserted in 1553 – is a bit of a disappointment. More interesting are the 'brods' (receipts for gifts of money or goods to the chapel, dating from the 16th to the 19th centuries) that wrap round the walls like a frieze, and the Deacon's Chair (1708).

Portfolio Gallery

43 Candlemaker Row, EH1 (220 1911/ portfolio@ednet.co.uk). Bus 23, 28, 45. **Open** noon-5.30pm Tue-Sat; closed Mon, Sun; *Festival* extended hours (phone for details). **Admission** free. **Credit** V. **Map** p309 F6.

Somewhat tucked away just off Grassmarket and overlooking Greyfriars cemetery is Scotland's leading photography and photography-related gallery. A two-level, small-scale, bright white space, Portfolio has been up and running since 1988. The emphasis is resolutely on the contemporary, and the notorious photographer of dead flesh Andres Serrano has shown in the space along with Helen Chadwick, Avi Holtzman and John Stezaker. The gallery also produces a quarterly catalogue of contemporary photography in Britain, entitled *Portfolio*.

Grassmarket

There has been a market in the Grassmarket since at least 1477 – a 1977 plaque on a rock there commemorates the 500th anniversary of the date it received its Charter from James III. Down King's Stables Road at the Grassmarket's north-west corner, gardens provided the raw material for a vegetable market from the 12th century while the Grassmarket itself held livestock sales. King's Stables Road was the site of a medieval tournament ground, begun when England's Edward III occupied the Castle in the 1330s, and finished by David II when Scotland regained the Castle.

But the Grassmarket also has a darker history. It was a frequent venue for executions, the most famous being the Porteous lynching (1736), given literary form in Sir Walter Scott's *The Heart of Midlothian*. John Porteous was an unpopular captain of the town guard. On 14 April 1736, he was in charge of the execution of two smugglers in the Grassmarket. Sensing trouble, he sealed off the area with guardsmen but went ahead with the hanging. The mob threw stones, Porteous ordered his men to open fire: three in the crowd were killed and a dozen

wounded. Porteous was tried for murder and found guilty. He was to be hanged on 20 July, but a royal warrant from Queen Caroline reprieved him. Not for long, though. A mob broke into the Old Tolbooth on the Royal Mile on 19 July, dragged Porteous down to the Grassmarket and hanged him. He was buried in Greyfriars, and there's still an entrance called Porteous Pend at the south-west corner of the Grassmarket, next to Mary Mallinson Antiques. On the north side of the Grassmarket, now a row of pubs and restaurants, the White Hart Inn is where Robert Burns supposedly wrote *Ae Fond Kiss* and the protagonist in Iain Banks' *Complicity* gets some hints about the whereabouts of a dismembered body.

The street leaving the Grassmarket on the way to Lothian Road is **West Port**, former home to murderers Burke and Hare who sold their victims to university anatomists (1827-8). At the bottom of West Port, opposite the Fiddlers Pub, is the **Vennel**: a steep lane leading up to Lauriston Place that runs along one of the best-preserved sections of the Flodden Wall. At the top of West Port, at the junction of High Riggs and East Fountainbridge, is **Main Point**. At one time this was a key exit from Edinburgh, with roads leading to Glasgow, Stirling and the south-west. In 1770, a rather pleasant house was built on the site, now surrounded by tenements and more modern buildings. But back then it took the common name given to any residence at an apex – a gusset house. This particular gusset house looks a little shabby these days and its ground floor is occupied by the far from reputable Burke & Hare pub.

The area has some excellent second-hand bookshops, many of which have very good sections devoted to Edinburgh and Scotland. Going up Lady Lawson Street from West Bow, the Sculpture Court of the **Edinburgh College of Art** (*see below*) is through the large gates on the left-hand side. At the top of the street, on the corner with Lauriston Place, the red-brick **Lothian & Borders Firestation** (*see page 80*) is now the force's administrative headquarters. Turning to the right, Lauriston Place leads down to Tollcross, while turning left takes you back, past the entrance to **George Heriot's School** (*see page 80*) towards Forrest Road and Greyfriars. Opposite the school, the rather over-romantic buildings on the right are the Royal Infirmary, designed by David Bryce, with help from Florence Nightingale, in 1870.

Edinburgh College of Art

Lauriston Place, EH3 (221 6032/www.eca.ac.uk). Bus 23, 28, 45. **Open** 10am-8pm Mon-Thur; 10am-5pm Fri; 10am-2pm Sat; closed Sun; *Festival* 10am-5pm daily. **Admission** free. **No credit cards**. **Map** p309 E6.

The Edinburgh College of Art operates a year-round programme of exhibitions. For many, the highlight is the annual degree shows in June, when the public can eye up (and purchase) future art stars. The college puts on regular shows by artists from all over the world, taking in everything from photography to installations.

George Heriot's School

Lauriston Place, EH3 (229 7263). Bus 23, 28, 45. **Open** June, July, 1st 2 weeks Aug. Phone to book and to confirm dates. **Admission** free. **Map** p309 F6.
School prefects give historical tours of this fine 17th-century building. Heriot, a goldsmith and jeweller to the court of James I, was known as the Jinglin' Geordie. His original legacy was for the education of 'puir, fatherless bairns' but the school was used in its early days as a military hospital for Cromwell's troops.

Lothian & Borders Firestation

Lauriston Place, EH3 (228 2401) Bus 23, 28, 45. **Open** by appointment 10am-1pm, 2-4pm Mon-Fri; closed Sat, Sun. **Admission** free. **Map** p309 E6.
Built in 1898, the firestation is not normally open to the public, as the small collection of historic fire equipment in the old garage and stables of the station has no full-time curator. Fire officers are, however, happy to give tours to schools and those with a special interest in the history of firefighting.

Chambers Street

Opposite Greyfriars, the plain but graceful lines of the new **Museum of Scotland** (*see page 81*) mask a warren of winding corridors that open up on spectacular drops and huge spaces. The roof and turret restaurant give spectacular views of Arthur's Seat and the Castle. Next door along Chambers Street, the **Royal Museum** (*see page 81*), designed by Captain Francis Fowke and completed in 1888, is along far more conventional, Victorian lines. Although they are distinct entities, the two museums are linked inside and there is joint entry. Across from the imposing steps up to the Royal Museum is the **Matthew Architecture Gallery** (*see below*).

Younger than the universities of St Andrews or Glasgow, **Edinburgh University** dates from 1582. **Old College**, now its central focus, occupies the original site and backs onto Chambers Street. Entrance to the main courtyard is either through the small entrance to the **Talbot Rice Gallery** (*see page 81*), up West College Street, or through the rather more monumental arch on Nicolson Street. It was built by Robert Adam, who started the work in 1789, and William Playfair, who finished it after the interruption of the Napoleonic Wars. Rowand Anderson added the landmark dome in 1883. Certain areas of Old College are accessible to the public, notably the **Playfair Library** (where guided tours in summer show off one of

the city's finest classical interiors) and the old **Upper Museum** (now part of the Talbot Rice Gallery). The Upper Museum features a table from Napoleon's lodgings on St Helena with a cigar burn made, allegedly, by the Corsican snowbird himself. For details of how to join these tours contact the **University of Edinburgh Centre** (*see page 81*).

For even older buildings that are now part of the University, enthusiasts can go hunting down the bottom of Infirmary Street, off South Bridge. Through the gates at the foot of the street are the **Old High School** (1777) and **Old Surgeon's Hall** (1697). Adjacent are Victorian premises that once housed the wards of the Royal Infirmary where Joseph Lister discovered the benefits of antiseptic surgery. **'New' Surgeon's Hall** was built in 1832 on Nicolson Street, a stone's throw from Old College. This building is home to the Royal College of Surgeons of Edinburgh and was another William Playfair design. Access is limited but can be gained via the **Sir Jules Thorn Exhibition of the History of Surgery** (which also houses the **Dental Museum**; *see page 81*) and the **Museum of Pathology & Anatomy** (*see below*), whose displays are not for the weak of stomach.

Matthew Architecture Gallery

20 Chambers Street, EH1 (650 2342/ matthew.gallery@ed.ac.uk). Bus 23, 28, 40, 45. **Open** exhibitions 10am-4.30pm Mon-Fri (phone to confirm); closed Sat, Sun. **Admission** free. **No credit cards. Map** p309 F6.
Housed in the University of Edinburgh's School of Architecture, this one-time student common room has fast become Scotland's leading architectural gallery. Opened in 1992, the gallery, named after a former professor, Sir Robert Matthew, showcases work by top Scottish architectural practices and touring shows from all over the world. The gallery has also successfully ventured into solo shows by international names such as Siah Armajani and Per Kirkeby.

Museum of Pathology & Anatomy

Playfair Hall, Royal College of Surgeons of Edinburgh, 18 Nicolson Street, EH8 (527 1649/ www.rcsed.ac.uk/geninfo/museums.asp). Bus 7, 8, 21, 31, 80. **Open** viewing by appointment only to groups of 12-24. **Admission** phone for details. **No credit cards. Map** p310 G6.
Housed in Playfair's magnificent and well-preserved Royal College of Surgeons (opened in 1832) this is a working museum for the study of human disease. The collections of pathological anatomy – grouped according to the parts of the human body – are there to display diseases, abnormalities and deformities. Close perusal by the lay person with a sense of imagination is quite distressing. Public admission is by booking well in advance only and in groups of at least 12. The guide is chosen according to the knowledge of the visitors. No admission for anyone under the age of 15.

Museum of Scotland/Royal Museum

Chambers Street, EH1 (225 7534). Bus 23, 28, 40, 45. **Open** 10am-5pm Mon, Wed-Sat; 10am-8pm Tue; noon-5pm Sun. **Admission** £3 (£8 annual season ticket); £1.50 concessions (£5 annual season ticket); £15 family annual season ticket; free under-18s; free 4.30-8pm Tue. **Credit** *shop* MC, V. **Map** p309 F6.

There is joint entry to both these museums. The new Museum of Scotland, designed by Benson and Forsyth in 1998, houses all the Scottish artefacts owned by the National Museums of Scotland, many of which were previously on display in the Portrait Gallery. The displays wind up from the basement, where Scotland's geological beginnings are shown, to the top floors which are dedicated to the 20th century. The policy of covering only those eras for which there are artefacts to display makes for some breaks in the continuity of the history of the people of Scotland and some rather strange omissions, particularly amongst those Scottish leaders who were defeated by the English. There is a huge amount to see, however, and it is displayed in such a way as to provide a genuine understanding of its historical context. There are free, daily tours of Scottish highlights at 2.15pm, with themed tours at 3.15pm.

The Royal Museum boasts lofty Victorian galleries and a beautiful atrium. All the favourites of the Victorian museum-makers art are here with more besides: geology, anthropology, fossils, taxonomy, costumes, Chinese art and industry are all well represented and displayed. Some areas, such as the stuffed animals, are of the traditional improve-your-mind Victorian variety, but others, like the

Funky interior of the **Museum of Scotland.**

interactive shark display, are innovative. The temporary exhibitions and frequent lectures are usually excellent. There are free daily tours at 2.30pm (not Thursdays, and at 3.30pm on Sundays). With three cafes and a well-stocked shop, the museums are perfect for wet weather.

Sir Jules Thorn Exhibition of the History of Surgery/Dental Museum

9 Hill Square, EH8 (527 1649/ www.rcsed.ac.uk/geninfo/museums.asp). Bus 7, 8, 21, 31, 80. **Open** 2-4pm Mon-Fri; closed Sat, Sun. **Admission** free. **Map** p310 G6.

Tucked away in the square behind Surgeons Hall, this hidden treasure of Edinburgh's museums tells the history of surgery in the city since 1505, when the Barber Surgeons were granted a Charter. In providing the links between the growth of Edinburgh and increases in medical knowledge of its surgeons and anatomists, the exhibition manages to say a lot about both city and profession. There's quite a bit to read, but the exhibits are well displayed – if occasionally, out of necessity, on the macabre side. The floor above the Sir Jules Thorn Exhibition is dedicated to modern surgical practice. The Dental Museum takes up an adjoining room and, although not as well laid out, provides telling insights to the history of dentistry for anyone prepared to read between the lines.

Talbot Rice Gallery

Old College, South Bridge, EH8 (650 2211). Bus 7, 8, 21, 31, 80. **Open** 10am-5pm Tue-Sat; closed Mon, Sun; *Festival* 10am-5pm Mon-Sat; closed Sun. **Admission** free. **No credit cards. Map** p310 G6.

Situated just off William Playfair's grand and stately Old Quad, which was built for the University of Edinburgh in the early 1800s, is the relatively recent addition of the Talbot Rice Gallery. Opened in 1975, the gallery is named after the University's Watson Gordon Professor of Fine Art, the late David Talbot Rice, famed for his writings on Islamic art. Although it houses the University's Torrie Collection, consisting of Dutch and Italian old masters, the greatest part of the gallery is given over to temporary exhibitions. It is a vast and lofty space with balcony galleries, staging exhibitions ranging from solo shows of established Scottish artists to group shows of recent graduates.

University of Edinburgh Centre

7-11 Nicolson Street, EH8 (650 2252/ communications.office@ed.ac.uk/www.ed.ac.uk). Bus 7, 8, 21, 31, 80. **Open** 9.15am-5pm Mon-Fri; closed Sat, Sun. **Map** p310 G6.

The shop-front for all things related to Edinburgh University, including tours of the Old College.

Bristo & George Squares

Not all of the University of Edinburgh's buildings are as historically rich as the **Old College**. The arts and social science campus at

Thur, Fri, Sun; *Festival* 2-5pm Mon-Fri; closed Sat,
Sun. **Admission** free. **Map** p309 F6.
The University's collection of musical instruments
is over 1,000 strong and shows how the design of
individual instruments has evolved. It includes a few
choice oddities such as a clarinet-cum-walking-stick,
as well as a good selection of bagpipes. The newly
opened Sound Laboratory uses a variety of real
instruments, including a trumpet and a clarinet,
together with computer read-outs to demonstrate
how sound is generated.

The southern suburbs

South Edinburgh is dotted with large green
spaces, notably the **Meadows**, **Blackford
Hill** and the **Braid Hills**. But before the late
18th-century population explosion that saw
Edinburgh expand beyond the Old Town, the
whole area south of North Meadow Walk was
open country. The Meadows' Burgh Loch
supplied the city's (somewhat brackish) water.
At times of low rainfall, the water level
dropped, turning the loch into a swamp. A
piped supply was started from Comiston in
1676 and Burgh Loch was drained, eventually
leaving the Meadows as they appear now – a
great big sports park. It's easy to pick up casual
games of football here on Sunday afternoons.

In 1886 the Meadows was the site of the
ambitious International Exhibition of Industry,
which was housed in a huge temporary structure
at the western end. It did, however, leave the city
several permanent souvenirs including the whale
jawbones at Jawbone Walk on Melville Drive,
which were a gift from the Zetland and Fair Isle
Knitting Stand, and the memorial pillars where
Melville Drive joins Brougham Place. Down
Causewayside from the east end of the Meadows
is a refurbished garage that was designed in the
1930s international modern style by Sir Basil
Spence. Also to the east, on the other side of
South Clark Street on the way towards Arthur's
Seat, lies the area of St Leonard's. This largely
residential area does not have much of note, but
is the home to Iain Rankin's fictional detective:
Inspector Rebus, who is stationed at **St
Leonard's Police Station**. Besides writing
strong genre, detective fiction, Rankin has an
excellent sense of Edinburgh, and his Rebus
novels provide a different view of the city from
that normally portrayed.

South of the old Burgh Loch of the Meadows
lay the Burgh Muir, or town heath, given to
Edinburgh in 1128 by David I. Merchiston
Castle lay at the western edge of this open
countryside that sprawled south towards the
Pentlands. But the heath's days were numbered:
while the upper classes moved north out of the
Old Town in the early 19th century, the middle

Sir Basil Spence's 1930s garage.

George Square is home to a phalanx of ugly
1960s blocks. Their erection caused quite a fuss
as most of the 18th-century square was
demolished to make room for them, although the
library was designed by Sir Basil Spence. The
original tenements on the west side of the square
give a hint of what it was like when Sir Walter
Scott spent his early years there (at No.25).

Just to the north and east of George Square, the
empty block now used as a car park marks the
old area of Bristo, which was also demolished to
make way for university buildings. Facing Bristo
Square – a favourite spot for skateboarders – are
Teviot Row Student Union, the rather
pompous **McEwan Hall** (1897), which was
gifted to the university by local brewing magnate
Sir William McEwan and is used for ceremonial
occasions, and the classical **Reid Concert Hall**,
which houses the **Edinburgh University
Collection of Historic Musical Instruments**
(*see below*). Conveniently nearby, in West
Nicolson Street, is **Peartree House** (*see page
160*), a 17th-century building that is now a pub
with a capacious beer garden.

Edinburgh University Collection of
Historic Musical Instruments

*Reid Concert Hall, Bristo Square, EH8 (650 2423/
www.music.ed.ac.uk/euchmi). Bus 23, 28, 40, 45.*
Open 3-5pm Wed; 10am-1pm Sat; closed Mon, Tue,

Mellowing in the **Meadows**. *See page 82.*

classes moved south to build the suburbs of Bruntsfield, Marchmont, Morningside and the Grange on its grassy reaches. Ironically, in the 16th and 17th centuries (and possibly as early as the 1400s, when the plague first came to Scotland), the Burgh Muir was where the dying victims of epidemics would be banished to expire. Its other role was as a rallying ground for Scots armies. The royal standard was pitched in the Bore Stone (a rock with a hole in it) on the Burgh Muir, then carried off at the head of the army. This last happened before the Scottish defeat at Flodden (1513). The Bore Stone is now displayed on a plinth on Morningside Road by the old church at the corner of Newbattle Terrace. It was fixed there in 1852 by Sir John Stuart Forbes, who claimed he had rescued it from the indignity of lying prone in a field. Just around the corner, on Newbattle Terrace, is the **Dominion** cinema (*see page 197*). The rather bleak façade is forgiven because of its fine art deco interior.

Marchmont was built between 1876 and 1914 in Scottish baronial style. The cobbled sweep of Warrander Park Road gives a general idea, although the area now has a student ghetto flavour. Nearby, on Whitehouse Loan and incorporated into James Gillespie's High School, is **Bruntsfield House**: a 16th-century landmark on the old Burgh Muir.

Grange Cemetery on Beaufort Road is the city's neatest burial ground. Both Thomas Chalmers and Thomas Guthrie, who helped found the Free Kirk in 1843, are here. One imagines that neither would have approved of the fictional goings-on at St Trinian's, the louche school for girls created by cartoonist Ronald Searle and immortalised in a series of 1960s films. They were inspired by a pair of schoolgirls

from the real St Trinian's at neighbouring Palmerston Road – a short-lived establishment at No.10 that opened in 1922, moved over to Dalkeith Road, then closed in 1946.

Craigmillar & Merchiston

Sitting cheek by jowl with one of the city's shabbiest housing schemes are the impressive remains of the 14th-century **Craigmillar Castle** (*see below*). The approach from Niddrie Mains Road through the housing estates of Niddrie and Craigmillar reveals a side of Edinburgh that most visitors don't see.

At the south-western extreme of the Burgh Muir another act of academic vandalism was perpetrated in the 1960s, this time by Napier College of Commerce and Technology (now Napier University), when it constructed its appalling Colinton Road campus around **Merchiston Castle**. The 15th-century L-plan tower house once had such features as a moat and a secret passage. Early in its history it fell into the hands of the Napier family, of whom John Napier (1550-1617) – mathematician and inventor of logarithms – is the most celebrated scion. In the 1830s Merchiston Castle became a school, but a century later it fell into disuse, until Napier College took it over.

Craigmillar Castle

Craigmillar Castle Road, off Old Dalkeith Road, EH16 (661 4445). Bus 2, 21, 33. **Open** *June-Sept* 9.30am-6.30pm daily; *Oct-May* 9.30pm-4.30pm Mon-Wed, Sat; 9.30am-12.30pm Thur; 2-4.30pm Sun; closed Fri. **Admission** £2; 75p-£1.50 concessions. **Credit** AmEx, MC, V.

This substantial and atmospheric ruin is now managed by Historic Scotland. An L-shaped tower house, surrounded by a later curtain wall, it was razed by

Craigmillar Castle – a former hangout of Mary, Queen of Scots. *See page 83.*

the Earl of Hertford after the English invasion of 1544, but later refurbished. The castle was a favourite spot for Mary, Queen of Scots, who retreated there after the murder of her favourite, David Rizzio, in 1566. Because of the large number of French people in Mary's court who took up residence in the surrounding area, the region immediately to the south of the castle became known as 'Little France'.

Blackford

Sitting on top of Blackford Hill like a twin teacake tribute to Victorian empiricism is the **Royal Observatory** (*see below*). It took over the work of the observatory on Calton Hill when light pollution there became too great in the late 19th century. When the new building was completed in 1895 it was well outside the city boundary. It has a well-designed visitors centre that allows access to the flat roof between the domes from where there is an excellent view of the city's northern aspect (there are a couple of small telescopes for anyone who wants a close-up). Every Friday night during the winter, weather permitting, there's a public observing session with a six-inch refracting telescope.

Blackford Hill itself makes for a good Sunday afternoon stroll and, down on its south side, is the **Hermitage of Braid**, a gentler walk by the Braid Burn. A late 18th-century villa in the middle of the Hermitage acts as a countryside information centre and has a rudimentary tearoom in its basement. Herons have been sighted hereabouts – it's the kind of bucolic vale where you can forget you're in a city. Farther south still lie the Braid Hills, with two golf courses and yet another great view of Edinburgh and beyond (on a clear day you can see Ben Lomond). Access is either via Braid Hills Drive

or left off Braid Road heading south on the way to the suburb of Buckstone. Turn the other way down Braid Road, heading back to Morningside, and you pass the spot where the last public execution for highway robbery took place in Edinburgh. In December 1814, two men mugged a man delivering a horse to the city from the Borders. They said all they got was four pence. The victim said he lost £5, bread and a spleuchan (tobacco pouch). The sad pair were strung up outside where 66 Braid Road now stands – in the roadway, all that's visible are two recessed squares where the gibbet was fixed. Stick around for any length of time absorbing the atmosphere and curtains twitch: they keep a tight grip on their spleuchans in these parts still.

Royal Observatory

Blackford Hill, EH9 (information line 668 8370/ visitors centre 668 8405/www.roe.ac.uk/vc). Bus 24, 38, 41, 41A. **Open** *information line 2-4pm Mon-Fri; visitors centre 10am-5pm Mon-Sat; noon-5pm Sun; group visits by arrangement.* **Admission** £3.50; £2-£2.50 concessions; £8 family; £1 disabled. **Credit** MC, V.

When light pollution became too strong on Calton Hill, the Royal Observatory was moved south of the city to Blackford Hill. Today, the city has grown out to meet the Observatory, which gives picturesque views of Edinburgh from the south. Although there are telescope sessions on winter Friday evenings – weather permitting – it is not a working observatory but an important centre for the scientists who carry out research around the world using the UK's telescopes. The extensive visitors centre exhibitions are excellent, however, and will intrigue even those with only a faint interest in science for hours. Basic astronomical science is clearly explained, the history of astronomy in Edinburgh intriguingly told and the universe beautifully illustrated.

West Edinburgh

Boozing and banking have replaced brewing and barges as the principal attractions of this largely residential part of the city.

Most parts of Edinburgh are well known and well defined, with their own attractions for the visitor. Not so West Edinburgh, the part of the city stretching away from Lothian Road towards the bypass and the airport, which is often neglected by visitors. Much of the area is residential, but it does contrast some of the old economic engines of the city, such as brewing or canals, with the newer ones, particularly finance. There are also reminders of Edinburgh life that pre-date the last millennium.

Lothian Road

At the foot of Lothian Road, there are two churches. The obvious and slightly squat one is **St John's**, a great Episcopalian theme park with assorted shops in the basement. Consecrated in 1818, its stained glass is reckoned to be the finest collection under one roof in the whole of Scotland. Technically fine that is, as its relentless, 19th-century worthiness can overwhelm. The window best suited to contemporary tastes is in the chapel (built in 1935). It is a muted blue and purple affair showing Christ praying by the Sea of Galilee.

Next door is **St Cuthbert's**, named after a Northumbrian who beat the drum for early Christianity. He died in 687 and, as legend has it, a church was built here soon after. According to the history books, however, the first recorded church on the site was built in the 12th century when David I granted lands for the purpose. Its colourful history includes getting caught up in various sieges of Edinburgh Castle; it was occupied by Cromwell's troops in 1650, then Bonnie Prince Charlie's in 1745. Not surprisingly, the building has gone through many incarnations: the current one only dates back to 1894, although the steeple was built in 1789. The graveyard provides a shady retreat in the heart of the city for the footsore tourist. Other inhabitants include artist Alexander Nasmyth (who painted the famous portrait of Robert Burns), the logarithm inventor John Napier and the city's original drugs writer, Thomas de Quincey. He penned *Confessions of an English Opium Eater* in 1822, beating Irvine Welsh to the punch by around 170 years. Some 19th-century inhabitants tended to spend rather less time entombed, however, as their bodies

Standard Life (*p86*), *interesting plaza.*

were the targets of grave robbers. The lookout tower on the corner of Lothian Road and King's Stables Road is a reminder of those times.

Inside, St Cuthbert's has a large frieze behind the apse, based on Leonardo's *Last Supper*. Other assorted artwork and one of its stained-glass windows was commissioned from Tiffany's in New York. All very un-Presbyterian.

Opposite the churches is the secular temple to expensive overnighting, the **Caledonian Hotel** (*see page 105*). This great, red-stone edifice was frowned upon by natives when it appeared in 1903 as something more suited to vulgarian Glasgow. It was originally a railway hotel; the adjacent station closed in 1965, though the frieze over the former station entrance survives in the foyer by the hotel bistro.

Lothian Road itself, which dates to the 1780s, comes alive at night with the overflow from its pubs and bars. Many are far from salubrious and the road has a long history of hedonism – it was a favourite haunt of the young Robert Louis Stevenson, escaping the bourgeois claustrophobia of his New Town home. Rather less earthy entertainment is given at the **Usher Hall** (*see page 202*), which was built in 1914 with a £100,000 gift from the brewer Andrew Usher. Edinburgh's premier concert hall, it was recently extensively refurbished with all-new heating and wiring after the ceiling developed a rather unfortunate tendency to fall down. It is situated between the **Royal Lyceum** theatre (*see page 221*), with its glass façade and opulent auditorium, and the **Traverse Theatre** (*see page 221*) which, with a rather more modern practicality, is housed in the purpose-built basement of the modern offices of Saltire Court. The **Traverse Bar** (*see page161*) is a recommended place to find refreshment at any time of day or evening.

The Exchange

As the 20th century worked its way to a moneyed close, the area around the West Approach Road and Lothian Road saw a £350-million construction extravaganza described by the city's public relations team of the time, in predictably overblown terms, as Edinburgh's most important since the New Town.

First on the scene, in 1985 and before a formal development strategy had been hatched, was the almost Romanian façade (Ceauçescu era) of the **Sheraton Grand Hotel** (*see page 117*). In 1988, the city council launched a plan to promote the area as the **Exchange**, a new financial district. Investment managers Baillie Gifford sited Rutland Court, with its mirror-shades chic, on the West Approach Road in 1991, but the heart of the new area was to be the emblematic **Edinburgh International Conference Centre**. Designed by Terry Farrell, this opened on Morrison Street in 1995 and resembles an ambitious upturned engine part.

Soon the big names were moving in. Scotland's largest company, **Standard Life**, opted for new headquarters on Lothian Road in 1997, while the **Clydesdale Bank** erected its Plaza on the other side of the West Approach Road. The overall effect is reminiscent of London's Broadgate but with less Gordon Gecko sociopathy. The Standard Life building, by the Michael Laird Partnership, made an attempt at incorporating more creative elements, courtesy of sculptor John Maine (gates, entrance) and artist Jane Kelly (lights, railings). But the latest arrival, on the corner of Morrison Street and Semple Street, beats them all for sheer verve. The **Scottish Widows** headquarters by Glasgow's Building Design Partnership, completed in 1998, has a main crescent block that begs to house something more interesting than a pensions management company. But that's what generated the cash to pay for this kind of architecture in the first place.

The canal might not link up to Glasgow any more, but there's plenty of room for everyone.

Fountainbridge

Before the railways made an impact on the city, the last word in 19th-century transport was the Union Canal. The combined efforts of French stonemasons and Irish navvies helped build the waterway, which was completed in 1822 and ran from Lothian Road to Camelon near Falkirk in West Lothian, where it linked up with the Forth & Clyde Canal to Glasgow. In from West Lothian came passengers, coal and building materials; out from the city went merchants' goods, horse manure and more passengers, although not always in the same barge.

The original terminus of Port Hopetoun was at the site of Lothian House on Lothian Road, now home to the **ABC Film Centre** (*see page 196*). A close scrutiny of the building reveals decorative elements commemorating canal life. But as railways captured the zeitgeist of the age, and the Edinburgh and Glasgow Railway Company bought up the waterway in 1848, the canal was allowed to decay and commercial traffic died out after the 1860s. Port Hopetoun was drained and built upon in 1922, while the canal itself was officially mothballed in the 1960s, and parts were built over. The canal now ends at Fountainbridge and can be reached along Gilmore Park, next door to the Fountain Brewery where the old Leamington Lift Bridge now sits.

The canal towpath has become an alternative, if down-at-heel, route out of the city centre for joggers, walkers and cyclists. It provides intriguing glimpses of industrial relics on its way past Polworth and Colinton to the aqueduct at Slateford where it joins the **Water of Leith Walkway** (*see page 67*). The only traffic on the canal itself is from rowing boats and waterfowl. Eco-friendly recreational water transport is en vogue, however, and the Millennium Link, a project to reopen both the Union and the Forth & Clyde Canals, will create a continuous waterway between Edinburgh and Glasgow once again. Although there's no completion date set, owing to the engineering challenges thrown up by the project, most of the money is in place.

Rather less environmentally sound entertainment takes place in the Fountainpark leisure complex. Thrown together with all the bright, modern dullness of airport architectural vernacular, it is home to several large nightclubs and bars, a bowling alley, a 13-screen cinema, and the **Shaping a Nation** visitor attraction (*see below*).

Shaping a Nation

Fountainpark, Dundee Street, EH11 (229 1706). Bus 1, 22, 28, 34, 35, 35A. **Open** 10am-5pm Mon-Sat; 11am-5pm Sun. **Admission** £5.50; £4 concessions; £16 family. **Credit** MC, V. **Map** p308 B7.
With a modern hands-on approach to Scottish history, this attraction ('museum' is too old-fashioned a word) provides plenty to amuse those with more limited attention spans. Beside the displays about the great Scottish inventors and feats of Scottish engineering, there are interactive quizzes on all aspects of Scotland and access points to interactive computer programmes about Scottish history. It is in these latter, which include a wealth of historical documents from the Treaty of Edinburgh to Donald Dewar's speech at the opening of the Scottish Parliament in 1999, that the place does more than scratch the surface of history. The tour ends with a ten-minute iWERKS flight-simulator-type ride over Scotland's lochs and monuments.

Dalry & Gorgie

The West of Edinburgh was once a bucolic stretch of farms and small hamlets, with the area in immediate proximity to the Castle being given over to market gardening from the 12th century at the latest, and probably before. Such rural tranquillity hardly seems credible given the riot of tenements and late-20th-century developments that are crammed into the area now, but seek out some of the older buildings, and the picture of a time when life was rather slower than today gradually emerges.

Down Distillery Lane, for instance, off Dalry Road at Haymarket, there's a beautiful 18th-century mansion called **Easter Dalry House** (now an office) – Haymarket Station is in what used to be its garden. Further out along Dalry Road, on Orwell Place, is **Dalry House** – a survivor from the early 17th century. Hidden away in a residential warren, it is hard to imagine this beige-harled effort as an old Scots manor in extensive grounds. Although the height of respectability these days (it is run by Age Concern), one former owner, John Chiesley, wasn't quite so douce. He was executed for murder in 1689, then buried in the back garden.

Even further out, just off the western end of Gorgie Road, sits the architectural mishmash of Saughton Prison, Edinburgh's lock-up since 1919. Its ghoulish claim to fame is as the site of the city's most recent execution. A total of four men have been dispatched at Saughton, proving that the 20th century was not all that less liberal than the 17th. The last to go, George Alexander Robertson, was found guilty of murder and hanged in June 1954. His and the three other bodies lie buried inside the precincts of the jail.

Still at the end of Gorgie Road, but behind the Shell petrol station, is **Stenhouse Mansion**. This three-storey block was built in 1623 and would once have stood out obviously in a meander of the Water of Leith. Now it is run by Historic Scotland (668 8600) as a conservation and restoration centre, and is so well hidden that few locals even know it's there. The motto above the door reads, 'Blisit be God for all his giftis', a grace from the days when the master of the house, Patrick Eleis, could have looked back at the Castle, two-and-a-half miles (four kilometres) away over open land.

Slateford

At the height of the 19th-century beer frenzy, Edinburgh had over 40 breweries. Now there are just two. The biggest is the **Fountain Brewery** on Fountainbridge (not open to visitors), part of Scottish & Newcastle's empire and a manufacturing centre for two million barrels of iconic fizz each year, including McEwan's Export, McEwan's Lager and Younger's Tartan Special. Its huge, purple-lit chimney looms over the whole area at night and is also responsible for the pungent smell of yeast that hangs over West Edinburgh from time to time.

On the corner of Angle Park Terrace and Henderson Terrace is a famous Edinburgh institution: the Athletic Arms, popularly known as the Diggers, which has served the best pint of McEwan's 80/- in the city since formica was modern and Eric Clapton was cutting edge. The unremarkable Dalry Cemetery next door is where the pub's nickname comes from as the gravediggers used to pop in after work. A little further out at the start of Slateford Road is **North Merchiston Cemetery**, which was left to decay during years of private ownership

although it is now being cleaned up by the local authority. There's something particularly affecting about the unkempt North Merchiston, with its sprinkling of simple headstones for young men who died in World Wars I and II. The overall impact is far greater and more melancholic than at neighbouring Dalry.

Further out in Slateford Road, the **Caledonian Brewery** (*see below*) is a modern success story. Formerly owned by English brewer Vaux, it was to be closed in 1987 but was saved by a local management buy out. The business focused on real ales and now its Caledonian 80/- and Deuchars IPA win awards. Caledonian's Victorian red-brick buildings host ceilidhs on Saturday nights and an annual beer festival (*see page 96*). **The Caley Sample Room** (*see page 162*) is the best place to drink them.

Caledonian Brewery

Heritage Centre, 42 Slateford Road, EH11 (623 8066/www.caledonian-brewery.co.uk). Bus 28, 35, 35A or Slateford rail. **Open** Tours 11.30am, 12.30pm, 2.30pm and by arrangement. **Admission** £5. **Credit** AmEx, MC, V.

A near-disastrous fire in 1994 allowed this forward-thinking brewery, which still uses original brewing methods, to build a visitors centre and let the public in. Real ale fans will thrill at the open coppers, still fired by direct flame and the last of their kind still working. Real history buffs, meanwhile, will take more interest in the feel for Edinburgh's social life that the visitors centre gives. All, no doubt, will find tasting the ales brewed there even more interesting.

Looking west along Shandwick Place towards Haymarket and **Dalry**. *See page 87.*

Leith

Proudly independent, Leith is looking up as its dock area is regenerated and the *Royal Yacht Britannia* comes to stay.

A town bearing the motto 'persevere', Leith was for centuries the most important port in Scotland, providing trading links with the Netherlands, France, Portugal and the Mediterranean, as well as being a great shipbuilding town. It has always made use of its economic importance to the capital to square up to its dominant neighbour. Although the history of Leith and Edinburgh are inextricably linked, the people of the former have always felt a sense of separateness from those of the latter and have traditionally cast themselves as tenacious underdogs, ready to correct anyone who assumes they're from Edinburgh.

This bad feeling can be traced back to 1329 when Robert the Bruce included Leith in his Charter to Edinburgh. This gave the city control over the harbour to the extent that the captain of a ship berthed at Leith could not unload any cargo until the correct taxes had been paid three miles (five kilometres) inland at the Edinburgh Tolbooth. In a further Charter of 1428, James I gave Edinburgh the right to exact tolls from boats entering the port. Edinburgh controlled all of Leith's foreign trade until 1833 and the resentment became bitter. There were, however, a few years of separation. When the first modern docks were laid out in the early 1800s they cost so much that Edinburgh had to declare itself bankrupt. The docks were effectively nationalised in 1825. In 1833, an Act of Parliament gave Leith its independence as a parliamentary burgh. But the town never managed to generate enough income to sustain itself and amalgamation became increasingly likely after World War I. Not that it was popular with Leithers: in 1919 a last-ditch, toothless referendum was carried out in which Leithers voted 29,891 to 5,357 against amalgamation. But financial constraints were against them, and Edinburgh and Leith were merged in 1920.

Politics aside, Edinburgh and Leith have physically merged into one along **Leith Walk**, the mile-long thoroughfare that links the two. The **Boundary Bar** (379 Leith Walk; 554 2296) opposite Pilrig Church marks the point where Edinburgh and Leith join and the dividing line cuts through the middle of the bar. Legend, sadly apocryphal, has it that the resentment felt by Leithers was so deeply ingrained that drinkers on the Leith side wouldn't even cross to the other side of the bar at closing time to take advantage of Edinburgh's later opening times.

Leith Walk

Entering Leith down Leith Walk from Edinburgh city centre brings you straight to the **Kirkgate**. The historic hub of the town has been torn down and replaced with this faceless shopping arcade backing on to high-rise flats. In Leith, you're never far from a town planner's bungle.

Diagonally across from the Kirkgate are a supermarket and the aquatic playground **Leith Waterworld** (currently closed for renovation; *see below*). They stand on the site once occupied by Leith Central Station. Although it is now demolished, the abandoned station was part of the inspiration for *Trainspotting*. The hard drugs scene of the 1980s, as featured in Irvine Welsh's novel, threatened to tar Leith's reputation permanently, but the town's continuing regeneration is helping it to shake off its image as a junkie-ridden place in permanent industrial decline. The conversion of bonded warehouses into loft space is only the latest stage of a transformation that has also seen the advent of designer bars and cafés along the shorefront.

Leith Waterworld

377 Easter Road, EH6 (555 6000). Bus 7, 10, 16, 22. **Open** *school holidays* 10am-5pm daily; *term time* 10.30am-5.30pm Wed; 10am-5.30pm Thur-Sun; closed Mon, Tue. **Admission** £2.30; £1.40-£1.80 concessions; £5.50 family. **No credit cards**. **Map** p311 Jz.

This leisure pool is the best in Edinburgh – when it's not closed for repairs – and great for families. Attractions include the full range of wave machines, river runs, bubble beds, water slides, flumes and a learner lagoon.

Leith Links

To the east of the Kirkgate, at the foot of Easter Road, lie the green spaces of **Leith Links**. As Leith's traditional common land, the Links have been used for everything from cattle-grazing to archery contests. The Links also have a strong claim to be the home of golf, although the game has been prohibited here since 1907. While it is reported that, in 1593, the golf course on the Links was second only to St Andrews in seniority, the game's first set of rules was formulated in Leith. The Links also have more tragic associations. In 1560, the English army dug in here and raised artillery to besiege the town. Two of the gun emplacements, **Giants Brae** and **Lady Fyfe's Brae**, can still be seen as grassy mounds. Nowadays, the Links are mainly used for dog-walking, weekend football games and for visiting fairs.

Down Constitution Street, towards Bernard Street and the Shore, is South Leith Parish Church, which was rebuilt after being destroyed by cannon fire in the 1560 siege. Subtle ornaments to the architecture begin to reflect the maritime nature of the area and, among such fine pubs as **Homes** and **Nobles** (with beautiful stained-glass windows; 44A Constitution Street; 554 2024), the **Port O'Leith** (*see page 162*) has a true maritime atmosphere. Inside this cosy local is a huge array of flags and memorabilia, left to the bar by grateful seamen.

Signs of civic prosperity are visible in buildings like **Leith Assembly Rooms** and, round the corner in Bernard Street, the elegant, domed **Old Leith Bank**. The more upmarket of the new businesses that flooded into Leith during its regeneration in the 1980s are concentrated around this area, Leith's financial centre. For refreshment, the **Carriers Quarters** pub (42 Bernard Street; 554 4166), built in 1785 and barely changed since then, is a marvellous haven, particularly on winter nights.

The Shore

The Shore, the street overlooking the Water of Leith, is where Leith's regeneration is most apparent. The area has been lovingly restored, with new and appropriate buildings added. It boasts a run of fine bars and restaurants. Between the bright and airy **Raj Indian** restaurant (88-91 Henderson Street; 553 3980) at the junction of the Shore and Henderson Street, and **Malmaison**, a breathtakingly restored seamen's mission (now a hotel and restaurant; *see pages 111* and *125*), there are ample opportunities for good dining.

The **King's Wark** pub (*see page 162*) on the corner of the Shore and Bernard Street is the only remnant of James I's 'wark'. This was a storage point for cargo destined for royal use, which was begun around 1428, when James extended the port, and added to by subsequent monarchs until, at one time, it covered several blocks.

In the streets between the Shore and Constitution Street you can imagine the haphazard tangle of narrow alleys from

Malmaison – hotel, restaurant and landmark in one.

It's a **Shore** thing. *See page 90.*

centuries past, despite the smart new apartment blocks and business premises that thrive there now. It is here that the port's first loft spaces opened, and were quickly snapped up by affluent professionals with bohemian aspirations. Historically, the most notable building is **Provost Lambs House**, which is of uncertain age but great character. The Shore comes into its own on summer evenings when al fresco drinking, normally anathema to the Scots, seems perfectly natural.

The docks are still working commercially and access to some areas is limited. Signs indicate which parts these are, so it is easy to wander around, although it is quite a distance from one end to the other. The Tall Ships Race, which docked at Leith in 1996, gave the first real indication of the potential of the area for major events as thousands of people gathered to see the ocean-going sailing vessels.

Although no dock area is a sensible place to go wandering at pub closing time on a Friday or Saturday, Leith is less threatening than Lothian Road or the Cowgate up in the centre of Edinburgh at those times. Strangers to Leith should, however, exercise discretion when choosing their pubs and try to remain on the main thoroughfares later in the evening. Women on their own should certainly avoid Coburg Street and Coalhill at night lest they attract the attention of kerb-crawlers.

North & South Leith

Historically, Leith was split by the **Water of Leith**. The area to the west of the river mouth is called **North Leith** and to the east is **South Leith**. The river was described by Robert Louis Stevenson as 'that dirty Water of Leith'. Its reputation was well deserved but it has been cleaned up over the last 25 years. Even so, residents are complaining again about the scum and rubbish collecting at the bridges, and the fact that no one will take the responsibility to cleanse it. The **Water of Leith Walkway** (*see also page 67*), which starts at the northern end of the Sandport Place Bridge, follows the riverbank up to the heart of Edinburgh and is one of the best walks in the city.

Even if it is the centre of Leith's red-light district, **Coburg Street**, which connects the Shore with Ferry Road and runs parallel with the Water of Leith, is worth passing through in the daylight. Points of interest include the Dutch-style steeple of the ruined **Old St Ninian's Church** and the old **North Leith Churchyard**. A detour into **Couper Street**, opposite, brings you to **EASY** (Edinburgh Architectural Salvage Yard; *see page 164*), an Aladdin's cave of old fireplaces, pews, doors and other flotsam.

Straight over the bridge from Bernard Street, past the grand columns of Custom House and down Dock Place, lies **The Waterfront Wine**

Bar & Bistro (*see page 162*). It was one of the first attempts to lure solvent professionals to the area. It now has a branch of the Pierre Victoire chain of restaurants, the excellent fish restaurant **Skippers** (*see page 125*) and a trendy, over-designed café-bar, **Bar Sirius** (*see page 162*) for company.

Round the corner, on **Commercial Quay**, the developments have been far more dramatic. A row of bonded warehouses running almost the entire length of **Commercial Street** has been renovated into desirable apartments, upmarket shops and glass-fronted restaurants. Facing them, across the quayside, is the imposing piece of post-modern architecture that houses the former Scottish Office, now renamed the **Scottish Executive** in the aftermath of devolution. Its design certainly is uncompromising, and not to everyone's taste, but its boldness epitomises the spirit of redevelopment that has been taking place here, where the old and new interlock with surprising ease.

North Leith is best approached via **Great Junction Street**, which is a busy street of grocers, downmarket clothing shops, funeral directors and a couple of grim indoor markets. During shopping hours, it is usually thronging with senior citizens. Many of Leith's younger residents have been rehoused in outlying housing schemes.

One of the few sights off Great Junction Street is Junction Place's **Leith Victoria Swimming Pool** (*see page 93*), which opened in 1896. Left, down Bangor Street, is **Leith Mills**, where Scottish gifts, knitwear, golfing paraphernalia, a Clan Tartan centre and a café are all crammed into a warehouse space.

Over Junction Bridge, the corner of Ferry Road and North Junction Street is overlooked by a gable-end mural depicting the history of Leith. Symbolised as the final piece of a jigsaw and the target of some mud-slinging by local kids, a Sikh is pictured reaching to take the outstretched hand of the community. Most of the Sikhs in Edinburgh live in Leith, and their temple is in a converted church just back over the bridge and down Mill Lane towards the Shore. To the left of the mural are two grand but unfussy buildings, **Leith Library** and **Leith Theatre**, opened in 1932 and a superb example of economical design, with the theatre's portico following the curve of the library's semicircular reading room. Straight

Sikh and ye shall find a colourful mural describing the history of the area.

ahead is North Junction Street, where **Leith School of Art** inhabits the oldest Norwegian seamen's church outside Norway, a small Lutheran kirk dating from 1868.

The spire of **North Leith Parish Church** on Madeira Street, its impressive classical columns tucked away off the main road, marks the area where Leith Fort once stood. In 1779, John Paul Jones sailed up to Leith on a ship donated by the French and demanded £20,000 in compensation for British atrocities in America. A sudden storm forced him to cancel his plans, but the scare prompted the building of a fort housing 100 men, who, until its completion in 1809, were permanently encamped on the Links. Only guardhouses and parts of the wall remain, and on its site are the forbidding blocks of flats that inherited the name.

Leith Victoria Swimming Pool

Junction Place, EH6 (555 4728). Bus 7, 10, 34. **Open** phone for times. **Tickets** £1.40; 85p concessions. **No credit cards. Map** p311 Hz. A good basic 22-m (72-ft) swimming pool in one of Edinburgh's original Victorian bath houses, with hot baths and a sauna.

Ocean Terminal & Newhaven

The redevelopment of Leith has been so spirited and decisive that it was chosen as the final resting place for the **Royal Yacht Britannia** (*see below*), which covered more than a million miles in 40 years of ferrying the royal family around the world on state visits. She can be found just past the point where North Junction Street meets Lindsay Road, the continuation of Commercial Street.

The deck of the Britannia provides an excellent view of North Leith and the docks, particularly the ambitious new **Ocean Terminal** complex on the western side of Victoria Dock, which is due to open in autumn 2001 and is linked to the vessel's Visitor Centre by a covered walkway. Designed by Sir Terence Conran, the complex will contain – as well as an ocean terminal for cruise liners with state-of-the-art security and baggage handling – large retail stores, restaurants and bars, a 100-bedroom hotel and 100 flats and townhouses, an 'entertainment venue', health club facilities, a multiplex cinema and a museum, plus the inevitable conference facilities.

Following the shoreline west along Lindsay Road, past the gleaming white silos of **Chancelot Mill**, leads to the old fishing village of **Newhaven**. Much of the original village has been pulled down, but there are still some original fishermen's cottages in the streets near the shore. Up until the 20th century, Newhaven was a very insular community, thought to have descended from the intermarriage of locals and the craftsmen brought over from France, Scandinavia, Spain and Portugal by James III to build ships. Newhaven became famous for its sturdy and colourfully dressed fishwives who used to carry their creels full of fresh fish up to Edinburgh to sell every morning.

The once-flourishing **Fishmarket**, built in 1896, now uses only a fraction of the space that it once took up. The long red building has become home to a branch of Harry Ramsden's fish and chip shop, where, once a month, Scottish Opera and Northern Opera take turns to regale the punters with a bit of class, and the **Newhaven Heritage Museum** (*see below*). Although small, this is a vibrant community museum, renowned for its child-friendly exhibits, which has recordings of local residents recalling their working lives in the early 20th century. It is also a bit of a hangout for the older generation, who are more than happy to regale the interested visitor with stories.

Newhaven Heritage Museum

24 Pier Place, EH6 (551 4165). Bus 7, 10, 11, 16. **Open** noon-4.45pm daily. **Admission** free. **Map** p311 Ex. What this one-room museum lacks in size it makes up for in vitality. It needs to as it's quite a trek from the middle of town – east of Leith on the Forth shore, next to Harry Ramsden's – but one the fishwives made every day loaded down with their creels of fish to sell door-to-door round the city. The Newhaven living history project has done its job well and the recorded memories are vibrant and telling, although the accents might prove quite difficult to non-locals. The exhibits are a little wordy but child friendly.

Royal Yacht Britannia

Western Harbour, Leith Docks, EH6 (555 5566). Bus 10, 16, 22, 34 and dedicated shuttle bus service from Waverley Bridge. **Open** 10.30am-4.30pm daily. **Admission** £7.50; £5.75 OAPs; £3.75 concessions; £20 family. **Credit** AmEx, MC, V. **Map** p311 Gx. Even ardent Republicans could find a great deal of interest aboard the *Royal Yacht Britannia*, whether it's the Queen's telling passion for chintzy and flowery furniture coverings or the tiny cabin-space allocated to the admirals who captained the ship. The tradition of cleaning and polishing every item every day has continued, so that, even though the *Britannia* was decommissioned in 1997, setting foot on her is almost like stepping back to the 1950s – a revealing fact in itself. Small wonder that certain members of the royal family voiced a preference to see her scuttled rather than opened to the public.

Edinburgh by Season

OK, so it's known the world over for the Festival. Just don't forget that, whatever time of year you're here, there's plenty going on.

Sometimes it feels as if you're experiencing a whole year of seasons in a day in Edinburgh – such are the vagaries of the weather. Snow, sun, wind and rain can all have their hour during a walk around the city. Likewise, there is always something going on, whether it is a talk at the Royal Museum of Scotland, an organ recital at St Giles' Cathedral or a behind-the-scenes tour at the Traverse Theatre. All these things happen on an occasional basis but, probably influenced by the success of the Edinburgh International Festival itself, Edinburgh folk do have a penchant for grouping events into festivals. And of course, whichever event is taking place, there is an ingrained beauty to Edinburgh, whatever the weather.

For those events marked 'tbc', the exact date was yet to be confirmed as this guide went to press; always phone to check these first. Note that some events are free, while others charge admission: phone the relevant numbers for information.

Spring

Coats come off, scarves go back in the drawer and vegetation across the city bursts into bloom. The daffodils on Castle Hill, seen from Princes Street, would send Wordsworth searching for a better collective noun than 'host'. The cherry trees in St Andrew's Square and across the walks of the Meadows bring a secret smile to all that see them. As for the Royal Botanic Gardens, the rhododendra are a sight to behold. British Summer Time begins – and the clocks go forward an hour on the last Sunday in March: the 25th in 2001; 31st in 2002.

Easter Day is Sunday 15 April 2001 and Sunday 31 March 2002.

Edinburgh Science Festival

Various venues around Edinburgh
(information line 530 2001/box office 473 2070/
esf@scifest.demon.co.uk/
www.edinburghfestivals.co.uk). **Open** *information line* 9am-5pm Mon-Fri; closed Sat, Sun. **Dates** 7-17 April 2001; phone for 2002 dates.

Edinburgh has long been a city of scientific excellence: its scientifically minded children reach back to 1550 and the birth of Napier, the inventor of logarithms; and since the Enlightenment the city has been associated with the cutting edge of science,

thanks to the universities and the Scottish school system. The Science Festival, founded in 1987, is a bold and largely successful attempt to continue this trend by providing lectures and events that popularise all branches of science and technology. Without dumbing down, the Festival has become adept at putting a controversial and topical slant on the average of 220 events held in 40 venues around Edinburgh, thus ensuring maximum media exposure and continuing to attract scientific heavyweights from around the world. Much of its success must also be ascribed to the trick of presenting what could otherwise be dull and exceedingly dry material as part of a festival – which helps to put a positive slant on the presentations. The current trend is away from table-top experiments, towards more theatrical events, most of which take place in the family programme in the Assembly rooms.

Beltane

Calton Hill, EH7. Bus 3, 12, 16, 17, 24. **Times** 10pm-dawn. **Dates** 30 April annually. **Map** p307 G4.

As the winter nights shorten and the spring sap starts rising, in Edinburgh as elsewhere, people's thoughts turn to lust and wooing. Beltane captures some of this innate sensuality in a modern ritual, reinvented in 1988 by Angus Farquar of the radical art activists NVA. It takes place on Calton Hill from about 10pm, lasts until dawn and incorporates all sorts of fertility and seasonal rites, including the passage of winter into spring. The centrepiece of the night is the ritual procession of the May Queen to four elemental points around the hill, followed by the death and rebirth of the Green Man and the lighting of a huge bonfire. The ritual is slightly different every year, as the loose group of people who organise it changes. It can get crowded on the hill top. But the event, which makes liberal use of fire, dressing up, drumming and acting, is best enjoyed by those who stray from the role of spectator to participant – in however minor a way. This is the sort of anarchic night at which everyone can make their own impression: it won't do any harm to take a flask of whisky to toast the May Queen, something flammable to add to the bonfire and the inclination to stay up all night.

Edinburgh Independent Radical Book Fair

Organised by Word Power bookshop, 43 West Nicolson Street, South Edinburgh, EH8 (662 9112/ wordpower@free4all.co.uk). Bus 40-42, 46. **Dates** mid-May annually.

A long weekend, usually held in the Assembly Rooms on George Street. The event, organised by

Beltane – the rites place to be. *See page 94.*

Word Power bookshop (*see p167*), consists of readings, book launches, panel discussions and general promotion of books from small, independent and radical publishers.

Scottish International Children's Festival

Various city-centre theatres (information 225 8050/ www.edinburghfestivals.co.uk). **Open** *information* 9am-5pm Mon-Fri; closed Sat, Sun. **Dates** last week in May annually.

Taking children's theatre seriously does not mean serious theatre, but some of the best theatre for children in the world, all happening at the same time.

After a wash-out at the original site in Inverleith Park, the Festival moved to the city-centre theatres, like the Traverse and Royal Lyceum. Besides a strong international element, recent years have seen an increase in new writing for children. At its best, this is powerfully evocative stuff.

Summer

None of your 'I went to a matinée at the Filmhouse and missed the summer' for Edinburgh. While summer showers might wet you slightly, the long days more than

Public holidays

On public holidays and bank holidays many shops remain open, but public transport services are less frequent. On Christmas Day and New Year, however, most things close down.
New Year's Day Mon 1 Jan 2001; Tue 1 Jan 2002.
Bank Holiday Tue 2 Jan 2001; Wed 2 Jan 2002.
Spring Holiday Mon 9 Apr 2001; Mon 15 Apr 2002.
Good Friday Fri 13 Apr 2001; Fri 29 Mar 2002.
May Day Mon 7th May 2001; Mon 6 May 2002.

Victoria Day (Edinburgh only) Mon 21 May 2001; Mon 20 May 2002.
Spring Bank Holiday Mon 28 May 2001; Mon 27 May 2002.
Summer Bank Holiday Mon 7 Aug 2000; Mon 6 Aug 2001; Mon 5 Aug 2002.
Public Holiday (Edinburgh only) Mon 18 Sept 2000; Mon 17 Sept 2001; Mon 16 Sept 2002.
Christmas Day Mon 25 Dec 2000; Tue 25 Dec 2001; Wed 25 Dec 2002.
Boxing Day Tue 26 Dec 2000; Wed 26 Dec 2001; Wed 27 Dec 2002.

adequately make up for it. Around the end of June the nights are truly dark for no more than an hour – if, that is, the sky is clear.

Pride Scotland
The Meadows, South Edinburgh, EH3 (information line 556 8822). **Dates** June 2001, 2003. **Map** p309 F7.
Founded to 'celebrate the pride in the lifestyles of lesbian, gay, bisexual and transgender people, expressed in an annual march and festival', Pride Scotland is really an excuse for a whacking great knees up, usually on the last weekend in June. Not as outrageous as London Pride, it's still a great, affirming day out, with the partying continuing in the clubs and bars on Broughton Street into the wee small hours. In 2000 and 2002 Pride Scotland will be held at Glasgow Green.

Caledonian Beer Festival
Caledonian Brewery, 42 Slateford Road, West Edinburgh, EH14 (337 1286). **Bus** 28, 35, 35A/ *Slateford rail.* **Dates** first weekend in June annually.
Edinburgh's only independent brewery has a great deal to shout about with its fine selection of real ales. But that doesn't deter it from welcoming some 50 of its competitors' brews to join its own over a long weekend that is becoming a bit of a tradition with excellent catering and bands every evening.

Meadows Festival
The Meadows, South Edinburgh, EH3. **Bus** 24, 23, 28, 40, 45. **Dates** first weekend in June annually. **Map** p309 F7.
The walkways of the Meadows become lined with

stalls for this mini-festival, which also encompasses live musical entertainment, kids' amusements and fairground rides.

Royal Highland Show
Royal Highland Showground, Ingliston (information 335 6200/info@rhass.org.uk/www.rhass.org.uk). **Bus** *Scottish Citylink service 900/902 to Glasgow.* **Dates** 22-25 June 2000; 21-24 June 2001; 20-23 June 2002.
Held out at the Royal Highland Showground, Ingliston (ten miles/16km west of the city centre, near Edinburgh Airport), the Royal Highland Show is the biggest and probably the best place to see everything Scottish that is vaguely agricultural. This is where to go if you want to smell the animals that end up on your plates, see the machines that help grow the crops and ogle the food that results from all the farmers' efforts. The judged farm animal sections – all 400 of them – attract thousands of entries; there is some serious consumerism to be had – from combine harvesters to high-street goods; and the ring events are of top quality. It's a solid family day out for you and 150,000 other visitors.

T in the Park
Balado Airfield, by Kinross, Perthshire (information line 07000 113 114). **Dates** 8-9 July 2000; early July 2001, 2002 (tbc).
Scotland's big outdoor music festival is pulling in both the punters and the bands since starting in Strathclyde Park in 1994 and moving to a rural venue in Perthshire in 1997. As is the way with these things, nothing is confirmed until a month or so before the event, but expect the full range of festival names and a dedicated bus service from most

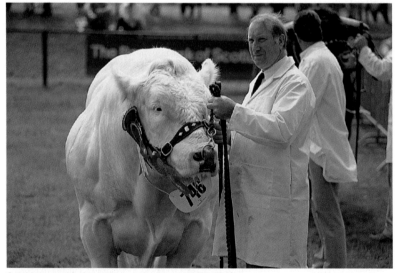

Catching up with the in-laws at the **Royal Highland Show**.

Scottish cities. Oasis, Underworld, the Prodigy, Ritchie Hawtin, and Nick Cave and Kylie Minogue have all trod the stages in years past.

The Festival

What is known, colloquially at least, as 'The Festival' is, in fact, a collection of six different festivals and events, each with its own distinct feel and organisation, but all held in Edinburgh during August.

Edinburgh International Festival

Various venues around Edinburgh; tickets from The Hub, 348 Castlehill, Royal Mile, EH1 (473 2001/ info@eif.co.uk/www.eif.co.uk). Bus 35, 35A. **Open** *The Hub* 9.30am-5.30pm daily. **Dates** 13 Aug-2 Sept 2000; 12 Aug-1 Sept 2001; 11-31 Aug 2002. **Map** p314 C3.

The first, although not, now, the biggest, of the six festivals was the Edinburgh International Festival. It was founded in 1947 following the concerted efforts of the Lord Provost John Falconer, Harry Wood of the British Council and Rudolph Bing, who became its first director. The major arts festivals of continental Europe were still in turmoil after World War II. The aim was, and still is, to 'provide the world with a centre where, year after year, all that is best in music, drama and the visual arts can be seen and heard in ideal surroundings'. Festival performances take place in most of the large venues around Edinburgh. The programme is published in April (phone the above number to order a copy). The offices of the EIF are in The Hub (*see p208*) on Castlehill, where the Ticket Centre sells tickets for most of Edinburgh's festivals.

Edinburgh International Film Festival

Most cinemas in Edinburgh, but centred at Filmhouse, 88 Lothian Road, EH3 (information 229 2550/2284051/info@edfilmfest.org.uk/ www.edfilmfest.org.uk). Bus 11, 15, 24. **Dates** 13-27 Aug 2000; 12-26 Aug 2001; 11-25 Aug 2002. **Map** p309 D6.

Immediately the folk at the Edinburgh Film Guild got wind of the plans for the International Festival they were incensed. A modern festival that did not celebrate film, the quintessential artistic medium of the 20th century? The Guild, with its founder Norman Wilson and the *Scotsman*'s film critic Forsyth Hardy at the controls, funded and staged the first Edinburgh International Festival of Documentary Films. Since 1947 it has broadened out from its tight documentary remit. Although it is no longer 'the only film festival worth a damn', as John Huston said in 1972, the two weeks of screenings are invariably a hotbed of young British filmmaking talent, an important showplace for new British and continental films and a forum for a Hollywood blockbuster or three to hold their European openings.

The Fringe

The Fringe Office, 180 High Street, Royal Mile, EH1 (226 5257/admin@edfringe.com/www.edfringe.com). Bus 35, 35A. **Open** *postal & Internet bookings* from early July; *box office* mid-July to end of EIF 10am-7pm daily. **Dates** 6-28 Aug 2000; 5-27 Aug 2001 (tbc); 4-26 Aug 2002 (tbc). **Map** p314 D3.

At the very first International Festival there were eight officially uninvited companies. But the term 'Fringe' was not used until 1948 when Robert Kemp wrote in the *Evening News* of 14 August that 'Round the fringe of official Festival drama there seems to be more private enterprise than ever before'. By the end of the 1950s, performers were describing themselves as being on the Fringe. From day one, the Fringe has been self-selecting. All a performer needs is a venue and enough money to buy a listing in the Fringe programme. Which means that the truly 'out-there' and avant-garde rub shoulders with the most steadfastly traditional, the really appalling with the most professional, the never-will-be hopefuls with the Gielguds of the next generation. Indeed, members of the Monty Python team performed in 1964 and Rowan Atkinson's review of 1977 closed after the first night as a flop. The Fringe certainly lives up to its reputation as the greatest arts festival in the world. In 1998, it decoupled itself from the EIF and now starts one week earlier.

Edinburgh Military Tattoo

Castle Esplanade, Royal Mile, EH1 (information 225 1188/edintattoo@edintattoo.co.uk/ www.edintattoo.co.uk). Bus 35, 35A. **Open** *information* 10am-4.30pm Mon-Fri; closed Sat, Sun; *Festival* 10am-9pm Mon-Fri; 10am-10.30pm Sat; 10am-4.30pm Sun. **Dates** 4-26 Aug 2000; 3-25 Aug 2001; 2-24 Aug 2002. **Map** p314 B3.

First performed in 1950 as the army's contribution to the Festival, the Tattoo has become its single most popular event, with 200,000 tickets sold every year. By show-time, there is rarely an empty seat on the temporary stands that line the Castle Esplanade. Although an overtly militaristic display, it is also a pageant of colour that uses its hundreds of performers and the Castle backdrop to stunning effect. Beware the tide of people entering and leaving the Tattoo in the early evening who cause serious traffic problems in the Royal Mile.

Book Festival

Charlotte Square Gardens, New Town, EH2 (information 228 5444/admin@edbookfest.co.uk/ www.edbookfest.co.uk). Bus 13, 19, 55, 82. **Open** *Festival* 9.30am-9pm daily. **Dates** 12-28 Aug 2000; 11-27 Aug 2001; 10-26 Aug 2002. **Map** p314 A1.

A relative newcomer to the Festival scene, the Book Festival occupies a tented village in the centre of Charlotte Square and usually takes place around the same time as the Film Festival. Notable for the number of authors it attracts and its lack of publishing trade professionals, it continues to grow and attract new audiences, particularly for its strong programme of children's events.

Sightseeing

Bet they're not really playing those instruments: the **Jazz & Blues Festival** belts 'em out.

Surviving the Festival

Getting through a full-blown encounter with the Edinburgh Festival can be compared to white-water rafting on particularly rocky rapids. You can do any amount of planning to make sure you'll come out of the experience alive, but once started, you don't have much control over what goes on – best just to cling in there and enjoy the ride.

The first directive of Festival-going is to make like a boy scout and be prepared. Get as many programmes as you can before coming to Edinburgh. If you're intent on seeing a specific performer or performance in the International Festival, particularly on the musical side, it is wise to buy those tickets early. The best seats for the big concerts sell out quickly.

If, however, you simply want a blast of top cultural entertainment to round off a few days of Fringe-going, then it is quite safe to wait until you arrive to choose your fancy.

The really hot tickets of every year's Festival are for the firework concert in

Princes Street Gardens, which takes place on the last Saturday of the Festival. These tickets are for the best seats of all, in the gardens themselves, and are mostly only available by postal application (contact the Hub on 473 2001), although a few are held back until the week before. The views are good, however, from all over town. Princes Street and the Mound offer the best close-up views, while North Bridge and Calton Hill allow for a bit more perspective.

Take a portable radio and tune in to the local station, Radio Forth (97.3 FM), which carries the concert live. Some people rate the view from even further afield – the Botanics or the far shore of Fife. But they don't get the full-on experience of the ground quaking as the big mortars thrust their pyrotechnic loads into the night sky.

Having procured the various festival programmes, peruse them thoroughly. This is the time to work out how the programmes – particularly the Fringe's – actually work. Make

Jazz & Blues Festival

Various venues around Edinburgh (tickets 668 2019/ information 467 5200/www.jazzmusic.co.uk). **Open** *information* 9am-5.30pm Mon-Fri; *ticket line* 10am-6pm daily. **Dates** 28 July-6 Aug 2000; 27 July-5 Aug 2001; 26 July-4 Aug 2002 (tbc).

Presenting 'the best of jazz to the biggest audience', the Festival covers most of its remit with the free Jazz on a Summer's Day in Princes Street Gardens and Mardi Grass in the Grassmarket. It also manages to cover the full range of jazz forms, in venues from the Playhouse to pubs and cabaret bars.

Autumn

As the haar – or sea mist – starts creeping up from the Forth and drizzles set in, Edinburgh folk's thoughts turn to indoor entertainment. Ceilidhs abound across the town. Much whisky is tasted and savoured. But that steel-grey sky still brings a remarkable beauty to the city. British Summer Time ends – and the clocks go back an hour – on the last Sunday in October: the 29th in 2000; 28th in 2001; and 27th in 2002.

Open Doors Day

Various buildings around Edinburgh. Details from Cockburn Association, Trunk's Close, 55 High Street, Royal Mile, EH1 (information 557 8686).

Open *information* 9am-5pm Mon-Fri, closed Sat, Sun. **Dates** 30 Sept 2000; 29 Sept 2001 (tbc).

On one day a year (usually the last Saturday in September) the Cockburn Association persuades the owners of many of Edinburgh's finest private buildings to open their doors to the public. The buildings that participate change every year, so contact the association for details.

Hallowe'en: Samhain

Parliament Square, High Street, Royal Mile, EH1. Bus 35, 35A. **Date** 31 Oct annually. **Map** p314 C3.

In recent years, the Beltane organisation (*see p94*) has attempted to revive the so-called quarter days of the ancient calendar. Samhain, which coincides with Hallowe'en, is the most obvious and members of the organisation take to the streets with much frenzied dancing and beating of drums.

Bonfire Night

Date 5 November annually.

Modern Scots have a certain ambivalence towards Guy Fawkes. The fact that his gunpowder plot of 1605 was against Scotland's own James IV is somehow masked by the fact that it was also against the English Parliament, a sentiment secretly supported in many a Scottish heart – at least up to the granting of the Scottish Parliament. But there again, any excuse for a party. The biggest firework displays are generously organised by the Council in Meadowbank Stadium (*see p217*).

In the middle of **The Fringe**. *See page 97.*

a wish list of must-see performances and perform some serious time management yourself. Make lists. Make more lists. A top tip is to work out an itinerary based around the Book and Film Festival events, which are mostly one-offs. You might even consider booking for both these festivals, as they are renowned for being places where authors and directors get to meet their public.

Having programmed every available second of your days in Edinburgh – performances start at breakfast time and finish well after most sane people are tucked snugly up in bed – work out how much it will all cost and how much time it will take to travel between each different venue. At this point you'll probably start daydreaming about a large bank error in your favour and the invention of a simultaneous matter transmitter.

It is wise not to book tickets for every show you want to see at this juncture. Your perceptions will change once you're in town. Also avoid shows that sell themselves on their nudity factor. It's a cheap form of publicity that masks more bad acting than it reveals naughty bits.

What will also change is the shape of your bottom. While the Festival and Fringe have evolved out of all recognition over the last 50 ►

Er... do I know you? **Edinburgh's Hogmanay**.

Winter

The nights are long, the days are dark and the wind can come howling in off the North Sea with a bitter Siberian after-taste. Visitors should pack accordingly – but be prepared for the odd day of deceptive sun. Exactly when the Edinburgh year begins depends on whether it is viewed from the aspect of a pessimist or an optimist. The former will choose 1 January – Ne'er Day – when most folk are reflecting on the hangover caused by the past night. The optimist will plump for Hogmanay itself: the last night of the year, the first of the new and cause for much public merrymaking.

Edinburgh's Hogmanay

Various venues around central Edinburgh (information 473 3800). **Dates** 29 Dec-1 Jan annually.

Hogmanay is New Year's Eve. The night when the people throughout Scotland take to the streets, meet by the market cross, kiss everyone within sight when the bells ring out and thence go 'first footing' with a lump of coal, a bun and a drop of the hard stuff. But Edinburgh became so notorious for its good-natured celebrations that in 1993 the City Council took paid advice from local entrepreneur Pete Irvine and instigated a three-day festival. Borrowing wisely and widely from Scottish tradition, Edinburgh's Hogmanay now features the

▶ Surviving the Festival (continued)

years, many of the seats have not. Before leaving make sure you pack something that can add just a little bit of comfort and padding. Don't bring something too soft or you will end up falling asleep, but that cross-stitch cushion Aunty Betty gave you for Christmas seven years ago will do fine. Also pack a few spare rolls of toilet paper, particularly if you're staying in a friend's flat.

Immediately on arrival make two purchases: the *Scotsman* and the *List*. The former carries more reviews than any other paper, the latter more previews and reviews than any other magazine; together they are a good way to start to understand the various time zones. Now you can find your accommodation, dump your kit and get going to your first show. You should also find yourself a good supply of very strong coffee. It is likely that you will need a large hit at regular intervals, as the pressure to overdo things will be intense. The

California Coffee Co (*see page 144*) and The Elephant House (*see page 145*) are both recommended.

There are two extremes of Festival-going: the itinerary-bound believer in firm plans and the laid-back follower of the coolest vibe. An itinerary allows you to remain focused and optimise your show-going potential. Waver towards this if time is limited or the number of shows you see is important. Hanging around in the bar after a show to find out what the best tips are can send you off to some unexpectedly groovy treats. Favour this option if you're in town for more than a weekend or the hipness factor of the shows you see means a lot to you.

The best time is to be had by holding both of these attitudes while making yourself aware of what the reviewers are saying. So be prepared to ignore all your lists. Although your first day in Edinburgh will leave you buzzing with cultural input and ready to drop after running from show to show, by the second day, you will be an old hand. Your opinion will be burning of a long boat, processions lit by firebrands, street theatre and several events for the more foolhardy and extrovert on Ne'er Day itself. This is Scottish hospitality at its best. Families with children are well catered for, while those without such ties are often in danger of meeting their life partners. Besides the official celebrations, every local place of revelry is ringing with clubs, ceilidhs, live acts, dancing and general merrymaking until the wee small hours. As the biggest winter festival in Europe, the main street party almost became a victim of its own success in 1996. A succession of mild winters, combined with the prospect of dancing drunkenly in the streets to top musical entertainers, provoked such a huge crowd that crushing almost caused a tragedy. In 1997, it was decided to limit the numbers in the town centre and make access from 8pm on New Year's Eve restricted to those with advance tickets. After the success and excess of the Millennium Hogmanay, the celebrations are be scaled down. No matter what is organised, however, this is a day when Edinburgh turns out, en masse, to party.

Turner Watercolours

National Gallery of Scotland, The Mound, New Town, EH2 (624 6200/nginfo@natgalscot.ac.uk/ www.natgalscot.ac.uk). Bus 3, 3A, 12, 16, 17. **Open** 10am-5pm Mon-Sat; noon-5pm Sun. **Dates** 1-31 Jan annually. **Map** p314 C2.

Over 40 Turner watercolours were bequeathed to the National Gallery of Scotland in 1900 by Henry Vaughan, who stipulated that they should only be exhibited in January when the light is at its weakest and therefore the least destructive to works of art on paper. They are exhibited every January at the National Gallery of Scotland (*see p57*) at the bottom of the Mound, along with Turner's illustrations of Thomas Campbell's poems.

Burns Night

Date 25 January annually.
It is the custom of Scots the world over to foregather on 25 January, consume the sacred foods – haggis, neeps (turnips) and tatties (potatoes) – sup of the sacred whisky and recite the sacred texts. For this night is the birthday of Robert 'Rabbie' Burns, Scotland's Bard. In Edinburgh, such Burns Suppers happen in private homes and among members of Burns associations and, in public, at restaurants and hotels around the town. It is best to get invited to someone's home if at all possible, otherwise things can appear over-formal (at least at the outset) or unbearably laced with tartan kitsch. If a native invitation is not forthcoming, do your best to find a few fellow travellers, grab a haggis supper each from the nearest chip shop, pass round the whisky (one bottle per person should just about do it) and read from a book of Burns' poems until the drink has loosened the tongues. Some of them are extremely bawdy, although *Tam o' Shanter* is a great story and the *Address to a Haggis* a true celebration of the working man.

sought from new arrivals and you will be able to compare your opinions with those in the papers.

One of the saddest trends over the last few years of the Festivals has been for Fringe-goers to concentrate on guaranteed laughs and hang around the big three comedy venues: the Gilded Balloon, the Pleasance and the Assembly Rooms. Which is all very well, but leaves the rest of the Fringe starved of an audience – and the potential audience itself bereft of some very fine performances.

It should be every Fringe-goer's duty, nay, desire, to see at least one idiosyncratic show in one wee hall on the edge of town. Not only might it be superb, but it will almost certainly be far cheaper than the central venues. Moreover, the kudos of having seen *Macbeth* performed in Scots at St Ninian's Hall is far greater than dozing through half an hour of duff stand-up at a London-programmed venue.

There are two problems with venues away from the centre of town. If you're the only member of the audience, do not panic: you owe the performers nothing. You have paid for your ticket and have every right to be entertained. And, if you're prepared to appear a bit strange and give a solo standing ovation at the end, the performers might buy you a drink. Besides, you had to overcome the second problem: getting there. A bicycle is useful if you're fit. Taxis are not too expensive if you're not. A good idea is to try a non-central venue after you've been around a few days. The walk will actually help you clear your brain of the Festival-induced psychosis that will have built up. You can often spend a whole day seeing a variety of genres, from comedy to straight theatre, by the same company in the one venue – an experience that carries its own special satisfactions.

Nor should Edinburgh's non-festival events be ignored. Club runners always try to attract the Festival crowd but, in the fast changing world of dance music, only the most mainstream can get their DJs booked far enough ahead to get in the Fringe brochure. Check out the flyers in central bars and pubs for some idea of what is really going on. As with the whole of the Festival, keeping your ear to the ground and your feet ready to go where the vibe is most appropriate is the best way to enjoy the rocky rapids of Edinburgh in August – with your sanity intact.

Consumer Edinburgh

Accommodation

Edinburgh's status as Festival City means there are now just about enough beds to go round. Just plan ahead if you're coming at a peak time.

As Edinburgh has played host to an increasing number of regular events, to complement the festivals, Hogmanay and Military Tattoo, it seems that barely a month has passed without another multi-million pound refurbishment or new hotel opening. Perhaps they fill up the slack times with the invading hordes of BBC period drama film crews who just can't get enough of all those Georgian terraces.

Edinburgh is one of those rare cities where intimate, traditional townhouse hotels are the norm and huge, modern bed banks are very much the exception. While it's hard to imagine any film crew setting up shots outside the Travelodge, such new-builds at least increase the range of Edinburgh's hotels to suit every taste and budget. This has created an increasingly competitive climate, where standards are pushed ever higher while rates are driven lower. Clearly, there can be only one true winner in this battle for custom.

INFORMATION & BOOKING

At certain times of the year, significant savings can be made if you're prepared to wait until the last minute before booking your room. Most clued-up hoteliers would rather sell their beds at a discount than leave them lying empty, so always ask if they have stand-by rates available. Bargain deals are increasingly commonplace – particularly from October to April – but watch out for those major events, which block out the whole city. If you're planning your visit during a major rugby international, Hogmanay, an international conference or anytime in August, our advice is simple: book early or pay dearly.

Hotels have been placed into the different catagories below according to the price of the cheapest double room, with breakfast – which will most probably be of a simple continental type. Room prices given include VAT and are the year-round rate. Many hotels, particularly the biggest, are owned by large hotel groups. The 'Chains' category is reserved for those hotel chains that preserve their own atmosphere wherever they are in the world.

Parking in Edinburgh can be very difficult, particularly in the centre of town and in residential areas. If you are travelling by car, you're advised to confirm with your hotel

The Balmoral. The best. *See page 105.*

that you will be able to find a parking space close by, especially if the parking is listed below as 'on street'.

Encouragingly, many hotels have **disabled rooms** and access; the Tourist Board (*see page 105*) will send you a list. Other advice is available from Disability Scotland and the Lothian Coalition of Disabled People (*see page 274*). Holiday accommodation solely for the disabled, their carers and their guide dogs is provided by **Trefoil House** (*see page 118*), which is to the west of the city.

The **Edinburgh & Lothians Tourist Board** is a useful resource: it can make reservations across the city from its office or by phone. Its brochure contains a list of all members and grades accommodation using a star rating system – based on the standard of furnishings and overall welcome.

Edinburgh & Lothians Tourist Board

*top floor of Waverley Shopping Centre, 3 Princes
Street, New Town, EH2 2QP (473 3800/fax 493
3881/esic@eltb.org/www.edinburgh.org). Bus 3, 3A,
12, 16, 17, 80.* **Open** *Oct-Mar* 9am-5pm Mon-Fri;
closed Sat, Sun; *Apr-Sept* 9am-7pm Mon-Fri; closed
Sat, Sun. **Credit** MC, V. **Booking fee** £3 plus 10%
deposit. **Map** p314 D2.

Hotels

Deluxe (£185 & above)

See also page 117 **Sheraton Grand Hotel.**

The Balmoral

*1 Princes Street, New Town, EH2 2EQ (556 2414/
fax 557 3747/reservations@thebalmoralhotel.com/
www.rfhotels.com/balmoral). Bus 3, 3A, 12, 16,
17, 80.* **Rates** *single* £160-£190; *double* £185-£280;
suite £400-£1,000. **Credit** AmEx, DC, MC, V.
Map p314 D2.
Traffic was brought to a standstill when crowds
gathered outside this 186-room landmark hotel at
the east end of Princes Street for a glimpse of band-
in-residence the Rolling Stones. Less-famous guests,
however, are just as likely to draw envious glances
from passers-by. Inside, the Balmoral has all the
trappings you would expect from a top-drawer,
classic hotel: marble floors, fine artworks, crystal
chandeliers and a high standard of service that is
always attentive but rarely intrusive. Sumptuous,
stylish and undoubtedly the most prestigious
address for those keen to impress. Nevertheless,
some of the small standard rooms do not justify
the overblown prices – like many designer labels,
you can find yourself paying for the name and
not for the product. If you have the means, fork out
the extra for a castle-view room or go the whole hog
and splash out on one of the huge suites – otherwise
you may wonder whether it's worth the expense
for the kudos alone.
Hotel services *Air-conditioning. Babysitting. Bars
(3). Beauty salon. Business services. Concierge.
Disabled: access, adapted rooms (4). Gym. No-
smoking rooms. Parking. Restaurants (3). Swimming
pool.* **Room services** *Dataport. Mini-bar.
Refrigerator. Room service (24-hr). TV: satellite.*

The Caledonian

*Princes Street, New Town, EH1 2AB (459 9988/
fax 225 6632/reservations@caledonianhotel.co.uk/
www.caledonianhotel.co.uk). Bus 3, 3A, 12, 16, 17.*
Rates *single* £155-£180; *double* £225-£325; *suite*
£360-£875. **Credit** AmEx, DC, MC, V. **Map** p314 A2.
Until very recently, the Grand Old Dame of Princes
Street was in danger of becoming as pathetic a
figure as Norma Desmond in *Sunset Boulevard*.
Trading primarily on reputation, the hotel had a
hard time convincing the public that she had more
to offer than a grandiose Edwardian façade at the
west end of the Street. Following extensive refurbishment, however, the huge hotel has been brought

back to its former glory. It steadfastly refuses to follow any current design trends, the result being that
the sense of a bygone Edwardian era is maintained
throughout: huge arched corridors lead past grand
staircases with stained-glass windows. Elegant,
opulent and more than a little ostentatious, the
Caledonian has a warm, luxurious feel, which is evi-
dent on every floor. A high standard of service has
made it a favourite of auspicious guests over the
years, including Sean Connery and Nelson Mandela.
After an investment of £8 million, the Old Dame is
back to her best.
Hotel services *Babysitting. Bar (3). Beauty salon.
Business services. Concierge. Disabled: access,
adapted rooms (4). Garden. Gym. Limousine service.
No-smoking rooms. Parking (not free). Restaurants
(3).* **Room service** *Dataport.
Mini-bar. Room service (24-hr). TV: satellite.*

George Intercontinental

*19-21 George Street, New Town, EH2 2PB (225
1251/fax 226 5644). Bus 8, 12, 16, 17, 25, 25A.*
Rates *single* £170-£195; *double* £190-£220; *suite*
£475-£650. **Credit** AmEx, DC, MC, V. **Map** p314 C1.
The George is conveniently located on Edinburgh's
smartest street in the town centre. The building
was designed by George Adam in 1775, and its
best feature is his trademark domed cupola in the
roof of the opulent Carvers restaurant (which is
renowned for its Sunday roasts). The east-wing
bedrooms are aimed at the corporate guest, while

We wish they all could be **The Caledonian**.

Consumer

the west wing has a softer 'classic country' style. The place is mobbed by the shoulder-pad set during the television festival in August. Le Chambertin restaurant has two AA stars and is a favourite for business lunches. Ten of the rooms have fully equipped office facilities.

Hotel services *Babysitting. Bar. Business services. Concierge. Disabled: access, adapted rooms (3). Gym. Limousine service. No-smoking rooms. Parking. Restaurants (2).* **Room services** *Dataport. Mini-bar. Refrigerator. Room service (24-hr). TV: satellite.*

The Howard

34 Great King Street, New Town, EH3 6QH (557 3500/fax 557 6515/reservations@thehoward.com/ www.thehoward.com). Bus 13, 23, 27. **Rates** *single £130-£135; double £245-£275; suite £325.* **Credit** AmEx, DC, MC, V. **Map** p306 E3.

This discreet terrace residence only reveals its identity through the brass plaque on the door. The hotel is a perfect example of how to successfully combine Georgian style and architecture with contemporary comfort and luxury. The breakfast room overlooks the cobbled street that was built as Edinburgh's 'second new town', and contains original 19th-century murals, some of which are so fragile they have been papered over to preserve them. Each of the 15 rooms is decorated individually – the Abercrombie Suite, for example, has a four-poster bed, while large bathrooms, state-of-the-art showers with steam jets and rolltop baths also feature. The excellent upmarket cuisine of 36, the Howard's restaurant, is an another reason to stay here.

Hotel services *Bar. Business services. No-smoking rooms. Parking. Restaurant.* **Room services** *Dataport. Room service (24-hr). TV: cable.*

Expensive (£110-£165)

Albany Hotel

39-43 Albany Street, New Town, EH1 3QY (556 0397/fax 557 6633/100414.1237@ compuserve.com). Bus 8. **Rates** *single £75-£95; double £135-£170; suite £165-£195, not incl breakfast.* **Credit** AmEx, MC, V. **Map** p306 F4.

Tucked away in a corner of the New Town, yet only minutes from Princes Street and the lively bars of Broughton, the Albany is a little gem with discreet charm. The Georgian-style rooms – all rich red fabrics and warm mahogany tones – are inviting and homely, although there is an element of over-kill with some of the period features. Quiet, intimate and with a high standard of personal service, this is a good hotel for a romantic weekend.

Hotel services *Babysitting. Bar. Business services. No-smoking rooms. Parking (on street). Restaurant.* **Room services** *Dataport. Mini-bar. Room service (7am-11pm). TV: satellite.*

The Bonham

35 Drumsheugh Gardens, New Town, EH3 7RN (226 6050/fax 226 6080/reserve@thebonham.com/

The best Hotels

For horses
The Caledonian (page 105), where singing cowboy Roy Rogers famously rode his trusty steed down the stairwell.

For rugby
Murrayfield is the place to see Scotland play, and there are plenty of budget B&Bs and guesthouses in Haymarket or Corstorphine. The **Jarvis Ellersly House Hotel** (page 111), however, is rather more refined.

For style fans
For minimal sleek chic, designer Amanda Rosa's **Malmaison** (page 111) and architect Andrew Doolan's **Point Hotel** (page 113) are where it's at.

For the view
Book a room on the south or east side of **The Balmoral** (page 105) for some of the best inner-city hotel views in the world.

For the nightlife
Cheep and cheerful the **Jurys Inn** (page 116) may be, and if you're only planning on sleeping during the day, even better.

For the musicals
Anything around Calton Hill or Broughton is close to the Playhouse, but the **Ailsa Craig Hotel** (page 114) gets our vote.

---

www.thebonham.com). Bus 13, 19, 40, 41, 41A 82. **Rates** *single £125-£135; double/twin £165-£225; suite £255-£295.* **Credit** AmEx, DC, MC, V. **Map** p308 C5.

This relatively new hotel made a massive impact among its more style-conscious visitors when it opened, with its contemporary blend of comfortable, light minimalism that is never too Starck. Neutral colours with some bright splashes and art deco furniture complement the high ceilings and cornices of the original Victorian building. Several Edinburgh hotels have attempted this fusion of modern style with traditional features, but few have achieved it as successfully as the Bonham. All this and a great location on a quiet, residential street in the West End: no wonder it was named the AA Hotel of the Year in Scotland in 1999.

Hotel services *Babysitting. Business services. Concierge. Disabled: access, adapted room. Limousine service. No-smoking rooms. Parking (on street). Restaurant.* **Room services** *Dataport. Mini-bar. Room service (24-hr). TV: cable, DVD.*

Channings

*12-16 South Learmonth Gardens, Stockbridge, EH4
1EZ (315 2226/fax 332 9631/central reservations
332 3232/reserve@channings.co.uk/
www.channings.co.uk). Bus 19, 82, 40, 41, 41A.*
Rates *single £110-£120; double/twin £125-£198; suite
£220-£235.* **Credit** AmEx, DC, MC, V. **Map** p305 B4.
At the time of writing this popular Edwardian terrace
hotel was undergoing a major revamp, bringing it
more in line with its sister hotels, the Bonham and the
Howard (for both, *see p107*). Gone is the flowery
chintz and the country cottage feel, although early
indications are that it will retain its homely character
and air of hushed intimacy. Starting with the lower
ground floor (which the owners refuse to call the basement), the rooms have been brought bang up to date
with stylish checker-board carpets and single-colour
fabrics in mushrooms and creams. The higher floors
have been updated rather than redesigned, but have
the advantage of terrific views of the famous Fettes
– the former school of James Bond and, er, Tony Blair.
Most striking of all is the new bar and restaurant,
with beech floors, rich red walls and brass fittings.
The Channings has always had a good reputation for
food, but now it has surroundings to match – a
brasserie in a chic '30s style. Swell.
Hotel services *Babysitting. Bar. Business services.
Garden. No-smoking rooms. Parking (on street).
Restaurant.* **Room services** *Dataport. Room service
(24-hr). TV: satellite.*

The Grange

*8 Whitehouse Terrace, Grange Loan,
South Edinburgh, EH9 2EU (667 5681/
fax 668 3300/grange-hotel@talk21.com/
www.grange-hotel-edinburgh.co.uk). Bus 40,
41, 41A.* **Rates** *single £70-£80; double £120-£135.*
Credit AmEx, MC, V.
Set within its own landscaped gardens in a sedate
part of Edinburgh, south of Bruntsfield, this impressive building in the Scots baronial style gives visitors a taste of the country even though it's in town.
It's a brisk mile-and-a-half walk to the centre of
town, but the Grange offers a rare sense of seclusion
and tranquillity, not to mention a rarer-still parking
space. Some of the decor and furnishings fall
into the curious middle ground between 'traditional
character' and just plain old fashioned, but there
can be no doubting the warmth of the welcome. Privately owned and personally run, this is a unique
hotel where good service is delivered out of courtesy,
not commercial concern.
Hotel services *Babysitting. Bar. Business services.
Garden. No-smoking rooms. Parking. Restaurant.*
Room services *Room service (24-hr). TV.*

Parliament House Hotel

*15 Calton Hill, EH1 3BJ (478 4000/fax 478 4001/
www.scotland-hotels.co.uk). Bus 1, 7, 11, 22, 34.*
Rates *single £90; double £130; suite £150, not incl
breakfast.* **Credit** AmEx, DC, MC, V. **Map** p307 G4.

You don't have to be an MSP to stay at the **Parliament House Hotel**.

Tucked away beside Calton Hill and moments from Princes Street, this hotel was named before it was decided to site the Scottish Parliament at Holyrood – not at the nearby Royal High School. The rooms are medium sized with comfortable furnishings. If the busy, navy-patterned wallpaper is too straining on the eye, there is a far more pleasing sight from the rooms at the front of the hotel – views across to Leith and the Forth. The newly opened, bright and cheerful basement café is the setting for full cooked breakfast. Dinners, meanwhile, are available in the neighbouring Café 1812.
Hotel services *Bar. Business services. Disabled: access, adapted rooms (3). Parking (on street). Restaurant.* **Room services** *Dataport. Mini-bar. Refrigerator. Room service (24-hr). TV.*

Prestonfield House Hotel

Priestfield Road, Prestonfield, South Edinburgh, EH16 5UT (668 3346/fax 668 3976/ prestonfield_house@compuserve.com). Bus 21, 33. **Rates** *single £145-£185; double £145-£245; suite £325-£490.* **Credit** AmEx, DC, MC, V.
Built in 1687 and former home to the Lord Provost, this country house nestling below Arthur's Seat is surrounded by parkland. The heavy cornicing and plasterwork on the ceilings (allegedly by the craftsmen who worked on the Palace of Holyroodhouse) give the house its Jacobean character. The hotel was recently extended to incorporate additional bedrooms, but, fortunately, the contemporary comfort of the new wing is very much in keeping with the atmosphere of the house. Access to the adjacent 18-hole golf course adds to the uniqueness of staying in a spacious, peaceful manor house with the city right on your doorstep.
Hotel services *Babysitting. Bar. Business services. Disabled: access, adapted rooms (2). Garden. No-smoking rooms. Parking. Restaurant.* **Room services** *Dataport. Room service (24 hours). TV: satellite.*

Roxburghe Hotel

38 Charlotte Square, New Town, EH2 4HG (240 5500/fax 240 555/info@roxburghe.macdonald/ hotels.co.uk). Bus 13, 19, 40, 41, 41A, 82. **Rates** *single £60-£130; double £110-£180; suite £210-£300, not incl breakfast.* **Credit** AmEx, DC, MC, V. **Map** p314 A1.
A major refurbishment of the 197-room Roxburghe, which cost more than building a new hotel from scratch, has paid off with this stunning cornerstone of Charlotte Square. The façade is still faithful to Robert Adam's Georgian design, but the interior has been totally transformed into a seamless blend of 19th-century elegance and 21st-century style. The huge leather armchairs sit comfortably on the stylish beechwood floors in the lobby, while the plush contemporary furnishings don't seem too out of place amidst the high ceilings and delicate cornices of the sizeable bedrooms. Locals may mourn the loss of some of the Roxburghe's original character and natural charm, but perhaps that's the price you pay for any major facelift.

Hotel services *Babysitting. Bars (2). Beauty salon. Business services. Concierge. Disabled: access, adapted rooms (6). Gym. No-smoking rooms. Parking (on street). Restaurants (2). Swimming pool.* **Room services** *Dataport. Mini-bar (on request). Refrigerator. Room service (24-hr). TV: satellite.*

Royal Scots Club

30 Abercromby Place, New Town, EH3 6QE (556 4270/fax 558 3769/royscotsclub@sol.co.uk/ www.scotsclub.co.uk). Bus 23, 27, 45. **Rates** *single £110; double £130; suite £190.* **Credit** AmEx, DC, MC, V. **Map** p306 E4.
Entering this classic Georgian townhouse, you'd be forgiven for thinking you'd walked into a gentleman's club. Well, you have. The Royal Scots Club was founded in 1919 as a tribute to those who fell in the Great War, and today the air of tranquillity and strong sense of history is palpable and genuine. The rooms, which were originally built for members wishing to stay overnight, have undergone extensive refurbishment in recent years. All have been tastefully furnished in a traditional style, some with four-poster beds and fine views towards the Firth of Forth. The cosy atmosphere and traditional features extend into every room, from the lounge with the real fire to the elegant restaurant. Here you'll find some fine Scottish fare and old-fashioned puddings (as opposed to 'desserts'). It's minutes away from Princes Street yet a million miles from the commercial modernity it represents.
Hotel services *Bar. Business services. Concierge. Garden. Gym. Parking (on street). Restaurant.* **Room services** *Room service (24-hr). TV: cable.*

Moderate (£70-£105)

See also page 116 **Crowne Plaza** *and page 117* **MacDonald Holyrood Hotel**.

17 Abercromby Place

17 Abercromby Place, New Town, EH3 6LB (557 8036/fax 558 3453/eirlys.lloyd@virgin.net/). Bus 23, 27, 45. **Rates** *single £50-£60; double £100-£120.* **Credit** MC, V. **Map** p306 E4.
The whole concept of townhouse hotels is at its apotheosis in Edinburgh. The Georgian New Town retains all of its original aspects of architecture, atmosphere and aloof gentility – which naturally rubs off on these establishments. The Lloyd family's townhouse is one of the best. Formerly the home of the distinguished architect William Playfair, it is located on one of the New Town's most sought-after cobbled streets, opposite Queen Street gardens. Five stunning floors retain their original features and display the family's impressive collection of antiques, oil paintings and tapestries. The nine rooms are large, with bay windows looking out onto the Forth estuary and Fife hills. Evening meals and pets allowed by arrangement.
Hotel services *Business services. Garden. No smoking. Parking (limited).* **Room services** *Dataport. TV: cable.*

Consumer

Thankfully, it costs less than your life savings to stay at **Bank Hotel**. *See page 111.*

Apex European Hotel

90 Haymarket Terrace, West Edinburgh, EH12 5LQ (474 3456/fax 474 3400/european@apexhotels.co.uk/ www.apexhotels.co.uk). Bus 12, 26, 31. **Rates** *single/ double* £90-£120 *(not incl breakfast).* **Credit** AmEx, DC, MC V. **Map** p308 B6.

The West End branch of Apex, this former office building was hastily converted to cope with over-spill from its more stylish sister hotel (*see below*). Still, you can't knock the prices, and the location is very convenient for Haymarket Station. Its street-level restaurant, Tabu, serves a three-course table d'hôte menu for a bargain £9.99.

Hotel services *Bar. Business services. Disabled: access, adapted rooms. Gym. No-smoking rooms. Parking (limited). Restaurant.* **Room services** *Dataport. Room service (24-hr). TV: satellite.*

Apex International Hotel

31-35 Grassmarket, South Edinburgh, EH1 2HS (300 3456/fax 220 5345/international@ apexhotels.co.uk/www.apexhotels.co.uk). Bus 2. **Rates** *double* £90-£180, *not incl breakfast.* **Credit** AmEx, DC, MC, V. **Map** p314 B3.

The Edinburgh-based Apex has put a spin on the concept of budget hotels – providing standard accommodation at a basic rate while managing to inject some style and individuality into the affair. Situated not far from the Castle, the 175-room Apex International has a sleek glass façade and boasts a fine view of the side of the Castle from its top-floor restaurant, Heights. All the rooms in the hotel are doubles; two-thirds have views of the Castle and two double beds (offering fantastic value for groups) and are therefore very popular.

Hotel services *Air-conditioning. Babysitting. Bar. Business services. Disabled: access. Limousine service. No-smoking rooms & floors. Parking. Restaurants (2). Swimming pool.* **Room services** *Dataport. Room service (24 hours). TV: satellite.*

Bank Hotel

1 South Bridge, Royal Mile, EH1 1LL (556 9940/ fax 622 6822). Bus 7, 8, 21, 31, 80. **Rates** *single* £65-£80; *double/twin* £75-£90; *family* £100-£130. **Credit** AmEx, DC, MC, V. **Map** p314 D3.

These are nine rooms above Logie Baird's Bar at the noisy intersection of the Royal Mile and Bridges in the historic Old Town. The mood is Gaelic, with wood panelling, dark tartan and mustard-coloured hallways. Each bedroom is individually themed around a famous Scot – the James Young Simpson room, for example, is filled with anatomical sketches, mock bookcases and collections of old potion bottles that reflect something of the character of the father of anaesthesiology. Cheesy? Perhaps. But it all works surprisingly well, and it's good to see a hotel with a more original approach to its Scottishness than an excess of tartan and Ceud Mille Failte signs at every turn. The bar is open round the clock.

Hotel services *Babysitting. Bar. Disabled: access. Parking. Restaurant.* **Room services** *Dataport. Room service (24-hr). TV: satellite.*

Carlton Greens Hotel

2 Carlton Terrace, Calton Hill, EH7 5DD (556 6570/ fax 557 6680/www.british-trust-hotels.co.uk). Bus 5, 15, 19, 26. **Rates** *single* £45-£55; *double* £90-£120. **Credit** MC, V. **Map** p307 J4.

A Georgian townhouse property tucked away in a quiet residential street under Calton Hill but only ten minutes' walk from the east end of Princes Street. A recent refurbishment has modernised the public areas but, like its sister hotel, Greens (*see p115*), this hotel offers good-quality rooms at a realistic price.

Hotel services *Bar. Business services. Disabled: adapted rooms (2). Garden. No-smoking rooms. Parking (on street). Restaurant.* **Room services** *Room service (8am-11pm). TV.*

Jarvis Ellersly House Hotel

Ellersly Road, Murrayfield, West Edinburgh, EH12 6HZ (337 6888/fax 313 2543/www.jarvis.co.uk). Bus 38. **Rates** *single* £39.50-£119; *double* £79-£139; *executive rooms* £134-£154, *not incl breakfast.* **Credit** AmEx, MC, V.

As you park the car on the gravel drive, stroll into the moss-covered exterior of this country house hotel and relax in front of the open fire in the wood-panelled bar, it's easy to forget that you're only twenty minutes west of the centre of town and just moments from Murrayfield Stadium. The patio doors at the back of the building lead onto a croquet lawn, which adds to the feeling that you've stumbled into a Merchant Ivory production... it's all very charming and – dare we say it? – English! The small and rather ordinary rooms are somewhat out of kilter with the rest of the hotel, but for a quiet retreat this is a popular choice for businessmen and tourists alike. Some rooms are suitable for disabled travellers, though they're not specifically adapted.

Hotel services *Bar. Business services. Disabled: access. Garden. No-smoking rooms. Parking. Restaurant.* **Room services** *Room service (24-hr). TV: satellite.*

Malmaison

1 Tower Place, Leith, EH6 7DB (555 6868/fax 468 5002/www.malmaison.com). Bus 10A, 16, 22, 35. **Rates** *single/double* £105-£140; *suite* £150-£165. **Credit** AmEx, DC, MC, V. **Map** p311 Jx.

This ex-seaman's mission on the Leith dockside, which dates from 1881, has been transformed by designer Amanda Rosa. The subtle style and sexy sophistication of this award-winning hotel have helped to breathe new life into Edinburgh's hotel trade by setting a new standard in chic, sleek decor at affordable prices. All bedrooms are decorated in either checks or wide stripes; the muted palette of coffee and cream through to navy and olive is stunningly effective. The best rooms are the suites at the front of the building and the four-poster rooms. Attention to detail is clearly a priority, as evidenced by the custom-made aromatherapy toiletries in the bathrooms and the CD choice in reception. The brasserie's chef, Lawrence Robertson, has won a loyal following for his wholesome, uncomplicated

New Town top rankin'

Visiting businessmen and conference delegates may prefer the modern facilities and anonymity of the larger, bed-bank hotels near the Edinburgh International Conference Centre, but this sort of bland uniformity hardly captures the spirit or charm of such an historic city. Edinburgh is awash with classic townhouse hotels, which, as they are part of the New Town development, are ideally located for the centre of town. They give a taste of the life that the New Town's first residents might have enjoyed when it was built – without the drawbacks of Georgian daily living.

The best, and most expensive, go out of their way to create a refined atmosphere, as fits the genteel architecture and furnishings. Such exclusive properties as **The Howard** (*see page 107*), on Great King Street, which was completed in 1820 when sedan chairs were still a common sight in Edinburgh, and the **Albany Hotel** (*see page 107*), on Albany Street, are good examples of these. But there are rather less ostentatious places to stay, such as **Melvin House Hotel** (*see below*) and **Greens Hotel** (*see page 115*), which are both fine examples of the townhouse style but without any stuffy pretentions. Those who prefer more modern design needn't feel excluded from the townhouse phenomenon: **The Bonham** (*see page 107*) is the epitome of contemporary style within its Georgian façade.

French-style food and the adjacent café serves vegetarian food throughout the day. Thoroughly recommended for its comfortable style and value for money. CD players in the rooms.
Hotel services *Babysitting. Bar. Business services. Disabled: access, adapted rooms (2). Garden. Parking. Restaurant.* **Room services** *Dataport. Mini-bar. Refrigerator. Room service (6am-10.30pm). TV: satellite.*

Melvin House Hotel

3 Rothesay Terrace, Westend, New Town, EH3 7RY (225 5084/226 5085/ reservations@melvinhouse.demon.co.uk/ www.melvinhouse.co.uk). Bus 13. **Rates** *single £65-£115; double £75-£160; suite £200.* **Credit** AmEx, DC, MC, V. **Map** p308 B5.
Former home of the founder of the *Scotsman* newspaper, Melvin House combines startling original features with modern home comforts. With its fine oak panelling, wonderful gallery library and beautifully carved staircase, this is the kind of house where you expect to find that Colonel Mustard 'dunnit' in the study with the rope. Privately owned, the hotel has a friendly, personal service more in keeping with a B&B than an upmarket hotel. The location is perfect – a quiet residential street, minutes from the West End and with fine views over the wonderful greenery of the Dean Village. After the traditional splendour of the public areas, the rooms are disappointingly modern, but this is a minor gripe. A real find.
Hotel services *Bar. Business services. No-smoking rooms. Parking (on street). Restaurant.* **Room services** *Room service (7am-11pm). TV.*

Point Hotel

34 Bread Street, South Edinburgh, EH3 9AF (221 5555/fax 221 9929/sales@point-hotel.co.uk/ www.point-hotel.co.uk). Bus 2, 11, 15, 24, 28, 28A.

Rates *single £80-£95; double/twin £100-£115; suite £180-195.* **Credit** AmEx, DC, MC, V. **Map** p309 D6.
Owned and designed by architect Andrew Doolan, this 140-room hotel is state-of-the-art metropolitan minimalism. Clean lines, sweeping curved walls and blocks of soft colour (a painter is in residence for touchups) give a feeling of fluidity and space. The coloured lighting adds to the soothing aura, while the white bedrooms, with their black leather furniture and low-level beds swathed in white linen, are oriental in their understated simplicity. The executive suites are huge, as are all of the bathrooms; some have square jacuzzis, which are lit internally and have a white leather headrest at each end. Environmentally friendly sensor heating clicks on as you enter the rooms, and some at the front of the hotel have Castle views. The ground-floor restaurant offers quality bistro dining for just £12.95 for three courses. The glass-fronted Monboddo bar is the place to see and be seen in (*see also p160*; don't bother with the food, though). Designer style at an off-the-peg price. Dataport in executive rooms.
Hotel services *Babysitting. Bar. Disabled: access, room adapted. No-smoking rooms. Parking (on street). Restaurant.* **Room services** *Room service (10am-10pm). TV.*

Royal Terrace Hotel

18 Royal Terrace, Calton Hill, EH7 5AQ (557 3222/ fax 557 5334/www.principalhotels.co.uk). Bus 5, 15, 19, 26. **Rates** *single £70-£125; double £90-£170; suite £170-£270.* **Credit** AmEx, DC, MC, V. **Map** p307 H4.
Designed by William Playfair in 1822, this quiet terrace sits beneath Calton Hill with views from the front towards Leith. The Georgian opulence (now a little faded) is echoed in the swags and flounces of the soft furnishings and chandeliers, while a contemporary touch in the form of a small gym and pool has been added in the basement. The courtyard

Consumer

garden is popular in the summer months with its life-size chess board and fountain. Rooms on the top floor are small due to the sloped attic ceilings.
Hotel services *Air-conditioning. Babysitting. Bar. Business services. Concierge. Disabled: access. Garden. Gym. Limousine service. No-smoking rooms. Parking (on street). Restaurant. Swimming pool.* **Room services** *Dataport. Mini-bar (on request). Room service (24-hr). TV: satellite.*

Simpsons Hotel

79 Lauriston Place, Tollcross, South Edinburgh, EH3 9HZ (622 7979/fax 622 7900/rez@simpsons-hotel.com/www.simpsons-hotel.com). Bus 16, 17, 23, 28. **Rates** *single £70-£80; double £80-£90; suite £110, not incl breakfast.* **Credit** AmEx, DC, MC, V.
Map p309 E7.

Unfussy and unpretentious, this is a smart, no-frills establishment. Formerly a maternity hospital, Simpsons has been reborn as a hotel which uses the building's characteristics to positive effect. Natural daylight in the window-lined corridors gives it a comfortable, airy feel rarely found in other hotels. Rooms are all of a fair size, with contemporary fabrics in pastels and greys – nothing spectacular, but comfortable and with all mod cons. There's no bar or restaurant, but breakfast and room service are provided by the Whereto? café over the road
Hotel services *Babysitting. Bar. Business services. Concierge. Disabled: access. Garden. Parking (on street). Restaurant.* **Room services** *Dataport. Room service (10am-10pm). TV: satellite.*

Tailors Hall Hotel

139 Cowgate, South Edinburgh, EH1 1JS (622 6800/fax 622 6822/www.festival-inns.co.uk). Bus 23, 28, 45. **Rates** *single £60-£80; double £70-£100; suite £100-£130.* **Credit** AmEx, DC, MC, V.
Map p314 D3.

Anyone wishing to turn up the volume on their Festival experience could do worse than make this their base. With its Cowgate location, two of the Fringe supervenues, the Pleasance and Gilded Balloon, are only five minutes walk away while the Three Sisters (*see p161*) – if not the most popular bar in town, certainly the busiest – is right under your feet. Built around a courtyard which acts as overspill from the bars, the 17th-century building houses a thoroughly modern interior. Rooms vary greatly in size and shape; all are comfortable and clean. Some are less noisy than others – ask for the new wing if you value your sleep. Whichever room you plump for, take solace in the fact that earplugs are provided free of charge in every room.
Hotel services *Bars (3). Business services. Disabled: access, adapted rooms (4). Parking (on street).* **Room services** *Room service (9am-9pm). TV.*

Budget (£60 or under)

See also **Holiday Inn Express Edinburgh-Leith** (*page 116*), **Hotel Ibis** (*page 116*) and **Jurys Inn** (*page 116*), **Travel Inn** (*page 117*) and **Travelodge** (*page 117*).

Ailsa Craig Hotel

24 Royal Terrace, Calton Hill, EH7 5AH (556 1022/ fax 556 6055/ailsacraighotel@ednet.co.uk/ www.townhousehotels.co.uk). Bus 5, 15, 19, 26. **Rates** *single £25-£55; double £45-£90; family rooms £90 (negotiable).* **Credit** AmEx, DC, MC, V.
Map p307 H4.

Like its sister hotel, Greenside, just a few doors down (9 Royal Terrace; 555 0022), Ailsa Craig boasts big, clean rooms, which have retained their original Georgian features. Though they're a bit on the basic side, some have views toward the Forth and all enjoy the quiet of this residential crescent. The rooms at Ailsa Craig tend to be bigger than those at Greenside, and some are kitted out with five beds. Both hotels are popular with people in town to see a show at the nearby Playhouse Theatre and with low-budget and student groups. Evening meals on request.
Hotel services *Bar. Garden. Parking (on street).* **Room services** *TV.*

Balfour Guest House

90-92 Pilrig Street, Broughton, EH6 5AY (554 2106/fax 554 3887/billmurray123@ netscapeonline.co.uk). Bus 7, 12, 16. **Rates** *single £20-£35; double £30-£60.* **Credit** AmEx, DC, MC, V.
Map p307 H1.

Isabel and Richard Cowe's large Georgian house is often full of visiting school parties enjoying their friendly hospitality. For groups, dinner can be provided in the basement dining room and packed lunches can be supplied on request, too. The rooms are all reasonably furnished. The central location with free parking makes this a popular choice for groups. Limited business services. No phone in rooms. Cable TV in lounge.
Hotel services *Babysitting. Bar. Disabled: access. Garden. No-smoking rooms. Parking (on street). Restaurant.* **Room services** *Room service (8am-9pm).*

Bar Java

48-50 Constitution Street, Leith, EH6 6RS (467 7527/fax 467 7528/carol2barjava.co.uk/ www.barjava.co.uk). Bus 16, 22, 34. **Rates** *single £25; double £50.* **Credit** AmEx, MC, V.
Map p311 Jz.

Near the rejuvenated Leith dock area and popular with Festival and Hogmanay performers. Ten rooms, each named after an island, sit above a funky bar. A beer garden out the back and interesting locals inside provide some character. Snacks and a wide variety of flavoured teas, coffees and smoothies are available all day. A great brunch is available on Sundays. Guests can also make use of the bar (*see p162*), café and satellite TV lounge.
Hotel services *Bar. Business services. Garden. Parking (on street). Restaurant.* **Room services** *TV.*

Claremont

14-15 Claremont Crescent, Broughton, EH7 4HX (556 1487/fax 556 7077). Bus 8. **Rates** *single £25-£35; double £50-£70.* **Credit** AmEx, MC, V.
Map p306 F2.

This hotel comprises two huge Georgian houses knocked into one. The reception area is sparse and the rooms are clean, comfortable and very large, with views of Arthur's Seat or the Forth. The place is a hive of activity, with quiz nights in the public bar and a disco downstairs. Full Scottish breakfast and evening meals are available, too. Parking is at the rear of the hotel.
Hotel services *Bars (2). Business services. Parking.*
Room services *TV.*

Frederick House Hotel

42 Frederick Street, New Town, EH2 1EX (226 1999/fax 624 7064/frederickhouse@ednet.co.uk/ www.townhousehotels.co.uk). Bus 28, 29, 29A, 80. **Rates** *single £40-£90; double £50-£120; suite £130-£220.* **Credit** AmEx, DC, MC, V.
Map p314 B1.
Bang in the centre of town, this hotel is well placed near St Andrew Square Bus Station and Waverley Rail Station. The listed building has been transformed from offices into five floors of bedrooms in patterned greens, gold and rouge; the best rooms are at the front of the hotel; the Skyline suite, meanwhile, has views to the Forth. Breakfast is taken in the Café Rouge brasserie opposite the hotel (and is included in the tariff).
Hotel services *Babysitting. Business services. No-smoking rooms. Parking (on street).* **Room services** *Dataport. Refrigerator. Room service (10am-10pm). TV: satellite.*

Greens Hotel

24 Eglinton Crescent, New Town, EH12 5BY (337 1565/fax 346 2990/greenshotel@hotmail.com). Bus 12, 13, 26, 31. **Rates** *single £50-£70; double £60-£110; superior £70-£120.* **Credit** AmEx, DC, MC, V.
Map p308 B6.
Just north of Haymarket Station, this Georgian townhouse makes for a warm, traditional hotel in a secluded residential street. Like its sister hotel, Carlton Greens (*see p111*), it is owned and managed by a charitable trust. The rooms offer good quality for the price.
Hotel services *Bar. Business services. Concierge. Disabled: access. Garden. Parking (on street). Restaurant.* **Room services** *Room service (24-hr). TV.*

Grosvenor Gardens Hotel

1 Grosvenor Gardens, New Town, EH12 5JU (313 3415/fax 346 8732/info@stayinedinburgh.com/ www.stayinedinburgh.com). Bus 12, 26, 31. **Rates** *single £45-£65; double £50-£135; family room £75-£200.* **Credit** MC, V. **Map** p308 B6.
Tucked away in a quiet cul-de-sac, this hotel is sumptuously swathed in cream, gold and pink. The eight large bedrooms have high ceilings and bay windows, but the en suite bathrooms are small. The place is immaculately kept and the mood is one of tranquillity and style.
Hotel services *Disabled: adapted room. Garden. No-smoking rooms. Parking (on street).* **Room services** *TV.*

Joppa Turrets Guest House

1 Lower Joppa, Portobello, EH15 2ER (669 5806/ fax 669 5806/stanley@joppaturrets.demon.co.uk/ www.joppaturrets.demon.co.uk). Bus 26, 26A. **Rates** *single/double £18-£35.* **Credit** MC, V.
Not ideal if you want to be right at the heart of things, but this well-run guesthouse is perfect if you're looking for a more peaceful location within easy reach of the city. It's a good example of the many guesthouses in the area, from when Portobello was where Edinburgh went on holiday, and is situated right on the beach three miles east of the centre. All five rooms have views over the Firth of Forth to the hills of Fife. There's unrestricted parking for those who have a car, and a tandem for hire from the friendly owners for those who don't. All rooms are non-smoking. Public phone available.
Hotel services *Garden. Parking (on street).* **Room services** *TV.*

Minto Hotel

16-18 Minto Street, Newington, South Edinburgh, EH9 9RG (668 1234/fax 662 4870). Bus 7, 8, 31, 80. **Rates** *single £25-£60; double £50-£95; family room £95-£120.* **Credit** AmEx, DC, MC, V.
A cheap stopover for groups, south past Newington Road. There's always a wedding or party taking place in the function suite; a piper calls every Saturday to pipe in the happy couple during the summer months. Heavily patterned in pinks and blues, the Minto is fairly basic but comfortable. It's the warmth of the welcome that makes regulars return.
Hotel services *Bar. Business services. Concierge. Disabled: access, adapted rooms (2). Garden. No-smoking rooms. Parking (limited). Restaurant. Swimming pool.* **Room services** *Dataport. Room service (7am-9.15pm). TV.*

Nova Hotel

5 Bruntsfield Crescent, South Edinburgh, EH10 4EZ (447 6437/fax 452 8126/jamie@scotland-hotels.demon.co.uk/www.novahotel.f9.co.uk). Bruntsfield buses. **Rates** *single £35-£55; double £60-£90; family room £80-£150.* **Credit** AmEx, DC, MC, V.
This Victorian building to the south of the city is just off Bruntsfield Links. Rooms vary in size – all are spacious, some are huge, with more than enough room for five single beds. The Nova has a pleasant and relaxing bar with the atmosphere and decor of a traditional pub – and there are plenty more pubs to choose from in the local area. The hotel is only ten minutes from the heart of town, so guests will never feel too far from the action.
Hotel services *Babysitting. Bar. Business services. Garden. No-smoking rooms. Parking. Restaurant.* **Room services** *Room service (24 hours). TV: satellite.*

Sutherland House

16 Esslemont Road, South Edinburgh, EH16 5PX (667 6626). Bus 7, 8, 31, 80. **Rates** *single/double £25-£35.* **No credit cards.**
Mayfield Road to the south of the city plays host to countless B&Bs of varying quality and price. For the

Consumer

best of both worlds, keep travelling south until you reach this wonderful three-bedroom property near the Cameron Toll shopping centre. With the style and comfort of a three-star hotel but the warmth and welcome of a guesthouse, the quiet sophistication of Sutherland House is disturbed only by the occasional bark from the owner's friendly dalmation (lesser spotted). It's not often you can describe a B&B as 'elegant'. This is one welcome exception.

Hotel services *Garden. No smoking. Parking (free).* **Room services** *TV.*

Town House Guesthouse

65 Gilmore Place, Tollcross, South Edinburgh, EH3 9NU (229 1985/susan@thetownhouse.com/ www.thetownhouse.com). Bus 10, 10A, 27. **Rates** *single £25-£36; double £48-£72.* **No credit cards.** **Map** p309 D7.

This detached Victorian house sits next to a church on a busy route into town. It's close to the major theatres and, hence, a popular Festival stopover. Spread over three floors, the house is very comfortable and run with pride by the amiable Susan Virtue. Everywhere is clean and well maintained, although the bathrooms tend to be on the small side. Also ask about the self-catering apartment in Newington, which can be rented for several nights or by the week. Note that there is no phone in the rooms.

Hotel services *No smoking. Parking (limited).* **Room services** *TV: cable.*

Chains

Crowne Plaza

80 High Street, Royal Mile, EH1 1TH (557 9797/ fax 557 9789/reservations@crowneplazaed.co.uk/ www.crowneplazaed.co.uk). Bus 35, 35A. **Rates** *single/double £110-£250; suites £250-£300.* **Credit** AmEx, DC, MC, V. **Map** p314 D3.

This turreted hotel may look like one of the original stone buildings on the Royal Mile but it was actually constructed at the beginning of the 1990s. Bustling and modern within, it provides all of the benefits associated with an American chain. Oasis have stayed here in the past but – and this might be telling – didn't feel moved to throw any televisions through the windows. The Great Scottish Hall occasionally hosts ceilidhs and there's regular live music in the Piano Bar downstairs. Advocates restaurant overlooks the cobbled High Street, while Carrubers bistro serves light lunches.

Hotel services *Babysitting. Bar. Business services. Concierge. Disabled: access, adapted rooms (3). Gym. Limousine service. No-smoking rooms & floors. Parking. Restaurants (2). Swimming pool.* **Room services** *Dataport. Mini-bar. Refrigerator. Room service (24-hr). TV: satellite.*

Holiday Inn Express Edinburgh-Leith

Britannia Way, Ocean Drive, Leith, EH6 6LA (555 4422/fax 555 4646/info@hiex-edinburgh.com/ www.hiex-edinburgh.com). Bus 10, 16, 22, 34.

Rates *twin/double/family room £57.50-£77.50.* **Credit** AmEx, DC, MC, V. **Map** p311 Gx.

The owners of this particular franchise couldn't believe their luck when the *Royal Yacht Britannia* became its new neighbour. Rather than looking out over a rather unsightly industrialised port, guests now enjoy views of one of the city's most popular new tourist attractions. The hotel itself has all the pros and cons that go with being purpose-built. It may be blocky and featureless, but the owners have at least tried to inject a little character. The furnishings are contemporary and the fittings could be an Ikea job-lot, while the shower-only bathrooms are a masterpiece of space-saving design. This being a limited service hotel, the restaurant only serves breakfast, but this is compensated by the room delivery service of menus from a variety of local eateries.

Hotel services *Bar. Business services. Disabled: access, adapted rooms (5). Garden. No-smoking rooms. Parking.* **Room services** *Dataport. TV: satellite.*

Hotel Ibis

6 Hunter Square, Royal Mile, EH1 1QW (240 7000/ fax 240 7007). Bus 7, 8, 21, 31, 80. **Rates** *single/double £49.50-£69.50; suite £70-£100.* **Credit** AmEx, DC, MC, V. **Map** p314 D3.

This international chain has a reputation for efficiency and good value, but the downside to this is a certain bland anonymity. Because of its bright, modern style, designed to appeal to homogenous tastes, you never really get to appreciate the fact that you're right in the heart of the Old Town in a historic European capital. Still, the rooms are comfortable and clean, the rates are reasonable and the location makes the Ibis an ideal launching pad for business or pleasure.

Hotel services *Air-conditioning. Babysitting. Bar. Business services. Disabled: access, adapted rooms (6). No-smoking rooms. Parking (not free).* **Room services** *Dataport. TV: cable.*

Jurys Inn

43 Jeffrey Street, Royal Mile, EH1 1DG (200 3300/ fax 200 0400/www.jurys.com). Bus 24, 35, 35A. **Rates** *£41-£104.* **Credit** AmEx, DC, MC, V. **Map** p310 G5.

This converted office block may not be the most attractive hotel in town, but few can match its ideal location for the short-term visitor. To the front lies Waverley Station, Princes Street and the New Town, while the wynd to the rear leads up into the heart of the Royal Mile. The rooms are all identical, with double beds as standard and inoffensive, soft-coloured furnishings. With sparse public facilities, the emphasis of the Jurys is firmly placed on going out rather than staying in, although the less adventurous might appreciate the pub-style bar. Some rooms are adapted partially for the disabled.

Hotel services *Bar. Business services. Disabled: access, adapted rooms (2). No-smoking rooms. Parking (on street). Restaurant.* **Room services** *Dataport. TV: satellite.*

Consumer

MacDonald Holyrood Hotel

81 Holyrood Road, Royal Mile, EH8 6AE (550 4500/fax 550 4545/www.macdonaldhotels.com). Bus 24, 25, 35, 35A. **Rates** *single £70-£160; double £89-£190; suite £120-£260.* **Credit** AmEx, DC, MC, V. **Map** p310 H5.

This brand-new hotel is located close to the offices of Scotsman Publications and the building site that is the new Scottish Parliament, so it comes as no surprise to find it has been built with business travellers in mind, with an impressive gym and a 14m pool. That said, it's also convenient for the Royal Mile, Dynamic Earth and Holyrood Palace. The brochure describes its look as 'a bold contemporary style harmonising with the historic area'. We say its a big yellow block. There's no denying the level of opulence and sophistication to which it aspires, however, with a marbled lobby and, on the Club Floor, the services of a butler who will attend to your every (legal) whim. **Hotel services** *Air-conditioning. Babysitting. Bars (2). Beauty salon. Business services. Concierge. Disabled: access, adapted rooms (16). Gym. No-smoking rooms. Parking. Restaurant. Swimming pool.* **Room services** *Dataport. Mini-bar. Refrigerator. Room service (24-hr). TV: cable.*

Sheraton Grand Hotel

1 Festival Square, Lothian Road, West Edinburgh, EH3 9SR (229 9131/fax 228 4510/ www.sheraton.com). Bus 11, 15, 22, 24. **Rates** *single £175-£200; double £215-£240; suite £300-£350, not incl breakfast.* **Credit** AmEx, DC, MC, V. **Map** p314 A3.

This imposing concrete hotel block next to the Edinburgh International Conference Centre is always swarming with business delegates. Recent modifications to create a more 'Scottish' ambience mean the staff now wear tartan uniforms. The accommodation is modern and the mood brisk – but the feeling that you could be anywhere in the world still remains. Marble, chandeliers and American cherrywood panelling abound in the large reception, where coolly efficient international staff bustle officiously. Each of the 260 rooms has the same decor, double glazing and air-conditioning. The Terrace conservatory restaurant overlooks the paved square and your food is stir-fried or grilled in front of you in the central cooking area. The adjacent Grill Room holds three AA stars and the French chef uses only fresh Scottish produce. **Hotel services** *Air-conditioning. Babysitting. Bar. Business services. Disabled: access, adapted rooms (2). Gym. Limousine service. No-smoking rooms. Parking. Restaurants (2). Swimming pool.* **Room services** *Dataport. Mini-bar. Refrigerator. Room service (24-hr). TV: Satellite.*

Travel Inn

1 Morrison Link, West Edinburgh, EH3 8DN (228 9819/fax 228 9836/www.travelinn.co.uk). Bus 3, 3A, 21, 25, 25A. **Rates** *£46.95.* **Credit** AmEx, DC, MC, V. **Map** p308 C6.

This colossal branch of Britain's largest budget hotel chain boasts one of the cheapest room rates in town. There are 282 rooms; all are priced at £46.95, can squeeze in two adults and two kids and are exactly

the same – right down to the light switches. The financial incentive obviously works because, despite being little more than a faceless, classless and bland slumber land, the hotel boasts a year-round occupancy rate of 97%. The ground-floor restaurant is open all day and carries through the formula with its informal catering and atmosphere. No room service or phones. **Hotel services** *Bar. Disabled: access, adapted rooms (15). No-smoking rooms. Parking (not free). Restaurant.* **Room services** *Dataport. TV.*

Travelodge

33 St Mary's Street, Royal Mile, EH1 1TA (557 6281/fax 557 3681/www.travelodge.co.uk). Bus 24, 25, 35, 35A. **Rates** *double/family £49.95, not incl breakfast.* **Credit** AmEx, DC, MC, V. **Map** 310 G5.

The biggest advantage of booking any one of the national chains is you know exactly what you're getting. This, however, is also the biggest drawback. If you want to capture something of the spirit of Edinburgh, look elsewhere. Nevertheless, if you want a fair-sized room that's comfortable, clean and moments from the Royal Mile then this is a good low-budget option that's well worth a look. **Hotel services** *Bar. Business services. Disabled: access, adapted rooms (11). No-smoking rooms. Parking (limited). Restaurant.* **Room services** *TV.*

Hostels

Rates given below are per person per night unless stated otherwise. The independent hostels do get very busy. If you intend staying out late, check about curfews when booking.

Scottish Youth Hostel Association

7 Glebe Crescent, Stirling, FK8 2JA (01786 891 400/fax 01786 891 333/central reservations 08701 553 255/groups@syha.org.uk/www.syha.org.uk). **Open** 9am-5pm Mon-Fri; closed Sat, Sun.

The SYHA will provide information on accommodation in its hostels around Scotland. To stay in them you have to be a member, but you can join when you arrive.

Castle Rock Hostel

15 Johnston Terrace, Royal Mile, EH1 2PW (225 9666/fax 226 5078/ castle-rock@scotlands-top-hotels.com/ www.macbackpackers.com). Bus 35, 35A. **Beds** 250. **Open** *reception* 24 hrs daily. **No curfew. Rates** £10.50-£12.30. **Credit** AmEx, MC, V. **Map** p314 B3.

Edinburgh Backpackers Hostel

65 Cockburn Street, Royal Mile, EH1 1BU (reception 220 1717/fax 220 5143/advance reservations 221 0022/fax 539 695/info@hoppo.com/ www.hoppo.com). Bus 7, 8, 21, 31, 80. **Beds** dorm 97; triple 1; double 4; twin 1. **Open** *reception* 24 hrs daily; *reservations* 9am-5.30pm Mon-Fri. **Rates** *dorm* low season £11.50; June £12; July £13; Aug, 27 Dec-1 Jan £14; *double/twin (per room)* low season £35; Aug £37.50; *triple (per room)* £49. **Credit** MC, V. **Map** p314 D3.

Edinburgh Bruntsfield Youth Hostel

7 Bruntsfield Crescent, South Edinburgh, EH10 4EZ (447 2994/fax 452 8588/www.syha.org.uk). Bus 11, 16, 17, 23. **Beds** 150. **Open** *reception* 7am-11pm daily. **Curfew** 2am. **Rates** (B&B) £11.75 SYHA members; £12.75 non-members. **Credit** MC, V.

Edinburgh Central Youth Hostel

Robertson's Close, Infirmary Street, South Edinburgh, EH1 1LY (337 1120/central reservations 08701 553 255/www.syha.org.uk). Bus 7, 8, 21, 31, 80. **Beds** 121. **Open** *reception* 7am-2am daily. **Curfew** 2am. **Rates** £14-£16.50. **Credit** MC, V. **Map** p310 G6. Available July-Sept only.

Edinburgh Eglinton Youth Hostel

18 Eglinton Crescent, Westend, New Town, EH12 5DD (337 1120/fax 313 2053/www.syha.org.uk). Bus 12, 13, 26, 31. **Beds** 160. **Open** *reception* 7am-midnight daily. **Curfew** 2am. **Rates** (B&B) *low season* £11.25 SYHA members; £13 non-members; July-Aug £12.75 SYHA members; £13.75 non-members. **Credit** MC, V. **Map** p308 B6.

Princes Street East Backpackers

5 West Register Street, New Town, EH2 2AA (556 6894/fax 557 3236/www.princessbackpackers.com). Bus 3, 3A, 12, 16, 17, 80. **Beds** 120. **Open** *reception* 24 hrs daily. **Rates** £9.50 (Festival rates vary). **Credit** MC, V. **Map** p314 D1.

Royal Mile Backpackers

105 High Street, Royal Mile, EH1 1SG (557 6120/fax 556 2981/hotels@scotlands-top-hostels.com). Bus 35, 35A. **Beds** 38. **Open** *reception* 7am-3am daily; 24-hr access. **Rates** £10.50-£12.50 (credit card surcharge of 30p). **Credit** AmEx, MC, V. **Map** p314 D3.

Camping & caravanning

Edinburgh Caravan Club Site

Marine Drive, Silverknowes, EH4 (312 6874/fax 336 4269). Bus 40, 41, 41A. **Open** *reception* 8am-8pm daily. **Rates** £4; £2.25 off-season; £1.20 children; electrical link £1.50; *plus tent* £3; *plus caravan* £6; **Parking** *car* £1.50; *motorbike* 50p. **Credit** MC, V.

Mortonhall Caravan Park

Frogston Road East, EH16 (664 1533/fax 664 5387). Bus 7, 11. **Open** *reception* 8am-10pm daily. **Rates** *pitch & 2 adults* £8.25-£12.75; *extra adult* £1. **Credit** AmEx, MC, V.

Disabled accommodation

Trefoil House

Gogarbank, Ratho, EH12 9DA (339 3148/fax 317 7271/info@trefoil.org.uk/www.trefoil.org.uk). SMT 37 bus. **Rates** full weekly board £250 *guest*; £231 *carer*; per night £45 guest; . Other rates on request. **No credit cards.**
Services *Bar. Business services. Disabled: access. Garden. Lift. No-smoking rooms. Swimming pool.*

Private apartments

Renting a flat is a popular form of accommodation during the Festival and Hogmanay – so, as always, it's best to book early. Alternatively, look in the Thursday property section of the *Scotsman*. The **Town House Guesthouse** (*see page 116*) also has an apartment for rent.

Canon Court Apartments

20 Canonmills, New Town, EH3 5LH (474 7000/fax 474 7001/info@canoncourt.co.uk/www.canoncourt.co.uk). Bus 8, 23 27. **Open** 8am-8pm Mon-Fri; 8.30am-2pm Sat, Sun. **Rates** *per night* £65-£170. **Credit** AmEx, MC, V. **Map** p306 E2.

Colin Hepburn

3 Abercorn Terrace, Portobello, EH15 (tel/fax 669 1044). Bus 26, 26A. **Open** 9am-10pm daily. **Rates** *weekly* £60-£350. **No credit cards.**

Glen House Apartments

101 Lauriston Place, EH3 9JB (228 4043/fax 229 8873/info@edinburgh-apartments.co.uk/www.edinburgh-apartments.co.uk). Bus 23, 28, 45. **Open** 9am-5.30pm Mon-Fri; closed Sat, Sun. **Rates** *weekly* £160-£700. **Credit** AmEx, DC, MC, V. **Map** p309 E7.

West End Apartments

2 Learmonth Terrace, EH4 1PQ (332 0717/226 6512/fax 226 6513/brian@sias.com/members.edinburgh.org/westend). Bus 19, 82, 40, 41, 41A. **Open** 9am-11pm daily. **Rates** *weekly* £200-£800. **No credit cards.** **Map** p305 B4.

Seasonal lets

Universities let out their halls of residence during student holidays. They can be out of town, but are a useful form of basic accommodation.

Carberry Tower Conference Centre

Musselburgh, EH21 8PY (665 3135/fax 653 2930/carberry@dial.pipex.com/www.dspace.dial.pipex.com/carberrry). **Beds** 90. **Rates** £28-£38 (B&B). **Credit** MC, V.

Edinburgh University Accommodation Service

18 Holyrood Park, Edinburgh South, EH16 5AY (667 1971/fax 668 3217). Phone for locations and rates. **Credit** MC, V. **Map** p310 J8.

Fet-Lor Youth Centre

122 Crewe Road South, EH4 2NY (332 4506). **Beds** 36. **Rates** £8 per person per night. Available during Festival only. **No credit cards.**

Heriot-Watt Conference Office

Heriot-Watt University, Riccarton campus, EH14 4AS (451 3669/fax 451 3199/www.hw.ac.uk). B&B accommodation. Phone for details of locations and rates. **Credit** MC, V.

Consumer

Edinburgh Backpackers
Hostel. *See page 117.*

Napier University Conference & Letting Services

219 Colinton Road, Craiglockhart, West Edinburgh, EH14 (455 4331/fax 455 4411/www.napier.ac.uk/ vacation.lets@napier.ac.uk/). **Rates** £300-£450 per week. City-centre locations. **Credit** MC, V.

Queen Margaret University College

Hospitality Services Department, Clerwood Terrace, EH12 (317 3310/fax 317 3169/www.qmuced.ac.uk). **Rates** (B&B) *single* £24-£27; *double* £36-£44. West of city centre. **No credit cards.**

Agencies

Factotum

40A Howe Street, New Town, EH3 6TH (220 1838/ fax 220 4342/factotum@easynet.co.uk/ www.factotum.co.uk). **Bus** 13, 28, 29, 80. **Open** 9am-5.30pm Mon-Fri; closed Sat, Sun. **Credit** MC, V. **Map** 3 D4.

Festival Flats

3 Linkylea Cottages, Gifford, East Lothian, EH41 4PE (01620 810 620/fax 01620 810 619/ festflats@aol.com). **Open** 9am-5pm Mon-Fri; closed Sat, Sun. **No credit cards.**

Greyfriars Property Services

29-30 George IV Bridge, EH1 (220 6009/fax 220 6008/david@greyprop.co.uk/www.greyprop.co.uk). **Bus** 23, 28, 45. **Open** 9.30am-12.30pm, 1.30-5.30pm Mon-Fri; closed Sat, Sun. **Credit** MC, V. **Map** p309 F6.

Mackay's Agency

30 Frederick Street, New Town, EH2 2JR (225 3539/fax 226 5284/www.mackay-scotland.co.uk). **Bus** 28, 29, 29A, 80. **Open** *office* 9am-5.30pm Mon-Fri; 9am-4pm Sat; 10am-3pm Sun. *Phone enquiries* 9am-8pm Mon-Fri. **Credit** MC, V. **Map** p314 B1.

Short notice

Festival Beds

(225 1101/www.festivalbeds.co.uk). **Open** 9am-5.30pm Mon-Fri; closed Sat, Sun.

If you arrive when the Festival is in full swing and you have nowhere to stay, then this is the place to contact for bed and breakfast in a private house; about 60 properties contribute. In the past, the occupancy rate has been as low as 50% during the Festival season, while people have been spotted sleeping on the streets. Which is not recommended, even in the summer.

Accommodation by area

Note that the following list does not include apartments, campsites, disabled accommodation or gay and lesbian hotels.

Royal Mile

Bank Hotel (*p111*); Castle Rock Hostel (*p117*); Crowne Plaza (*p116*); Edinburgh Backpackers Hostel (*p117*); Hotel Ibis (*p116*); Jurys Inn (*p116*); MacDonald Holyrood Hotel (*p117*); Royal Mile Backpackers (*p118*); Travelodge (*p117*).

New Town

17 Abercromby Place (*p109*); Albany Hotel (*p107*); The Balmoral (*p105*); The Bonham (*p107*); The Caledonian (*p105*); Edinburgh Eglinton Youth Hostel (*p118*); Frederick House Hotel (*p115*); George Intercontinental (*p105*); Greens Hotel (*p115*); Grosvenor Gardens Hotel (*p115*); The Howard (*p107*); Melvin House Hotel (*p113*); Princes Street East Backpackers (*p118*); Roxburghe Hotel (*p109*); Royal Scots Club (*p109*).

Stockbridge

Channings (*p108*).

Calton Hill & Broughton

Ailsa Craig Hotel (*p114*); Balfour Guest House (*p114*); Carlton Greens Hotel (*p111*); Claremont (*p114*); Greenside (see Ailsa Craig, *p114*) Parliament House Hotel (*p108*); Royal Terrace Hotel (*p113*).

South Edinburgh

Apex International Hotel (*p111*); Edinburgh Bruntsfield Youth Hostel (*p118*); Edinburgh Central Youth Hostel (*p118*); The Grange (*p108*); Minto Hotel (*p115*); Nova Hotel (*p115*); Point Hotel (*p113*); Prestonfield House Hotel (*p109*); Simpsons Hotel (*p114*); Sutherland House (*p115*); Tailors Hall Hotel (*p114*); Town House Guesthouse (*p116*).

West Edinburgh

Jarvis Ellersly House Hotel (*p111*); Apex European Hotel (*p111*); Sheraton Grand Hotel (*p117*); Travel Inn (*p117*).

Leith

Bar Java (*p114*); Holiday Inn Express Edinburgh-Leith (*p116*); Malmaison (*p111*).

Further afield

Joppa Turrets Guest House (*p115*).

Restaurants

While you won't be disappointed if you've come to try out haggis, there are plenty of cuisines from all corners of the planet to keep your tastebuds happy.

As Scotland tentatively emerged from the recession of the early '90s, Edinburgh began to experience something of a restaurant boom. Aided by the city's growing reputation as a year-round festival venue, new ventures of every conceivable type have sprung up in the years since.

Existing restaurateurs predictably complain that there are too many restaurants and that some of the newcomers are riding on the back of a year-round tourist trade. There is some truth in this and if the bubble bursts then something of a cull is on the cards. But right now the city's restaurant scene is buoyant and the good places heavily outnumber the indifferent, while the truly foul are few and far between.

Every point on the globe from Japan to California is represented in some form in Edinburgh's restaurants and, like any other British city, there are plenty of good Chinese, Indian and Italian places. As forScottish restaurants, these are a bit more difficult to define. Few of the places listed in the Scottish section of this chapter serve dishes that definitively belong to a Caledonian culinary tradition. Instead, they tend to use almost exclusively Scottish produce and prepare, season and serve it according to very wide-ranging influences. The food itself may be from the Highlands or the waters of the West Coast but it is likely to be Scottish with a nod to French, Spanish, North African or Pacific Rim ideas. In other words, they may serve haggis but it'll be wrapped in Greek filo pastry and served with a Chinese hoisin sauce on a bed of Irish champ. Generally, though by no means exclusively, it is in these restaurants that you're most likely to experience the finest meals.

During the Festival season (August to early September) many restaurants are open much later than indicated in the year-round times; these extended hours can change from year to year, so it's best to phone first to check.

PRACTICALITIES

Few places have strict dress codes these days; as a general rule, the pricier the joint, the smarter the clientele. It's only common sense that you don't turn up to Rhodes & Co wearing a string vest; but if you're unsure call ahead first.

Cosmo by name... *See page 128.*

It's standard practice to pay 10 per cent on top of the bill for service. Some restaurants will add this automatically (while insisting that it is 'optional'; so if service wasn't up to scratch you should deduct the charge). Be wary of places that include service on the bill and then leave the space for a gratuity empty on your credit card slip.

The average prices below are for a starter and a main course, excluding drinks and service, for one person.

American

Bell's Diner

7 St Stephen Street, Stockbridge, EH3 (225 8116). Bus 28, 29, 29A, 80. **Open** 6-10.30pm Mon-Fri, Sun; noon-10.30pm Sat. **Average** £9. **Credit** MC, V. **Map** p306 D3.

Burgers and steaks form the bulk of the menu at this tiny Stockbridge restaurant and it must be the only place in town that offers a slimmer's burger. Bell's has been around for more years than most people care to remember and no one seems to have tired of it yet. The beef and chicken burgers come in various sizes, and no less attention is paid to the veggie burgers.

The Buffalo Grill

14 Chapel Street, South Edinburgh, EH8 (667 7427). Bus 40-42, 46. **Open** noon-2pm, 6-10.15pm Mon-Fri; 6-10.15pm Sat; 5-10pm Sun. **Average** £16. **Credit** MC, V. **Map** p310 G7.

With every kind of steak, from Cajun to carpetbags, teriyakis to Delmonicos, and as many burger variations as you care to dream of, this is where it's at if you want to get busy on the beef. Almost every restaurant in Edinburgh offers a steak but this is the only place that offers them all. Although it isn't licensed (but there's no charge if you take your own bottle) this, the original branch, always seems fully booked, and the Stockbridge outpost is getting to be the same way.

Branch: 1 Raeburn Place, Stockbridge, EH4 (332 3864).

Mamma's

30 Grassmarket, South Edinburgh, EH1 (225 6464). Bus 2. **Open** noon-11pm Mon-Thur, Sun; noon-midnight Fri, Sat. **Average** £7.50. **Credit** MC, V. **Map** p314 B3.

Traditional American pizzas and panzerotti keep a surprisingly wide customer base smiling at these two restaurants. The pizzas go up to 16 inches and as well as all the usual toppings more off-the-wall ones such as haggis and cactus are offered. Both branches are fun and the flamboyant pizza chefs are the culinary equivalent of firecracker cocktail-bar staff.

Branch: 1 Howard Street, Inverleith Row, Stockbridge, EH3 (558 7177).

Caribbean

Caribbean Connection

3 Grove Street, West Edinburgh, EH3 (228 1345). Bus 3, 12, 25. **Open** 7-9.30pm Wed-Sat; closed Mon, Tue, Sun. **Average** £13.50. **Credit** MC, V. **Map** p308 C6.

Run by a cheery couple who spent many a year in the Caribbean, this great little joint looks like a roadside shack – all wooden planks and Jamaican bric-a-brac. The food is spicy and sweet; special mention must go to the wet jerk rub – barbecued chicken or pork marinated with herbs and spices. It's unlicensed, but they'll open your own bottle for nothing. Booking is as essential as the Bob Marley soundtrack.

Chinese

Chinese Home Cooking

34 West Preston Street, South Edinburgh, EH8 (668 4946). Bus 3, 7, 8, 31, 80. **Open** noon-2pm, 5.30-11.30pm Mon-Thur; 5.30-11.30pm Fri, Sat; 5.30-11pm Sun. **Average** £7. **No credit cards. Map** p310 H8.

While highly unlikely to ever trouble the Michelin inspectors, Chinese Home Cooking offers basic oriental standards at rock-bottom prices. Good for group parties and for filling up cheaply, but not ideal if you're looking to impress.

Dragon Way

74 South Clerk Street, South Edinburgh, EH8 (668 1328). Bus 7, 8, 31, 80. **Open** noon-2.30pm, 5pm-midnight daily.* **Average** £11. **Credit** AmEx, DC, MC, V. **Map** p310 H8.

The decor here is a riot of red and gold pagodas, dragons and flowers, which are only partially eclipsed by the indoor waterfall and fish pond. Seafood is the speciality but don't on any account overlook the crispy duck, which could make a grown man weep.

Loon Fung

2 Warriston Place, Inverleith Row, Stockbridge, EH3 (556 1781). Bus 8, 23, 27. **Open** noon-11.30pm Mon-Thur; noon-1am Fri; 2pm-1am Sat; 2pm-midnight Sun. **Average** £12. **Credit** AmEx, MC, V. **Map** p306 E2.

Down on Canonmills and handily placed for the Botanic Gardens, Loon Fung is one of Edinburgh's better Cantonese restaurants. There's a great selection of dim sum, and specials include baked crab in ginger sauce and steamed chicken with mushrooms. Often busy when everywhere else is deserted.

Oriental Dining Centre

8 Morrison Street, West Edinburgh, EH3 (221 1288). Bus 11, 15, 24. **Open** *Rainbow Arch* noon-11.30pm daily. *Noodle Shack* 5.30pm-2am daily. *Cellar Bar* noon-3am daily. **Average** *Rainbow Arch* £10; *Noodle Shack* £7; *Cellar Bar* £3. **Credit** AmEx, MC, V. **Map** p309 D6.

There are three different outlets under the umbrella of the Oriental Dining Centre. Rapid bowls of steaming udon noodles provide a quick refuelling stop at the upstairs Noodle Shack, while the ground-floor Rainbow Arch offers the full sit-down-and-banquet-till-you-burst option. The dim sum cellar bar is perhaps better known as a late night drum 'n' bass 'n' drinking jazz joint: Henry's Cellar Bar (*see p162*).

Fish

Café Royal Oyster Bar

17A West Register Street, New Town, EH1 (556 4124). Bus 3, 3A, 12, 16, 17, 80. **Open** noon-2pm, 7-10pm daily. **Average** £23. **Credit** AmEx, DC, MC, V. **Map** p314 D1.

Adjacent to the equally ornate Café Royal Circle Bar (*see p151*), this rather grand Victorian restaurant prides itself on classic fish dishes, which it does remarkably well. Not that customers have to go the whole hog and eat a full meal: half a dozen oysters will give any seafood lover a refreshing taste of the briney. It's a horrible word but 'classy' fits.

Creelers

3 Hunter Square, Royal Mile, EH1 (220 4447). Bus 7, 8, 21, 31, 80. **Open** noon-2.30pm, 5.30-

Fish list

The abundance of quality fish restaurants in Edinburgh is indicative of its position near the sea on the Firth of Forth. For the true Edinburgh fish experience you simply must visit a local fish and chip shop. Here, fish comes either as a 'supper' (that's fish and chips) or as a 'single' (but don't be surprised if you get a couple of chips with your fish).

What is unique to Edinburgh is that when the fish supper is ready to be wrapped you'll be offered sauce on it, not vinegar. Although this viscous, brown, vinegar-based concoction looks suspiciously as if it could contravene the United Nations chemical weapons limitation treaty, it adds a spicy zing to the supper and should be tried at least once. Edinburgh natives swear by it, but visitors can find the resulting finger-licking experience a bit messy. If you want vinegar, not sauce, just say 'salt and vinegar' when offered 'salt'n'sauce?' but beware, the offer can sound more like 'serasas?'.

The menu in Scottish fish and chip shops is slightly different to that south of the border. Besides fish, smoked sausage, pie or chicken, on offer are haggis, black pudding and white pudding. All are cooked in batter. Haggis is slightly spicy, black pudding is a blood-based sausage and white pudding is vegetarian.

Another quirk of the Scottish fish and chip shop is that none seem to be able to leave a bag of chips open so that you can eat them walking down the street. No matter how much you ask, it doesn't happen. Even at the best places, which include those listed below:

L'Alba D'Oro
5 Henderson Row, Stockbridge, EH5 (557 2580). Bus 23, 27. **Open** *Chip shop* 11.30am-1.30pm, 5pm-midnight Mon-Fri; 5pm-midnight Sat, Sun. *Pizzas* 11.30am-2.30pm, 5pm-midnight Mon-Fri; 5pm-midnight Sat, Sun. **No credit cards. Map** p306 D3.

L'Aquila Bianca
17 Raeburn Place, Stockbridge, EH4 (332 8433). Bus 28, 29, 29A, 80. **Open** 11.30am-1.30pm, 4.30pm-12.30am Mon-Thur, Sun; 4.30pm-1am Fri, Sat. **No credit cards. Map** p305 C3.

Clam Shell Fish & Chip Shop
148 High Street, Royal Mile, EH1 (225 4338). Bus 35, 35A. **Open** 11.30am-12.30am daily. **No credit cards. Map** p314 D3.

Concord Fish Bar
49 Home Street, South Edinburgh, EH3 (228 1182). Bus 11, 16, 17, 23. **Open** 11am-2pm, 4.30pm-2.30am Mon-Fri; 11am-4.30am Sat; 4.30pm-2.30am Sun. **No credit cards. Map** p309 D7.

Rapido
79 Broughton Street, Broughton, EH1 (556 2041). Bus 8. **Open** 11.30am-2pm, 4.30pm-1.30am Mon-Thur; 11.30am-2pm, 4.30pm-3am Fri, Sat. **No credit cards. Map** p306 F3.

10.30pm Mon-Thur; noon-2.30pm, 5.30-11pm Fri, Sat; 5.30-10.30pm Sun; closed Sun in winter. **Average** *bistro* £15; *restaurant* £25. **Credit** MC, V. **Map** p314 D3.

The couple who own this bistro and restaurant also have a branch and a smokehouse on the Isle of Arran. The husband also worked for years on the trawlers on the West Coast. The upshot of all this is that they are the ideal people to source the best fish and seafood. The bistro at the front is cheaper and more informal than the full restaurant in the back room. A typical dish would be fillet of cod with a black olive tapenade. Eating outside can be pleasant in the summer, if somewhat crowded during the Festival season. No smoking in the restaurant before 2pm at lunchtime or 9.30pm in the evening.

The Mussel Inn
61 Rose Street, New Town, EH2 (225 5979). Bus 3, 3A, 12, 16, 17. **Open** noon-3pm, 6-10pm Mon-Fri;

noon-10pm Sat; 1.30-10pm Sun. **Average** £12. **Credit** AmEx, DC, MC, V. **Map** p314 C1.

This is a kind of back to basics for seafood restaurants. The shellfish come direct from the farms of the owners and the food is prepared very simply and served in colourful surroundings, which are perfectly comfortable but don't boast too many frills. Kilo pots of mussels are a favourite and, when accompanied by a bowl of chips and mayo, it seems as if the world couldn't be a better place. Rather tempting choc pud as well, if you can face it.

The Shore
3-4 The Shore, Leith, EH6 (553 5080). Bus 1, 6, 10A, 32, 52. **Open** *Bar* 11am-midnight Mon-Sat; 12.30-11pm Sun. *Restaurant* noon-2.30pm, 6.30-10pm Mon-Sat; 12.30-3pm, 6.30-10pm Sun. **Average** £17. **Credit** AmEx, MC, V. **Map** p311 Jy.

Everyone in Edinburgh has their personal favourite from the several fish restaurants in Leith. They're

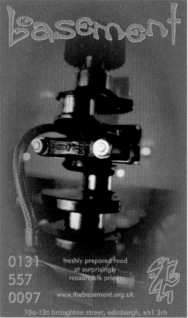

all pretty damn good, but the Shore may well be the most relaxed. Guests can eat in the restaurant proper or the more smoky environs of the bar, where regular folk and jazz sessions add another element to the experience. The fish dishes can be adventurous. Others to try in the immediate vicinity are the good-looking **Fishers**, 1 The Shore, EH6 (554 5666); the more intimate **Skippers**, 1A Dock Place, EH6 (554 1018) and the maritime themed **Ship On The Shore**, 24 The Shore, EH6 (555 0409).

French

Bleu

36-38 Victoria Street, Royal Mile, EH1 (226 1900). Bus 23, 28, 35, 45. **Open** noon-3pm, 6-11pm Mon-Sat; noon-4pm, 6-11pm Sun. **Average** £9. **Credit** DC, MC, V. **Map** p314 C3.

Taking to the extreme the idea that a little bit of what you fancy can only be beneficial, Bleu's menu is composed of *bouchées*, literally mouthfuls of food. Global tapas is perhaps a more helpful term. Typical examples include salmon and crab fish cakes, vegetable tempura and home-made duck confit. All three branches are very sleek.
Branches: 4 Union Street, Broughton, EH1 (557 8451); 8 Gloucester Street, New Town, EH3 (225 1037).

Le Café Saint-Honoré

34 North West Thistle Street Lane, New Town, EH2 (226 2211). Bus 23, 27. **Open** noon-2.15pm, 7-10pm Mon-Fri; 7-10pm Sat; closed Sun. **Average** £20. **Credit** AmEx, DC, MC, V. **Map** p314 B1.

Burnished mirrors, a checked floor and lots of wood panelling make this hard-to-find restaurant a dead ringer for a classic French bistro. The food is less obviously Gallic but certainly not to be sniffed at either. Apparently, this is where many of Edinburgh's other restaurant managers and chefs come on their nights off. Early diners might like to take advantage of the weekday 5-7pm reduced-price offers. Booking is advised for late suppers. No smoking in main dining area.

La Cuisine d'Odile

French Institute, 13 Randolph Crescent, New Town, EH3 (225 5685). Bus 13, 19, 55, 82. **Open** noon-2pm Tue-Sat; closed Mon, Sun. **Average** £6.95 (3-course set menu). **No credit cards. Map** p308 C5.

Some French restaurants are about as Gallic as le chewing gum. Odile's, set in the basement of the ever-active French Institute, is the real deal, even if it isn't licensed (corkage is £1). Odile works her home cooking around what was available that morning and tends to follow the season's produce – so it will be fresh, but a strawberry tart ain't going to feature in January. In fine weather, the outside tables provide a pleasant view of the large sweep of trees beyond the garden. Lunch only.

Duck's at Le Marché Noir

2-4 Eyre Place, New Town, EH3 (558 1608/ enquiries@ducks.co.uk/www.ducks.co.uk). Bus 23, 27.

The Apartment
Edinburgh's culinary cutting edge.
See page 127.

Black Bo's
Fresh designs on veggie favourites.
See page 136.

Café Royal Oyster Bar
Classic fish dishes in ornate surroundings.
See page 122.

Creelers
Fish, fresh from the owners' Arran smokehouse. See page 122.

La Cuisine d'Odile
Simple French food *comme il faut*.
See page 125.

Restaurant Martin Wishart
The Balmoral's head chef goes it alone.
See page 127.

Sweet Melinda's
Excellent fish, but the puds deserve special attention. See page 134.

The Tower
Decent food but an even better view.
See page 134.

The Witchery by the Castle
A long-standing Edinburgh favourite.
See page 135.

Yumi
Authentic Japanese food, at authentic Japanese prices. See page 129.

Open noon-2.30pm, 6.30-10pm Mon-Thur; noon-2.30pm, 6.30-10.30pm Fri; 6.30-10.30pm Sat; 6.30-10pm Sun. **Average** £20. **Credit** AmEx, DC, MC, V. **Map** p306 E3.

A well-established French/Scottish restaurant run by the unique Malcolm Duck, this New Town restaurant has one of the best wine lists in the city. The food is serious, with dishes like herb crumbed salmon and scallop *boudin* with creamed leeks and a tarragon beurre blanc taking considerable effort and expertise to create. Wine-tasting dinners are a regular feature.

Malmaison

1 Tower Place, Leith, EH6 (468 5001). Bus 10A, 16, 35, 35A. **Open** 7-10am, noon-2.30pm, 6-10.30pm daily. **Average** £15. **Credit** AmEx, DC, MC, V. **Map** p311 Jx.

Duck's
at Le Marché Noir
Restaurant

Contemporary Scottish Cuisine
with international flair

www.ducks.co.uk
enquiries@ducks.co.uk

Duck's
at Le Marché Noir

2/4 Eyre Place, Edinburgh, EH3 5EP
Tel: 0131 558 1608. Fax: 0131 556 0798

Malmaison may be one of Edinburgh's funkier hotels (*see p111*) but it has looked towards the old school of Parisian brasseries for its dining room. Serving staff in white aprons and black waistcoats, dark wood panelling and a pretty relaxed ambience complete the picture. The perennially popular steak-frites is something of a best seller.

Restaurant Martin Wishart

54 The Shore, Leith, EH6 (553 3557). Bus 10A, 16, 35, 35A. **Open** 12.30-2.30pm, 7-10pm Tue-Fri; 7-10pm Sat; closed Mon, Sun. **Average** £21. **Credit** MC, V. **Map** p311 Jy.

This small and sunny restaurant is entirely the baby of the eponymous owner. Formerly the head chef at Hadrian's at the Balmoral (*see p105*), he struck out on his own in 1999 and hasn't looked back. Classical French cooking with the occasional innovation is his forte. Booking is advisable.

Petit Paris

38 Grassmarket, South Edinburgh, EH1 (226 2442). Bus 2. **Open** noon-3pm, 5.30-10.30pm Mon-Thur, Sun; noon-3pm, 5.30-11pm Fri, Sat; closed Mon in winter. **Average** £15. **Credit** MC, V. **Map** p314 B3.

This vibey little place is a gem. Coq au vin, moules marinières and boeuf bourgignon all do their bit for the Auld Alliance. The day's specials are chalked up on a blackboard and it does cheap deals at lunchtime and in the early evening. The goat's cheese salad is sure to have you whistling the *Marseillaise* in double-quick time.

Pierre Victoire

10 Victoria Street, Royal Mile, EH1 (225 1721). Bus 23, 28, 35, 35A, 45. **Open** noon-3pm, 6-11pm daily. **Average** £10.50. **Credit** MC, V. **Map** p314 C3.

Most of the branches of the UK-wide chain of PVs have waved 'adieu' but the very first one is still trading here under its original name. The format is much the same: bistro decor and bistro food at decent prices. The cooking has had its up and downs, but seems to have settled at a reasonable standard.

The Vintner's Rooms

The Vaults, 87 Giles Street, Leith, EH6 (554 6767). Bus 10A, 35, 35A. **Open** noon-2pm, 7pm-midnight Mon-Sat; closed Sun. **Average** £25. **Credit** AmEx, MC, V. **Map** p311 Jy.

Perfect for a romantic night out, the Vintner's Rooms are housed in an ancient wine warehouse in Leith. Soft candle lighting and the best Scottish produce with a French undercurrent are the main selling points is one of Edinburgh's better restaurants. The adjacent bar is cheaper but can't match that intimate atmosphere. No smoking.

Global

The Apartment

11 Barclay Place, on Bruntsfield Place, South Edinburgh, EH10 (228 6456). Bus 11, 16, 17, 23. **Open** 6-11pm Mon-Fri; noon-3pm, 6-11pm Sat, Sun. **Average** £12. **Credit** DC, MC, V. **Map** p309 D8.

A seriously funky space that pulls off its minimalist styling well, the Apartment has nicked some of the best ideas from around the world and pulled them together neatly. The North African marinated spicy lamb balls with merguez and basil, wrapped in melted goat's cheese, are a real eye-opener and just one example of the kitchen's inventiveness. Fresh as it is, the Apartment attracts an older crowd as well as the capital's trend-setters. Worth a visit to see the cutting edge of Edinburgh's modern food scene.

Nicolson's

6a Nicolson Street, South Edinburgh, EH8 (557 4567). Bus 7, 8, 21, 31, 80. **Open** noon-3pm, 5-11pm daily. **Average** £15. **Credit** AmEx, MC, V. **Map** p310 G6.

An airy first-floor space with an art deco feel, Nicolson's menu runs from dishes such as gado gado to scallop and herb salad with fresh coconut and lime. The minute steaks are good too, for the less adventurous. While not the main point of a visit, the martinis bear closer investigation and this is the only place in the capital to sell the South American spirit pisco.

Polo Fusion

503 Lawnmarket, Royal Mile, EH1 (622 7722/ polofusion@cablenet.co.uk). Bus 35, 35A. **Open** noon-2pm, 6-10pm Tue-Sat; closed Mon, also closed Tue in winter. **Average** £18. **Credit** AmEx, DC, MC, V. **Map** p314 C3.

Edinburgh's first fusion cooking restaurant, Polo Fusion fits the global melting pot idea without being a flash in the pan. That so many different flavours would work on the one plate seems unlikely when reading the menu but the proof is in the tasting. The Pacific Rim, California and all the countries around the Med (and that includes Africa) make an appearance.

Indian

Britannia Spice

150 Commercial Street, Leith, EH6 (555 2255/ www.britanniaspice.com). Bus 10A, 16, 34. **Open** 12.15-2.15pm, 5-11.45pm daily. **Average** £15. **Credit** AmEx, DC, MC, V. **Map** p311 Jy.

Decked out like the nearby *Royal Yacht Britannia*, this new 150-cover restaurant serves up Thai, Sri Lankan, Nepalese and Bangladeshi dishes. The nautical theme of the decor is quite fun and the food is ship shape and Bristol fashion.

Kebab Mahal

7 Nicolson Square, South Edinburgh, EH8 (622 7228). Bus 7, 8, 21, 31, 80. **Open** noon-midnight Mon-Thur, Sun; noon-2am Fri, Sat. **Average** £7. **Credit** AmEx, DC, MC, V. **Map** p310 G6.

A late-night munchie pick-up point for many a tired and emotional reveller, the Kebab Mahal also has basic sit-in facilities. It is not the lap of luxury by any stretch of the imagination but cheap, quick

Consumer

and pretty decent curries and kebabs all do their job well. Legend has it that one of the staff once smiled. No alcohol.

Khushi's
16 Drummond Street, South Edinburgh, EH8 (556 8996). Bus 7, 8, 31, 80. **Open** noon-3pm, 5-9pm Mon-Thur; noon-3pm, 5-9.30pm Fri, Sat; closed Sun. **Average** £8. **No credit cards**. **Map** p310 G6.
Khushi's back-to-basics approach to curry won't find favour with those who like their dishes intensely rich or creamy but since it has been thriving for decades it's certainly doing something right. Cheap, cheerful and unlicensed (free corkage), it's a good spot to fill up for little money, although not everyone might like things quite so spartan.

Pataka
190 Causewayside, South Edinburgh, EH9 (668 1167). Bus 7, 8, 31, 80. **Open** noon-2pm, 5.30-11.30pm daily. **Average** £10. **Credit** AmEx, MC, V. **Map** p310 H8.
Charles Rennie Mackintosh and Indian food might not seem the most closely related of cousins but the Pataka has successfully married Chas's design sense with a more upmarket than usual range of dishes.

Mrs Uni's Kitchen
101 Dalry Road, Haymarket, West Edinburgh, EH11 (337 3852). Bus 3, 21, 25. **Open** noon-2pm, 5pm-midnight Mon-Sat. **Set dinner** £11.99. **Credit** MC, V. **Map** p308 B7.
Nobody comes here for the decor but the reputation of Mrs Uni's bargain buffets, billed as Asian home cooking, is growing. For this you can eat to your heart's content from a wide range of standards including lamb pashinda, mince and peas and a selection of sundry side dishes. It's unlicensed but there's no corkage charge.

Suruchi
14A Nicolson Street, South Edinburgh, EH8 (556 6583). Bus 7, 8, 21, 31, 80. **Open** noon-2pm, 5.30-11.30pm daily. **Average** £14. **Credit** DC, MC, V. **Map** p310 G6.
Handily situated across from the Festival Theatre, Suruchi makes an interesting change from the standard curry house menu, which doesn't vary much from Inverness to Islington. Proprietor Herman Rodrigues is a bit of a scholar of Indian cooking and is often over there digging up new recipes and spices, while priding himself in sourcing Scottish ingredients. Cultural evenings of Indian music and dance feature from time to time.

The Verandah
17 Dalry Road, Haymarket, West Edinburgh, EH11 (337 5828). Bus 3, 12, 25. **Open** 12.30-2.30pm, 5pm-midnight daily. **Average** £9. **Credit** AmEx, DC, MC, V. **Map** p308 B7.
In business for almost two decades, the Verandah specialises in Bangladeshi and North Indian cooking, with an emphasis on milder dishes. Subtle curries such as amer murgh, made from chicken, mango pulp and cream, are the norm, rather than culinary

napalm. Rather surreally, both Clint Eastwood and Cliff Richard have eaten here and the photos are on the wall to prove it.

Italian

Bar Napoli
75 Hanover Street, New Town, EH2 (225 2600). Bus 23, 27, 45. **Open** noon-2.30am daily. **Average** £8. **Credit** AmEx, DC, MC, V. **Map** p314 C1.
A Hanover Street special, Bar Napoli is a large pizza and pasta joint that has the added bonus of being open until 2.30am, seven days a week. Watching the staff making their own bread at lunchtimes is a pleasant way to pass the time, while munching on one of the house specials like *saltimbocca alla romana*.

Cosmo
58A North Castle Street, New Town, EH2 (226 6743). Bus 13, 19, 55, 82. **Open** 12.30-2.15pm, 7-10.45pm Mon-Fri; 7-10pm Sat; closed Sun. **Average** £23. **Credit** AmEx, MC, V. **Map** p314 B1.
Appealing to the more mature and better-heeled client, Cosmo is an Edinburgh institution, albeit one that doesn't like to shout. A million miles away from the usual pizza and pasta joints, Cosmo is all about classic Italian cooking, with an emphasis on fish. Trainers and a T-shirt are a definite no-no.

Est Est Est
135a George Street, New Town, EH2 (225 2555). Bus 13, 19, 55, 82. **Open** noon-11pm daily. **Average** £12. **Credit** AmEx, DC, MC, V. **Map** p314 A1.
Bright, brash and modern, this busy branch of a national chain likes to flaunt its assets. Young professionals, who perhaps want to see and be seen, have a fondness for its menu of slightly jazzed-up trattoria staples.

Ristorante Tinelli
139 Easter Road, Greenside, EH7 (652 1932). Bus 1, 35, 35A. **Open** noon-2.30pm, 6.30-11pm Mon-Sat; closed Sun. **Average** £12.50. **Credit** AmEx, DC, MC, V. **Map** p307 J3.
Not the most fashionable end of town and not the city's most promising exterior either, but Tinelli's has done good business over the years thanks to the Lombardy cooking and the eponymous owner's hospitality. Many of Edinburgh's married couples have fond memories of this place and wedding anniversaries are not an uncommon reason to come here.

La Rusticana
88-90 Hanover Street, New Town, EH2 (225 2227). Bus 23, 27, 45. **Open** noon-2pm, 5-11pm daily. **Average** £15. **Credit** AmEx, DC, MC, V. **Map** p314 C1.
While not quite Little Italy, Hanover Street is home to many of Edinburgh's more relaxed trattorias. La Rusticana is typical, with pizza, pasta and other standards served up in a bustling and vibrant atmosphere. Checked table cloths, murals of the

Italian Riviera and paintings of the Three Tenors are all present and correct, you'll be glad to hear. **Branch:** 25-27 Cockburn Street, Royal Mile, EH1 (225 2832).

Scalini

10 Melville Place, Queensferry Street, New Town, EH3 (220 2999). Bus 13, 19, 55, 82. **Open** noon-2.30pm, 6-10pm Mon-Sat; closed Sun. **Average** £15. **Credit** AmEx, DC, MC, V. **Map** p308 C5.

Scalini is an intimate, basement restaurant that tends to keep things simple rather than use over-complicated, fussy ideas. Silvio is the exuberant owner here and should you visit you will almost certainly make his acquaintance. No smoking.

Japanese

Tampopo

25A Thistle Street, New Town, EH2 (220 5254). Bus 23, 27. **Open** noon-2.30pm, 6-9pm Mon-Sat; noon-3pm Sun; closed Mon, Sun in winter. **Average** £10. **No credit cards. Map** p314 C1.

If Yumi is Edinburgh's exclusive Japanese restaurant then this unlicensed treat represents the fast food side of Japanese culture, with big bowls of noodles taking pride of place. It does sit-in or take away sushi and bento boxes.

Yumi

2 West Coates, West Edinburgh, EH12 (337 2173). Bus 12, 26, 31. **Open** 6.30-11pm Mon-Sat; closed Sun. **Average** £23. **Credit** DC, MC, V. **Map** p308 A6.

Now that Daruma-ya in Leith has said 'Sayonara' and packed its bags, Yumi is the only full-blown Japanese restaurant in town. Still, it doesn't cut any corners. To go the whole hog, book the Tatami room, put on a clean pair of socks and get acquainted with authentic Japanese cuisine. As you may imagine, it's not cheap.

Mexican

Blue Parrot Cantina

49 St Stephen Street, Stockbridge, EH3 (225 2941). Bus 28, 29, 29A, 80. **Open** 5-11pm Mon-Thur; noon-11pm Fri, Sat; 5-10.30pm Sun. **Average** £11.50. **Credit** MC, V. **Map** p306 D3.

A touch more adventurous than the usual fajita factories, this basement cantina on Stockbridge's boho St Stephen Street throws in the odd unexpected ingredient from time to time. Try the sautéed whole chillies or the Mexican steak.

Tex Mex

47 Hanover Street, New Town, EH2 (225 1796). Bus 23, 27, 45. **Open** noon-11pm Mon-Sat; 12.30-11pm Sun. **Average** £16. **Credit** AmEx, DC, MC, V. **Map** p314 C1.

The fiesta doesn't seem to stop very often around these parts of the city and that quiet evening with just the two of you is doomed before kick-off. On the other hand, if painting the town red is what's required then this is as good a place as any to start. As you may have guessed from the name, the food is Tex and indeed Mex, with all the usual tacos and quesadillas.

Viva Mexico – thankfully the food is more up to date than the photos. *See page 131.*

TOWER RESTAURANT

The Tower has a soigné ease rare in Scotland. Uniquely for a Museum this has become the hottest table in Edinburgh.
AA Gill, The Sunday Times

All Museum restaurants are hideous...how great to be proved wrong for once.
Giles Gordon.

The Tower serves food so sublime it eclipses the wine. Almost.
Iain Banks

Edinburgh's stunning rooftop restaurant and terrace with unique views of the castle and the skyline opens all day for lunch and dinner until late seven days.

RESERVATIONS 0131 225 3003

TOWER RESTAURANT
Museum of Scotland, Chambers Street
Edinburgh EH1 1JF
www.tower-restaurant.com

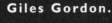

Viva Mexico
*41 Cockburn Street, Royal Mile, EH1 (226 5145/
judygon@tinyonline.co.uk). Bus 35, 35A.* **Open**
noon-2.30pm, 6.30-10.30pm Mon-Sat; 6.30-10pm
Sun. **Average** £11. **Credit** AmEx, DC, MC, V.
Map p314 D3.
All the Mexican staples that you might expect are
here. Head to the downstairs dining room for a
splendid collection of moustaches, courtesy of the
black and white photos. Those in the know give the
thumbs up to the Margaritas.

Scottish

36
*Howard Hotel, 36 Great King Street, New Town,
EH3 (556 3636). Bus 23, 27.* **Open** noon-2pm, 7-
10pm Mon-Fri; 7-10pm Sat; noon-2pm, 7-9.30pm Sun;
closed lunch in winter. **Average** £20. **Credit** AmEx,
DC, MC, V. **Map** p306 E3.
If 36 was a magazine, it would be something of a
cross between *Vogue*, with its sense of classic style
and *Wallpaper**, with its fresh attitude. Put more
straightforwardly, the place, in the basement of the
Howard Hotel (*see p107*), looks great, thanks to a
simple but highly effective use of coloured light and
shade. The food is just as stylish without being a
fashion victim. Think navarin of lamb rump with a
black olive and rosemary mash.
Channings and the Bonham are two other restaurants owned by the same company. They are similar in ethos to 36 but also retain their own distinct
identities. Channings Brasserie and Conservatory
serves dishes such as a ragoût of free-range
Aberdeenshire chicken with wild mushroom ravioli.
Pelham Hill, the chef at the Bonham, likes to experiment at the point where Scottish produce meets
Californian culinary ideas.
Branches: **Channings** 12 South Learmonth
Gardens, Dean, EH4 (315 2225); **The Bonham** 35
Drumsheugh Gardens, New Town, EH3 (226 6050).

The Atrium
*10 Cambridge Street, South Edinburgh, EH1 (228
8882). Bus 11, 15, 24.* **Open** noon-2pm, 6.30-10.30pm
Mon-Fri; 6.30-10.30pm Sat; closed Sun. **Average** £25.
Credit AmEx, DC, MC, V. **Map** p314 A3.
While Andrew Radford's empire has expanded
rapidly in the last three years and now encompasses four outlets (most notably the blue Bar Café;
see p157), he hasn't forsaken his first success story,
the Atrium. The food is innovative modern British
cuisine that uses carefully sourced Scottish ingredients. Attention to detail is paramount and the
decor is unconventional without putting the fright-
eners on the businessmen and older couples who
form a large proportion of the clientele.

Backstage Bistro
*22 Valleyfield Street, South Edinburgh, EH3 (229
1978). Bus 11, 16, 17, 23.* **Open** *July to mid-Sept*
noon-10pm daily; *mid-Sept to June* 5-11pm daily.
Average £12. **Credit** MC, V. **Map** p309 D7.

This unassuming little bistro is a favourite with the
audiences at the King's Theatre (*see p221*) around
the corner. Not surprisingly, there is a pre-theatre
menu from 5-7pm, at decent prices (one course for
£5.75 and three for £7.95). Breast of pheasant,
tuna steaks and cous cous-stuffed aubergines are
just three typical dishes. It's unlicensed, and there's
no charge for corkage.

Banks Restaurant
*Newington House, 10 Newington Road, South
Edinburgh, EH8 (667 0707). Bus 7, 8, 31, 80.*
Open *Grill Room* noon-2.30pm, 6-10.30pm
Tue-Sat; 12.30pm-10.30pm Sun; closed Mon.
A la carte noon-2.30pm, 6-10.30pm Tue-Sat;
closed Sun, Mon. **Average** *Grill Room* £15;
à la carte £20. **Credit** AmEx, MC, V.
Map p310 H8.
Within a couple of months of opening, this Georgian
townhouse was already garnering plaudits. Chef
patron Peter Banks has an impressive array of
awards to his name for previous culinary ventures
but it seems as though he has really hit the bullseye
with this one. The downstairs char-grill keeps it simple, with prime steaks and chunky chips, while
upstairs the likes of langoustine with sea bass
ravioli and a chive *velouté* rule the roost. Booking
is highly recommended.

The Dial
*44-46 George IV Bridge, South Edinburgh, EH1
(225 7179). Bus 23, 28, 45.* **Open** noon-3pm, 6pm-
11pm daily. **Average** £17. **Credit** AmEx, DC, MC,
V. **Map** p314 C3.
White walls, paper lanterns, twisting banisters and
translucent cutlery mean that the Dial's decor
makes as bold a statement as its menu. Top-notch
Scottish produce is given an eclectic treatment that
is, at times, reassuringly familiar (albeit with modern touches), and at others, totally unexpected. The
stir-fried salmon with mangetout, ginger and
coriander has more than a touch of the Pacific Rim
about it, while the ribeye Angus with mash and a
filo parcel of home-made pâté is conspicuously nu-
Scottish. The Dial is in a basement so it's easy to
miss the entrance.

Dubh Prais
*123B High Street, Royal Mile, EH1 (557 5732).
Bus 35, 35A.* **Open** noon-2pm, 6.30-10.30pm
Tue-Fri; 6.30-10.30pm Sat; closed Mon, Sun.
Average £18. **Credit** AmEx, MC, V.
Map p314 D3.
James McWilliams is the chef and owner of this
basement restaurant on the Royal Mile and he
reckons that he was serving Scottish cuisine before
anyone else even knew what it was. Well, he may
be right, but more pertinently the Dubh Prais (that's
'black pot' in Gaelic, fact fans) has long provided
a serious standard of food. Naturally, the raw
ingredients are the best that Scotland has to offer and
McWilliams treats them so as to allow their flavours
to shine through. Despite the prime location, this
is no tourist trap.

(Fitz)henry: a brasserie

19 Shore Place, Leith, EH6 (555 6625). Bus 10A, 35, 35A. **Open** 12.30-2.30pm, 6.30-10pm Mon-Thur; 12.30-2.30pm, 6.30-10.30pm Fri, Sat; closed Sun. **Average** £19. **Credit** AmEx, MC, V. **Map** p311 Jy.
One of only two restaurants in Edinburgh to be awarded a Michelin Bib Gourmand, this old warehouse has been elegantly decorated to create a unique atmosphere. Proprietor and professional maverick David Ramsden is equally idiosyncratic and has very definite ideas about food. Actually pinning down his kitchen's output to a concise definition isn't easy but French provincial cooking with more global flourishes is heading in the right direction. As this Guide went to press, Ramsden was making noises about moving up town, so phone first.

Haldanes

39A Albany Street, New Town, EH3 (556 8407). Bus 8, 12, 16, 17, 25. **Open** noon-1.30pm, 6-10pm Mon-Fri; 6-10pm Sat, Sun. **Average** £22. **Set menu** £25 3 courses. **Credit** AmEx DC, MC, V. **Map** p306 F4.
George Kelso is the chef-patron at this well-appointed and highly rated basement restaurant in the New Town. Scottish produce is very much to the fore (Haldanes is a member of the Scotch Beef Club) and Kelso is a keen proponent of preparing as much from scratch as possible. Haldanes has deliberately aimed for a country-house feel and this is helped by customers being able to retire to the lounge or study for after-dinner drinks and coffee.

Howie's

75 St Leonard's Street, South Edinburgh, EH8 (668 2917). Bus 2 21. **Open** 6-10pm Mon; noon-2pm, 6-10pm Tue-Sun. **Set menu** *lunch* £7.95; *dinner* £16.95 3 courses. **Credit** AmEx, MC, V. **Map** p310 H7.
Howie's four restaurants have long been sturdy mid-price favourites in the city. They are the kind of place that young courting couples might use for a first dinner date or older marrieds might use for a reliable meal out. Scottish produce forms the foundations of the menu and this is forged into the likes of fish cakes and pan-fried fillets of chicken with a Madeira and coriander jus. All the branches are comfortably laid-back but the Stockbridge one is the most chic looking.
Branches: 208 Bruntsfield Place, South Edinburgh EH10 (221 1777); 63 Dalry Road, West Edinburgh, EH11 (313 3334); 4 Glanville Place, Kerr Street, Stockbridge, EH3 (225 5553).

Igg's

15 Jeffrey Street, Royal Mile, EH1 (557 8184). Bus 35, 35A. **Open** *restaurant* noon-2.30pm, 6-10.30pm Mon-Sat; closed Sun. *Barioja* 11am-11pm Mon-Sat; closed Sun. **Average** *restaurant* £21. **Credit** AmEx, DC, MC, V. **Map** 310 G5.
'Plush' is a suitable term for the food at Iggy Campos'

The extraordinary light-fitting at the acclaimed **Banks Restaurant**.
See page 131.

place. He sources all of his meat from the organic farm at Stobo Castle and then his chefs perform wonders with it. Tapas are the stock in trade at lunchtimes. He recently opened a more informal tapas bar, Barioja, next door, which had teething problems. We expect that Señor Campos will sort these out.

Jackson's Restaurant

209 High Street, Royal Mile, EH1 (225 1793). Bus 35, 35A. **Open** noon-2.30pm, 6-10.30pm daily. **Average** £19. **Credit** AmEx, DC, MC, V. **Map** p314 D3.
Since Jackson's decor has a number of points in common with a Scottish hunting lodge, it is fitting that the fruits of hunting, shooting and fishing as well as careful cattle-rearing should feature so heavily on the menu. It is all done well and, while tourists are far from being the only ones to dine from the white linen, the chatter in here is a cosmopolitan mix of tongues.

Keepers

13B Dundas Street, New Town, EH3 (556 5707). Bus 23, 27. **Open** noon-2pm, 6-10pm Tue-Fri; 6-10pm Sat; closed Mon, Sun. **Average** £17.50. **Credit** AmEx, MC, V. **Map** p306 E4.
Deep in the New Town, this basement restaurant consists of interconnected, candle-lit cellars that are ideal for that gaze-into-each-other's-eyes occasion. The Scottish staples of beef, game and salmon are all treated with a steady panache. Saddle of rabbit with a vermouth and truffle sauce is the sort of dish the chef excels with.

The Marque

19 Causewayside, South Edinburgh, EH9 (466 6660). Bus 42, 46. **Open** 11.45am-2pm, 5.45-10pm Tue-Thur; 11.45am-2pm, 5.45-11pm Fri; 12.30-2pm, 5.45-11pm Sat; 12.30-2pm, 5.45-10pm Sun. **Average** £18. **Credit** MC, V. **Map** p310 H8.
Aiming towards the top of Edinburgh's restaurant jungle, this relatively recent newcomer is getting it right. Without unnecessary fad or faff, the Marque looks a bit further afield for many of its influences than other 'Scottish' restaurants and you may find spices from the Far East pepping up your breast of Bresse chicken. The cheese selection comes with great chutneys and pickles. Tempting as it is, stealing the beautiful cutlery is frowned upon. Good-value pre- and post-theatre menus.

Martin's

70 Rose Street North Lane, New Town, EH2 (225 3106). Bus 3, 3A, 12, 16, 17. **Open** noon-2pm, 7-10pm Tue-Fri; 7-10pm Sat; closed Mon, Sun & 24 Dec-23 Jan. **Average** £25. **Credit** AmEx, DC, MC, V. **Map** p314 B1.
Worth the effort but not easy to find, Martin Irons' restaurant is a showcase for Scottish produce and he realised the value of attentive sourcing and organic ingredients years before most. From the vegetables to the lamb and the fish, Irons insists that as far as possible everything is just as nature intended. The reward for his persistence has been an enviable reputation since he opened in '83. No smoking unless a private booking.

Consumer

Number One, The Restaurant

The Balmoral Hotel, 1 Princes Street, New Town, EH1 (557 6727). Bus 3, 3A, 12, 16, 17, 80. **Open** noon-2pm, 7-10pm Mon-Thur; noon-2pm, 7-10.30pm Fri; 7-10.30pm Sat; 7-10pm Sun. **Set lunch** £16.95 2 courses; £19.95 3 courses. **Set dinner** £35 3 courses. **Credit** AmEx, DC, MC, V. **Map** p314 D2.

The flagship restaurant in what many consider to be Edinburgh's grandest hotel, Number One is a very special occasion restaurant for the majority. This is reflected in the unstinting use of luxury ingredients and in the sophisticated techniques of head chef Jeff Bland. The decor is a subtle and sumptuous exercise in oriental design and the wine list will keep the most demanding oenophile intrigued. Bland is also in charge of the kitchens at the more relaxed and less expensive Hadrian's at the Balmoral (557 5000).

Off the Wall

11 South College Street, South Edinburgh, EH8 (667 1597). Bus 7, 8, 21, 31, 80. **Open** noon-2pm, 5.30-11pm Mon-Sat; closed Sun. **Average** £25. **Credit** AmEx, DC, MC, V. **Map** p310 G6.

The decor at this pocket-sized restaurant has been much improved since the last edition and could almost claim to do justice to the quality of food here. The staple ingredients of Scotland's natural larder make their customary appearances on the menu but they are used deftly in such dishes as the saddle of lamb with black pudding and the beef with a beetroot gratin.

Rhodes & Co

3 Rose Street, New Town, EH3 (220 9190). Bus 3, 3A, 12, 16, 17, 80. **Open** noon-2.30pm, 6-10.30pm Mon-Sat; noon-2.30pm Sun. **Average** £14. **Credit** AmEx, DC, MC, V. **Map** 314 C1.

Celebrity chef Gary Rhodes has many admirers and a fair share of detractors but at present the former have the upper hand over the latter if business is anything to go by. Since modern British food is Rhodes' forte, this brasserie doesn't strictly fit in the Scottish category but it is closer in ethos to most of the restaurants in this section than any other. Expertly executed comfort food may seem like faint praise but isn't intended to be. Poached egg benedict with local ham, tournedos au poivre with chips (hurray!) and salt and peppered duck breast with spicy plums fit the bill.

The Rock Restaurant

78 Commercial Street, Leith, EH6 (555 2225). Bus 10A, 16. **Open** noon-2.30pm, 6-10.30pm Mon-Sat; 12.30-2.30pm, 6-10.30pm Sun. **Average** £25. **Credit** AmEx, DC, MC, V. **Map** p311 Jy.

The Rock has a clean, minimalist look that is matched by incredible concentration in the open-plan kitchen. It's a combination that makes it the most sophisticated place on Commercial Street's restaurant row. Typical starters are chillied squid and balsamic dressed potatoes or seared seabass on hiniman sauce, while the main courses boast the likes of oven roasted duck breast glazed with orange Shiraz sauce. The natural habitat of expense account execs, the Rock has just started offering early evening deals that

put it more firmly within the reach of everybody else. Book a lunch table for four or more and staff will arrange transport within Leith and the New Town.

Stac Polly

8-10 Grindlay Street, South Edinburgh, EH3 (229 5405). Bus 11, 15, 24. **Open** noon-2pm, 6-10.30pm Mon-Fri; 6-10.30pm Sat; 6-10pm Sun. **Average** £22. **Credit** AmEx, MC, V. **Map** p314 A3.

Named after the mountain in the far north, the two Stac Pollys are decked out so as to simulate the natural colour scheme of the countryside around Ullapool (only not so wet, naturally). The haggis and filo pastry starter has a reputation that is taking on a life of its own, and for each one sold 50p is donated to the upkeep of the paths on the real mountain. Philanthropy aside, main courses like the saddle of venison on a black pudding risotto warrant closer inspection.
Branch: 29-33 Dublin Street, New Town, EH3 (556 2231).

Sweet Melinda's

11 Roseneath Street, South Edinburgh, EH9 (229 7953). Bus 40, 41, 41A. **Open** noon-2pm, 7-10pm Tue-Sat; closed Mon, Sun. **Average** £15. **Credit** MC, V. **Map** p309 F8.

One of only two notable restaurants in the culinary desert of Marchmont, Sweet Melinda's is a charming, one-roomed find that majors in seafood and game. Among the starters, the Thai fish cakes with sweet chilli dipping sauce are big sellers, while the char-grilled tuna steaks with salsa verde add zest to the mains. Lunchtimes offer scaled-down dishes along the same lines as the dinner menu, at roughly half the price, and there is always a vegetarian option.

The Tower

Museum of Scotland, Chambers Street, South Edinburgh, EH1 (225 3003). Bus 23, 28, 45. **Open** noon-11pm daily (from 10am for coffee). **Average** £25. **Credit** AmEx, DC, MC, V. **Map** p309 F6.

Situated like an eagle's nest at the top of the new Museum of Scotland, the Tower has incomparable views of Edinburgh. By night, when the castle is flood-lit, it is almost enough to make you forget about the food. But not for long. Oysters, crabs' claws, lobster and seafood platters battle it out with chargrilled rib-eye steaks, tuna and green bean salads, carpaccios of beef and a deluxe interpretation of the much-besmirched prawn cocktail. The surroundings are elegant and sophisticated. No smoking.

Winter Glen

3A1 Dundas Street, New Town, EH3 (477 7060). Bus 23, 27. **Open** noon-2pm, 6.30pm-late Mon-Sat; closed Sun. **Average** *Mon-Thur* £23; *Fri, Sat* £30. **Credit** AmEx, MC, V. **Map** p306 E4.

Another of Edinburgh's New Town basement establishments, Winter Glen distinguishes itself by winning countless awards. The menu changes about once a month but expect the likes of marinated seafood and Scottish smoked salmon, and breast of chicken stuffed with woodland mushrooms finished with a carrot and cumin sauce.

The Witchery by the Castle

352 Castlehill, Royal Mile, EH1 (225 5613). Bus 35 35A. **Open** noon-4pm, 5.30-11.30pm daily. **Average** £25. **Credit** AmEx, DC, MC, V. **Map** p314 C3.

Now in its third decade, the Witchery is one of Edinburgh's most atmospheric restaurants. The dining area comprises the wood-panelled Witchery itself and the beamed Secret Garden. Its location and looks make it justifiably popular with visitors but the lavish menus also ensure repeat custom from a regular, local clientele. Opulent and historic surroundings, professional service and what must count as the Domesday Book of wine lists are obvious attractions, which must share billing with the food. The menu alters every now and then but roasted fillet of Aberdeen Angus with a brioche crust and winter chanterelles leave a lasting impression. Few can eat here every day but the cheaper early and late evening menus make the experience more accessible.

WOW Brasserie

2 Broughton Place, Broughton, EH1 (558 8868). Bus 8. **Open** *summer* 11am-midnight daily; *winter* noon-2.30pm, 6-10pm Tue-Fri; noon-4pm, 6-11pm Sat; noon-4pm Sun; closed Mon. **Average** £15. **Credit** DC, MC, V. Map p306 F3.

The decor here is more hip designer label to the sturdy tweeds of many in this section but the food is resolutely Scottish. WOW is rapidly and justifiably gaining a reputation for its excellent ingredients. Starters, for example, include a warm gateau of Stornoway black pudding and woodland mushrooms, while the loin of lamb with sweet potato mash is pointedly from Killiecronan. It is still early days for this place and, unlike good bars, good food outlets don't seem to naturally thrive on Broughton Street. Because of this, getting a table midweek is often easy, although the weekend proves more difficult.

Spanish

Tapas Olé

10 Eyre Place, New Town, EH3 (556 2754). Bus 23, 27. **Open** 11am-11pm daily. **Average** £10. **Credit** MC, V. **Map** p306 E3.

Sweet Melinda's: an oasis in a culinary desert. *See page 134.*

Neither branch of Tapas Olé holds back on the party spirit although the original branch on Eyre Place has a basement dining area in which to put the more raucous parties. Best enjoyed with friends and a few bottles of wine, Tapas Olé provides a relaxed and chatty atmosphere in which to fill up with hot tapas. It is also cheaper to get to than Andalucia.

Branch: 4 Forrest Road, South Edinburgh, EH3 (225 7069).

The Tapas Tree

1 Forth Street, Broughton, EH1 (556 7118). Bus 8. **Open** 11am-11pm daily. **Average** £10. **Credit** AmEx, DC, MC, V. **Map** p307 G3.

One of a kind when it first opened, the Tapas Tree now has competition but still holds its more senior position well. The upstairs area is quite small but best if dining *à deux*, while the bigger downstairs room lends itself to large-scale celebrations. Chorizo, patatas bravas, chillied prawns and so on give a taste of the Iberian experience. Despite its pretty rapid turnover, booking at the weekends will save a long wait. Live music on Mondays and Thursdays.

Swiss

Denzler's

121 Constitution Street, Leith, EH6 (554 3268). Bus 16. **Open** noon-2pm, 6.30-10pm Tue-Fri; 6.30-10.30pm Sat; closed Mon, Sun. **Average** £15. **Credit** AmEx, DC, MC, V. **Map** p311 Jz.

Much like Switzerland, Denzler's is a well-established, comfortable and respectable kind of place, although you don't need to be a tax exile to eat here. Naturally, both cheese and meat fondues feature prominently on the menu but there is also space for central European relations of the gnocchi, noodle and dumpling families. When it comes to dessert, apple strudel is the only way to go.

Thai

Ayutthaya

14B Nicolson Street, South Edinburgh, EH8 (556 9351). Bus 7, 8, 21, 31, 80. **Open** noon-2.30pm, 5.30-11pm daily. **Average** £12. **Credit** AmEx, DC, MC, V. **Map** p310 G6.

The venue may be small but the menu is extensive at the Ayutthaya, opposite the Festival Theatre. Old favourites like tom yum soup, satays and green curries are much in evidence but it's worth exploring a little off the beaten track. The gai yang – a whole, small chicken marinated in honey and spices, grilled and served with a sweet chilli sauce – is one such dish.

Branch: Sukhothai 23 Brougham Place, Tollcross, South Edinburgh EH3 (229 1537).

Siam Erawan

48 Howe Street, New Town, EH3 (226 3675). Bus 28, 29, 29A, 80. **Open** noon-2.30pm, 6-11pm Mon-Sat; 6-10.30pm Sun. **Average** £12. **Credit** MC, V. **Map** p306 D4.

The Erawan on Howe Street is the original restaurant in a rapidly growing Edinburgh empire. Its looks are fading a bit but many still prefer its charms to those of its smarter offspring. There are differences between the menus of the various branches, but you can count on their yum specialities – a cooking technique whereby meat and seafood are very quickly cooked in a spice and stock combination, giving the dishes a unique hot and sour flavour. For something unusual try the curried roast duck with grapes, sweet basil and toasted spices.

Branches: **Erawan Express** 176 Rose Street, New Town, EH2 (220 0059); **Erawan Oriental** 14 South St Andrew Street, New Town, EH1 (556 4242).

Vegetarian

Bann's

5 Hunter Square, Royal Mile, EH1 (226 1112). Bus 35, 35A. **Open** noon-11pm Mon-Fri; 10am-11pm Sat, Sun. **Average** £12.50. **Credit** AmEx, MC, V. **Map** p314 D3.

Handily placed for the Royal Mile, Bann's is an informal vegetarian café producing everything from smoothies to sit-down all-night meals. Sushi, veggie haggis, Thai noodles and avocado wraps will keep the home fires burning during the winter, while the salads and focaccia offer lighter alternatives in summer.

Black Bo's

57-61 Blackfriars Street, Royal Mile, EH1 (557 6136). Bus 35, 35A. **Open** 6-10.30pm Mon-Thur, Sun; noon-2.30pm, 6-10.30pm Fri, Sat. **Average** £16. **Credit** MC, V. **Map** p310 G5.

Very much a vegetarian restaurant, as opposed to a café or diner, Bo's keeps on graciously accepting the praise that's heaped on it with a modest curtsy. Pinning down exactly what it does isn't easy because it changes constantly depending on the whim of Albert, the chef patron. Veggie bean bakes and nut loafs don't get a look in. *See also p148.*

Henderson's Salad Table

94 Hanover Street, New Town, EH2 (225 2131). Bus 23, 27, 45. **Open** 8am-10.30pm Mon-Sat; closed Sun. **Average** £8. **Credit** AmEx, MC, V. **Map** p314 C1.

Founded at a time when vegetarians were seen as basketcases, Henderson's is now having the last laugh as an ever-increasing proportion of the population come round to the idea. The original basement salad table is still going strong and around the corner there is the relative newcomer, Henderson's Bistro. The Bistro is a touch more comfortable, open on Sundays and also does free tapas during the week from 5-7pm to entice the afterwork tipplers. Above the Salad Table is Henderson's deli.

Branch: Henderson's Bistro 25 Thistle Street, New Town, EH2 (225 2605).

Isabel's

83 Clerk Street, South Edinburgh, EH8 (662 4014). Bus 7, 8, 31, 80. **Open** 11am-6.30pm Mon, Thur, Fri; 11am-5.30pm Tue, Wed, Sat; closed Sun. **Average** £5. **No credit cards.** **Map** p310 G7.

Nestled under the Nature's Gate health-food shop, Isabel's offers a low-priced lunch and dinner menu. The sweet stuff is the best bet, with great carrot cake, date slices, chocolate cakes and banana loaf. Juices, herbal teas, coffee and hot chocolates are also available. As well as the likes of veggie burgers and houmous, Isabel prepares one hot, and, it must be said, tasty, meal every day. Gluten-free and vegan diets can also be catered for. There's no licence but no corkage charge either. No smoking.

Kalpna

2-3 St Patrick Square, South Edinburgh, EH8 (667 9890). Bus 7, 8, 31, 80. **Open** *summer* noon-2pm, 5.30-11pm Mon-Sat; 5.30-11pm Sun; *winter* noon-2pm, 5.30-11pm Mon-Fri; 5.30-11pm Sat; closed Sun. **Average** £12. **Credit** MC, V. **Map** p310 G7.

A familiar and long-standing friend to Edinburgh's lovers of vegetarian and Indian food, the Kalpna offers a £5 buffet lunch and every Wednesday

night it hosts the evergreen regional buffet for a very reasonable £8.95. Chow down on the likes of the mild but filling khumb masala: mushrooms cooked in coconut milk with tomatoes, coriander, onions and garlic. No smoking.

Susie's Wholefood Diner

51-53 West Nicolson Street, South Edinburgh, EH8 (667 8729). Bus 40-42, 46. **Open** 10am-8pm Mon; 10am-9pm Tue-Sat; noon-6pm Sun. **Average** £6. **No credit cards.** **Map** p310 G6.

A firm fixture on the lunch circuit for many of the students at the nearby Edinburgh University, Susie's is a laidback, self-service diner that runs the full gamut of veggie delights from felafel and soups to chillies, curries and bakes. The caring, sharing '90s may well have been a media invention but there is a definite communal atmosphere to Susie's. The noticeboard is handy for flatshare notices, yoga classes and all kinds of knit-your-own consciousness lessons.

Restaurants by area

Royal Mile

Bann's (*p136*); **Black Bo's** (*p136*); **Bleu** (*p125*); **Creelers** (*p122*); **Dubh Prais** (*p131*); **Igg's** (*p133*); **Jackson's Restaurant** (*p133*); **Pierre Victoire** (*p127*); **Polo Fusion** (*p127*); **La Rusticana** (branch; *p129*); **Viva Mexico** (*p131*); **The Witchery by the Castle** (*p135*).

New Town

36 (*p131*); **Bar Napoli** (*p128*); **Bleu** (branch; *p125*); **The Bonham** (see 36; *p131*); **Café Royal Oyster Bar** (*p122*); **Le Café Saint-Honoré** (*p125*); **Cosmo** (*p128*); **La Cuisine d'Odile** (*p125*); **Duck's at Le Marché Noir** (*p125*); **Erawan Express** (branch of Siam Erawan; *p136*); **Erawan Oriental** (branch of Siam Erawan; *p136*); **Est Est Est** (*p128*); **Haldanes** (*p133*); **Henderson's Bistro** (branch of Henderson's Salad Table; *p136*); **Henderson's Salad Table** (*p136*); **Keepers** (*p133*); **Martin's** (*p133*); **The Mussel Inn** (*p123*); **Number One, The Restaurant** (*p134*); **Rhodes & Co** (*p134*); **La Rusticana** (*p128*); **Scalini** (*p129*); **Siam Erawan** (*p136*); **Stac Polly** (branch; *p134*); **Tampopo** (*p129*); **Tapas Olé** (*p135*); **Tex Mex** (*p129*); **Winter Glen** (*p134*).

Stockbridge

Bell's Diner (*p121*); **Blue Parrot Cantina** (*p129*); **Buffalo Grill** (branch; *p122*); **Channings** (see 36; *p131*); **Howie's** (branch; *p133*); **Loon Fung** (*p122*); **Mamma's** (branch; *p122*).

Calton Hill & Broughton

Bleu (branch; *p125*); **Ristorante Tinelli** (*p128*); **The Tapas Tree** (*p136*); **WOW Brasserie** (*p135*).

South Edinburgh

The Apartment (*p127*); **The Atrium** (*p131*); **Ayutthaya** (*p136*); **Backstage Bistro** (*p131*); **Banks Restaurant** (*p131*); **The Buffalo Grill** (*p122*); **Chinese Home Cooking** (*p122*); **The Dial** (*p131*); **Dragon Way** (*p122*); **Howie's** (*p133*); **Isabel's** (*p136*); **Kalpna** (*p137*); **Kebab Mahal** (*p127*); **Khushi's** (*p128*); **Mamma's** (*p122*); **The Marque** (*p133*); **Nicolson's** (*p127*); **Off the Wall** (*p134*); **Pataka** (*p128*); **Petit Paris** (*p127*); **Stac Polly** (*p134*); **Sukhothai** (branch of Ayutthaya; *p136*); **Suruchi** (*p128*); **Susie's Wholefood Diner** (*p137*); **Sweet Melinda's** (*p134*); **Tapas Olé** (branch; *p136*); **The Tower** (*p134*).

West Edinburgh

Caribbean Connection (*p122*); **Howie's** (branch; *p133*); **Mrs Uni's Kitchen** (*p128*); **Oriental Dining Centre** (*p122*); **The Verandah** (*p128*); **Yumi** (*p129*).

Leith

Britannia Spice (*p127*); **Denzler's** (*p136*); **(Fitz)henry: a brasserie** (*p133*); **Malmaison** (*p125*); **Restaurant Martin Wishart** (*p127*); **The Rock Restaurant** (*p134*); **The Shore** (*p123*); **The Vintner's Rooms** (*p127*).

Consumer

Cafés & Bistros

The first coffeehouse in Edinburgh, opened in 1673, was a novelty. Now you can pick up a hot cup of stimulating joe on any street corner.

Such is the importance of the traditional boozer in Edinburgh, you'd be forgiven for thinking there was no danger of it ever developing anything resembling a café culture. Far from it. The city has never been averse to the lure of caffeine, and does, in fact, boast a vibrant coffee life, from twee teashops at one end of the spectrum to late-night and laid-back hotspots favoured by clubbers at the other end. Also included in this chapter are informal bistros where you can just pop in for a coffee or a glass of wine but which also offer more substantial meals.

The times given here are for all the year around. During the Festival, opening hours become more fluid, so to speak, as establishments often remain open according to their eager publics' demands.

Royal Mile

Byzantium

9 Victoria Street, EH1 (226 1448). Bus 23, 28, 35, 35A, 45. **Open** 10am-5.30pm Mon-Sat; closed Sun. **No credit cards. Map** p314 C3.
In the airy top floor of Byzantium antiques and crafts market, built inside a converted church, this Indian-influenced café provides a welcome point of calm in the middle of town. In addition to meat curries it offers a vegetarian buffet at lunchtime for just £3.50.

Café Hub

Castlehill, EH1 (473 2067). Bus 35, 35A. **Open** 9.30am-6pm daily; *Apr-Sept* 9.30am-11pm daily. **Credit** AmEx, MC, V. **Map** p314 C3.
An integral part of The Hub (*see p208*), Edinburgh's Festival Centre, this bright yellow café is run by the team responsible for the city's highly successful blue Bar Café and Atrium restaurant. The terrace allows for all-day sipping and munching. From early-bird breakfasts to civilised nightcaps, the menu is a balanced selection of open sandwiches, saucy salads, baked dishes and juicy steaks. Alternatively, if you just need a restorative cup of coffee then this is welcome and tasty relief.

The Cafeteria

Fruitmarket Gallery, 45 Market Street, EH1 (226 1843). Bus 7, 8, 21, 24, 31, 80. **Open** 11am-5pm Mon-Sat; noon-5pm Sun. **Credit** DC, MC, V. **Map** p314 D2.
Big baguette melts are the order of the day in the café of the Fruitmarket, possibly Edinburgh's

hippest art gallery (*see p49*). Fresh Danishes keep the mid-morning grazers happy and there is always a selection of gateaux for the more leisurely afternoon browser. But it's lunchtimes that see the real action, with staff aiming to fill up customers with pasta and melts in under an hour. No smoking.

Clarinda's

69 Canongate, EH8 (557 1888). Bus 24, 35, 35A. **Open** 9am-4.45pm Mon-Sat; 10am-4.45pm Sun. **No credit cards. Map** p310 G5.
Not one to change merely for the sake of change, Clarinda's seems to have always been a feature on the oft-volatile Royal Mile catering scene. Home-baking is the name of the game here and this place is sure to find approval in the hearts of those who appreciate the beauty of a well-turned-out bun.

Common Grounds

2-3 North Bank Street, EH1 (226 1416). Bus 23, 28, 35, 35A, 45. **Open** 9am-10pm Mon-Fri; 10am-8pm Sat, Sun. **Credit** AmEx, MC, V. **Map** p314 C3.
More than just an American-style coffeehouse with umpteen different types of joe, Common Grounds is also the venue for regular live music events, usually of a rootsy bent. It can get quite steamy over the two floors, making it a pleasant spot for wasting away a winter afternoon.

Elephant's Sufficiency

170 High Street, EH1 (220 0666). Bus 35, 35A. **Open** *winter* 8am-5pm Mon-Fri; 9am-5pm Sat-Sun; *summer* 8am-10pm Mon-Fri; 9am-10pm Sat, Sun. **No credit cards. Map** p314 D3.
Very usefully located on the Royal Mile, this little café is a good place to sit outside in the summer and watch the passing wildlife. Lawyers and MSPs from the nearby courts and Parliament are among the customers getting stuck into the usual soups and sandwiches. As far as possible, only Scottish ingredients are used – but special mention must go the bacon and Camembert roll.

Lianachan

15 Blackfriars Street, EH1 (556 6922). Bus 35, 35A. **Open** 11am-7pm Tue-Thur; 10am-10pm Fri, Sat; noon-6pm Sun. **No credit cards. Map** p310 G5.
With a name meaning 'wee meadow' in Gaelic, it is perhaps no surprise that this café is strong on organic teas and fresh fruit juices. There is also a Greek theme at work on the menu, with baklava and moussaka making their presence felt. It's a laid-back kind of place, with New Age and '60s music adding something to the exhibits of local artists on the walls.

Lower Aisle Restaurant

St Giles' Cathedral, High Street, EH1 (225 5147).
Bus 35, 35A. **Open** 9.30am-4.30pm Mon-Fri;
10am-2pm Sun; closed Sat (except during Festival
when open as weekdays). **No credit cards.**
Map p314 D3.

Set in the vaults of St Giles' Cathedral, the Lower
Aisle ain't exactly the place for a party but it is
handy for a simple and filling lunch, especially if you
like baked potatoes.

Pâtisserie Florentin

8 St Giles Street, EH1 (225 6267). Bus 23, 28, 35,
35A, 45. **Open** 7am-9pm daily. **No credit cards.**
Map p314 C3.

It may not have the sparkle it once possessed and
indeed in a certain light it can even look ragged
around the edges, but Florentin's is still a top spot
for a coffee and a croissant. Those with a penchant
for wickedness will head for the cake counter, where
thousands of calories are contained in single chocolate and cream creations.
Branch: 5 North West Circus Place, New Town,
EH2 (220 0225).

New Town

A Table

4 Howe Street, EH3 (220 5355). Bus 13, 28, 29, 80.
Open 8.30am-5.30pm Mon-Fri; 10am-6pm Sat; 10am-
4pm Sun. **Credit** MC, V. **Map** p306 D4.

A self-styled French farmhouse café, this new addition to the city's caffeine scene is big on wholesome,
organic food. Most of the dishes are very simple, from
plates of charcuterie to organic yoghurts. Customers
sit around one large table, making for a cosy and
distinctly un-British atmosphere. In keeping with the
farmhouse idea, it all looks suitably rustic.

Brown's

131-133 George Street, EH2 (225 4442). Bus 13,
19, 55, 82. **Open** noon-11.30pm Mon-Thur, Sun;
noon-midnight Fri, Sat. **Credit** AmEx, MC, V.
Map p314 A1.

A respectable and well-mannered bistro, Brown's is
part of a small national chain. The food is reliable
and there is little to frighten the less-adventurous
palate. The signature dish is steak, mushroom and
Guinness pie. There is a small bar next to the main
dining area but the emphasis is much more on
eating than drinking.

Café Rouge

43 Frederick Street, EH2 (225 4515). Bus 28, 29,
80. **Open** 7.30am-11pm Mon-Sat; 8am-11pm Sun.
Credit AmEx, MC, V. **Map** p314 B1.

As part of the UK-wide chain of French restaurants,
Café Rouge is stereotypically Gallic in both its looks
and menus. That it doesn't make its waiting staff
wear stripy tops and strings of onions may well
qualify for minor miracle status. Still, for those
moments when only a bourgignon, steak frites or
moules marinières will do, then they've got them.
The (loud) live jazz on a Saturday night (8.30-
10.30pm) adds to the experience.

Cyberia

88 Hanover Street, EH2 (220 4403/
edinburgh@cybersurf.co.uk/www.cybersurf.co.uk).

Clarinda's – a golden oldie on the city's café scene. *See page 138.*

Bus 23, 27, 45. **Open** 10am-10pm daily. **No credit cards. Map** p314 C1.

Email and Internet access along with IT training and tuition make this place stand out from most of Edinburgh's other caffeine providers. But it is not just webheads who get wired up here: passing shoppers who just fancy a snack pop in too.

Glass & Thompson

2 Dundas Street, EH3 (557 0909). Bus 23, 27, 45. **Open** 8.30am-5.30pm Mon-Sat; 11am-4.30pm Sun. **Credit** AmEx, MC, V. **Map** p306 E4.

If a café could be said to be very 'New Town' then this is it. Glass & Thompson is conspicuously smart and serves fine delicatessen food with a definite continental flavour.

James Thin Booksellers Café

57 George Street, EH2 (225 4495). Bus 19, 55, 82. **Open** 8am-5pm Mon-Sat; 11.15am-4.30pm Sun. **No credit cards. Map** p314 B1.

Contrary to what you may think, it's not just book browsers who use this well-established café. Local office workers have their lunch here while a more mature clientele set down their shopping bags and take a much-needed break.

Laigh Bake House

117A Hanover Street, EH2 (225 1552). Bus 23, 27, 45. **Open** 8am-4pm Mon-Sat; closed Sun. **No credit cards. Map** p314 C1.

'If it ain't broke, don't fix it' could be the motto here. OK, so the Laigh has taken to using organic ingredients for its baking, but otherwise, nothing has changed for years in what is widely reputed to be one of Edinburgh's most venerable cafés. All that's missing is a sighting of the ghost of Robert Louis Stevenson.

Palm Court

The Balmoral Hotel, 1 Princes Street, EH1 (556 2414). Bus 3, 3A, 12, 16, 17, 80. **Open** 10am-6pm daily; *coffee* 10am-noon; *afternoon tea* 3-5pm; *lunch* noon-2.30pm. **Credit** AmEx, DC, MC, V. **Map** p314 D2.

Go on, spoil yourself. Quite possibly Edinburgh's grandest hotel, the Balmoral lays on a slap-up afternoon tea. There are no crusts on the sandwiches here and the cake selection can lead to agonies of indecision. While staff might not throw you out if you turn up in jeans and a T-shirt, you'll be the only one dressed that way.

The Place to Eat

2nd floor, John Lewis, St James Centre, EH1 (556 9121). Bus 1, 11, 22, 34. **Open** 9.30am-5.15pm Tue, Wed, Fri; 9.45am-7.15pm Thur; 9.30am-5.45pm Sat; closed Mon, Sun. **Credit** MC, V. **Map** p307 G4.

The self-service food here plays second fiddle to the fantastic vistas across the Firth of Forth and on to the Kingdom of Fife. On a fine, clear day, a quick latte and a ten-minute gaze at the view can make you feel like a god. No smoking.

Queen Street Café at the Scottish National Portrait Gallery

1 Queen Street, EH2 (557 2844). Bus 8, 12, 16, 17, 25. **Open** 10am-4pm Mon-Sat; noon-4.30pm Sun. **No credit cards. Map** p306 F4.

If not quite a venerable Edinburgh institution then this place at least has a feeling of gentle tradition. Good for a gossip and a scone even if the pictures of stern Scottish founding fathers in the Portrait Gallery (*see p60*) can be a bit unsettling.

Starbucks

Waterstone's, 128 Princes Street, EH2 (226 3610). Bus 3, 3A, 12, 16, 17. **Open** 8.30am-7pm Mon-Sat; 10.30am-6pm Sun. **Credit** AmEx, MC, V. **Map** p314 A2.

Starbucks may be the same the world over but at least you know that you will get a reasonable cup of coffee. This branch has the added attraction of giving a fine view of Edinburgh Castle. No smoking. **Branches:** throughout the city.

Stockbridge

Café Newton

Dean Gallery, 72 Belford Road, EH4 (624 6273). Bus 13. **Open** 10am-4.30pm Mon-Sat; noon-4.30pm Sun. **No credit cards. Map** p308 A5.

Big bowls of soup mopped up with chunks of crusty bread sell well here although they face stiff competition from the toasted focaccia. Food aside, the most startling feature of this smallish café is its use as an extra room to the Dean Gallery (*see p69*). Paolozzi's huge plaster of Newton in thoughtful pose dominates the room and a silver eagle is perched atop the coffee machine.

The Gallery Café

Scottish National Gallery of Modern Art, 74 Belford Road, EH4 (624 6309). Bus 13. **Open** 10am-4.30pm Mon-Sat; noon-4.30pm Sun. **No credit cards. Map** p308 A5.

Perennially popular, and not just with the city's art hounds visiting the gallery (*see p69*). The real value of this place becomes apparent on fine summer days when people take their snacks outside and soak up the rays in peace.

River Café

36 Deanhaugh Street, EH4 (332 3322). Bus 28, 29, 29A, 80. **Open** 9am-6pm Mon-Sat; 11am-6pm Sun. **No credit cards. Map** p305 C3.

One of a little row of eating places, the River Café at first appears to be a conventional Scottish café offering all the usual soups and sarnies. Closer inspection reveals a more intriguing array of Persian dishes such as kuftleh meatballs, and Mexican chimichangas and fajitas.

The Terrace Café

Royal Botanic Garden, Inverleith Row, EH3 (552 0616). Bus 8, 23, 27. **Open** 9.30am-6pm daily (earlier closing times Oct-Apr; phone for details). **Credit** MC, V. **Map** p305 C2.

The service
has changed a lot
over the years.

It now features
the words
'enjoy your meal'.

New restaurant, old church, divine food.
Open daily 9.30am-11.00pm
Reservations 0131 473 2067
Non-Smoking
The Hub, Castlehill, Edinburgh EH1 2NE.

cafe Hub
EDINBURGH'S FESTIVAL CENTRE
Main sponsor BANK OF SCOTLAND

The Botanics (*see pp68-9* **Green fingers & glass-houses**) are a popular spot for an afternoon wander and the café next to Inverleith House (*see p66*) is a handy pitstop. The real beauty is the view over the city with the castle dominating the skyline. No smoking, except on the terrace.

Calton Hill & Broughton

Blue Moon Café

36 Broughton Street, EH1 (556 2788). Bus 8. **Open** 11am-11.30pm Mon-Thur, Sun; 9.30am-11.30am Fri, Sat. **Credit** MC, V. **Map** p306 F3.

At the heart of Edinburgh's pink triangle, this gay-run but straight-friendly café bar is a popular meeting and eating place both during the day and at weekends, when the atmosphere steps up a gear to accommodate the high spirits of the clubbing brigade. There is a smaller, connected room looking directly out onto Broughton Street. This seems to have opened and shut several times in the last year or so but its various incarnations have filled much the same role as the Blue Moon itself.

Café Libra

5A Union Street, EH1 (556 9602). Bus 7, 12, 16. **Open** 9am-4pm Tue-Fri; 10am-4pm Sat; 11am-3pm Sun; closed Mon. **No credit cards. Map** p307 G3.

A small basement joint seating around 20 people, Café Libra may not boast interior design by the latest style guru but it does do the all-day breakfasts, toasties and omelettes that are the mark of a real and lovingly run caff.

Lost Sock Diner

11 East London Street, EH7 (557 6097). Bus 8. **Open** 9am-4pm Mon; 9am-10pm Tue-Fri; 10am-10pm Sat; 11am-5pm Sun. **No credit cards. Map** p306 F3.

Adjacent to a launderette (hence the name), this is a funky little neighbourhood diner that dishes up burgers, nachos, cooked breakfasts, sandwiches and the like. In the evening, dishes such as poached salmon are added. It attracts a youthful crowd (the bank of TVs showing MTV may have something to do with it), and is often mobbed for weekend brunch.

Mediterraneo

73 Broughton Street, EH1 (557 6900). Bus 8. **Open** *June-Sept* 8.30am-6pm Mon-Thur; 8.30am-9.30pm Fri, Sat; 9.30am-5pm Sun; *Oct-May* 8.30am-6pm Mon-Sat; 9.30am-5pm Sun. **Credit** MC, V. **Map** p306 F3.

Not only does it do a thriving lunchtime trade in takeaway baguettes, but family-run Mediterraneo also has a pleasant diner area. Most of the food displays the owners' Italian roots and, without meaning, to sound risqué, they can do things with grapes and a piccante sausage that your tastebuds wouldn't dare dream about.

Smoke Stack

53-55 Broughton Street, EH1 (556 6032). Bus 8. **Open** noon-2.30pm, 6-10.30pm Mon-Fri; noon-10.30pm Sat; closed Sun. **Credit** AmEx, DC, MC, V. **Map** p306 F3.

Sister restaurant to the bohemian Basement bar across the road, the Smoke Stack is a lively and hip char-grill joint. Steaks, burgers, ribs and barbecue chicken are the staples, and there's ample provision for vegetarians too.

Valvona & Crolla

19 Elm Row, EH7 (556 6066). Bus 7, 12, 16. **Open** 8am-5pm Mon-Sat; closed Sun. **Credit** AmEx, MC, V. **Map** p307 G3.

This family-run bistro is in the rear of the famed deli (*see p177*). The temptation to loosen the purse strings before even entering the dining area is immense, yet firm resolution will be rewarded – let the staff show you what they can do with such ingredients. The virtues of great Italian cooking are shown to their best advantage so getting a table at lunchtimes and over the weekend isn't easy. Informal, friendly and, for many, the best café/bistro in town. No smoking.

Arthur's Seat & Duddingston

The Engine Shed

19 St Leonard's Lane, EH8 (662 0040). Bus 2, 21. **Open** 10.30am-3.30pm Mon-Thur; 10.30am-2.30pm Fri; 10.30am-4pm Sat; 11.30am-4pm Sun. **No credit cards. Map** p310 H7.

Somewhat off the main drag but handy for a hike up Arthur's Seat, the Engine Shed is a vegetarian café that also serves vegan meals. Fresh bread is baked on the premises. No smoking.

California Coffee Co. *See page 144.*

Consumer

South Edinburgh

The Arches Bistro

66-67 South Bridge, EH1 (556 0200). Bus 7, 8, 21, 31, 80. **Open** noon-2.30pm, 5-10pm Mon-Thur; noon-2.30pm, 5-10.30pm Fri, Sat; summer also open Sun (phone for details). **Credit** AmEx, DC, MC, V. **Map** p310 G6.

Given its location, almost directly opposite the Festival Theatre, it's no surprise that a fair proportion of the clientele at this family-run restaurant are of a theatrical bent. The menu is comprised of reliable bistro standards with the occasional nod to Italian ideas.

Black Medicine Co

2 Nicolson Street, EH8 (622 7209). Bus 7, 8, 21, 31, 80. **Open** 8am-8pm Mon-Sat; 9am-8pm Sun. **Credit** MC, V. **Map** 310 G6.

The black medicine in question is the range of coffees that are served up in this rather rugged-looking place. The walls are rough stone and the furniture is chunky and wooden, giving the whole place a bit of an outdoorsy feel. It's comfy enough though and the large windows offer excellent opportunities for talent-spotting.

The Bookstop Café

4 Teviot Place, EH1 (225 5298). Bus 23, 28, 45. **Open** 10am-7pm Mon-Fri; 10am-6pm Sat; noon-6pm Sun. **Credit** DC, MC, V. **Map** p309 F6.

A small, independently run bookshop and café; the hiss of the Gaggia and the sound of muffins being munched are the only things disturbing the browsing of the bookworms. Thoughtfully sited next to one of Edinburgh University's main drags, the Bookstop Café seems to have found a niche from which it can compete with the big chains. Not surprisingly, there's a good Scottish literature section.

Café Grande

184 Bruntsfield Place, EH10 (228 1188). Bus 11, 16, 17, 23. **Open** 9am-11pm Mon-Wed; 9am-midnight Thur-Sat; 10am-10pm Sun. **Credit** MC, V. **Map** p309 D8.

Recently refurbished in warm red tones, this place has something of a dual personality. By day, it's a cosy two-roomed café selling cakes, pastries, burgers and breakfasts. At night, the menu switches to more substantial fare, with dishes such as Thai pork curry.

California Coffee Co

St Patrick's Square, EH8 (228 5001). Bus 7, 8, 31, 80. **Open** 7.45am-9pm Mon-Fri; 10am-9pm Sat, Sun. **No credit cards. Map** p310 G7.

Dr Who got it wrong. Turning former police boxes into time-travelling Tardises is a waste of resources when they can be turned into al-fresco coffee booths. The coffee-making people, or *baristas* if you want to get cosmopolitan, can rustle up your java juice any which way. Great for warming your hands on a bitter summer morning. Its latest wheeze is a coffee cart on George Street.

Branches: throughout the city.

Chatterbox Tea Room

1 East Preston Street, EH8 (667 9406). Bus 7, 8, 31, 80. **Open** 8.30am-6.30pm Mon-Fri; 9am-6pm Sat; 10am-6pm Sun. **No credit cards. Map** p310 H8.

Favorit's a favourite virtually round the clock. *See page 145.*

Cafés for arts lovers

The Cafeteria
There's not much fruit at the Fruitmarket Gallery any more, just the best touring art shows with top melts and pasta. See page 138.

Café Hub
Top-class food, to complement the opulent headquarters of the Edinburgh International Festival. See page 138.

Café Newton
Sit around the Paolozzi sculptures and munch on some delicate dishes at the Dean Gallery. See page 141.

Festival Theatre Café
Nice nosh for music lovers in the glassy and classy foyer of Scotland's opera house. See page 145.

Filmhouse Bar
With a bit of a swinging '60s feel to it, this is a prime point for contemplating those arthouse releases. See page 146.

Gallery Café
This might be a gallery of modern art, but there's nothing like an old-fashioned cup of tea in the garden. See page 141.

Queen Street Café at the Scottish National Portrait Gallery
Don't be put off by all those Scottish worthies in the rooms upstairs – they're just jealous of your scones. See page 141.

The Terrace Café
The place to catch up on a little botany, before perusing the art in the Botanics' Inverleith House. See page 141.

Millennia have come and gone, Scotland has gained its own Parliament, but Chatterbox remains. This small traditional tearoom has a strong core regular locals as well as visitors from the nearby Commonwealth swimming pool and student residences.

The Elephant House
21 George IV Bridge, EH1 (220 5355). Bus 23, 28, 45. **Open** 8am-11pm Mon-Fri; 9am-11pm Sat, Sun. **Credit** MC, V. **Map** p314 C3.
A popular and spacious café, packed with all sorts of figurines of, yes, elephants. In term time, it's busy with students idling over a cup of coffee while pretending to study – or bunking off from the nearby National Library. The back room looks up to the Castle, should you fancy a room with a view. No smoking in the front room.

Elephants & Bagels
37 Marshall Street, Nicolson Square, EH8 (668 4404). Bus 7, 8, 21, 31, 80. **Open** 8am-6pm Mon-Fri; 10am-5pm Sat, Sun. **Credit** MC, V. **Map** p310 G6.
The baby sister operation to the Elephant House, the E&B doesn't sell many pachyderms but it's big on the bagel side of the equation. Popular with students, who often take away their goodies for impromptu picnics at nearby George Square during the summer.

Favorit
19-20 Teviot Place, EH1 (220 6880). Bus 23, 28, 45. **Open** 8am-3am daily. **Credit** AmEx, MC, V. **Map** p309 F6.
With its long opening hours, Favorit provides everything from breakfast for workers in a hurry to nightcaps for clapped-out clubbers. The sandwiches have a definite American flavour, with pastrami and

Gruyère on rye being typical. It also acts as a deli and gadget shop, so if you drop in for a smoothie, don't be too surprised if you walk out with a new espresso machine. The decor is as cool as the concept. **Branch**: 30-32 Leven Street, Tollcross, South Edinburgh, EH3 (221 1800).

Festival Theatre Café
13-29 Nicolson Street, EH8 (662 1112). Bus 7, 8, 21, 31, 80. **Open** 10am-6pm daily. **Map** p310 G6.
There are two ways to look at the appearance of the Festival Theatre café. The huge glass plates that front the theatre (*see p204*) either allow customers to watch everyone wander past or they make them feel as if they're in a goldfish bowl. Not the best-kept wine list in town, but popular with local workers for lunch. No smoking.

Helios Fountain
7 Grassmarket, EH1 (229 7884). Bus 2. **Open** 10am-6pm Mon-Sat; noon-5pm Sun. **Credit** MC, V. **Map** p314 B3.
Set at the back of a New Age craft- and bookshop, Helios is somewhat aloof from the raucous boozers that make up most of the Grassmarket. Vegetarian bakes and salads are the staple diet here and are very reasonably priced. As a self-service affair, the staff could sometimes do with shifting the used plates a bit quicker but Helios isn't the sort of place where anyone is going to kick up a fuss. No smoking.

Kaffe Politik
146-148 Marchmont Road, EH9 (446 9873). Bus 24, 40, 41, 41A. **Open** 10am-10pm daily. **Map** p309 F8.
Prior to this place popping up a few years back, Marchmont was very badly served for cafés. Now

it has one of the best-looking caffs in the city. Black and white photos of assorted politicos cover one wall and gaze balefully over the assorted students and locals as they sup smoothies, dither over which speciality tea to have next and munch on the wonderful home-baked goodies.

Lucas
16 Morningside Road, EH10 (446 0233). Bus 11, 16, 17, 23. **Open** 9am-10pm daily. **Credit** DC, MC, V.
Famed for the ice-cream at its Musselburgh café, this recently opened Edinburgh branch south down Bruntsfield Place also offers a range of club sandwiches, panini melts and pizzas. But who needs sensible food when there are nut sundaes, Caribbean longboats and snowballs this good to be enjoyed?

Metropole
33 Newington Road, EH9 (668 4999). Bus 7, 8, 31, 80. **Open** 10am-11pm daily. **No credit cards.** **Map** p310 H8.
Deep in the heart of studentland, this converted bank lends an air of faded grandeur to the simple act of sipping a cappuccino. Metropole is a firm believer in the idea that variety is the spice of life and the adventurous customer could come in here every day for a month and still not sample all the speciality teas and coffees. No smoking.

Ndebele
57 Home Street, Tollcross, EH3 (221 1141). Bus 11, 16, 17, 23. **Open** 10am-10pm daily. **No credit cards.** **Map** p309 D7.
Instantly popular from the moment it opened its doors a few years back, this African-themed café is genuinely different from everything else you'll find in Edinburgh. Where else can you get speciality South African sausages?

Pigs Bistro
41 West Nicolson Street, EH8 (667 6676). Bus 7, 8, 21, 31, 80. **Open** noon-2pm, 6-10pm Mon-Sat; closed Sun. **Credit** AmEx, MC, V. **Map** p310 G6.
Close to Edinburgh University and therefore correspondingly popular with students, Pigs Bistro is an informal, fun place. The menu is as bright and breezy as the decor, with pork, steak and duck being given light and modern treatments. Good value and good times for all are on the cards here. BYOB.

Web 13
13 Bread Street, EH3 (229 8883). Bus 2, 11, 15, 24. **Open** 9am-10pm daily. **Credit** MC, V. **Map** 309 D6.
As the name suggests, this is a terminal for people wanting to plug into cyberspace. Not surprisingly, it offers all the Net access and facilities that you could want. Obviously, man cannot live on virtual reality alone and surfers can munch to their hearts content while they browse.

Whereto?
103 High Riggs, EH3 (229 6886/ whereto@why.co.uk/www.why.co.uk/where).

Bus 23, 28, 45. **Open** 9am-9pm Mon-Fri; 8am-10pm Sat, Sun. **Credit** MC, V. **Map** p309 D7.
Diversification is apparently the key to the future and it is a message that has been taken to heart here. As well as Mac and PC facilities, Whereto? provides IT training and, through its sister company Whynot?, courses in business and personal development. As if that wasn't enough, it also runs a programme of outdoor activities from the café. Appropriately, it looks like an Alpine lodge; it serves the sort of healthy food that you might find in a Sierra Nevada ski resort.

West Edinburgh

Cornerstone Café
St John's Church, corner of Princes Street & Lothian Road, EH2 (229 0212). Bus 3, 3A, 12, 16, 17. **Open** 9.30am-4pm Mon-Sat; closed Sun. **No credit cards.** **Map** p314 A2.
A popular lunchtime haunt of weary shoppers and office workers, the Cornerstone Café is housed in the vaults of St John's and serves up reasonable salads, baked spuds and the like. In the summer, people seem to like sitting on the terrace outside and peering into the adjacent cemetery. No smoking.

Costa
35 Shandwick Place, EH2 (221 9306). Bus 3, 3A, 12 25. **Open** 7.30am-7pm Mon-Fri; 8am-7pm Sat; 10am-5pm Sun. **Credit** MC, V. **Map** 308 C5.
New branches of Costa are springing up at a rate of knots but this was the chain's first real coffee house in Edinburgh. As well as preparing your coffee any which way you choose to name, it also has terminals for anyone who fancies a whizz on the web. **Branches:** throughout the city.

Filmhouse Bar
88 Lothian Road, EH3 (229 5932). Bruntsfield buses. **Open** 10am-11.30pm Mon-Thur, Sun; 10am-12.30am Fri, Sat. **Food served** noon-10pm daily. **Map** p314 A3.
Not the place to spend an entire evening carousing, but The Filmhouse *(see p197)* is hassle-free and a convivial place to meet before a movie. Tuck into all sorts of grub including burgers, cakes, vegetarian and vegan dishes. The place comes into its own during the Film Festival, when starspotting adds a certain piquancy.

Leith

Daniel's Bistro
88 Commercial Street, EH6 (553 5933). Bus 10A, 16. **Open** 9am-10pm daily. **Credit** MC, V. **Map** p311 Jy.
One of the better places among the row of restaurants on the quayside, Daniel's deals in authentic food from Alsace. Hearty raclettes, confits of duck and choucroutes all take pride of place on the menu. The setting is light, bright and modern. There's also a no-smoking conservatory.

Bars & Pubs

We choose the best places to booze.

Soaking up the rays at **EH1**. *See page 148.*

Edinburgh is a drinker's town and can cater for visitors seeking a contemplative afternoon pint just as well as it can for those who want to rip it up until the early hours. The licensing hours are among the most liberal in Britain, with most pubs serving until midnight, many until 1am and some as late as 3am (those listed below where relevant, and others during the Festival). Shiftworkers, early tipplers and the daft brushes who never quite made it home from the night before can then restart at 5am in a handful of the city's more colourful bars.

The pub scene in Edinburgh is evolving very quickly. There are still plenty of linoleum-floored old men's boozers but most new openings are 'style bars', which hold interior design to be at least as important as the condition of the ale. Another phenomenon is the rise of the off-the-peg chain bar. Some drinkers bemoan the fact that the Wetherspoons, All Bar One and Firkin chains are destroying individuality, but their popularity is proof that they do provide what a substantial portion of the drinking public wants. Whatever changes come about, a handful of the old Edinburgh 'howffs' will stay. (This old Scots word is probably derived from the Dutch word for courtyard – 'hof' – and can be used to refer to any regular meeting place, but it most commonly means a pub). Such strongholds of gleaming brass, groaning gantries and time-worn bars are as much a part of Edinburgh's fabric as the Castle, Princes Street and a slight sniff of superiority.

Visitors with a hankering for these types of places might like to join the **McEwan's 80/-Edinburgh Literary Pub Tour** (*see page 52*), which takes in some of the bars made famous by the likes of Burns, Stevenson and Scott.

Many pubs have come up to speed with the provision of a bit more than a pie with your pint. When no starting time is given for service of food, assume it will be available from when the pub opens.

Royal Mile

Bannerman's Bar

212 Cowgate, EH1 (556 3254). Bus 7, 8, 21, 31, 80. **Open** 5pm-1am Mon-Thur; noon-1am, Fri, Sat; 11am-1am Sun. **Food served** until 10pm daily. **Map** p314 D3.

Once a real ale pub that was as down to earth as the subterranean caverns it occupies, Bannerman's has now transformed itself into a pre-club bar. However, while you can scrub up an old dog, you can't teach it new tricks and despite the DJ decks and brightly coloured bottles of alcofizz in the fridge, Bannerman's is still an atmospheric treat with a real fire.

Baracoa

7 Victoria Street, EH1 (225 5846). Bus 23, 28, 45. **Open** 11am-1am Mon-Sat; noon-1am Sun. **Food served** until 9pm daily. **Map** p314 C3.

A Cuban restaurant and bar, Baracoa can get full of Latin spirit, especially rum, as the night wears on. In summer, they open the large windows onto Victoria Street and the fiesta mood spills out. Young and fun although the cooking doesn't always hit the mark.

Black Bo's

57-61 Blackfriars Street, EH1 (557 6136). Bus 35, 35A. **Open** 4pm-1am Mon-Sat; 6pm-1am Sun. **Map** p310 G5.

A mainstay in the life of any self-respecting bohemian, Bo's, more often than not, is where it's at. The place is tiny and by about 10pm is usually packed and enveloped in a thick fug of blue smoke. DJs play unobtrusive selections of Latin, house and hip hop and the emphasis is on convivial and half-cut banter.

The Bow Bar

80 West Bow, EH1 (226 7667). Bus 2. **Open** 11am-11.30pm Mon-Sat; 2-11pm Sun. **Map** p314 C3.

A firm bastion of tradition against anything tainted with the curse of the wine bar, the Bow Bar does real ale, real whisky and real conversation. The staff wear their white aprons as a badge of their professionalism and remain vigilant for any potential threat to the status quo.

Carwash

11-13 North Bank Street, EH1 (220 0054). Bus 23, 28, 45. **Open** noon-1am Mon-Sat; 6pm-1am Sun. **Food served** noon-5.30pm Mon-Sat. **Map** p314 C3.

Lava lamps, bubble chairs and disco hits of yesteryear on the sound system mean that stepping into Carwash is like reliving the '70s – except that the prices have gone up. The cocktails are reasonable and the pool table and table football up the stairs are useful if you run out of conversation. Fear not – perms and flares aren't obligatory.

The City Café

19 Blair Street, EH1 (220 0125). Bus 7, 8, 21, 31, 80. **Open** 11am-1am daily. **Food served** 11am-10pm daily. **Map** p314 D3.

Twelve years after it opened, the City Café has strong claims to being Edinburgh's first style bar, even if the stylish have moved on. Done out like an American diner with a chrome-topped bar, fans on the ceiling and a section of booth seating, it still pulls in a steady crowd. At the weekends, it's where many of the hard-core clubbers congregate before hitting the bright lights. DJs do their thing downstairs at the weekends.

Doric Tavern & McGuffie's Bar

15-16 Market Street, EH1 (225 1084). Bus 7, 8, 21, 24, 31, 80. **Open** *Doric Tavern* noon-1am Mon-Sat; 12.30pm-1am Sun. *McGuffie's Bar* 11am-1am Mon-Thur; 10am-1am Fri, Sat; closed Sun (except during the Festival). **Food served** noon-6pm Mon-Sat. **Map** p314 D2.

Both a bar and a bistro, the Doric Tavern used to be a second home for many of the journalists who worked at the adjacent *Scotsman* premises but, at the end of 1999, the newspaper relocated. A new set of more smartly dressed professionals have taken their place, ransacking the long wine list and gassing over a lemon sole. Highly variable work from local artists lines the walls. McGuffie's Bar downstairs has fewer frills.

EH1

197 High Street, EH1 (220 5277). Bus 35, 35A. **Open** 9.30am-1am Mon-Fri; 9am-1am Sat, Sun. **Food served** until 7pm daily. **Map** p314 D3.

A trendy city-centre bar that practically sits on the crossroads of the Bridges and the Royal Mile, EH1 is a magnet for stylish twenty- and thirtysomethings, plus tourists. In summer the area outside is usually full of people happily munching in the sun. When night falls, it all becomes a little cooler and DJs add to the ambience.

Finnegan's Wake

9B Victoria Street, EH1 (226 3816). Bus 23, 28, 45. **Open** noon-1am Mon-Sat; 12.30pm-1am Sun. **Map** p314 C3.

Incredibly popular, with queues up the street at the weekend, this Irish-themed bar is stuffed with all sorts of green-tinged odds and sods. The main attraction is the nightly live bands, which give the young and mainly student-based clientele the chance to get close to a member of the opposite sex under the cover of dancing.

The Jolly Judge

7a James Court, Lawnmarket, EH1 (225 2669). Bus 35, 35A. **Open** noon-midnight Mon, Thur-Sat; noon-11pm Tue, Wed, Sun. **Food served** noon-2pm daily. **Map** p314 C3.

The name may seem like an oxymoron but this warm wee pub is worth seeking out. It's just off the Lawnmarket and right on the tourist trail. It has a homely feel to it, courtesy of its open fire and friendly staff. Its compact size actually makes it seem like sitting in somebody's living room.

Last Drop Tavern

74-78 Grassmarket, EH1 (225 4851). Bus 2. **Open** 11am-1am Mon-Sat; 12.30pm-1am Sun. **Food served** noon-7.30pm; snacks until close. **Map** p314 C3.

Another student favourite on the Grassmarket drinking strip, the Last Drop takes its name from its location beside the former city gallows. Lunching outside in the summer sun can be fun but the evenings are always more lively affairs. As to the weekends, be prepared to party.

The best Pubs to party at

Any Grassmarket pub
The weekend starts on Thursday and the hangover lasts till Wednesday. The **Last Drop Tavern** (pictured) is a good example.

The Basement
Subterranean shenanigans are a regular feature. See page 155.

Peartree House
A beer garden, sun and students make for an oft-boisterous mix. See page 160.

The Three Sisters
Pints, pulling and dancing, although not necessarily in that order. See page 161.

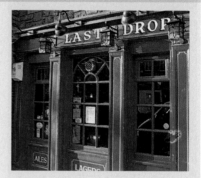

Logie Baird's
Bank Hotel, 1 South Bridge, EH1 (556 9940). Bus 7, 8, 21, 31, 80. **Open** 9am-1am daily. **Food served** 9am-6pm daily. **Map** p314 D3.
An intriguing place, Logie Baird's has a second seating area on top of the island bar. Popular with tourists, lawyers from the nearby courts and local office folk, it's not really the kind of place for a ripper of a party but more of a one for sober suits and gentle conversation.

Maggie Dickson's
92 Grassmarket, EH1 (225 6601). Bus 2. **Open** 11am-1am daily. **Food served** 11am-8pm daily. **Map** p314 B3.
Smaller than most of the bars on the Grassmarket, Maggie Dickson's has a distinct haunted house feel to it, with dark wood and morbid fittings. The customers are much the same as in the rest of the strip, though, with tourists dropping in during the day and young locals turning up for the night shift. Packed at the weekend.

The Malt Shovel Inn
11-15 Cockburn Street, EH1 (225 6843). Bus 24, 35, 35A. **Open** 11am-12.30am Mon-Thur, Sun; 11am-1am Fri, Sat. **Food served** noon-6pm daily. **Map** p314 D2.
A certain pride in its real ales has helped make the Malt Shovel the chosen venue for a few afterwork jars. It's a deceptively large space, with the sociable drinkers sticking by the imposing bar while couples and groups tend to colonise the partitioned tables towards the back.

The Mitre
133 High Street, EH1 (524 0071). Bus 35, 35A. **Open** 11am-midnight Mon-Thur, Sun; 11am-1am Fri, Sat. **Food served** noon-9pm daily. **Map** p310 G5.
Recently refurbished, the Mitre is a large spacious pub with a correspondingly huge bar. It has a prime

position on the Royal Mile and come the balmy days of July (ha ha!) the windows at the front are opened out for a daring if doomed stab at continental chic.

The Royal Mile Tavern
127 High Street, EH1 (557 9681). Bus 35, 35A. **Open** 11am-11pm Mon-Thur; 11am-midnight Fri, Sat; noon-11pm Sun. **Food served** until 9pm daily. **Map** p310 G5.
A touch more elegant or perhaps more formal than its neighbours on either side, the Royal Mile Tavern looks almost as regal and staid as the name suggests. Polished brass, a carpet on the floor and old black and white prints set the tone. There's a quiet bistro at the back where the food is better than you might expect.

Siglo
184 Cowgate, EH1 (240 2850). Bus 7, 8, 21, 31, 80. **Open** noon-1am daily. **Food served** noon-10pm Mon-Thur, Sun; noon-9pm Fri, Sat. **Map** p314 D3.
This newish fun pub is big, brash and bright. There are happy hours most nights of the week and DJs to spin the party tunes du jour. Siglo being Spanish for 'century', there is a Spanish element to the food, with tapas and paella making an appearance. The cocktail list is long and lethal.

The Tass
1 High Street, EH1 (556 6338). Bus 24, 35, 35A. **Open** 11am-midnight Mon-Thur; 11am-1am Fri, Sat; 11am-midnight Sun. **Food served** noon-8pm Mon-Sat. **Map** p310 G5.
When it's quiet, it is absolutely deathly in here but folk sessions and lunchtime food promos do their bit to raise the atmosphere. The sausage and mash could feed a family of four.

Whistle Binkies
6 Niddry Street, EH1 (557 5114). Bus 7, 8, 21, 31, 80. **Open** 7pm-3am daily. **Map** p314 D3.
A splendid late night drinking den that bears witness

The **Café Royal** will have something to suit you, whether it's the Bistro Bar or the Circle Bar.

to much beery bonhomie, Whistle Binkies owes much of its success to its live music policy. Seven days a week, bands of varying persuasions provide a lively background to many a saucy chat-up line. Below the main bar area there is a row of little rooms for more covert shenanigans.

The World's End

4 High Street, EH1 (556 3628). Bus 24, 35, 35A.
Open 11am-1am Mon-Sat; 12.30pm-1am Sun.
Food served noon-9pm Mon-Sat; 12.30-9pm Sun.
Map p310 G5.
So named (though perhaps rather dramatically) because the furthest wall from the bar used to mark the city's boundary, the World's End is a snug and traditional pub. The tiny kitchen works miracles at lunchtimes and in the evenings there is a pleasant mix of locals and backpackers from nearby hostels.

New Town

All Bar One

9 George Street, EH2 (226 9971). Bus 8, 12, 16, 17, 25. **Open** 11.30am-midnight Mon-Thur; 11.30am-1am Fri, Sat; 12.30-11pm Sun. **Food served** noon-10pm daily. **Map** p314 C1.
Edinburgh's two branches of this national chain are booming. Allegedly designed to make bars more attractive to women, All Bar One outlets boast big windows, good wine selections and bistro-style menus. In other words, they're the antithesis of dark, smelly boozers. But you do pay for your gentility.
Branch: Exchange Plaza, Lothian Road, West Edinburgh, EH3 (221 7951).

Bar 38

126-128 George Street, EH2 (220 6180). Bus 13, 19, 55, 82. **Open** 10am-1am Mon-Sat; 10am-midnight Sun. **Food served** 10am-9.30pm daily. **Map** p314 A1.
The unisex toilets have made the unmentionable the biggest talking point in here but there's more to the place than the plumbing. The ubiquitous blond wood fittings are offset by some remarkable cloth sculptures, which give the place some character. The modern bar food has its fans and it witnesses an enthusiastic after-work crowd.

Café Royal Bistro Bar

17 West Register Street, EH2 (557 4792). Bus 3, 12, 16, 17, 80. **Open** 11am-1am daily. **Food served** 11am-5pm Mon-Fri. **Map** p314 D1.
Popular with ruddy-faced members of the rugby community when there is an international on, this first-floor bar also plays host to the occasional left-field concert and the whey-faced indie kids who tend to frequent them.

Café Royal Circle Bar

19 West Register Street, EH2 (556 1884). Bus 3, 12, 16, 17, 80. **Open** 11am-11pm Mon-Wed, Sun; 11am-midnight Thur; 11am-1am Fri, Sat.
Map p314 D1.
The huge island bar and tiled scenes of toil on the back wall are the key features of this historic bar. An amiable place for an ale or two (and bar snacks after 7pm), it has large booth seating, which makes conversation easier if you're in a crowd. Used by a more mature crowd rather than young clubbers, the Café Royal is soundtracked by the murmur

The Dome – better than home.

of conversation. Incongruously, the floor of the gents' toilets is often swimming. For the oyster bar, see p122.

The Cumberland Bar

1 Cumberland Street, EH3 (558 3134). Bus 19A, 23, 27, 37, 47 buses. **Open** noon-11.30pm Mon-Wed; noon-midnight Thur-Sat; *summer also* 12.30-10pm Sun. **Food served** noon-2pm Mon-Sat; 12.30-3pm Sun. **Map** p306 E3.

Those whose parents were a generation before the baby boomers might imagine this is where their fathers could have drunk. That distinctly Edinburgh brand of respectability and tradition is indelibly stamped here in the gleaming real ale pumps and the old, burnished mirrors advertising long-forgotten brands of fags. There's a small beer garden that occasionally catches some sun, and the pies are good.

The Dome

14 George Street, EH2 (624 8624). Bus 8, 12, 16, 17, 25. **Open** noon-11.30pm Mon-Thur, Sun; noon-1am Fri, Sat. **Food served** noon-11pm daily. **Map** p314 C1.

It's difficult to think of a more spectacular bar in Edinburgh than the Dome, housed in a former bank headquarters. The island bar in the centre is surrounded by wicker chairs and assorted bits of leaf and frond, while the mezzanine area at the back serves good bistro food. The wine list keeps winning awards and the cocktail bar to the side of the main

entrance is worth a visit as well. It seems to attract the young and well-heeled and one can imagine it being a footballer's or hairdresser's dream (but don't let that put you off).

The Drum & Monkey

80 Queen Street, EH2 (538 8111). Bus 13, 19, 55, 82. **Open** noon-11pm Mon-Thur; noon-midnight Fri, Sat; closed Sun. **Food served** noon-8pm Mon-Fri; noon-4pm Sat. **Map** p306 D4.

Located just a pin-striped stride from Edinburgh's financial district, the Drum & Monkey has the look of a gentleman's club, all wing-backed leather seats and low lighting. Adding weight to the 'old boy' theme is the fact that it sells the stoutly named Old Wallop ale, and staff know how to mix a bally good Bloody Mary. That's tradition for you.

Fibber Magee's

24 Howe Street, EH3 (220 2376). Bus 28, 29, 29A, 80. **Open** 11am-11pm Mon; 11am-midnight Tue, Wed; 11am-1am Thur, Fri; 10am-1am Sat; 10am-midnight Sun. **Food served** until 6pm daily. **Map** 306 D4.

Young New Town dwellers provide the main custom of this dark Irish bar. And they provide a lot of it. It is often busy and almost always loud. And not exactly cheap either.

Indigo Yard

7 Charlotte Lane, EH2 (220 5603). Bus 3, 3A, 12, 16, 17. **Open** 8.30am-1am daily. **Food served** 8.30am-10pm daily. **Map** p308 C5.

This incredibly popular West End bar partially comprises an old courtyard that's been covered by a huge glass canopy. It's an arresting sight, although most people are too busy hoovering up their lunch, slurping coffee or knocking back an after-work beer or three to pay much attention. As much a bistro as a bar, it serves everything from breakfast to supper. The menus are international in outlook and the food is pretty good.

The Kenilworth

152-154 Rose Street, EH2 (226 4385). Bus 3, 12, 16, 17. **Open** 10am-11pm Mon-Thur; 9am-12.45am Fri, Sat; 12.30-11pm Sun. **Food served** as opening times. **Map** p314 B1.

Perhaps Rose Street's most striking bar, the Kenilworth is housed in a listed building and boasts tiled walls, an Edwardian ceiling and remarkable stained glass windows. They just don't build 'em like this any more.

Milne's Bar

35 Hanover Street, EH2 (225 6738). Bus 23, 27, 45. **Open** 11am-11.30pm Mon-Wed; 11am-midnight Thur; 11am-1am Fri, Sat; 12.30-11.30pm Sun. **Food served** 11am-9.30pm daily; from 12.30pm Sun. **Map** p314 C1.

A winding, almost maze-like pub, Milne's runs higgledy-piggledy over three levels, all of which are covered in plain but pleasant dark wood. Pictures of members of Scotland's literary Renaissance such as Hugh MacDiarmid, who were wont to meet here for heated debate, abound.

Penny Black

17 West Register Street, EH2 (556 1106). Bus 3, 3A, 12, 16, 17, 80. **Open** 5am-6.30pm Mon-Thur; 5am-10.30pm Fri, Sat; closed Sun. **Map** p314 D1.

This isn't the last word in salubrious surroundings and the range of drinks won't exactly bowl you over but it does open at 5am. While the rest of the city sleeps or thinks about going to bed, the Penny Black is open for business and dishing up the bevvy. Nothing beats a pint of heavy to kick start the day.

The Rose Street Brewery

55 Rose Street, EH2 (220 1227). Bus 3, 12, 16, 17, 80. **Open** 11am-11pm Mon-Thur; 11am-midnight Fri, Sat; 12.30-9pm Sun. **Food served** 11am-9pm Mon-Sat; 12.30-9pm Sun. **Map** p314 B1.

Unfortunately it has stopped brewing its own beer on the premises but the Rose Street Brewery is still well-liked by tourists and thirsty shoppers. The cross-beamed interior gives it a certain old charm.

Ryan's

2 Hope Street, EH2 (226 6669). Bus 3, 3A, 12, 16, 17. **Open** 11am-1am Mon-Sat; 12.30pm-1am Sun (bar only). **Food served** until 10pm daily. **Map** p314 A1.

Perhaps the archetypal West End bar, Ryan's is a big hit with local office workers (and Friday night is the one where they let off steam). It does a good trade in lunches and coffees during the day and there is a small bistro downstairs.

The Standing Order

62-66 George Street, EH2 (225 4460). Bus 13, 19, 55, 82. **Open** 11am-1am Mon-Sat; 12.30pm-1am Sun. **Food served** until 11pm daily. **Map** p314 B1.

One of the increasingly sprawling Wetherspoon's empire, the Standing Order is housed in a former bank and follows the company's concept of no live

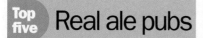

Top five Real ale pubs

The Bow Bar

No-nonsense service from staff who take pride in their work. See page 148.

The Caley Sample Room

The full range of Caledonian beers under one roof. See page 162.

Cask & Barrel

A good range of guest ales and great Deuchar's IPA. See page 155.

The Cumberland Bar

Old school in the New Town. See page 152.

Hogshead

Not the best-looking but a great real ale selection. See page 159.

music, cheap beer and food, lots of no smoking areas and comfortable if sanitised surroundings. Purists moan but the public love them.

Whighams Wine Cellar

13 Hope Street, EH2 (225 8674). Bus 13, 19, 55, 82. **Open** noon-midnight Mon-Thur; noon-1am Fri, Sat; closed Sun. **Food served** noon-10pm Mon-Thur; noon-9pm Fri, Sat. **Map** p314 A1.

Not so much a cellar as a series of little vaults, Whighams is where nearby business people come to lunch, and play afterwards. The food is upmarket Scottish game and seafood while the wine list roams the globe.

Stockbridge

The Antiquary

72-78 St Stephen Street, EH3 (225 2858). Bus 28, 29, 29A, 80. **Open** 11.30am-12.30am Mon-Wed; 11.30am-1am Thur-Sat; 11am-12.30am Sun. **Food served** 11.30am-2.30pm Mon-Sat; 11.30am-2.30pm Sun. **Map** p306 D3.

Open fires, unreconstructed decor and quiz nights every Wednesday make this a charming and uncomplicated part of any Stockbridge pub crawl. Its three rooms are housed in interlinked basements and all are as comfy as they are basic.

The Bailie

2-4 St Stephen Street, EH3 (225 4673). Bus 28, 29, 29A, 80. **Open** 11am-midnight Mon-Thur; 11am-1am Fri, Sat; 12.30-11pm Sun. **Food served** 11am-5pm daily. **Map** p306 D3.

Another Stockbridge institution, The Bailie is a dark and smoky basement bar that boasts numerous crepuscular crannies in which to hide away with a pint. While phrases like 'interior design' are considered blasphemous in here, the food is several notches above that served by many traditional boozers. The stir-fried shredded beef beats the more customary Scotch pie hands down.

Bert's Bar

2-4 Raeburn Place, EH4 (332 6345). Bus 28, 29, 29A, 80. **Open** 11am-midnight Mon-Thur; 11am-1am Fri, Sat; 12.30-11pm Sun. **Food served** 11am-midnight; 12.30-11pm Sun. **Map** p305 C3.

A respectable, wood-panelled bar of the old school, with no piped music, Bert's is known for its beer and pies. Hailed as things of beauty by pie connoisseurs the city over, its pastry delights come in multiple varieties and taste like heaven when dipped in brown sauce and washed down with a pint of IPA. The William Street branch is a welcome shelter for weary West End shoppers.

Branch: 29-31 William Street, New Town, EH3 (225 5748).

Maison Hector

47 Deanhaugh Street, EH3 (332 5328). Bus 28, 29, 29A, 80. **Open** 11am-midnight Mon-Wed; 11am-1am Thur, Fri; 10.30am-1am Sat; 10.30am-midnight Sun. **Food served** until 10.30pm daily. **Map** p305 C3.

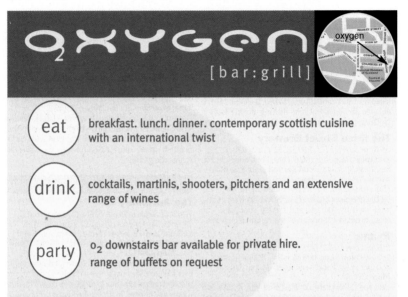

You don't have to be old to appreciate the simple but endearing **Antiquary**. *See page 153.*

Long a favourite with Stockbridge's more cosmopolitan inhabitants, Maison Hector is a great place for lounging around in. Lots of candles, cocktails – including wicked Margaritas – and deep seats encourage sloth. It is especially popular at the weekends, when the kitchen cooks up brunch dishes such as eggs benedict. There's a bistro area towards the back serving grilled red mullet and the like.

The Watershed

44 St Stephen Street, EH3 (220 3774). Bus 28, 29, 29A, 80. **Open** 10am-12.30pm Mon-Thur, Sun; 10am-1am Fri, Sat. **Food served** 10am-7pm Mon-Sat; 10am-5pm Sun. **Map** p306 D3.

This basement bar with funky fittings is probably the most trendy bar in Stockbridge. The young at heart are seemingly attracted by its laid-back attitude. (The fact that breakfast is served until 10pm should clue you in).

Calton Hill & Broughton

The Barony Bar

81-85 Broughton Street, EH1 (557 0546). Bus 8. **Open** 11am-midnight Mon-Thur; 11am-12.30am Fri, Sat; 12.30-11pm Sun. **Food served** as opening times. **Map** p306 F3.

The area's late twenty- and early thirtysomething professionals quaff their cask ale here in faux-traditional surroundings. Polished pumps, old wood and an open fire make for a cosy spot although come the weekends it's often so rammed that getting to the bar is a bit of an expedition. Special mention must go to the puff pastry pies.

Baroque

39-41 Broughton Street, EH1 (557 0627). Bus 8. **Open** 10am-1am Mon-Sat; noon-1am Sun. **Food served** 11am-10pm Mon-Thur; 11am-8pm, Fri, Sat; 11am-10pm Sun. **Map** p306 F3.

Gaudí's work is the inspiration for Baroque's look, which is to say the bar's designer was not shy of splashing out with the bright colours. One of Broughton Street's flashiest bars, it draws in a young and lively crowd. In the summer, the large windows are opened out making this an agreeable place for a mid-afternoon swally.

The Basement

10A-12A Broughton Street, EH1 (557 0097). Bus 8. **Open** noon-1am daily. **Food served** noon-10pm daily. **Map** p306 F3.

When Broughton Street first started becoming hip, much of its kudos came courtesy of the Basement. It's a funny, dark place with tables made from bits of old machinery, giving it a pseudo-industrial feel. The crowd are young, good natured, slightly left field and fond of a drink. The bar staff wear Hawaiian shirts that are as loud as the music and can be daunting if you're suffering from a hangover. There's Tex-Mex grub at the weekends and reasonable bistro food during the week.

Cask & Barrel

115 Broughton Street, EH1 (556 3132). 7A, 8, 8A, 9, 9A, 19, 39 buses. **Open** 11am-12.30am Mon-Wed, Sun; 11am-1am Thur-Sat. **Food served** noon-2pm daily. **Map** p306 F3.

A real-ale-lover's idea of heaven, the Cask was refurbished in 1999 but still looks as though nothing has changed for decades. Prints of old Broughton Street line the nicotine-coloured walls and the staff exhibit the kind of fast efficiency that seemed to have died out years ago. Pies, samosas and filled rolls are all on hand to soak up the drink.

Catwalk Café
2 Picardy Place, EH1 (478 7771). Leith Walk buses. **Open** 11am-1am daily. **Food served** noon-7pm daily. **Map** p307 G4.
A style bar with a capital S, Catwalk Café is either artfully minimal or deadly clinical depending on your point of view. It's popular with the young and beautiful but you might feel out of place if you have last week's haircut. Often busy and always mobbed at weekends, when DJs deliver the rhythms, it's also a good spot for a mid-afternoon coffee, especially when the sun is streaming through the glass frontage.

Habana
22 Greenside Place, EH1 (558 1270). Leith Walk buses. **Open** noon-1am daily. **Food served** noon-6pm daily. **Map** 307 G4.
One of a burgeoning number of Cuban-themed bars that have opened in the capital, Habana is partial to a sinuous salsa soundtrack. Other than being exotic, it is difficult to see what the fake animal skin seat covers have to do with Cuba but it all makes perfect sense after you've spent some time getting acquainted with the rum-based cocktail list.

Mathers Bar
25 Broughton Street, EH1 (556 6754). 7A, 8, 8A, 9, 9A, 19, 39 buses. **Open** 11am-midnight Mon-Thur; 11am-12.30am Fri, Sat; 12.30-11pm Sun. **Food served** until 10pm daily. **Map** p306 F3.

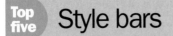

Top five Style bars

blue Bar Café
Chic minimalism for the slightly more mature trendsetter. See page 157.

The City Café
Over a decade old but still cooler than many of the young pretenders will ever be. See page 148.

Henry's Cellar Bar
Unstylish to look at but possibly *the* late-night place to hang cool. See page 162.

Iguana
Night-time hangout for the cooler club lizard. See page 160.

Oxygen Bar & Grill
Two pints of lager, a packet of crisps, and a canister of pure O_2 for the driver please. See page 160.

One of Broughton Street's old guard, Mathers is a homely cask ale boozer where the beer pumps are kept polished, the air is often redolent of cigars and the footie is the main topic of gruff conversation. A gem, in other words.

The Outhouse
12A Broughton Street Lane, EH1 (557 6668). 7A, 8, 8A, 9, 9A, 19, 39 buses. **Open** noon-1am Mon-Sat; 12.30pm-1am Sun. **Food served** noon-3pm daily. **Map** p306 E3.
Just off Broughton Street but just as chic as any of the bars on the main drag, the Outhouse's main attraction in the summer months is its zen beer garden and boules pitch. What's zen about it isn't immediately apparent but exhaust-fume-free outside drinking is not to be sniffed at, so to speak.

Phoenix Bar
46 Broughton Street, EH1 (557 0234). 7A, 8, 8A, 9, 9A, 19, 39 buses. **Open** 8am-1am Mon-Sat; 12.30pm-1am Sun. **Map** p306 F3.
The salty locals and Home Counties students who drink here make for a volatile and sometimes explosive mix, which means that the Phoenix is not for the faint of heart. In its favour, the drink is among the cheapest in town and there are some genuine characters knocking about.

Pivo Caffé
2-6 Calton Road, EH8 (557 2925). Bus 1, 11, 22, 34. **Open** 10am-1am daily. **Food served** noon-6pm daily; snacks till 10pm. **Map** p307 G4.
Recently revamped as a slice of Prague, the former St James Oyster Bar has been endlessly improved. Old pictures of Prague show off the city in its best light while four draught beers and a huge list of bottled beers demonstrate the prowess of its brewers. The brass bar is an eye-catcher, as are the brass kittens climbing the beer founts. Snacky food of a Czech flavour is available.

Arthur's Seat & Duddingston

The Sheep Heid Inn
43 The Causeway, Duddingston, EH15 (656 6951). Bus 4, 42, 46. **Open** 11am-11pm Mon-Wed; 11am-midnight Thur-Sat; 12.30-11pm Sun. **Food served** until 8pm daily.
A visit to the Sheep Heid Inn, one of Edinburgh's oldest pubs, is a relaxing way to finish off any expeditions up Arthur's Seat. People go for the calm atmosphere, the beer garden and the venerable skittle alley (a real blast from the past), which can be hired out by the hour.

South Edinburgh

Bar Ce Lona
2-8 West Crosscauseway, EH8 (662 8860). Bus 40, 41, 42, 46. **Open** 11am-11pm Mon, Sun; 11am-midnight Thur; 11am-1am Fri, Sat. **Food served** noon-9pm Mon-Fri; noon-8pm Sat, Sun. **Map** p310 G7.

Get frisky for some whisky at **Bennet's**.

Although one of Edinburgh's newest bars, Bar Ce Lona looks pretty much like any other generic style bar – with blond wood and a vague Mediterranean theme being the distinguishing factors. Still, it seems to be a happy hunting ground for the youngish, vogueish professionals and students who come here. DJs up the ante at the weekends and the food is of the contemporary global variety.

Bar Kohl
54 George IV Bridge, EH1 (225 6936). Bus 23, 28, 45. **Open** noon-1am Mon-Sat; closed Sun. **Food served** noon-2.30pm Mon-Sat. **Map** p314 C3.
Vodka and hip hop are the motivating factors behind this family-run bar, although not necessarily in that order. Those who are baggy of trouser and fly of demeanour congregate here to inspect the latest imported hip hop cuts. There's also an amazing range of flavoured and rare vodkas.

Bennet's Bar
8 Leven Street, Tollcross, EH3 (229 5143). Bus 11, 16, 17, 23. **Open** 11am-11.30pm Mon-Wed; 11am-12.30am Thur-Sat; 7-11pm Sun. **Food served** noon-2pm Mon-Sat. **Map** p309 D7.
Right next to the King's Theatre, Bennet's boasts the most amazing carved wooden gantry, stained-glass windows, a tiny snug, loads of mirrors and maps laid into the table tops. It should be made into a national monument to Edinburgh howfs. The

adjoining Green Room, which mops up any overspill, is much less attractive, although after you've sampled a few of the dozens of malt whiskies on offer you may not care.

Biddy Mulligan's
94-96 Grassmarket, EH1 (220 1246). Bus 2. **Open** 9am-1am daily. **Food served** 9am-8pm daily. **Map** p314 B3.
Despite its Irish theme, Biddy Mulligan's is much like any other bar on the Grassmarket drinking strip. In term time, it's packed with students seven days a week. On weekends, the students are joined by stag parties and crowds of lads in neatly ironed, untucked Polo shirts. During the day, sitting outside in the sun and sipping a pint is pleasant; the evenings tend to be more raucous. As the bar staff's T-shirts proclaim, somewhat ominously, 'Everyone has to learn to drink somewhere'.

Bliss
253-255 Cowgate, EH1 (557 2780). Bus 7, 8, 21, 31, 80. **Open** 4.30pm-1am daily. **Map** p314 D3.
Multiple cheap drinks promos are the main selling point at this small bar that's aimed at the younger after-work crowd. At the weekends, it's a popular pre-club haunt, with a tiny dancefloor catering for those who can't wait to start capering. Tacky isn't quite the word but let's just say that when this place opened, its advertising featured the image of a well-filled bra with the word 'Bliss' transposed across.

blue Bar Café
10 Cambridge Street, EH1 (221 1222). Bus 11, 15, 24. **Open** 11.30am-midnight Mon, Tue, Sun; 11.30am-1am Wed-Sat. **Food served** noon-11pm daily. **Map** p314 A3.
A chic and grown-up style bar upstairs from the **Traverse Bar** (*see p161*), blue is the preferred hangout for Edinburgh's smart and fashionable professionals. It boasts loads of whiskies and a fantastic bottled beer selection but, most importantly, it takes great pride in making its cocktails properly. Blue does a good trade in modern bistro food, with the gourmet sausages on Puy lentils being especially favoured. In case you're wondering, the lower case 'b' of blue serves to emphasise the joint's understated style, sweetie.

The Cameo Bar
38 Home Street, EH3 (228 4141). Bus 11, 16, 17, 23. **Open** 12.30-11pm Mon-Wed, Sun; 12.30pm-1am Thur-Sat. **Map** p309 D7.
Compact and bijou are the by-words at this pine-dressed cinema bar. It's handy for pre- or post-movie philosophising, and there are usually works by local artists and photographers spicing up the walls if the film hasn't moved you to conversation.

The Canny Man's
237 Morningside Road, EH10 (447 1484). Bus 11, 16, 17, 23. **Open** noon-midnight Mon-Sat; 12.30-11pm Sun. **Food served** noon-3.30pm daily.
Always a law unto itself, the Canny Man's has been in

CAFÉ ROUGE
RESTAURANT   BAR   CAFE

Ouvert 7 Jours

Monday - Saturday 7.30 a.m. Last Orders 11 p.m.
Sunday 7.30 a.m. Last Orders 10.30 p.m.

Fresh French food at value for money prices

BREAKFAST · CAPPUCCINO · PATISSERIE · TEA
MENU PRIX FIXE · LUNCH · MENU RAPIDE · WINES
BAGUETTES · BEERS · COCKTAILS · DINNER

TELEPHONE : (0131) 225 4515

Pub etiquette

A few hints and pointers for happy boozing or 'going on the peeve', as the activity is sometimes known in Edinburgh.

Apart from standard, or 'cooking', lager, all **beers** are ordered by either their proprietary name or as 60, 70, 80 or 90 shilling. These figures refer to the duty historically payable on a cask of ale and varied according to its strength. Nowadays they denote different styles but 60 shilling is still the lightest in alcohol and 90 shilling the strongest. Both 60 and 90 are quite rare today. Just to confuse matters further, 80 shilling is sometimes called heavy and 70 shilling special.

Other common styles are the hoppy IPA, an abbreviation of India Pale Ale, and Export. As well as the usual multinational breweries, Edinburgh is supplied by a number of independent Scottish outfits whose beers can be excellent. Names to look out for include Edinburgh's Caledonian, Dunbar's Belhaven, the Broughton Brewery in the Borders and Alloa's Maclay and Company.

As to **whisky**, some of the blended brands are very good but none of them match the complexity of a good single malt. Ignore the macho talk about neat whisky being the only way to drink the stuff. The addition of half as much again water opens up the flavours and bouquet of the whisky, but the exact amount is a matter of taste, so add gently and by degrees. The addition of cola or any other fizzy stuff is rightly frowned upon as a perverse abomination.

A word of warning: never use the word 'bouquet' in a pub where the barman has asked to see your tattoos before serving you. **Table service** is rare in Edinburgh's pubs and you will almost always have to go to the bar yourself. Even when the sun is shining and people are sat at tables outside you will wait forever to be served. **Tipping** the bar staff is the exception rather than the rule although occasionally adding 'and one for yourself' at the end of your order will make them very happy.

Consumer

business since Victoria was on the throne. The publican knows what he likes and what he doesn't like. If he doesn't like what you are wearing then you won't get served. It's safe to say that green hair, clashing dungarees and a T-shirt featuring Bart Simpson mooning won't meet with approval (and quite right too). The tremendous collection of genuine bric-a-brac and oddities nailed to the wall make it worth the effort of securing entry.

The Cas Rock

104 West Port, EH3 (229 4341). Bus 2, 11, 15, 24. **Open** noon-midnight Mon-Thur; noon-1am Fri, Sat; 12.30pm-midnight Sun. **Map** p309 D6.
A second home to many of the city's scruffier musicians, the Cas is one of the main venues for up-and-coming bands of an alternative persuasion. Idlewild, Ballboy and Ganger have all played here in recent times and if you've never heard of them then you probably have no cause to visit the Cas. The two pool tables are handy if the bands are unlistenable. *See also p206.*

Cellar No.1

1A Chambers Street, EH1 (220 4298). Bus 7, 8, 21, 31, 80. **Open** noon-1am Mon-Wed; noon-3am Thur-Sat; 6pm-1am Sun. **Food served** noon-10pm Mon-Sat; 6-10pm Sun. **Map** p310 G6.
While office workers use it for lunch and coffee breaks during the day, this basement hangout pulls in a more studenty crowd in the evenings. It does a good range of wines and features regular live music, usually of a jazzy nature.

Dr Watt's Library

3 Robertson's Close, EH1 (557 3768). Bus 7, 8, 21, 31, 80. **Open** 11am-1am daily. **Food served** noon-3pm daily; *summer* noon-7pm daily. **Map** p310 G6.
Dr Watt's Library is housed on the ground floor of a students' residence, so it's no surprise that it's often full of scholars researching the effects of alcohol on the brain. Young, loud and better inside than out.

Greyfriars Bobby Bar

34A Candlemaker Row, EH1 (225 8328). Bus 23, 28, 45. **Open** 11am-1am Mon-Sat; 12.30pm-1am Sun. **Food served** 11am-8pm Mon-Sat; 12.30-8pm Sun. **Map** p309 F6.
Taking its name from the faithful terrier whose statue stands outside, Greyfriars Bobby is a comfortable pub that makes a convenient stop-off point for refreshments after a session at the nearby museum. The pub grub is reasonably priced.

Hogshead

30-32 Bread Street, EH3 (221 0575). Bus 2, 11, 15, 24. **Open** 11am-1am daily. **Food served** noon-9pm daily. **Map** p314 A3.
Real ale and a good wine selection attract a busy and mixed clientele to the Hogshead. There are a lot of students in the evenings but it's by no means exclusively a student pub. OK, so it's not the most attractive-looking pub and wouldn't seem too out of place as part of a motorway service station, but it has its plus points. Perhaps most notable of these is the food: the Cumberland sausages and mash hit the spot. **Branch**: 133 Rose Street, EH2 (226 1224).

Iguana

41 Lothian Street, EH1 (220 4288). Bus 23, 28, 40, 45. **Open** *9am-1am daily.* **Food served** *9am-10pm daily.* **Map** *p309 F6.*

A thoroughly modern and sleek-looking bar that caters to a young and hip crowd. Iguana is just a hop, skip and a stumble from Edinburgh University's main campus, so students are no rarity. It's also a popular pre-club venue, where DJs rev up the temperature. The food has a definite global slant and leaves traditional pub grub standing.

International Bar

15 Brougham Place, EH3 (229 6815). Bus 11, 16, 17, 23, 24. **Open** *9am-1am Mon-Sat; 12.30pm-1am Sun.* **Map** *p309 E7.*

Unflustered by the rise of the style bar, the IB, as it is known to regulars, has ploughed the same unfussy furrow for years. Tourists are the exception rather than the norm but if you want to see a regular neighbourhood pub come in anyway – the locals don't bite.

The Maltings Ale House

81-85 St Leonard's Street, EH8 (667 5946). Bus 2, 21. **Open** *noon-1am Mon-Sat; 12.30pm-1am Sun.* **Map** *p310 H7.*

This bar's proximity to one of the city's largest student residences ensures that there is usually a young and upbeat buzz about the place. Most of the decor comprises flyers and posters advertising clubs and gigs. There's not much more to it other than a good, relaxed atmosphere.

Maxies Bistro

32B West Nicolson Street, EH8 (667 0845). Bus 7, 8, 21, 31, 80. **Open** *11am-midnight Mon-Thur; 11am-1am Fri, Sat; closed Sun.* **Food served** *noon-3pm, 5-11pm Mon-Sat.* **Map** *p310 G6.*

This whitewashed cellar bar is a cosy home from home for many of the academics at the adjacent Edinburgh University and it does a brisk lunchtime trade. Though the term might seem a bit dated now, Maxies is definitely one of Edinburgh's few wine bars and very civilised it is too. Great for a quiet weekend night out with a seat almost guaranteed.

The Meadow Bar

42 Buccleuch Street, EH8 (667 6907). Bus 40, 41, 42, 46. **Open** *noon-1am daily.* **Food served** *noon-3pm daily.* **Map** *p310 G7.*

Once an old man's spit and fag ash boozer, the two-floor Moo Bar, as it is known to its adherents, pulls in a young studenty crowd. Strange metal sculptures, low lighting and lower slung seating make this a cross between a living room and a private club. Scenes of prehistoric stick men hunting buffalos are painted on the walls.

Monboddo

The Point Hotel, 34 Bread Street, EH3 (221 5555). Bus 2, 11, 15, 24. **Open** *10am-midnight Mon-Thur, Sun; 10am-1am Fri, Sat.* **Food served** *10am-10pm Mon-Thur, Sun; 10am-5pm Fri; 10am-8pm Sat.* **Map** *p314 A3.*

Not so much a style bar as an art bar, Monboddo is decorated with rather startling pieces of modern sculpture, while the sky-high gantry is bursting with intriguing bottles – a sight to warm any tippler's heart. It's all very Manhattan (or at least it would like to be).

Montpeliers

159-161 Bruntsfield Place, EH10 (229 3115). Bus 11, 16, 17, 23. **Open** *9am-1am daily.* **Food served** *9am-10pm daily.* **Map** *p309 D8.*

A rapid success story from the day it opened, Montpeliers is a well-located bar bistro that provides decent pastas, salads and sandwiches as well as fancier fish stews and char-grilled chunks. It is very respectable during the day and then lets its hair down a bit in the evening.

Negociants

45-47 Lothian Street, EH1 (225 6313). Bus 23, 28, 40, 45. **Open** *9am-3am daily.* **Food served** *9am-2.30am daily.* **Map** *p309 F6.*

Late opening, table service and an impressive selection of foreign beers and cocktails make Negociants a buzzy bar for the later reveller of a more genteel bent. It also does a reasonable array of snacky foods. The drawback is the often-slow service as too few harassed waitresses run around too many tables.

The Old Fire Station

52 West Port, EH1 (228 4543). Bus 2. **Open** *11am-1am daily.* **Food served** *11am-9pm daily.* **Map** *p309 E6.*

Split into three different levels, the Old Fire Station is something of a party pub and can get quite excitable at the weekends. Ghosts and the fire service are the dual themes running through the decor, with black and white prints of old Hammer movies providing the former and old fire-fighting equipment the latter.

Oxygen Bar & Grill

3 Infirmary Street, EH1 (557 9997). Bus 7, 8, 21, 31, 80. **Open** *11am-midnight daily.* **Food served** *10am-10pm daily.* **Map** *p310 G6.*

A seriously sleek-looking bar and grill, Oxygen's unique selling point is the fact that it sells canisters of pure oxygen. If that sounds like a load of hot air then the cocktail list is stunning and the food is very now. Downstairs is another bar where the music is louder and dancing isn't frowned upon. Groovy.

Peartree House

38 West Nicolson Street, EH8 (667 7533). Bus 40, 41, 42, 46. **Open** *11am-midnight Mon-Thur; 11am-1am Fri, Sat; 12.30pm-midnight Sun.* **Food served** *noon-2.30pm Mon-Sat; 12.30-2.30pm Sun.* **Map** *p310 G7.*

Boasting the city's biggest beer garden, the Peartree has sunk many a promising academic career at the adjacent university. When the sun is shining and exams grow near it is a great place to get softly dazed and confused. Inside there are big sofas for sprawling across.

Air today, gone tomorrow? The **Oxygen Bar & Grill** seems set to stay afloat. *See page 160.*

The Royal Oak

1 Infirmary Street, EH1 (557 2976). Bus 7, 8, 21, 31, 80. **Open** *9am-2am Mon-Sat; 12.30pm-2am Sun.* **Map** p310 G6.

Once the thrapples are well enough oiled with whisky and beer, spontaneous outbreaks of traditional singing and fiddle often strike up at the Royal Oak. Open sessions are held every night and there is no better place to see the grassroots folk tradition up close. Forget the tartan nonsense and Highland dinners that some venues put on for tourists: this is the real thing.

Sandy Bell's

25 Forrest Road, EH1 (225 2751). Bus 23, 28, 40, 45. **Open** *11am-12.30am Mon-Sat; 12.30-11pm Sun.* **Map** p309 F6.

Real ales and – some say – one of the best pints of 80/- in Edinburgh are reliable attractions at this old men's bar. The other draw is the impromptu folk sessions that sometimes get going in the back room.

Scruffy Murphy's

49-50 George IV Bridge, EH1 (225 1681). Bus 23, 28, 45. **Open** *11am-1am Mon-Sat; 12.30pm-1am Sun.* **Food served** *11am-6pm Mon-Sat; 12.30-6pm Sun.* **Map** p309 F6.

Yet another of the seemingly unstoppable Irish theme bars. Pleasant enough, though, and often very busy. The food is all hot Eire.

The Three Sisters

139 Cowgate, EH1 (622 6800). Bus 7, 8, 21, 31, 80. **Open** *9am-1am daily.* **Food served** *till late.* **Map** p314 D3.

Offering an Irish bar (complete with snugs that look

like confessionals), a Gothic bar and a modern style bar all under the one roof has been a sure route to success for the Three Sisters complex. The popularity of its open-air courtyard as a drinking venue only cements the bars' profitability. At the weekend, queues extend up the Cowgate as hopeful party animals take their chances. Come the next morning, if you buy a full cooked breakfast before 11am then they'll even throw in a free Bloody Mary or a pint of Guinness.

Traverse Bar

14 Cambridge Street, EH1 (228 5383). Bus 11, 15, 24. **Open** *10.30am-midnight Mon-Wed; 10.30am-1am Thur-Sat; 6pm-midnight Sun.* **Food served** *noon-8pm Mon-Sat; 6pm-midnight Sun.* **Map** p314 A3.

Gossip, scandal and completely unfounded rumours about the theatre world nearly all originate here. Not only is this network central in luvvie land, but it is also deservedly popular with the young at heart. Regular drinks promos and a healthy buzz help loosen tongues.

Uluru

133 Lothian Road, EH3 (228 5407). Bus 11, 15, 24. **Open** *11am-12.30am Mon-Thur; 11.30am-1am Fri, Sat; 10.30am-midnight Sun.* **Food served** *as opening times.* **Map** p309 D6.

Playing on a vague Aboriginal theme, this place is decked out with lots of wood and sand-coloured decor for that 'Outback on Lothian Road' feel. Uluru has deliberately set out to be different from the other pubs on Lothian Road, not all of which are in anyway either pleasant or welcoming. So far at least it seems to be working.

West Edinburgh

The Caley Sample Room
58 Angle Park Terrace, EH11 (337 7204). Bus 1, 28, 34, 35, 35A. **Open** 11am-midnight Mon-Thur; 11am-1am Fri, Sat; 12.30pm-midnight Sun. **Map** p308 A8.
Although somewhat barn-like, the Caley Sample Room is usually bustling with beery good cheer. It sells the full range of cask ales crafted in the nearby Caledonian Brewery and sports fans often avail themselves of the facilities before, during and after matches at either Murrayfield or Tynecastle.

Cuba Norte
192 Morrison Street, EH3 (221 1430). Bus 3, 3A, 12, 25, 25A. **Open** noon-1am daily. **Food served** noon-10.30pm daily. **Map** p308 C6.
The first in what is becoming a growing number of Cuban restaurants in Edinburgh, Cuba Norte manages to be a bar, restaurant and no-holds barred fiesta joint. The *mojitos* will set you up for the Miami-Cuban menu and, after puffing on a Cohiba, you can shake off the calories with some dancefloor salsa. Can be wild at the weekend.

Henry's Cellar Bar
8-16A Morrison Street, EH3 (538 7385). Bus 11, 15, 24. **Open** noon-3am daily. **Food served** 1-10.45pm daily. **Map** p309 D6.
Underground Edinburgh comes alive here. This is actually a dim sum restaurant but as night falls the emphasis switches to drinking and exploring musical fusions. There are live music and jamming sessions every night although the young crowd often seems more intent on getting the next round in than listening to the latest nu-jazz 'n' bass experiment. Well worth a visit for the hipper night owl.

Leith

Bar Sirius
7-10 Dock Place, EH6 (555 3344). Bus 10A, 16. **Open** 11am-midnight Mon-Wed; 11.30am-1am Thur-Sat; noon-1am Sun. **Food served** 11.30am-9pm. **Map** p311 Jy.
Leith's first designer bar is home to a youngish, dressed-up crowd who don't mind shouting over the music at the weekend. The wire-backed chairs and low-slung sofas were modish when the place opened a few years back but it's beginning to look a little worn around the edges now. Nevertheless, it's still very popular and its global menu is worth a look.

The Bourse Café Bar Gallery
28 Bernard Street, EH6 (476 8080). Bus 16, 35, 35A. **Open** 8am-11pm Mon-Wed; 8am-midnight Thur, Fri; 9am-midnight Sat; 9am-11pm Sun. **Food served** until 10pm. **Map** p311 Ky.
Leith's latest designer bar – its huge lightshades dominate the room – is strong on its food, which looks to the four corners of the earth for its inspiration. The emphasis switches to the bar side of the operation in the evening.

Club Java
39 Commercial Street, EH6 (555 5622). Bus 10A, 16. **Open** noon-midnight Mon-Thur; noon-2am Fri, Sat; noon-6pm Sun. **Food served** noon-10pm Mon-Sat; noon-6pm Sun. **Map** p311 Jy.
The owners have tried to cover all the entertainment bases with Club Java, and have largely succeeded. Over two floors of a converted church, there is a bar, a restaurant, semi-private dining rooms and a dancefloor. At the time of writing, salsa classes were just getting off the ground, so to speak, and given the current trend for all things Latin they seem pretty likely to continue. Sister to the similarly funky Bar Java in Leith.
Branch: Bar Java 39 Constitution Street, Leith, EH6 (467 7527).

King's Wark
36 The Shore, EH6 (554 9260). Bus 10A, 35, 35A. **Open** noon-11pm Mon-Thur; noon-midnight Fri, Sat; 11am-11pm Sun. **Food served** noon-10pm daily. **Map** p311 Jy.
Considerably older than many of the neighbouring pubs (and they're no spring chickens), the King's Wark is an integral part of Leith and proud of it. Not the kind of place to ask for a Flaming Lamborghini cocktail but the food is quite special.

The Pond
2 Bath Road, EH6 (467 3825). Bus 16, 35, 35A. **Open** 4pm-1am Mon-Thur; 2pm-1am Fri-Sun.
One of Edinburgh's more oddball bars, The Pond could be described as future retro but that would be more than a shade pretentious, which just isn't the place's style. One of the people behind it is Murray, a man who has overseen some of the city's most left-field clubs. There is a car in the pond out the back – if you don't believe us, go and check it out for yourself.

Port O'Leith Bar
58 Constitution Street, EH6 (554 3568). Bus 16. **Open** 9am-12.45am Mon-Sat; 12.30pm-12.45am Sun. **Map** p311 Jz.
A fine Leith tradition – legend has it that this is a home away from home for any old seadog who happens to be in port. No frills, no fuss and lots of steady drinking are the orders from the bridge. It may not be the last word in contemporary design but it is as open and friendly a boozer as you are likely to find anywhere in the city.

The Waterfront Wine Bar & Bistro
1C Dock Place, EH6 (554 7427). Bus 10A, 16. **Open** noon-11pm Mon-Thur; noon-midnight Fri, Sat; 12.30-11pm Sun. **Food served** until 9.30pm daily. **Map** p311 Jy.
A paddle steamer waiting room in a former life, the Waterfront has been converted into a cosy bistro and bar. Nautical charts and other unidentifiable maritime bits are scattered about for a spot of sea-going charm. The food here is very good and the vine-covered conservatory by the water is the best place to eat it.

Shops & Services

Tartan, cashmere and whisky might be what Edinburgh is renowned for, but there's plenty more shopping to be had along the broad streets and narrow wynds.

The traditional charm of shopping in Edinburgh has been threatened by the arrival of national chain stores and out-of-town shopping malls over the past couple of decades. Yet, largely because of the city's idiosyncratic character, city-centre shopping has managed to survive. A myriad of specialist and independent outlets sell everything from broomsticks to Beanie Bears in an atmosphere that can encompass the cosmopolitan, the quaint or the laid-back in the turning of a corner. There's no need to rush around shopping 'til you drop, either, as most shops are concentrated around the centre of the city. Instead, do as the locals do, and wander.

Unsurprisingly, the heart of the capital around **Princes Street** is also the shopping mecca of the city. It helps that the shops are all on the north side of the street, giving shoppers fantastic views of the Castle and Old Town. Once dominated by family-run institutions, of which **Jenners** is the last, proud remnant, this bustling thoroughfare is now home to a mixture of upmarket and high-street names that spill over into the surrounding streets. It's a pleasant place to shop, apart from on Saturday afternoons when it seems as if the entire population of the city has descended en masse in a consumerist frenzy. The traditional elegance of **George Street**, two blocks to the north, offers a welcome respite from the hubbub, with an eclectic range of reassuringly expensive shops. Browsing can be a pleasure in itself, with many shops retaining their original character and charm, yet even the most old-fashioned looking of establishments is far from fuddy-duddy.

Away from the main shopping areas, a kaleidoscopic range of wares can be discovered in the most unlikely of settings, thanks, in particular, to the city's reputation for antiques and second-hand goods. **Thistle Street, Broughton Street, Victoria Street** and **Causewayside** are all home to clusters of fascinating and funky junk shops. Veer off the Rose Street and Royal Mile tourist trails of tacky souvenirs and there are plenty of unusual gift opportunities, especially in **Cockburn Street** and the **Grassmarket**.

Much of the enjoyment of Edinburgh's cosy consumer culture is down to the lingering village feel to many of the areas. Districts such as **Morningside**, **Tollcross** and **Stockbridge** are pretty much self-contained. Residents still do their daily shopping locally and each area has its own grocer, florist, chemist and post office. Butchers' and fishmongers' also continue to survive, despite the sustained growth of vegetarianism, and many are worth visiting just to admire the traditional decor.

The city's attitude to consumerism has relaxed gradually with the adoption of continental flexible trading hours. Most shops are usually open from 9am to 6pm but in recent years many have started to stay open late on Thursdays. And, amid much clerical consternation, Sunday trading has started to creep in, though usually only from noon. Opening times listed below are year-round, but be aware that branches may keep different hours and that many shops stay open longer during the Festival.

Retro Interiors: cool kitsch. *See page 164.*

Antiques

Causewayside

Sciennes, South Edinburgh. Bus 40, 41, 42, 46.
Map p310 H8.

A series of around a dozen antique shops line the first few blocks of this road, which goes south from the west end of the Meadows. Most specialise in pre-'50s furniture but there are also plenty of curios for collectors among the crockery and other ornaments. The wry sign above the Antiques Fine Art Gallery says it all: 'Connoisseurs to the Impecunious Gentry'.

Edinburgh Architectural Salvage Yard

Unit 6, Couper Street, Leith, EH6 (554 7077/ enquire@easy-arch-salv.co.uk/ www.easy-arch-salv.co.uk). Bus 10, 22, 16.
Open 9am-5pm Mon-Sat; closed Sun.
Credit MC, V. **Map** p311 Hy.

A treasure chest of artefacts from a bygone era. Church pews, Victorian rolltop baths and sundials are among the dazzling curiosities in this large warehouse, while the gangways connecting the different floors make it feel like you're navigating the cargo hold of an old sailing ship.

Just Junk

87 Broughton Street, Broughton, EH1 (557 4385/ www.firebelly.demon.co.uk/junk). Bus 8. **Open** 10.30am-6.30pm Tue-Sat; noon-4pm Sun; closed Mon.
Credit MC, V. **Map** p306 F3.

Furniture and clothes from the 1940s to the '60s dominate both the ramshackle exterior and small but neat interior of Just Junk, while the ever-changing window display normally offers at least one eye-catching oddity worth investigating.

Retro Interiors

36 St Mary's Street, Royal Mile, EH1 (558 9090). Bus 24, 25, 35, 35A. **Open** 10.30am-5.30pm Tue-Sat; closed Mon, Sun. **No credit cards. Map** p310 G5.

Undoubtedly the best place for high-quality authentic furnishings from the '50s to the '70s for fans of exotica, kitsch and op-art decor. Most of the stock in the two floors of this attractively laid-out shop is in mint condition, and priced as such, and there are genuine rarities to be found.

Arts & entertainment

Books

There are regular Meet the Author events at **Waterstone's** and **James Thin**, advertised in the shops' window displays and the *List* magazine. Book early for Waterstone's, where even the free events are ticketed (some cost around £2, but this is often redeemable against the book being publicised). James Thin events are usually free and unticketed, but arrive early to ensure entry.

Avizandum

56A Candlemaker Row, South Edinburgh, EH1 (220 3373/elizabeth@avizandum.com). Bus 2, 23, 28, 45.
Open 9.30am-6pm Mon-Fri; 10am-1pm Sat; closed Sun. **Credit** AmEx, MC, V. **Map** p309 F6.

Specialist law bookshop, run by a lawyer, with an encyclopedic stock for professionals and plenty of reference materials and information for non-lawyers.

Bauermeister Booksellers

19 George IV Bridge, South Edinburgh, EH1 (226 5561/enquiries@bauermeister.co.uk). Bus 23, 28, 45.
Open 9am-8pm Mon-Fri; 9am-5.30pm Sat; noon-5pm Sun. **Credit** AmEx, MC, V. **Map** p314 C3.

Tourist guidebooks, maps, magazines, and educational and cut-price fiction titles dominate the two floors of this respectable mainstream bookshop near the Royal Mile.

Beyond Words

42-44 Cockburn Street, Royal Mile, EH1 (226 6636/ info@beyondwords.co.uk/www.beyondwords.co.uk). Bus 7, 8, 21, 31, 80. **Open** 10am-6pm Tue-Sat; noon-5pm Mon, Sun. **Credit** MC, V. **Map** p314 D3.

A small, tranquil shop devoted to photography, useful for finding more off-beat visual mementos of Scotland than the standard tourist titles. Discreet pine benches around the foot of the shelves invite the casual browser.

Body & Soul Bookshop

52 Hamilton Place, Stockbridge, EH3 (226 3066/ info@bodyandsoulbookshop.co.uk/ www.bodyandsoulbooks.com). Bus 35, 35A.
Open 10am-6pm Mon-Sat; *Dec also* 1-5pm Sun.
Credit AmEx, MC, V. **Map** p306 D3.

Relaxed, scented and pleasant shop selling an interesting range of books, magazines, CDs and gifts related to alternative health, New Age spirituality and gay and lesbian lifestyles. Body & Soul also owns *Being*, Scotland's leading mind, body and spirit magazine.

Branch: 166 Bruntsfield Place, South Edinburgh, EH10 (228 6906).

The Cooks Bookshop

118 West Bow, Royal Mile, EH1(226 4445/ www.cooks-book-shop.co.uk). Bus 2, 23, 28, 45.
Open 10.30am-5.30pm Mon-Sat; closed Sun.
Credit AmEx, MC, V. **Map** p314 C3.

Clarissa Dickson-Wright's snug nook of a bookshop is filled with new and second-hand cookery titles covering almost every imaginable edible concoction. Many are connected to her hugely successful *Two Fat Ladies* television cookery programme. A pleasantly ramshackle layout and old-fashioned fireplaces add to the cosy home kitchen feel of the place.

Deadhead Comics

*27 Candlemaker Row, South Edinburgh, EH1 (226 2774/webmaster@monstersquad.co.uk/ www.monstersquad.co.uk). Bus 23, 28, 45.***Open** 10am-6pm Mon-Sat; 12.30-5.30pm Sun.
Credit MC, V. **Map** p309 F6.

Easily recognisable by the luminous yellow exterior,

One-stop shopping

Shopping malls are the same the world over and these ones do their job as well as any. If they should fail, however, there's always the mighty Jenners (*see page 171*).

Cameron Toll

6 Lady Road, South Edinburgh, EH1 (666 2777). Bus 3, 8, 33, 80. **Open** 8am-8pm Mon-Thur, Sat; 8am-10pm Fri; 9am-6pm Sun. **Credit** varies.

Just ten minutes on the bus from Newington, this large shopping complex is dominated by Sainsbury's, but has around 50 other high-street outlets dealing in gifts, household accessories, travel, beauty supplies and fashion.

Gyle Centre

South Gyle Broadway, West Edinburgh, EH12 (539 8828). Bus 22. **Open** 8am-10pm Mon-Fri; 8am-8pm Sat; 9am-7pm Sun. **Credit** varies.

Built to meet the needs of the fast-growing capital, this is a little out of town but easy to find, located as it is on the main route out of the city close to the airport. Chain stores such as Marks & Spencer, Boots and Sainsbury's are laid out along with smaller fashion and gift shops in an airy, attractive and surprisingly intimate mall.

Princes Mall

Princes Street (east end), New Town, EH1 (557 3759). Bus 3, 3A, 12, 16, 17, 80. **Open** 8.30am-6pm Mon-Wed, Fri, Sat; 8.30am-7pm Thur; 11am-5pm Sun; *Festival & Dec* extended hours; phone for details. **Credit** varies. **Map** p314 D2.

Opened on the site of an old fruit and veg market in 1984 as the Waverley Centre,

the mall has a horrible, crude concrete exterior which encroaches vulgarly on to the glorious vista from the east end of Princes Street. Inside, however, it is three bland and airy floors of shop-a-holics delight. Outlets selling designer gear, CDs and bargain books sit alongside one-off shops specialising in Scottish gifts, upmarket jewellery and educational science toys. The ground floor has cafés and fast-food outlets to suit most tastes.

St James Centre

Leith Street, New Town, EH1 (557 0050). Bus 1, 11, 22, 34. **Open** 7.30am-6.30pm Mon-Wed, Fri, Sat; 7.30am-8.30pm Thur; noon-5pm Sun. **Credit** varies. **Map** p307 G4.

It might look like a concrete grey fortress but the St James Centre is undoubtedly handy, set near Waverley Station at the east end of Princes Street. It is accessible from St Andrews Bus Station, there are two entrances on Leith Street and one, over the bridge from Calton Hill. At its heart is John Lewis, but there are dozens of shops that cater for both basic needs and general whims, with smaller outlets of major names dealing in electrical goods, fashion, sports equipment, gifts, stationery and chocolate treats. Photo-booths and business card-printing machines are located near the bus station entrance. Snack food outlets and a seating area upstairs at the Leith Street entrance provide a welcome rest-stop.

Consumer

this friendly comic shop has helpful staff and a large range of Marvel and DC titles, plus fantasy card games and role-playing figures. Especially good for independent and small press titles.

James Thin

53-59 South Bridge, South Edinburgh, EH1 (556 6743/enquiries@jthin.co.uk/www.jamesthin.co.uk). Bus 7, 8, 21, 31, 80. **Open** 9am-10pm Mon, Wed-Fri; 9.30am-10pm Tue; 9am-5.30pm Sat; 11am-5pm Sun. **Credit** AmEx, MC, V. **Map** p310 G6.

Since 1848 Thin's has been a reliable source of mainstream titles across a broad range of educational and recreational subject areas. There are also some cult surprises to be found.
Branches: throughout the city.

McNaughtans

3A Haddington Place, Leith Walk, Broughton, EH7 (556 5897/mcnbooks@globalnet.co.uk). Bus 7, 12, 16. **Open** 9.30am-5.30pm Tue-Sat; closed Mon, Sun. **Credit** MC, V. **Map** p307 G3.

Tucked away at lower-ground level at the top of Leith Walk, this gloomy-looking bookshop is actually full of high-quality second-hand literary treasures. Browsers are welcome.

Tills Bookshop

1 Hope Park Crescent (Buccleuch Street), South Edinburgh, EH8 (667 0895). Bus 40, 42, 46. **Open** noon-7.30pm Mon-Fri; 11am-6pm Sat; noon-5.30pm Sun. **No credit cards.** **Map** p310 G7.

This small, bright shop is a favourite hangout for students and beatniks of all ages. In addition to a

good stock of second-hand philosophy and criticism textbooks you'll find classic and pulp fiction. There's also a well-sussed sideline in original posters from cult films, which line the walls.

Waterstone's

128 Princes Street, New Town, EH2 (226 2666/www.waterstones.co.uk). Bus 3, 3A, 12, 16, 17, 80. **Open** 8.30am-8pm Mon-Sat; 10.30am-7pm Sun. **Credit** AmEx, DC, MC, V. **Map** p314 A2.

Three attractive spacious floors of titles separated into specialist areas, each kept bang up to date by knowledgeable staff who are happy to advise customers. This branch is also home to a Seattle Coffee Company café, which offers fine views of Princes Street Gardens and the Castle.

Branches: 13-14 Princes Street, New Town, EH1 (556 3034); 83 George Street, New Town, EH2 (225 3436).

West Port Books

145 West Port, South Edinburgh, EH1 (229 4431). Bus 2, 28, 28A. **Open** 10.30am-5pm Mon-Fri; 11.30am-5pm Sat; closed Sun. **Credit** MC, V. **Map** p309 E6.

A fantastically labyrinthian second-hand bookshop near the Grassmarket, laid out in a warren of rooms on two floors, and overflowing with second-hand and remaindered books, classical records and sheet titles. Especially good for art books.

Word Power

43 West Nicolson Street, South Edinburgh, EH8 (662 9112). Bus 7, 8, 21, 31, 80. **Open** 10am-6pm Mon-Fri; 10.30am-6pm Sat; *Dec also* noon-4pm Sun. **Credit** AmEx, MC, V. **Map** p310 G6.

The only radical bookshop in Edinburgh, and well-established as a vibrant centre for the capital's alternative writing scene. Holds an extensive stock of women's, gay and alternative books, magazines and fanzines packed into a small but bright space. The owner also hosts the Radical Book Fair every year around the middle of May.

Music & video

Alphabet Video

22 Marchmont Road, South Edinburgh, EH9 (229 5136). Bus 24, 40, 41. **Open** 2-10pm Mon-Fri, Sun; noon-midnight Sat. **No credit cards**. **Map** p309 F8.

Excellent selection of mainstream, independent, classic and cult films from £1 for a two-day hire. To to become a video club member (£5 charge), take along two bits of ID with your name and address. If the film you want is not listed among the 4,000 titles in stock, Mark Alphabet will happily try and search it out for you. Beautiful tropical fish add to the pleasure of browsing in this idiosyncratic shop.

Avalanche

17 West Nicolson Street, South Edinburgh, EH8 (668 2374/avalanche.records@virgin.net/ www.avalancherecords.co.uk). Bus 7, 8, 21, 31, 80. **Open** 10am-6pm Mon-Sat; noon-6pm Sun. **Credit** MC, V. **Map** p310 G6.

Kevin Buckle's record shop opened in 1983 and is now a Scottish indie institution, with an eclectic budget range of new and second-hand vinyl and CDs. Especially good for more obscure finds, and particularly devoted to New Zealand bands.

Branches: 28 Lady Lawson Street, South Edinburgh, EH3 (228 1939); 63 Cockburn Street, Royal Mile, EH1 (225 3939).

Backbeat

31 East Crosscauseway, South Edinburgh, EH8 (668 2666). Bus 7, 8, 21, 31, 80. **Open** 10am-5.30pm Mon-Sat; 12.30pm-6.30pm Sun. **Credit** MC, V. **Map** p310 G7.

Collectors of rare vinyl and obscure CD re-issues will gasp in amazement at this mecca of aural delights hidden away behind Clerk Street. Frequent trips abroad by the owner ensure that there is always a huge selection of quality jazz, soul, blues, '60s and '70s sounds from around the world, yet the prices are easily within any visitor's budget.

FOPP

55 Cockburn Street, Royal Mile, EH1 (220 0133/ www.fopp.co.uk). Bus 7, 8, 21, 31, 80. **Open** 9.30am-7pm Mon-Sat; 11am-6pm Sun. **Credit** AmEx, DC, MC, V. **Map** p314 D3.

This bright, modern shop has a reputation for indie and dance vinyl and CDs, but is also excellent for jazz, soul, ska and world music sounds, with plenty of special offers among the two floors of well-organised stock.

Ripping Music & Tickets

91 South Bridge, Royal Mile, EH1 (226 7010). Bus 7, 8, 21, 31, 80. **Open** 9.30am-6.30pm Mon-Wed, Fri; 9am-7pm Thur; 9am-Sat; noon-5.30pm Sun. **Credit** MC, V. **Map** p314 D3.

Tickets for rock and pop gigs in Edinburgh and Glasgow are available here. There's an additional 50p booking fee on every ticket bought.

Uber-Disko

36 Cockburn Street, Royal Mile, EH1 (226 2134). Bus 7, 8, 21, 31, 80. **Open** 10am-6pm Mon-Sat; noon-4pm Sun. **Credit** AmEx, MC, V. **Map** p314 D3.

Small, sparse and sometimes intimidating, but this is a well-respected name for house and techno sounds nonetheless.

Underground Solushun

9 Cockburn Street, Royal Mile, EH1 (226 2242/ www.earcandy.co.uk). Bus 7, 8, 21, 31, 80. **Open** 10am-6pm Mon-Wed, Sat; 10am-7pm Thur, Fri; noon-5pm Sun. **Credit** MC, V. **Map** p314 D3.

Unbeatable for vinyl dance imports, with a huge choice of house, garage, techno and jungle sounds. The staff are happy to answer your questions, play requests and give tips for a top night of clubbing.

Virgin Megastore

124-125 Princes Street, New Town, EH2 (220 2230/edinburgh.virgin@virgin.net). Bus 3, 3A, 12, 16, 17. **Open** 9am-6pm Mon, Wed, Fri, Sat; 9.30am-6pm Tue; 9am-8pm Thur; 11am-6pm Sun. **Credit** AmEx, MC, V. **Map** p314 A2.

Consumer

Sounds good

Recent years have seen a boom in Scottish folk music, with bands like Martyn Bennett and Capercaillie introducing a worldwide dance music audience to the sounds of such traditional Celtic instruments as the fiddle and the pipes. Of course, you could simply enjoy this type of music at one of the many folk nights around the city (*see pages 207-208*), or indeed just watch the pipers in any of the popular tourist spots, but for those who want to take a piece of Scotland's musical culture home with them, and perhaps impress (or scare) friends and neighbours, there are several good places to find out more.

Bagpipes Galore

118 Canongate, Royal Mile, EH8 (556 4073/ www.bagpipe.co.uk). Bus 35, 35A. **Open** 9.30am-5.30pm Mon-Sat; *June-Aug also* noon-4pm Sun. **Credit** AmEx, MC, V. **Map** p310 G5.

Ideal for both beginners and experts, with a huge range of new and second-hand pipes ranging from plain models from £550 up to lavish old-fashioned ivory makes. It's also a good place to come for accessories, including a comprehensive selection of reeds and Gore-tex pipe bags. The starter tutor kit is especially good value, with a chanter for £20 and accompanying book and CD for £10, while those who feel a bit more adventurous can try the practice pipes at £97.

Blackfriars Folk Music Shop

49 Blackfriars Street, Royal Mile, EH1 (557 3090/scotfolk@compuserve.com/ www.scotfolk.org). Bus 35, 35A. **Open** 9.30am-5.30pm Mon-Sat; *Dec* Sun also noon-4pm. **Credit** AmEx, MC, V. **Map** p310 G5.

An intriguing range of bagpipes, bodhrans, fiddles, harps, whistles, recordings, sheet music, accessories and magazines fill this small, neat and unassuming shop. Staff are knowledgeable about all aspects of traditional music, and can advise on anything from which type of instrument to choose to ideas for tunes.

Mev Taylors

212 Morrison Street, West Edinburgh, EH3 (229 7454/mevtaylors@aol.com/ www.mevtaylors.co.uk). Bus 3, 3A, 12, 25. **Open** 9.30am-5.30pm Mon-Sat; closed Sun. **Credit** AmEx, MC, V. **Map** p308 C6.

As well as being Scotland's biggest saxophone centre, this well-known music shop features a wide range of fiddles and smaller ceilidh-size accordions, as well as penny whistles and a good selection of mainstream folk sheet music.

Rae MacIntosh

6 Queensferry Street, New Town, EH2 (225 1171). Bus 13, 19, 55, 82. **Open** 9am-5.30pm Mon-Fri; 9am-5pm Sat; closed Sun. **Credit** AmEx, MC, V. **Map** p308 C5.

Three floors of records, CDs, videos and games slap bang in the centre of town. It's the largest selection in the city, but also the most expensive. Virgin also sells tickets for rock and pop gigs (credit card bookings: 220 3234).

Sport & outdoor

Blacks Outdoor Leisure

13-14 Elm Row, Broughton, EH7 (556 3491/ www.blacks.co.uk). Bus 7, 12, 17. **Open** 9.30am-6pm Mon, Wed, Fri; 10am-6pm Tue; 9.30am-7pm Thur; 9am-5.30pm Sat; *Dec also* noon-5pm Sun. **Credit** AmEx, MC, V. **Map** p306 G3.

Trendy rucksacks, clothes and equipment for hikers, skiers and ramblers are sold in this two-floor emporium. The tent department is especially worth checking out.

Branch: 24 Frederick Street, New Town, EH2 (225 8686).

Millets

12 Frederick Street, New Town, EH2 (220 1551). Bus 28, 29, 29A, 80. **Open** 9am-5.30pm Mon-Wed, Fri, Sat; 9am-6.30pm Thur; *Festival & Dec also* 11.30am-5pm Sun. **Credit** AmEx, MC, V. **Map** p314 B1.

City-centre outlet with an excellent range of budget-priced outdoor gear – especially tents and rucksacks – on two floors.

Tiso

115-123 Rose Street, New Town, EH2 (225 9486/ mail@tiso.co.uk/www.tiso.co.uk). Bus 3, 3A, 12, 16, 17. **Open** 9.30am-5.30pm Mon, Wed, Fri, Sat; 10am-5.30pm Tue; 9.30am-7.30pm Thur; noon-5pm Sun. **Credit** AmEx, MC, V. **Map** p314 B1.

Four floors of outdoor, sports and survival equipment, clothes and accessories. A popular outlet for pros but also ideal for beginners, with knowledge-able, helpful staff.

Branch: 41 Commercial Street, Leith, EH6 (554 0804).

Piping up: Scottish music is booming.

Well-priced chanters, bodhrans and penny whistles are among the eclectic range of instruments available to try and buy in this invitingly cosy shop. The main attraction is the large, well-organised stock of sheet music, spanning sounds from obscure reels to modern folk heroes such as Aly Bain. The approachable staff are happy to help if you want to find a certain piece, even if you can only hum a few bars of it.

Varsity Music

8A-10A Nicolson Street, South Edinburgh, EH8 (0800 614151). Bus 7, 8, 21, 31, 80. **Open** 9am-5.30pm Mon-Sat; closed Sun. **Credit** AmEx, DC, V. **Map** p310 G6.
A good selection of accordions from £200, fiddles from £70, fiddle and popular ceilidh collection music, as well as fiddle tuition books.

Toys & games

Aha Ha Ha

99 West Bow, Royal Mile, EH1 (220 5252). Bus 2, 23, 28, 45. **Open** 10am-6pm Mon-Sat; *Festival & Dec also* noon-4pm Sun. **Credit** AmEx, MC, V. **Map** p314 C3.
The oversized Groucho moustache and glasses over the front door are only the tip of the chuckles to be found in this cheap and infinitely cheerful shop. Jokes, novelties, disguises and trashy wigs fill the bright interior.

Balloon & Party Shop

3 Viewforth Gardens, off Bruntsfield Place, South Edinburgh, EH10 (229 9686/ www.balloonandparty.co.uk). Bus 11, 16, 17, 23. **Open** 10am-6pm Mon-Fri; 10am-5.30pm Sat; noon-4pm Sun. **Credit** AmEx, MC, V. **Map** p309 D8.
Unassuming small outlet selling banners and all

manner of balloons and accessories to make your party go with a swing. A useful decoration service is also available.

Early Learning Centre

67-79 Shandwick Place, West Edinburgh, EH2 (228 3244/www.elc.co.uk). Bus 3, 3A, 12, 25, 25A. **Open** 9am-5.30pm Mon-Sat; noon-4pm Sun. **Credit** AmEx, MC, V. **Map** p308 C5.
Safe, educational and well-priced toys, games and playsets for tots, toddlers and pre-pubescents. There's even a play area for the kids (and no doubt their parents) to test them out. Especially good for children's art equipment.
Branches: 61 St James Centre, New Town, EH1 (558 1330); Gyle Shopping Centre, South Gyle Broadway, West Edinburgh, EH12 (538 7172).

Games Workshop

136 High Street, Royal Mile, EH1 (220 6540/ www.games-workshop.com). Bus 35, 35A. **Open** 10am-6pm Mon, Tue; 10am-8pm Wed, Thur; 10am-6pm Fri, Sat; 10am-6pm Sun; *Dec also* open daily from 9am. **Credit** MC, V. **Map** p314 D3.
War-gaming figures and accessories plus regular workshops and battle enactments on a table-top fantasy kingdom.

Monkey Business

167 Morrison Street, West Edinburgh, EH3 (228 6636). Bus 3, 12, 25, 25A. **Open** 10am-5.30pm Mon-Sat; closed Sun. **No credit cards. Map** p308 C6.
Bouncy castles available for hire from £50 per day, with free delivery, set-up and collection. Also on offer are fancy dress hire, fireworks and a smaller selection of jokes, novelties, wigs and masks.

Toys Galore

193 Morningside Road, South Edinburgh, EH10 (447 1006). Bus 11, 16, 17, 23. **Open** *Jan, Feb* 9am-5pm Mon-Sat; *Mar-Dec* 9am-5.30pm Mon-Sat; closed Sun. **Credit** AmEx, MC, V.
Choc-a-bloc full of top toy names, all at pocket-money prices.

Wonderland

97 Lothian Road, South Edinburgh, EH3 (229 6428/www.wonderlandmodels.com). Bus 11, 15, 24. **Open** 9.30am-6pm Mon-Fri; 9am-6pm Sat; *Dec also*

Aha Ha Ha – just one big joke.

Consumer

Cashmere
Soft, sensual and hard wearing.

Caithness crystal
Glass, cut to let the light glisten.

Clan tartans
Rugs are great, but kilts are better.

Rare malt whiskies
A single malt at cask strength is unique.

Selkirk bannock
The scrummy teacake from the Borders town.

Haggis
Well, if you can't catch one yourself...

---

noon-5pm Sun. **Credit** AmEx, MC, V. **Map** p314 A3.
A paradise for kids of all ages, with a breathtaking range of model cars, trains and planes, plus horror, sci-fi and cult favourite action figures.

Auctions

Christies, Scotland
5 Wemyss Place, New Town, EH3 (225 4756/ www.christies.com). Bus 13, 19, 55, 82. **Open** 9am-1pm, 2-5pm Mon-Fri; closed Sat, Sun. **No credit cards. Map** p306 D4.
Antiques and paintings auctioned at various times and dates, usually listed in the window. Free auction estimates as well as advice on probate and insurance valuations are also offered.

Curiosity shops

The Edinburgh Dolls House Shop
44 Leven Street, Tollcross, South Edinburgh, EH1 (622 7890/www.intermart.co.uk/dollshouse). Bus 11, 16, 17, 23. **Open** 10am-5.30pm Mon-Sat; closed Sun. **Credit** AmEx, MC, V. **Map** p309 D7.
A miniaturised world of painted and unpainted dolls' houses and accessories to go with them. A decorating service is also available.

The Jolly Roger
137 Rose Street, New Town EH2 (226 3497). Bus 3, 3A, 12, 16, 17 **Open** 9.30am-5.30pm Mon-Sat; closed Sun. **Credit** MC, V. **Map** p314 B1.
Household accessories, games and beautiful ornaments in brass and wood for the sailing enthusiast.

Mr Wood's Fossils
5 Cowgatehead, Grassmarket, EH1 (220 1344/ mwfossils@cablenet.co.uk/ www.mrwoodsfossils.co.uk). Bus 2, 23, 28, 45. **Open** 10am-5.30pm Mon-Sat; closed Sun. **Credit** AmEx, MC, V. **Map** p314 C3.
A low-key alternative treasure trove of archaeological fossils and crystals to decorate the home.

The Pipe Shop
92 Leith Walk, Leith, EH6 (553 3561/ alan@thepipeshop.co.uk/www.thepipeshop.co.uk). Bus 7, 12, 16. **Open** 8.45am-6pm Mon-Sat; closed Sun. **Credit** AmEx, MC, V. **Map** p307 J1.

This well-established, down-to-earth puffer's paradise sells pipes, cigarettes and tobaccos. Its cigars come from Cuba, Honduras and other countries.

Robert Cresser
40 Victoria Street, Royal Mile, EH1 (225 2181). Bus 23, 28, 45. **Open** 9.30am-5pm Mon-Sat (*Festival* open until 6.30pm); closed Sun. **No credit cards. Map** p314 C3.
Generations of Edinburgh families have bought their brushes and brooms at Robert Cresser, and the dark Dickensian interior and product list have barely changed in over a century.

Wind Things
11 Cowgatehead, Grassmarket, South Edinburgh, EH1 (622 7032/shop@windthings.co.uk/ www.windthings.co.uk). Bus 2. **Open** 10am-5.30pm Mon-Sat; *Festival & Dec also* 10am-5.30pm Sun. **Credit** AmEx, MC, V. **Map** p314 C3.
All kinds of kites, circus props and practical guides as to their use.

Department stores

Most of the major department stores – Debenhams, Frasers, Marks & Spencer, Bhs and Boots – are on Princes Street, but **Jenners**, the grand old man of the main city drag, undoubtedly towers above the rest, with its mock-classical façade and several floors of luxury clothes, toys, food, beauty products and household accessories. For everyday quality goods, **John Lewis**, accessible either from within the St James Centre or from Leith Street at the east end of Princes Street, is the local favourite. The store prides itself on its service and prices, whether you're after a hi-fi or a bin.

Bhs
64 Princes Street, New Town, EH2 (226 2621). Bus 3, 3A, 12, 16, 17, 80. **Open** 9am-5.30pm Mon-Wed; 9am-8pm Thur; 9am-6pm Fri, Sat; noon-5pm Sun. **Credit** AmEx, MC, V. **Map** p314 C2.

Debenhams
109-112 Princes Street, New Town, EH2 (225 1320/www.debenhams.com). Bus 3, 3A, 12, 16, 17. **Open** 9.30am-6pm Mon-Wed; 9.30am-8pm Thur;

9.30am-7pm Fri; 9am-6pm Sat; noon-5pm Sun (hours vary according to season). **Credit** AmEx, DC, MC, V. **Map** p314 B2.

Frasers
145 Princes Street, New Town, EH2 (225 2472). Bus 3, 3A, 12, 16, 17. **Open** 9am-5.30pm Mon-Wed, Fri; 9am-7.30pm Thur; 9am-6pm Sat; 11am-5.30pm Sun. **Credit** AmEx, MC, V. **Map** p314 A2.

John Lewis
69 St James Centre, New Town, EH1 (556 9121/ www.johnlewis.co.uk). Bus 1, 11, 22, 34. **Open** 9am-5.30pm Tue, Wed, Fri; 9am-7.30pm Thur; 9am-6pm Sat; closed Mon, Sun; Dec hours vary; phone for details.* **Credit** MC, V. **Map** p306 G4.

Marks & Spencer
53 Princes Street, New Town, EH2 (225 2301/ www.marks-and-spencer.co.uk). Bus 3, 3A, 12, 16, 17, 80. **Open** 9.30am-5.30pm (*food* 7am-7.30pm) Mon, Tue; 9.30am-5pm (*food* 7am-7.30pm) Wed; 9am-8am Thur; 9am-6pm (*food* 9am-7pm) Fri; 9am-6pm Sat; noon-5pm Sun. **No credit cards.** **Map** p314 C2.
This branch has menswear, childrenswear and food. **Branches**: 21 Gyle Avenue, EH12 (317 1333); *homeware* 104 Princes Street, New Town, EH2 (225 5765); *womenswear* 91 Princes Street, New Town, EH2 (225 2301).

Jenners
48 Princes Street, New Town, EH2 (225 2442). Bus 3, 3A, 12, 16, 17, 80. **Open** 9.30am-5.30pm (*food* 7pm) Mon, Tue; 9am-5.30pm (*food* 7pm) Wed; 9am-8pm Thur; 9am-6pm (*food* 7pm) Fri, Sat; noon-5pm Sun (hours vary according to season; phone for details). **Credit** AmEx, DC, MC, V. **Map** p314 C2.
Opened in 1895, this is the world's oldest independent store, and famously known as the Harrods of Scotland. With six stately floors of merchandise including international designerwear, a huge toy department and a food hall replete with exquisite Scottish and international delicacies, as well as facilities including a hairdresser's, beauty salon, photographic studio and posting facilities, it's almost a self-contained village and easily a day trip in itself.

Fashion

Big Ideas
96 West Bow, Grassmarket, Royal Mile, EH1 (226 2532/www.bigideasforladies.co.uk). Bus 2, 23, 28, 45. **Open** 10am-5.30pm Mon-Sat; closed Sun. **Credit** AmEx, MC, V. **Map** p314 C3.
A stock of upmarket continental labels provides a refreshingly bright and eye-catching range of daytime and eveningwear for women of size 16 and upwards. Don't miss the permanent sale rails in the branch down the road at 116 West Bow (220 4656), which also has a further range of casualwear.

Corniche
2 Jeffrey Street, Royal Mile, EH1 (556 3707/ nina@corniche.fsbusiness.co.uk). Bus 24, 35, 35A. **Open** 10am-5.30pm Mon-Sat; *Festival & Dec also*

noon-4pm Sun. **Credit** AmEx, MC, V. **Map** p310 G5.
The quietly hip ethnic decor of this spacious outlet complements a discerning range of women's designerwear by the likes of Vivienne Westwood, Jean-Paul Gaultier and Alexander McQueen. Keep an eye out for the regular end-of-line specials.
Branch: *menswear* 12 Jeffrey Street EH1 (557 8333).

Crombie Retail Ltd
63 George Street, New Town, EH2 (226 1612/ www.crombie.co.uk). Bus 13, 19, 55, 82. **Open** 9am-5.30pm Mon-Wed, Fri; 9am-7pm Thur; 9am-6pm Sat; closed Sun. **Credit** AmEx, MC, V. **Map** p314 C1.
Renowned worldwide for almost 200 years for the classic Crombie coat, beloved of American presidents, teddy boys and the characters in *Lock, Stock & Two Smoking Barrels*, the oak-panelled elegance of this gentlemen's outfitters sums up the classic, genteel appeal of the city. A Crombie, either single or double-breasted, will set you back £495. The refined atmosphere and service, however, cannot be priced.

Cruise
14 St Mary's Street, Royal Mile, EH1 (556 2532). Bus 24, 35, 35A. **Open** 10am-6pm Mon-Wed, Fri; 10am-7pm Thur; 9am-6pm Sat; 1-5pm Sun. **Credit** AmEx, DC, MC, V. **Map** p310 G5.
With designers such as Stone Island, Armani, Dolce & Gabbana and Hugo Boss – and prices to match – it's no wonder that this well-established outlet is

Mr Wood's Fossils. *See page 170.*

Consumer

TimeOut

'THE GREATEST LONDON AUTHORITY'

www.timeout.com

a favourite with both well-heeled clubbers and upmarket hipsters. Would-be fashion victims will also love the minimalist, whitewashed surroundings and pampered service.
Branch: 94 George Street, New Town, EH1 (226 3524).

Cult Clothing

7-9 North Bridge, Royal Mile, EH1 (556 5003). Bus 7, 8, 21, 31, 80. **Open** 9.30am-6pm Mon-Wed, Fri, Sat; 10am-7pm Thur; noon-5pm Sun. **Credit** AmEx, MC, V. **Map** p314 D2.
Possibly the hippest of the clubwear shops in Edinburgh, and the loudest, with a thumping instore soundtrack to match the trendy Custard Shop, Addict, Carhartt and Mambo gear. Prices, however, are affordable. Combat trousers start at around £20.

Karen Millen

53 George Street, New Town, EH2 (220 1589/ enquiries@karenmillen.co.uk). Bus 13, 19, 55, 82. **Open** 10am-6pm Mon-Wed, Fri, Sat; 10am-7pm Thur; noon-5pm Sun. **Credit** AmEx, DC, MC, V. **Map** p314 B1.
Gorgeous dresses, jumpers and coats from the London-based designer in minimalist whitewashed surroundings.

Momentum Surf Shop

22 Bruntsfield Place, South Edinburgh, EH10 (229 6665/momentum@surfzone.co.uk/ www.commercepark.co.uk/momentum). Bus 11, 16, 17, 23. **Open** 10am-6pm Mon-Sat; *Festival & Dec* also 10am-6pm Sun. **Credit** MC, V. **Map** p309 D8.
Well-priced, high-quality skateboarding and surf-wear for fashion-conscious sporty types.

Pie in the Sky

21 Cockburn Street, Royal Mile, EH1 (220 1477/ pieskylim@aol.com). Bus 7, 8, 21, 31, 80. **Open** 9.30am-6pm Mon-Wed, Fri; 9.30am-7pm Thur; 9.30am-6pm Sat; noon-5pm Sun. **Credit** AmEx, MC, V. **Map** p314 D3.
Well-established student haunt close to Waverley Station specialising in cheap tie-dye and rainbow clothes, hats, bags, jewellery and incense.

Sheeps Clothing For Ewe

46 High Street, Royal Mile, EH1 (557 9721/ jennifer@bhanley.freeserve.co.uk). Bus 35, 35A. **Open** *Oct-Apr* 10am-6pm daily; *May-Sept* 10am-8pm daily. **Credit** AmEx, DC, MC, V. **Map** p310 G5.
One of the few Scottish outlets stocking the N Peal and Barrie designer cashmere labels, and exclusive in Edinburgh. High-quality cashmere garments, plus Kangol hats, wraps and a popular range of Celtic jewellery complete the picture.

TK Maxx

Meadowbank Retail Park, London Road, EH7 (661 6611). Bus 5, 15, 19, 26. **Open** 10am-8pm Mon-Fri; 9am-6pm Sat; 11am-5pm Sun. **Credit** AmEx, MC, V.
A massive warehouse of end-of-line bargain-priced stock from names such as Prada and Red or Dead. Raking through the rails nearly always pays off.

Jenners – an institution. *See page 171.*

Children

New & Junior Profile

88-92 Raeburn Place, Stockbridge, EH4 (332 7928). Bus 28, 29, 29A, 80. **Open** 9am-5.30pm Mon-Sat; closed Sun. **Credit** MC, V. **Map** p305 C3.
Pretty and practical clothes in bright colours and folksy designs for babies to eight-year-olds, all at mid-range prices.

Shoos

8 Teviot Place, South Edinburgh, EH1 (220 4626). Bus 23, 28, 40, 45. **Open** 9.30am-5pm Mon-Fri; 9am-5.30pm Sat; closed Sun. **Credit** MC, V. **Map** p309 F6.
Small shop specialising in Start-Rite shoes.

Topsy Turvy

18 William Street, New Town, EH3 (225 2643). Bus 3, 3A, 12, 25, 25A. **Open** 10am-5pm Mon; 9.30am-5.30pm Tue-Sat; closed Sun. **Credit** AmEx, MC, V. **Map** p308 C6.
A cosy West End outlet with tots-to-teens designer clothes from Germany, France and Holland.

Dress hire

Highland Laddie

6 Hutchison Terrace, South Edinburgh, EH14 (455 7505). Slateford rail. **Open** 9.30am-5pm Mon-Sat; closed Sun. **No credit cards**.
Tartan for men and children with good, old-fashioned service and attention to detail. Expect to pay around £50 for a full adult outfit – jacket, waistcoat

Consumer

and shoes – while a miniaturised version for kids is from £32-£40.
Branch: Highlander 30-32 Haymarket Terrace, South Edinburgh, EH3 (313 2863).

McCalls of the Royal Mile

11 High Street, Royal Mile, EH1 (557 3979/ freephone 0800 056 3056). Bus 35, 35A. **Open** 9am-5.30pm Mon-Wed, Fri, Sat; 9am-7.30pm Thur; noon-4pm Sun; closed Tue. **Credit** AmEx, MC, V. **Map** p310 G5.
Hires out Highland dress for children, with a toybox available to keep them amused. Set price of £29.50 for everything bar the shirt and insurance.

No.19

19 Grassmarket, Royal Mile, EH1 (225 7391). Bus 35, 35A. **Open** 10.30am-5.30pm Mon-Sat; closed Sun. **Credit** AmEx, DC, MC, V. **Map** p314 B3.
All the upmarket evening dresses here are one-off designs, made on the premises and available for three-day hire from £60.

Fetish

Leather & Lace

8 Drummond Street, South Edinburgh, EH8 (557 9413). Bus 7, 8, 21, 31, 80. **Open** 10am-9pm Mon-Sat; noon-9pm Sun. **Credit** MC, V. **Map** p310 G6.
Home to a wide range of magazines, toys and equipment for those with an ever-active imagination to match their ever-active bedroom lives. If the knotty problem of restraint comes up, the friendly staff can point you in the right direction. Big video section.

Whiplash Trash

53 Cockburn Street, Royal Mile, EH1 (226 1005). Bus 7, 8, 21, 31, 80. **Open** 10.30am-5.30pm Mon-Wed, Fri, Sat; 10.30am-6pm Thur; closed Sun. **No credit cards. Map** p314 D3.
Good range of PVC, leather and rubber gear.

Jewellery

Hamilton & Inches

87 George Street, New Town, EH2 (225 4898/ www.hamiltonandinches.com). Bus 13, 19, 55, 82. **Open** 9.30am-5.30pm Mon-Fri, 9.30am-5pm Sat; closed Sun. **Credit** AmEx, MC, V. **Map** p314 B1.
The reputation of this upmarket jeweller's, which opened in 1866, recently gained it the patronage of none other than Tiffany of New York. The late-Georgian interior, with its gilded columns and ornate plasterwork, is just as awe-inspiring as the glittering gems themselves.

Joseph Bonnar

72 Thistle Street, New Town, EH2 (226 2811). Bus 13, 19, 55, 82. **Open** 10.30am-5pm Mon-Sat; closed Sun. **Credit** MC, V. **Map** p314 C1.
Renowned antique jeweller with an extensive selection in elegant and intimate velvet surroundings. Prices range from around £50 up to £20,000.

Scottish Gems

24 High Street, Royal Mile, EH1 (557 5731). Bus 35, 35A. **Open** *June-Aug* 10am-6pm Mon-Sat; 11am-4pm Sun; *Sept-May* 10am-5.30pm Mon-Sat; closed Sun. **Credit** AmEx, DC, MC, V. **Map** p310 G5.
Modern Scottish jewellery including well-crafted Celtic wedding rings from £20.
Branch: 162 Morningside Road, South Edinburgh, EH10 (447 5579).

Second-hand

15 The Grassmarket

15 Grassmarket, South Edinburgh, EH1 (226 3087). Bus 2. **Open** noon-6pm Mon-Fri; 10.30am-5.30pm Sat; closed Sun; *Festival* noon-8pm Mon-Sat; 2-6pm Sun. **No credit cards. Map** p309 E6.
This small cavern-like shop offers period lace, linen and velvet curtains, in addition to pre-1950s men's suits, tweed jackets and an impressive selection of trilby hats.

WM Armstrong & Son

83 Grassmarket, South Edinburgh, EH1 (220 5557/ bren@nathans.demon.co.uk). Bus 2, 23, 28, 45. **Open** 10am-5.30pm Mon-Thur; 10am-6pm Fri, Sat; noon-6pm Sun. **Credit** MC, V. **Map** p314 C3.
The oldest second-hand shop in the capital was originally set up as a gentlemen's outfitter in the Cowgate in 1840, but is now the city's leading retrowear chain, despite the emphasis on quantity rather than quality. New stock arrives daily and prices start from £15 for evening dresses, £10 for jeans, and £15 for a leather jacket, £20 for cashmere sweaters; it also stocks kiltwear. The Rusty Zip outlet sometimes offers one-off, half-price, one-day sales.
Branches: 313 Cowgate, South Edinburgh, EH1 (556 5977); 64-66 Clerk St, South Edinburgh, EH8 (667 3056); **Rusty Zip** 14 Teviot Place, South Edinburgh, EH1 (226 4634).

Flip of Hollywood

59-61 South Bridge, South Edinburgh, EH1 (556 4966). Bus 7, 8, 21, 31, 80. **Open** 9.30am-5.30pm Mon-Wed; 9.30am-6pm Thur-Sat; *Festival also* noon-5pm Sun. **Credit** MC, V. **Map** p310 G6.
This branch of the national chain of American clothing shops has seen better days, but is still worth checking out for the extensive range of well-priced second-hand jeans, cords, cowboy shirts and suede jackets.

Herman Brown

151 West Port, South Edinburgh, EH1 (228 2589). Bus 2, 28, 28A. **Open** noon-6pm Mon-Sat; closed Sun. **Credit** AmEx, MC, V. **Map** p309 E6.
The decorative kitsch bric-a-brac and lamps are as much of a feature as the well-made clothes in this classy retro shop. Prices start from around £3 for tops and less than £10 for dresses, while authentic period items cost more. An eye-catching range of quirky jewellery and a good selection of bags and accessories should complete that perfect outfit.

A fishy business

With a coastal setting on the Firth of Forth, it's no surprise that the capital has a reputation for seafood. In times gone by, the fishing villages along the coast, primarily the port of Leith, brought in their hauls from the North Sea and the fishwives of Newhaven would bring the fresh catch up to Edinburgh every morning to sell at the kitchen doors of the houses of the well-to-do. Salmon was a dish for the poor and something like two million oysters were harvested every year from the oyster beds in the Firth. Although the fishing villages are gone, the fishing industry is in decline and North Sea fish stocks are depleted, the reputation remains. It is enhanced by the old-fashioned charm of many of the remaining fishmongers around town, some of which retain their original 1930s decor.

Carnies Fish

75 Nicolson Street, South Edinburgh, EH8 (668 2900). Bus 7, 8, 21, 31, 80. **Open** *5am-6pm Tue-Sat; closed Mon, Sun.* **No credit cards. Map** *p310 G6.*
A clean, bright modern shop, but full of character, especially the staff. Fresh catches come in from all over Scotland every day.

Eddie's Seafood Market

7 Roseneath Street, South Edinburgh, EH9 (229 4207). Bus 24, 40, 41 41A. **Open** *8.30am-6pm Tue-Sat; closed Mon, Sun.* **No credit cards. Map** *p309 F8.*
A large, bright minimalist shop, full of the bustle and noise of a real market, thanks to the ever-vocal staff. Its fish is fresh and the range wide.

George Armstrong

80 Raeburn Place, Stockbridge, EH4 (315 2033). Bus 28, 29, 29A, 80. **Open** *7am-5.30pm Mon-Fri; 7am-5pm Sat; closed Sun.* **No credit cards. Map** *p305 C3.*
Specialists in smoked salmon and all-local catches, but it also imports swordfish and other upmarket varieties from as far away as Ecuador.

Neptunes

23 Leven Street, South Edinburgh, EH3 (229 2160). Bus 11, 16, 17, 23. **Open** *8am-5.30pm Tue-Fri; 8am-5pm Sat; closed Mon, Sun.* **No credit cards. Map** *p309 D7.*
An art deco seafood specialist with a range of fish as colourful and exotic as the fish nets and bright plastic lobsters that decorate it.

Something Fishy

16A Broughton Street, Broughton, EH1 (556 7614). Bus 8. **Open** *7am-6pm Tue-Sat (phone to check); closed Mon, Sun.* **No credit cards. Map** *p306 F3.*
The queue often stretches out of the door of this authentic '30s shop. The locals know it as the place for fresh supplies of mainstays.

Shoes

Barnets Shoes

7 High Street, Royal Mile, EH1 (556 3577). Bus 24, 35, 35A. **Open** *9am-5.15pm Mon-Sat; closed Sun.* **Credit** *AmEx, MC, V.* **Map** *p310 G5.*
Small and low-key, this is an unassuming purveyor of high-quality workwear and outdoor shoes and boots at budget prices. Possibly the ultimate recommendation – in terms of comfort at least – is that this is where the local traffic wardens shop for their shoes.

Schuh

6 Frederick Street, New Town, EH2 (220 0290/ www.schuh.co.uk). Bus 28, 29, 29A, 80. **Open** *9am-6pm Mon-Wed; 9am-8pm Thur; 9am-6pm Fri, Sat; noon-5pm Sun.* **Credit** *AmEx, MC, V.* **Map** *p314 B1.*
The large central outlet of this popular Scottish chain has a fantastic range of trendy own-make and brand-name shoes, boots and trainers, including many outrageous styles. This is the place to go if you need either a pair of purple velvet, 16-hole Docs or red, patent leather thigh-high boots. Look out for the price-slashing winter and summer sales.
Branch: 32 North Bridge, Royal Mile, EH2 (225 6552).

Specialist

Edinburgh Woollen Mill

453 Lawnmarket, Royal Mile, EH1 (225 1525). Bus 35, 35A. **Open** *Jan-Mar 9.30am-5.30pm Mon-Sat; 11am-5pm Sun; Apr-Dec 9am-7pm Mon-Fri; 9am-6pm Sat; 11am-5pm Sun.* **Credit** *AmEx, MC, V.* **Map** *p314 C3.*
Well-established woollenwear outlet, with branches scattered around the city, selling good-quality

Consumer

traditional clothes, shawls, rugs and scarves, all at affordable prices.
Branches: 62 Princes Street, New Town, EH2 (225 4966); 139 Princes Street, New Town, EH2 (226 3840).

Kinloch Anderson

Commercial Street/Dock Street, Leith, EH6 (555 1390/enquiries@kinlochanderson.com/ www.kinlochanderson.com). Bus 10, 16, 22. **Open** *mid-Oct to mid-Apr* 9am-5pm Mon-Sat; closed Sun; *mid-Apr to mid-Oct* 9am-5.30pm Mon-Sat; closed Sun. **Credit** AmEx, DC, MC, V. **Map** p311 Jy.
Renowned since 1868 as makers and retailers of Highland dress. This rather spartan retail shop, deep in the heart of Leith, is low on atmosphere but offers a full range of traditional tartan clothes and kilts at reasonable prices.

Tattoos & body piercing

Bills Tattoo Studio

72 Elm Row, Broughton, EH7 (556 5954). Bus 7, 12, 16. **Open** 8.30am-5pm Mon, Tue, Thur, Fri; 7.30am-5pm Sat; closed Wed, Sun. **No credit cards**. **Map** p306 G3.
Traditional tattoo and piercing parlour. Bill might appear a bit abrasive at first, but he won't let you walk out with anything you'll regret later. Prices start from £15 for both tattoos and piercing.

Tribe Body Manipulations

47 West Nicolson St, South Edinburgh, EH6 (622 7220). Bus 7, 8, 21, 31, 80. **Open** noon-6pm Tue-Sat; closed Sun, Mon. **No credit cards**. **Map** p310 G5.
Alternative tattoos and piercing of any body parts you care to think of in a small, friendly shop, which also stocks a wide range of original body jewellery. Prices from £20 for tattoos. Appointment necessary.

Food & drink

Delicatessens

Margiotta

77 Warrender Park Road, South Edinburgh, EH9 (229 2869). Bus 24, 40, 41, 41A. **Open** 7.30am-10pm Mon-Sat; 8am-9pm Sun. **Credit** MC, V. **Map** p309 F8.
Although the prices are generally around a fifth more than you'd pay elsewhere, with branches throughout the Old and New Towns this well-stocked deli is extremely handy for those moments when you just have to have some red pesto and everywhere else is shut.
Branches: throughout the city.

Peckhams

155-159 Bruntsfield Place, South Edinburgh, EH10 (229 7054). Bus 11, 16, 17, 23. **Open** 8am-midnight Mon-Sat; 9am-midnight Sun. **Credit** MC, V. **Map** p309 D8.
This huge grocer's, south-west of the centre has shelves up to the ceiling, full of tempting luxuries. It's

WM Armstrong (*p174*) and branch **Rusty Zip**.

a one-stop shop for exotic sweet and savoury delicacies and drinks. Licensed to sell alcohol until midnight. **Branch**: Unit 12, Waverley Rail Station, New Town, EH1 (557 9050).

Valvona & Crolla

19 Elm Row, Broughton, EH7 (556 6066/ www.valvonacrolla.co.uk). Bus 7, 12, 16. **Open** 8am-6pm Mon-Wed; 8am-7.30pm Thur, Fri; 8am-6pm Sat; closed Sun. **Credit** AmEx, MC, V. **Map** p306 G3.

Run by the families of Valvona and Crolla since the 1930s, this long narrow Italian food shop is famed for the mouthwatering range of Mediterranean delicacies that cram the shelves. In recent years it has risen to the challenge of the big supermarkets by going upmarket, concentrating on speciality goods. Fresh mozzarella and plump Sicilian tomatoes are imported overnight from Italy, and its exotic range of spirits and liqueurs now includes the demon Absinthe. Thankfully everything remains reasonably priced.

Drink

Better Beverage Company

43 William Street, New Town, EH3 (538 7180). Bus 3, 3A, 12, 25. **Open** 10am-5pm Mon, Sat; 10am-6pm Tue-Fri; closed Sun. **No credit cards.** **Map** p308 C6.

The friendly staff of this intimate West End outlet could turn anyone into a coffee lover, while the great quality range of beans will satisfy even the most discerning connoisseur.

Oddbins

223 High Street, Royal Mile, EH1 (220 3516/ www.oddbins.co.uk). Bus 35, 35A. **Open** 11am-9pm Mon-Thur; 9am-10pm Fri; 10am-10pm Sat; 12.30-8pm Sun. **Credit** AmEx, MC, V. **Map** p314 D3.

Best of the chain liquor retailers, with eager assistants, a huge range of beers, wines and liqueurs, plus more whiskies than any of its English branches, including the occasional cask-strength single malt. The sandwich boards outside give details of tastings. **Branches**: throughout the city.

Peter Green & Co

37A-B Warrender Park Road, South Edinburgh, EH9 (229 5925). Bus 24, 40, 41, 41A. **Open** 9.30am-6.30pm Tue-Thur; 9.30am-7.30pm Fri; 9.30am-7pm Sat; closed Mon, Sun. **Credit** AmEx, MC, V. **Map** p309 F8.

Diverse selection of wines and over 100 whiskies. Tastings take place on most Friday nights from 4.30pm to 7.30pm.

Royal Mile Whiskies

379 High Street, Royal Mile, EH1 (225 3383/ whiskies@demon.co.uk). Bus 35, 35A. **Open** 10am-6pm Mon-Sat; 12.30-6pm Sun. **Credit** AmEx, MC, V. **Map** p314 C3.

Traditional façade and a classic range of whiskies inside, with over 300 varieties available to tantalise the tastebuds. The free tastings during peak season on Saturday afternoons should whet the appetite.

Scotch Malt Whisky Society

The Vaults, 87 Giles Street, Leith, EH6 (554 3451/ www.smws.com). Bus 10A, 22, 35, 35A. **Open** 10am-5pm Mon-Wed; 10am-11pm Thur, Fri; 10.30am-11pm Sat; closed Sun. **Credit** AmEx, MC, V. **Map** p311 Jy.

Unique malt whiskies, bottled direct from single casks, available to members only. If you're a bit of a whisky buff, forget the commercial malts, phone for a tasting programme and join the Society. The pleasure you get from it will more than compensate for the membership fee of £75 for the first year (which includes a bottle of whisky and full tasting notes) and £25 per year thereafter.

Scotch Whisky Heritage Centre

354 Castlehill, Royal Mile, EH1 (220 0441/ enquiry@whisky-heritage.co.uk/ www.whisky-heritage.co.uk). Bus 35, 35A. **Open** 10am-6pm daily (licensed from 12.30pm on Sundays). **Credit** AmEx, DC, MC, V. **Map** p314 C3.

Try before you buy from the broad range of commercial whiskies at the centre's friendly bar and gift shop, which are open to all, whether or not you want to go on the accompanying tour (*see p43*).

Ethnic

Lupe Pinto's Deli

24 Leven Street, South Edinburgh, EH3 (228 6241/ www.lupepintos.com). Bus 11, 16, 17, 23. **Open** 10am-6pm Mon-Sat; closed Sun. **Credit** MC, V. **Map** p309 D7.

Every inch of available space in this small shop is crammed with Mexican, Spanish and Caribbean products. Whether you want authentic salsa or a string of chillies, they're all here. And if they're not, you can be sure the dedicated staff will try to order them. It also has a national mail order service.

Pats Chung Ying Chinese Supermarket

199-201 Leith Walk, Leith, EH6 (554 0358). Bus 7, 12, 16. **Open** 10am-6pm daily. **Credit** MC, V. **Map** p307 H2.

An exquisite smorgasbord of frozen, fresh and packaged Chinese foods in a vast, modern shop.

Fruit & veg

Argyle Place

Marchmont, South Edinburgh, EH9 (no phone). Bus 24, 40, 41, 41A. **Credit** varies. **Map** p309 F8.

A busy strip of fruit and veg shops on the south side of the city, where locals go for the cheap produce.

Health & vegetarian

Holland & Barrett

18 Nicolson Street, South Edinburgh, EH8 (667 6002). Bus 7, 8, 21, 31, 80. **Open** 9am-5.30pm Mon-Sat; closed Sun. **Credit** AmEx, MC, V. **Map** p310 G6.

Consumer

This well-established shop is good for basic vegetarian supplies and health supplements. Its range of products is constantly updated.

Nature's Gate

*83 Clerk Street, South Edinburgh, EH8 (668 2067).
Bus 7, 8, 31, 80.* **Open** 10am-7pm Mon, Wed, Thur,
Fri; 10am-6pm Tue, Sat; noon-4pm Sun. **Credit** MC,
V. **Map** p310 G7.
A wide range of vegetarian and vegan foods is sold
at Nature's Gate. There's an impressive selection of
organic wines and beers to top it all off.

Real Foods

*37 Broughton Street, Broughton, EH1 (557 1911/
admin@realfoods.freeserve.co.uk). Bus 8.* **Open** 9am-
7pm Mon-Wed, Fri; 9am-8.30pm Thur; 9am-6.30pm
Sat; 10am-6pm Sun. **Credit** MC, V. **Map** p306 F3.
A veritable one-stop supermarket for the vegetarian,
vegan and organic consumer, even if the prices are
not always cheap.
Branches: 8 Brougham Place, South Edinburgh,
EH3 (228 1201); **The Organic Shop** 47 Broughton
Street, Broughton, EH1 (556 1772).

Late-night grocers

Late opening and all-night grocers seem to
move on regularly, but these chain stores have
stayed the course.

Alldays

*91-93 Nicolson Street, South Edinburgh, EH8 (667
7481). Bus 7, 8, 21, 31, 80.* **Open** 24 hrs daily.
Credit MC, V. **Map** p310 G6.

Late-night munchies can be satisfied here with a
wide range of food and drink mainstays and treats.
Branches: 126 Marchmont Road, South Edinburgh,
EH9 (447 0353); 127-129 Corstorphine Road, West
Edinburgh, EH12 (337 1039).

Costcutter

*125 Lothian Road, South Edinburgh, EH3 (622
7191). Bus 11, 15, 24.* **Open** 24 hrs daily.
Credit MC, V. **Map** p314 A3.
Costcutter stocks a basic range of grocery and
household supplies.
Branch: 44-46 South Bridge, South Edinburgh, EH1
(622 7162).

Sainsbury's

*185 Craigleith Road, Blackhall, EH4 (332 0704/
www.sainsburys.co.uk). Bus 29, 29A, 82.* **Open** 8am-
10pm Mon-Thur; 8am-midnight Fri; 8am-9.30pm Sat;
9am-7pm Sun. **Credit** AmEx, MC, V.
This well-known supermarket by the junction of
Craigleith and Queensferry Roads, west beyond
Stockbridge, has an extensive range of quality produce and household supplies. Other facilities include
a coffee shop, three ATMs, a Supasnaps, a Sketchley
dry cleaner's, free parking and assistance for people
with mobility difficulties.

Specialist

Caseys Confectioners

*52 St Mary's Street, Royal Mile, EH1 (556 6082).
Bus 24, 25, 35, 35A.* **Open** 9am-5.30pm Mon-Fri;
9.30am-5.30pm Sat; closed Sun. **No credit cards**.
Map p310 G5.

We defy you to leave **Valvona & Crolla** empty-handed. *See page 177.*

Only the prices have changed in this old-fashioned sweet shop since it first opened in 1954. It still has a picture-postcard, art deco exterior while, inside, there are racks of colourfully filled jars of mouth-watering sweets, handmade on the premises. Go on, splash out on a 50p bag of Berwick Cockles and saunter up the Pleasance.

Branch: 28 East Norton Place, Abbeyhill, EH7 (no phone).

Crombies of Edinburgh
97-101 Broughton Street, Broughton, EH1 (557 0111). Bus 8. **Open** 8am-6pm Mon-Thur; 8am-7pm Fri; 8am-5pm Sat; closed Sun. **Credit** MC, V. **Map** p306 F3.

Top-quality meats from local farms, but it's the extensive and inventive range of pies and sausages that get the queues stretching out of the door. Try a venison, wild boar and apple sausage in your Sunday fry up and you'll soon taste why.

Iain Mellis Cheesemonger
30A Victoria Street, Royal Mile, EH1 (226 6215). Bus 23, 28, 45. **Open** 9.30am-6pm Mon-Fri; 9.30am-6pm Sat; noon-5pm Sun **Credit** MC, V. **Map** p314 C3.

Only the most olfactorily challenged of passers-by could miss the pungent odour from this small, galley-shaped cheesemonger, situated just a step away from the Royal Mile. Organic food and veg-etables are also sold. Try a slice of Gubbeen.

Branch: 205 Bruntsfield Place, South Edinburgh, EH10 (447 8889).

MacSweens of Edinburgh
Dryden Rd, Loanhead, EH20 (440 2555/ haggis@macsween.co.uk/www.macsween.co.uk). Bus 81A, 87, 88. **Open** 8.30am-5pm Mon-Fri; closed Sat, Sun. **Credit** MC, V.

So dedicated are the MacSweens to their haggis that every single batch is tasted by one of the family. Vegetarian haggis is also available. Also stocked in Peckhams (*see p176*) and Jenners (*see p171*).

Mr Boni's
4 Lochrin Buildings, Tollcross, South Edinburgh, EH3 (229 5319). Bus 11, 16, 17, 23. **Open** 10.30am-10.30pm Mon-Thur; 10.30am-11pm Fri, Sat; noon-10.30pm Sun. **Credit** AmEx, MC, V. **Map** p309 D7.

This family-run ice-cream institution opened 75 years ago and Mr Boni, the grandson of the founder, is still dreaming up new recipes to add to the rota of 300 imaginative flavours available, all of which are made from fresh, natural ingredients. Pooh Bear Crunch is a bestseller.

Health & beauty

Cosmetics & toiletries

Lush
44 Princes Street, New Town, EH2 (557 3177). Bus 3, 3A, 12, 16, 17, 80. **Open** 9.30am-6.15pm Mon-

Casey's Confectioners – sweet all over.

Wed, Fri, Sat; 9.30am-8pm Thur; noon-5pm Sun. **Credit** AmEx, MC, V. **Map** p314 D1.

Fresh ingredients are the name of the game at this store. Decked out to look more like a deli than a cos-metics store, it even sells its soaps in wedges, sliced at the counter like lumps of cheese. Just don't eat them when you get home.

Neal's Yard Remedies
46A George Street, New Town, EH2 (226 3223). Bus 13, 19, 55, 82. **Open** 10am-6pm Mon-Sat; Sun varies; phone for details. **Credit** MC, V. **Map** p314 C1.

These fab-smelling alternative lotions and potions in their distinctive dark blue bottles showcase the benefits of various herbs and oils. Pricey but worth it. Book in at the treatment room if you'd rather someone else pamper you.

Hairdressers

Cheynes
46 George Street, New Town, EH2 (220 0777/ www.cheynes.com). Bus 13, 19, 55, 82. **Open** 9am-5.15pm Mon-Wed, Fri; 9am-6.30pm Thur; 9am-4.30pm Sat; closed Sun. **Credit** AmEx, MC, V. **Map** p314 C2.

Popular Edinburgh chain of hairdressers' for men and women, well known for quality hair cuts, perms and colourings. Prices start from around £19.50. Appointments necessary.

Branches: 57 South Bridge, South Edinburgh, EH1 (556 0108); 45A York Place, New Town, EH1 (558 1010); 77 Lothian Road, South Edinburgh, EH3 (228 9977); 3 Drumsheugh Place, Queensferry Street, New Town, EH3 (225 2234).

Patersons SA
129 Lothian Road, South Edinburgh, EH3 (228 5252). Bus 11, 15, 24. **Open** 9am-6pm Mon-Wed, Fri; 10.30am-7.30pm Thur; 9am-4.30pm Sat; closed Sun. **Credit** AmEx, MC, V. **Map** p314 A3.

Bright, comfortable and gay-friendly hairdresser's, which was so popular it had to open up another

Consumer

branch round the corner. Prices start at £22 for a cut. **Branches:** 6-8 Bread Street, South Edinburgh, EH3 (229 5151); 134 High Street, Dalkeith (660 5722).

Woods the Barbers

12 Drummond Street, South Edinburgh, EH8 (556 6716). Bus 7, 8, 21, 31, 80. **Open** 8.30am-5pm Mon, Tue, Thur, Fri; 9am-1pm Wed; 8.30am-4pm Sat; closed Sun. **No credit cards. Map** p310 G6.
A classic barber's in the south of the city that's great for a quick cut. Prices start at a very reasonable £4.50 for a short back and sides.

Household

Habitat

32 Shandwick Place, New Town, EH2 (225 9151/ www.habitat.net). Bus 3, 3A, 12, 25, 25A. **Open** 9am-5.30pm Mon-Wed, Fri; 9am-7pm Thur; 9am-6pm Sat; 11.30am-5.30pm Sun; *Dec* extended hours; phone for details. **Credit** AmEx, MC, V. **Map** p308 C5.
Popular household chain store with affordable, attractive furnishings and furniture on three laid-back, roomy floors at the west end of Princes Street.

Ikea

Straiton Road, Loanhead, South Edinburgh, EH20 (448 0500/www.ikea.com). Bus 81A, 87, 88. **Open** 10am-8pm Mon-Fri; 10am-6pm Sat, Sun. **Credit** MC, V.
The long-awaited Scottish branch of the phenomenally successful Swedish chain is as popular as the rest, despite being some way out of the city centre. Sleek, modern furnishings for every part of the home are laid out on two massive floors, but be prepared for the no-frills do-it-yourself service and long queues that go with the exceptionally low prices.

Inhouse

28 Howe Street, New Town, EH3 (225 2888/ www.inhousenet.co.uk). Bus 13, 28, 29, 29A, 80. **Open** 9.30am-6pm Mon-Wed, Fri; 10am-7pm Thur; 9.30am-5.30pm Sat; *Festival also* noon-5pm Sun. **Credit** MC, V. **Map** p306 D4.
Two floors of designer names such as Alessi plus high-street brands, with delightful trinkets to catch the eye at every turn. Upstairs is mainly larger furniture, with prices around £400 for a chair; downstairs is the real Santa's grotto, ideal for practical but unusual household furnishings and accessories.

James Gray & Son

89 George Street, New Town, EH2 (225 7381). Bus 13, 19, 55, 82. **Open** 9am-5.30pm Mon-Sat; *Dec also* 11am-5pm Sun. **Credit** AmEx, MC, V. **Map** p314 B1.
Traditional city-centre ironmongers and hardware shop with an extensive range of quality goods for the home and garden, although not exactly the cheapest around.

Lakeland

52 George Street, New Town, EH2 (220 3947). Bus 13, 55, 19, 82. **Open** 9am-5.30pm Mon-Wed, Fri, Sat; 9.30am-5.30pm Thur; *Dec also* noon-5pm Sun. **Credit** MC, V. **Map** p314 B1.

Tartan up the Royal Mile

At one time, the only place in Edinburgh providing that singular element of an authentic Scottish holiday – the Scottish novelty shop – was at the top of the Royal Mile, on the way up to Castlehill. There they clustered like a gang of wee radges round the door of the chippy. In recent years, however, the shops have grown bolder and put themselves about a bit, notably down the High Street towards where the new Scottish Parliament building will be – perhaps in the hope that the MSPs will be tempted to prove their dedication to Scotland's tartan heritage with the straggly red locks of a 'see-you-Jimmy' bonnet or a T-shirt declaring 'I'm a wee monster'. Princes Street also has plenty of gift shops selling tartan teatowels and other kitsch items, but the best and most tasteless are still to be found on the Royal Mile. The bargains are better and, in the summer months, the shops at the top of the Mile stay open until they've run out of tourists to serve.

Plaid

318 Lawnmarket, Royal Mile, EH1 (no phone). Bus 35, 35A. **Open** 9am-6pm daily; *Festival* 9am-10pm daily. **Credit** AmEx, DC, MC, V. **Map** p314 C3.
Plaid tops the tackometer rating with an extensive stock that seems to leave no household item untouched by tartan.

Royal Mile Sepia

116 Canongate, Royal Mile, EH8 (557 8945/ royalmilesepia@talk21.com). Bus 24, 35, 35A. **Open** 10am-6pm daily. **Credit** AmEx, MC, V. **Map** p310 G2.
Great for the been there, done that, taken the picture tourist. You don 18th-century Highland costumes, have your picture taken, then wait while the dozen prints are developed. Costs £12.50 each, for a minimum of two people.

The Scotland Shop

18-20 High Street, Royal Mile (557 2030). **Open** 9.30am-6pm Mon-Sat; 11am-6pm Sun.

Consumer

Two floors with every kitchen accessory you could ever need, and many more eccentric inventions you would never have thought you needed, never mind existed: a chrome banana tree, anyone?

Markets

Greenside Place Car Boot Sale

Level 2 in car park off Leith Street, Broughton, EH1 (no phone). Bus 1, 11, 22, 34. **Open** 10am-2pm Sun; closed Mon-Sat. **No credit cards. Map** p307 G4.

With room for up to 300 car boot stalls, run by a mixture of professional traders and ordinary folk clearing out their attic, this is a mecca for bargain hunters, the kind of place where you really could find an antique vase worth thousands for only £1 among the bric-a-brac, antiques and junk on offer. Haggling is acceptable, although by no means always expected. The car boot sale is not dangerous, but, like any other place with crowds, look out for pickpockets and keep your valuables close at hand.

Ingliston Market

Off Glasgow Road (A8), West Edinburgh, past Edinburgh Airport (no phone). Scottish Citylink service 900/902 to Glasgow. **Open** 10am-4pm Sun; closed Mon-Sat. **Credit** varies.

Probably the nearest Edinburgh has to a Barras set-up, with around 100 traders selling mostly clothes, household and electrical goods and hippie paraphernalia in an outdoor field, plus a car boot sale alongside with anything from 20 to 200 cars

Cuddly Scottish Terrier toy

Kilted furry Scotsman

Piper doll

Tartan tickling stick

Whisky-flavoured condoms

(depending on the weather). If you want a cheap fleece, novelty clock or lighter, then this place will offer the best prices. Just make sure you check the quality first.

Credit AmEx, MC. V. **Map** p310 G5.

Fearsome Braveheart-styled swords, cutlasses and equally scary tartan porcelain dolls bedeck the window of the Scotland Shop. But the neat interior also contains a wide range of reasonably priced and rather more low-key Scottish paraphernalia.

The Tartan Gift Shop

54 High Street, Royal Mile, EH1 (558 3187). Bus 35, 35A. **Open** 9am-5pm Mon-Sat; 11am-4.30pm Sun. **Credit** MC, V. **Map** p310 G5.

A small, traditional shop aimed mainly at men, with a large stock of kiltwear accessories, golf balls, engraved hip flasks and ornamental knives. Also good for cheaper good-quality tartan rugs and tartan household accessories.

Thistle Do Nicely

2 Upper Bow, Royal Mile (no phone). Bus 35, 35A. **Open** 9am-6pm daily; *Festival* 9am-

10pm daily. **Credit** AmEx, DC, MC, V. **Map** p314 C3.

A mix of true tat with more upmarket gifts, all crammed into a tiny, attractive nook of a shop.

Whigmaleeries Ltd

328 Lawnmarket, Royal Mile, EH1 (no phone). Bus 35, 35A. **Open** 9am-6pm daily; *Festival* 9am-10pm daily. **Credit** AmEx, DC, MC, V. **Map** p314 C3.

Reproduction weapons, jewellery and a family history research service in impressively elegant surroundings.

White Dove

140 High Street, Royal Mile, EH1 (220 1566/www.white-dove.co.uk). Bus 35, 35A. **Open** 10am-6pm Mon-Sat; 11am-6pm Sun. **Credit** AmEx, DC, MC, V. **Map** p314 D2.

A fine range of tacky novelties in the back (past the wizard and troll fantasy figures). The place to come for the obligatory whisky-flavoured condoms.

New Street Indoor Sunday Market

Waverley Car Park, New Street, Royal Mile EH8 (no phone). Bus 35, 35A. **Open** 10am-4pm Sun; closed Mon-Sat. **No credit cards. Map** p310 G5.
There are more traders than cars here, unless Greenside (*see above*) is full, when the spillover to here can make Sunday morning bargain hunting something of a marathon.

Specialist & gifts

Aitken Dott & Son/Miller Graphics

36 North Bridge, Royal Mile, EH1 (225 1006/ millers.graphics@btinternet.com). Bus 7, 8, 21, 31, 80. **Open** 9am-5.30pm Mon-Sat; closed Sun. **Credit** AmEx, MC, V. **Map** p314 D2.
Centrally located professional stationery suppliers. It's split into two parts, with the basement specialising in paper and card of all shades, sizes and weights, as well as printing and photocopying facilities. Upstairs is a wide selection of paints, pens, gift cards and stationery.

Crystal Clear

52 Cockburn Street, Royal Mile, EH1 (226 7888/ wildwoodbooks@yahoo.com). Bus 7, 8, 21, 31, 80. **Open** 10am-6pm Mon-Wed, Fri, Sat; 10am-7pm Thur; noon-5pm Sun. **Credit** MC, V. **Map** p314 D3.
Tiny but atmospheric shop packed with intriguing books and crystals, Buddhist singing bowls, wind chimes and relaxation tapes. Owner Thom McCarthy has done it all, from running a shopping empire to living in a monastery for ten years. Now he's back to running a shop, and is often around to offer friendly and knowledgeable advice.
Branch: **Wildwood Books** 16 High Street, Royal Mile, EH1 (557 4888).

Digger

35 West Nicolson Street, South Edinburgh, EH8 (668 1802). Bus 7, 8, 21, 31, 80. **Open** 10am-6pm Mon-Sat; closed Sun. **Credit** AmEx, MC, V. **Map** p310 G6.
A small, colourful shop brimming over with well-priced crafts including wind chimes, wooden Indian carvings and mirrors, as well as plenty of amusing and pretty pocket-money gift ideas.

Eden

37-39 Cockburn Street, Royal Mile, EH1 (220 3372). Bus 7, 8, 21, 31, 80. **Open** 9.30am-6pm Mon-Wed, Fri, Sat; 9.30am-7pm Thur; noon-5pm Sun. **Credit** AmEx, MC, V. **Map** p314 D3.
Ethnic wooden crafts and textiles plus brightly coloured oddities such as inflatable chairs and furry personal organisers.

The Edinburgh Floatarium

29 North West Circus Place, Stockbridge, EH3 (225 3350/edinburgh.floatarium@scotland.com). Bus 28, 29, 29A, 80. **Open** 9am-8pm Mon-Fri; 9am-6pm Sat; 9.30am-4pm Sun. **Credit** MC, V. **Map** p306 D4.

The sea salt floats (£22) are the main attraction here, among various beauty and health treatments. The shop at the front also sells a wide selection of New Age books, crystals and gifts.

George Waterston & Sons

35 George Street, New Town, EH2 (225 5690). Bus 13, 19, 55, 82. **Open** 9am-5.30pm Mon-Wed, Fri, Sat; 9am-6.30pm Thur; *Festival & Dec also* noon-5pm Sun. **Credit** MC, V. **Map** p314 B1.
This centrally located veteran stationer, which was established way back in 1752, sells a wide range of cards and writing supplies in its split-level shop. It also offers excellent facilities for printing personalised stationery.

Halibut and Herring

89 Westbow, Royal Mile, EH1 (226 7472). Bus 23, 28, 45. **Open** 10am-6pm Mon-Sat; noon-5pm Sun. **Credit** MC, V. **Map** p314 C3.
Clockwork diving submarines, op-art see-through shower curtains and a colourful range of soaps and ceramics made in a workshop in Musselburgh have established this small new chain of shops as a firm local favourite for quirky bathroom treats.
Branches: 31 Raeburn Place, Stockbridge, EH4 (332 5687); 108 Bruntsfield Place, South Edinburgh, EH10 (229 2669).

Helios Fountain

7 Grassmarket, South Edinburgh, EH1 (229 7884/ 622 7173). Bus 2. **Open** 10am-6pm Mon-Sat; noon-5pm Sun. **Credit** MC, V. **Map** p314 B3.
Celtic jewellery, crafts, trinkets and a huge selection of beads for necklaces or bracelets are the order of the day at Helios Fountain. There's also a good stock of vegetarian, vegan and New Age books.

Kick Ass

34 Cockburn Street, Royal Mile, EH1 (622 7318/ kickassposters.co.uk). Bus 7, 8, 21, 31, 80. **Open** 9.30am-6pm Mon-Wed, Fri, Sat; 9.30am-7pm Thur, noon-5pm Sun. **Credit** MC, V. **Map** p314 D3.
Home to an eclectic selection of postcards ranging from the Simpsons to saucy 3D winking ladies.

Paper Tiger

53 Lothian Road, South Edinburgh, EH1 (228 2790). Bus 11, 15, 24. **Open** 9.30am-6pm Mon-Wed, Fri; 9.30am-6.30pm Thur; 9.30am-6pm Sat; *Festival & Dec* 9am-6.30pm Mon-Sat; noon-5pm Sun. **Credit** MC, V. **Map** p314 A3.
Funky designs of cards, envelopes, wrapping paper, diaries and notebooks.
Branch: 16 Stafford Street, New Town, EH3 (226 2390).

Round the World

15 NW Circus Place, Stockbridge, EH3 (225 7800). Bus 28, 29, 29A, 80. **Open** 10am-6pm Mon-Sat; closed Sun. **Credit** MC, V. **Map** p306 D3.
Housed in a former bank, this sleek, modern emporium of hipness is full of trendy designer furniture and gifts. There's also a coffee shop.

Studio One

10-16 Stafford Street, New Town, EH3 (226 5812).
Bus 3, 3A, 12, 25, 25A. **Open** 9.30am-6pm
Mon-Wed, Fri; 9.30am-6.30pm Thur; 9.30am-
5.30pm Sat; noon-5pm Sun. **Credit** MC, V.
Map p308 C5.
Popular basement shop filled with ethnic and
trendy gifts and household furnishings. The children's nook is good for pocket-money curiosities
and novelties. The Morningside Road branch is a
cook's paradise, with a good range of quality
kitchen utensils and crockery.
Branch: 71 Morningside Road, South Edinburgh,
EH10 (447 0452).

The Whole Works

Jacksons Close, 209 Lawnmarket, Royal Mile, EH1
(225 8092/www.wholeworks.co.uk). Bus 35, 35A.
Open 9am-8pm Mon-Fri; 9am-5pm Sat; closed Sun.
No credit cards. Map p314 C2.
Stress management, counselling, acupuncture,
aromatherapy, dreamwork, chiropractic, reiki and
shiatsu are just some of the treatments on offer at
this alternative therapy centre.

Services

Chemists

Boots

101-103 Princes Street, New Town, EH2 (225 8331/
www.boots.co.uk). Bus 3, 3A, 12, 16, 17. **Open** 9am-
6pm Mon-Wed, Fri, Sat; 9am-7.30pm Thur; noon-5pm
Sun. **Credit** MC, V. **Map** p314 B2.
This is Edinburgh's largest branch of the reliable
old favourite.
Branches: throughout the city.

Napiers Dispensary

1 Teviot Place, South Edinburgh, EH1 (225 5542).
Bus 23, 28, 40, 45. **Open** 10am-5.30pm Mon;
9am-5.30pm Tue-Sat; closed Sun. **Credit** MC, V.
Map p309 F6.
Established in 1860, this respected medical herbal-
ist is well stocked with homeopathic medicines and
books, vitamin supplements, organic and ecological
toiletries, essential oils, herbal teas and Bach flower
remedies. The staff are informed and helpful, while
the clinic next door offers a range of services from
acupuncture and homeopathy to psychotherapy and
osteopathy, as well as herbal treatments.
Branches: Napiers Clinic 18 Bristo Place, South
Edinburgh, EH1 (225 5542); 35 Hamilton Place,
Stockbridge, EH3 (315 2130).

Cleaning & repair

Canonmills Launderette

7-8 Huntly Street, Brandon Terrace, New Town,
EH3 (556 3199). Bus 8, 23, 27. **Open** 8am-
8pm Mon-Fri; 8am-5pm Sat; 9pm-5pm Sun.
Credit MC, V. **Map** p306 G2.

Same-day dry-cleaning service for items that arrive
before noon. Prices range from £3 to £5 per item,
while a wash costs £3.

Kleen Cleaners

10 St Mary's Street, Royal Mile, EH1 (556 4337).
Bus 24, 25, 35, 35A. **Open** 8.30am-6pm Mon-Fri;
10am-1pm Sat; closed Sun. **No credit cards**.
Map p310 G5.
Dry cleaning, plus speedy repairs and alterations.

Electronic supplies

Tandy

27 North Bridge, Royal Mile, EH1 (556 0301/
www.tandy.co.uk). Bus 7, 8, 21, 31, 80. **Open** 9am-
5.30pm Mon-Sat; noon-4.30pm Sun. **Credit** AmEx,
MC, V. **Map** p314 D3.
Centrally located suppliers of electronic equipment,
accessories and parts, with an extensive range at
favourable prices.

Florists

Clare Florist

Jenners, 54 Princes Street, New Town, EH2
(225 7145)/www.clareflorist.com). Bus 4, 44, 28.
Open 9.30-5.30pm Mon-Sat; closed Sun. **Credit**
AmEx, DC, MC, V. **Map** 314 C2.
A good selection of classic blooms.
Branch: 18-20 Easter Road, Leith, EH7 (659 6596);
4 Hutchison Terrace, South Edinburgh, EH2
(538 5799).

Narcissus

50A Broughton Street, Broughton, EH1 (478 7447).
Bus 8. **Open** 9am-6pm Mon-Sat; 11am-5pm Sun.
Credit AmEx, DC, MC, V. **Map** p306 F3.
This small, low-key shop sells a select range of simple but exotic blooms and plants, including impressively tall cacti, all at reasonable prices. It also offers
a full range of services, including international and
national deliveries.

Iain Mellis Cheesemonger. *See page 179.*

Foreign newspapers

International Newsagents
351 High Street, Royal Mile, EH1 (225 4827). Bus 35, 35A. **Open** 6am-6pm Mon-Fri; 7am-6pm Sat; 9am-4pm Sun; *Festival* 6pm-midnight Mon-Fri; 6am-1am Sat, Sun. **Credit** MC, V. **Map** p314 C3.
French, Spanish, German and American daily newspapers, in addition to an extensive range of European magazines.

Internet & email

Cyberia
88 Hanover Street, New Town, EH2 (220 4403/edinburgh@cybersurf.co.uk/www.cybersurf.co.uk). Bus 23, 27, 45. **Open** 10am-10pm daily.
No credit cards. Map p314 C1.
Spacious Internet café with coffee, snacks and a licensed bar. Surfing costs £2.50 per half-hour (£2 concs) and email accounts start at £12 per month. The public email drop-box facility means friends can send you messages via Cyberia's email address. Your mail will be kept on a list displayed in the café for two weeks; collection costs 50p per mail.

Web 13
13 Bread Street, South Edinburgh, EH3 (229 8883/ian@web13.co.uk/www.web13.co.uk). Bus 2, 28, 28A. **Open** 9am-10pm daily. **Credit** V. **Map** p314 A3.
Accessible and friendly cyber-café in the financial district. It offers the full range of Internet and web training, so beginners needn't miss out. Surfing costs from £1 for 20 minutes, £3 for an hour. A ten-minute beginners' guide to using the Internet is also available, priced £2.50. The all-day café has an extensive and cheap menu.

Mobile phones

Carphone Warehouse
25 Princes Street, New Town, EH2 (558 7020/www.carphonewarehouse.co.uk). Bus 3, 3A, 12, 16, 17. **Open** 9am-6pm Mon-Wed, Fri, Sat; 9am-7pm Thur; 11am-5pm Sun. **Credit** AmEx, MC, V. **Map** p314 D2.
Carphone Warehouse offers a vast, well-priced selection of mobile phones and pagers.
Branches: 62 Haymarket Terrace, West Edinburgh, EH12 (337 6771); 24 Dalziel Place, London Road, Abbeyhill, EH6 (661 7005); 25 Shandwick Place, West Edinburgh, EH2 (228 4360).

Opticians

Dollond & Aitchison
50 St James Centre, New Town, EH1 (558 1149/www.dolland.co.uk). Bus 1, 11, 22, 34. **Open** 9am-6pm Mon-Wed, Fri, Sat; 9am-8pm Thur; closed Sun. **Credit** AmEx, MC, V. **Map** p307 G4.
Wide range of quality frames. Most repairs can be done on the premises on the same day.

Branches: 56 Newington Road, South Edinburgh, EH9 (667 6442); 61 London Road, Greenside, EH6 (653 0806); Cameron Toll, South Edinburgh, EH16 (664 2545).

Vision Express
Units 12-14, St James Centre, New Town, EH1 (556 5656/www.visionexpress.co.uk). Bus 1, 11, 22, 34. **Open** 9am-5.30pm Mon-Wed, Fri, Sat; 9am-7pm Thur; noon-5pm Sun. **Credit** MC, V. **Map** p307 G4.
Huge selection of spectacles to choose from, most ready within an hour. Prices from £48 for single-vision lenses.

Photocopying

Most newsagents, independent chemists and art shops offer cheap (although not necessarily good-quality) photocopying, with charges from 4p for an A4 copy. Look out for the yellow and black signs hanging outside shops.

Photo-processing

There are numerous branches of photo-processing shops such as **SupaSnaps** around the city, but chemists are generally cheaper and offer all the same facilities, including one-hour processing (note, though, that this service normally carries a premium).

SupaSnaps
94-96 South Bridge, New Town, EH1 (225 9250). Bus 7, 8, 21, 31, 80. **Open** 9am-5.30pm Mon-Sat; closed Sun. **Credit** AmEx, MC, V. **Map** p314 D3.

Travel

Edinburgh Travel Centre
3 Bristo Square, South Edinburgh, EH8 (668 2221). Bus 23, 28, 40, 45. **Open** 9am-5pm Mon-Wed, Fri; 10am-5pm Thur; closed Sat, Sun. **Credit** AmEx, MC, V. **Map** p310 G6.
Specialists in student travel.

Haggis Backpackers
60 High Street, Royal Mile, EH1 (557 9393/haggis@radicaltravel.com). Bus 35, 35A. **Open** 8am-late daily. **Credit** MC, V. **Map** p310 G5.
Interesting, off-beat and laid-back tour operator run by travellers for travellers.

Usit Campus
53 Forrest Road, South Edinburgh, EH1 (telesales 668 3303/www.usitworld.com). Bus 23, 28, 45. **Open** 9am-5.30pm Mon-Wed, Fri; 10am-5.30pm Thur; 10am-1pm Sat; closed Sun. **Credit** AmEx, MC, V. **Map** p309 F6.
Popular Southside student and youth travel agent. It's especially excellent for adventure travel, but be prepared for long queues, no matter what time of day you turn up.
Branch: 2 South Clerk Street, EH8 (667 9488).

Arts & Entertainment

Feature boxes

Art Galleries

Although the city's commercial galleries might not have the profile of its public collections, that's no excuse to miss out on these gems.

Edinburgh might be well endowed with strong art collections, displayed in the public galleries (which are listed within the relevant Sightseeing chapters, *pages 39-93*), but in the commercial field, the city has had more of a reputation for the archetypal, twee Scottish landscape than anything else. It is a reputation that has not been helped by Glasgow's notoriety as a robust hotbed of young talent – which rather left poor old Edinburgh resting on its conservative laurels.

Nowadays, while publicly funded galleries like the **Fruitmarket** (*see page 49*) and **Inverleith House** (*see page 66*) are happy to put on shows by contemporary artists from across Scotland, so the commercial galleries are beginning to show and sell artworks that reflect the growing vitality of Scottish artists. Commercial spaces such as the **Nexus Galleries** (*see page 187*) are built upon the idea that buying art is not only for the terminally hip or the helplessly moneyed. The popular trends of contemporary art have also been acknowledged by the likes of the **Bellevue Gallery** (*see below*), which shows artwork used in the design of

posters and club flyers. Galleries such as **WASP Gallery** (*see page 188*) and **Edinburgh Printmakers** (*see page 187*) also continue to thrive as places where the artists who use the associated studios can sell their work.

The douce Scottish landscape can still be bought, of course, and there is no inherent harm in doing so. **Bourne Fine Art** and the **Leith Gallery** (for both, *see page 187*) are testaments to its enduring appeal. It is just that there is much more to Scottish artists. And, whatever you do, don't call the current popularity of Scottish artists the 'Scottish phenomenon' or worse, the 'tartan renaissance'. The modern art world, as opposed to the world of modern art, would never be as parochial as that.

Bellevue Gallery

4 Bellevue Crescent, Broughton, EH3 (557 1663/ art@pixi.demon.co.uk/www.pixi.demon.co.uk). Bus 8. **Open** *noon-6pm Tue-Sat or by appointment; closed Sun & mid-end Sept.* **Admission** *free (generally).* **Credit** *MC, V.* **Map** *p306 F3.*
Situated just beyond Broughton Street, this privately owned gallery fills the ground floor of a lovely con-

The **Bellevue Gallery**, showing contemporary art in refined surroundings.

verted New Town terraced house. An expanse of polished floors and bright white walls, the Bellevue is one of Edinburgh's rare commercial galleries specialising solely in contemporary art, even going so far as to stage exhibitions of club flyers and poster artwork. Both solo and group shows by newcomers and established artists alike feature on the programme.

Bourne Fine Art

6 Dundas Street, New Town, EH3 (557 4050/
bournefineart@enterprise.net/
www.bournefineart.com). Bus 23, 27. **Open**
10am-6pm Mon-Fri; 11am-2pm Sat; closed Sun;
Festival 10am-6pm Mon-Fri; 11am-4pm Sat;
closed Sun. **Admission** free. **No credit cards.**
Map p306 E3.

Dundas Street, one of the New Town's busiest thoroughfares, is home to many of Edinburgh's commercial, upmarket galleries. One of the grandest is Bourne Fine Art, with its bow-windowed façade. The gallery specialises in traditional Scottish landscapes and portraiture by artists from the 1700s through to the 1950s, and its line-up of artists includes luminaries such as Sir David Wilkie, Sir William MacTaggart and JD Cadell in addition to a host of lesser-knowns. More recently the gallery has started to stage the occasional show of work by contemporary artists.

Edinburgh Printmakers

23 Union Street, Broughton, EH1 (557 2479/
www.edinburgh-printmakers.co.uk). Bus 7, 12,
16. **Open** 10am-6pm Tue-Sat; closed Mon,
Sun. **Admission** free. **Credit** MC, V.
Map p307 G3.

Scotland has a strong printmaking tradition, and Edinburgh Printmakers, which was founded in 1967, is probably the country's leading gallery dedicated to exhibiting work by contemporary printmakers. The gallery consists of three exhibition spaces and has recently branched out into showing work in media other than printmaking. But as one of the gallery windows overlooks the workshop, it's still possible to witness printing work in action.

Ingleby Gallery

6 Carlton Terrace, Calton Hill, EH7 (556 4441/
inglebygallery@dial.pipex.com). Bus 25. **Open** 10am-
5pm Wed-Sat; closed Mon, Tue, Sun; *Festival also*
10am-5pm Mon, Tue. **Admission** free. **Credit** MC,
V. **Map** p307 J4.

This classy gallery is housed in one of William Playfair's grand townhouses that look out onto the Palace of Holyroodhouse and Arthur's Seat. Doubling up as a family home, the Ingleby is a space that has consciously moved away from the 'white cube' look. It's one of Edinburgh's few commercial galleries specialising in contemporary art, and boasts a range of work that extends from established British greats such as Howard Hodgkin, Andy Goldsworthy and Callum Innes through to lesser-known artists. Ceramics and sculpture also make an appearance in the gallery's rolling programme of exhibitions.

One of Graham Dean's prints, shown at **Edinburgh Printmakers**.

Ink Tank

30 St Stephen Street, Stockbridge, EH3 (226 5449/
inktank@ednet.co.uk/www.ink-tank.co.uk). Bus 28,
29, 29A, 80. **Open** 9am-6pm Mon-Fri; by
appointment Sat, Sun. **Admission** free.
No credit cards. Map p306 D3.

A tiny gallery situated to the north of Princes Street in Stockbridge, Ink Tank is also a graphic design business. Setting out to promote innovative work by both recent art graduates and more established artists, this is a good place to witness the crossover between art and design.

The Leith Gallery

65 The Shore, Leith, EH6 (553 5255/
info@the.leithgallery.co.uk/www.the-leith-gallery.co.uk).
Bus 10A, 22, 35,35A. **Open** 11am-5pm Tue-Fri,
11am-4pm Sat; closed Mon, Sun; *Festival* extended
hours (phone for details). **Admission** free. **Credit**
AmEx, MC, V. **Map** p305 Jy.

A successful commercial gallery overlooking Leith harbour and specialising in contemporary Scottish art. There are no aspirations towards championing the avant-garde, so expect to find landscapes, still lifes and slightly saucy beach scenes by a diverse range of Scotland-based artists.

Nexus Galleries

61 Bread Street, South Edinburgh, EH3 (477 4524/
info@nexusgalleries.co.uk/www.nexusgalleries.co.uk).
Bus 2, 28, 35, 35A. **Open** 10am-6pm Mon-Sat; closed
Sun; *Festival* extended hours (phone for details).
Admission free. **Credit** MC, V. **Map** p314 A3.

The latest addition to Edinburgh's contemporary art scene is the Nexus Galleries. Funded by a city property developer, whose aim is to raise the profile of the Bread Street area, Nexus consists of three separate commercial gallery spaces. Each one is devoted to showing work by young and emerging artists who are based in Scotland but whose work is in a range of different media, from jewellery and lighting through to the rather more conventional painting and sculpture.

Open Eye Gallery

75-79 Cumberland Street, New Town, EH3 (557 1020/open.eye@virgin.net/www.openeyegallery.co.uk). Bus 13, 23, 27. **Open** 10am-6pm Mon-Fri; 10am-4pm Sat; closed Sun. **Admission** free. **No credit cards. Map** p306 E3.

Situated on one of the New Town's quieter streets, the Open Eye has built up a reputation as a vibrant commercial gallery since it opened in 1980. Exhibitions change every three weeks and feature artists drawn from Scotland and further afield. Paintings jostle for attention alongside ceramics, jewellery and sculpture. From beach scenes through to street scenes, the paintings tend away from the cutting edge, while the jewellery and ceramics are often a sure step away from high-street conventionality. The Eye Two gallery has a more contemporary, minimalist feel to it, with an emphasis on prints and funky ceramics.

Branch: Eye Two 66 Cumberland Street, New Town, EH3 (558 9872).

Patriothall/WASP Gallery

Patriothall Studios, off 48 Hamilton Place, Stockbridge, EH3 (225 1289). Bus 35, 35A. **Open** noon-5pm Mon-Fri; noon-6pm Sat, Sun; *Festival* noon-6pm daily. **Admission** free. **No credit cards. Map** p306 D3.

Slightly off the beaten track is this informal exhibition space. The shows predominantly feature work by the artists based in the 60 or so studios found under the same roof and, as work is often for sale, this is the place to take a look at young talent and consider making a purchase.

The Sable Gallery

29b Dundas Street, New Town, EH3 (467 3937/sable@cableinet.co.uk). Bus 23, 27. **Open** 11am-7pm Mon-Fri; closed Sat, Sun. **Admission** free. **Credit** MC, V. **Map** p306 E3.

This basement gallery has recently joined the band of commercial galleries that lie along Dundas Street. A two-room space, the exhibitions range from group shows by local and international artists to solo shows by emerging artists.

Scottish Gallery

16 Dundas Street, New Town, EH3 (558 1200/mail@scottish-gallery.co.uk). Bus 23, 27. **Open** 10am-6pm Mon-Fri; 10am-4pm Sat; closed Sun. **Admission** free. **Credit** AmEx, MC, V. **Map** p306 E4.

With a history dating back to 1842, the Scottish Gallery is the country's oldest commercial gallery. Situated on Dundas Street, the heart of Edinburgh's commercial gallery quarter, the gallery has, over the years, shown work by many of the country's leading artists. Today the emphasis is on contemporary and fairly established artists. A downstairs gallery is given over to ceramics and jewellery made by some of the country's most exciting designers.

A work by Gerry Dudgeon on show at the **Nexus Galleries**. *See page 187.*

Trips Out of Town

Trips Out of Town

Some people come to Edinburgh for the nightlife, plenty come to look at the place and millions come for the Festival, but any who never venture out of the capital just don't realise what a beautiful, wild and rugged country Scotland can be.

Having made it to Edinburgh, it would be a shame to leave without glimpsing something of the rest of Scotland. There are many fine places within easy striking distance of the capital in Lothian, Fife and the Borders, which, if they aren't quite the Highlands and Islands, at least give an introduction to life beyond the capital. And, if you've got a bit more time, it is possible to get right out into the wilds with comparative ease. Then, of course, there is Glasgow, Scotland's largest city and Edinburgh's rival, and only 50 minutes away from the capital by train. It makes an easy day trip for shopping or sightseeing and has its own cultural and nightlife to be proud of.

PLANNING A TRIP

The best place to start is the **Edinburgh & Lothians Tourist Board** on Princes Street. However, while the staff are helpful, they are only able to provide information, not give an opinion, which can be irritating if you want to find out the pros and cons of one destination over another. But if you're pretty sure of where you want to go, it is the best place to find out how to get there and what to see when you arrive.

A good map is invaluable, not only for getting an idea of distances but also to see if a particular place is within easy reach of, say, the coast or good walking territory. Ordnance Survey (OS) has the whole of Great Britain mapped in intimate detail. The two series that are likely to prove of greatest use are the Landranger (scale 1:50,000) and the Pathfinder (scale 1:25,000).

Edinburgh & Lothians Tourist Board

3 Princes Street, New Town, EH2 (473 3800/ www.edinburgh.org). Bus 3, 3A, 12, 16, 17. **Open** *May, June, Sept* 9am-7pm Mon-Sat; 10am-7pm Sun; *July, Aug* 9am-8pm Mon-Sat; 10am-8pm Sun; *Nov-Mar, Apr, Oct* 9am-6pm Mon-Sat; 10am-6pm Sun. **Map** p314 D2.

The Stationery Office Bookshop

71 Lothian Road, South Edinburgh, EH3 (228 4181/ www.itsofficial.net). Bus 11, 15, 24. **Open** 9am-5pm Mon-Fri; 10am-5pm Sat; closed Sun. **Credit** MC, V. **Map** p314 A3.

Sells OS maps covering the whole of Scotland, plus a good selection of the more esoteric guides to the country's monuments, including some published by Historic Scotland. Business and computing books are also stocked. The official outlet for government publications.

GETTING AROUND

Transport can sometimes be a problem. Some of the more remote rural areas are lucky if they're served by two buses. A week. If you are going to use the public bus service you should ensure you can make it back to Edinburgh when you need to. Scotland's rail system is fairly efficient and provides a network of trains to most of the larger towns but rarely to smaller places. Hiring your own transport is often the best option as it allows you to follow your curiosity and explore more out-of-the-way areas. For details of **Waverley Railway Station** and **St Andrew Square Bus Station** in Edinburgh, *see page 272*. The latter is closed for refurbishment in May 2000. Until it is reopened in 2003, long-distance bus services and those to Glasgow and Fife will leave from the south side of St Andrew Square. Local services and those to the Lothians will leave from Waterloo Place. Details of bicycle, car and motorbike hire are given on *pages 275-6*.

ORGANISED TOURS

If you are going further afield, several companies organise tours. Many of these are rather sedate and involve a lot of sitting on a coach while the country rolls past and a tour guide rolls out a spiel. There are several companies that will tailor a tour to suit your needs if you are in a large group. Others cater for independent travellers, either alone or in small groups (*see page 184*).

MOUNTAINS & REMOTE AREAS

Scotland's mountains are incredibly beautiful and provide pleasure for thousands of people. They are the sort of places that you can wander into without having to make too much effort. But, while you can often travel for miles along benign tracks, you can also wander off into places that can be highly dangerous with perturbing ease. Always observe the basic rules – accidents do happen but their effects can be minimised. Always tell someone where you are going and what time you plan to get back. Take

a map, a compass and a torch. Wear suitable footwear and take waterproofs. Carry a water bottle (which you can refill from a burn or small stream if necessary) and emergency rations. The real problem is that the weather can change very quickly, so if it looks like turning bad, get off the mountain quickly. Reputable sports and outdoor equipment shops (*see page 168*) will be able to give advice on mountain conditions. Everyone should always observe these precautions if they are planning on taking a walk away from the beaten track.

There 284 peaks over the height of 914 metres (3,000 feet) in Scotland, called 'Munros' after Sir Hugh Munro, who first counted their number in 1891. While Munro-bagging – attempting to climb every single one – is a great sport, it can lead to dangerous situations, particularly when the desire to get to the top of the mountain stops the climber realising that the need to get off it has become more urgent.

MIDGES

The Highlands of Scotland hold one natural terror for humankind: the midge. Tiny it may be, but never doubt its voracious appetite for fresh human blood. They breed on boggy

ground, prefer still days and are at their worst between late May and early August.

The good news is that, although they can make you itch and a cloud of them might be enough to drive you mad, their tiny bites rarely swell up and they do not transmit any diseases to humans. The bad news is that no one has found a repellent for them that works. However, they are deterred by citronella and herb oils such as thyme or bog myrtle. They also prefer dark- to light-coloured clothing and detest smoke.

HOW THIS CHAPTER IS ARRANGED

This chapter has been split into three broad areas. **Glasgow** is a short guide to the city, its culture, history and sightseeing. The **Day Trips** section gives an overview of those areas around Edinburgh that are close enough to make a viable day out – ie the Lothians, Fife, the Borders and Stirling. In the **Further Afield** section, there is basic information about getting to the more far-flung destinations for which at least an overnight stay is called for: Dundee & Angus, Perthshire, Grampian & Aberdeen, Highlands, Argyle, Ayrshire and Dumfries & Galloway.

Glasgow

Scotland's biggest city more than matches up to Edinburgh, with architecture, shops and entertainment that can turn its east coast rival green with envy.

A webcam view of the recently revamped George Square, at the heart of Glasgow's city centre, was recently voted one of the world's ten most 'image-rich' live websites. The accolade is a triumph for a city that has had more stabs at reinventing itself than Madonna. And that's just in the last ten years. The city's tenure in 1999 as UK City of Architecture and Design certainly consolidated the richness of its physical image, which is based on its bountiful architectural heritage. Image, in Glasgow terms, however, goes way beyond bricks and mortar. A renaissance of style has been a major factor in explaining the city's burgeoning allure. This rebirth of Glasgow as a designer city, as much as any architectural or cultural regeneration, has helped to sideline the pervading but dated post-war image of 'no mean city' – when drunkenness and violence seemed to be the two main qualities attributed to Glaswegians by outsiders. Although some negative traits will possibly never change – the city's poor heart disease record and its sectarian divisions remain – there has never been a better time to appreciate Glasgow's riches.

Scotland's largest city, with a population of 623,000, lies a mere 50 miles (80 kilometres) west of Edinburgh along the M8 – an hour's journey by car, or 50 minutes by train. For many, that modest distance is enough to place Scotland's two main cities poles apart. Rather than celebrate their differences and co-exist peacefully, Glasgow and Edinburgh traditionally 'enjoy' the splenetic relationship of warring neighbours. Denizens of Edinburgh refer to 'Weegie soap-dodgers'; Glaswegians trumpet their city's friendly reputation – in contrast to Edinburgh's aloof coldness. And so the sweeping generalisations persist.

Although it boasts as rich a history as its east coast neighbour, Glasgow is not as ensnared by its own heritage as the tourist-pleasing Edinburgh. The annual Celtic Connections festival in January is not, for example, simply a festival of the traditional, but an exploration of new forms of folk music. Glaswegians are proud of their social, political and industrial histories and convictions run deep for many of Glasgow's staunchly socialist population. The city's size and personality are its main advantages: it is large and dynamic

George Street, at the heart of the city.

enough to always be offering new experiences for its residents, yet it is intimate enough for no one to feel lost or alienated. Glasgow's reputation for friendliness prompted the Council to mark it as the 'Friendly City', to warmly invite visitors. Besides ignominiously replacing the city's previous marketing icon, Mr Happy, if the campaign lacks imagination it at least gets straight to the point of the city's enduring appeal.

SCRUBBING UP WELL

For its friendliness and the renewed confidence in its cool credentials, Glasgow, it seems, is reaping the rewards. Its successful tenancy as European City of Culture in 1990 – when big-name artists visited the city, new cultural venues sprang up and bars and clubs opened late into the night – kick-started a decade that saw Glasgow blossom to become the UK's hippest urban centre outside London. This position at the vanguard of cool was consolidated by 1999's architecture and design fest, which not only created a focus for its architectural identity but was instrumental in providing a launchpad for local designers. One area their influence can be felt is in the proliferating 'style' bar and club scene – hotspots like Air Organic, Strata, Tun Ton and Balsa are bars designed by the local young and hip for the local young and hip.

If Glaswegians are conscious of where they want to look good, they are equally tuned in to what it takes to look good in the first place. Recent years have seen an influx of designer clothing retailers to the city. With a choice of Versace, Armani, Hugo Boss and home-grown style emporium Cruise for all their Paul Smith and Prada needs, it's no surprise that moneyed Glaswegians wear their labels with pride. Nor are they in danger of eclipsing the dynamic street style culture, fuelled by local clubby designers and superlative retro-clothing shops.

Trendiness in music is harder to pin down. The best acts are so cool they shun fashion and get on with making idiosyncratic records and blitzing the nation's venues. Bands like Travis, Mogwai, and Belle and Sebastian are among Britain's rock and pop vanguard; venues such as the 13th Note, Nice'n'Sleazy and King Tut's carry on supporting the new wave of rising stars.

EARLIEST TIMES

Glasgow's appearance has always been a product of its position and fortunes. The earliest, prehistoric, settlement was at the lowest ford on the Clyde, which continued in use right up to the Roman invasion of AD 80. The Romans were looking for a stable northern frontier and built part of their Antonine Wall where the northern suburbs now stand. After they left in AD 163, few facts are known about the area, until St Mungo, the city's patron saint, was given land called 'glas cau' or 'the green hollow' by the King of Strathclyde in the early seventh century.

Takin' the Mac

The legacy of Charles Rennie Mackintosh looms large over the city of Glasgow. City-centre bins, benches and just about every other street accessory designed for or after 1990 is an ersatz variation on a Mackintosh stylistic theme, affectionately known as 'Mockintosh'. Mockintosh mania aside, the city is the best – some would say only – place to experience the work of one of the most original and dynamic architects and designers of the late 19th and early 20th centuries.

Mackintosh's greatest public buildings can be seen in and around Glasgow and some of the most important are reviewed on pages 228-238. The **Martyrs' Public School** (1896), just north of the Cathedral, is an example of his early architectural style. A stone's throw from each other in the city centre are the **Glasgow Herald Building** (see page 233) and **Daily Record Building** (1901). The latter is one of the hidden treasures of the city centre, combining curvilinear, art nouveau forms with geometric patterns set into glazed brick. It can only be viewed from Renfield and St Vincent Lanes. The

Scotland Street School Museum (see page 236) is best seen at night to appreciate the full illuminated impact of its glass Scots-baronial-type turrets.

Although Mackintosh is most often associated with the **Willow Tearoom** (see page 231), his *pièce de résistance* is undoubtedly the **Glasgow School of Art** (see page 233). Meanwhile the house he designed, but never saw built, is the **House for an Art Lover** (see page 236).

Mackintosh's other masterpiece is **Hill House** (West Upper Colquhoun Street, 01436 673900/ www.nts.org.uk; open Apr-Oct 1.30-5pm daily but phone first to check), which involves a trip to Helensburgh, 45 minutes by train outside Glasgow (trains leave from Queen Street Station every half hour). Walter Blackie, director of the well-known Glasgow publishers, commissioned not only the house and garden but much of the furniture and all of the interior fittings and decorative schemes. Today, the rooms seem as modern as they must have been in 1904 when the Blackie family moved in.

Trips Out of Town

Often seen in Glasgow: old versus new.

commissioning of the public buildings to the west of George Square and the city's self-confidence lead to the 1888 International Exhibition in Kelvingrove Park. But it was a city that was as impoverished as it was wealthy. A huge influx of immigrants from Ireland and the Highlands resulted in chronic overcrowding of the new tenements. While the population rose to 500,000, with over half the workforce employed in shipbuilding and manufacturing, crime and disease both flourished.

The 20th century was a time of industrial decline and consequent rise in worker action. The radical socialist group, the Red Clydesiders, organised their first strike in 1915 as shipyards, geared to maximum capacity, faced a post-war slump. While some of the greatest liners of the 20th century, including the *QE2* and the *Royal Yacht Britannia,* were launched into the Clyde, by the 1960s and 1970s shipyards along the length of the river were closing down. Today, all that remains is the 50-metre (164-foot) high Finnieston Crane and a legacy of left-wing, radical politics in a city that knows how to change with the times and make sure that its position on the cutting edge will ensure its future prosperity.

A religious settlement grew on this site, where Glasgow Cathedral stands today, while another grew around the fishing trade a mile south on the northern bank of the river.

Trade drove the area's expansion for much of the second millennium. Referred to as a city in 1172, it exported hides, wool, herring and salmon – and, by the 1500s, it had grown to a single development of some 5,000 inhabitants. It kept on expanding as coal, cloth and Clyde red herrings were shipped to France and Ireland in exchange for meal, oats, butter, salt and pepper.

While Glaswegians fervently opposed the 1707 Act of Union, the opportunities for trade proved their boon. As the closest British port to the West Indies and America, the city became rich by trading in tobacco and the Merchant City began to be built eastwards of the existing centre. But when the American colonies revolted against British rule in 1775, the traders had to re-invent themselves as manufacturers, paving the way for the Industrial Revolution to make its first home in the city.

During the 19th century, Glaswegians created more wealth from industries that made full use of the local iron and coal deposits, while building an elegant Victorian expansion to their city, more in keeping with the needs of their businesses. No expense was spared in the

Sightseeing

City centre

Glasgow's small but perfectly formed city centre is laid out in a grid pattern, not unlike that of that other great second city, Chicago. It is also, in common with Chicago, a definitively 19th-century city. The Clyde River, historically the main artery along which the city's wealth flowed, also leads to the physical and symbolic heart of the city in the shape of George Square, a former swamp. The magnificent **City Chambers**, opened by Queen Victoria in 1888, to the east of the square, is the most potent representation of Glasgow's former status as the 'second city' of her vast empire.

MERCHANT CITY
Spreading away from the south-east of George Square is the **Merchant City**, formerly the centre for Glasgow's sugar and tobacco traders, who brought the city its prosperity in the early 19th century. As the city's trading prowess declined in the late 19th and early 20th centuries and heavy industry became king, the Merchant City's pre-eminence also waned and the area suffered. The yuppie years of the 1980s, however, not usually given credit for anything other than shoulder pads and greed, heralded the beginning of the renaissance of the area, and it is now impossible to walk about

here without passing one trendy bar, bistro, brasserie or another. Designer clothes meccas also dominate in swanky shopping areas such as the **Italian Centre**.

Ingram Street, the main thoroughfare, connects the Merchant City to the city centre proper and culminates in **Royal Exchange Square**. The **Gallery of Modern Art**, GOMA (*see page 232*), is at the heart of the square. Since opening in 1996 it has attracted a record amount of controversy and disapproval for its populist selection policy. It has also attracted a record number of visitors.

CANDLERIGGS

Candleriggs, or Merchant City East, as the more upwardly mobile denizens of the area would describe it, is home to the city's more understated and charming live venues, such as the **City Hall** (*see page 239*). **Café Gandolfi** (*see page 240*), on Albion Street, is another charmer, and a Glasgow café institution, characterised by its homely wooden interior designed by Tim Stead. To the south lies Trongate, marked by the **Tolbooth Steeple** at the intersection of five roads. Next to it, the **Mercat Cross** is a 1929 copy of the original that marked the first Glasgow market in the 12th century. Turning eastwards into Trongate, which forms the beginning of Argyle Street, the

The City Chambers. *See page 228.*

clock steeple belongs to the Tron Theatre. The steeple is all that remains of the original church, which was burned down in 1793 by members of the local branch of the Hellfire Club. The huge **St Enoch Centre** (*see page 246*) helps to make Argyle Street Glasgow's best mainstream shopping drag. Opposite is the **Argyle Arcade**, an attractive and airy Victorian glass-roofed throughfare, lined with jewellers' shops, which links through to **Buchanan Street**, the discerning shopper's paradise.

ART & ANTIQUES

To the south of Argyle Street, Chisholm Street and Parnie Street are worth more than a passing glance, not only for the unorthodox but eye-catching marriage of red/blonde sandstone tenements, but for the quirkiest shopping area in the city: tattoos, comics, signed footballs and tropical fish are among the many goods on offer. The adjoining King Street is a centre for art galleries and collectives of a similarly conceptual persuasion, such as the **Transmission Gallery**, **Art Exposure**, **Glasgow Print Studio** and **Streetlevel Gallery**. With a number of studios above the galleries themselves, this is one of the more bohemian, buzzing parts of the city centre. King Street swerves and culminates in King's Court, a must for the serious second-hand and vintage clothes shopper. **Paddy's Market** lies just over the road, a traditional market whose romance is tarnished by the daily detritus left behind. Along the gentle curve of the railway line towards the Clyde are three of Glasgow's most established and well-loved drinking dens. The **Victoria Bar** and **Clutha Vaults**, like the 250-year-old **Scotia Bar** (for all three, *see page 241*) on Stockwell Street, are a mecca for folk music and traditional Scottish culture. Together they are known affectionately as the 'Stockwell Triangle'. And on a good day the Stockwell Triangle does, indeed, make people disappear. At least until their hangovers subside.

NAUTICAL INFLUENCES

Down by the riverside, the Clyde Walkway is a good excuse for a pleasant stroll underneath the numerous city-centre bridges. The nearby **Riverside Club** is another of Glasgow's fine institutions, and rightly famous for its weekend ceilidh dances. Close to the Clyde stands Central Station, a magnificent feat of Victorian engineering and recently restored to something of its former glory. In the renovated railway arches beneath the station is **The Arches**, home to the hippest music, club and theatre happenings in Glasgow. In this vicinity are also some of the most notable city-centre buildings,

Trips Out of Town

BUILT IN 1911 AND RESTORED IN 1999 DURING GLASGOW'S
YEAR AS UK CITY OF ARCHITECTURE & DESIGN, ARTHOUSE IS A FUSION
OF CLASSICAL ARCHITECTURE AND MODERN INTERIOR DESIGN.

THE LISTED INTERIOR HAS BEEN GIVEN A CONTEMPORARY TWIST
CREATING A MODERN CLASSIC, MAKING ARTHOUSE THE
MOST DISTINCTIVE HOTEL IN THE CITY.

ARTHOUSE HOTEL.
65 BEDROOMS. 2 RESTAURANTS. 2 BARS.
MEETINGS. FUNCTIONS. HAIR & BEAUTY.

ArtHouse Hotel, 129 Bath Street, Glasgow G2 2SY Tel: 0141 221 6789 Bookings: 0141 572 6000
Fax: 0141 221 6777 Email: info@arthousehotel.com www.arthousehotel.com

including the Egyptian Halls by Alexander 'Greek' Thomson (*see page 232* **It's all Greek to me**). Although it is one of Thomson's most handsome façades, plans to clean and consolidate the building remain unresolved, so it looks criminally neglected. One block along, on Mitchell Street, is Charles Rennie Mackintosh's first public building (1895) built to house the *Glasgow Herald*. It is now, after a spectacular makeover, home to **The Lighthouse**, Scotland's Centre for Architecture, Design and the City (*see page 233*). Nearby, the **Odeon City Centre Cinema** (*see page 238*) has also undergone a major facelift to reveal one of the most charming of the few remaining art-deco façades in the city.

SHOPPING STOPS

The pedestrianised **Buchanan Street** is an area of rather more upmarket shops. At the very north of the street, past the **Buchanan Galleries**, is the **Royal Concert Hall**, another of Glasgow's least impressive monoliths. **Sauchiehall Street** is legendary – the mere mention of it can bring a tear to the eye of an expatriate Glaswegian. It has also become a byword for crowded. It is worth visiting, however, to view the **Willow Tearoom** (1904), the only remaining tearoom designed by Charles Rennie Mackintosh for the formidable Kate Cranston, a pioneer of the genteel tearoom society so prevalent in Glasgow in the late 19th century. They retain their simple and understated façade as well as many of their original features in the Salon de Luxe. The venue of the recent ground-breaking and definitive Mackintosh exhibition, the **McLellan Galleries**, is close by. It is currently home to the **Centre for Contemporary Arts** (*see page 232*), which hosts a range of touring and temporary shows from new artists and international celebrities. The eight-storey **Baird Hall of Residence**, further west along Sauchiehall Street, is an eye-catching splash of art deco, its verve rivalled only slightly by the truck protruding from the wall above the **Garage** (*see page 244*), the popular rock and club venue situated close by.

GARNETHILL

A sharp incline to the north of Sauchiehall Street leads up to Garnethill, a mainly residential area that is the centre of Glasgow's Chinese community and also contains Garnethill Synagogue, the oldest Jewish place of worship in the city. The **Glasgow School of Art** (*see page 233*), Mackintosh's masterpiece and the best reason to visit the city, balances on this perilously steep hill. Over the brow, on Buccleuch Street, is **Tenement House**

Pop in for some char at the **Willow Tearoom**, the only remaining tearoom by Mackintosh.

Trips Out of Town

(*see page 233*), the preserved home of Agnes Toward, who lived there from 1911 to 1965 without changing the interior.

Westwards is **Cowcaddens**, an area recognised principally as the home of Scottish Television. The **Glasgow Film Theatre** (*see page 238*) is the hub of much of the activity of the Scottish Film Industry, which also has a base in Glasgow and which has enjoyed something of a renaissance recently with the likes of Peter Mullan's *Orphans* and Lynne Ramsay's *Ratcatcher*. Cowcaddens boasts many of the city's best-known theatre and drama centres. The area is dominated by the attractive modern brick and glass edifice of the **Royal Scottish Academy of Music & Drama** (*see page 239*), which hosts a variety of concerts and recitals; opposite lies the **Theatre Royal** (*see page 239*), home of Scottish Opera and Scottish Ballet production premières; and finally, the **Pavilion Theatre** (*see page 239*), the place for nostalgia seekers everywhere, with cheery, end-of-the-pier type shows.

Centre for Contemporary Arts

McLellan Galleries, 270 Sauchiehall Street, G2 (0141 332 7521/box office 332 0522/ www.cca-glasgow.com). Cowcaddens tube. **Open** *Gallery* 10am-6pm Mon-Sat; 11am-5pm Sun. *Centre* 9am-9pm Mon-Thur; 9am-midnight Fri; 10am-midnight Sat; 11am-9pm Sun. **Admission** free. **Credit** MC, V. **Map** p302 C2.

Glasgow's focus for contemporary visual, performance and multimedia art. Currently housed in the McLellan Galleries until a new state-of-the-art refurbishment is completed in 2001.

Gallery of Modern Art

Queen Street, G1 (0141 229 1996). Buchanan St tube. **Open** 10am-5pm Mon-Thur, Sat; 11am-5pm Fri, Sun. **Admission** free. **Credit** AmEx, DC, MC, V. **Map** p303 D3.

Glasgow architect David Hamilton was responsible for the portico addition to the Cunninghame Mansion (1778), now home to a lively, eclectic and controversial modern art collection. The two-tier café has terrific views of the city's skyline and good-value fare.

It's all Greek to me

Alexander 'Greek' Thomson (1817-75) probably contributed more than any other single architect to the defining Victorian character of Glasgow's architecture. He earned the nickname 'Greek' through his use of the architectural language of the ancient Greeks, adding elements of Egyptian and Oriental architecture, while making striking use of new materials such as plate glass and iron. With the unmitigated success of the Glasgow 1999 exhibition 'Alexander Thomson: The Unknown Genius', which was the inaugural presentation at **The Lighthouse** (*see page 233*), he has finally gained his deserved recognition alongside Mackintosh as local architectural hero. A tour of Thomson's architectural legacy is an excellent way to explore the city as a whole, both north and south of the river.

Of all the buildings Thomson designed, about two-thirds remain, the rest of them falling victim to Glasgow's infamous demolition programmes. Must-sees include the magnificent, classical-fronted warehouse and office developments in the city centre such as the **Egyptian Halls** (1871) on Union Street and the **Grosvenor Building** (1861) on Gordon Street. His domestic terraces of note include **Great Western Terrace** (1867) – Glasgow's grandest terrace – and **Moray Place**, where Thomson himself lived and died.

His most most striking villa is **Holmwood House** (1858) in Cathcart, which combines the classical and picturesque while, arguably, anticipating Frank Lloyd Wright's **Prairie Houses** (1901-10) with their low-pitched roof and overhanging eaves. An image of Homwood House's spectacular cupola appears, along with the architect himself, on the Clydesdale Bank's £20 note. Finally, Thomson built three churches, or monumental temples, which were described by American historian Henry-Russell Hitchcock as 'three of the finest Romanic-Classical churches in the world'. Of the two remaining (Queens Park Church was bombed by the Luftwaffe), **Caledonia Road Church** (1856) on Cathcart Road is only a shell, which stands neglected 'like a gigantic exclamation mark at the edge of the Gorbals', according to a disgruntled reader of Glasgow's **Evening Times**. However, **St Vincent Street Church** (1859) survives intact and stands as one of the most recognisable landmarks in the city with its amazing mix of Greek-, Egyptian- and Indian-style motifs. An incredible feat considering the architect had never even made it across the English Channel, let alone visited any of these inspirational countries. St Vincent Street Church has recently joined the Taj Mahal as one of the 100 most-endangered sites on the World Monuments Watch List.

Glasgow School of Art

167 Renfrew Street, G3 (0141 353 4500/
www.gsa.ac.uk). Cowcaddens tube/Queen St rail.
Open *Tours* 11am, 2pm Mon-Fri; 10.30am,
11.30am Sat; closed Sun. **Shop** 10am-5pm
Mon-Fri; 10am-noon Sat; closed Sun. **Tours** £5;
£3 concessions; free under-10s. **Credit** AmEx,
MC, V. **Map** p303 D2.
Charles Rennie Mackintosh's masterpiece and an
icon of 20th-century design. The must-see views,
of what is a must-see item on any tour of Glasgow,
are the façades of the north and west wings,
and particularly the library beyond. The interior is
only open to the public on guided tours but is well
worth taking the trouble to see.

The Lighthouse

11 Mitchell Lane, G1 (0141 221 6362/
www.thelighthouse.co.uk). St Enoch or Buchanan
St tube/Central Station rail. **Open** 10.30am-5.30pm
Mon, Wed, Fri, Sat; 11am-5.30pm Tue; 10.30am-7pm
Thur; noon-5pm Sun. **Admission** free. *Mackintosh
Interpretation Centre* £2.50; £1.50-£2 concessions.
Map p303 D3.
Charles Rennie Mackintosh's *Glasgow Herald* build-
ing has metamorphosed into the snappily named
Lighthouse, Scotland's Centre for Architecture,
Design and the City, one of the major flagship pro-
jects of Glasgow's reign as UK City of Architecture
and Design in 1999. It's a great place to come, to see,
and to hang out.

Tenement House

145 Buccleuch Street, G3 (0141 333 0183/
www.nts.org.uk). Cowcaddens tube. **Open** *Mar-Oct*
2-5pm daily; closed Nov-Feb. **Admission** £3.50;
£2.50 concessions; free under-18s with adult
(maximum three) during 2000; free NT members.
No credit cards. Map p302 C1.
The preserved home of Agnes Toward provides a
fascinating snapshot of Glasgow tenement living.
Agnes was a renowned hoarder, and the interior is
crammed with artefacts from her time.

Old Town & East End

East of the shopping thoroughfares and chic
bars and restaurants of the Merchant City beats
the city's historic heart, where the area known
as **Glasgow Cross** fans eastwards from the
intersection of Trongate, Gallowgate, High
Street and Saltmarket.

This area was the old centre of the city
before the 19th-century surge westwards and,
although it lacks the social vibrancy of the
Merchant City, it has rich pickings for anyone
with an interest in Glaswegian history. The
city was effectively founded at the point where
the Molendinar Burn flowed into the Clyde,
now the site of the High Court. Further up
the Saltmarket, at the point where it becomes
the High Street, stands the quintessential
symbol of old Glasgow: the 39-metre

(126-foot) **Tolbooth Steeple** (1626). Here
royal proclamations were read and condemned
prisoners were hanged. It was to here that
Bonnie Prince Charlie marched his troops in
1745 and it was where farmers and, later,
merchants met to talk shop. Nowadays, it
serves as a focal point on Hogmanay when its
bells ring in the new year.

DEAR GREEN PLACE

Saltmarket stretches south from the steeple to
the river, with the **McLennan Arch** on the
left. Originally the main entrance to the
Ingram Street Assembly Rooms, the arch now
marks the entrance to the city's most famous
public space, **Glasgow Green**. This stretch of
parkland may look unspectacular but, as
Europe's oldest public park, it supports over
800 years of memories and experiences. It
doubled as both fair site and hanging place
and has also been a drying green for the local
wash-houses. According to the terms of a 14th-
century charter, the Green can only be used as
a place of leisure: the annual Bonfire Night
fireworks display, Glasgow Fair Festival and
rock concerts have honoured this. The
People's Palace and the **Winter Gardens**
(for both, *see page 234*) are the main
permanent attractions on the Green.
Renaissance Venice makes a striking
appearance opposite the People's Palace, in the
guise of one of the city's most quirky
buildings, **Templeton's Carpet Factory**
(1889). Designed by William Leiper, and based
on the Doges' Palace, the building is one of the
finest examples of decorative brickwork in
existence, and a rare find in an essentially
stone city. Just off the Green where it borders
on Greendyke Street is the **Homes for the
Future** development, one of the cornerstone
projects of Glasgow's year as the UK City of
Architecture and Design. This ambitious
housing development has managed to reclaim
the lost urban spaces north of the Green with
some of the most handsomely modern and
cutting-edge architecture in the city.

Templeton's Carpet Factory – a beauty.

Necropolis, up close and personal.

BARRAS BARGAINS

To the north-west of the Green lie the twin thoroughfares of **Gallowgate** and **London Road**. A stroll here after dark can be a hair-raising experience, but these two streets form the boundary for Glasgow's famous weekend market, the **Barras**, which is a whole Sunday morning bargain-hunting expedition in itself. The biggest and most popular of Glasgow's ballrooms, the famous **Barrowland**, adjoins the market. Unveiled on Christmas Eve 1934, it subsequently had its huge neon sign taken down during World War II after German planes used it to navigate by. Its current fame rests on the fact that it is *the* venue for rock concerts in the city, and indeed Scotland. Just look for the unmissable neon sign.

There is little for the sightseer further east, although, for about half the city's population, Parkhead is synonymous with the agony and ecstasy of supporting Glasgow Celtic Football Club, whose stadium, **Celtic Park**, dominates the area.

Snaking up the High Street, north of the Gallowgate, a cluster of attractions including the **Cathedral**, **Necropolis**, **Provand's Lordship** and the **St Mungo Museum of Religious Life & Art** are sadly, but vitally, all that remains at the heart of the medieval city. All these places are listed below.

Glasgow Cathedral

Castle Street, G4 (0141 552 6891/0988). High St rail. **Open** *Apr-Sept* 9.30am-6pm Mon-Sat; 2-5pm Sun; *Oct-Mar* 9.30am-4pm Mon-Sat; 2-4pm Sun. **Admission** free. **Map** p303 F2.
Glasgow's patron saint, St Mungo, whose tomb can be found in the crypt, founded Glasgow Cathedral in 543 on burial ground consecrated by St Ninian. Parts of the current building date from the 12th century, making it one of Scotland's oldest medieval churches. Unfortunately, it has been subject to brutal alteration over the centuries, with the Victorians lopping off two towers on the west front for aesthetic reasons. It's no blockbuster as cathedrals go, but it is bold, unfussy and quite scary at night when viewed from the dramatic rise to the south-east.

Necropolis

Glasgow Necropolis Cemetery, 50 Cathedral Square, G4 (0141 552 3145). High St rail. **Open** 24hrs daily. **Admission** free. **Map** p303 F2.
Scotland's first non-denominational 'hygienic' graveyard was inspired by the famed Père Lachaise cemetery in Paris to give the industrialists and merchants of the 19th century a dignified resting place.

The People's Palace/Winter Gardens

Glasgow Green, G4 (0141 554 0223). Bridgeton rail. **Open** 10am-5pm Mon-Thur, Sat; 11am-5pm Fri, Sun. **Admission** free. **Map** p303 F4.
The red sandstone People's Palace, built in 1898, originally served as a municipal and cultural centre for the city's working class. It now houses one of Glasgow's most cherished exhibitions, covering all aspects of Glaswegian life, particularly its social and industrial history. The adjoining Winter Gardens was severely damaged by fire in 1998.

Provand's Lordship

3 Castle Street, G4 (0141 553 2557). High St rail. **Open** phone for details. **Map** p303 F2.
Glasgow's oldest (1471) and only medieval house. Another claim to fame is that Mary Queen of Scots is believed to have slept here. Due to open in late 2000 following extensive refurbishment.

St Mungo Museum of Religious Life & Art

2 Castle Street, G4 (0141 553 2557). High St rail. **Open** 10am-5pm Mon-Sat; 11am-5pm Sun. **Admission** free. **Map** p303 F2.
The main reason to visit this museum is to see Dali's awesome *Christ of St John of the Cross*. Despite Glasgow's undesirable sectarian predilections, this is a multi-faith museum with its own Zen garden for some instant karma.

South Side

The West End may be the city's bohemian hub, but the **South Side**, with its rich ethnic diversity, is probably the city's most cosmopolitan area. Most of the South Side is residential, encompassing many different and disparate communities, from the affluent Newton Mearns to the rather less affluent housing estate of Castlemilk and, most infamously, the **Gorbals**.

GORBALS

The Gorbals has a colourful history. It was a leper colony before becoming one of Glasgow's first suburbs in the 19th century. Its name has been translated variously as 'beautiful town' and 'rough plot of ground'. Its desirability as a residential area has fluctuated too. The surrounding greenbelt made the Gorbals fashionable at first, but the arrival of industry and immigrants led to slum overcrowding. With the subsequent obliteration of the tenements, to make way for the high-rise flats that still dominate the area, the community disappeared as well. Only recently, with the construction of the 'New

Outside the **People's Palace**. *See page 234.*

Gorbals Village', are these disastrous post-war housing initiatives being rectified. Nevertheless, the area can proudly boast one of best theatres in Britain. The **Citizens' Theatre** was founded in 1943 by James Bridie as a theatre for the people, and it is justly world famous for its risk-taking and cutting-edge productions – Glasgow's theatre-goers are equally impressed by its unfeasibly low ticket prices.

The district of **Govan** nestles next to the river and shares many similarities to the Gorbals, namely medieval roots, a population explosion in the 19th century, a rough reputation and current redevelopment. Its most famous inhabitant is TV's string vest-wearing philosopher Rab C Nesbitt.

South Side landmarks worth more than a passing glance are Mackintosh's **Scotland Street School Museum** (*see page 236*) and, on a Saturday night, the **Grand Ole Opry** (*see page 244*).

PARK LIFE

The South Side is dotted with the largest parks in a city that boasts more parks per head of population than anywhere else in Europe. These include **Bellahouston**, where the Pope said mass in 1982 and where you will find a version of Mackintosh's **House for an Art Lover** (*see page 236*). In **Pollok Park**, Glasgow's largest park – at 146 hectares (361 acres) – and probably most beautiful, are the main attractions south of the river: **Pollok House** and the **Burrell Collection** (for both, *see page 236*).

Some of the best examples of Alexander 'Greek' Thomson's architecture (*see page 232* **It's all Greek to me**) can also be found in the South Side. The **Caledonia Road Church** in the Gorbals was inspired by the Acropolis but its future has remained uncertain since a fire in 1965 destroyed the painted interior, leaving only the portico and tower intact. The **double villa** in Mansionhouse Road, Langside, was built in 1856, shortly before **Holmwood House** (*see page 236*) in Netherlee, which is regarded as Thomson's finest villa. The Thomson-designed terraces of Regent Park in the district of Strathbungo, to the west of Queen's Park, have been designated a conservation area since the 1970s. Both Thomson and Mackintosh lived there.

No round-up of the attractions south of the city would be complete without mention of its stadiums: **Ibrox** (*see page 238*), home of Glasgow Rangers Football Club and the **National Stadium** at Hampden Park, home to Scotland's national football team.

Burrell Collection

Pollok Park, 2060 Pollokshaws Road, G43 (0141 287 2550). Pollokshaws West rail, then 10-min walk. **Open** 10am-5pm Mon-Thur, Sat; 11am-5pm Fri, Sun. **Admission** free. **Map** p301.

Sir William Burrell gifted his prodigious collection of art and artefacts to the city of Glasgow in 1944. One of the jewels in Glasgow's cultural crown, the collection encompasses treasures from ancient Egypt, Greece and Rome and ceramics from various Chinese dynasties as well as European decorative arts including rare tapestries and stained glass. It also boasts one of the finest collections of Impressionist and Post-Impressionist paintings and drawings in the world. Try to come on a sunny day – the interior courtyard illustrates that natural light is the essential material of good architecture.

Holmwood House

61-63 Netherlee Road, G44 (0141 637 2129/ www.nts.org.uk). Cathcart rail. **Open** *Apr-Oct* 1.30-5.30pm daily; access may be restricted at peak times. Groups must pre-book. **Admission** £3.20; £2.20 concessions; free children. **No credit cards**. **Map** p301.

Alexander Thomson's finest and most elaborate villa. Visitors can see the progress being made on the conservation and restoration of the architect's richly ornamental classical interior. Unmissable.

House for an Art Lover

10 Dumbreck Road, G41 (0141 353 4791/ www.houseforanartlover.co.uk). **Open** *Apr-1 Oct* 10am-4pm Mon-Thur, Sun; 10am-3pm Sat; closed Fri; *2 Oct-Mar* 10am-4pm Sat, Sun; closed Mon-Fri. **Admission** £3.50; £2.50 concessions. **Credit** MC, V. **Map** p301.

Built to the plans Mackintosh submitted to a German architectural competition in 1901, the house has finally been completed. Rooms include the Main Hall, Dining Room, Music Room and Oval Room (although Mackintosh included the latter in his plans he never added any details). The main impression is one of space and light. There's also a shop and a café and exhibitions are held throughout the year.

Pollok House

Pollok Park, 2060 Pollokshaws Road, G43 (0141 616 6410/www.nts.org.uk). Pollokshaws West rail, then 10-min walk. **Open** *Apr-Oct* 10am-5pm daily; *Nov-Mar* 11am-4pm daily. **Admission** £4; £3 concessions; free children. **Credit** MC, V. **Map** p301.

This magnificent 18th-century mansion houses the Stirling Maxwell Collection of Spanish and European paintings, in addition to one of the finest collections of works by William Blake.

Scotland Street School Museum

225 Scotland Street, G5 (0141 287 0500/ www.glasgow.gov.uk). Shields Rd tube. **Open** *from Aug 2000* 10am-5pm Mon-Thur, Sat; 11am-5pm Sun. **Admission** free. **Map** p302 B4.

A real Mackintosh treat, this majestic school

The lovely **Botanic Gardens**. *See page 237.*

building is now a museum, offering an insight into Glaswegian schooling in the first half of the 20th century. Closed until August 2000.

West End

The huge dome and imposing façade of the **Mitchell Library** (*see page 238*), Europe's largest reference library, unofficially divides the West End from the city centre. The West End, it has to be said, has a character all of its own. A dual personality has evolved through its role as the soft play area for the city's huge student population and as the happy hunting ground for the bourgeois and the bohemian, or bourgeois bohemian (as probably best describes the quintessential Westender). All this adds up, as you might imagine, to a cornucopia of bars, bistros, and brasseries – and a lot more besides.

GREAT WESTERN

One of the main arteries serving the West End is the never-ending Great Western Road, built in 1836 after relentless pressure from Glasgow's middle classes, who wanted a route out of the overcrowded, industry-polluted city centre. Now it contributes to that pollution. To the south, the domestic terrace buildings of this period are among the city's most superb architectural features and it is well worth taking a leisurely stroll around them. Highlights are **Park Circus** (1857-63) and **Park Terrace** (1855). Further west, flanking Great Western Road, **Great Western Terrace** (1867) is the definitive Glasgow terrace designed by Alexander 'Greek' Thomson (*see page 232* **It's all Greek to me**).

Escape northwards and the hidden curiosity of the Glasgow branch of the **Forth & Clyde Canal Path** becomes apparent. Although not the most salubrious area, on a sunny day this stretch makes for an unusual walk. The walkway, which dates back to 1790, eventually leads upstream to the West Highland Way, Scotland's first long-distance footpath, which ends 92 miles (147 kilometres) away in Fort William. A popular turn-off is at Fir Park, Firhill Road, the home of Partick Football Club, the city's 'third' football team, and a stone's throw away from the Queen's Cross Church (1898), the headquarters of the Charles Rennie Mackintosh Society and Mackintosh's only church. Downstream the walkway follows the River Kelvin towards the **Botanic Gardens** (*see below*).

THE HEART OF THE WEST END

The Botanic Gardens is the place to be seen during Glasgow's short summer. But Byres Road, just beyond the main gates of the Gardens, is the real heart of the West End, both for shopping and for students. The road itself is pretty impressive in its own right. Radiating from the main thoroughfare can be found the lanes (Ashton, Dowanside and Cresswell), which are a must for second-hand and vintage clothes and unusual gifts. Arguably the comfiest cinema in the city, **The Grosvenor** (*see page 238*), can also be found in this hub, as well as a plethora of cafés and bars, which range from the cheap and cheerful to the swanky. The **Cottier Theatre** (*see page 239*) is a striking church conversion, and one of the few arts venues – and beer gardens – to be found outside the city centre.

The University of Glasgow dominates this area, and indeed the whole of the West End skyline, in its own overwhelming Gothic revivalist kind of way. The bizarre concrete façade of the Mackintosh House at the **Hunterian Art Gallery & Museum**, next door (*see page 238*), forms a strange but tantalising juxtaposition. To the east of the University is the 34-hectare (85-acre) Kelvingrove Park. First laid out as pleasure grounds in the 1850s, on a hot day it becomes instantly packed; on the other 364 days of the year, it is an oasis of calm. The red sandstone confection that is the **Art Gallery &**

Museum, Kelvingrove (*see below*), was built to hold the 1901 International Exhibition and dominates the southern end of the park. The nearby **Museum of Transport** on Argyle Street (*see page 238*) completes the picture of the West End Museum Mile.

Art Gallery & Museum, Kelvingrove

Kelvingrove, G3 (0141 287 2700/ www.glasgow.gov.uk). Kelvinhall tube/Partick rail. **Open** 10am-5pm Mon-Thur, Sat; 11am-5pm Fri, Sun. **Admission** free. **Map** p301.
The current display has essentially remained the same for decades, providing a 'thrill of the old'. Home to a world-class permanent collection of fine art, including 17th-century Dutch paintings, the Impressionists, and Scottish art and artefacts among them works by the Glasgow Boys' School and Mackintosh.

Botanic Gardens & Kibble Palace

730 Great West Road, G12 (0141 334 2422/ www.glasgow.gov.uk). Hillhead tube. **Open** *Palace* Apr-Oct 10am-4.45pm daily; Nov-Mar 10am-4.15pm daily. *Tropical glasshouse* 1-4.15pm Sat; noon-4.15pm Sun; closed Mon-Fri. *Gardens* 7am-dusk daily. **Admission** free. **Map** p301.
The gardens are dominated by the huge dome of Kibble Palace. A beautiful feat of Victorian engineering, it was originally a conservatory built for

Museum of Transport. *See page 238.*

eccentric John Kibble, who is said to have brought it from his estate on the shores of Loch Long, up the River Clyde on a huge raft drawn by a steamboat. Its greenhouses contain many rare species, palm trees and tropical plants.

Hunterian Art Gallery & Museum

University of Glasgow, Hillhead Street, G12 (0141 330 5431/www.gla.ac.uk/Museum). Hillhead tube. **Open** 9.30am-5pm Mon-Sat; closed Sun. *Mackintosh House* also closed 12.30-1.30pm Mon-Sat. **Admission** free. **Map** p301.

Scotland's largest print collection, including the finest works on paper by Mackintosh. The gallery leads to the Mackintosh House, and includes a recreation of the architect's home in Southpark Avenue, where he lived from 1906 to 1914. Built in 1807, the Hunterian is Scotland's oldest public museum, and among its archaeological treasures are several dinosaurs – as befits the Scottish Centre for Dinosaur Research.

Mitchell Library

North Street, G3 (0141 287 2999/ www.mitchelllibrary.gov.uk). Charing Cross rail. **Open** 9am-8pm Mon-Thur; 9am-5pm Fri, Sat; closed Sun. **Map** p302 B2.

With over one million books and documents, this is the largest reference library in Europe. The Glasgow and Burns Collections are invaluable for researchers.

Museum of Transport

1 Bunhouse Road, Kelvinhall, G3 (0141 287 2720). Kelvinhall tube/Partick rail. **Open** 10am-5pm Mon-Thur, Sat; 11am-5pm Fri, Sun. **Admission** free. **Credit** AmEx, MC, V. **Map** p301.

This is one of Britain's better transport museums. The Clyde Room celebrates, as well as mourns, Glasgow's shipbuilding industry. Home to the Museum of Football while its permanent venue is being completed at Hampden Park.

Entertainment

Glaswegians are not known for holding back when it comes to a party. And equally, there is plenty of international-class cultural entertainment to be had, whether the drama is on the stage or the football field.

TICKETS & INFORMATION

For **listings information**, call the venues direct or peruse the *List* (published fortnightly) or the *Glasgow Evening Times*. Glasgow City Council's website (www.glasgow.gov.uk) has a relatively useful events page divided into sections for theatre, music, sport, visual arts, family and festivals. The **Ticket Centre** is also useful.

Ticket Centre

Candleriggs, City centre, G1 (0141 287 5511/ 7777). Buchanan St tube, then 5-min walk. **Open** *office* 9.30am-6.30pm Mon-Sat; 10am-5pm Sun;

phoneline 9am-9pm Mon-Sat; 10am-5pm Sun. **Credit** AmEx, MC, V. **Map** p303 E3.

Sells tickets for venues and events for a booking fee.

Cinema

Glasgow Film Theatre

12 Rose Street, City centre, G3 (0141 332 8128/ www.gft.org.uk). Cowcaddens tube. **Admission** £3.75-£4.75; £1.75-£3.25 concessions. **Credit** AmEx, MC, V. **Map** 302 C2.

The place to see independent, arthouse and foreign releases. The former Cosmo cinema has been refurbished to enhance its art deco look. Café Cosmo in the foyer is a convenient spot to refuel before a film.

The Grosvenor

Ashton Lane, Hillhead, West End, G12 (credit card bookings 0141 339 4298/ www.caledoniancinemas.co.uk). Hillhead tube. **Open** *box office* 11am-7pm Mon-Sat; 1-7pm Sun. **Admission** £4; £2-£3 concessions. **Credit** AmEx, MC, V. **Map** p301.

A West End institution, this small, two-screen cinema programmes a strong mix of mainstream and arthouse movies.

Odeon City Centre Cinema

56 Renfield Street, City centre, G2 (0141 332 3413/credit card bookings 0870 5050 007/ www.odeon.co.uk). Queen St tube. **Admission** £4.25-£4.75. **Credit** AmEx, MC,V. **Map** p303 D2.

The last remaining big traditional city-centre cinema in Glasgow. The films are mainstream and it gets packed on weekends. But with six screens there is a reasonable choice.

Football

The Old Firm rivalry between the giants of Scottish football, Celtic and Rangers, is as legendary as the sectarianism of their supporters. Celtic's are Catholics, Rangers' are Protestant. Celtic play at Celtic Park, Rangers at Ibrox. The national team plays at the recently refurbished Hampden Park, which will be the site of the **Museum of Football** (which is currently at the Museum of Transport; *see above*).

Celtic Park

95 Kerrydale Street, G40 (0141 551 8653/ www.celticfc.co.uk). Bell Grove rail. **Admission** £16-£25. **Credit** MC, V. **Map** p301.

Hampden Park

Somerville Drive, G42 (0141 649 9256/ www.scottishfa.co.uk). King Park or Mount Florida rail. **Admission** prices vary. **Credit** MC, V. **Map** p301.

Ibrox

Edmiston Drive, G51 (0870 600 1993/ www.rangers.co.uk). Ibrox tube. **Admission** £17-£22. **Credit** MC, V. **Map** p301.

Music

City Hall

*Candleriggs, City centre, G1 (0141 287 5511).
Buchanan St tube/Queen St rail.* **Open** *box office*
9am-9pm Mon-Sat; 10am-5pm Sun. **Admission** free-
£15. **Credit** AmEx, MC, V. **Map** p303 E3
Although superseded by the Royal Concert Hall, the
City Hall is nevertheless still used by the Scottish
Chamber Orchestra.

Royal Concert Hall

*2 Sauchiehall Street, City centre, G2 (0141 353
8000/grch.com/www.grch.com). Buchanan St
tube.* **Open** *box office* 10am-6pm Mon-Sat; 1-6pm
Sun. **Admission** £8-£25. **Credit** AmEx, MC, V.
Map p303 D2.
While this is one of Glasgow's least impressive
monoliths, it is home to the Royal Scottish National
Orchestra and, for the last three weeks of every
January, to Celtic Connections. Started in 1994, Celtic
Connections is now one of the world's biggest and
most prestigious roots festivals, with a music policy encompassing old, new, traditional and modern
forms in a craic-fuelled frenzy.

Royal Scottish Academy of Music & Drama

*100 Renfrew Street, City centre, G2 (0141 332
4101/5057 box office/www.rsamd.ac.uk).
Cowcaddens tube.* **Open** phone for details of
performances. **Admission** £4-£5. **Credit** MC, V.
Map p303 D2.
There are two halls in this busy venue, which holds
recitals and masterclasses and hosts guest soloists.

Scottish Exhibition & Conference Centre

*Finniestoun Quay, G3 (0141 248 3000/
www.secc.co.uk). Exhibition Centre rail.* **Open** varies.
Admission varies. **Credit** AmEx, MC, V.
A soulless, aircraft hangar of an arena, which is the
main venue for the biggest touring rock groups and
stars who come to Scotland. The 3,000-seat
Armadillo auditorium provides all the intimacies
required by the more mature performers. By day, the
SECC is host to a variety of major exhibitions.

Theatre

Citizens' Theatre

*119 Gorbals Street, South Side, G5 (0141 429
0022). Bridge St tube.* **Open** *box office* 10am-
6pm Mon-Sat; closed Sun. **Admission** £10; £3
concessions. **Credit** MC, V. **Map** p303 D4.
Risk-taking and lively productions of new theatre
are the hallmarks of the 'Citz'. Even the Edinburgh
critics like it. The 600-seat main theatre concentrates
on British and foreign work, while the Circle and
Stalls studios (120 and 60 seats respectively) cram
the audience right up next to the actors for sometimes brilliant, sometimes awful, but always worth
seeing, new or obscure plays.

Cottier Theatre

*93 Hyndland Street, West End, G12 (0141 357
3868/cottierth@aol.com). Kelvinhall tube.* **Open**
box office 4.15-8pm Mon-Sat; closed Sun.
Admission £6; £4 concessions. **Credit** AmEx,
MC, V. **Map** p301.
An unusual venue, this beautifully converted church
shows a mix of cabaret, comedy and small-scale
touring shows. It can be draughty, but the beer garden is unique in Glasgow.

King's Theatre

*294 Bath Street, City centre, G2 (0141 287 5511/
www.citylive.org). Charing Cross rail.* **Open**
box office 10am-6pm Mon-Sat; closed Sun.
Admission £8.50-£12.50. **Credit** AmEx, MC, V.
Map p302 C2.
Glasgow's own musical home, where the local amateur shows alternate with big touring productions.

Pavilion Theatre

*121 Renfield Street, City centre, G2 (0141 332
1846/www.paviliontheatre.co.uk). Cowcaddens tube.*
Open *box office* 10am-8pm Mon-Sat; closed Sun.
Admission £6.50-£14. **Credit** AmEx, MC, V.
Map p303 D2.
If it's the Krankies, end-of-the-pier nostalgia and big
traditional comics you're after, then you've come to
the right place.

Theatre Royal

*282 Hope Street, City centre, G2 (0141 332 9000/
www.theatreroyalglasgow.com). Cowcaddens tube.*
Open *box office* 10am-6pm Mon-Sat; closed Sun.
Admission £3.50-£45.50. **Credit** AmEx, MC, V.
Map p303 D2.
Home of Scottish Opera and Scottish Ballet, this is
culture central, particularly when the larger touring
productions from the likes of the Royal Shakespeare
Company are in town.

Tron Theatre

*63 Trongate, City centre, G1 (0141 552 4267/
www.tron.co.uk). St Enoch tube.* **Open** *box office*
10am-9pm Mon-Sat; closed Sun except on
performance days. **Admission** £3-£9; £3-£5
concessions. **Credit** MC, V. **Map** p303 E3.
This small theatre has recently been refurbished and
puts on a good mix of small touring productions and
its own shows. The restaurant and bar come highly recommended.

Where to eat & drink

Not surprisingly, given its size, Glasgow has a
wide choice of eateries and hostelries. Below
we choose the best of them. Average prices –
the approximate cost of a starter and main
course for one person, excluding drinks and
service – are given below for those places
that serve food.
   The café and restaurant at the **Cathedral
House Hotel** (*see page 247*) are also
highly recommended.

Stop off at **The Rogano** for some fishy delights in art deco surroundings. *See page 241.*

City centre

Bar 91

91 Candleriggs, G1 (0141 552 5211). Argyle St rail. **Open** 11am-midnight Mon-Sat; 12.30pm-midnight Sun. **Credit** MC, V. **Map** p303 E3.

A staple of any Merchant City pub crawl. Ideal for twenty- and thirtysomethings who enjoy stylish surroundings but baulk at the idea of trendier-than-thou style-bar culture. A respectable lunch prospect, too.

Café Gandolfi

64 Albion Street, G1 (0141 552 6813). Argyle St or High St rail. **Open** 9am-11.30pm Mon-Sat; noon-11.30pm Sun. **Average** £14. **Credit** MC, V. **Map** p303 E3.

Well-established port of call in the Merchant City, with a large and devoted following.

China Sea

12 Renfield Street, G2 (0141 221 2719). St Enoch tube. **Open** noon-midnight Mon-Sat; 2pm-midnight Sun. **Average** £10. **Credit** AmEx, MC, V. **Map** p303 D2.

This attractively traditional and unaffected Chinese restaurant offers an excellent two-course lunch menu for under a fiver.

Corinthian

191 Ingram Street, G1 (0141 552 1101/ corinthian@g1group.co.uk). Buchanan St tube. **Open** noon-3am daily. **Average** £12. **Credit** AmEx, MC, V. **Map** p303 E3.

Housed in what was described by the *Guardian* as 'Glasgow's finest Grade-A listed building', the Corinthian houses a piano bar, cocktail bar and the most opulent main bar in the city.

Delmonica's

68 Virginia Street, G1 (0141 552 4803). St Enoch tube. **Open** noon-midnight daily. **Credit** MC, V. **Map** p303 E3.

Spacious bar renowned as a gay hangout with a straight-friendly policy. A fun drinking experience, with extensive happy hours, DJs and karaoke.

Fratelli Sarti

21 Bath Street, G2 (0141 204 0440). Buchanan St tube. **Open** 8am-10.30pm Mon-Sat (licence until 1am); noon-10.30pm Sun. **Average** £12. **Credit** AmEx, DC, MC, V. **Map** p303 D2.

Priding itself on its '100% authentic Italian' motto, this family-run restaurant, and its Wellington Street branch, are exactly that. This charming eatery straddles the restaurant/bistro/deli dividing lines.

Often busy, especially at weekends, so advance booking is advisable.
Branch: 133 Wellington Street, G2 (enquiries 0141 248 2228/bookings 0141 204 0440).

The Griffin

266 Bath Street, G2 (0141 331 5171). Charing Cross rail. **Open** 11am-midnight Mon-Sat; 12.30pm-midnight Sun. **Average** £7.50.
Credit MC, V. **Map** p302 C2.
Few pubs in Glasgow have a genuinely varied clientele, but this is one of them. With the King's Theatre (*see p239*) across the road, it's ideal for a pre- or post-performance tipple. Sturdy bar food is available at lunchtime.

The Horseshoe

17 Drury Street, G2 (0141 229 5711). Buchanan St tube. **Open** 11am-midnight Mon-Sat; 12.30pm-midnight Sun. **Set lunch** (three courses, Mon-Sat) £2.80. **No credit cards. Map** p303 D3.
In a city of drinking institutions, this is the one to end them all. It boasts the longest continuous bar in the UK – as the *Guinness Book of Records* attests. More important is the friendly atmosphere of its traditional surroundings. Famed also for its ridiculously cheap three-course lunches.

The Rogano

11 Exchange Place, Buchanan Street, G1 (0141 248 4055). Buchanan St tube or Queen St rail. **Open** *Restaurant* noon-2.30pm, 6.30-10.30pm daily. *Café* noon-11pm Mon-Thur, Sun; noon-midnight Fri, Sat. **Average** *restaurant* £30; *café* £15. **Credit** AmEx, DC, MC, V. **Map** p303 D3.
A fabulous example of art deco style and a must-visit. The restaurant's menu is traditional, with fish a forté. Downstairs, Café Rogano has a slightly more modern menu, which is also highly recommended. No smoking before 2pm at lunch or 10pm at dinner.

The Scotia

112 Stockwell Street, G1 (0141 552 8681). St Enoch tube/Argyle St rail. **Open** 11am-midnight Mon-Sat; 12.30pm-midnight Sun. **Credit** MC, V. **Map** p303 D3.
This traditional bar, situated close to the river, claims to be Glasgow's oldest public house. It is the busiest and most famous of the three bars that make up the so-called Stockwell Triangle – the other two are the **Victoria Bar** (159 Bridgegate; 0141 552 6040) and the **Clutha Vaults** (167 Stockwell Street; 0141 552 7520).

Old Town & East End

The Saracen Head

209 Gallowgate, G1 (0141 552 1660). High St rail. **Open** 11am-11pm Mon-Thur; 8am-midnight Fri, Sat; 12.30-11pm Sun. **No credit cards. Map** p303 F3.
A glorious spit-and-sawdust bar that has nevertheless begun submitting to the karaoke onslaught. As it is usefully situated for pre- and post-Barrowland drinks, the clientele tends to change according to who is playing across the road.

South Side

The Battlefield Rest

55 Battlefield Road, G42 (0141 636 6955). Mount Florida rail, then 5-min walk. **Open** 10am-10pm Mon-Sat; closed Sun. **Average** £12. **Credit** AmEx, MC, V. **Map** p301.
This green-and-white tiled restaurant used to be a tramworkers' bothy. Now it successfully blends Scots and Italian cultures and cuisine and is popular with discerning South Siders.

The Burrell Café & Restaurant

Pollok Country Park, G43 (0141 632 3910). Pollokshaws West rail, then 10-min walk. **Open** *Café* 10am-4.30pm Mon-Thur, Sat; 11am-4.30pm Fri, Sun. *Restaurant* noon-4pm daily. **Average** *restaurant* £8. **Credit** AmEx, MC, V. **Map** p301.
Self-service café and more upmarket restaurant in a gloriously light and airy setting. The food is good, but the views are better. No smoking.

Café Sergei

67 Bridge Street, G5 (0141 429 1547). Bridge St tube. **Open** noon-2.30pm, 5-11pm (licence until 1am) Mon-Sat; 6-11pm Sun. **Average** *lunch* £5; *dinner* £13.50. **Credit** AmEx, MC, V. **Map** p303 D4.
The popular and lively Café Sergei serves Greek and Mediterranean cuisine to a varied clientele. On Fridays, it's dance night: for £17.50 per head, patrons are treated to a three-course meal plus coffee, dance demonstrations (Greek and ceilidh dancing) and audience participation.

Cul De Sac Southside

1179 Pollokshaws Road, G41 (0141 649 4717/ www.bigbeat.co.uk). Pollokshields East rail. **Open** noon-2.30pm, 5-8.30pm (licence until 1am) Mon-Thur; noon-9pm (licence until 1am) Sat, Sun. **Average** £12.50. **Credit** AmEx, DC, MC, V. **Map** p301.
The stylish South Side branch of this West End institution attracts an older crowd wanting an alternative to the spit-and-sawdust local hostelries and to indulge in a spot of discerning dining.
Branch: 44-6 Ashton Lane, G12 (0141 334 6688).

Heraghty's

708 Pollokshaws Road, G41 (0141 423 0380). Pollokshields East rail. **Open** 11am-11pm Mon-Thur; 11am-midnight Fri, Sat; 12.30-11pm Sun. **No credit cards. Map** p301.
This authentic Irish bar on the South Side is the place to head to watch a Celtic match on the box or to listen to some genuine Irish blarney, rather than the manufactured flavour of the city centre's Irish theme bars.

West End

Air Organic

36 Kelvingrove Street G3 (0141 564 5200/bar 564 5201). Kelvinhall tube, then 10-min walk. **Open** 11am-11pm Mon-Thur, Sun; 11am-midnight Fri, Sat.

Trips Out of Town

Restaurant opens at noon daily. **Average** £18.
Credit AmEx, MC, V. **Map** p302 A2.
Minimalist chic restaurant and bar with a pan-Asian menu. Popular with trendy West Enders.

The Halt Bar
160 Woodlands Road, G3 (0141 564 1527).
Kelvinbridge tube. **Open** 11am-11pm Mon-Thur; 11am-midnight Fri, Sat; 12.30-11pm Sun.
No credit cards. Map p302 B1.
Another well-loved traditional bar.

Mother India
28 Westminster Terrace, Sauchiehall Street, G3
(0141 221 1663). Kelvinhall tube, then 10-min
walk. **Open** noon-2pm, 5.30-11pm Mon-Thur; noon-2pm, 5-11.30pm Fri; noon-11.30 Sat; 5-11pm Sun.
Average £12.50. **Corkage** 85p. **Credit** MC, V.
Map p302 A2.
Excellent authentic Indian home cooking in relaxed, no-fuss surroundings make this one of the most popular Indian restaurants in the city. A must-stop for vegetarians. BYOB.

Nairns
13 Woodside Crescent, G3 (0141 353 0707/
www.nairns.co.uk). Charing Cross rail/tube, then 10-min walk. **Open** 11am-1.45pm, 6-9.45pm Mon-Sat; closed Sun. **Set menu** *lunch* £13.50 (two courses), £17 (three courses); *dinner* £27.50 (three courses).
Credit AmEx, DC, MC, V. **Map** 302 B1.
Nick Nairn casts a long shadow in the world of Scottish cuisine. The food at his restaurant is contemporary Scottish, taking on board influences from North Africa, the Mediterranean and Asia. This is relaxed dining and, for the quality on offer, the prices are pretty hard to beat.

One Devonshire Gardens
1 Devonshire Gardens, G12 (0141 339 2001/
www.one-devonshire-gardens.com). Hillhead tube.
Open noon-2pm, 7.15-10pm Mon-Fri, Sun; 7.15-10pm Sat. **Average** £40 (four courses). **Credit** AmEx, DC, MC, V. **Map** p301.
A truly special, luxurious occasion; the food is excellent, entirely worthy of its Michelin one star (the only one in Glasgow) and fairly priced. No smoking.

Stravaigin
28-30 Gibson Street, G12 (0141 334 2665/
www.stravaigin.com). Kelvinbridge tube. **Open**
Café-bar 11am-11pm Mon-Sat; 12.30-11pm Sun.
Restaurant noon-2.30pm, 5-11pm Fri, Sat; 5-11pm Tue-Thur, Sun; closed Mon. **Average** £24.
Credit AmEx, DC, MC, V. **Map** p301.
A former winner of Restaurant of the Year by the Chefs Association. Good honest Scottish produce with an exotic twist. The bar menu is also excellent.

The Ubiquitous Chip
12 Ashton Lane, G12 (0141 334 5007/
www.ubiquitouschip.co.uk). Hillhead tube. **Open**
noon-2.30pm, 5.30-11pm Mon-Sat; 12.30-2.30pm, 6.30-11pm Sun. **Set menu** *lunch* £18.95-£23.95; *dinner* £27.95-£32.95. **Credit** AmEx, DC, MC, V.
Map p301.

Housed in a converted mews stable, the Ubiquitous Chip is a Glasgow institution. The constantly evolving menu makes use of seasonal Scottish produce. The bar attracts an older crowd than the other Ashton Lane bars, and achieves that rare feat of being civilised and boisterous at the same time. An excellent wine and malt whisky selection.

Uisge Beatha
232 Woodlands Road, G3 (0141 564 1596).
Kelvinbridge tube. **Open** 11am-11pm Mon-Thur; 11am-midnight Fri, Sat; 12.30-11pm Sun. **Map** p302 A1.
A tasteful Scottish bar that looks like a Highland hunting lodge. The Uisge Beatha, meaning 'water of life' (whisky), manages to incorporate tartan, stuffed stags' heads and log fires into the decor without being naff. The varied clientele is testament to its enduring popularity.

University Café
87 Byres Road, G11 (0141 339 5217). Hillhead or Kelvinhall tube. **Open** 9am-10pm Mon, Wed-Fri; 9am-10.30pm Sat; 10am-10pm Sun; closed Tue.
Average £3. **No credit cards. Map** p301.
Famous for its fab 1950s-style decor and hearty food. The ice-cream has won innumerable awards.

Nightlife

As the capital of cool, Glasgow has everything from designer-orientated superclubs to truly underground venues. It leads the British explosion of the pre-club bar scene and, with **King Tut's** and the **Barrowland**, knocks Edinburgh into a booming bass-bin when it comes to live gigs.

Clubs

The Arches
30 Midland Street, City centre. G1 (0141 221 4001/
info@thearches.co.uk/www.thearches.co.uk). St Enoch tube/Central Station rail. **Open** 10pm-3am Fri; 11pm-4am Sat; closed Mon-Thur, Sun. *Box office* 10am-8pm Mon-Fri; noon-8pm Sat; closed Sun. **Admission** varies. **Credit** MC, V. **Map** 303 D3.
One of the city's largest clubs, situated in renovated railway arches beneath Central Station. A rotating selection of local promoters host the Saturday night clubs, which are mostly of a hard house/techno persuasion. Fridays get hot and sweaty.

Bennet's
80-90 Glassford Street, City centre, G1 (0141 552 5761). St Enoch tube. **Open** 11.30pm-3am Tue-Sun; closed Mon. **Admission** £2.50-£6; £1.50-£5 concessions. **No credit cards. Map** p303 E3.
Long-established gay club.

The Sub Club
22 Jamaica Street, City centre, G1 (0141 248 4600/
www.subclub.co.uk). St Enoch tube. **Open** 11pm-3am Wed-Fri, Sun; 11pm-5am Sat; closed Mon, Tue.

Trips Out of Town

Admission £4-£10; £3-£6 concessions.
No credit cards. Map p303 D3.
This ten-year-old club is one of the best in the whole
of Scotland for deep house on a Saturday night,
while Fridays offer harder house and techno. The
Sunday club, Optimo, is renowned for being musically daring.

The Tunnel

*84 Mitchell Street, City centre, G1 (0141 204 1000/
www.tunnel.co.uk). Central Station rail.* **Open** 11pm-
3.30am Thur, Fri; 10.30pm-4am Sat; closed Mon-
Wed, Sun. **Admission** £4-£9; £3-£7 concessions.
No credit cards. Map p303 D3.
The Tunnel is as near to a superclub as you get
in Glasgow, regularly welcoming the biggest names
on the dance circuit. A dressy crowd inhabits
this stunning venue, which, not surprisingly, has a
fairly strict door policy.

Pre-club & club bars

The 13th Note

*50-60 King Street, City centre, G1 (0141 553 1638)
& 260 Clyde Street, G1 (0141 243 2177). St Enoch
tube.* **Open** *Café-bar* noon-midnight Mon-Sat;
closed Sun. *Club* 11pm-3am Wed, Thur, Sun; 9pm-
3am Fri, Sat; closed Mon, Tue. **Average** *Café-bar*
£7-£10. **Credit** MC, V. **Admission** *Club* free-£4.
No credit cards. Map p303 E3.
A grassroots institution that has recently spread its
wings to become a cosy art-deco café-bar (on King
Street) and a laid-back club (Clyde Street). Both host
cheap nights of live music and most of Glasgow's

hip new bands such as Mogwai and the Delgados
started life (and still hang out) here. The vegan café
stops serving at 10pm, but the music continues.

Bar 10

*10 Mitchell Lane, City centre, G1 (0141 572 1448/
www.bar10.co.uk). St Enoch tube, then 5-min walk.*
Open 10am-midnight daily. **Average** *lunch* £5.
Credit MC, V. **Map** p303 D3.
The grandaddy of the Glasgow 'style' bars and still
cutting the mustard. This city-centre mecca for clubbers is a favourite of the gay community. Also ideal
for a post-Lighthouse libation or a leisurely, languid
lunch (no food in the evenings).

Nice'n'Sleazy

*421 Sauchiehall Street, City centre, G2 (0141 333
0900). Charing Cross rail.* **Open** 11.30am-11.45pm
Mon-Sat; 12.30-11.45pm Sun. **No credit cards.**
Map p302 C2.
Sleazys is perfect for those looking for the young and
funky who want to bypass the pretensions of the
style-bar set. It's a great place to find out about the
local band scene – many of them either drink in the
bar or play in the scarlet dive venue downstairs.

The Polo Lounge

*84 Wilson Street, City centre, G1 (0141 553 1221/
www.pololounge.co.uk). Buchanan St tube, then
5-min walk.* **Open** 5pm-1am Mon-Thur; 5pm-3am
Fri; noon-3am Sat, Sun. **Credit** AmEx, DC, MC, V.
Map p303 E3.
Just round the corner from Delmonica's (*see p240*),
the Polo Lounge is a more recent and very welcome
addition to Glasgow's gay bar scene. There's a club

Glasgow's nod to Vegas: **Barrowland**. *See page 244.*

downstairs, but the large bar area on the ground floor is equally popular. As the name suggests, it has a luxurious imperial feel.

Rock & pop venues

Barrowland

244 Gallowgate, East End, G4 (0141 552 4601/ barras@zoom.co.uk). Argyle St rail. **Open** phone for details. **Admission** £7-£25. **No credit cards**. **Map** p303 F3.
Once a ballroom, now this is one of Scotland's top concert venues for the bigger, but nonetheless still hip and happening rock and dance acts. It might be a bit of a dive, but the atmosphere is electric.

The Garage

490 Sauchiehall Street, City centre, G2 (0141 332 1120/www.cplweb.com). Charing Cross rail. **Open** 11pm-3am Mon-Fri, Sun; 10.30pm-3am Sat. **Admission** £2-£6. **No credit cards**. **Map** p302 C2.
The place to see live bands before they make the leap to the Barrowland.

King Tut's Wah Wah Hut

272A St Vincent Street, City centre, G2 (0141 221 5279). Central Station rail. **Open** noon-midnight Mon-Sat; closed Sun. **Admission** £3.50-£10. **No credit cards**. **Map** p302 C2.
Rock history remembers this as the venue where Oasis was spotted and signed. With only 350 capacity it might be small, but it's a hot spot on the indie touring circuit.

Folk & country venues

Grand Ole Opry

2-4 Govan Road, South Side, G51 (0141 429 5396). Shields Road tube. **Open** 6.30pm-12.30am Fri-Sun; closed Mon-Thur. **Admission** £2.50. **No credit cards**. **Map** p302 A4.
A Glaswegian institution nestling south of the river. Country fans of all ages don their gingham and denim and gather each weekend in this tacky hall, decorated in confederate memorabilia, to imbibe cheap liquor, line-dance to the live band, witness the fake shoot-out and, in a surreal twist, play bingo. Not for the faint-hearted.

Riverside Club

33 Fox Street, City centre, G1 (0141 248 3144). St Enoch tube. **Open** 7.30-11pm Thur; 7.30pm-midnight Fri, Sat; closed Mon-Wed, Sun. **Admission** £4-£6. **No credit cards**. **Map** p303 D3.
The weekend ceilidh dances consistently attract a lively and youthful crowd. Arrive early for a seat.

Shopping

Glasgow's reputation as a style-conscious city goes way back to the 18th and 19th centuries when the Tobacco Lords would prioritise the purchase of the 'right' clothing over feeding

their families. Glaswegians still wear their labels with pride and when Giorgio and Gianni wondered which city in Britain, other than London, would provide the most fertile ground for their growing empires, Glasgow was it.

The Merchant City exerts a particularly strong pull upon the Versace and Armani-clad McGlitterati, with seriously label-friendly zones such as the **Italian Centre**. As the largest independent designer retailer in Britain, **Cruise** offers the best range of men and women's gear in the city. Hip urban warriors are also well served in the area, with **Concrete Skates** and **Dr Jives** providing your underground labels and local clubby designer gear.

There isn't one shopping area like London's Oxford Street in Glasgow: there are three. **Argyle Street** has the edge over **Sauchiehall Street** for scale and quality, with the biggest choice of high-street chains, large department stores such as **Debenhams** and Europe's largest glass-covered shopping area, the **St Enoch Centre**. Once the loudest and proudest of Glasgow's shopping centres, the St Enoch has been spectacularly eclipsed by the recent appearance of the **Buchanan Galleries** super-mall. This shopping city within a city perches at the pinnacle of **Buchanan Street**, Glasgow's classic shopping thoroughfare. A must for discerning shoppers, the street boasts stylish stores such as **House of Fraser** and quality retailers ranging from **Hugo Boss** to **Diesel**. The jewel in its crown is **Princes Square**, a place to exercise the credit card with caution.

For the credit card-less and retro-cool dudes, second-hand and vintage clothes outlets are ubiquitous around the city. The best are in the **King's Court Arcade** at the bottom of King Street and, unsurprisingly, there are a whole host of them in 'studentsville', aka the **West End**. Cresswell, Ruthven and Downanhill Lanes, off **Byres Road**, are a must for indie kids or those of the gently alternative persuasion. **Decourcis Arcade** in Cresswell Lane is also perfect for gifts, knick-knacks and what-nots.

West End lane culture also attracts the bookish consumer. Gems include the **Voltaire & Rousseau** second-hand and antiquarian bookshop, and, back on the beaten track, **John Smith & Son**, Scotland's sole national bookseller, which has branches throughout the city and is one of the best outlets for new Scottish fiction. Its Byres Road branch contains a music department with something of a reputation for attracting budding indie stars. **Fopp Records**, **Missing Records** and **23rd Precinct** complete the city's essential sounds shopping circuit.

Children

Big ideas for the littl'uns.

Princes Street Gardens. *See page 190.*

Edinburgh is great from a kid's point of view. Where else does the High Street begin with a fantasy castle, slope down past a queen's palace and end up at a volcanic mountain? Not only are many of the interesting sights within walking distance of each other, but it is also a pretty good city for walking around with children in tow as, in spite of the hills and traffic, most of the pavements are wide enough to let kids trot along at their own pace without having to grab them out of danger all the time. If short legs get tired, the popular alternative is a big black taxi. Fares are reasonable, there are seats for five passengers, all with seatbelts, and pushchairs don't need to be folded. On buses and trains, under-fives go free and fives-to-15s pay 50p. The open-top guided tour buses, although more expensive, allow you to get on and off all day for the price of a single ticket.

Those with only a day or two in Edinburgh are best off sticking to **Edinburgh Castle** and the **Royal Mile** area. Older kids will love the city's ghostly guided tours (*see page 52* **Witches & wynds**; check which ones are suitable for them first). Those staying longer could try **Edinburgh Zoo**, **Deep Sea World**, **Inchcolm Island**, **Dalkeith County Park**, **Butterfly & Insect World** or, in warmer weather, the clean beach at **Gullane** (all are listed in this chapter). An invaluable guidebook is *Edinburgh for Under Fives*, available from most local bookshops. The **Edinburgh Tourist Board** will send out information on current children's events and staff can provide detailed information about suitable accommodation for families over the phone.

Sights listed in **bold** are described in more detail elsewhere in the guide (*see* **Index**).

Events & entertainment

Many of the annual events listed in the **Edinburgh by Season** chapter include activities for kids. **Hogmanay**, the **Edinburgh Science Festival**, the **Scottish International Children's Festival**, the **Royal Highland Show**, **Meadows Festival**, **Edinburgh Festival** and **Fringe**, and the **Book Festival** are all particularly good.

Netherbow Arts Centre (*see page 221*) often stages plays aimed at children. Most other theatres have some sort of pantomime or children's show at Christmas. There is always an excellent reinterpretation of a classic fairy or folk story aimed at five-to-ten year olds at the **Royal Lyceum**. The **Theatre Workshop** produces an alternative, often ethnically based, show for the over-fives, while the **Traverse Theatre**'s offering usually includes a singalong for small children. For the traditional Scottish panto, complete with dancing girls, dame, best boy and plenty of glitter, the **King's Theatre** comes up trumps.

The **Odeon** cinema runs the Movie Mob on Saturday mornings for kids. The new **Virgin** complex at Fountainpark has films for kids, bowling and a Turbo Ride. The **Filmhouse**, meanwhile, often has programmes that are as suitable for children as they are for grown-ups. Also worth checking out is the **City Art Centre**, which hosts the sort of blockbuster exhibitions that are staged to attract children and has a café with high chairs.

Exploring

Royal Mile & Arthur's Seat

There is plenty to keep the most boisterous kids occupied at **Edinburgh Castle**. Give yourself a couple of hours and get there in good time for the one o'clock gun, which is fired daily (except Sunday) with a satisfyingly big bang and puff of smoke by a stiffly marching artilleryman. The castle is still an army HQ so there are plenty of real soldiers about, which adds to the atmosphere. There are lots of open rocky spaces for scrambling around on, some scary precipices to peer over, very exciting dungeony bits and very boring military museums (although small boys have a peculiar fascination with the latter). The teeny church often has weddings at weekends and the spacious café has dull but child-friendly food.

The **Royal Mile** itself is riddled with alleyways and courtyards that are great for exploring – quite a few lead to open spaces that are good for a run-about or a picnic. **Dunbar's Close**, 137 Canongate, with its secluded 17th-century garden, is a particularly good find.

Worth considering for older kids on a sunny day is the **Camera Obscura**, which has some scary holograms and good telescopes, while the **Brass Rubbing Centre** is a great rainy day standby. The **Museum of Childhood**, **The People's Story** and the **Huntly House Museum** are three free museums in the High Street/Canongate area. The Museum of Childhood can be a little disappointing for wee ones because it is full of marvellous toys they can't get their hands on, but the shop has plenty to choose from. The People's Story is fun, with lots of life-size figures, noises and even smells, but the presentation of local history in the Huntly House Museum is a bit dry.

The **Palace of Holyroodhouse** is best seen by guided tour, and can be a bit boring for little ones, although the grounds are nice. Nearby is **Our Dynamic Earth**, which has good facilities and a café and where kids can experience a rainforest and touch an iceberg – very educational and good fun. From here, the base of **Arthur's Seat** is just a short walk away. To the left is **St Mary's Loch**, with loads of swans and a large area that's particularly suitable for the flying of kites, gliding of frisbees, kicking around of footballs and general letting off of steam. The climb to the top of Arthur's Seat is quite straightforward, but it is a long haul with quite a scramble at the end. If it's likely to prove too much for weaker legs, get a taxi up to Dunsapie Loch, climb the last bit of hill and then walk down instead.

How cute is little **Greyfriars Bobby**?

South Edinburgh

The **Royal Museum of Scotland** and its new sister museum, the **Museum of Scotland**, are perfect for wet days. They have loads of space, massive stuffed animals, indoor goldfish ponds, buttons to push, a roof terrace, three eating areas and lockers to stash pushchairs and coats. The Discovery Centre for children is useful, but is sometimes booked for school parties, so phone ahead. On Saturdays and Sundays there are 'Quickies for Kids' – ten-minute talks on anything from bats to buttons.

At the far west end of Chambers Street is the dog statue of **Greyfriars Bobby**. If he's too cute for the older kids, then **Greyfriars Kirkyard** itself might prove more interesting. South along Forrest Road and Middle Meadow Walk lies the **Meadows**, a big grassy space with three playgrounds: one at each end and a toddler park in the middle. Funfairs are held here from time to time. It's a great place to let off steam but watch out for dog mess and speeding students on bikes.

New Town & north Edinburgh

Princes Street Gardens is a brilliant antidote to the surrounding shops. Not only is there lots of open space, ice-cream vans and a playground at the West End, but it also has a railway line running through the middle. You can even get the train drivers to hoot if you wave like mad from the clear-sided bridge behind the Ross Band Stand.

At the east end of Princes Street is **Calton Hill**, with its row of Greek columns on top. It is a good open space for fresh air and views if you haven't the energy or time for Arthur's Seat. There are a couple of visitor attractions, monuments and lots of grass, but it is not very clean and only just accessible by pushchair from Waterloo Place – if you don't mind bumping up the first flight of steps.

Further to the north, the **Royal Botanic Garden** is a godsend for children and their minders. Not only does it have acres of grass, no cars and absolutely no dog mess, but there are loads of feedable squirrels and ducks, glasshouses with huge goldfish, a gift shop and a café with high chairs, an outdoor eating area and nappy-changing facilities. The Exhibition Hall, past the Glasshouse Experience, has some good hands-on educational exhibitions for those who get bored looking at plants. There's also a playground opposite the West Gate, hidden behind hedges in **Inverleith Park**.

To the west, the **Scottish National Gallery of Modern Art** and the new **Dean Gallery** sit across the road from each other, surrounded by huge grassy spaces that are perfect for using up excess energy brought on by too much culture. The Dean Gallery, a former orphanage, will probably appeal to kids most as it has a Paolozzi's massive metal giant and a replica of his chaotic studio. But it is worth crossing the road to the Scottish National Gallery of Modern Art for the café, which is bigger than the Dean's and has seating outside.

From the galleries you can access the **Water of Leith walkway**, a delightful ribbon of riverside paths that meander through the city to the docks. The best bit starts from the bridge on Belford Road, opposite the Hilton International, and goes downstream via the Dean Village to India Place in Stockbridge. A good itinerary is

to visit the Scottish National Gallery of Modern Art and leave through the path to the rear, then follow the waterside walk downstream past the Hilton and end up in Stockbridge. St Stephen Street has lots of little eateries but the real burgers at **Bell's Diner** (*see page 121*) usually prove popular all round. Maps and information can be obtained from the **Water of Leith Conservation Trust**.

The Shore area in **Leith** can be interesting for those with older children who are not likely to run off and fall in the water. But be warned, the docks are huge and wandering round them can be very time consuming, although the **Royal Yacht Britannia** makes them worth a visit. To the west is **Newhaven**, with its pretty harbour and the **Newhaven Heritage Museum**, where kids get to dress up as fishermen and fishwives.

Out of town

A half-hour train ride from Waverley Station brings you to the small East Lothian town of **North Berwick**, with its harbour, summer boat trips to the Bass Rock, ice-cream shops, Sea Bird Centre, rockpools and a shallow sea-water paddling pool on the sandy beach. **Gullane**, an hour's drive or bus ride east of the city, has a good clean beach with toilets. Eight miles (13 kilometres) south-east of town is **Dalkeith Country Park** (654 1666; buses to Dalkeith), which is open between March and October and some winter weekends. It is an astonishing adventure playground for children over four, with elevated walkways, a good café, woodland paths, intriguing riverside tunnels and flying foxes. The seabirds and ancient monastic ruins of **Inchcolm Island and Abbey**, together with the ferry boat trip to get there, are sure lures for kids. Take the Maid of the Forth boat from South Queensferry, which also stops at **Deep Sea World** (24-hour information line 331 4857). The most exciting castles close to Edinburgh are **Linlithgow Palace** (01506 844600) in West Lothian and **Tantallon Castle** (01620 892 727) in East Lothian. Both have dizzying drops, so hang on to the kids.

Outdoor adventures

Animal encounters

Some of the following are a bit of a way out of town, but all are surefire crowd-pleasers.

Bird of Prey Centre

Dobbies Garden World, Lasswade, Midlothian, EH18 (654 1720). Bus 3. **Open** *summer* 11am-5pm daily; *winter* 11am-4pm daily. **Admission** £2.50; £1.25 children; £1.25 concessions. **No credit cards.**

'Hawks away!' at the **Bird of Prey Centre**.

Half-an-hour's bus ride away from Princes Street, the Bird of Prey Centre is on the same site as Butterfly & Insect World (*see below*), so if aerial violence doesn't get 'em, aerial elegance will. Flying displays take place every day at 1.30pm and 3pm. There's a café nearby.

Butterfly & Insect World
Dobbies Garden World, Lasswade, Midlothian, EH18 (663 4932). Bus 3. **Open** *summer* 9am-5.30pm daily; *winter* 9.30am-5pm daily. **Admission** £3.95; £2.85 children, concessions; £12 family; free under-3s. **Credit** MC, V.
There are butterflies hatching all year round in these heated greenhouses near the Bird of Prey Centre (*see above*). Brave hearts might prefer the creepy-crawlies, including scorpions and tarantulas.

Cramond village
Bus 40, 40A, 41, 41A. **Ferry** *Apr-Sept* 9am-7pm Mon-Thur, Sat, Sun; closed Fri; *Oct-Mar* 10am-4pm Mon-Thur, Sat, Sun; closed Fri.
A few miles to the west of Edinburgh, where the River Almond flows out into the Forth, this little village makes a diverting day excursion. There are plenty of different things to do, although none are too taxing. The Roman fort is very much a flattened ruin and will take a good deal of imagination to conjure up, but Roman statuary has been found in the river. Cramond Island is only accessible at low tide and makes a good venue for a picnic – so long as you get the timing right. There is a tiny ferry across the Almond (60p adults; children free) leading to woodlands and a coastal path along the Forth, which is suitable for pushchairs. While the Firth isn't a great place to swim, the foreshore at Cramond is good for paddling. There is a child-friendly pub and bistro by the edge of the river, and Lauriston Castle (*see below*) is just down the road.

Deep Sea World
North Queensferry, Fife, KY11 (01383 411 411). North Queensferry rail, then 10-min walk. **Open** 10am-6pm daily. **Admission** £6.25; £3.95 children; £4.50 concessions; £16.75 family. **Credit** MC, V.
An award-winning fishy paradise where you go under the sea. Aquariums with lots of educational bits, a fish pool where you can put your hands in and feel the fish (and attendants who tell you all about it as you do), films, educational lectures, and a café. You can even get to feed the sharks, or just observe as the divers do it (every half hour).

Edinburgh Zoo
Corstorphine Road, West Edinburgh, EH12 (334 9171/www.edinburghzoo.org.uk). Bus 12, 31, 26. **Open** *Apr-Sept* 9am-6pm daily; *Oct, Mar* 9am-5pm daily; *Nov-Jan* 9am-4.30pm daily. **Admission** £6.80; £3.80 3s-14s; £3.80-£4.80 concessions; £19-£23.50 family; free under-3s; group rates on request. **Credit** MC, V.
Loads of animals, including all the favourites (pandas, hippos, snakes), but the zoo's principal claim to fame is its army of penguins, the most assembled in

It's a kids' day out at **Lauriston Castle**.

captivity anywhere. The penguin parade, at 2pm every day between March and October, is one of Edinburgh's most bizarre sights. There's also an Education Centre, which runs touchy-feely sessions where they tell you about the animals and let you handle them (usually rabbits, snakes, chinchillas and so on) – they're great fun and really popular.

Gorgie City Farm
Gorgie Road, South Edinburgh, EH11 (337 4262). Bus 3, 3A, 21, 25, 25A. **Open** *summer* 9.30am-4.30pm daily; *winter* 9.30am-4pm daily. **Admission** free.
A lovely informal spot for much younger children, with all the farmyard faves, a playground and a good café with high chairs.

Lauriston Castle
Cramond Road South, Davidsons Mains, Crammond, EH4 (336 2060). Bus 40, 41, 41A. **Open** *Apr-Oct* 11am-5pm Mon-Thur, Sat, Sun; closed Fri; *Nov-Mar* 2-4pm Sat, Sun; closed Mon-Fri. **Admission** *house* £4.50; £3 concessions; *grounds* free. **No credit cards.**
Set in large, reasonably well-kept grounds on the way to Cramond, this 16th-century fortified house was left to the nation by William Reid, an enthusiastic antiques collector who furnished it throughout with Edwardian period furniture. Young children probably won't appreciate the guided tours of the house (hourly), with its exquisite and unique interiors, but there are plenty of lawns to run about on and a meadow to throw frisbees around on.

Indoor activities

For **sports centres** *see page 217*; for **ice-rinks** *see page 218*.

Play centres

Charlie Chalks
Scottish Brewers Fayre, Newhaven Quay, Newhaven, Leith, EH10 (555 1570). Bus 7, 10, 11, 16. **Open** 11am-9pm Mon-Sat; noon-9pm Sun. **Admission** £1 per hour. **Credit** MC, V. **Map** p311 Ex.

A large and exciting indoor play area attached to a pub/restaurant, with a safe section for toddlers. Near the Newhaven Heritage Museum (*see p93*).

Clambers at the Royal Commonwealth Pool
21 Dalkeith Road, South Edinburgh, EH16 (667 7211). Bus 2, 14, 21, 33. **Open** *3s-8s* 10am-5pm Mon-Fri; 10am-5pm Sat, Sun; *under-3s* 10am-1pm Mon-Fri; closed Sat, Sun. **Admission** *45-min session* £1.45. **No credit cards. Map** p310 J8.
A large, safe enclosed play area with soft play, a climbing wall and a café. *See also p218.*

The Games Workshop
for listings see p169.
Kids can get to grips with the great selection of board games and models, including Warhammer.

Play away

Of the following playgrounds, **Princes Street Gardens** has no swings, and **Scotland Yard** has activities on Saturday mornings for kids with special needs.

Bruntsfield Links & the Meadows
Off Melville Drive, South Edinburgh, EH3. Bus 24. **Maps** p309 E7 and p310 G7.

Canonmills
Eyre Place, New Town, EH3. Bus 23, 27. **Map** p306 E3.

Inverleith Park
Arboretum Place, Stockbridge, EH3. Bus 28, 29, 29A, 80. **Map** p305 C2.

Leith Links
John's Place, Foot of Leith Walk, Leith, EH6. Bus 16, 35, 35A. **Map** p311 Kz.

Montgomery Street
Montgomery Place, off Leith Walk, Greenside, EH7. Bus 5, 15, 19, 26. **Map** p307 H3.

Pilrig Park
Off Pilrig Street, Leith Walk, Leith, EH6. Bus 7, 12, 16. **Map** p307 G1.

Princes Street Gardens
West Princes Street Gardens, New Town, EH2. West entrance, opposite Gap. Bus 3, 3A, 12, 16, 17. **Map** p314 A2.

Scotland Yard
Scotland Street, New Town, EH2. Bus 23, 27. **Map** 306 E3.

Wednesday night is Fantasy Night, Games Night is on a Thursday, Saturday features games from 1pm, while Sunday is for beginners (from 10am).

The Jelly Club
unit 10B Peffermill Industrial Estate, Peffermill Road, South Edinburgh, EH16 (652 0212/ www.jellyclub.co.uk). **Open** 10am-7pm daily. **Admission** *2-hour session* £2.25-£3.95. **Credit** MC, V.
A club for children aged 12 and under, with good facilities, though toddlers need close supervision. Kids can get to grips with the massive barn, with soft play, abseiling, a pedal car circuit, chutes and ball pools. The large café has a wide range of food.

Laserquest
28 Bread Street, South Edinburgh, EH3 (221 0000). **Open** 11am-11pm Mon-Sat; 11am-8pm Sun. **Admission** *per game* £3.50 before 6pm; £4.50 after 6pm. **No credit cards. Map** p309 D6.
A great place for kids and their parents to release all that pent-up energy: you can zap them and they can zap you back, and you still go home in one piece.

Little Marco's at Marco's Leisure Centre
55 Grove Street, West Edinburgh, EH3 (228 2141). Bus 1, 28, 34, 35, 35A. **Open** 9.30am-5.30pm (last admission) daily. **Admission** *1½-hour session* £2 under-4s; £3.50 over-4s; £2 children with special needs. **Credit** MC, V. **Map** p308 C7.
A soft play area best suited to the over-fives (maximum age ten). Note that children must be supervised.

Swimming
Edinburgh has some great swimming pools, although the atmospheric Victorian ones were not designed with children in mind. The main ones usually sell arm bands and floats. All have crèches that take bookings. Of the pools listed on page 218, the **Royal Commonwealth Pool** is best for kids as it has flumes (open from 2.30pm) and a children's pool.

Eating out
Pubs that serve full meals are allowed to let children in until 8pm, although this is at the bar staff's discretion.

Places children will really like
There are several chain inns around the city fringes where a play shed has been tacked onto a pub/diner. Although these are hardly inspiring and the food can be indifferent, they do provide some kid-free moments. The newest and best is **Charlie Chalks** (*see page 192*). The **Cramond Inn** (Glebe Road, Cramond Village, EH4; 336 2035), **Lauriston Farm Brewers Fayre** (Lauriston Farm Road,

All the following serve really good food in an adult atmosphere but still welcome children.

blue Bar Café
Sophisticated, blond wood and glass, high chairs, wonderful food, half portions and plenty of space. See page 157.

Café Hub
The nearest decent food to the Castle. Café Hub also has high chairs and nappy-changing facilities. See page 138.

The Dome
A former bank of grand proportions, with the sort of white-aproned waiters who whip out a high chair and wipe it down for you. And then offer to heat the baby food. See page 152.

The Outhouse
A trendy bar/restaurant with tables in an open-air courtyard that also has a boules court. Just off Broughton Street. No high chairs. See page 156.

Silverknowes, EH4; 312 7071) and **Hunter's Tryst Restaurant** (97 Oxgangs Road, Oxgangs, EH13; 445 3132) are more typical.

Slightly better food is available at **Umberto's** (2 Bonnington Road Lane, Leith, EH6; 554 1314), where booth tables form a train, no one minds the kids running around and there's an outdoor playground. **Guiliano's** on the Shore in Leith (554 5272) is another, less gimmicky Italian place; children can create their own pizzas. **Mammas**, near the Royal Botanic Garden (1 Howard Street; 558 7177), also does great pizzas in a relaxed atmosphere. For sit-down fish and chips, **Harry Ramsden's** (Pier Place, Newhaven; 551 5566) is best.

Along the Royal Mile

The lower part of the Royal Mile is becoming less of a culinary a desert than it once was: new eating places are popping up all over the place along the Canongate now that building of the new Parliament is under way and Our Dynamic Earth is complete.

On the High Street, **Di Placido's** Italian deli (No.36-38; 557 2286) has great sarnies to take away, plus a few tables on the streets outside. Nearby, at No.43, is the **Netherbow Arts Centre** (556 2647), whose café dishes up nutritious soups and great scones; it rates very high on the child-friendly stakes, with an outdoor courtyard, high chairs and a nappy-changing area. Further up the High Street, at No.235, is the **Filling Station** (226 2488), a large American-style diner, with the added bonuses of high chairs and a nappy-changing area. Up by the Castle, are the **Café Hub** (see page 138) and the Italian restaurant **Lorenzo's** (226 2426) at 5 Johnston Terrace. If it's pizzas the kids are hankering after, head for North Bridge towards the middle of the

Royal Mile, where you'll find **Pizza Express** at No.23 (557 6411) and **Pizza Hut** on the other side (No.46; 226 3038). Both have branches across Edinburgh; Pizza Hut's are concentrated in the New Town.

Practicalities for parents

Babysitting/childminding

The top hotels provide their own babysitting and/or childminding facilities. **Edinburgh Crèche Co-op** (553 2116, 9am-5pm Mon-Fri) provides a babysitting service in your room, will take the child(ren) out for the day and provide mobile crèches for parties and so on. **Emergency Mums** (447 7744, 8.45am-6pm Mon-Fri; 07970 442428 24 hours daily) and **Guardian** (343 3870; 9am-8pm daily) will look after the kids in your home or hotel.

Equipment hire

Baby Equipment Hire (337 7016; 9am-9pm daily) will deliver pushchairs, cots, backpacks, car seats and more.

Shopping

The best toy shop is in **Jenners** department store on Princes Street (see page 171). For baby supplies there are branches of **Boots** on Princes Street (see page 183). The **St James Centre** (see page 165) has an **Early Learning Centre** (see page 169), **Boots** and **John Lewis** (see page 171), which has a café and baby-changing facilities. **Argos** on North Bridge, EH1 (558 1474) sells really cheap pushchairs. **Safeway**, on Pilton Drive, EH5 (315 4970), has a great crèche for two- to ten-year olds. The **Gyle Centre** (see page 165) has crèches for kids of three months to eight years.

Film

Our pick of where to see the flicks.

The cream of Scotland's talent? Robert Carlyle at the **Edinburgh International Film Festival**.

Considering its modest size, Edinburgh's presence on the silver screen is actually quite strong – and that's even after discounting a certain 007. Sean Connery, probably the most famous Scot in the world, drove his milk float up Fountainbridge before finding fame as James Bond. Although Connery comes back to open the odd film such as *Entrapment*, which had its glittering world première at the **Edinburgh International Film Festival** (*see page 97*), he is more likely to be found pacing the greens and fairways of Scotland's upmarket golf courses.

Edinburgh has been seen in the predictable tourist-oriented short films over the years, and has also witnessed the Disney-tastic excesses of the likes of *Greyfriars Bobby* (1961), which tells the story of the wee Highland Terrier who stayed near the grave of his master in Greyfriars Churchyard for 14 years after he died in 1858.

But there is a small group of movies in which, as David Bruce points out in his book *Scotland the Movie*, the character of Edinburgh is integral to the feel of the film. *The Battle of the Sexes* (1959) depicts the city as 'cold, hidebound, reactionary and harbouring homicidal tendencies'. Not an altogether fair analysis,

but one that Peter Sellers uses to great comedic effect. And also one that is portrayed in *The Prime of Miss Jean Brodie* (1968), adapted from the book by Muriel Spark, which won Maggie Smith the Oscar for Best Actress in 1969.

Part of the problem in portraying Edinburgh is that it is simply too pretty a place. Which is why, when the darker side of life is addressed, the tourist end of town has been spurned for the down-at-heel outer estates. And they have been well reflected. *Conquest of the South Pole* (1989) caught the depression of unemployment in a peculiarly fascinating light when it portrayed a group of unemployed lads in Leith re-enacting Amundsen's Polar journey. Similarly, *Shallow Grave* (1994), the first film from the *Trainspotting* production team, reflected the zeitgeist of the early 1990s when yuppie greed seemed capable of anything.

The grim but surreal heroin epic *Trainspotting* (1996) was the international smash that put Edinburgh squarely on the cinematic map, despite the fact that it was mostly shot in Glasgow. It was swiftly followed by *Mary Reilly* (1996), a reworking of the Jekyll and Hyde story, for which Julia Roberts and John Malkovich spent a few days filming in

The Dominion – giving the multiplexes a run for their money. *See page 197.*

Edinburgh. Unfortunately *The Acid House* (1999), author Irvine Welsh's follow-up to *Trainspotting*, in no way emulated the success of its predecessor, although it did at least sustain the city's profile for a while longer.

The people of Edinburgh should probably have been content with that, but there is still a healthy interest in the city itself and adaptations of works by Edinburgh-based authors. Jonny Lee Miller played the lead in *Complicity* (2000), a big-screen adaptation of Iain Banks's best-selling tale of gruesome murders in and around Edinburgh. A film version of Edinburgh author JK Rowling's spectacularly successful *Harry Potter and the Philosopher's Stone* is to be made by Hollywood director Chris Columbus. Hopes have even been raised of Ewan McGregor and Leonardo Di Caprio starring together in a film about the Bay City Rollers, one of Edinburgh's proudest exports – and if that doesn't make Edinburgh the hippest city of cinema, it's hard to know what would.

The real problem with shooting movies in Edinburgh is that the Scottish film industry has its institutional and practical bases in Glasgow. Edinburgh might have the longest-running film festival in the world, but Glasgow has the government-funded Scottish Film and Locate in Scotland, as well as all the studios. And, while there has been talk of a film studio opening on the outskirts of Edinburgh in a scheme which is championed by Sean Connery, it looks as though, even if a studio complex does open, it will end up going to Glasgow instead.

PRACTICAL INFORMATION

Film programmes change on Fridays. Full listings are carried in the *List* magazine. The *Edinburgh Evening News* and the *Scotsman* run limited listings. Films are classified as: (U) – for universal viewing; (PG) – parental guidance advised for young children; (12), (15) and (18) – no entry for those aged under 12, 15 and 18 respectively. Most of the city's cinemas have disabled access and toilets, but it's always best to phone to check first.

Cinemas

The newly opened **Virgin Megaplex** in Sean Connery's old stomping ground of Fountainbridge has brought Edinburgh's total number of cinema screens to 52, a dozen more than there were half a century ago, although that profusion hasn't done much to increase choice, with the city's three multiplexes running practically identical mainstream fare. But saturation point may have been reached: the managers of most of the existing cinemas are warning that the two twelve-screen multiplexes planned for Greenside Place and Ocean Terminal in Leith will be too much of a good thing, and that job losses and closures are likely to result.

ABC Film Centre

120 Lothian Road, South Edinburgh, EH3 (228 1638/recorded info 229 3030/credit card bookings 228 1638). Bus 11, 15, 22, 24. **Tickets** £3-£4 before 6pm; £4.20-£5.20 after 6pm; £3-£3.30 concessions. **Credit** AmEx, MC, V. **Map** p309 D6. Mainly commercial fare is on show at this city-centre, three-screen cinema. Although the building is getting a bit tatty around the edges, the size of the screens more than compensates. Screen One has the best atmosphere in town when packed out on a Friday night for the latest blockbuster. The bar doesn't look as if it has changed much since the cinema was opened as the Regal in 1938.

ABC Multiplex
Westside Plaza, 120 Wester Hailes Road, Wester Hailes, West Edinburgh, EH14 (453 1569/recorded info 442 2200/credit card bookings 453 2494). Bus 3, 3A, 33. **Tickets** £3.20-£3.80 before 6pm; £4.50-£5.20 after 6pm; £3.20 concessions. **Credit** AmEx, MC, V.

A modern, eight-screen multiplex out to the west of the city centre. A licensed bar is open every evening. Refreshments are also served in an ice-cream bar – coffee, soft drinks, ice-cream, snacks and sweets should cater for most tastes.

The Cameo
38 Home Street, South Edinburgh, EH3 (228 4141/recorded info 228 2800/credit card bookings 228 4141). Bus 11, 16, 17, 23. **Tickets** £2-£5.20; £2-£3 Mon; £3.50 concessions. **Credit** MC, V. **Map** p309 D7.

A comfy, cheerful and friendly independent, run from London but showing the imaginative end of the cinematic spectrum. Screen One's airline seats are comfortably spacious and the top-quality sound is cranked right up for the late-night screenings (Thur-Sat) of modern cult movies. Screens Two and Three, on the other hand, are the size of seatback screens on a plane, but the sightlines are good enough. Before 11pm, drinks from the trendy bar may be taken into the film. Top-quality ice-cream – but pricey. *See also p157.*

The Dominion
18 Newbattle Terrace, Morningside, South Edinburgh, EH10 (447 4771/recorded info 447 2660/447 8450/credit card bookings 447 4771). Bus 11, 16, 17, 23. **Tickets** £3.50-£4.20 before 6pm; £4.70-£5.70 after 6pm; £3.50 concessions before 6pm, all day Mon. **Credit** MC, V.

Cinema-going as she used to be sung! This independent is still run by the Cameron family for whom it was built in 1938. They have a hands-on approach to their cinema and like to make sure their customers are always satisfied. The building is classic art deco, although it's now divided into four screens. Screen One's Pullman seats are probably the comfiest in town. The screening policy is in keeping with the douce location in Morningside and oriented towards family entertainment, although commercial realities do not preclude the odd 18-rated film. Hot snacks are available before 6pm in the basement café bar, which stays open until the end of the last film. Drinks may taken into the cinema.

The Filmhouse
88 Lothian Road, South Edinburgh, EH3 (228 2688). Bus 11, 15, 22, 24. **Tickets** £3.20 matinée; £4.20 before 7pm; £5.20 after 7pm; £1.80-£3.80 concessions; *Fri matinée* £2.20; £1.20 concessions. **Credit** MC, V. **Map** p314 A3.

The British Film Institute's representative cinema in Edinburgh, which means top-quality movies from around the world, the big current arthouse releases and regular screenings for classic movies – although they tend to have short runs. Screen One's sound

system is state of the art and powerful. Screen Three's sound system manages to drown out the noise of the projector. The Filmhouse is the centre for the Edinburgh International Film Festival and has a relentless round of themed mini-festivals throughout the year including French, Italian, gay and Australian. The bar is laid-back and convivial (*see page 146*).

Lumiere
Royal Museum, Chambers Street, South Edinburgh, EH1 (247 4219). Bus 23, 28, 40, 45. **Tickets** £4.50; £2.50 concessions. **Credit** MC, V. **Map** p309 F6.

This small screen in the lecture hall area of the Royal Museum shows a selection of vintage and contemporary classic movies on Fridays, Saturdays and Sundays. The children's matinées programme is particularly strong.

The Odeon
7 Clerk Street, South Edinburgh, EH8 (667 0971/recorded info & credit card bookings 08705 050007). Bus 7, 8, 31, 80. **Tickets** £4.50-£4.90; £3.50 concessions; £2 Sat morning kids' show. **Credit** AmEx, DC, MC, V. **Map** p310 G7.

This centrally located member of the Odeon chain has five screens. It shows the big commercial movies, with shows for kids on Saturday mornings (at 9.30am; no entry without a child) and grown-up late-nighters on Fridays and Saturdays. Screen One is huge; all of them are reasonably appointed. Check which seat you're being allocated when you get your ticket or you'll get stuck in the corner. A café-bar is open in the evenings and drinks can be taken into the film.

The UCI
Kinnaird Park, Newcraighall Road, Newcraighall, South Edinburgh, EH15 (669 0777/recorded info 08700 102030/credit card bookings 08700 102030). Bus 14, 14B, 32, 52. **Tickets** £5.20; £4.20 before 5pm Mon-Fri, before 3pm Sat, Sun. **Credit** AmEx, MC, V.

Modern 12-screener multiplex in the Kinnaird Shopping Park about 20 minutes out of Edinburgh. It lacks the atmosphere of the older cinemas, but has good equipment and shows more films for longer runs than its in-town rivals. A good selection of sweet concessions for munchies during the films.

Virgin Megaplex
Fountain Park, 65 Dundee Street, West Edinburgh, EH11 (recorded info & credit card bookings 0870 902 0417). Bus 1, 28, 34, 35, 35A. **Tickets** £5.25; £3.75 concessions (Mon-Fri only). **Credit** AmEx, MC, V. **Map** p308 B8.

Edinburgh's newest cinema boasts 13 screens, including the three-storey-high, crystal-sharp Iwerks screen, which comes into its own showing mountaineering and undersea shorts, and the Premier Screen, a private, bookable room with reclining double-seats and tables and its own bar and cloakroom. It's part of the Fountain Park complex of nightclubs, restaurants and a bowling alley, and although the cinemas are comfy, with ample leg-room, it scores no higher in ambience than the average multiplex. It has a café-bar and the usual food stalls.

Gay & Lesbian

Everyone's out and about on the streets of Edinburgh – but not all the battles are won and there is still a nasty nip of homophobia in the air.

Edinburgh has a thriving, vibrant and relatively open gay and lesbian community, which has added a strong commercial element to its sound political front over the years since a gay age of consent was finally adopted into Scots Law in 1980. Nowhere is this clearer than the bars, cafés, clubs and shops in the area surrounding Broughton Street, Picardy Place and the top of Leith Walk, which is known as the 'Pink Triangle'. Together they provide a cohesive and successful source of entertainment and information.

The majority of Edinburgh's straight community are not just tolerant of the gay and lesbian community, but are happy to live together. For a while in the '90s, it seemed as if most of the battles had been won and, indeed, the age of consent was lowered to 18. An attempt by the Bank of Scotland to go into commercial partnership with the anti-gay American TV Evangelist Pat Robertson was attacked with such a furore that the bank decided not to go ahead with the deal. But then, in 2000, when the Labour Party majority in the Scottish Parliament tried to implement an election commitment and repeal the so-called Section 28 – a law put in place during the 1980s, in an attempt to ban any teaching about homosexuality in schools – the bigots came out to play. The 'Keep the Clause' campaign combined with a level of hostility towards the Labour Party and some hysterical advertising to create a new climate of homophobia in Scotland as a whole. Reports of violence to gay individuals have risen and there is a certain part of the society in which it is becoming acceptable to be anti-gay once again.

Not that it is all gloom and doom. Lobbying on Scottish law goes both ways. And the community's sense of optimism and confidence is obvious from such large-scale productions as the twice-yearly Switchboard Ceilidh held in February and October at The Assembly Rooms (*see page 96*) and the mammoth organising feat behind Pride Scotland, alternating between Edinburgh and Glasgow in June. Then there are the regular events like 'Oot On Tuesday', at the Stand Comedy Club (*see page 213*) on the second Tuesday of the month, which draws the best gay comics from across the UK and packs the punters in.

There is plenty of information available for the gay visitor without having to look too hard. Posters and flyers advertising all kinds of events can be found at every venue, as can the free papers, including *Scotsgay* (*see also page 283*), *NOW* and *Cruise*. The best place to look is the **Lesbian, Gay and Bisexual Centre** (60 Broughton Street, 478 7069), which also has services such as Massage for Health (pager 01426 396953). If you want to check events before leaving home, phone the **Gay Switchboard** or **Lesbian Line** (for both, *see page 280*).

Health & safety

Outright Scotland, the country's main political campaigning group, has been working for some years with Lothian and Borders Police. The **Gay and Lesbian Liaison Committee** ensures that the police will deal fairly and without prejudice with gay and lesbian complaints. There is a Gay and Lesbian Liaison Officer, who provides a direct contact for the community and is based at **Gayfield Square Police Station** at the top of Leith Walk (Gayfield Square, 556 9270; open 24 hours daily). The police are also instigating an open surgery with the gay community.

Areas within the Pink Triangle, including the bit used as a cruising ground between Regent Road and London Road, are policed for the safety of gay men. Cruising areas outside this are not patrolled in this way, although Warriston Cemetery is a cruising ground of long-standing and is relatively safe – but should be avoided at night. Steer well clear of Calton Hill. It is notoriously dangerous. Go for the view during the day.

For gay and lesbian helplines and information on health issues, *see page 280*.

Accommodation

All the guesthouses listed here are either gay- or lesbian-run or gay friendly. A certain level of behaviour is expected (no cruising other guests), but they don't have any restrictions about late entry or who you're travelling with. The rates are for B&B. *See also page 289* for women-friendly accommodation.

Kilts, six-packs and other bad habits at **Pride Scotland**. *See page 96.*

Ardmor House

74 Pilrig Street, Broughton, EH6 (tel/fax
554 4944/robin@ardmorhouse.freeserve.co.uk/
www.ardmorhouse.freeserve.co.uk). Bus 7, 12, 16.
Rates £25-£40. **No credit cards. Map** p307 H2.
A stylish Victorian townhouse near the city centre
with five beautifully decorated rooms. The gay
owners welcome both gay and straight guests.
Hotel services *No smoking. Parking.* **Room
services** *TV.*

Garlands Guest House

48 Pilrig Street, Broughton, EH6 (tel/fax
554 4205/bill@garlands.demon.co.uk/
www.garlands.demon.co.uk). Bus 7, 12, 16.
Rates £25-£40. **Credit** MC, V. **Map** p307 H2.
A clean and comfortable gay- and straight-friendly
place to stay. It's relatively close to the fun on
Broughton Street, and a 'realistic' 15-minute walk
from the centre of town.
Hotel services *No smoking. Parking.* **Room
services** *TV.*

Mansfield House

57 Dublin Street, New Town, EH3 (556 7980/
fax 466 1315). Bus 8, 12, 16, 17. **Rates** £30-£40.
Credit MC, V. **Map** p306 F3.
Set in the heart of Edinburgh's Georgian New Town,
this substantial guesthouse has nine rooms with
lovely decor. It's very clean and always busy, so
book in advance.
Room services *Refrigerator. TV.*

Portobello House

2 Pittville Street, Portobello, EH15 (669 6067/
fax 657 9194/portobello.house@virgin.net/
freespace.virgin.net/portobello.house/index.htm).
Bus 26. **Rates** from £20. **Credit** V.
Although it's well out of town in the seaside district
of Portobello, this hotel is clean, gay- and straight-
friendly and within easy reach of the city centre by
public transport. Special diets catered for.
Hotel services *Garden. Parking.* **Room
services** *TV.*

Rimswell House Hotel

33 Mayfield Gardens, South Edinburgh, EH9 (tel/fax
667 5851). Bus 7, 8, 31, 80. **Rates** from £20.
Credit MC, V.
On a long drag of hotels and guesthouses on the
south side of the city, the Rimswell is not an exclusively gay establishment. There is disabled access
with assistance.
Room services *TV.*

Letting agency

Clouds Accommodation Agency

16 Forth Street, Broughton, EH1 (550 3808/fax 550
3807/cloudsacc@aol.com). Bus 8. **Open** 9am-6pm
Mon-Fri; noon-5pm Sat; closed Sun. **No credit
cards. Map** p307 G3.
A gay-friendly agency that can provide longer lets
and flatshares.

You knew just what I was there for – the **Blue Moon Café**.

Cafés

Blue Moon Café
See p143 for listings.
The longest-running gay establishment in Edinburgh, the Blue Moon deserves its good reputation for its varied menu and friendly service.

C32 Café
32C Broughton Street, Broughton, EH1 (557 2012). Bus 8. **Open** 10am-11pm daily. **Map** p307 F3.
Stylish gay-friendly licensed café with an extensive menu including a good choice of veggie dishes.

Nexus Café Bar
Lesbian, Gay and Bisexual Centre, 60 Broughton Street, Broughton, EH1 (478 7069). Bus 8. **Open** 11am-11pm daily. **Credit** AmEx, MC, V. **Map** p306 F3.
This great licensed café is friendly and inviting, and has email access (5p per min). In the same building as, but separate from, the LGB Centre, it is a good spot to pass a quiet afternoon or meet before clubbing.

Clubs

The best clubs in Edinburgh are mixed – that is gay, lesbian and straight – and the city has a good reputation for bringing together people who want to party in an environment where sexuality is not an issue. Wilkie House has become a staple, lead by the ever-strong Joy. Many of the pubs on Broughton Street have decks and DJs, and if you don't make it out of the area, you can always fall into **CC Blooms** (*see page 201*). Clubs come and go, but the following should endure in one form or another. All venues are listed in the **Nightlife** chapter.

Divine Divas
A women-only night, held monthly on Fridays at **The Venue**. All profits go to Lesbian Line.

Icons
The first Sunday of the month, at **Club Mercado**. The club's dance troupe perform current and older gay anthems to the amusement of the young crowd. Dress as your favourite icon for extra fun. A shuttle bus runs from **Planet Out** (*see p201*).

Joy
The legendary 'gay club for happy people' is as busy and as lively as ever and now runs once a month on a Saturday at **Wilkie House**. It boasts top guest DJs and a music policy that tends towards the heavier end of house.

Luvely
Runs monthly in **Wilkie House**, two weeks after Joy (*see above*). A fun night out for anyone who is gay, glam or trendy. Lads are strictly not welcome. Big house tunes and glorious fun.

Queer Sunday
Every Sunday at opulent ex-casino **E2K**. It's everything from cheesy disco to handbag house upstairs with easy listening and karaoke downstairs. Often plays host to a live PA.

Shebang
A mixed club held at **Wilkie House**, monthly on Saturdays, with an all-female DJ line up. Uplifting house music.

Tackno
On the last Sunday of the month, Trendy Wendy attracts an extrovert, mixed crowd to her dressing-up theme nights of trashy disco and '70s kitsch at **Club Mercado**.

Taste
An up-for-it and mixed crowd come to **Wilkie House** every Sunday. Hedonism incarnate – if you like your house music to be pumping and uplifting. Dress to sweat, as well as to be seen.

Escort services

Edinburgh Gay Escorts

19A Albany Street, Broughton, EH1 (558 1011/
www.edinburghgayescorts.co.uk).
Provides gay and lesbian escorts throughout Scotland
as well as tours of Edinburgh and its environs.

Pubs

Again, the bars on **Broughton Street** (*see
pages 155-6*) are the places to see and be seen,
but there are plenty of other less sceney places
around town. The **Traverse Bar** (*see page
161*) and **Black Bo's** (*see page 148*) are
always fun without being too out there. For
that, you'll have to end up in a messy heap on
the floor of **CC Blooms** (*see below*) – and
dahling, you won't be the first. Or the last.

CC Blooms

*23 Greenside Place, Leith Walk, Broughton, EH1
(556 9331). Bus 7, 12, 16.* **Open** 6pm-3am daily.
Admission free. **Map** p307 G3.
The dancefloor of this busy gay bar gets mobbed at
weekends. Everything from karaoke to disco, house
and striptease is on offer. This tends to be where
those who want to play hard but forgot to stop
drinking hard end up – no matter their sexuality.

The Claremont

*133-135 East Claremont Street, Broughton, EH7
(556 5662/www.scifipub99.freeserve.co.uk). Bus 8.*
Open 11am-1am daily. **Map** p306 F2.
A friendly mixed place run by two gay men. It occasionally hosts theme nights and also has a restaurant.

Habanas

*22 Greenside Place, Leith Walk, Broughton, EH1
(558 1270/cafehabanas@homail.com). Bus 7, 12, 16.*
Open noon-1am daily. **Map** p307 G3.
A mixed stylish bar serving a wide selection of
drinks including coffees and herb teas.

Hot Stuff

*89 Rose Street Lane North, New Town, EH2 (225
7651). Bus 3, 3A, 12, 16, 17.* **Open** noon-1am daily.
Map p314 B1.
This vibrant '70s disco bar, off the beaten track and
run by the fantastically named drag queen Sheila
Blige, attracts the city's TV/TS community.

The Newtown Bar

*26B Dublin Street, New Town, EH3 (538 7775). Bus
8, 12, 16, 17.* **Open** noon-1am Mon-Thur, Sun; noon-
2am Fri, Sat. **Map** p306 F4.
A well-appointed bar with a neighbourhood feel and
friendly staff. Downstairs is Intense, a heavy cruise
bar known for its warren of rooms and leather nights.

Planet Out

*6 Baxter's Place, Leith Walk, Broughton, EH1 (524
0061). Bus 7, 12, 16.* **Open** 4pm-1am Mon-Fri; 2pm-
1am Sat, Sun. **Map** p307 G3.

Attracts a very mixed crowd, who tend to be slightly
older during the week and younger at weekends.
Women, in particular, favour the place.

Stag & Turret

*1-7 Montrose Terrace, Calton Hill, EH7 (478 7231).
Bus 5, 15, 19, 35, 35A.* **Open** noon-1am Mon-Sat;
12.30pm-1am Sun. **Map** p307 J4.
Though it's a bit out of the way, this small
friendly place is well patronised.

Shops

Atomix

*Lesbian, Gay and Bisexual Centre, 60 Broughton
Street, Broughton, EH1 (558 8174).* **Open** 11am-
7pm daily. **Credit** MC, V. **Map** p306 F3.
Specialises in men's and women's club clothes and
fetish wear as well as gifts, videos, books and toys.

Fantasies

*8B Drummond Street, South Edinburgh, EH8 (557
8336). Bus 7, 8, 21, 31, 80.* **Open** 10am-9pm Mon-
Sat; noon-9pm Sun. **Credit** MC, V. **Map** p310 G6.
Downstairs in a sex shop, Fantasies has everything
a guy might want to expand his nightlife.

Out of the Blue

*Basement of Blue Moon Café, 36 Broughton Street,
EH1 (478 7048). Bus 8.* **Open** noon-7pm daily.
Credit MC, V. **Map** p306 F3.
The UK's biggest gay and lesbian store outside
London sells books, mags, videos, gifts and clothes.

Hot spots

The two best places to head if you want to
work up a sweat, or more.

No.18

*18 Albert Place, Leith Walk, Broughton, EH7
(553 3222/www.no.18sauna.co.uk). Bus 7,
12, 16.* **Open** noon-10pm Mon-Sat; 2-10pm
Sun. **Admission** £8; £5 concessions.
No credit cards. Map p307 H2.
Edinburgh's longest established gay sauna is
clean, well run and as safe a place as you'll
get. The crowd is mixed and very friendly.

The Townhouse

*53 East Claremont Street, Broughton, EH1
(556 6116/www.townhouse-sauna.co.uk).
Bus 8.* **Open** noon-11pm daily. **Admission**
membership £2, plus £8, £5 concessions.
Map p306 F2.
The newly opened Townhouse offers sauna,
steam room, jacuzzi, tanning booths, gym,
Intranet café, bar, Kruze video zone and
male to male massage. Clean, comfortable
and professional.

Arts & Entertainment

Music:
Classical & Opera

From the grand opera of the Festival Theatre to organ recitals in St Giles' or chamber music in the Queen's Hall, Edinburgh is music to your ears.

Edinburgh's output of home-grown music might well be overshadowed by the month-long glut of artistic overindulgence that is the **Edinburgh International Festival** (*see page 97*), but that doesn't mean the city's music lovers have to make do with meagre rations for the rest of the year.

BUYING TICKETS

Tickets for many major venues can be booked through the **Ticketline** network (220 4349; 10am-8pm Mon-Sat; 11am-6pm Sun); otherwise contact individual box offices listed under the relevant venues.

Classical music

There are stunning performances from Scotland's own classical companies all through the year. Although two of the main national companies, the **Royal Scottish National Orchestra** (RSNO) and the orchestra of the **Scottish Opera**, have their administrative bases in Glasgow, they perform regular seasons in the capital. The Edinburgh-based **Scottish Chamber Orchestra** (SCO) is still enjoying a sensational relationship with principal conductor Joseph Swensen and performs throughout Scotland, but gives more concerts in Edinburgh than elsewhere. One of Europe's finest chamber orchestras, the SCO is renowned not only for the quality of its performances but also for its imaginative programming and commissioning policy, and its education work. Conductor Laureate Sir Charles Mackerras has initiated the orchestra's move into period performance, with natural trumpets and calf-skinned timpani being heard with increasing frequency. It is to be hoped that this side of the orchestra's work will be further developed in the future. The **BBC Scottish Symphony Orchestra** makes occasional forays from the west for one-off events, often featuring music by a specific composer.

The best orchestral venue in the city is the splendid **Usher Hall** (Cambridge Street), which was built in 1914 with £100,000 gifted to

the city for the purpose by the beer magnate Andrew Usher. Sadly, the hall has been out of commission for some time, undergoing a £9-million refurbishment. It will open for the Edinburgh International Festival in 2000, close again for more renovations, and then (in theory) reopen permanently in December 2000. Outside the Festival, full symphony orchestra performances now take place in the **Edinburgh Festival Theatre** (*see page 204*), where a specially designed acoustic shell has improved the acoustic for concerts, although it is not an ideal solution for the 90-strong RSNO. Relocated to the Festival Theatre until the Usher Hall renovations are complete, the RSNO puts on a summer Proms season, which brings popular symphonic classics including, as one might expect, nights of Tchaikovsky, Vienna and film music. The RSNO's winter season repertoire mixes the familiar with the less familiar; international soloists and conductors add variety and interest.

The **Queen's Hall** (*see below*) is a short distance south of the Festival Theatre in a converted Georgian church. The Hall is just right for chamber music but is becoming too small as the rehearsing and performing base of the SCO. The Main Hall of **The Hub** (*see page 208*) is being used for a variety of different concerts, mostly informal. Although the setting is spectacular, the acoustics aren't up to much.

Venues

Queen's Hall

Clerk Street, South Edinburgh, EH8 (box office 668 2019/admin 668 3456/queenshall@cableinet.co.uk). Bus 7, 8, 31, 80. **Open** *box office* 10am-5.30pm Mon-Sat (until start of performance on performance days); 1hr before performance Sun. **Telesales** 10am-5pm, 5.30pm on performance nights. **Admission** £2-£25. **Credit** AmEx, DC, MC, V. **Map** p310 H7.

A converted church seating 800 people – albeit on rather uncomfortable old pews. Aside from providing a home for the SCO (*see above*), it also hosts a wide variety of concerts from ensembles and groups of all shapes and sizes. Contemporary and classical

The BBC Scottish Symphony Orchestra at play at the **Queen's Hall**. *See page 202.*

chamber music can be heard to great effect here and there are two first-class Steinways in residence. Amateur, youth and school concerts are held regularly and there are short seasons of Wednesday afternoon tea concerts when an extended interval is filled with delicious home-made scones and cakes.

University of Edinburgh

(concert secretary 650 2423/music@ed.ac.uk/ www.ed.ac.uk). Bus 23, 28, 45. **Open** *9am-5pm Mon-Fri; closed Sat, Sun.*

The University is an excellent source of free concerts during term-time. High-quality lunchtime chamber music recitals on Tuesdays at the **Reid Concert Hall** complement Friday lunchtime organ recitals next door at the **McEwan Hall** (both at Bristo Square, South Edinburgh; Oct-May 1.10-1.55pm), where a more unusual repertoire is programmed. Reid Hall also houses the unique **Edinburgh University Collection of Historic Musical Instruments** (*see p82*). The working exhibits of the **Russell Collection of Early Keyboard Instruments** (*see p55*), just down the road at the 18th-century St Cecilia's Hall in the Cowgate, are used for public performance once a year.

CHURCHES

Many of Edinburgh's churches are suitable for concerts and, indeed, many are used for this purpose during the Fringe. The following are the main ones used during the rest of the year. Where a charge is sometimes made, this is indicated, although the church may not charge for all events and certainly not for services.

Greyfriars Tolbooth & Highland Kirk

2 Greyfriars Place, Candlemaker Row, South Edinburgh, EH1 (225 1900/www.greyfriarskirk.com). Bus 23, 28, 35, 35A, 45. **Open** *Apr-Oct 10.30am-4.30pm Mon-Fri, Sun; 10.30am-2.30pm Sat; Nov-Mar 1.30pm-3.30pm Thur; all year morning service 11am Sun; Gaelic service 12.30pm Sun.* **Admission** £4-£6. **Map** p309 F6.

Choral concerts by professional groups such as Cappella Nova and the Dunedin Consort are often held here. The Kirk produces the quarterly *Greyfriars Programme,* which lists all the events – except for those taking place during the Festival –

and can be picked up from a tourist information centre or information points at pubs and hotels.

St Giles' Cathedral

Parliament Square, Royal Mile, EH1 (visitors centre 225 9442). Bus 35, 35A. **Open** *spring-autumn 9am-7pm daily; winter 9am-5pm daily; all year organ recitals 6pm Sun.* **Admission** £4-£6. **Map** p314 D3.

Boasts an amazing Rieger organ installed in 1992. In addition to the regular concerts during spring, summer and autumn there is an hour of free music on a Sunday at 6pm. It's always best to phone to check before you set off.

St John's Episcopal Church

Princes Street, New Town, EH2 (229 7565). Bus 3, 3A, 12, 16, 17. **Open** *Eucharist 9.45am Sun; matins 11.15am Sun; choral evensong 6pm Sun.* **Admission** free. **Map** p314 A2.

Right at the west end of Princes Street, this church has a splendid acoustic and is host to a variety of musical happenings.

St Mary's Episcopal Cathedral

Palmerston Place, New Town, EH12 (225 6293/ www.cathedral.net). Bus 3, 3A, 12, 25, 25A. **Open** *summer 9am-9pm; winter 9am-6pm; all year choral evensong 5.30pm Mon-Wed, Fri; 3.30pm Sun; choral Eucharist 5.30pm Thur, 10.30am Sun.* **Admission** free. **Map** p308 B6.

At the west end of the city, this is another favourite for organ recitals. Its own choir – the first in Britain to include girl as well as boy trebles – sings at evensong on weekdays during term-time as well as at Sunday services. During the summer, a programme of visiting choirs is offered. Ring the cathedral for more information.

Stockbridge Parish Church

Saxe Coburg Street, Stockbridge, EH3 (332 0122). Bus 35, 35A. **Open** *phone for details.* **Admission** £2-£5. **Map** p306 D3.

The only regularly used concert venue on the north side of the city. Similar in size and architecture to the Queen's Hall (*see p202*), it is used by the Edinburgh Quartet, a number of choirs and for various one-offs. There are no regular concerts, but there is a free mailing list and the church's monthly magazine, the *Bridge*, includes musical events.

Arts & Entertainment

A reflection of the city's classical music scene at the **Edinburgh Festival Theatre**.

Opera

For many years the weakest part of Edinburgh's claim to staging the world's greatest arts festival was its lack of a truly grand-scale, fully appointed space for opera. This somewhat glaring gap was more than handsomely filled in 1994 when the 1,900-seat **Edinburgh Festival Theatre** (*see below*) was opened. The Council-backed refurbishment of this former Victorian variety house included the restoration of the interior to its original, opulent glory, the introduction of state-of-the-art technical specifications and the addition of an emphatically modern, three-storey-high, glass frontage housing the box office, café and bars.

   Scottish Opera stages around eight different operas each year, mixing past successes with new productions that are generally innovative and often noted for discovering emerging young talent. After struggling with debt during the '90s, the company was sent over the edge in 1999 by a particularly well received, but expensive, production of Verdi's *Macbeth*, directed by Luc Bondi. It is now in a joint management deal with Scottish Ballet. This has not stymied future plans and the complete Ring Cycle is being mounted in collaboration with the Edinburgh International Festival: *Das Rheingold* in 2000; *Die Walküre* in 2001; *Siegfried* in 2002; and the complete cycle including *Götterdämmerung* in 2003. Recent commissions have included operas by Scottish composers James MacMillan and Judith Weir.

Venues

Edinburgh Festival Theatre

13-29 Nicolson Street, South Edinburgh, EH8 (box office 529 6000/admin 662 1112/tickets@eft.co.uk/ www.eft.co.uk). Bus 7, 8, 21, 31, 80. **Open** *box office/telesales* performance days 11am-8pm Mon-Sat; 4pm-curtain-up Sun; non-performance days 10am-6pm Mon-Sat; closed Sun. **Admission** *opera* £5-£45.50; *other* £4.50-£22.50. **Credit** AmEx, DC, MC, V. **Map** p310 G6.

After years of debating the idea of building a new opera house in Edinburgh, the various powers-that-be got their act together to bring the old Empire Theatre back to artistic life in 1994. The fact that it has a decent-sized pit, one of the largest stages in Europe and an acoustic that is perfect for singers has made it as popular with the public as it is with the performers from Scottish Opera – which now uses it for all its Edinburgh performances. Otherwise it is used by Scottish Ballet when it is in Edinburgh. Generally the theatre's management, which also runs the King's Theatre (*see page 221*), has a policy of booking a wide range of productions, from high-fallutin' dance to bawdy comics. Touring companies and the local amateur grand opera society also use the theatre, as do some visiting orchestras and choirs.

   The coffee and wine are good-enough quality, but interval queuing can be a bore, so remember to order in advance. If not, the Café Lucia at ground level will probably provide the quickest service as staff are more plentiful there. Advance booking is advisable for the best seats – the circle has especially good sightlines.

Music: Rock, Folk & Jazz

From the fiddles and reels of the ceilidhs to Tommy Smith's cool jazz, there's more to Edinburgh's music scene than the Bay City Rollers.

Ocean Colour Scene belting out the tunes at Edinburgh's Hogmanay.

Rock, pop & dance

Leaving to one side the colossal impact of the Bay City Rollers in the 1970s, in rock and pop music terms, the capital has always been upstaged by its old rival Glasgow. In the sense of long-term commercial success, Edinburgh's recent past is a catalogue of also-rans like Win and Goodbye Mr Mackenzie, whose backup vocalist Shirley Manson nonetheless found fame fronting Garbage, and whose guitarist, 'Big' John Duncan, reached the lofty heights of playing second guitar with Nirvana on their final tour. There are the odd, proud exceptions. The Proclaimers have achieved international recognition with a sound that owes as much to Memphis as it does to the vocal and lyrical tradition of their homeland. Opportunity also knocked for pop-reggae singer Finley Quaye, who in 1998 won the Best Solo Male Brit Award for his debut album.

The fact that Edinburgh has a relatively small population means that, despite its importance as a capital city, there hasn't been a record industry infrastructure strong enough to compete with the bigger cities. Local record labels are small, hand-to-mouth businesses with very limited clout, and the music business (such as it is) could do with a focal point to rally around. Even the burst of activity in the late '90s that invigorated the scene with such bands as Idlewild, Annie Christian and Magicdrive – as well as the rather smoother sounds of singing sisters Gina and Sylvia Rae in the Lanterns – failed to lead to bigger and better things. And V2's Equipe Ecosse, the first major label subsidiary to base its head office in Scotland, now seems on the verge of wrapping up its operation for good.

But even though Edinburgh acts have scored low on the commercial potential scale, the innovative spirit that infused such early-1980s bands as Josef K and the

Arts & Entertainment

Fire Engines still sparks the city. There is a history of maverick combos whose music is frequently as interesting as, if not more interesting than, their counterparts' in the west, not least former Fire Engine Davey Henderson's current outfit The Nectarine No.9, or the bizarre, medieval-inspired songs of Dominic Waxing Lyrical. Bands from Edinburgh might find it hard to scale the corporate ladder, but that doesn't mean you can't pop into one of the smaller venues and hear some fine, spirited, often inspired bands. And, interestingly, they rarely have anything but their city of origin in common. There isn't, and never has been, an 'Edinburgh sound'.

The dance scene is in good health, with re-mix artists like Huggy (Burger Queen), George T (Tribal Funktion) and Aqua Bassino making their names on the national and international house music circuits, with George Mac (Manga) forging ahead in the drum'n'bass world.

There's no shortage of guitar bands either. The latest crop include The Cherry Fire Ashes, Huckleberry and Solaris. And their number is constantly being augmented. Regular Edinburgh audiences know that if any band fails to last the course there'll be another one along in a minute.

For years, Edinburgh has been bypassed in favour of Glasgow by big and medium-sized bands due to the city's lack of suitable venues, a frustrating state of affairs which forces fans to travel 40 miles to see them. This trend may be about to turn, however, with the opening of **The Corn Exchange** (*see below*), which is intended to be an East Coast counterpart to Glasgow's legendary Barrowland, and with the **Edinburgh Playhouse** (*see page 221*) tentatively relaxing its policy of block-booking big-budget musicals to allow the occasional, suitably prestigious performer to grace its stage.

Venues

The Attic

Dyer's Close, 71 Cowgate, Royal Mile, EH1 (225 8382). Bus 7, 8, 21, 31, 80. **Open** varies Mon-Wed; 8pm-3am Thur-Sun. **Admission** £3-£6.50. **No credit cards. Map** p309 F6.

The somewhat dingy upstairs room of a pub, the Attic is nevertheless the current place to see up-and-coming local bands as well as cool indie bands from further afield, some of them fairly well-known.

La Belle Angele

For listings see p211.

The concrete walls and floor of the long L-shaped main room can be a bit of a downer, but the effect is mitigated with arty flourishes. Cool enough to be

Bagpipes and beats from **Martyn Bennett**.

used by record companies for Scottish showcases, La Belle hosted the debut Edinburgh performances of Oasis, Radiohead and Jeff Buckley.

The Cas Rock

For listings see p159.

For all the love-hate relationship that its patrons have with it, the Cas Rock is practically an institution, a small space specialising in the noisiest, most obscure bands ever to crawl out from under a stone – along with some of the most exciting local talent. The site is threatened with being bulldozed and replaced with a big hotel, so get the noise while you can.

The Corn Exchange

11 Newmarket Road, off Chesser Avenue, West Edinburgh, EH14 (477 3500/www.ece.uk.com). Bus 28, 35, 35A. **Times** vary. **Admission** £8-£20. **Credit** AmEx, MC, V.

Out on the west side of the city, The Corn Exchange is Edinburgh's attempt to create its own equivalent of Glasgow's hallowed Barrowland Ballroom. With a capacity of 2,500, and a lot of money spent to ensure its acoustic qualities, it's certainly an atmospheric, enjoyable place to see a band. Gigs have been sporadic so far, however, so it hasn't had much chance to prove itself or foster brand loyalty. A great venue with a lot of hard work ahead of it.

The Liquid Room

For listings see p211.

Now used regularly by the better local bands and some illustrious out-of-towners, the Liquid Room's reputation has seriously risen along with the scale of the bands it attracts. The upstairs bar and gallery give a great view of the stage.

The Venue

For listings see p211.

The main floor is a classic dark and dingy rock dive that has expanded over the years but retains the atmosphere that small-to-medium-sized touring rock bands thrive on. When big names are playing, the dancefloor can get very packed and sweaty. Local, triple-band packages are a staple of its programme, and sometimes sell surprisingly well.

Folk & roots

If Edinburgh's rock scene is a bit low key, the folk scene is flourishing like never before. Scotland has witnessed a remarkable flowering of folk and roots-based music in recent years, with Edinburgh firmly at its epicentre. The political potency of traditional music may have diminished since the banning of the bagpipes – on pain of death – as an instrument of war following the 1745 Jacobite Rebellion, yet the popular debate over cultural identity in the run-up to the new Parliament has undoubtedly been the key catalyst in folk music renaissance. Add to this the widespread interest in acoustic and 'ethnic' music, fostered by the world-beat vogue, and you get a new generation of sounds that embodies Scotland's revitalised self-confidence.

This is inventive stuff, too. Bands like Shooglenifty, Martyn Bennett, the Tartan Amoebas and the Peatbog Faeries blend traditional forms with all manner of rock, dance, jazz and global influences to create music that leaves hoary old finger-in-the-ear folk stereotypes floundering in the dust.

As the undisputed hub of all this cosmopolitan crossover, Edinburgh has become a folk music mecca for those in the know. Edinburgh-born musicians are outnumbered by emigré Highlanders and Hebrideans, folk from Fife and the north-east, and a good sprinkling of Orcadians and Shetlanders for good measure. All of whom add their own traditions to the melting pot. As does the vibrant local jazz and club circuit and the wealth of international cross-currents jointly supplied by the Festival, tourism and an extensive academic community. All told, a recipe for some exhilarating musical adventures.

Cutting-edge fusions aside, Edinburgh's folk scene has many other faces: pipers in full Highland dress busk on Princes Street; 'traditional' Scottish evenings play nightly during the summer in the big chain hotels; a cappella singers and instrumental duos perform in pub cellars; and the ceilidhs at **The Assembly Rooms** (*see page 208*) are routinely packed out with sweatily mad-for-it revellers. The city's musicians cater for the genre's full spectrum of tastes.

Paradoxically the music can take some seeking out. Decent gigs are often thin on the ground. Edinburgh may be abundantly supplied with performers, but the kind of small and mid-scale venues generally best suited to their skills seem to be stuck in the rock and house music circuit. **The Bongo Club** and **Whistle Binkies** (for both, *see page 208*) are honorable exceptions, with an eclectic and frequently interwoven mix of live local acts and club nights, often with an experimental twist.

The Edinburgh Folk Club at the Pleasance offers a solid and reasonably diverse diet of traditional and contemporary sounds every Wednesday in the Cabaret Bar except when the Pleasance is taken over by the Fringe in summer. Among the bigger venues, the Main Hall of **The Hub** (*see page 208*), the **Edinburgh Festival Theatre** (*see page 204*), the **Queen's Hall** (*see page 202*) and **The Assembly Rooms** (*see page 208*) all stage occasional gigs by Celtic and world-music acts. The last-mentioned is also home to a highly popular monthly series of ceilidhs, held throughout the spring and autumn.

Authentic informal pub sessions tend, by definition, to be spontaneous and are therefore moveable feasts. Some pubs can generally be relied on for a tune, however. **The Royal Oak** on Infirmary Street; **Sandy Bell's** on Forrest Road (for both, *see page 161*); **Ensign Ewart** on the Lawnmarket (225 7440); the **Shore Bar** on the Shore, Leith (225 2751); and the **Hebrides** on Market Street (220 4213) are all good bets for a session.

Another sweaty folk sesh in the city.

Venues

The Blind Poet

32C West Nicolson Street, South Edinburgh, EH8 (667 0876/www.blindpoet.fsbusiness.co.uk). Bus 7, 8, 21, 31, 80. **Open** 11am-1am Mon-Fri; noon-1am Sat; 6pm-1am Sun. **Map** p310 G6.

A small but attractive pub to the south of the city centre, the Blind Poet offers music in the form of folk and traditional residencies.

The Bongo Club

For listings see p211.
Not fancy by any means, this small venue is run as a charity by a hugely eclectic and fiercely independent collective who will put on any kind of music from left-field classical to dance to the hinterlands of post-rock. It really comes to life during the Festival, but there are gigs on here most weeks.

The Hub

348 Castlehill, Royal Mile, EH1 (tickets 473 2000). Bus 35, 35A. **Open** varies. **Admission** varies. **Credit** AmEx, DC, MC, V. **Map** p314 C3.
The Main Hall of The Hub, with its striking textile covered walls, is a good-looking venue for a variety of concerts, from classical to folk and jazz. The acoustics of the room, which was the Assembly Hall for the Church of Scotland, are rather too echoing for any great clarity, however.

Whistle Binkies

For listings see p149.
Popular pub with the rootsy and traditional fraternity, usually featuring sessions from 8-11pm and late-night bands.

Jazz

Edinburgh has nurtured a respectable roster of important jazz musicians over the years, including the iconoclastic clarinetist Sandy Brown and the Royal High Gang of the late 1950s, and saxophonist Tommy Smith, considered the most important jazz musician Scotland has ever produced. If they have sometimes seemed to thrive more in spite of than thanks to the city's jazz scene (or simply had to go elsewhere), that is not unique to Edinburgh, and provision for jazz has often been better than in many bigger cities.

The current scene ranges from Dixieland in pubs to international jazz at the **Queen's Hall** (*see below*), where Assembly Direct promotes international artists, albeit less frequently than in the past. The local late-night club scene that mushroomed in the late 1990s is still active despite some enforced changes, centred on the Jazz Joint at **Henry's Cellar Bar** (*see below*), where DJ Tinku runs the gigs (jazz-hip hop fusion is a speciality, but acoustic jazz gets an occasional look in – actually hearing it in this noisy basement can be another matter), and **The Bongo Club** (*see above*).

A newcomer to the scene, the Jazz Trane, launched at the beginning of the new century in the **St Bride's Centre** (*see page 222*). The Freddie King Quintet is the house band at the

once-a-month club here, with special guests brought in from further afield, including the odd American soloist as well as known British names. There are also a number of well-established free residencies in pubs and restaurants, covering various styles of jazz.

Early August ushers in the **Edinburgh Jazz & Blues Festival** (*see page 99*). Once focused almost entirely on traditional and mainstream jazz, the festival now has a much more wide-ranging remit. The principal concerts are held at the **Queen's Hall** (*see below*) and **The Hub** (*see above*), with smaller club-style venues at places like **The Liquid Room** (*see page 206*), often with genuine name artists (the likes of Greg Osby, Bobby Watson, David Sanchez, Martin Taylor and Tommy Smith all featured in the 1999 programme).

The Leith Jazz Festival is a much more modest event in musical terms, but provides a convivial weekend (usually early in June) when the pubs and restaurants around the Shore move into raucous swing mode. The events are free, and there is a genuine buzz around the port, especially if the rain stays away.

Venues

The Assembly Rooms

54 George Street, New Town, EH2 (box office 220 4349/admin 220 4348). Bus 23, 27, 45. **Open** *box office* 10am-5pm Mon-Sat; till 8pm performance nights; *admin* 10am-5pm Mon-Fri; closed Sat, Sun. **Admission** £2-£25. **Credit** AmEx, DC, MC, V. **Map** p314 B1.
Beyond the Festival, this former Georgian society rendezvous retains its faintly Jane Austen-esque aura. The ceiling of the main room is too high, so the acoustics can go awry, along with the atmosphere. On the other hand, the large ballroom across the landing, with chandeliers and a civilised atmosphere, can make even the scuzziest of crowds feel special. Hosts a monthly ceilidh on the last Friday of the month from October to May, and the occasional rock, folk, jazz and world-music gigs by Scottish and international artists.

Henry's Cellar Bar

For listings see p211.
Kulu's Jazz Joint is an excellent club where the live music displays Kulu's eclectic tastes and booking policy. Depending which night you go, you could be regaled with free jazz, hip hop, Latin, funk or even Asian drum'n'bass. Some of the best DJs in the city man the decks too.

Queen's Hall

For listings see p202.
A converted Georgian church that has played host to some big names in every sphere of music. The atmosphere is intimate, but the hard wooden pews leave something to be desired in the comfort stakes.

Nightlife

With its cackling comedy and crucial clubbing, Edinburgh is the place to cut loose, let rip, and have fun, fun, fun.

Disco Inferno at **The Assembly Rooms**. See page 211.

From house to disco, dressing up to dressing down, Edinburgh offers a plateful of fun to the late-night party animal. Yet, if all they had to go on was the tourist board's cosy, tartan image of the city, even the most inveterate seekers of nightlife would be forgiven for pausing before partaking of their nocturnal pleasures in Edinburgh.

Those with a smattering of literary or cinematic knowledge would, however, have an inkling that, behind the elegant façade and grey, moral rectitude, there lies something a little more interesting. Once the sun has set, the wildlife comes out to play.

But nightlife takes many forms and after-dark pleasures are far from a modern phenomenon. Although Robert Louis Stevenson is reputed to have based his *Strange Case of Dr Jekyll and Mr Hyde* on the grisly history of Deacon Brodie, it is more likely that the primary inspiration came from

his own experiences. Late at night, he would steal away from the drawing rooms of the New Town to purchase his pleasures up Lothian Road, in the Old Town and down in Leith. This was Edinburgh's knicker-free posterior guarded by the warming fur coat. 'I love night in the city,' he wrote, 'the lighted streets and the swinging gait of harlots. I love cool pale morning, in the empty by-streets…'

Nowadays, the purchasing of fleshy pleasures has been banished to the city's saunas, which are licensed under the city health and safety regulations, much to the outrage of the moral minority. While this certainly makes life safer and less unhealthy for workers in the sex industry, it does not reduce exploitation. The uncharitable would also argue that it allows the great and good of Edinburgh to indulge themselves with ease and in private. The viewing of flesh continues, but not in private, at a couple of seedy dives in the West Bow and a lap-dancing bar in Tollcross.

Which is neither the wholesome image the Tourist Board would like to present nor a typical representation of Edinburgh at play, although it is one at which the city's comics are wont to laugh. But whatever your mood and whatever your predilection, this is a city where the night-time is the right time for dancing.

Pre-club bars

Edinburgh has style, although not in the same self-consciously designer-led conspicuousness of Glasgow. It's more discreet and based on taste and individuality – not the ability to spot a label before it becomes hip. The most obvious face of the style bar culture is in the rise and rise of the pre-club bar: places that stay open until 1am, have a pair of decks in the corner and the nous to hire someone to use them rather than just sticking on the latest mix CD.

Of the bars listed in the **Bars & Pubs** chapter, **Pivo Caffé** (*see page 156*) is convenient for The Venue and Studio 24. Up on the Royal Mile, **The City Café** and **EH1** (for both, *see page 148*) are close to Wilkie House, The Vaults (15 Niddry Street, EH1) and La Belle Angele, as is **Iguana** (*see page 160*) to the south. For those places that make you want to stay all night, upstairs at **The Meadow Bar** (*see page 160*) is a good bet for some interesting beats and breaks, while **Black Bo's** (*see page 148*) adds a sense of down-at-heel sophistication to a night on the town. **CC Blooms** (*see page 201*) is gay-oriented but caters to straights too.

Clubs

Edinburgh's club scene is thriving. Though the city is small enough to have kept out the supermarket attitudes of the super-club, it is at the same time large enough to have a wealth of home-grown talent. Tribal Funktion, Joy, Taste, Tackno, Manga and Disco Inferno have all made their individual marks on the cluberati over the years without becoming stale. New clubs are constantly springing up. What Edinburgh lacks, though, is the motivating and unifying force of a strong independent record label along the lines of Glasgow's Soma. Instead, there is a good number of DJs, all talented in their chosen areas of dance music, who are dedicated to creating a name for themselves in the city and in Scotland, rather than around the world. This is as true for the cutting-edge dance clubs as it is for the retro-cool.

Too much orange squash?

Thanks to Scotland's halfway decent licensing hours, at the same time that London is struggling home with a lager carry-out and a greasy kebab, Edinburgh is just getting into the swing of things and deciding which club to go to. The down side is that, except under special circumstances, the guardians of the city's moral fibre have decreed that 1.30am is the time you have to be in the club and that 3am is the absolute limit. A somewhat annoying decision, to say the least.

In general terms, Friday-night clubs tend to be about going out, getting sweaty and dancing the tensions of the week away. Saturday nights see a far more sartorially elegant approach. Sunday clubs cater for those full-on party animals who can afford to ignore Monday morning. Weekday clubbing tends more towards the alcohol-fuelled boogie than a hard-core fest.

Because of the ephemeral nature of the club scene, no written guide will ever be up to date, even the *List*'s club information, which is not always as reliable as the rest of its listings. Club runners do spend a lot on advertising, however. Flyers piled in the trendier bars like The City Café (*see page 148*) and in record shops help point out the rest. Underground Solushun (*see page 167*) is always a good place to hang out – the staff are friendly and know their stuff.

Club nights come and go. Those mentioned here have a reasonable chance of lasting. Prices vary wildly, with most venues charging little if at all midweek. The higher prices are for non-members on Fridays and Saturdays. Expect to pay even more during the Festival, when clubs also tend to extend their opening hours.

The Assembly Rooms

for listings see p208.
As well as gigs and ceilidhs, The Assembly Rooms hosts occasional special one-off nights for clubs, such as Vegas and Disco Inferno.

The Attic

Dyer's Close, Cowgate, Royal Mile, EH1 (225 8382). Bus 7, 8, 21, 31, 80. **Open** 11pm-3am Fri-Sun; Mon-Wed phone for times; closed Thur. **Admission** £2-£4. **No credit cards. Map** p309 F6.
A smallish space that doubles as a live venue for the indie rock scene in the early evening. The clubs tend to be student-oriented in a retro-pop vein, with a bit of dance thrown in midweek.

La Belle Angele

11 Hasties Close, Cowgate, Royal Mile, EH1 (225 7536). Bus 7, 8, 21, 31, 80. **Open** 8pm-3am Thur-Sun; closed Mon-Wed. **Admission** £5-£12. **No credit cards. Map** p314 D3.
For a while, this former gallery, tucked away in a little square at the end of a close and surrounded by centuries-old buildings, had little but the (excellent) drum'n'bass night Manga to recommend it. But with a renovation and an increase of capacity to 500, it's now the new home of the groovy and eclectic Lizzard Lounge, which helped make the now-defunct Café Graffiti Edinburgh's most essential night out, Futuristica, the current venture of Joseph Malik, one of Graffiti's star DJs, and Radio Babylon.

The Bongo Club

14 New Street, Royal Mile, EH8 (office 556 5204/bar 558 7604/www.outoftheblue.uk). Bus 35, 35A. **Open** 10pm-3am Thur-Sun; closed Mon-Wed. **Admission** £3-£7. **No credit cards. Map** p310 G5.
A multimedia arts space above an old bus station that can hit a truly underground vibe with dub reggae from the mighty Messenger Sound System (fortnightly, Sat). Otherwise, it's pretty bohemian and highly eclectic. The accent is away from house music towards the beats and breaks. An adjoining café is open from 11am to 6pm Mon-Fri.

The Citrus

40-42 Grindlay Street, South Edinburgh, EH3 (622 7086/www.citrus-club.co.uk). Bus 11, 15, 22, 24. **Open** 11pm-3am Thur, Sat, Sun; 10.30pm-3am Fri; closed Mon-Wed. **Admission** £2-£4. **No credit cards. Map** p314 A3.
Small, indie and retro-oriented club that does well from its student clientele.

Club Mercado

36-39 Market Street, Royal Mile, EH1 (226 4224). Bus 35. **Open** 5pm-3am Fri; 11pm-4am Sat; 11pm-3am Sun; closed Mon-Thur. **Admission** free-£10. **No credit cards. Map** p314 D2.
A venue where the emphasis is on sheer fun, and one that tends towards celebrating the kitsch and cheesy, especially with the marvellous Tackno on the last Sunday of the month. Be warned of the Friday night after-work office party of TFI Friday.

E2K

14 Picardy Place, Broughton, EH1 (478 7434). Bus 7, 12, 16. **Open** 11pm-3am Mon-Thur, Sat; 10.30pm-3am Fri; 10pm-3am Sun. **Admission** £2-£8. **No credit cards. Map** p307 G4.
This glamorous ex-casino is the venue for everything from the people's favourite, Vegas (retro-kitsch and groovy tunes), to the house and garage night Substantial, which was praised by DJ Danny Rampling as 'one of the finest nights in the land', (both monthly, Saturdays) as well as one-off events from the outrageous bondage and fetish club Sin.

Henry's Cellar Bar

8 Morrison Street, West Edinburgh, EH3 (538 7385). Bus 11, 15, 22, 24. **Open** 10pm-3am daily. **Admission** £3-£5. **No credit cards. Map** p309 D6.
Despite the name, Kulu's Jazz Joint is a haven for all types of good music, both live and on record. Depending which night you go on, you could be regaled with free jazz, hip hop, Latin, funk or Asian drum'n'bass. Underground bohemian cool.

The Liquid Room

9C Victoria Street, Royal Mile, EH1 (225 2564/www.liquidroom.com). Bus 23, 28, 35, 35A, 45. **Open** 10.30pm-3am Wed-Sun; closed Mon, Tue. **Admission** £2-£11. **No credit cards. Map** p314 C3.
Aimed at students midweek, and also the venue for the venerable indie crossover club Evol. On Saturday nights, Yogi Haughton keeps the crowd going well into the early hours of Sunday morning with disco, funk, Latin and jazz.

Studio 24

24 Calton Road, Calton Hill, EH8 (558 3758). Bus 24, 25, 35, 35A. **Open** 11pm-3am Wed; 10pm-3am Thur; 10.30pm-3am Fri, Sat; closed Mon, Tue, Sun. **Admission** £1-£7. **No credit cards. Map** p310 H5.
Studio 24 has a concrete-floored barn downstairs, while the upstairs is more intimate and has a better dancefloor. The programme covers virtually everything, from various goth/industrial/indie nights to trance, hard house and techno. This is where you're likely to find some old-school tartan techno in the house with the whistle posse still giving it large at 180 bpm.

The Venue

17-21 Calton Road, Calton Hill, EH8 (557 3073/www.edinburghvenue.com). Bus 1, 7, 11, 22, 34. **Open** 10.30pm-3am Fri, Sat. **Admission** £3-£9. **No credit cards. Map** p310 G5.
Three floors that can be run independently from each other. The Cooler is a surprisingly warm chill-out zone; the ground floor is the dark embodiment of a truly underground venue; and the top floor has bright lights and a well-sprung dancefloor. Among the numerous clubs that The Venue hosts, Saturdays alternate between the underground house of Tribal Funktion (superb) and the drunken antics of Disco Inferno, the original retro-disco drinking den.

Wilkie House

207 Cowgate, Royal Mile, EH1 (225 2935). Bus 7, 8, 21, 31, 80. **Open** *10.30pm-3am Wed-Sun; closed Mon, Tue.* **Admission** *£3-£10.* **No credit cards.** **Map** *p314 D3.*

A good, airy space with bar and balcony overlooking the well-sprung dancefloor. Fridays have jostled into the trance and techno market. Saturdays alternate between four classy, housed-up monthly nights. Joy, the happy club for gay people, with a pumping nu-NRG soundtrack leads the way. Taste on Sundays is hard-house hedonism incarnate, while clubs on other nights range from indie and big beat to mainstream dance. There's a chill-out room upstairs to the back. Used as a theatre venue during the Festival.

Discos

Edinburgh's wildlife is at its most obvious in the West End, Lothian Road, the Grassmarket, the Cowgate and the newly opened Fountainpark. All of these throng with revellers on Friday and Saturday nights. Not much changes: bare-legged girls with high heels, even higher hemlines and WonderBra busts queue nonchalantly for clubs and teeter out of pubs. The lads, sporting chinos, checked shirts and too much aftershave, stagger and pose manfully in their wake. These are the lands of the discotheque, where the meat-market mentality never went away. A night out starts with a group of pals getting tanked up on as much alcohol as they are able, as cheaply as possible, then boogying down to some chart and party sounds before having carnal knowledge of a member of the opposite sex. Mega pubs such as the **Three Sisters** (*see page 161*) or the pubs on the Grassmarket are the sort of places where such shenanigans normally start out.

The Ark

3 Semple Street, Tollcross, South Edinburgh, EH3 (229 7733). Bus 1, 28, 34, 35, 35A. **Open** *10pm-3am daily.* **Admission** *£2-£5.* **No credit cards.** **Map** *p309 D7.*

The Ark caters to the well-dressed, older crowd and early-evening office workers, while its drinks promos, understandably, attract the city's students.

The Cavendish

3 West Tollcross, Tollcross, South Edinburgh, EH3 (228 3252). Bus 11, 16, 17, 23. **Open** *9.30pm-3am Wed; 10pm-3am Thur-Sat; 11pm-3am Sun; closed Mon, Tue.* **Admission** *£4-£6.* **No credit cards.** **Map** *p309 D7.*

This was once a roller disco, with springy floor, and, rather fittingly, the management now restricts the music to 1960s and '70s nostalgia sounds. Its saving grace is that the upstairs is the current home of the Mambo Club, a long-running reggae, funk and soul night. In the main area downstairs (respectably dressed over-25s only) there is enviable seating for those who'd rather drink and talk.

Eros/Elite

Fountainpark, 65 Dundee Street, West Edinburgh, EH11 (228 1661/www.nightclub.co.uk). Bus 1, 28, 34, 35, 35A. **Open** *9.30pm-3am Wed-Sun; closed Mon, Tue.* **Admission** *£2-£5 before midnight; £4-£7 after midnight.* **Credit** *MC, V.* **Map** *p308 B8.*

Part of the new Fountainpark leisure development with a 2,100 capacity. Mainstream party music and chart anthems are played for smart but casual people (no trainers allowed). Buses bring in the punters from all over Scotland. Scary.

Gaia

28 King's Stables Road, South Edinburgh, EH1 (229 7986). Bus 11, 15, 22, 24. **Open** *10pm-3am Wed, Thur; 9pm-3am Fri-Sun; closed Mon, Tue.* **Admission** *£2-£4.* **No credit cards.** **Map** *p314 B3.*

Gaia gets packed with students, who are kept off the streets and dancing very drunkenly on the regular cheap drinks promo nights to a mix of indie pop, house, Latin and breakbeats.

Po Na Na

43B Frederick Street, New Town, EH2 (226 2224). Bus 28, 29, 80. **Open** *10pm-3am Mon, Tue, Sun; 9pm-3am Wed-Fri; 8pm-3am Sat.* **Admission** *£3 after 11pm Fri, Sat.* **Credit** *(over £15) AmEx, MC, V.* **Map** *p314 B1.*

An after-work drinking hole for local office workers in the early evening, this warren of alcoves below Café Rouge (*see p139*) picks up the clubby crowd mid-evening. After 11pm, when the DJ gets to work, the dancefloor gets hot and sweaty. The sounds can be crucial, even if the clientele isn't always so.

Revolution

31 Lothian Road, West Edinburgh, EH1 (229 7670). Bus 11, 15, 22, 24. **Open** *10pm-3am Wed-Sat; closed Mon, Tue, Sun.* **Admission** *£3-£7.* **No credit cards.** **Map** *p314 A2.*

A £2.5-million facelift might have left this massive venue with an impressively grand interior, including four bars and a swooping lighting rig, but the clientele and their behaviour haven't changed much from its former incarnation as Century 2000: white stilettos, loads of testosterone and fights in the girls' loos are the order of the evening. Lots of drinks promos and a steady stream of charty dance anthems.

Comedy

For three weeks in August, Edinburgh becomes the undisputed laughter capital of Britain, if not the world. Comedy is probably the best-known face of the **Festival Fringe** (*see page 97*). Yet, for a long time, the funny crowd seemed unable to get to grips with the year-round Edinburgh audience. Attempts by one aspiring promoter after another to establish some kind of ongoing venture foundered on the rocks of scant resources, remoteness from the stand-up circuit's London hub and perceived audience apathy.

One unique retail experience not to be missed is the weekend rummage. The **Barras Market**, held in the buildings and lanes behind the Gallowgate every Sunday morning, specialises in designer labels (although these are more likely to originate from Possil than Paris), bric-a-brac, antiques and coronary-inducing fast food. In fact anything of saleable value. It's a Glasgow institution and great fun. **Paddy's Market** is along the same lines, and in the same part of town, but further down the sliding scale. It's not for the faint-hearted but essential for second-hand Richard Clayderman LPs.

Shops

23rd Precinct
23 Bath Street, City centre, G2 (0141 332 4806). Buchanan St tube. **Open** 10am-6pm Mon-Sat; noon-5pm Sun. **Credit** AmEx, DC, MC, V. **Map** 303 D2.

Concrete Skates
20 Wilson Street, City centre, G1 (0141 552 0222). Buchanan St tube. **Open** 10.30am-6pm Mon-Sat; noon-5pm Sun. **Credit** MC, V. **Map** p303 E3.

Cruise
180 Ingram Street, City centre, G1 (0141 572 3232). Buchanan St tube. **Open** 10am-6pm Mon-Wed, Fri; 10am-7pm Thur; 9am-6pm Sat; 1-5pm Sun. **Credit** AmEx, DC, MC, V. **Map** p303 E3.

Debenhams
97 Argyle Street, City centre, G2 (0141 221 0088). St Enoch tube. **Open** 9am-6pm Mon-Wed; 9am-8pm Thur; 9am-7pm Fri, Sat; 11am-6pm Sun. **Credit** AmEx, DC, MC, V. **Map** p303 D3.

Diesel
116-120 Buchanan Street, City centre, G2 (0141 221 5255/www.diesel.com). Buchanan St or St Enoch tube. **Open** 10am-6pm Mon-Wed, Fri; 10am-7pm Thur; 9.30am-6pm Sat; noon-5pm Sun. **Credit** AmEx, MC, V. **Map** p303 D3.

Dr Jives
111-113 Candleriggs, City centre, G1 (0141 552 5451/www.drjives.com). Queen St rail. **Open** 10am-6pm Mon-Sat; noon-5pm Sun. **Credit** AmEx, DC, MC, V. **Map** p303 E3.

Shopping in style at **Princes Square**. *See page 246.*

Trips Out of Town

Fopp Records
358 Byres Road, West End, G12 (0141 357 0774).
Hillhead tube. **Open** 9.30am-7pm Mon-Sat; 11am-
6pm Sun. **Credit** AmEx, MC, V. **Map** p301.

House of Fraser
*21-45 Buchanan Street, City centre, G1 (0141 221
3880).* *St Enoch tube.* **Open** 9.30am-6pm Mon-Wed,
Fri; 9.30am-8pm Thur; 9am-6pm Sat; noon-5.30pm
Sun. **Credit** AmEx, DC, MC, V. **Map** p303 D3.

Hugo Boss
*55-79 Buchanan Street, City centre, G1 (0141 221
7168).* *Buchanan St or St Enoch tube.* **Open** 9.30am-
6pm Mon-Wed, Fri, Sat; 9.30am-7pm Thur; noon-5pm
Sun. **Credit** AmEx, DC, MC, V. **Map** p303 D3.

John Smith & Son
*57 St Vincent Street, City centre G2 (0141 221
7472/www.johnsmith.co.uk).* *Buchanan St tube.*
Open 9am-6pm Mon-Sat; noon-4pm Sun. **Credit**
AmEx, MC, V. **Map** p303 D2.
Branch: 252 Byres Road, West End, G12 (0141 334
2769).

Missing Records
*9-11 Wellington Street, City centre, G2 (0141 248
1661).* *Central Station rail.* **Open** 8.30am-6.30pm
Mon; 9.30am-6.30pm Tue-Sat; 11am-6pm Sun.
Credit MC, V. **Map** p302 C3.
Branch: 685 Great Western Road, West End, G11
(0141 400 2270).

Voltaire & Rousseau
18 Otago Lane, West End, G12 (0141 339 1811).
Kelvinbridge tube. **Open** 10am-6pm Mon-Sat; closed
Sun. **No credit cards**. **Map** p302 A1.

Shopping centres & arcades

Buchanan Galleries
*220 Buchanan Street, City centre, G1 (0141 333
9898).* *Buchanan St tube.* **Open** 9am-6pm Mon-Wed,
Fri, Sat; 9am-8pm Thur; 11am-5pm Sun. **Credit**
varies. **Map** p303 D2.

Decourcis Arcade
Cresswell Lane, West End, G2 (0141 334 6959).
Hillhead tube. **Open** 11am-5.30pm daily. **Credit**
varies. **Map** p301.

Italian Centre
7 John Street, City centre, G1 (0141 552 6368).
Buchanan St tube/Queen St rail. **Open** 8am-6pm
Mon-Sat; closed Sun. **Credit** varies. **Map** p303 E3.

Princes Square
*48 Buchanan Street, City centre, G1 (0141 221
0324).* *St Enoch tube.* **Open** 9am-7pm Mon-Sat;
11.30am-5.30pm Sun. **Credit** varies. **Map** p303 D3.

St Enoch Centre
*55 St Enoch's Square, City centre, G1 (0141 204
3900).* *St Enoch tube.* **Open** 9am-6pm Mon-Wed, Fri,
Sat; 9am-8pm Thur; 11am-5.30pm Sun. **Credit**
varies. **Map** p303 D3.

Where to stay
With increasing conference and tourist trades,
Glasgow has a wide range of places to stay.

City centre

ArtHouse Hotel
*129 Bath Street, G2 2SY (0141 221 6789/fax 0141
221 6777/www.arthousehotel.com).* *Buchanan St
tube/Central Station rail.* **Rates** £90-£140. **Credit**
AmEx, DC, MC, V. **Map** p302 C2.
Recently opened hip hotel/restaurant/bar where the
beautiful people go to stay and play.

Brunswick Merchant City Hotel
*106-108 Brunswick Street, G1 1TF
(0141 552 0001/fax 0141 552 1551/
www.scotland2000.com/brunswick).* *Buchanan St
tube.* **Rates** £65-£95. **Credit** AmEx, DC, MC, V.
Map p303 E3.
State-of-the-art landmark hotel in the Merchant City.
Highly recommended.

Glasgow Hilton
*1 William Street, G3 8HT (0141 204 5555/fax 0141
204 5004/www.hilton.com).* *Bus 62, 64/Central
Station rail.* **Rates** £170-£210. **Credit** AmEx, DC,
MC, V. **Map** p302 C2.
Rates reflect the jet-set quality guest you get at this
300-room chain hotel.

Lodge Inn Hotel
*10 Elmbank Gardens, G2 4PP (0141 221 1000/
fax 0141 248 1000).* *Charing Cross rail.*
Rates £44.95 per room. **Credit** AmEx, DC, MC, V.
Map p302 B2.
Great views of the city from the upper floors and
handy for the bars and restaurants in nearby
Sauchiehall Street.

Malmaison
*278 West George Street, G2 4LL (0141 572 1000/
fax 0141 572 1002/www.malmaison.com).* *Buchanan
St tube.* **Rates** £105-£165. **Credit** AmEx, DC, MC,
V. **Map** p302 C2.
A very stylish converted church with a high quo-
tient of celebrity guests – Keanu Reeves and Ewan
McGregor have checked in in the past.

The Old School House
*194 Renfrew Street, G3 7TF (0141 332 7600/
fax 0141 332 8684/www.hotelsglasgow.com).*
Cowcaddens tube. **Rates** £30-£75. **Credit** MC, V.
Map p302 C2.
Built to house a Tobacco Lord in the 19th century.
Good value for money and the added bonus of being
within view of the Glasgow School of Art. Part of
the McMillan group, which also owns the Town
House Hotel (*see below*).

Quality Central Hotel
*99 Gordon Street, G1 3SF (0141 221 9680/fax 0141
226 3948/central reservations 0800 444 444/*

admin@gb627.u-net.com). Central Station rail.
Rates £75-£120. **Credit** AmEx, DC, MC, V.
Map p303 D3.
A product of Glasgow's halcyon era as the second city of the Empire, this 200-plus-room hotel rises proudly above Central Station and is popular with overseas visitors.

Old Town & East End

Cathedral House Hotel
28-32 Cathedral Square, G4 OXA (0141 552 3519/ fax 0141 552 2444). High St rail, then 2, 2A, 37 buses. **Rates** £49-£69. **Credit** AmEx, MC, V.
Map p303 F2.
This minimalist Scottish chic hotel began its life in 1877 as a halfway house for a local prison, before being transformed into the regional diocese head-quarters of the Catholic Church. The split-level café bar downstairs is a popular lunching spot for local professionals, while the first-floor restaurant is one of Glasgow's best-kept secrets.

South Side

Regent Guest House
44 Regent Park Square, G41 2AG (0141 422 1199/ fax 0141 423 7531). Queens Park or Pollokshields West rail, then 5-min walk. **Rates** £20-£40. **Credit** AmEx, MC, V. **Map** p301.
This neatly furnished, family-run guesthouse is well priced, if unremarkable. It is situated in a leafy, residential area and ideal for a pilgrimage to Pollok Park.

West End

The Albion Hotel
407 North Woodside Road, G20 6NN (0141 339 8620/fax 0141 334 8159/ www.smoothHound.co.uk/hotels/albionho.html). Kelvinbridge tube. **Rates** £44-£85. **Credit** AmEx, DC, MC, V. **Map** p301.
Fine views of the River Kelvin are one of the attractions at this above-average B&B.

Hillview Hotel
18 Hillhead Street, G12 8PY (0141 334 5585/ fax 0141 339 6955). Hillhead tube. **Rates** £23-£60. **Credit** MC, V. **Map** p301.
There is an unaffected, homespun feel to this young, family-run hotel. Ideal for the bar/bistro bonanza that is Byres Road.

One Devonshire Gardens
1 Devonshire Gardens, G12 0UX (0141 339 2001/ fax 0141 337 1663/onedevonshire@btconnect.com/ www.one-devonshire-gardens.co.uk). Bus 11, 20, 51, 66. **Rates** £145-£230 (weekend rates on request). **Credit** AmEx, DC, MC, V. **Map** p301.
Glasgow's most exclusive hotel (some rooms have four-poster beds), with a restaurant to match (*see p242*). Worth every penny.

Town House Hotel
21 Royal Crescent, G3 7SL (0141 332 9009/ fax 0141 353 9604/www.hotelsglasgow.com). Bus 42, 57, 57A. **Rates** £23-£70. **Credit** MC, V. **Map** p302 A2.
This excellent value-for-money hotel is in palatial surroundings. Well placed for Kelvingrove Park and the West End.

Hostels, apartments & seasonal lets

Berkeley Globetrotters Independent Hostel
56 Berkeley Street, West End, G3 7DX (0141 221 7880/fax 0141 204 3986). Charing Cross rail, then 5-min walk. **Rates** from £9.50 per night; from £56 per week. **No credit cards. Map** p302 B2.
No frills, but plenty of friendly advice and company to survive on. Twelve dormitory rooms and two private, with 81 beds in total. Conveniently located in city centre and West End.

Glasgow Youth Hostel
7-8 Park Terrace, West End, G3 6BY (0141 332 3004/fax 0141 332 5007/glasgow@syha.org.uk). Bus 11, 44, 59, then 5-min walk. **Rates** £11.25 (under-18s), £12.75 (over-18s). **No credit cards. Map** p302 A1.
A Georgian townhouse and formerly a hotel, which accounts for the en-suite-as-standard facilities in this popular hostel. Most rooms have five to eight beds. The standard YHA rate includes continental breakfast. Meals for groups can be booked in advance. Note that non-SYHA members pay an extra £1, and that rates increase by £1 in July and August. There are 160 beds in total.

University of Glasgow
3 The Square, University Avenue, West End, G12 (0141 330 5385/fax 0141 334 5465/ conf@gla.ac.uk). Hillhead tube, then 5-min walk. **Open** *office* 9am-5pm Mon-Fri; closed Sat, Sun. **Map** p301.
A wide range of affordable accommodation to let, mainly during student holidays (July-Sept).

University of Strathclyde
50 Richmond Street, G1 1XF (0141 553 4148/fax 0141 548 4149). Bus 6, 8, 41. **Open** *office* 9am-5pm Mon-Fri; closed Sat, Sun. **Map** p303 E2.
A range of affordable accommodation to let, mainly during student holidays.

West End Apartments
401 North Woodside Road, West End, G20 6NN (0141 342 4060/fax 0141 334 8159/ www.smoothHound.co.uk/hotels/westendhtml). Kelvinbridge tube. **Open** *office* 9am-5pm Mon-Fri; closed Sat, Sun. **Rates** £252-£357 per week (nightly rate on request). **Credit** MC, V. **Map** p301.
Four apartments housed in an elegant, sandstone building in Kelvinbridge.

Trips Out of Town

Getting there

From the airport

Glasgow Airport (0141 887 1111) is 8 miles (14km) south-west of the city, at Junction 28 of the M8. Buses leave the airport for the city every 15min during the day, and about every 30min after 6pm and on Sundays. The 25-min journey costs £3. A taxi will take about 20min and cost about £13.

By car

Infamous for its all-ensnaring motorway system, Glasgow is actually easy to access by car. The M8 from Edinburgh delivers you into the heart of the city. Take exit 15 for the East End and Old Town, 16 for Garnethill, 18 for the West End, 19 for the City centre and 20 for the South Side.

By bus or coach

Long-distance buses arrive at and depart from **Buchanan Street Bus Station** (0141 332 7133 Killermont Street, Map p303 D2). There are buses to and from Edinburgh every half hour and from London every hour.

By train

Glasgow has two main-line train stations. **Queen Street Station** (West George Street, Map p303 D2) serves Edinburgh (trains every 15min) and the north of Scotland. **Central Station** (Gordon Street, Map p302 D3) serves the West Coast and south to England. The stations are centrally located and within walking distance of each other. For all rail enquiries call the national number: 0345 484950.

Getting around

Central Glasgow is easy to negotiate on foot, but you'll need to use public transport if you're going much further afield. Nearly all the listings in this chapter refer only to the tube or train network for reasons of space. However, the frequent **bus** service that runs throughout the city is well signposted at the regular bus stops. Glasgow is also served by a fleet of capacious black **taxis**. They're cheap, but conveniently disappear just as the clubs turn out at 3am. As for **trains**, besides the inter-city services, there is a good network of low-level trains serving Glasgow's suburbs, which is run by Scotrail. The **tube** system, affectionately known as the 'Clockwork Orange', is a single, circular line that loops between the centre and the West End.

St Enoch Travel Centre

St Enoch Square, G1 (0141 226 4826). St Enoch tube. **Open** 9am-5pm Mon-Sat; closed Sun. **Map** p303 D3.
The convenient, one-stop information service for finding out about Glasgow's tube, train and bus services.

Car rental

Glasgow is a good starting point to head for the West coast of Scotland. It's easy to pick up a car at the airport from **Europcar/BCR**.

Europcar/BCR *Terminal Building, Glasgow Airport, Inchinnan Road, Paisley, PA3 2RP (0141 887 0414).* **Open** 7am-10.30pm daily. **Credit** AmEx, DC, MC, V. **Rentals** (subject to change; ring to confirm) start from £57 per day, £189 weekly.

Tourist information

Greater Glasgow & Clyde Valley Tourist Board

11 George Square, G2 (reservations 0141 221 0049/general enquiries 0141 204 4400/ fax 0141 221 3524/enquiries@seeglasgow.com/ www.seeglasgow.com). Buchanan St tube. **Open** *Apr, May* 9am-6pm Mon-Sat; 10am-6pm Sun; *June* 9am-7pm Mon-Sat; 10am-6pm Sun; *July, Aug* 9am-8pm Mon-Sat; 10am-6pm Sun; *Sept* 9am-7pm Mon-Sat; 10am-6pm Sun; *Oct-Mar* 9am-6pm Mon-Sat; closed Sun. **Booking fee** £2, plus 10% deposit. **Credit** MC, V. **Map** p303 E2.
The tourist board will take credit-card bookings for accommodation throughout the city. It also answers general enquiries about sightseeing and events and supplies details of special rates in its brochure.

Communication

Post offices

There are post offices throughout the city, the majority operating within usual shop hours. To get information about your nearest one, call the helpline on 0345 223 344 (9am-6pm Mon-Fri; 8.30am-4pm Sat). A late-opening post office near the city centre, which offers all the usual postal facilities as well as a bureau de change, is **Anniesland** (900 Crow Road, G13, 0141 954 8661, open 8am-10pm Mon-Sat; 9am-8pm Sun).

Telephones

The area phone code for Glasgow and its environs is 0141.

Health

The two infirmaries listed below have 24-hour accident and emergency departments.

Glasgow Dental NHS Trust

378 Sauchiehall Street (0141 211 9600). Sauchiehall St buses. **Open** *emergency clinic* 9am-3pm Mon-Fri; closed Sat, Sun. **Map** p302 C2.

Glasgow Royal Infirmary NHS Trust

84 Castle Street, G4 (0141 211 4000). High St rail, then 2, 2A, 37 buses. **Map** p303 F2.

Western Infirmary NHS Trust

Dumbarton Road, G11 (0141 211 2000). Kelvinhall tube.

Sir Bernard Chumley takes to the stage, courtesy of the **Gilded Balloon**.

In 1995, one small club with big ideas and bucketloads of determination – step forward **The Stand**, and take a bow – altered the picture dramatically. At first, gigs were staged in hired pub basements, but after three years the rapidly snowballing operation moved into its own custom-designed premises in the New Town. With its main-house bills lining up newcomers and rising talents alongside more tried-and-tested acts, the Stand has encouraged the emergence of a home-grown scene backed by a consistent audience base. It has forged links with the UK circuit and some of Ireland's finest comedic exports, and is on the point of expanding into Glasgow. In the face of such stiff competition, other clubs often still struggle, despite featuring big-name acts and sometimes stronger bills.

Specific talent inevitably comes and goes, but local comics to look out for include Bob Doolally, Joe Heenan and Susan Morrison... and don't leave town without catching the inspired lunacy of Allan Miller, regular host of The Stand's Sunday night show.

As well as all this indigenous activity, the TV-boosted big guns of the UK-wide comedy scene periodically pass through on tour, usually playing the **Queen's Hall** (*see page 202*) or the **Traverse Theatre** (*see page 221*). Full details of comedy is given in the *List* and on *www.ScottishComedy.com*.

Comedy at La Belle Angele
La Belle Angele, Hasties Close, Royal Mile, EH1 (225 7536/www.gilded-balloon.co.uk). Bus 7, 8, 11, 21, 31, 80. **Admission** £8. **No credit cards.** **Map** p314 D3.
A new club, held on the second Saturday of every month. The bill usually features a mixture of local acts with at least one well-established headliner. It is run by the Gilded Balloon, which is one of the major players on the Fringe comedy circuit and also organises tours and one-off gigs over the year. *See also p206.*

The Stand
5 York Place, New Town, EH1 (enquiries 558 7373/ box office 558 7272/www.thestand.co.uk). Bus 8, 12, 16, 17, 25, 25A. **Open** *café-bar* noon-midnight Mon-Fri; noon-1am Sat, Sun. *Red Raw* 8-10pm Mon. *Theme nights* (Gay, Connoisseur and Benefit Shows) 9-11pm Tue. *Rhymes and Misdemeanours/Skitters/ Gardyloo* 7-8pm Wed. *World of Comedy Quiz Show* 9-11.30pm Wed. *Comedy acts* 9-11pm Thur; 9-11.15pm Fri; 9-11.30pm Sat. *Pint Size Comedy* (short acts) 8-10pm Sun. **Admission** £1 Mon; £5-£6 Tue; £4 Wed; £4 Thur; £6 (£5 concessions) Fri; £7 (£4 concessions) Sat; £2.50 Sun. **Credit** MC, V. **Map** p306 F4.
Housed in a former insurance company document store, The Stand's basement premises comprise two performance spaces. The main cabaret bar is decked out in blues and brick reds, and holds audiences of up to 160, while the rather barer studio space can squeeze in around half that number.

Arts & Entertainment

Sport & Fitness

Even when Hibs and Hearts aren't top of the football league, Edinburgh has some first-class leisure facilities in which to let off steam.

Whether Edinburgh can be classed as a 'sporting' city is a moot point. Its citizens are so preoccupied with football, rugby and golf that when success in these particular fields is proving elusive, pessimism clouds their perception of all sports. Which is a shame, as the city regularly scores some notable successes in the so-called 'minor sports'. Compared to many other cities, Edinburgh's sports fans can be ambivalent and unambitious. Nor is much of the city's wealth invested in sport.

That said, for a relatively small city, Edinburgh has consistently punched above its weight in terms of the number of world and Olympic champions it has produced over the years. And when its football teams do well – as Heart of Midlothian Football Club did in 1998 by winning the Scottish Cup and Hibernian Football Club did when it won the League Cup in 1991 – the city's success-starved football supporters come to line the streets by the tens of thousands to hail their heroes.

Edinburgh Leisure (557 5457), which manages the city's sports and leisure facilities, can provide details of further activities and sports venues. Another useful contact is **sportscotland** (317 7200/www.sportscotland.org.uk), which doubles up as the headquarters for a number of sports, such as basketball and hockey.

American football

American football has been played at an amateur level in Scotland for years, but the arrival of the **Scottish Claymores** – fully professional and with a strong NFL presence – put the sport on the map. The team is now the UK's only pro football team, following the demise of the London Monarchs; a sprinkling of Scottish players has also helped establish a vibrant relationship with the public. The Claymores play in the NFL Europe league between April and June. Home games are played at both **Murrayfield Stadium** (*see page 219*) in Edinburgh and **Hampden Park** (*see page 238*) in Glasgow.

Scottish Claymores

(office) 205 St Vincent Street, Glasgow, G2 (0141 222 3800/ticket hotline 0500 353535/ www.claymores.co.uk). **Open** 9am-6pm Mon-Fri; closed Sat, Sun. **Tickets** £12 adults; £4-£6 concessions. **Credit** AmEx, MC, V.

Basketball

The recently founded **Edinburgh Rocks** is the only Scottish franchise in the Great Britain-wide Dairylea Dunkers Championship. This might explain why the club's fans are the most passionate in the league. Home games are played most Sunday afternoons during the September-May season, from 5pm, at **The Quarry**, the self-styled basketball court at **Meadowbank Sports Centre** (*see page 217*). Outdoor and indoor courts can be booked at the MSC.

Cricket

Scotland did not win a game during the 1999 World Cup; it should have defeated Bangladesh but at least gave the mighty Australia a fright. The presence of a national side is helping to develop the game in Scotland, however, and the appointment of a full-time national coach, former England Test bowler Mike Hendrick, has helped, as has a new national league structure at club level. Surprisingly, there are more cricket clubs than rugby clubs in Scotland. The **Scottish Cricket Union** (317 7247/www.scu.org.uk) is a useful contact.

Cycling

The City of Edinburgh team is Britain's crack track outfit, based at the velodrome at the **Meadowbank Sports Centre** (*see page 217*). In the 1999 Great Britain senior championships it picked up a hatful of medals and two of its riders were part of the three-man team that won the silver in the Olympic Sprint event during the 1999 World Championships. Highlights of the local track calendar include the East of Scotland Grand Prix (end of June) and the Festival meeting (mid-August). Both incorporate British League events. The velodrome is also home to the **Scottish**

Day Trips

The sights to see if you don't want to go all the way.

The beach at **Gullane**, East Lothian.
See page 250.

East Lothian

East Lothian stretches east of Edinburgh, fringed to the north by the Firth of Forth and the North Sea and to the south by the Lammermuir Hills. It is within easy striking distance of the capital and, although the main A1 to England cuts through this predominantly flat and not always exciting landscape, breaking away along the coastal route or smaller inland roads is rewarding.

The bulk of Traprain Law, an ancient volcanic plug, dominates the lowlands of East Lothian. It was once home to the Pictish tribe of Votadini, and the name Lothian is derived from King Loth, a sixth-century Pictish ruler. By the mid-fifth century the area was under the rule of the Angles, until Malcolm II took the territory for Scotland in 1018. It was no easy claim. In the centuries that followed, English armies and land-greedy nobles backed by bank-rolling monarchs made numerous forays into the area, leaving a trail of destruction. In 1216 King John of England burned the principal towns of Dunbar

and Haddington, while castles such as Dirleton, Hailes and Tantallon became ever-sturdier defences.

Nevertheless, warring aside, the area enjoyed prosperity and its rich and fertile land led it to be dubbed 'the bread basket of Lothian'. The royal burgh of Haddington flourished and the villages of Aberlady, Athelstaneford and East Linton grew up. Today these villages, along with the coastal towns of North Berwick and Dunbar, continue to thrive and hold on to their good looks. The coast itself, with its sandy beaches of Gullane and Yellowcraig and views across to Fife, has some good walks; the Aberlady Bird Sanctuary and the John Muir Country Park provide signposted trails.

North of the A1

Just off the A1, and almost seamlessly attached to Edinburgh, is **Musselburgh**, known since the early 14th century as the 'honest toun', a sobriquet gained when townsfolk refused to claim the reward for recovering the body of the Earl of Moray. Its handsome **Tolbooth** dates from 1591. After the **Musselburgh Race Course**, the coast road turns off along the B1348 and passes the **Prestongrange Mining Museum**, which is a minimal but nonetheless interesting reminder of the local industry. The unglamorous villages of **Cockenzie** and **Prestonpans** follow on in quick succession. Just to the south is where Bonny Prince Charlie routed the English at the Battle of Prestonpans in 1745.

Beyond the village of **Longniddry**, the full picturesque roll of the East Lothian coast takes off. A mile before Aberlady is **Gosford House**. Although only the central core remains of the original building designed by Robert Adam in the 18th century, its three-storey, Italian-style 19th-century marble hall is a fabulous statement of opulence. **Aberlady** itself has a neat line-up of almshouses and its fine 15th-century church houses a notable 18th-century memorial to one Lady Elibank by the sculptor Canova. A mile outside the village, on the tiny back road to Drem, is the **Myreton Motor Museum**, a privately owned hotchpotch of lovingly restored vehicles, bicycles and motoring memorabilia.

The **Aberlady Wildlife Sanctuary** is reached by crossing the footbridge from the car park just east from the village of Aberlady. Its sandy mudflats and dunes are a good spot to see wading birds and are popular with naturalists. The beach at **Gullane** is a favourite with families, while golf fanatics will recognise the name as the course where the Scottish Open is sometimes played.

Five miles on, standing picturesquely at the heart of the pretty village of **Dirleton**, is **Dirleton Castle**, which originally dates from the 13th century but was rebuilt and modified in the 14th and 16th centuries. Its garden still has its old bowling green as well as an early 20th-century Arts and Crafts garden and a restored Victorian garden.

North Berwick Law, a massive carbuncle of volcanic rock, stands sentry-like over the lively coastal town of **North Berwick**. The town was once known as the Salem of Scotland: nearly 100 people, including the Earl of Bothwell, the husband of Mary, Queen of Scots, were arrested for taking part in the now-infamous Witches' Sabbat held in the old kirk in 1590. The story goes that over 200 witches (women and men) sailed to North Berwick in sieves in a plot to kill King James VI. Many of the so-called witches were burnt to death on Edinburgh's Castle Rock.

By the late 19th century, however, North Berwick had reinvented itself as a popular holiday destination. The now-redundant '30s lido is a testament to the bathing era – which is also remembered in the **North Berwick Museum**. The **Bass Rock**, another vast lump of volcanic basalt, lies three and half miles offshore. A one-time prison, fortress and monastic retreat, today it is home to thousands of gannets. Their Latin name, sula bassana, is taken from the rock's name. Regular boat trips around the rock leave from North Berwick harbour, but landings must be arranged in advance (01620 893863). You can see gannets all season, but May and June are the best time for guillemots, razorbills and puffins.

The area to the south of North Berwick has several places of interest. Standing proud over the landscape is the **Hopetoun Monument**, a slender tower built in 1824 on the Garleton Hills in memory of the fourth Earl of Hopetoun. Take a torch if you intend climbing to the top of the tower. The village of **Athelstaneford**, nearby on the B1343. The legend goes that here in 832, the leader of the Pictish army, King Angus, saw a mass of white clouds form a diagonal cross prior to his battle with a mighty Saxon force headed by Athelstan. Angus believed the cross to be a sign from St Andrew and vowed that he would declare him patron saint of Scotland if his army was victorious. It was. St Andrew duly became patron saint and the St Andrew's

Bass Rock and, nearby, **Tantallon Castle**. *see page 251.*

cross, or Saltire, became the Scottish flag. Today it's the oldest flag in Europe and the Commonwealth. In Athelstaneford's churchyard there is a 1965 memorial to the flag's birth and a Flag Heritage Centre, housed in a 16th-century dovecote. Athelstaneford itself was built in the 18th century by one Sir David Kinloch as a model village for his estate workers.

Moving east again is the **National Museum of Flight** at East Fortune Airfield, a popular destination for family outings. Exhibits, the oldest of which is a 1896 glider, are housed in a converted hangar. The attractive village of East Linton was the birthplace of the 19th-century engineer John Rennie, who designed London's Waterloo and Southwark bridges.

The coast between North Berwick and the attractive nature reserve of **Tyninghamme Links**, which has a gentle walk out to St Baldreds Cradle, is dominated by **Tantallon Castle**, a formidable, mainly 14th-century, cliff-edge fortification. The castle's rose-coloured stone ramparts command splendid views of the Bass Rock.

The next coastal town is the robust-looking old fishing town of **Dunbar**, with its wide high street and 17th-century stone Town House. Reputedly, this is the sunniest place in Scotland. Its ruined castle stands just above the harbour and was the resting place on a number of occasions for Mary, Queen of Scots. In 1650 the Battle of Dunbar, which saw Oliver Cromwell defeat the Covenanters, was fought to the south-east of the town.

The famous conservationist John Muir is the town's most noted son. Born in 1838, he is remembered in the **John Muir House**. When he was three, his family emigrated to America, where Muir went on to become a naturalist and the founding father of the US national parks. The **John Muir Country Park** is a vast stretch of land containing salt marshes, lagoons and a long sandy beach that lies north-west of Dunbar just outside Belhaven. It is home to a wide variety of birds and wildlife. Belhaven itself was once the port for Dunbar, but the independent **Belhaven Brewery**, founded in 1719 by local monks, sets it apart. While distilleries have their 'angel's share', Belhaven boasts the ghosts of drunk monks. The Volunteer Arms in the village is the best place to sample the exceptionally smooth 80/-.

Belhaven Brewery

Brewery Lane, Dunbar (01368 862734). **Open** pre-booked guided tours only. **Admission** £3; no under-14s allowed. **No credit cards.**

Dirleton Castle & Gardens

Dirleton (01620 850330). **Open** *Apr-Sept* 9.30am-6.30pm daily; *Oct-Mar* 9.30am-4.30pm Mon-Sat; 2-4.30pm Sun. **Admission** £2.50; £1-£1.90 concessions. **Credit** AmEx, MC, V.

Gosford House

Longniddry (01875 870201). **Open** *July-early Aug* 2-5pm Wed-Sun; closed Mon, Tue. **Admission** £4; £1 concessions. **No credit cards.**

John Muir House

126 High Street, Dunbar (01368 862585). **Open** *June-Sept* 11am-1pm Mon-Sat; 2-5pm Sun. **Admission** free.

Myreton Motor Museum

Aberlady (01875 870288). **Open** *Oct-Easter* 10am-5pm daily; *Easter-Sept* 10am-6pm daily. **Admission** £3; £1-£2 concessions. **No credit cards.**

National Museum of Flight

East Fortune Airfield, East Fortune (01620 880308). **Open** 10.30am-5pm daily. **Admission** £3; £1.50 concessions; free under-18s. **Credit** MC, V.

North Berwick Museum

School Road (01620 895457). **Open** *Apr-Oct* 11pm-5pm daily; closed Nov-Mar. **Admission** free.

Prestongrange Mining Museum

on the B1348 coast road between Musselburgh & Prestonpans (0131 6532 904). **Open** *Apr-Oct* 11am-4pm daily; closed Nov-Mar. **Admission** free.

Tantallon Castle

off the A198, 3 miles east of North Berwick (01620 892727). **Open** *Apr-Sept* 9.30am-4.30pm Mon-Wed; 9.30am-12.30pm Thur; 2-4.30pm Sun; closed Fri, Sat. **Admission** £2.50; £1-£1.90 concessions. **Credit** AmEx, MC, V.

South of the A1

Although ravaged by the warring English on a number of occasions in the Middle Ages, the royal burgh of **Haddington** is today an elegantly well-heeled market town, lying 13 miles east of Edinburgh on the A1. The birthplace of Alexander II in 1198 and of John Knox, architect of the Scottish reformation, in 1515, the town is spaciously ranged around a main high street and boasts 284 listed buildings. The 14th-century **St Mary's Collegiate Church** is particularly impressive and houses the tomb of Jane Welsh, the wife of the 19th-century writer Thomas Carlyle and an intellectual in her own right. The **Jane Welsh Carlyle Museum** is in her childhood home on Lodge Street.

To the east of Haddington is **Hailes Castle**. Dating from the 13th century, it started life as a manor house, expanding its guest facilities to

Trips Out of Town

incorporate two vaulted pit prisons. A mile south of the town is **Lennoxlove House**. It was originally called Lethington Tower but its name was changed in 1702 to 'Lennox love to Blantyre' for Frances, Duchess of Lennox, a famous beauty who never even lived there. Still further south of Haddington is the toy-town-like model village of **Gifford**, built by the Marquis of Tweeddale in the 18th century for his estate workers. John Witherspoon, the first moderator of the Presbyterian Church of America and the only clergyman to sign the American Declaration of Independence, was born here. An interesting eatery is the **Goblin Ha'** (*see below*), which is signposted by a levitating yogic goblin. It gets its name from an underground chamber at the now-ruined Yester Castle, which was romantically described by Sir Walter Scott in his novel *Marmion*.

The **Lammermuir Hills** are easily accessible from nearby Longyester, from where there is a track up to the Hopes Reservoir. Scoffed at by those who would never deign to climb anything less than a Munro (*see page 225*), the Lammermuirs, with their good covering of heather and sheep, are nonetheless handsome. Sir Walter Scott, ever the man with an eye for a good bit of scenery, even found them inspirational. He penned the sorrowful tale *The Bride of Lammermuir*, which was later turned into an opera, *Lucia de Lammermuir*, by the composer Donizetti. East along the A6903 back to Edinburgh the **Glenkinchie Distillery**, the most southerly in Scotland and the source of one of United Distillers' six 'classic' malts.

Glenkinchie Distillery Visitors Centre
Pencaitland (01875 342004). **Open** 9.30am-4pm Mon-Fri; closed Sat, Sun; *Easter, May bank holiday, July, Aug also* 9.30am-5pm Sat; noon-5pm Sun. **Admission** £3; free under-18s. **Credit** AmEx, MC, V.

Hailes Castle
one and a half miles south west of East Linton (0131 668 8800). **Open** all year. **Admission** free.

Jane Welsh Carlyle Museum
Lodge Street, Haddington (01620 823738). **Open** *Apr-Sept* 2-5pm Wed-Sat; closed Mon, Tue, Sun and Oct-Mar. **Admission** £1.50; £1 concessions. **No credit cards**.

Lennoxlove House
Lennoxlove, Haddington (01620 823720). **Open** *Easter-Oct* 2-4.30pm Wed, Thur, Sun; occasional Sat (phone to check); closed Mon, Tue, Fri. **Admission** £4; £2 concessions. **No credit cards**.

Where to eat

North of the A1
Luca's in Musselburgh, EH21 (32 High Street, 665 2237, open daily) is home to the best ice-cream on the east coast.

South of the A1
Hearty fare is dished up at the **Goblin Ha' Hotel** in Gifford (Main Street, 01620 810244), a hotel-cum-inn dating back to the 18th century. In Haddington, **Poldrate Restaurant** (Tyne House, 01620 826882, closed Mon, Sun) is a beautifully renovated mill with an imaginative menu. Clarissa Dickson Wright (of *Two Fat Ladies* TV cookery show fame) runs the **Garden Café** (closed Mon, Sat, Sun) at Lennoxlove House.

Where to stay

North of the A1
In North Berwick, the **Tantallon Inn** (Marine Parade, 01620 892238) has double rooms for £28-£34. **Browns Hotel** in Haddington (1 West Road, 01620 822254) has single rooms for £65, and doubles for £90.

South of the A1
The **Eaglescairnie Mains** (01620 810491) in Gifford is a lovely old farmhouse bed and breakfast; rates from £25.

Getting there

By bicycle
Cycling is a viable mode of travel (cycles can be put on trains, but may require pre-booking), with some signposted routes and designated trails (mostly along disused railway lines) leaving Edinburgh.

By bus
East Lothian is served by Eastern Scottish buses from St Andrew Square Bus Station in Edinburgh. During refurbishment of the bus station (May 2000-2003), buses leave from Waterloo Place.

By car
Take the A1 out of Edinburgh towards Haddington. The coastal route is signposted at regular intervals.

By train
A local train branch line runs from Edinburgh's Haymarket, through Waverley to Musselburgh, Prestonpans, Longniddry, Drem and North Berwick. Some East Coast mainline services call at Dunbar.

Tourist information

In **Dunbar**, the tourist information office is situated at 143A High Street (01368 863353, closed Sun). The office in **Musselburgh** is at the Granada Service Station, off the A1 (0131 653 6172, open daily). Also try the one in **North Berwick** (Quality Street, 01620 892197, closed Sun).

Midlothian

Wildlife and rural solitude are surprisingly easy to find in the vicinity of Edinburgh. The graciously curvaceous **Pentland Hills** lie just south of city on the A702, and are particularly easy to reach. Lord Cockburn, the 19th-century conservationist, dubbed the hills, which covers 22,000 acres, 'paradise'. Today they form the **Pentland Hills Regional Park**. There's a golf course, dry ski slope and country park at the hills' eastern end, but travel further along the A702 to reach the Iron-Age fort of **Castle Law Hill** for more unadulterated ruralness. Oliver Cromwell was not impressed by the hills. In 1650 he complained about the lack of trees: he wished to hang a sergeant for stealing a cloak but could not find the necessary branch. Today, however, **Glencorse Reservoir** is a picturesque spot surrounded by Scots pines. Just beyond is **Rullion Green**, where in November 1666, 900 Covenanters were defeated by the Royalist army under General Tam Dalyell. It is possible to walk for some distance in the Pentlands but it's best to take a map (*see page 224*).

Carlops, further along on the A702, with its handsome line-up of sturdy stone cottages, was once renowned as a meeting place for witches. It also briefly marked the border between Scotland and England, after the defeat of the Scots at the battle of Neville's Cross in 1346.

One of Scotland's most enigmatic buildings lies just six miles (ten kilometres) south of Edinburgh. **Rosslyn Chapel**, founded in 1446 by Sir William St Clair, a prince of Orkney, is a fantastic blend of pagan, Celtic, Christian and Masonic symbolism. Hardly a stone surface has been spared from the stonemason's hand. Apparently there are more 'green men' than in any other building in Britain – over 100 have been counted – and there is a bizarre twisted pillar for which its maker is said to have been killed. Questions abound. Why are there carvings of new world plants, such as Indian corn, carved over 100 years before Columbus is said to have discovered America? Was the chapel built as a copy of Solomon's Temple in Jerusalem and therefore has little connection with Christianity? What lies beneath its floors – the Scrolls of the original Temple, the Ark of the Covenant, the true Stone of Destiny, 20 barons or Knights Templar or even the head of John the Baptist? And where is the secret entrance to the crypt? The chapel is currently undergoing extensive restoration but it is possible to climb the external scaffolding and view the chapel from on high.

Carvings in **Rosslyn Chapel.**

Next to the chapel is a former inn, which in its time offered refreshments to the likes of Samuel Johnson, James Boswell and William Wordsworth. They were taken not only with the chapel but with the ruins of Rosslyn Castle and the woodlands of Roslin Glen, which lie a stone's throw away. And, adding to the time-honoured mysteries of the area, Dolly, the first cloned sheep, was born at the nearby Roslin Institute. Hardly surprising, some would say.

Though architecturally unremarkable, the town of **Dalkeith** has a fine **Country Park** (01316 541666) surrounding the 18th-century **Dalkeith House**, which is now owned by the University of Wisconsin. The bridge spanning the River Esk was designed by Robert Adam in 1792. Although visual reminders of the area's industrial past are few, the **Scottish Mining Museum** is an attempt to keep that heritage in mind, with its purpose-built, three-storey visitor centre, featuring interactive exhibitions and a hands-on operations centre. Older ruins have proved more permanent and **Crichton Castle** near Pathhead is quite a spectacular ruin; its most impressive features were built in 1591 for the Earl of Bowthwell.

Crichton Castle
south-west of Pathhead, off A68 (01875 320017). **Open** *Apr-Sept* 9.30am-6.30pm daily; closed Oct-Mar. **Admission** £1.80; 75p-£1.30 concessions. **No credit cards.**

Rosslyn Chapel
Roslin (0131 4402159). **Open** 10am-5pm Mon-Sat; noon-4.45pm Sun. **Admission** £3.50; £1-£3 concessions. **Credit** MC, V.

Scottish Mining Museum
Lady Victoria Colliery, Newtongrange, Midlothian; nine miles south of Edinburgh on the A7 (0131 663 7519). **Open** 10am-5pm daily. **Admission** £4; £2.20 concessions. **Credit** MC, V.

Where to eat & stay

The **Allan Ramsey Hotel** in Carlops (01968 660258, open daily) is an old inn with accommodation, bar meals and a restaurant. Just a few minutes' walk from Rosslyn Chapel, the **Original Hotel** in Roslin (0131 440 2384) has rooms from £45. Dalkeith's **County Hotel**, 152 High Street (0131 663 3495) is a luxury townhouse hotel whose rooms start at £45.

Getting there

By bus
Buses leave from St Andrew Square for the Pentland Hills, Roslin and Dalkeith. During refurbishment of the bus station (May 2000-2003), buses leave from Waterloo Place.

By car
Take the A701 to Rosslyn or the A702 to the Pentland Hills. Dalkeith is on the A7.

Tourist information

There's a tourist office at the **Scottish Mining Museum** (*see above*).

West Lothian

To the west of Edinburgh, the needs of coal mining and heavy industry are remembered in the old slag heaps or 'bings' of **Livingston** and **Bathgate**. Closer to Edinburgh, just south of the airport, the village of **Ratho** is home to the **Edinburgh Canal Centre**. The centre remembers the uses of the Union Canal, built by, amongst many others, the notorious grave-robbers Burke and Hare.

The best parts of West Lothian are closer to the Forth. Along the A90, and just off the B924 to South Queensferry, in the village of **Dalmeny**, is **St Cuthbert's**. One of the finest Norman churches in Scotland, the carvings on the south door and a gruesome line-up of gargoyles are particularly eye-catching. Overlooking the Forth is **Dalmeny House**, a Gothic revival mansion designed by William Wilkins in 1814 and home of the Earls of Rosebery. It boasts the obligatory grand interior and, somewhat incongrously, an extensive collection of Napoleon memorabilia.

Named after Queen Margaret, wife of Malcolm III, **South Queensferry** lies just beyond. It is an excellent place to view the magnificent **Forth Rail** and **Forth Road bridges**. Built between 1883-1890 and just over a mile long, 50,000 tons of rust-red steel make up the Forth Rail Bridge, which is still considered one of the world's great engineering achievements. The small **South Queensferry Museum** (0131 331 5545) offers an interesting insight into the history of the bridges and of the village, including the annual custom of the 'Burry Man', who every July parades the village for nine hours wearing a costume made of burrs. A ferry from South Queensferry goes to **Inchcolm Abbey**. Founded in 1123, it comprises a fine clutch of monastic buildings spectacularly located on Incholm Island in the Firth of Forth.

West of South Queensferry is the knowingly grandiose **Hopetoun House**. Designed by William Bruce in 1699 for Charles Hope, the first Earl of Hopetoun, and enlarged by William Adam in 1721, it stands elegantly swathed in parkland overlooking the Firth of Forth. Further west still is **Blackness Castle**, used by Zefferelli in his film version of *Hamlet*. Its

Trips Out of Town

The fading glow at **St Michael's Church** and **Linlithgow Palace**.

stark walls have crumbled somewhat since they were built in the 1440s but the view across the Forth from the promontory on which they stand is still spectacular. Inland, the **House of the Binns** is the ancient seat of the Dalyells and dates from the 17th century.

Four miles south, just off the M9, is the attractive royal burgh of **Linlithgow**, famed for its royal palace overlooking Linlithgow Loch. Back in the 17th century, the town nearly found itself capital of Scotland. That honour denied, it still manages to thrive, though its high street has been somewhat blighted by brutish new buildings. But **Linlithgow Palace** is a stunner. The palace began life as a mere manor house, but in the 14th century Edward I of England kicked off a series of extensions. Later came a succession of Scottish monarchs and further palace improvements. The central courtyard, with its 16th-century fountain, is a statement of courtly grandeur, while the north façade, built by James V, has a definite hint of the French Renaissance. And, importantly for devotees to the various bedchambers she stayed in, Mary, Queen of Scots was born in the palace in 1542.

Neighbouring the palace is **St Michael's Church**. Dating back to the 13th century, it is considered one of the finest in Scotland. Its skeletal-like aluminium spire is a surprisingly effective addition from the 1960s. Mary, Queen of Scots was probably baptised here, while her grandfather, James IV, is said to have had a

vision here warning him not to go to war with England. He died shortly afterwards at Flodden, as did the majority of his 10,000-strong army. His wife, Margaret Tudor, waited in vain for his return in what is now called Queen Margaret's Bower, in the north-west of the palace.

South of Linlithgow, the history just keeps on rolling. **Cairnpapple Hill**, near **Torphichen**, is a burial site dating from 3000BC, with some of Scotland's most important prehistoric remains. The hill also gives good views over the surrounding country. The **Torphichen Preceptory** is a 13th-century tower with transepts built by the Knights Hospitaller of the Order of St John of Jerusalem.

Just north of Linlithgow lies the once-thriving town of Bo'ness, which today looks more than a little frayed at the edges. It does, however, boast an attraction for steam fanatics in the **Bo'ness & Kinneil Railway**, along which steam trains run the seven-mile round trip to the Birkhill Claymines where there is a guided tour. In contrast, **Grangemouth**, its near neighbour, is resolutely 21st century. Overlooking the Firth of Forth, its oil refineries, host of fire-throwing funnels and shiny pipes create an industrial landscape fit for the space age. Journey through here at night and the special effects really take off.

Inland from Grangemouth is the seemingly unremarkable village of **Bonnybridge**. Remains of the Antonine Wall – the Romans' most northerly defence and intended to keep the wild Highlanders out of the Empire – are visible at a number of signposted spots, though a generous imagination is needed to conjure up their former glory. Imagination of a more fanciful nature is required to sum up Bonnybridge's more recent claim to fame – Unidentified Flying Objects. Since 1992, when one Councillor Billy Buchanan took up the concerns of a local businessman who had sighted a UFO, the village, depressed at its industrial decline, has understandably hyped its reputation as a centre for extra-terrestrial activity. A 'window area', as some UFO experts believe. According to Buchanan, about 6,000 people have seen unexplained lights, including a Toblerone-shaped object reported by Andy Swan, a cable layer for Scottish Power, in 1994. In true *X-Files* style, Buchanan believes that the nation is not taking it seriously. In the name of spreading the word, he has faxed Tony Blair and released *The Lights of Bonnybridge*, which he has sung outside London's Number Ten.

Blackness Castle
4 miles north of Linlithgow on the A904 (01506 834807). **Open** *Apr-Sept* 9.30am-6.30pm daily; *Oct-Mar* 9.30am-4.30pm Mon-Wed, Sat; 9.30am-12.30pm Thur; 2-4.30pm Sun; closed Fri. **Admission** £2; 75p-£1.50 concessions. **No credit cards.**

Bo'ness & Kinneil Railway
Bo'ness (01506 822298). **Open** *Apr-Oct* 11am-4.15pm Sat, Sun; closed Mon-Fri and Nov-Mar. **Admission** £4; £2-£3 concessions; £10 family; *other attractions including locomotive museum* £7.50; £3.50-£5.50 concessions; £18.50 family. **Credit** MC, V.

Cairnpapple Hill
near Torphichen off the A89 (01506 634622). **Open** *Apr-Sept* 9.30am-6.30pm daily; closed Oct-Mar. **Admission** £1.50; 50p-£1.10 concessions. **No credit cards.**

Dalmeny House
South Queensferry (0131 331 1888). **Open** *July, Aug* 2-5.30pm Mon, Tue, Sun; closed Wed-Sat; closed Sept-June. **Admission** £4, £2 concessions. **No credit cards.**

Edinburgh Canal Centre
Ratho, near Edinburgh airport (0131 333 1320/1251). **Open** *sightseeing cruises* June-Aug 2.30pm daily; Mar-May, Sept, Oct 2.30pm Sat, Sun. **Admission** £4.50; £2.50 concessions. **Credit** AmEx, DC, MC, V.

Hopetoun House
South Queensferry, West Lothian (0131 331 2451). **Open** *Apr-Sept* 10am-5.30pm daily; closed Oct-Mar. **Admission** £5.30; £2.70-£4.70 concessions. **Credit** DC, MC, V.

Glorious **Falkland Palace**. *See page 258.*

House of the Binns
off A904, 4 miles east of Linlithgow (01506 834255). **Open** *House* May-Sept 1.30-5pm Mon-Thur; Sat, Sun; closed Fri. *Park* Apr-Oct 10am-7pm daily; Nov-Mar 10am-4pm daily. **Admission** *house* £4; £3 concessions; *park* free. **No credit cards.**

Inchcolm Abbey
Inchcolm Island, Firth of Forth (ferry company 0131 331 4857). **Open** reached by ferry from South Queensferry; *Apr, May, June, Sept, Oct* sailings Sat, Sun; July, Aug daily. Timings change so check in advance. **Admission** *ferry trip and abbey* £9.50; £4 concessions. **No credit cards.**

Linlithgow Palace
Kirkgate, Linlithgow (01506 842896). **Open** *Apr-Sept* 9.30am-6.30pm; *Oct-Mar* 9.30am-4.30pm Mon-Sat; 2-4.30pm Sun. **Admission** £2.50; £1-£1.90 concessions. **Credit** AmEx, MC, V.

Torphichen Preceptory
Torphichen. **Open** *Apr-Sept* 11am-5pm Sat; 2-5pm Sun; closed Mon-Fri and Oct-Mar. **Admission** free.

Where to eat

In South Queensferry, the **Hawes Inn** (0131 331 1990), which was immortalised by Robert Louis Stevenson in *Kidnapped*, serves food every day. The **Ratho Inn** (0131 333 1320) in

Ratho, has two canal boat restaurants and a restaurant on land. The **Hopetoun House** tea shop near South Queensferry is very well thought of by tea-cake aficionados.

Where to stay

Uphall Houston House in Uphall (01506 853831) isn't exactly a bargain, with single rooms for £140 and doubles for £160. A cheaper option is the **Thornton** in Edinburgh Road, Linlithgow (01506 844693), a large Victorian house with B&B rates for £22-£27.

Getting there

By bus
A regular bus service departs St Andrew Square. During refurbishment of the bus station (May 2000-2003), bus services leave South St Andrew Square.

By car
Take the A902 west of Edinburgh, then the B974 for South Queensferry. Take the M9 for Linlithgow.

By train
Trains regularly depart from Waverley and Haymarket Stations in Edinburgh for South Queensferry, Bo'ness and Linlithgow.

Tourist information

In **Linlithgow**, the tourist information office is at Burgh Hall, The Cross (01506 844600). There's also an office in **Bo'ness**, at the Seaview car park (01539 442895). Both offices are open daily.

Fife

Fife has an image problem: much of its landscape is uninspiring. Yet it would harsh to dismiss the Kingdom, as it is still known locally. Lying north of Edinburgh and sandwiched between the Firth of Forth and the Firth of Tay, it juts out, peninsula-like, into the North Sea. A Pictish stronghold in the eighth and ninth centuries, with its capital at Abernethy (in today's Perthshire), many of Fife's place-names still bear witness to that era and include the word 'pit'. Later the towns of Dunfermline and St Andrews grew up as major centres of Christianity.

Dunfermline was once a seat of Scottish royals, a stop-off for pilgrims travelling north to St Andrews, and a pilgrim centre in its own right. Today the town can be somewhat intimidating, fortified as it is by roundabouts and ring rounds. Yet at its core, **Dunfermline Abbey** has one of the finest Norman naves in Scotland. Founded by Queen Margaret, wife of Malcolm III, in 1070, Margaret had Benedictine monks sent up from Canterbury to help establish a monastic community here. It was Margaret's son, the pious David I, who did much to extend the Abbey. The nave was begun in 1128 and with its zig-zag patterned piers is reminiscent of Durham Cathedral. Robert the Bruce was buried before the high altar in 1329, save for his heart, which was cut out and, legend says, buried at Melrose Abbey (*see page 260*). At the eastern end of the Abbey is the ruinous Chapel of St Margaret. Here Queen Margaret who was canonised after her death in 1093 is buried. Neighbouring the Abbey are the stately

Crail Harbour in the **East Neuk** of Fife. *See page 258.*

Trips Out of Town

St Andrews – par for the course.

remains of the palace. Originally a guesthouse serving the monastery, it was rebuilt in the 16th century by James VI and is where Charles I was born. The nearby **Abbot House Heritage Centre** (01383 733266), an interesting 15th-century building in itself, provides a good introduction to Dunfermline's history.

In more recent times, the industrialist and benefactor Andrew Carnegie was born in Dunfermline in 1835. He made his fortune in the US and given his name to numerous libraries and concert halls around the world. He gifted the gardens of Pittencrieff Glen, just next to Dunfermline Palace, to the town in 1903.

Lying west of Dunfermline is **Culross**. Standing just on the Forth of Firth, it is perhaps the most handsome of the Fife burghs. Once an important port, today it is under the guardianship of the National Trust of Scotland. The site of an abbey, palace and numerous sturdy stone houses, Culross's former wealth is obvious. Today there is a slight sense of it being set in aspic, yet its charm wins through.

North-east of Dunfermline, nestling beside the Lomond Hills with cobbled streets and weavers' cottages, is the royal burgh of Falkland. It is home to **Falkland Palace**, which was the favoured home of James V while his daughter, Mary, Queen of Scots, hunted the surrounding country. In the grounds is one of the few remaining 'real' tennis courts, dating from 1539. Further east again, the **Hill of Tarvit Mansionhouse** near Cupar has a good

collection of French furniture in a house rebuilt in 1901 by the architect Sir Robert Lorimer.

The largish town of **Kirkcaldy** stretches along the south coast of Fife. While not particularly picturesque, it was the birthplace of the Adam dynasty of architects and Adam Smith, who penned *A Wealth of Nations* in 1776. Heading north, the coast really comes into its own around **Largo Bay**. This stretch of coastline up to St Andrews is known as **East Neuk**, but is also goes by the name 'fringe of gold'. Its fishing villages were once some of the wealthiest in Scotland. **Pittenweem** has a slight bohemian air to it and hosts an arts festival every August while **Crail**, the oldest fishing village in East Neuk, is well-served by a host of crows-stepped and red-tiled houses. Crail's churchyard is also worth pausing at, boasting as it does a number of carved memorials.

St Andrews, looking out over the North Sea, is a proud sort of place – arguably with good reason. According to legend, the bones of Christ's apostle Andrew were brought here by St Rule sometime after the fourth century. A cathedral was built in the apostle's honour and while St Andrew later became Scotland's patron saint, the town became its ecclesiastical capital. Yet it is a place that trades in diversity. The royal burgh is home to Scotland's oldest university, founded in 1412, and to the Royal & Ancient Golf Club. Founded in 1754, it's the big chief of the golfing world, determining the rules of the game.

Abbot House Heritage Centre
Maygate, Dunfermline (01383 733266). **Open**
10am-5pm daily. **Admission** £3; £2 concessions;
free children. **Credit** MC V.

Falkland Palace
High Street, Falkland (01337857 397). **Open** *Apr-Oct* 11am-5.30pm Mon-Sat (last entry 4.30pm); 1.30-
5.30pm Sun (last entry 4.30pm); closed Nov-Mar.
Admission *Palace & gardens* £5; £3.50
concessions; *gardens only* £2.50; £1.70 concessions.
No credit cards.

Hill of Tarvit Mansionhouse
Cupar (01334 653127). **Open** *Apr-June, Sept*
1.30-5.30pm daily (last entry 4.45pm); *July, Aug*
11am-5.30pm daily; *Oct* 1.30-5.30pm Sat, Sun (last
entry 4.45pm). *Garden & grounds* Apr-Sept
9.30am-9pm daily; Oct-Mar 9.30am-4.30pm daily.
Admission £4; £1-£3 concessions;
grounds only £1. **No credit cards.**

Where to eat

For hot and hearty lunches, **Brambles**
(5 College Street, St Andrews, 01334 475380,
open daily) is unbeatable. Seafood lovers,
meanwhile, might like to try **The Cellar**
in **Anstruther** (24 East Green, 01333 310378,
closed Mon, Tue in winter). If you're visiting
Dunfermline Abbey, pop next door to the
Abbot House Heritage Centre, (01383
733266, open daily), a small café offering
tasty snacks.

Where to stay

In Dunfermline, the **Dawaar House Hotel**,
(126 Grieve Street, 01383 721886) has single
and double rooms for £35-£50. The St Andrews
Inn, (Lathones, by Largoward, 01334 840494)
has rooms for £62 (single) and £80 (double).
In Falkland, the **Covenanter Hotel** (The
Square, 01337 857224), which has single and
double rooms for £24 to £39, is recommended.

Getting there

By bus
Buses depart from Edinburgh's St Andrew Square
for Dunfermline and St Andrews. Stagecoach (01592
261461) provides a bus service around Fife,
including the service from Leuchars to St Andrews.

By car
Take the A90 out of Edinburgh then the M90.
Take the A823 for Dunfermline; the A921 for
the coastal route. For St Andrews take the A91
from the M90.

By train
Trains depart Edinburgh Waverley for Dunfermline,
Kirkcaldy and Leuchars.

Tourist information

A good website for accessing tourist
information on the area is
www.standrews.co.uk. The tourist information
office in the Scottish Fisheries Museum,
Harbour Head, **Anstruther** (01333 311073), is
open from April to September, as is the office
the Museum & Heritage Centre, Marketgait,
Crail (01333 450869) and the one in
Dunfermline, at 13/15 Maygate (01383
720999). The **Kirkcaldy**, the tourist
information office (19 Whytecauseway, 01592
267775) is open all year, as is the office in **St
Andrews** (70 Market Street, 01334 472021).

The Borders

Pastoral landscapes, a handsome coastline,
picturesque towns and a host of abbeys make
the Borders a fascinating stretch of Scotland. It
might have a slightly picture-postcard
prettiness, yet by dint of neighbouring England,
the area witnessed much warring over the
centuries. It was under the rule of Northumbria
until Malcolm II took the land for Scotland in
the early 11th century. David I founded the
powerful abbeys of Kelso, Melrose, Jedburgh
and Dryburgh in the 12th century. As potent
symbols of Scotland's rule, they, and many of
the border towns, were frequently raided by the
English. Inter-nation warfare aside, the Border
Reivers, family-based groups of cattle thieves
and land-grabbers, further ensured that life in
these parts was far from lacking in action.

Peebles is the closest Borders town to
Edinburgh and nestles, somewhat smugly,
beside the River Tweed. The obligatory woollen
shops aside, the town does offer up the odd
surprise. In the **Tweeddale Museum & Art
Gallery** on the High Street there are impressive
plaster copies of the Parthenon Frieze (just
don't call them the Elgin Marbles) together
with a copy of a frieze executed by the
celebrated 19th-century Danish sculptor,
Bertel Thorvaldsen for the Palazzo Quirinale
in Rome. But if getting plastered in the
colloquial sense of the word is more appealing,
the Bridge Inn has character, and some
interesting old photos of Peebles.

More architecturally vigorous, just west of
Peebles off the A72 and standing proud over the
River Tweed, is the 14th-century **Neidpath
Castle**. Understandably it inspired both
William Wordsworth and Sir Walter Scott to
pen a few lines. From here there are a number of
well-signposted riverside walks. Further west is
the **Dawyck Botanic Garden**, an outstation
of the Royal Botanic Garden in Edinburgh.
Travelling east of Peebles on the A72 is the

small and rather town of **Innerleithen**. It found brief fortune in 1822 when a Dr Fyfe relaunched it as a Victorian spa town. He claimed its waters could benefit sufferers of scurvy through to sterility. The place found further fame as the setting for Scott's novel, *St Ronan's Well*. St Ronan, the patron saint of Innerleithen, is traditionally depicted attacking Satan with a crook (Cleiking the De'il) and Cleikum Ceremonies are still held at St Ronan's Border Games in July.

Just outside Innerleithen is the truly handsome, 1,000-year-old, **Traquair House**. Acclaimed as the oldest inhabited house in Scotland, over the centuries it has served as a court for William the Lion, a hunting lodge for Scottish royalty, a refuge for Catholic priests and acted as a stronghold of Jacobite sentiment. The ever-bed-hopping Mary, Queen of Scots not only stayed here in 1566 but possibly embroidered one of its bedspreads. Two centuries later, in 1745, the clearly optimistic fifth Earl of Traquair wished his guest, one Prince Charles Edward Stuart, a safe journey into battle and rashly promised that he would not reopen Traquair's great gates until the Stuarts were restored to the throne. They have remained closed ever since and today visitors use the 'temporary' drive. The grounds include an impressive maze, a croquet lawn, a number of craft workshops in the old stables and a brewery.

Galashiels, though not an attractive Borders town, does have a buzz. With a population of nearly 14,000, it is the second largest town in the Borders, and continues to be the manufacturing centre of tweed (the word derives from a misreading of tweel, the Scottish word for twill, not, as if often assumed, from the River Tweed). **Loch Carron** is one of only four textile manufacturers to have survived from the 30 that once stood in Galashiels and has a small museum devoted to tweed and tartan. Nearby is **Melrose Abbey**, reputed to be the resting place of Robert the Bruce's heart. Founded in 1136 by Cisterian monks from Rievaulx in Yorkshire, it was all but destroyed by the English in 1385 but remains one of the most picturesque Border abbeys.

Unsurprisingly, the history-packed Borders appealed to Sir Walter Scott, the tireless promoter of Scotland's past. **Abbotsford**, just outside Melrose, was his home and it's an appropriately romantic affair. Overlooking the Tweed, this Gothic-cum-Scottish baronial pile is stuffed with relics including Rob Roy's gun, Montrose's sword and Prince Charlie's quaich. Always one for a good view, Scott frequently praised the nearby Eildon Hills, the legendary burial ground of King Arthur. You can see what he saw by visiting 'Scott's View', a few miles east of Melrose. Meanwhile nearby, another

Eyemouth harbour. *See page 261.*

hero, William Wallace, is celebrated with the gargantuan Wallace Statue.

Fittingly, the now-serene **Dryburgh Abbey** besides the Tweed is the burial site of Scott. Founded in 1150 by the White Canons of the French Premonstratensian Order, and sacked by the English in the 1540s, here the phrase 'romantic ruins' really comes into its own.

Selkirk is a pretty town just south of Galashiels on the A7, where Scott was Sheriff of Selkirkshire from 1799 to 1832. Selkirk is also famous for its bannock, a rich currant loaf. There are several bakeries in town, but Camerons on the High Street bakes the best. At the Fleece pub, The Rolling Stones were purportedly refused service as their hair was too long!

Kelso, with its capacious town square and fine 1816 Court House, has a slight Gallic air. Standing at the point where the Teviot meets the Tweed, it is indisputably attractive, Kelso Abbey being perhaps the finest of the Border abbeys. Founded in 1128 by David I for a community of French monks from Tiron, near Chartres, it is today the most incomplete border abbey, being virtually destroyed in 1545. Yet what remains – principally the west façade and transept – offers a staggering show of Norman and Gothic architecture. According to local legend, a horseshoe embedded in Roxburgh Street (outside Safeway) is said to have come off Bonny Prince Charlie's horse, when he visited the town in 1745.

Pomp and many a good circumstance are brought to mind at **Floors Castle** (01573 223333). Overlooking the Tweed, it is Scotland's largest inhabited castle and home to the Duke of Roxburgh. Designed by William Adam in 1721, it was flamboyantly remodelled by William Playfair in the mid-19th century and as befits such architecture houses a wealth of treasures. Those less-fortunate, namely French, prisoners of war from the Battle of Waterloo, built the high stone wall that surrounds the grounds.

Further display of good fortune is given in **Mellerstain House** (01573 410225). Begun in 1725 by William Adam and completed by his son Robert, many believe its interior marks the zenith of his career. Certainly it is one of the most intact Adam interiors. Unusually, Adam also landscaped the grounds – note the alignment of the lake and the folly on the hill. The Italian-style terrace gardens were added in 1911.

Jedburgh is not the most good-looking of Border towns. Once a tweed-making centre tweed, today its principal export is coathangers. **Mary, Queen of Scots House** is a 16th-century bastel house that provides everything you ever wanted to know about the woman herself. Jedburgh's abbey is the best preserved in the Borders though its setting besides a busy road is far from scenic. It was founded soon after 1138 for the Augustinian order, and after the Reformation (1560) was used as a parish church.

Duns has the dubious honour of being the birthplace of John Duns Scotus. A medieval scholar who taught philosophy at the University of Paris, his teachings were discredited and his name became associated with stupidity, and thanks to him we have the word 'dunce'. The town honours him in the shape of a statue and plaque. James Hutton (1726-97), now known as the father of the science of geology, was a rather brighter Duns man. He described the Borders as 'the most important geological site in the world' and challenged the theory of Creation.

South of Duns on the banks on the Tweed is **Coldstream**. Here Edward I crossed into Scotland in 1296, establishing a route for numerous other English and Scots armies. Its military associations were further strengthened by one General Monk, who raised the famous Coldstream Guards here in 1659.

Heading north-east you reach the rugged coastline of the North Sea. **Eyemouth**, one time stronghold of tobacco and booze smuggling, is not the most picturesque of fishing villages, but it's worth stopping at the **Eyemouth Museum** to look at the Eyemouth Tapestry. It commemorates the 1881 fishing disaster when 189 local fishermen were drowned. The next fishing village north is **St Abb's**, which has the full quota of picture postcard prettiness. North of the port, the cliffs rise up to **St Abb's Head**. There is a well-trodden pathway to the cliff edge, the whole of the headland being a nature reserve and, during spring, home to guillemots, razorbills and puffins. Further north again is **Sicar Point** where Hutton finally formulated his 'Theory of the Earth' in 1788.

Abbotsford
Melrose (01896 752043). **Open** *Apr, May, Oct* 10am-5pm Mon-Sat; 2-5pm Sun; *June-Sept* 10am-5pm Sun. **Admission** £3.80; £1.90 concessions. **No credit cards**.

Daywyck Botanic Garden
on B712, Stobo, Peebles. (01721 760254). **Open** *Mar-Oct* 9.30am-6pm daily; closed Nov-Feb. **Admission** £3; £1-£2.50 concessions; £7 family. **Credit** MC, V.

Eyemouth Museum
Auld Kirk, Eyemouth (01890 750678). **Open** *Easter-Oct* 10am-5pm Mon-Sat; 11am-1pm Sun (11am-4pm July, Aug); closed Nov-Easter. **Admission** £1.75; £1.25 concessions. **Credit** MC V.

Floors Castle
Roxburgh Estates, Kelso (01573 223333). **Open** *Easter-Oct* 10am-4.30pm daily; closed Nov-Easter. **Admission** £5; £3-£4.50 concessions. **No credit cards**.

Loch Carron
Waverley Mills, Huddersfield Street, Galashiels (01896 752091). **Open** 9am-5pm Mon-Sat; *June-Sept also* noon-5pm Sun. **Admission** £2.50. **Credit** AmEx, DC, MC, V.

Mellerstain House
Gordon, Berwickshire (01573 410225). **Open** *Easter-Sept* 12.30-5pm Mon-Fri, Sun; closed Sat; **Admission** £4.50; £2-£3.50 concessions. **Credit** MC, V.

Traquair House
Innerleithen (01896 830323/www.traquair.co.uk). **Open** *late Apr-Oct* 12.30-5.30pm daily (10.30am-5.30pm June-Aug). **Admission** £5.20; £2.60-£4 concessions. **Credit** DC, MC V.

Tweeddale Museum and Gallery
Chambers Institute, High Street, Peebles (01721 724820). **Open** 10am-noon, 2-5pm Mon-Fri; *Easter-Oct also* 10am-1pm, 2-4pm Sat; closed Sun. **Admission** free. **No credit cards**.

Abbotsford, Scott's former gaff.

Mary, Queen of Scots House

High Street, Jedburgh (01835 863331). **Open** *Mar,
Nov* 10.30am-4.45pm Mon-Sat; 1-4pm Sun; *Apr, Oct*
10am-4.30pm Mon-Sat; noon-4.30pm Sun; *June-Aug*
10am-4.30pm Mon-Sat; 10.30am-4.30pm Sun.
Admission £2; £1 concessions. **No credit cards.**

Where to eat

In Innerleithen, the **Traquair Arms Hotel**
(01896 830229, open daily) is a characterful pub-
hotel serving food. A picturesque choice is the
Tibbie Shiels Inn, St Mary's Loch (01750
42231, closed Mon-Wed in winter), an old haunt
for writers that overlooks the loch. **Kailzie
Gardens**, near Peebles (01721 720007, open
daily) is a fine tea shop set in courtyard and
serving up good home baking. Try the **Ship
Hotel** (Harbour Road, Eyemouth, 01890
750224), which serves food daily.

Where to stay

In Peebles, the **Peebles Hydro Hotel** (01721
720602, single rooms £95; doubles £150) is
recommended for its great views of the town
and for its facilities – swimming pool,
whirlpool, tennis courts, and a health and
beauty salon. For B&B in an 18th-century
farmhouse, contact Mrs Debby Playfair at
Morebattle Tofts, Kelso (01573 440364,
single £19, doubles £40, open Apr-Oct).
George & Abbotsford Hotel,
High Street, Melrose (01896 822308) has single
rooms for £30-£53; doubles from £60.
Philipburn House (Selkirk, 01750 720747)
has single rooms for £79.50; doubles £99.50.
Rooms at **Castle Rock Guest House**,
Murrayfield (01890 771715), meanwhile, go for
£23-£25 (single and double). **Garth House**,
7 Market Street, Coldstream, (01890 882477) has
rooms from £16. In Duns, **Barniken House
Hotel**, 18 Murray Street (01361 882466) has
singles for £27-£30; doubles £30. There's also
self-catering accommodation in the grounds of
Duns Castle (01361 883211).

Getting there

By bus

Buses depart from St Andrew Square, Edinburgh.
During refurbishment of the bus station (May 2000-
2003), buses leave South St Andrew Square.

By car

Take the A701 out of Edinburgh, then the A703 to
Peebles.

By train

The nearest train station to the Borders is Berwick-
upon-Tweed, from where buses go to Galashiels
and other destinations.

Tourist information

The tourist information centres at **Galashiels**
(St John Street,01896 755551) and Drumlanrig's
Tower, **Hawick** (01450 372547) are open from
Easter to October. Also try the centres at
Jedburgh (Murray's Green, 01835 863435),
Kelso (Town House, The Square, 01573
223464), **Melrose Abbey House** (01896
822555) **Peebles** (23 High Street, 01721 720138)
and Halliwell's House, **Selkirk** (01750 20054).

Stirling

According to an ancient saying, 'To hold
Stirling is to hold Scotland'. Standing just
above the River Forth with the Ochil Hills
and the Grampian Mountains lying to the north,
it is strategically placed at the meeting of
Scotland's Highlands and Lowlands. Two
of the most significant battles against
English rule took place nearby: in 1297
William Wallace defeated the English at
the Battle of Stirling Bridge and in 1314
at **Bannockburn**, Robert the Bruce beat
Edward II's forces. Today, this once-powerful
town is unassuming. **Stirling Castle** crowns
the Old Town and remains a magnificent
testament to past times. Yet the busier town
centre, enlivened by students from the just-out-
of-town university, not to blow the heritage
trumpet too loudly.

Holding tight onto rocky remnants of
ancient volcanic activity, **Stirling Castle**
is a both robust fortification and a stately
royal palace. Castle Rock was probably first
occupied in the 600s, yet today's castle dates
mainly from the 15th and 16th centuries.
Over the years it has been the centre of
numerous 'tug of wars' with the English and
witnessed numerous royal comings and
goings. Alexander I died here in 1124 and James
II was born within its walls. Mary, Queen of
Scots was crowned here and her son James VI
(later James I of England) was christened in the
castle's chapel. By the early 18th century,
however, it had lost much of its importance,
becoming a military barracks.

Castle Wynd sweeps down from the castle
and passes **Argyll's Lodgings**. One of
Scotland's most stunning examples of a 17th-
century grand townhouse, it was once home to
the dukes of Argyll. There is a definite French
château feel to the place, particularly in the
turreted courtyard. Over the way is Mar's
Wark, the impressive stone remains of what
was once a grand Renaissance-style house built
by the Earl of Mar. Neighbouring it is the
Church of the Holy Rude, which has one of the
few surviving medieval timber roofs in

A **Stirling** example of a castle. *See page 262.*

Scotland. Here James VI was crowned in 1567.
Next door is Cowane's Hospital, a flamboyant-
looking affair built by a wealthy merchant
in the mid-17th century.

Beyond Stirling Old Bridge, and about a mile
north-east of the town, is the **National
Wallace Monument**. Dominating the
skyline, this stone tower commemorates Sir
William Wallace, hero of the Battle of Stirling
Bridge, and star of the film *Braveheart*.
Funded by public subscriptions, and built
in the Scottish baronial style, it opened in
1860 and houses Wallace memorabilia
including his double-edged sword. **Bridge
of Allan**, a couple of miles out of Stirling, is
genteel sort place. Once a popular spa town,
today it is well-furnished with tea shops.
About ten miles east is **Castle Campbell**, the
so-called 'Castle of Gloom', which comes up
trumps for its spectacular location, just at the
head of Dollar Glen.

Dunblane, a smallish town to the north
of Stirling, has a fine cathedral and makes
a good starting point for touring the
nearby Ochil Hills. Just beyond is **Doune**,
once a pistol-making centre, today it is known
for its castle, which overlooks the River
Teith. The town's bridge was built by one
James Spittal in the 16th century. Refused
passage on the ferry due to lack of funds,
Spittal funded the bridge out of spite, to
put the ferryman out a job.

Argyll's Lodgings

Castle Wynd (01786 450000). **Open** *summer*
9.30am-6pm daily; *winter* 9.30am-5pm daily.
Admission *Argyll's Lodging & Castle* £6; £1.50-
£4.50 concessions; *Argyll's Lodgings only* £2.80;
£1.20 concessions. **Credit** AmEx, DC, MC, V.

Bannockburn Heritage Centre

*Glasgow Road, off the A91, 2 miles south of Stirling
(01786 812664).* **Open** *site* all year. *Heritage centre*
Mar, Nov-late Dec 11am-4.30pm daily; Apr-Oct 10am-
5.30pm daily. **Admission** £2.50; £1.70 concessions;
free under-18s. **Credit** DC, MC, V.

National Wallace Monument

*Abbey Craig, off A91, 1 mile north-east of Stirling.
(01789 472140).* **Open** all year.

Stirling Castle

Castle Esplanade, Stirling (01786 450000).
Open *summer* 9.30am-5.15pm daily; *winter*
9.30am-4.15pm daily. **Admission** *Castle &
Argyll's Lodgings* £6, £1.50-£4.50 concessions.
Credit AmEx, MC, V.

Where to eat

Two recommended choices in Stirling are the
Barnton Bar & Bistro (3 Barnton Street,
01786 461698, open daily) and the **Hogs Head**
(2 Baker Street, 01786 448722, open daily).

Where to stay

Accommodation-wise, Stirling has a few decent
options. Among them are the **Golden Lion** (8
King Street, 01786 475351, single roosm £65-£81,
double £45-£55), a handsome hotel dating back
to 1876. A cheaper option is the **youth hostel**
on St John Street (01786 473442) £11.25-£12.75;
members only (you can join at the hostel).

Getting there

By bus
Buses depart St Andrew Square. During
refurbishment of the bus station (May 2000-2003)
buses leave from South St Andrew Square.

By car
Stirling lies 40 miles north of Edinburgh. Take the
A8 then M9 leaving at junction 9.

By train
Trains depart Waverley and Haymarket Stations.

Tourist information

There are tourist information centres at the
Pirnhall Motorway Service Area, M9,
junction 9 (01786 814111, open Apr-Oct), and
two in **Stirling** (41 Dumbarton Road, 01786
475019; Castle Esplanade (01786 479901).

Further Afield

The hills, the glens and the bonny, bonny banks.

Dundee & Angus

Dundonians still call it the City of Apathy, but the tourist board hails the City of Discovery. Situated on the north bank of the Tay, Dundee, with a population of 150,300, has received a makeover in recent years, successfully bringing in new technology-based industries, while the opening of **Dundee Contemporary Arts** arts centre, with galleries, cinema and café, has further fuelled a vibrant arts scene. In short, Dundee, is a gutsy city that has had its fair share of ups and downs. It was stormed by the forces of Henry VIII, by Montrose in 1645 and by Cromwell's General Monk during the Civil War.

The city once thrived on the three Js: Jute, Journalism and Jam, together with shipbuilding. The jute industry today has been whittled down to a mere two companies, the jam has shifted production to Manchester and only journalism continues to flourish in the form of DC Thomson & Co, the publishers who own Britain's largest comic paper empire. The only reminder of the shipbuilding industry is the **RRS Discovery**. It was the ship in which Captain Scott made his first expedition to the Antarctic, in 1901.

Angus stretches to the north of Dundee. On the coast is **Arbroath**, an attractive fishing village that resonates with history. In 1320, a declaration of independence was signed in **Arbroath Abbey** after Robert the Bruce's victory over the English at Bannockburn (*see page 262*). Today the abbey is a majestic ruin. Further north is **Lunan Bay**, with fine sandy beaches and a spectacular cliff edge topped by the 15th-century **Red Castle**.

The area is replete with **Pictish** artefacts, which are explained at the **Pictavia** centre, devoted to the life and times of the Pictish people. Good castles to visit in the area include **Glamis**, the legendary setting for Shakespeare's *Macbeth*. **Kirriemore** is the home town of *Peter Pan* author JM Barrie. Behind the town, the glens of **Isla**, **Clova**, **Prosen**, **Lethnot** and **Esk** go up into the **Grampian Mountains** and include ten Munros (*see page 225*). Even if you're not up to bagging one, it is worth taking a slow scenic drive along their narrow roads.

Dundee Contemporary Arts
Nethergate (01382 432000). **Open** 10.30am-midnight daily. **Galleries** close 5.30pm Mon-Thur, Sun; 8pm Fri, Sat.

Glamis Castle
Glamis village, by Forfar (01307 840393). **Open** *Apr-Nov* 10.30am-5.30pm daily; closed Dec-Mar. **Admission** *house & grounds* £6; £3-£4.50 concessions; *grounds only* £3; £1.30-£1.50 concessions. **Credit** MC, V.

Pictavia
near Brechin off the A90 (no phone). **Open** 9am-5pm Mon-Sat; 10am-5pm Sun; summer open until 6pm. **Admission** £3.25; £2.25 concessions. **No credit cards.**

RRS Discovery
Discovery Point, Discovery Quay (01382 201245). **Open** *Nov-Mar* 10am-4pm Mon-Sat; 11am-4pm Sun; *Apr-Oct* 10am-5pm Mon-Sat; 11am-5pm Sun. **Admission** £5; £4.15 concessions. **Credit** MC, V.

Where to eat

The **Jute Café**, at Dundee Contemporary Arts (Nethergate, 01382 432 000, closed Mon) has good views over the Tay. The whole **Angus** area is well geared up to tourist tea-room stops, but **Visocchi's** in Broughty Ferry (40 Gray Street, 01382 779297) serves excellent ice-cream.

Where to stay

In Dundee, the **Swallow Hotel** (Kingsway West, Invergowrie, 01382 641122) is part of a clean, modern chain with single rooms for £70 and doubles from £90. Also in the city, **Restalrig Guest House** (69 Clepington Road, 01382 455412) is cheaper – a single room costs £23 and a double £36. Near Arbroath, the **Chance Inn**, Inverkeilor (01241 830308) has rates starting at £20 for both single and double rooms.

Getting there

By air
Dundee has a small airport to the west of the city.

By bus
Buses depart from St Andrew Square, Edinburgh.

The cream of the crop – **Scone Palace**.

By car

Take the A90 out of Edinburgh, then the M90, returning to the A90 at Perth.

By train

Trains depart from Edinburgh Waverley for Dundee, Arbroath and Montrose on their way to Aberdeen.

Tourist information

Dundee's tourist office is at 21 Castle Street (01382 527527/www.angusanddundee.co.uk). Other useful offices include the one at Brechin Castle Centre, Haughmuir, **Brechin** (01356 623050, open Apr-Sept). If you're in **Forfar**, go to 40 East High Street (01307 467876, open Apr-Sept). **Kirriemuir**, meanwhile, has a tourist information office at Cumberland Close (01575 574097, open Apr-Sept).

Perthshire

Perthshire is perhaps the most stately of Scotland's regions. Well-heeled and scenically wealthy too, it has attracted numerous visitors over the centuries. The Romans built one of their largest stations in Britain at **Ardoch** in the second century. In the ninth century, after Kenneth MacAlpine merged the land of the Picts in the east with the western kingdom of Dalriada, Perth became capital of the embryonic nation of Scotland. The nearby Moot-Hill, neighbouring what was Scone Abbey, and now **Scone Palace**, witnessed the crowning of a succession of early monarchs. It was also home, until its removal to Westminster Abbey by Edward I in 1297, of one of Scotland's most potent national symbols: the Stone of Destiny, which was returned to Scotland in 1997 and is now in Edinburgh Castle.

Another, more recent monarch – who did much to popularise 'the romance of Scotland' – fell in love with Perthshire. Queen Victoria was indeed amused, and Queen's View on Loch Tummel is named after her. Unsurprisingly, Perthshire, renowned for its shooting, and

salmon fishing on the River Tay, has attracted a good share of stately piles, with **Blair Castle** epitomising the Scottish baronial style of turrets and crenellations.

There is a touch of the tartan theme-park to some parts of Perthshire. **Pitlochry** is a pleasant town but rather stuffed with woollen mills and tartan paraphernalia. However, **Dunkeld**, the site of a monastery founded by St Columba in the sixth century and home to handsome ruins of a cathedral overlooking the Tay, does not overplay the heritage card. **Perth**, likewise, has not lost itself down memory lane. Also bordering the Tay, the city's good looks prompted Walter Scott to write *The Fair Maid of Perth*. Today, high-street chain stores have elbowed their way into the royal burgh, making it very much a working town.

Towns aside, Perthshire is good for outdoor amusements. To the north lies the **Spittal of Glenshee**, a winter ski resort and part of the massive Grampian Mountain range. North of Pitlochry is the pass of **Killiecrankie**, where the Jacobites defeated the English forces in 1689. Perthshire is also well-served on the tree front. To the west of Dunkeld is the vast **Tummel Forest Park** and numerous lochs. At **Fortingall**, to the west of Aberfeldy and near Loch Tay, stands an ancient yew tree which, at 3,000 years old, is believed to be the oldest tree in Europe.

Blair Castle

Blair Atholl, nr Pitlochry (01796 481207).
Open *Apr-Oct* 10am-6pm daily (last entry 5pm); closed Nov-Mar. **Admission** £6; £4 concessions. **No credit cards.**

Killiecrankie

Pitlochry off the B8079 (no phone). **Open** *visitor centre, shop & snack bar* Apr-Oct 10am-5.30pm daily; closed Nov-Mar. **Admission** £1. **No credit cards.**

Scone Palace

Perth (01738 552300/sconepalace@cqm.co.uk).
Open *Apr-Oct* 9.30am-5.15pm daily (last entry 4.45pm). **Admission** £5.60; £3.30-£4.80 concessions; *grounds only* £2.70; £1.50 concessions. **Credit** MC, V.

Where to eat

Recommended eateries in the area include the **Atholl Arms Hotel** at Blair Atholl (01796 481205) and the **Farleyer Hotel & Bistro**, Weem, near Aberfeldy (01887 820332), which serves lunches in its bistro and more formal dinners in its dining room. **Patrick's Wine Bar**, at Speygate, near Perth (01738 620539) is another winner. All serve food daily.

Trips Out of Town

Where to stay

Ptarmigan House, at Blair Atholl (01796 481269), is a former shooting lodge with rooms from £20. The **Atholl Arms Hotel** (Tay Terrace, Dunkeld, 01350 727219) has rooms from £40-£70. In Perth, **Beechgrove Guest House** (Dundee Road, 01738 636147) has single rooms for £25-£30 and doubles from £40.

Getting there

By bus
Buses depart Edinburgh's St Andrew Square.

By car
Take the M90 north to Perth.

By train
Trains go from Edinburgh's Waverley Station to Perth.

Tourist information

Perth's tourist information office, at Lower City Mills, West Mill Street (01738 450600), and **Pitlochry**'s, at 22 Atholl Road (01796 472215), are open all year – as are **Crieff**'s office at the town hall on the High Street (01764 652578), and **Dunkeld**'s at The Cross (01350 727688).

Grampian & Aberdeen

Over a 100 miles north-east of Edinburgh, **Grampian** is a shoulder-like hunk of land, named after the **Grampian Mountains** that rise up from Perthshire in the south. There are more summits standing at over 4,000 feet here than anywhere else in Scotland – Grampian's best-known mountain range is the **Cairngorms**. To the north and east, the slopes give way to the North Sea coastline.

Good-looking landscape aside, this is the place to go for whisky distilleries and turreted castles. It's a veritable haven for themed 'tourist trails'; there is even a Victorian heritage trail around Royal Deeside, thanks to the fact that Queen Victoria's husband, Prince Albert, bought nearby **Balmoral Castle** in 1852 (access only to the grounds and a display of paintings in the ballroom). Whisky and Victoriana are combined at the **Dallas Dhu Distillery** near Forres, a preserved Victorian distillery.

Grampian's capital is **Aberdeen**, the 'Granite City' and Scotland's third largest. Standing on the estuaries of the Rivers Dee and Don, it has long known wealth, though the North Sea oil boom of the 1970s is now firmly in the past. Yet a mood of civic pride remains –

Aberdeen has repeatedly won Britain in Bloom awards. Union Street is the thoroughly confident main street. Its 17th-century **Mercat Cross** was paid for out of the city's wine guild fund, while the rugged Provost **Ross's House**, dating from 1593, is the city's oldest building. The nearby **Marischal College**, part of the city's university, is an elaborate, pinnacled 19th-century affair.

From Aberdeen, it is wise to decide where you want to head for. Many of the whisky distilleries flanking the River Spey offer tours and a tempting 'wee dram'. Castle bagging is best done west of Aberdeen. The imposing **Corgarff Castle**, near Strathdon, was used by the military to combat whisky smuggling, once a roaring business. For clan history, further south is **Braemar Castle**, a rather forbidding edifice and ancestral home of the Farquharsons.

As to the east coast, south of Aberdeen near Stonehaven is **Fowlsheugh**, an RSPB reserve which is mainland Britain's largest seabird colony. Further north is **Cruden Bay**, with sandy beaches, and **Slain Castle**, said to have inspired Bram Stroker's *Dracula*.

Balmoral Castle
Ballater (013397 42334/info@balmoral-castle.co.uk). **Open** *mid-Apr to July* 10am-5pm daily; closed Aug-mid-Apr. **Admission** £4; £1-£3 concessions. **Credit** MC, V.

Braemar Castle
Braemar (013397 41219). **Open** *Apr-Oct* 10am-6pm Mon-Thur, Sat, Sun; *July, Aug also* Fri; closed Nov-Mar. **Admission** £3; £1-£2.50 concessions. **No credit cards.**

Corgarff Castle
Strathdon on the A939 (01975 651460). **Open** *Apr-Sept* 9.30am-6.30pm daily; *Oct-Mar* 9.30am-4.30pm Sat; 2-4.30pm Sun. **Admission** £2.50; £1-£1.90 concessions. **No credit cards.**

Dallas Dhu Distillery
1 mile south of Forres on the A940 (01309 676548). **Open** *Apr-Sept* 9.30am-6.30pm daily; *Oct-Mar* 9.30am-4.30pm Mon-Wed, Fri, Sat; 9.30am-12.30pm Thur; 2-4.30pm Sun. **Admission** £3; £1-£2.50 concessions. **Credit** AmEx, DC, MC, V.

Where to eat

Fjord Inn, Fisherford, east of Huntly (01464 841232, daily except Mon, Tue) serves good pub grub in a casual setting. **The Grant Arms**, The Square, Monymusk, 20 miles east of Aberdeen (01467 651226) has food every day. **Silver Darling**, Pocraquay, Aberdeen (01224 576229), is one of Aberdeenshire's finest seafood restaurants.

Where to stay

In **Aberdeen**, the Queen's Hotel (51-53 Queen's Road, 01224 209999) has single rooms (£35-£70) and doubles (£50-£80). **Aspen Lodge Hotel**, Braemar Road, Ballater (013397 55486) has singles for £18-£28; doubles for £18-£30. Dufftown's **Tannochbrae Guest House** (22 Fife Street, 01340 820541) is another good option; rates (single and double) are £17.50-£22.50. In Elgin, the **Braelossie Hotel & Restaurant** (2 Sherriffmill Road, 01343 547181) has singles and doubles from £30-£40.

Getting there

By air
Aberdeen has an international airport. Flights depart from Edinburgh airport.

By bus
Coaches depart St Andrew Square Bus Station (St Andrew Square during refurbishment) in Edinburgh.

By car
Take the M90 to Perth, then the Deeside tourist route (A93), the faster A90 or the coastal route (A92) from Dundee.

By train
Trains go direct from Glasgow and Edinburgh's Waverley Station to Aberdeen.

Tourist information

The tourist information centres at **Aberdeen** (St Nicholas House, Broad Street, 01224 632727), **Stonehaven** (66 Allardice Street, 01569 762806) and **Braemar** (The Mews, Mar Road, 01339 741600) are open all year.

Highlands

If Scotland had a soul it would doubtless reside in the Highlands. The most northerly stretch of Scotland, circled by the islands of Orkney, Shetland, Skye and the Hebrides, is a land tangled with both lament and romance.

Some of Scotland's most resonant moments in history have been played out here. **Glencoe** is indelibly linked with the Glencoe Massacre of 1692, when members of the MacDonald Clan were killed for not swearing quick allegiance to the Crown. **Glenfinnian**, at the head of Loch Shiel, was where Bonny, Prince Charles raised the Jacobite standard in 1745. A year later at **Culloden Moor**, east of Inverness, his forces were defeated by the Duke of Cumberland. Later, from the 1780s to the mid-19th century,

thousands of Highlanders were forcefully evicted by rent-greedy landowners in the Highland Clearances. Many headed for the Americas and Australia.

The scenery here can be staggering. There are the white sand beaches of the west coast – on a sunny day they are said not to be dissimilar from those of the Caribbean – the drama of **Ben Nevis**, which at 4406ft, is the highest mountain in Britain; countless lochs; the ancient forest of Glen Affric or the wilder coast around Caithness.

Today there is still a sense of Highland spirit. The most northern point of mainland Scotland, **John O'Groats**, is nearly 300 miles from Edinburgh and the Highlands are, in many ways, far removed from the Lowlands. Yet, despite fears of 'theme-park tartan heritage', the Highlands and Islands hold fast to their integrity.

Culloden Moor
5 miles east of Inverness (01463 790607). **Open** *Site* all year. *Visitor centre* Feb, Mar, Nov, Dec 10am-4pm daily; Apr-Oct 9am-6pm daily. **Admission** *visitor centre & Old Leanach Cottage* £3.50; £1-£2.50 concessions. **No credit cards.**

Glencoe
off the A82, 17 miles south of Fort William (01855 811307). **Open** *Site* all year. *Visitor centre* Mar, Apr, Sep, Oct 10am-5pm daily; May-Aug 9.30am-5.30pm daily. **Admission** *Visitor Centre* 50p; 30p concessions. **Credit** DC, MC, V.

Where to eat

The **Three Chimneys** restaurant and house by Colbost, Dunvegan (01470 511258) has award-winning food and is a great place to stay. **The Tables** at Dunvegan (01470 521414) serves great food in dilapidated splendour. **Kinacarra Restaurant** (Kinlochmoidart, 01967 431238) has amazing food in a spectacular setting (reservations recommended).

Where to stay

Glencoe Guesthouse, Strathlachlan, near Glencoe (01855 811244), has rooms from £17-£24. The **Glen Mhor Hotel**, (9-12 Ness Bank, Inverness, 01463 234308), is another option in the area, with singles for £45-£65 and doubles from £58. In Fort William, **Distillery House**, (Nevisbridge, North Road, 01397 700103) has single and double rooms from £20. Thurso's **Waterside House** (3 Janet Street, 01847 894751) offers single and double rooms (rates start at £16).

Getting there

By air
There are airports at Wick and Inverness.

Trips Out of Town

By bus
Coaches depart St Andrew Square, Edinburgh.

By car
Take the M8 to Glasgow then the A82 to Fort
William or Inverness. Take the M9 to Stirling then
A9 to Inverness or Thurso.

By train
Trains depart Edinburgh Waverley for Fort William
and Inverness.

Tourist information

A useful website is www.host.co.uk, with
information on the Highlands & Islands. At
Aviemore, the tourist information office is at
Grampian Road (01479 810363). On the **Isle of
Skye**, the office in **Broadford** (01471 822361)
is open from April to October and the
Dunvegan office at 2 Lochside (01470 521581),
is open from April to September. In Fort
William try the Cameron Centre (Cameron
Square, 01397 703781), or the office in Inverness
(Castle Wynd, 01463 234353). And, if you're lost
in **John O'Groats**, there's a tourist
information office on County Road (01955
611373), open from April to October.

Argyll

Topographically, Argyll is brilliantly
undisciplined. A jagged coastline, a host of
outlying islands, lochs that carve through the
landscape and, in the north, the high peak of
Ben Cruachan, make it a scenery-buff's dream.

Lying on the west coast of Scotland, north of
Glasgow, Argyll has been a stopping-off point
for various peoples, thanks in part to its
proximity to Ireland. In the Dark Ages, Irish
Celts arrived forming the Kingdom of Dalriada.
In the sixth century the Christian missionary St
Columba landed at the southern tip of the
Kintyre peninsula. In the centuries that
followed power was grabbed by the Norsemen
and, later still, various clans battled it out for
territory. All this has bequeathed Argyll with a
wealth of historic sites. **Kilmartin Glen** in
particular is home to numerous Bronze-Age
monuments and **Kilmartin House** is probably
the best place to start an exploration of the
area's prehistoric treasures.

A worthwhile port of call is the pretty village
of **Inveraray** where **Inveraray Castle**, the
fairy-tale-cum-château-style home to the Dukes
of Argyll, overlooks **Loch Fyne**, a stretch of
water renowned for its oysters. Heading south
into **Kintyre**, the roads get quieter, save for
traffic heading for the ferries from Kennacraig
to Islay and Jura. **Jura** is the quieter of the two
islands. The author George Orwell stayed here

People come to **Mull** to mull things over.

while writing the 20th-century classic *1984*.
Islay is home to strong, peaty malt whisky.

The tiny **Iona** lies to the south-west of the
much larger island of **Mull**. St Columba
founded a monastery on Iona in 563 and
pilgrims have travelled to the island ever since.
It is also the site of Scotland's oldest burial
ground, **St Oran's Cemetery**, in which lie
over 40 early Scottish kings, including Duncan,
who was murdered by Macbeth in 1040.

In the north of Argyll is the busy town of
Oban. A bustling town and port (ferries leave
here for the islands of Mull, Coll, Tiree and
Colonsay), it is geared up for tourists with
attractions like **Dunstaffnage Castle**, where
Flora MacDonald, helpmate of Bonny Prince
Charlie, was once imprisoned.

Dunstaffnage Castle
nr Oban (01631 562465). **Open** *Apr-Sept* 9.30am-
6pm daily; *Oct-Mar* 9.30am-4.30pm Mon-Sat; 2-
4.30pm Sun. **Admission** £2; 75p-£1.50 concessions.
Credit AmEx, MC, V.

Inveraray Castle
Inveraray (01499 302203). **Open** *Apr-June, Sept,
Oct* 10am-1pm, 2-5.45pm Mon-Thur, Sat; 1-5.45pm
Sun; closed Fri; *July, Aug* 10am-5.45pm daily; closed
Nov-Mar. **Admission** £4.50; £2.50-£3.50
concessions; £12 family. **Credit** MC, V.

Kilmartin House
Kilmartin (01546 510278/www.kht.org.uk).
Open 10am-5.30pm daily. **Admission** £3.90;
£1.20-£3.10 concessions; £5.10-£9 family.
Credit AmEx, MC, V.

Where to eat

In Crinan, the **Crinan Hotel** (01546 830261)
serves decent food daily. Bar food can be
had at the **Anchor Hotel** (Harbour Street,
Tarbet (01880 820577) and at the **Tayvallich
Inn** in **Tayvallich** (01546 870282, closed Mon
in winter). The **Waterfront** (1 Railway Pier,
Oban, 01631 563110, closed Jan to mid-Mar)
dishes up Scottish cooking with a
Mediterranean influence.

Where to stay

Decent accommodation choices in the area include **Achnadrish House** on the Isle of Mull (01688 400388, open Mar-Nov and by request), whose rates start at £20. The **Glenrigh Guest House** (Corran Esplanade, 01631 562991, Oban) is a similarly priced option. Also try the **Argyll Hotel**, Front Street, Inveraray (01499 302466), with single rooms from £40-£55, and doubles from £64. On the Isle of Islay, **Glenmachrie** (Port Ellen, 01496 302560) has single rooms from £40 and doubles from £60. The **Gallery of Lorne Inn** (01852 500284, Adfern, single rooms £35-£45, doubles £70-£90) overlooks Loch Craignish.

Getting there

By bus

Buses depart St Andrew Square, Edinburgh, for Oban.

By car

Take the M8 to Glasgow, then the A82 to Arrochar. To head south take the A83. North to Oban take the A82 then A85.

By train

Trains depart Glasgow's Central Station for Oban.

Tourist Information

There's an office at **Bowmore**, Isle of Islay (01496 810254). There's also a tourist information centre at Craignure on the **Isle of Mull** (01680 812377), **Inveraray** (Front Street,01499 302063) and **Oban** (Argyll Square, 01631 563122). All of the offices are open year-round.

Ayrshire

The major lure of Ayrshire is Robert Burns. Courtesy of the Rabbie Burns Heritage Trail, you can follow in the poet's footsteps and, if you have the head for it, echo his drinking habits. From celebratory monuments to pubs in which he drank and locations that inspired him, such a tour will get you to some of Ayrshire's brightest spots even if you're not a great fan of Scotland's bard.

For 'Burns Country' head south. The overspill of industrialisation has marked the north, leaving it a little short on glamour. From Ardrossan, south-west of Glasgow, the 20-mile long **Isle of Arran** is only an hour's ferry ride. Robert the Bruce stopped off there en route to Turnberry and the Wars of Independence in 1306 and it has attracted tourists almost ever since. Nowadays it's **Brodick Castle**, in its award-winning estate, that brings them here.

They also come to enjoy the great outdoors – which is conveniently accessible. From Arran's highest peak, **Goat Fell** (2,868 feet) you get fine views of the slender peninsula of Kintyre.

The mainland coastal route south from Kilmarnock goes via the happy-go-lucky resort of **Troon**. Busy **Ayr** has a somewhat forlorn seafront. At **Prestwick**, Elvis took his only steps on British soil, stopping off at the airport en route to sing to the US forces in Germany. **Alloway** is where Burns was born, in **Burns' Cottage**, in 1759. There's a Grecian-style Burns Monument and the **Brig O'Doon**, spanning the River Doon, is the setting for his *Tam O'Shanter*.

Further south beyond Maybole is **Culzean Castle**, Robert Adam's famed 18th-century castle perched on cliffs above the Firth of Clyde. Inland, past Dalmellington, there is more mountainous landscape. **Loch Doon**, on the fringes of The Glenkens, is positively scenic.

Brodick Castle & Country Park

Isle of Arran (01770 302202). Ferries depart Ardrossan and Claonig, Kintyre; for times call 01475 650100. **Open** *Apr-June, Sept, Oct* 11am-4.30pm daily; *July, Aug* 11am-5pm daily. *Grounds* 9.30am-sunset daily. **Admission** £6; £4 concessions; *grounds* £2.50; £1.70 concessions. **Credit** MC, V.

Burns' Cottage

Alloway (01292 441215). **Open** *Apr-Oct* 9am-6pm daily; *Nov-Mar* 10am-4pm Mon-Sat; noon-4pm Sun. **Admission** £4.25; £2 concessions. **No credit cards.**

Culzean Castle & Country Park

nr Maybole on A719 (01655 884455). **Open** *Apr-Oct* 10.30am-5.30pm daily; closed Nov-Mar. *Grounds* 9.30am-sunset daily. **Admission** £7; £5 concessions; *grounds* £3.50; £2.50 concessions. **Credit** MC, V.

Where to eat

Nardini's (Esplanade, Largs, 01475 674555, open daily) is a famed café serving, some say, the best ices in Scotland and much more in its art deco lounge. The **Kinloch Hotel**, Blackwaterfoot, Isle of Arran (01770 860444) is also open daily for food. In Troon, the **Marine Hotel** (Crosbie Road, 01292 314444) offers lunch and dinner every day, and has views out onto Troon's famous golf course.

Where to stay

In Ayr, **Abbotsford Hotel** (14 Corsehill Road, 01292 261506) offers single and double rooms, starting at £35. **Strathwhillan House,** Brodick, Arran (01770 302331) has decent rooms for £16 (single) and £32-£50 (double). The **Arran Glen Cloy Farm Guesthouse**, Brodick (01770 302351) has singles and doubles from £22.

Trips Out of Town

Getting there

By bus
Buses for Ayrshire depart from Buchanan Street Bus Station, Glasgow.

By car
Take the M8 to Glasgow then the M77/A77 to Ayr.

By train
Trains leave from Central Station, Glasgow for Ayr, Irvine, Troon and Ardrossan.

Tourist information

Brodick, on the Isle of Arran, has a year-round tourist information office on the pier (01770 302140). **Kilmarnock**'s office (62 Bank Street, 01563 539090) is open from Easter to October.

Dumfries & Galloway

Dumfries & Galloway lends itself to easy definition. A horizontal finger of land, it briefly touches England in the south-east, but most of its southern and western edges border the coast. The finger-like south-westerly peninsular is less than 25 miles from Ireland. To the north lies Ayrshire and Southern Uplands. This makes for a place that you rarely head through – save to Stranraer, the ferry port for Ireland. But if it is off the tourist track, the area hardly wants for history, scenery or sites.

The east is busiest. **Dumfries** is a bustling and not exactly beautiful town, famed for being the home of Rabbie Burns for five years until his death in 1796. It is really only worth a visit to do the Burns trail and take in **Burns' House** or the **Robert Burns Centre**. The west is quieter and the landscape unfolds. Part bogland, part mountainous, part covered in trees by, in particular Galloway Forest, an air of independence hangs over Galloway which, incidentally, means 'land of the strange Gaels'. In the Middle Ages it was reluctant to forge an alliance with the Scottish crown, and was governed instead by powerful local families. In the 17th century, many Gallovians were Covenanters who were martyred defending their religious rights.

Christianity has strong roots here. In the late fourth century, St Ninian, a Galloway man, returned from Rome and introduced Christianity to Scotland, building a small church at **Whithorn** in the very south. **St Ninian's Priory**, built in the 12th century, stands near the site of St Ninian's earlier church, which was known as Candida Casa.

To the north there is good walking to be had. **Merrick** and the **Rhinns of Kells**, north of Newton Stewart, offer good and usually quiet walks for both the serious hillwalker and the more casual saunterer.

Burns' House
Burns Street, Dumfries (01387 255297). **Open** *Apr-Sept* 10am-5pm Mon-Sat; 2-5pm Sun; *Oct-Mar* 10am-5pm Tue-Sat; closed Sun. **Admission** free.

Robert Burns Centre
Mill Road, Dumfries (01387 264808). **Open** *Apr-Sept* 10am-8pm Mon-Sat; 2-5pm Sun; *Oct-Mar* 10am-1pm, 2-5pm Tue-Sat; closed Sun. **Admission** free; *audio-visual display* £1.20; 60p concessions.

Where to eat

In Dumfries, the **Globe Inn**, High Street (01387 252335) is open daily for breakfast and lunch, and also for dinner in summer. A former drinking hole of Burns, it is now stuffed with memorabilia. On the Isle of Whithorn, the **Steam Packet** on the harbour (01988 500334) is open daily. Also worth a visit is the **Selkirk Arms** (Old High Street, Kirkcudbright, 01557 330402, open daily).

Where to stay

Comlongon Castle, Clarencefield, near Dumfries, (01387 870283, closed Jan) has single rooms for £45 and doubles from £100. The **Anchor Hotel** (Kippford, 01556 620205) has singles for £24 and doubles for £52. Overlooking the River Ur in Kirkcudbright is a townhouse B&B (3 High Street, 01557 3307851), with single rooms (£30) and doubles (£50). The **Moffat House Hotel** (The Square, Moffat, 01683 220039) has singles for £57 and doubles for £88. And in Whithorn, **Belmont** (St John Street, 01988 500890) has singles for £18; doubles £40.

Getting there

By bus
Buses leave for Dumfries from St Andrew Square.

By car
Take the A702 out of Edinburgh, to the M74 southbound. Follow signs for Dumfries.

By train
There are no direct trains from Edinburgh. Trains leave from Glasgow for Dumfries and Stranraer.

Tourist information

Dumfries has a year-round tourist information centre at 64 Whitesands (01387 253862). **Kirkcudbright**'s office is at Harbour Square (01557 330494) and is open from Easter to October, as is **Moffat**'s at Churchgate (01683 220620).

Directory

Feature boxes

Directory

Getting Around

By air

Edinburgh Airport

EH12 (333 1000). About 10 miles (16km) west of the city centre, north of Glasgow Road.
Edinburgh Airport is about 20 minutes' drive from Princes Street. The airport services flights from the Continent and English airports. Flights also leave Edinburgh for the north and Highlands and Islands of Scotland. The cheapest way to travel to and from the airport is by the dedicated **Airline 100** bus service (*see below*). The quickest way to travel from the airport, on the other hand, is by **Edinburgh Airport Taxis** (344 3344). The service covers every flight in and out of the airport (from approximately 5am-11pm); journey time is 15-20 minutes, although this rises to 30 minutes during rush hours (7.30-9.30am and 4.30-7pm Mon-Fri). The fare is about £12-£14, depending on the time of day and the number of passengers. All taxis in the city have one seat adapted for disabled passengers (*see also p274*).

Airline 100

555 6363
These blue and white buses stop at Gogarburn, Maybury, Corstorphine, Edinburgh Zoo, Murrayfield and the West End. Buses leave the airport 5.30am-midnight daily; the service from Waverley Bridge runs 6am-10pm Mon-Fri; 6.45am-10pm Sat, Sun. Buses are double-deckers with ample luggage space. Collapsible wheelchairs can be carried but, due to union regulations, staff are unable to physically assist disabled customers (for safety reasons). Tickets cost £3.30 adult (£2 5s-15s) one way; £5 adult (£3 child) day return; free under-5s; Airline Day Saver £4.20 adult (£2.65 child) allows one journey to or from the airport and unlimited travel for the whole day on the **Lothian Regional Transport** (LRT) bus network (*see p273*).

By bus/coach

St Andrew Square Bus Station

Clyde Street, New Town, EH1. Bus 8, 12, 16, 17, 25, 25A. **Map** p314 D1/p306 F4.
Coaches arriving in Edinburgh from England and Wales are run by Britain's most extensive coach network, **National Express** (0990 808080). Coaches serving the whole of Scotland are run by **Scottish Citylink** (0990 505050). **St Andrew Bus Station**, in the city centre, closed in May 2000 to be redeveloped as a new bus station and upmarket retail unit. Reopening is planned for late 2003. Until then buses to Glasgow and Fife and long-distance bus services have been relocated to the south side of St Andrew Square, while East Lothian buses are running from Waterloo Place.

By train

Haymarket Station

Haymarket, West Edinburgh, EH12 (train information 0345 484950). Bus 3, 3A, 12, 25. **Map** p308 B6.
On the main line to Glasgow. Most trains travelling north and west from Waverley stop here, as do local services to West Lothian.

Waverley Station

Waverley Bridge, New Town, EH1 (train information 0345 484950). Bus 3, 12, 16, 17, 80. **Map** p314 D2.
Edinburgh's central railway station serves the East Coast main lines to London and Aberdeen. Scotrail services leave for destinations throughout Scotland, including a shuttle service to Glasgow and connections to the West Coast. Local services go to East and West Lothian.

Getting around Edinburgh

Edinburgh is best explored on foot to fully appreciate the beauty, elegance, charm and contrasts of the city centre and its environs. Walking around Edinburgh is safe and can provide a rewarding experience, but do exercise the usual caution at night (*see page 289*). Individuals with a nervous disposition should avoid the areas of the city with abundant and rowdy nightlife such as Lothian Road and the Cowgate. A useful way to orient yourself and get an overview of the major tourist sights is on one of the guided bus tours (*see page36*) or themed walking tours (*see page 52* **Witches & wynds**).

Getting around the centre of Edinburgh by bus is reasonably fast and reliable. Driving can be more hassle than it's worth, especially as city-centre parking can prove problematic. Taxis are numerous, if rather pricey. Cycling, on the other hand, is a fast and efficient way of getting around, both in the city centre and further afield (*see page 275* **Wheel life**).

The City of Edinburgh Council's **Greenways** scheme, introduced in 1997, has made public transport more efficient in the city centre. All the major routes into the city centre are covered by the scheme: Greenways road lanes are painted green with red road markings. Signs at the roadside show when and where stopping is permitted; buses, licensed taxis and cycles all have unrestricted access to green lanes at all times; private vehicles have restricted access during rush hours and at peak times.

Public transport

Buses

Edinburgh has extensive bus networks that give ready access to most of the city day and night. The City of Edinburgh Council runs a free 24-hour telephone enquiry line, Traveline, on 0800 232323. The ubiquitous maroon and white buses are run by Lothian Regional Transport (LRT), which has a seven-day telephone Enquiry Line, on 555 6363 (local calls). **LRT Travelshops** provide free maps and details of all local public transport services in Lothian.

Throughout this guide, we have listed LRT buses only. As some parts of town, such as Princes Street, are served by as many as 20 different routes, we have kept the number listed for each sight to a minimum. Routes have been chosen for their frequency and area covered.

Edinburgh's other main bus company is **FirstBus**, which incorporates SMT, Eastern Scottish, Lowland Omnibuses and Midland Scottish. For information call 663 9233.

LRT Travelshops

27 Hanover Street, New Town, EH2 (554 4494). Bus 23, 27, 45. **Open** 8.30am-6pm Mon-Sat; closed Sun. **Map** p314 C1.
Waverley Bridge. Bus 3, 12, 16, 17. **Open** *Apr-Oct* 8am-7.15pm Mon-Sat; 9am-4.30pm Sun; *Nov-Mar* 9am-4.30pm Tue-Sat. **Map** p314 D2.

Night buses

Night buses run seven days a week from about midnight-4am Mon-Thur, Sun nights and midnight-3am Fri, Sat. There is a flat fare of £1.60 which allows one transfer to be made to another night service at Waverley Bridge, on production of a valid ticket. A free map and timetable can be picked up at LRT Travelshops.

Scotrail

Most rail services in Scotland are run by **Scotrail**. Details of services and fares are available from National Rail Enquiry Scheme (0345 484950, 24 hours daily). The information desk in Waverley Station (*see page 272*) has timetables and details of discount travel, season tickets and international travel.

Fares & travelcards

Bus fares are based on a stage system; fare stages are listed on individual service timetables. Bus drivers don't give change, so ensure you have the correct fare before boarding. There is no on-the-spot fine for travelling without a valid ticket or pass but action may be taken later.

Prices, offers and concessions are subject to change so contact an LRT Travelshop for information.

Adult fares

Single journey tickets start from 50p (1-2 stages). Travelling 3-8 stages, which will get you across the city centre, costs 80p; 9-13 stages 90p; 14- or more stages £1. A Day Saver multiple journey ticket, purchased from the driver of the first bus you board, costs £2.20 and allows unlimited travel around the LRT network for a day. An off-peak Bargain Day Saver costs £1.40 and is valid after 9.30am on weekdays and all day at weekends.

Child fares

Children under five travel free (up to a maximum of two children per adult passenger). Children's fares are charged for ages 5 to 15 inclusive. Photo ID cards, if desired, can be purchased for £1 from the LRT Travelshop at 27 Hanover Street upon production of a birth certificate. Child fares are a flat fare of 50p per journey. A Child Day Saver ticket is £1.50 and a Bargain Day Saver is 70p.

Ridacard

The Ridacard gives unlimited travel on ordinary LRT services but is not valid on night buses, services to special events, Airline 100 buses or tours. For adults, a 1-week Ridacard costs £10.50, 2 weeks £21, 4 weeks £30; Junior Ridacards (ages 5-15 inclusive) are 1-week £6.50, 2 weeks £13, 4 weeks £18. You can buy Ridacards at LRT Travelshops (you need a passport-sized photo to do so).

Touristcard

A Touristcard is more flexible for the visitor to Edinburgh than the Ridacard. In addition to unlimited travel on all LRT city bus services, including the Edinburgh Classic Tour (*see p36*), the Touristcard offers reductions on LRT coach tours and discounts on city restaurants and tourist attractions. The prices of Touristcards are: for 2 days £13 (£7 child), 3 days £15 (£8.50), 4 days £17 (£10), 5 days £19 (£11.50), 6 days £21 (£13), 7 days £23 (£14.50).

Tokens

LRT Travelshops sell travel tokens in denominations of 10p, 25p, 30p and 50p. If a Day Saver, Ridacard or Touristcard is not financially worthwhile, tokens can avoid the need to search for change.

Sightseeing tours

See page 36.

Taxis

Black cabs

Edinburgh's licensed taxis are black cabs. When a taxi's yellow For Hire light is on, you can stop it in the street. Many taxi companies will take credit cards, but check when you book or get in. Taxis can be found in the *Yellow Pages*; larger companies with facilities for the disabled traveller and a 24-hour service are **Capital Castle Taxis** (228 2555), **Central Radio Taxis** (229 2468), **City Cabs** (228 1211) and **Radio Cabs** (225 9000).

Minicabs

Minicabs (saloon cars) are generally cheaper than black cabs, but the drivers are unlicensed and may be uninsured; minicabs are not permitted to use the Greenways routes. Private-hire companies with facilities for disabled passengers include **Bluebird Private Hire** (467

Directory

7770), **Dunedin Private Hire** (229 6661) and **Persevere Private Hire** (555 3377/553 7711). It's a good idea to call round first to get the best price.

Complaints or compliments about a taxicab or private hire company journey can be made to The Cab Inspector, The Cab Office, 33 Murrayburn Road, Wester Hailes, Edinburgh, EH14 2TF (529 5800). Make a note of the date and time of the journey and the licence number of the vehicle.

Driving

In conjunction with the Greenways Scheme (*see page 272*), a system of one-way streets and pedestrian-only areas is being introduced into the city centre. This will no doubt make driving in the centre more frustrating. As it is, driving in Edinburgh is often a time-consuming, difficult business. Princes Street has limited access for private vehicles and is best avoided if possible; a knock-on effect of this is that the surrounding roads are becoming increasingly busy: slow-moving traffic is the norm, especially during rush hours (7.30-9.30am, 4.30-7pm Mon-Fri). In addition to overcrowded roads and traffic jams you will find stringent parking restrictions, and the whole driving process could well leave you feeling harassed and frustrated. If you park illegally, you will probably get a £40 parking ticket (£20 if it is paid within a fortnight); if your car is causing an obstruction, it may be towed away and impounded (*see below*). The good news is that in Scotland the clamping of vehicles has been ruled illegal; don't let that lull you into a false sense of security, however, as zealous traffic wardens patrol the city centre.

Vehicle removal

If your car has been impounded, a fee of £105 is levied for removal, plus a £12 storage fee for every day the vehicle remains uncollected. This is in addition to the £40 parking ticket. Impounded cars are taken to the **Edinburgh Car Compound**, which keeps a log of all impounded cars. If your car has been stolen you should report it at once to the police.

Edinburgh Car Compound
14-16 Beaverhall Road, Broughton, EH7 (557 5244). Bus 8, 23, 27. **Open** 7am-8pm Mon-Wed; 7am-11pm Thur-Sat; 9am-11am Sun. **Credit** MC V. **Map** p306 F2.

24-hour car parks

Greenside Car Park
Greenside Row, Broughton, EH1 (558 3518). **Map** p307 G4.

National Car Parks
Castle Terrace, South Edinburgh, EH1 (229 2870). **Map** p314 A3.

St James Centre
Leith Street, New Town, EH1 (556 5066). **Map** p307 G4.

Breakdown services

If you are a member of a motoring organisation in your home country, check to see if it has a reciprocal agreement with a British organisation.

AA (Automobile Association)
Fanum House, Upper Ground Street, Basingstoke, Hampshire RG21 (enquiries 0990 444444/breakdown 0800 887766/insurance 0800 444777/new membership 0800 919595). **Open** 24 hours daily. **Credit** MC, V.
You can call the AA if you break down and become a member on the spot for £123. The first year's roadside service membership starts at £40. Its information line (0990 500600) gives information on International Driving Permits, route maps, Roadwatch and Weatherwatch.

Environmental Transport Association
Freepost KT 4021, Weybridge, Surrey, KT13 8RS (0193 282 8882). **Open** *Office* 8am-6pm Mon-Fri; 9am-4pm Sat; closed Sun. *Breakdown service* 24hrs daily. **Credit** MC, V.
The green alternative, if you don't want part of your membership fees to be used for lobbying the government into building more roads, as happens with the AA and RAC. Basic membership is £20 per year for individuals and £25 for families.

RAC
Great Park Road, Bristol, BS12 4QN (enquiries 0990 722722/breakdown 0800 828282/motor insurance 0800 678000/new membership 0800 550550/www.rac.co.uk). **Open** *Office* 9am-5pm Mon-Fri; closed Sat, Sun. *Breakdown service* 24hrs daily. **Credit** AmEx, MC, V.
Membership costs from £39 to £130, plus £75 for European cover.

Disabled travellers

For travellers with mobility difficulties, Edinburgh City Council publishes the booklet *Transport in Edinburgh: A Guide for Disabled People*. This gives information on transport accessibility and services and assistance available to disabled people; it also includes a list of useful contact addresses and phone numbers. The booklet can be picked up free of charge from **Lothian Regional Transport Travelshops** (*see page 273*) or requested from Traveline on 0800 232323 (free calls) or 225 3858 (local calls). In addition, the **Lothian Coalition of Disabled People**, Norton Park, Albion Road, EH6 (475 2360/fax 475 2392) may be able to give information and advice. Lothian Regional Transport is replacing all its buses with low-floor versions, but currently the only routes with a reliable low-floor service are the Nos.44 and 26 along Princes Street. Black cabs can take wheelchairs and the minicabs listed below have facilities for disabled passengers.

Transport hire

Bicycles

See below **Wheel life**.

Cars

To hire a car you must have at least one years driving experience and be in possession of a current full driving licence with no serious endorsements. Overseas visitors, particularly those whose national driving licence is not readily readable by English speakers, are recommended to acquire an International Driving Licence before travel.

Prices for car hire vary considerably between companies, and may be subject to change, so ring round to find the deal that suits you best. A few of the more reputable companies are given on page 276. Be sure to check exactly what insurance is included in the price. Also ask about special deals when booking.

Wheel life

Do not be put off by Edinburgh hills: it is a great place to cycle around, thanks to some successful lobbying by the local cycle campaign, **Spokes** (232 Dalry Road, EH11, 313 2114/ www.spokes.org.uk). The city council has invested wisely in both off-road cycle paths and road-edge cycle lanes. Although it is not compulsory for motorists to observe the latter, the lanes ease the flow of cyclists during rush hours and make some of the more tricky roads safer. Cyclists can travel freely along all the bus lanes – including Princes Street.

Admittedly, some of the hills are a bit strenuous – but it is quite acceptable to walk up them – and the strong winds in winter can make exposed spots like North Bridge rather treacherous. Be sensible when tethering a bike in the street: the Grassmarket, Rose Street and other pub-infested areas are prone to bouts of drunken vandalism and, as everywhere, theft is a problem. Otherwise, the only real worries for those cyclists not on mountain bikes are the cobbled streets around the New Town, which can give buttocks a bit of a buffeting.

The joy of cycling in Edinburgh is that you can fly from one side of town to the other in minutes – even when the streets are blocked during the Festival. A bike also makes areas outside the city centre remarkably accessible. Spokes produces three cycle maps which show all the cycle routes and cycle paths for Edinburgh, Midlothian and West Lothian respectively; the maps cost £4.95 each and are available from Spokes or from bike shops. There are good paths out to Cramond from Roseburn, out towards East Lothian, starting at the Innocent Cycle Path in Holyrood Park, and a bike is the perfect way to explore the Water of Leith walkway.

BikeTrax Cycle Hire

11 Lochrin Place, South Edinburgh, EH3 (228 6333/ www.biketrax.co.uk). Bus 11, 16, 17, 23. **Open** May-Oct 9.30am-6pm Mon-Sat, noon-5pm Sun; Nov-Apr 9.30am-5.30pm Mon-Sat; closed Sun. **Hire** £10 first day; £20 second day; £50 seven days. **Deposit** £100 per bike. **Credit** V, MC. **Map** p309 D7. A wide range of cycles, helmets, child seats, trailers, car racks; maps and guides for sale.

Edinburgh Bicycle Co-operative

8 Alvanley Terrace, Whitehouse Loan, South Edinburgh, EH9 (228 1368/www.edinburgh-bicycle.co.uk). Bus 11, 16, 17. **Open** summer 10am-7pm Mon-Fri; 10am-6pm Sat, Sun; winter 10am-6pm Mon-Wed, Fri-Sun; 10am-7pm Thur. **Credit** AmEx, DC. MC, V. **Map** p309 D8. Extensive equipment and own-brand bikes for sale. Friendly, helpful staff. Repair service.

Edinburgh Cycle Hire

29 Blackfriars Street, Royal Mile, EH1 (556 5560/ www.cyclescotland.co.uk). Bus 35, 35A. **Open** May-Oct 9am-9pm daily; Nov-Apr 10am-6pm daily. **Hire** from £10 first day; weekly rates and discounts available. **Deposit** £100 per bike. **Credit** AmEx, DC, MC, V (for deposit); cash/ cheque preferred for rental. **Map** p310 G5. Mountain bikes, road bikes, city tourers and tandems are all available – with helmets and locks included as standard – plus panniers, trailers and lightweight tents. Anatomically-designed gel saddles can be fitted to all bikes. In addition to renting you the pedal-power, staff can also sell you maps, suggest routes and offer a range of day excursions and longer tour-packages to suit all pockets.

Directory

Arnold Clark
553 Gorgie Road, West Edinburgh, EH11 (444 1852). **Open** 8am-8pm Mon-Fri; 8am-5pm Sat; 11am-5pm Sun. **Credit** AmEx, DC, MC, V.

A full range of vehicles is available for hire. One-way rates upon request; corporate accounts; free courtesy coach to and from Edinburgh Airport (from Bankhead Ave branch only). Cheapest rental rates are £16 per day; £39 weekend; £80 seven days. You must be aged between 23 and 75 to hire here; a deposit of £100 is required.
Branches: 64 Craigentinny North Avenue, EH6 (553 3323); 16 Bankhead Drive, EH11 (458 1501); Lochrin Place, EH3 (228 4747)

Hertz
Edinburgh Airport, EH12 (333 1019/central reservations 0990 996 699). **Open** *Phone line* 24hrs daily. *Office* 7am-10.30pm daily. **Credit** AmEx, DC, MC, V.

A wide range of manual and automatic vehicles; corporate accounts; one-way rates; collection and delivery. Cheapest rental, all inclusive, is £41.73 per day; £59.36 weekend; £201 seven days. You must be 25 or over.
Branches: 10 Picardy Place, EH1 (556 8311/8312); Waverley Station, EH1 (557 5272).

National Car Rental
Edinburgh Airport (333 1922/central reservations 0990 365365). **Open** *Phone line* 24hrs daily. *Office* 6.45am-10pm Mon-Fri; 8am-10pm Sat, Sun. **Credit** AmEx, DC, MC, V.

A wide range of manual and automatic vehicles, one-way rates and a delivery and collection service. The cheapest rental, all inclusive, is £32.66 per day; £53.35 weekend; £135 seven days. To hire, you must be 21 years of age or more.

Motorbikes

Alvins
9B Springfield Street (off Leith Walk), Leith, EH6 (555 1636). **Open** 9am-5.30pm Mon-Fri; 9am-5pm Sat; closed Sun. **Credit** MC, V. **Map** p307 H1.

You will need a full driving licence, and you must be aged 25 or over to hire from here. Hire rates are inclusive of VAT, insurance and breakdown recovery service. Waterproofs and luggage may be hired, but you will need to purchase or bring your own helmet. Other services offered here are bike sales, parts and accessories and a workshop. Sample hire rates are: GS 500 Suzuki £55 per day (aged 30 and over), £65 per day (25-29 years); RG 900 Suzuki £80 per day (30 years and over), £90 per day (25-29 years). Harley-Davidson rates on request. There's a non-refundable deposit of £50 upon booking; £350 refundable credit card deposit on collection.

Left luggage

Edinburgh Airport
344 3486. **Open** 6am-10pm daily. Located outside the main terminal building, opposite parking zone E.

St Andrew Bus Station
There was no information available at the time of going to press on where left luggage will be relocated while the bus station is closed.

Waverley Train Station
550 2711. **Open** 24 hrs daily. Adjacent to Platform 11.

Lost property

Always inform the nearest police station if you lose anything (to validate insurance claims). A lost passport should also be reported to your embassy or consul (*see page 278*). The main lost property offices for items left on public transport are listed below.

Airport

Edinburgh Airport
344 3486. **Open** 6am-10pm daily. The lost property office is located outside the main terminal building, opposite parking zone E. For items lost on the plane, contact the airline or handling agents.

Bus

Lothian Region Transport
Lost Property Office, 1-4 Shrub Place (Leith Walk opposite Albert Street), Leith, EH6 (554 4492). Bus 7, 12, 16. **Open** 10am-1.30pm Mon-Fri; closed Sat, Sun. **Map** p307 H2.

Taxis

Edinburgh Police Headquarters
Fettes Avenue, Stockbridge, EH4 (311 3141). Bus 28, 29, 80. **Open** 8am-5pm Mon-Fri; closed Sat, Sun. **Map** p305 A3.

All property that has been lost in a registered black cab, as well as in the street or in shops, gets sent here.

Train stations

If items have been lost in railway stations or trains in Scotland, contact the individual station (see the phone book for numbers).

Resources A-Z

Information

Edinburgh Chamber of Commerce & Enterprise
152 Morrison Street, West Edinburgh, EH3 8EB (477 7000/fax 477 7002/www.ecce.org). Bus 2, 28. **Open** 9am-5pm Mon-Fri; closed Sat, Sun. **Map** p308 C6.

One of the fastest-growing Chambers in the United Kingdom, with international trade near the top of its agenda.

Lothian & Edinburgh Enterprise Ltd
Apex House, 99 Haymarket Terrace, West Edinburgh, EH12 5HD (313 4000/fax 313 6120/www.leel.co.uk). Bus 3, 3A, 21, 25. **Open** 9am-5pm Mon-Fri; closed Sat, Sun. **Map** p308 B6.

A government-funded economic development, training and environmental improvement agency with responsibility for the Lothians (which include Edinburgh).

Scottish Executive
St Andrew's House, Regent Road, Calton Hill, EH1 3DG (556 8400/www.scotland.gov.uk). Bus 3, 12, 16, 17. **Open** 8.30am-5pm Mon-Fri; closed Sat, Sun. **Map** p307 G4.

This is a good starting point from which to reach the relevant department, such as Enterprise & Tourism or Economic & Industrial Affairs.

Moonlighting at **Murrayfield** golf course. *See page 216.*

Cyclists' Union (652 0187/
www.btinternet.com/~scottish.cycling),
which can advise on all the cycling sports,
from mountain biking to track disciplines.

Football

The Scottish football season runs from
August to May with three main domestic
competitions: the League, the Cup and the
League Cup. The two professional football
clubs in Edinburgh, **Heart of Midlothian**,
to the west of Edinburgh, and **Hibernian**,
to the east of the city centre, have both
been perennial underachievers. The Glasgow
clubs, **Celtic** and **Rangers** (collectively
known as the Old Firm), soak up the lion's
share of the trophies. There isn't nearly
the same money swilling around the
Edinburgh pair as there is around the Old
Firm and, equally, not the same poisonous
rivalry. The new-look Scottish Premier
League has brought all-seater stadia and a
decline in the sectarian bigotry that is
associated with the Old Firm – a combination
that is encouraging more families to attend

matches. Most games are pay-at-the-turnstile,
but it is advisable to phone and confirm first.
Old Firm games and local derbies are likely
to be all-ticket. There is a flourishing
amateur and semi-professional scene
throughout the city and the women's game
is growing steadily. It is easy to get a
kickabout on the grass any weekend; the
Meadows on a Sunday afternoon is the best
bet, but the area in Holyrood Park near
Holyroodhouse and overlooked by Arthur's
Seat is the most spectacular setting.

Heart of Midlothian FC

*Tynecastle Park, Gorgie Road, West Edinburgh,
EH11 (200 7200/shop 200 7211/tickets 200 7209/
www.hearts.co.uk). Bus 3, 3A, 21, 25, 25A.* **Open**
shop 9.30am-5.30pm Mon-Fri; 9.30am-3pm
matchdays. **Tickets** £16-£18; £8-£9 concessions.
Credit MC, V.

Hibernian FC

*Easter Road Stadium, Albion Place, Abbeyhill,
EH7 (661 2159/shop 656 7078/www.hibs.co.uk).
Bus 35, 35A.* **Open** *shop* 9am-5pm Tue-Fri;
9.30am-3pm, 4.45pm-5.15pm matchdays.
Tickets £13-£18; £8 concessions. **Credit**
AmEx, MC, V. **Map** p307 J2.

Footie fun in **Holyrood Park**. *See page 215.*

Golf

Scotland is a great place for golf and Edinburgh has numerous courses both within and outside the city boundary. **St Andrews**, the home of the game's governing body, the Royal and Ancient, and venue for the 2000 Open, is an hour-and-a-half's drive away. Some of the finest links courses in the world are along the coast in East Lothian, including **Muirfield**, a regular venue for the Open. Nearer the city, **Musselburgh Links** has hosted some of the first Open championships and Mary, Queen of Scots is said to have 'hit a golf ball' there as early as 1567. Golf is very much a people's game in Scotland. While there are a few snooty clubs, the majority welcome visitors with open arms. But don't turn up to a course and expect to play straightaway as demand often outstrips supply – so make sure you book in advance.

The **Edinburgh & Lothians Tourist Board** offers a discount pass (a seven-day pass costs £5, giving an average discount £3-£5 per course; phone for details on 473 3800 or check out the website at www.edinburgh.org) for the single-minded golfer hoping to cram in as many rounds at as many courses as possible.

Braids

Braid Hills Approach Road, South Edinburgh, EH10 (447 6666). Bus 11, 15. **Open** dawn-dusk daily. **Green fee** £9.20-£11 per round. **Club hire** £10.70; £10 deposit. **No credit cards**.
Not one but two municipal courses. Braids One is among the best in south-east Scotland, with great holes and a superb view.

Gullane

West Links Road, Gullane, East Lothian, EH31 (01620 842255). Bus SMT 124. **Open** dawn-dusk daily. **Green fee** £16-£72 per round; £25-£87 per day. **Club hire** £20 per round. **Credit** AmEx, MC, V.
Three courses (though access by the public to Gullane One is limited) and, no matter what time of year, the greens are always in excellent condition. The third course is the shortest, but the fairways are narrower. A beer at the nearby Old Clubhouse makes a pleasant end to the day.

Lothianburn

Biggar Road, Hillend, South Edinburgh, EH10 (445 2288) Bus 4. **Open** dawn-dusk daily. **Green fee** *midweek* £14 per round; £22 per day; *weekend* £22 per round; £27 per day. **Club hire** £10. **Credit** MC, V.
A hillside course, again affording great views of the city. One of the cheaper private courses to play.

Mortonhall

Braid Road, South Edinburgh, EH10 (447 5185). Bus 11, 15. **Open** dawn-dusk daily. **Green fee** £30 per round; £40 per day. **Club hire** by prior arrangement. **Credit** V.
A private course in the Braid hills.

Muirfield

The Honourable Company of Edinburgh Golfers, Muirfield, Gullane, EH31 (01620 842123). Bus SMT 124. **Open** to visitors dawn-dusk Tue, Thur. **Green fee** £80 per round; £105 per day.
Book six months in advance (one year for summer) to play this prestigious course. There's a minimum handicap to play: 18 (men), 24 (women).

Murrayfield

43 Murrayfield Road, EH12 (337 3479). Bus 13. **Open** dawn-dusk Mon-Fri (last tee-off 4.30pm). **Green fee** £30 per round; £35 per day. **Club hire** £14. **No credit cards**.
The sixth hole is the best for views of the city. Closed to visitors at weekends.

Musselburgh Links

Balcarres Road, Musselburgh, EH21 (665 5438). Bus 26, 44. **Open** dawn-dusk daily. **Green fee** £7.50; £4 concessions. **No club hire. No credit cards**.
Historic nine holes in the middle of the racecourse. You can travel back in time by hiring a set of hickory clubs and guttie balls for £28.

St Andrews

West Sands Road, St Andrews, Fife, KY16 (01334 466666/www.standrews.org.uk). **Green fee** in high season (after 1 Apr) £17-£80.
Europe's biggest golf complex, with six courses – Old, New, Jubilee, Eden, Strathtyrum and Balgrove (nine holes). There are also two non-members clubhouses and a driving range. You can book a day ahead for the Jubilee, Eden and Strathtyrum courses; at the New and Balgrove courses it is first come-first served (fitting in with tee times booked in advance). A ballot is available for tee times on the Old course – phone by 2pm the day before (or Saturday if for Monday). Otherwise, reserve at least six months ahead. For Old and New courses the minimum handicap required is 24 (men) and 36 (women).

Driving ranges

Braid Hills

Liberton Drive, South Edinburgh, EH16 (658 1111/ www.braidhillsgolf.co.uk). Bus 31. **Open** 10am-9pm Mon-Fri; 9am-6pm Sat, 10am-6pm Sun. **Cost** £2.50 per 50 balls. **Credit** MC, V.

Port Royal

Eastfield Road, Ingliston, Edinburgh Airport, EH28 (333 4377). Bus 100. **Open** 10am-9pm daily; *winter* closes 6pm Fri-Sun. **Cost** £2 per basket of 45 balls; pitch & putt £4; £3 concessions.

Gyms & fitness centres

Body Talk Health & Fitness Centre

7-9 Ponton Street, West Edinburgh, EH3 (228 2426). Bus 11, 16, 17, 23 . **Open** 7am-10pm Mon-Fri; 9am-6pm Sat, Sun. **Admission** £3.75; membership from £25 per month. **Credit** MC, V. **Map** p309 D7.
The centre has a gym, a beauty room and sunbeds.
Branch: 54A Fountainbridge, West Edinburgh, EH3 (228 2426).

Esporta Health & Fitness Club

Fountainpark, 65 Dundee Street, West Edinburgh, EH11 (221 1793/www.esporta.co.uk). Bus 1, 28, 34, 35. **Open** 6.30am-11.30pm Mon-Fri; 8am-10pm Sat, Sun. **Members only**. **Credit** MC, V. **Map** p308 B7.
Esporta has a 25-m pool, sauna, steam rooms, two spa baths, gym, two aerobics studios, spinning studios, children's leisure facilities and a restaurant.

Meadowbank Sports Centre & Stadium

139 London Road, Abbeyhill, EH7 (661 5351). Bus 5, 19, 14, 26, 26A, 45. **Open** 9.30am-10.30pm Mon; 9am-10.30pm Tue-Sun.
Opened for the Commonwealth Games in 1970, this large, council-run centre has facilities for badminton, squash, basketball and football, as well as a velodrome. There are classes for children, adults and the over-50s in everything from archery to martial arts. Phone for more information on rates and classes. Telephone bookings for members only.

Next Generation

Newhaven Harbour, Leith, EH6 (554 5000/ www.nextgenerationclubs.co.uk). Bus 7, 10, 11, 16. **Open** 6.30am-11.30pm daily. **Members & their guests only**. **Credit** MC, V. **Map** p311 Ex.
Squash, badminton, gym, celsius spa, basketball, mini climbing wall, beach volleyball, indoor and outdoor swimming and tennis, crèche and restaurants.

Pleasance Sports Centre

46 Pleasance, South Edinburgh, EH8 (650 2585). Bus 60. **Open** 8.30am-9.30pm Mon-Fri; 8.50am-5.30pm Sat; 9.50am-5.30pm Sun. **Credit** MC, V. **Map** p310 G6.
This facility is attached to the University of Edinburgh, so there is a split in availability: during term time it is open only to members and their guests; during vacations it is open to the public (£4 per session or £137 annual membership).

Horse racing

The sport of kings takes place at five racecourses in Scotland. **Musselburgh** is the closest at six miles (ten kilometres) east of Edinburgh city centre. Further afield, the rural courses of **Perth**, to the north, and **Kelso**, to the south, make a pleasant day out. **Ayr**, on the west coast, stages the bigger races in Scotland, such as the Scottish Grand National. **Hamilton**, meanwhile, is an award winner.

Ayr

2 Whitletts Road, Ayr, KA8 (01292 264179). **Admission** from £7 (stand from £14). **Credit** MC, V.
Scotland's premier course hosts 25 meetings per year. A slightly more expensive Club Badge provides entry to the pleasant Western House at the bottom of the course. The biggest events in the calendar are the Scottish Grand National (April) and the Ladbroke Ayr Gold Cup (September). Telephone prebooking only.

Hamilton

Bothwell Rd, Hamilton, ML3 (01698 283806/ www.hamilton-park.co.uk). **Admission** £8-15. **Credit** MC, V.
Scotland's most urban course hosts about 18 meetings a year, many in the evening, and is known as the 'Royal Ascot of the north'. Advice: dress to thrill. Telephone prebooking only.

Kelso

18-20 Glendale Rd, Wooler (01668 281611). **Admission** £7-£15. **Credit** MC, V.
Wonderful traditions in rural splendour. The Tin Hut bar is no more than a chicken shed, but the locals seem to like it. About 12 meetings per year. The biggest events of the year are the Bank of Scotland Novices Hurdle (March) and the Scottish Borders National (April).

Musselburgh

Linkfield Road, Musselburgh, EH21 (665 2859/ www.musselburgh-racecourse.co.uk). Bus 26, 44.

Admission £7-£12; £4 concessions; free accompanied under-16s. **No credit cards**.
Scotland's oldest racecourse hosts 22 meetings per year, some in the evening, which are well attended. The Pinkie Bar was opened in 1997 by the legendary jockey Lester Piggott. Popular events include the Saints and Sinners charity meet at the end of February and Gold Cup day in June.

Perth
Scone Palace Park, Perth, PH2 (01738 551597/ www.perth-races.co.uk). **Admission** £4-£15. **No credit cards**.
Frequently voted the 'best small racecourse in the north', Perth hosts about ten meetings per year. Enjoy the garden party atmosphere and maybe catch a pre-meet game of polo. The biggest event of the year is the Perth Festival in April.

Ice-skating

Murrayfield Ice Rink
Riversdale Crescent, West Edinburgh, EH12 (337 6933). Bus 3, 3A, 12, 25, 25A. **Open** 2.30-4pm daily; various times for beginners, group tuition. **Admission** (includes skate hire) £3 Mon-Fri; £3.50 Sat, Sun. **No credit cards**.
The rink is home to the Edinburgh Capitals ice hockey team. The unlicensed café is open on Wednesdays, Fridays and at the weekend. Friday and Saturday nights attract a young crowd for the disco skating (7.30-10.30pm; £4.50).

Rock climbing

Meadowbank Sports Centre (*see page 217*) has a wall constructed mainly of brick.

Alien Rock
8 Pier Place, Newhaven, Leith, EH6 (552 7211). Bus 7, 10, 11, 16, 25A. **Open** *summer* noon-10pm Mon-Fri; 10am-7pm Sat, Sun; *winter* noon-11pm Mon-Thur; noon-10pm Fri; 10am-9pm Sat, Sun. **Admission** *peak* £5; *off-peak* (before 4pm Mon-Fri, after 5pm Sat, Sun) £3.50; £2 concessions. **No credit cards**. **Map** p311 Ex.
A 10m-high wall located in a former church. All the necessary equipment is available for hire, including footwear. A two-hour introductory course for novices costs £18, including equipment hire. There is also a café, shop and a bouldering room with a 4m-high wall.

National Rock Climbing Centre of Scotland
Ratho Quarry, West Edinburgh, EH28 (no phone/ www.nrcc.co.uk). **Open** from December 2000.
Once completed, this will be the biggest outdoor pursuits training centre of its kind in Europe, with 2,500m (8,200ft) of indoor surfaces, 5,000m (16,400ft) of outdoor surfaces and a specialist gym for adventure sports. Restaurant, lecture facilities, tuition, guiding service and accommodation also available.

Rugby union

Union is the preferred code of rugby in Scotland. The national team plays at **Murrayfield Stadium**. Tickets are very hard to come by for these games and must be booked well in advance. As a centre of rugby, Edinburgh differs from other parts of the country because its club scene is so closely linked to a group of

Splashing out

Edinburgh boasts a range of excellent swimming pools. Many are a legacy from the city's far-sighted Victorian forebears, including **Warrender Baths** in Marchmont and **Glenogle Swim Centre** in Stockbridge. All these pools are run by Edinburgh Leisure (*see page 214*).

Glenogle Swim Centre
Glenogle Road, Stockbridge, EH3 (343 6376). Bus 28, 29, 29A, 80. **Open** (phone first to confirm) 8am-7.40pm Mon-Fri; 10am-3.40pm Sat; 9am-3.40pm Sun. **Admission** *pool* £1.50-£1.70; *sauna* £3.30-£3.60*.No credit cards*. **Map** p305 C3.

Portobello Swim Centre
57 The Promenade, off Bellfield Street, EH15 (669 6888). Bus 2, 20, 26, 42, 46. **Open** *pool* 7am-2pm, 3-9pm Mon; 7am-9pm Tue-Fri; 9am-3.40pm Sat, Sun. *Turkish baths women* 3pm-9pm Mon; 9am-9pm Wed; *men* 9am-9pm Tue, Thur; *mixed* 9am-9pm Fri, 9am-4pm Sat, Sun. **Admission** *pool* £1.50-£1.70; *Turkish baths* £5.20. **No credit cards**.

Royal Commonwealth Pool
21 Dalkeith Road, South Edinburgh, EH16 (667 7211). Bus 2, 14, 21, 33. **Open** 6am-9.30pm Mon-Fri; 6am-4.30pm Sat; 10am-4.30pm Sun. **Admission** *pool* £2.10-£2.70; *sauna* £5.40-£6.60. **No credit cards**. **Map** p310 J8.
Built for the 1970 Commonwealth Games and housing Olympic-size swimming and diving pools, fitness and sauna suites. Flumes in operation after 2.30pm Monday to Friday, all day Sat, Sun.

Warrender Baths
Thirlestane Road, Marchmont, South Edinburgh, EH9 (447 0052). Bus 24, 40, 41. **Open** 8am-9pm Mon-Fri; 9am-3.40pm Sat, Sun. **Admission** *pool* £1.50-£1.70; *sauna* £3.30-£3.60. **No credit cards**.

Scottish Science Library, National Library of Scotland

33 Salisbury Place, South Edinburgh EH9 (667 9554/fax 466 3810/ www.nls.uk). Bus 40, 41, 42, 46. **Open** 9.30am-5pm Mon, Tue, Thur, Fri; 10am-8.30pm Wed; closed Sat, Sun. **Map** p310 H8.

Scottish Business Information Service (SCOTBIS) is part of the Scottish Science Library and is dedicated to providing up-to-date information to the scientific, technical, and business communities, via a combination of electronic and conventional printed sources. Internet access, CD-Roms, annual company reports, large market research collection.

Conferences

Edinburgh Convention Bureau

4 Rothesay Terrace, New Town, EH3 (473 3666/fax 473 3636/ www.edinburgh.org/conference). Bus 13. **Open** 9am-5pm Mon-Fri; closed Sat, Sun. **Map** p308 B5.

Part of the business and tourism division of the Edinburgh & Lothians Tourist Board, the ECB offers impartial advice on finding a conference venue and help with the organisation.

Edinburgh International Conference Centre

The Exchange, 150 Morrison Street, West Edinburgh, EH3 (300 3000/ www.eicc.co.uk). Bus 2, 28. **Open** *telephone enquiries & office* 8am-6pm Mon-Fri; closed Sat, Sun. **Map** p308 C6.

In the modern surroundings of the city's new financial centre, the Exchange can accommodate up to 1,200 delegates and offers in-house catering as well as business services.

Equipment hire

PC World

1-17 Glasgow Road, West Edinburgh, EH12 (334 5953/ fax 334 6169/www.pcworld.co.uk). Bus 12, 31. **Open** 9am-8pm Mon-Fri; 9am-6pm Sat; 10.30am-5pm Sun.

PC World doesn't hire out equipment, but has a dedicated business centre within the store – PC World Business Direct – with a stock of 12,000 lines.

Sound & Vision AV

11B South Gyle Crescent, West Edinburgh, EH12(334 3324/fax 316 4975/www.sound-and-vision.co.uk). Bus 22. **Open** 8.30am-5.30pm Mon-Fri; closed Sat, Sun.

Will hire out anything required for a presentation, including PCs, and can produce graphics. Also has the unique (in the UK) service of a van full of equipment ready to go in case of emergencies.

Import & export

Companies House

Argyle House, 37 Castle Terrace, South Edinburgh, EH1 (535 5800/ fax 535 5820). Bus 11, 15, 24. **Open** 9am-5pm Mon-Fri; closed Sat, Sun. **Map** p314 A3.

Companies House incorporates new limited companies, and to export goods you must be registered here. It also has information on Scottish companies and foreign companies registered in Scotland.

Customs & Excise

Glasgow office, 21 India Street, Glasgow G2 4PZ (0345 442266/fax 0141 303 3408). **Open** 8.30am-5pm Mon-Thur, 9am-4.30pm Fri; closed Sat, Sun.

The Glasgow office deals with all Scottish import/export licences and information as well as enquiries about VAT.

Office space

Edinburgh Office Business Centre & Conference Venue

16-26 Forth Street, Broughton, EH1 (550 3700/fax 550 3701). Bus 8. **Open** 8.30am-5.30pm Mon-Thur; 8.30am-5pm Fri; closed Sat, Sun. **Map** p307 G3.

Over 60 office spaces, ranging from 85 to 775sq ft. Rates start at £150 per month.

Regus

Conference House, The Exchange, 152 Morrison Street, West Edinburgh, EH3 8EB (200 6000/fax 200 6200/www.regus.com). Bus 2, 28. **Open** 8.30am-6pm Mon-Fri; closed Sat, Sun. **Map** p308 C6.

Conference House contains one- to 67-person office suites, starting at £1,000 per month. A fully furnished office can be provided, with phones, PCs, secretarial support and catering. Conference space can also be hired by the day or hour. Its website allows you to see round offices and book online.

Rutland Square House

12 Rutland Square, New Town, EH1 2BB (228 2281/fax 228 3637). Bus 3, 12, 25. **Open** 8.30am-5.30pm Mon-Fri; closed Sat, Sun. **Map** p308 C6.

Twelve fully furnished offices, from £400 per month. All are hired out on a three-month minimum basis.

Secretarial

Alva Business Centre

82 Great King Street, New Town, EH3 6QU (225 5718/fax 557 2861/ alvaedin@aol.com). Bus 13. **Open** 9am-5pm Mon-Fri; closed Sat, Sun. **Map** p306 E3.

Doesn't actually hire out staff, but provides secretarial and word-processing services, as well as photocopying, document binding, faxes, translation and interpreting (with prior notice). Email can be forwarded here too.

Office Angels

95 George Street, New Town, EH2 3ES (226 6112/fax 220 6850/ edinburgh@office-angels.com). Bus 13, 19, 55. **Open** 8.30am-6pm Mon-Fri; closed Sat, Sun. **Map** p314 B1.

Hires out staff right through from the mailroom to PAs . Does not have qualified accountants and IT specialists on its books and only hires to offices, not businesses run from a private address.

Reed Employment

13 Frederick Street, New Town, EH2 2BY (226 3687/fax 247 5900/ www.reed.co.uk). Bus 3, 12, 16, 17. **Open** 8am-6pm Mon-Fri; closed Sat, Sun. **Map** p314 B1.

Reed supplies office, secretarial, call centre and catering staff. The office at 25 Frederick Street, EH2 2ND (226 3686/fax 225 5817) deals with accountancy staff.

Translation

Berlitz

24-26 Frederick Street, New Town, EH2 2JR (226 7198/fax 225 2918). Bus 3, 12, 16. **Open** 9am-5pm Mon-Fri; closed Sat, Sun. **Map** p314 B1

Berlitz will translate out of or into any language under the sun. Phone for rates.

Integrated Language Services

School of Languages, Heriot-Watt University, Riccarton, EH14 4AS (451 3159/fax 451 3160). Bus 45. **Open** 9am-5pm Mon-Fri; closed Sat, Sun.

All European languages and most others can be translated. ILS also supplies interpreters and all necessary interpreting equipment for conferences. Rates on request.

Directory

Consuls

For a full list of foreign consular offices in Edinburgh consult the phone book or *Yellow Pages* under Consuls and/or Embassies.

American Consulate General

3 Regent Terrace, Calton Hill, EH7 (556 8315/fax 557 6023/ www.usembassy.org/scotland). Bus 25. **Open** *Telephone enquiries* 8.30am-noon, 1-5pm Mon-Fri; closed Sat, Sun. *Personal callers* (emergencies only) 1-4pm Mon-Fri or by appointment; closed Sat, Sun. **Map** p307 H4.
Offers a limited service such as assistance with repatriation, return of bodies, hospitalisation and arrest, as well as giving out general information, advice and official forms. It does not issue visas or replacement passports. For replacement passports telephone 020 7499 9000; for visa enquiries telephone 09068 200290 (recorded message service, calls charged at 60p per minute at all times) or 09061 500590 (operator, calls charged at £1.50 per minute).

Australian Consulate

37 George St, New Town, EH2 (624 3333). Bus 13, 19, 55, 82. **Open** phone for times. **Map** p314 C1.
The Australian Consulate is based in a small commercial office in George Street and provides basic services only where a personal appearance is required, such as driving licence renewal and witnessing of documents. For visa enquiries call 09001 600333 and for other migration enquiries call Australia House in London (020 7379 4334).

Consulate General of the Federal Republic of Germany

16 Eglinton Crescent, New Town, EH12 (337 2323/fax 346 1578/ 113315.565@compuserve.com). Bus 3, 3A, 12, 25, 25A. **Open** 9am-noon, by appointment 1-3pm Mon-Fri; closed Sat, Sun. **Map** p308 B6.
Comprehensive service including visas.

French Consulate General

11 Randolph Crescent, New Town, EH3 (general enquiries only 225 7954/fax 225 8975/visa enquiries 220 6324/visa enquiry line 0891 600215/passports 225 3377/legal 220 0141). Bus 13, 19, 55, 82. **Open** *Visas* 9.30am-11.30am.

Passports/ID cards 9.30am-1pm, by appointment 2-5pm, Mon-Fri; closed Sat, Sun. **Map** p315 C5.

Italian Consulate General

32 Melville Street, New Town, EH3 (226 3631/220 3695/fax 226 6260/ consedimb@consedimb.demon.co.uk). Bus 3, 3A, 12, 25, 25A. **Open** *Telephone enquiries* 9.30am-5.30pm Mon-Fri; closed Sat, Sun. *Personal callers* 9.30am-12.30pm Mon-Fri; closed Sat, Sun. **Map** L5. Emergency calls are redirected via the main phone number.

Spanish Consulate

63 North Castle Street, New Town, EH2 (220 1843/fax 226 4568/visas 09001 600123). Bus 13, 19, 55, 82. **Open** *Telephone enquiries* 9am-3pm, (9am-noon visas only) Mon-Fri; closed Sat, Sun. *Personal callers* 9am-noon 1-3pm Mon-Fri; closed Sat, Sun. **Map** p314 B1.

Customs

When entering the UK, non-EU citizens and anyone buying duty-free goods have the following import limits:

● 200 cigarettes or 100 cigarillos or 250 grams (8.82 ounces) of tobacco
● 2 litres still table wine plus either 1 litre spirits or strong liqueurs (over 22% alcohol by volume) or 2 litres fortified wine (under 22% abv), sparkling wine or other liqueurs
● 60cc/ml perfume
● 250cc/ml toilet water
● Other goods to the value of: £75 for EU citizens purchasing from another EU country or £145 for travellers arriving from outside the EU

The import of meat, poultry, fruit, plants, flowers and protected animals is restricted or forbidden; there are no restrictions on the import or export of currency.

Since the Single European Market agreement came into force at the beginning of 1993, people over the age of 17 arriving from an EU country have been able to import unlimited goods for their own personal use, if bought tax-paid (ie not duty-free).

However, the law sets out guidance levels for what is for personal use (and it's not as much as you might expect or hope), so if you exceed them

you must be able to satisfy officials that the goods are not for resale. Just remember, they've heard it all before.

HM Customs & Excise

Edinburgh Airport, EH12 (344 3196). **Open** 6am-11pm daily.

Disabled travellers

The older parts of Edinburgh can be hard for wheelchair users to get around: listed buildings are not allowed to widen their entrances or add ramps, and parts of the Old Town have very narrow pavements. However, equal opportunity legislation requires new buildings to be fully accessible – step forward the Festival Theatre and the new Museum of Scotland. The newer taxis can all take wheelchairs and the bus fleet is gradually being upgraded to low-floor models, though currently routes reliably plied by these are only the Nos.44 and 26. For more information, contact one of the following organisations.

Disability Scotland

Princes House, 5 Shandwick Place, New Town, EH2 4RG (229 8632/ fax 229 5168/ www.disabilityscotland.org.uk). Bus 3, 3A, 12, 16, 17. **Open** *Phone enquiries* 9am-1pm Mon-Fri; closed Sat, Sun. *Office* 9am-5pm Mon-Fri; closed Sat, Sun. **Map** p308 C5.
Scotland's primary disabled agency can advise travellers on access and other facilities throughout the country. It can also refer you to specialist agencies.

Lothian Coalition of Disabled People

Norton Park, 57 Albion Road, Calton Hill, EH7 (475 2360/fax 475 2392/enquiries@lcodp.demon.co.uk). **Open** *telephone enquiries* 9am-5pm Mon-Fri; closed Sat, Sun.
Publishes the free *Access Guide to Edinburgh.* Phone for a copy.

Emergencies

In the event of a serious accident, fire or incident, call **999** and specify whether you require ambulance, fire service or police.

Health

National Health Service (NHS) treatment is free if you fall into one of the following categories:

● European Union (EU) nationals, plus those of Iceland, Norway and Liechtenstein.
● European Economic Area (EEA) nationals living in an EEA state.
● Nationals/residents of countries with which the UK has a reciprocal agreement.
● Anyone who at time of receiving treatment has been in the UK for the previous 12 months.
● Anyone who has come the UK to take up permanent residence.
● Students on full-time recognised courses of study from anywhere in the world.
● Refugees and others seeking refuge in the UK.
● Anyone formally detained by the Immigration Authorities.

There are no NHS charges for the following:

● Treatment in accident and emergency departments.
● Emergency ambulance transport.
● Diagnosis and treatment of certain communicable diseases, including STDs.
● Family planning services.
● Compulsory psychiatric treatment.

If you do not fit into any of the above categories, but wish to find out if you may still qualify for free treatment, contact:

Primary Care Department

Lothian Health, Stevenson House, 555 Gorgie Road, West Edinburgh, EH11 (536 9000). Bus 3. 3A, 21, 25, 25A.

Accident & emergency

The 24-hour casualty department serving Edinburgh is located at:

Royal Infirmary of Edinburgh

Lauriston Place, South Edinburgh, EH3 (536 4000). Bus 23, 28, 45. **Map** *p309 F7.*

Chemists

Many drugs cannot be bought over the counter. A pharmacist will dispense medicines on receipt of a prescription from a doctor. An NHS prescription costs £6 per item at present. A late-opening dispensing chemist is **Boots** (48 Shandwick Place, New Town, EH2 (225 6757, open 8am-9pm Mon-Fri, 8am-7pm Sat, 10am-5pm Sun, Map p308 C5). *See also page 183.*

Contraception & abortion

Abortions are free to British citizens on the National Health Service (NHS). This also applies to EU residents and foreign nationals living, working or studying in Britain. Two doctors must agree that an abortion is justified within the terms of the Abortion Act 1967, as amended, whether it is on the NHS or not. If you decide to go private, contact one of the organisations below.

Lothian Brook Advisory Centre

5 Castle Terrace, South Edinburgh, EH2 (229 3596). Bus 11, 15, 24. **Open** *noon-6pm Mon-Thur; noon-3.30pm Fri; noon-2.30pm Sat. No appointment necessary.* **Map** *p314 A3.*
Advice on contraception, sexual problems and abortion with referral to an NHS hospital or private clinic. Contraception, sexual advice and counselling for young people under 25, including pregnancy advice and emergency contraception. For visitors based outside most Scottish regions, a £15 consultation fee is payable, plus any prescription costs.

Family Planning & Well Women Services

18 Dean Terrace, Stockbridge, EH4 (332 7941). Bus 28, 29, 80. **Open** *Switchboard 8.30am-7.30pm Mon-Thur; 9.30am-4pm Fri; closed Sat, Sun. Young people's clinic 9.30am-1pm Sat; closed Mon-Fri, Sun.* **Map** *p305 C3.*
Confidential advice, contraceptive provision and pregnancy tests. As an NHS-run clinic, covered under the European Union E111 scheme, it provides most services free, though some charges may apply to overseas visitors. Clinics give contraception advice, abortion referral, post-termination counselling, pre-menstrual syndrome advice and support, menopause information, psycho-sexual counselling, vasectomy operations and female sterilisation advice. Note that, except in emergencies, you must make an appointment first. The young persons' clinic is for under-25s.

Dental services

Dental care is free only to UK citizens in certain categories. All other patients, NHS or private, must pay; certain categories of people from some countries may be eligible for reduced dental costs. For advice, and to find an NHS dentist, contact the Primary Care Department (*see above*). Emergency dental treatment can be obtained at:

Edinburgh Dental Institute

Lauriston Building, Lauriston Place, South Edinburgh, EH3 (536 4900). Bus 23, 28, 45. **Open** *9am-3pm Mon-Fri; closed Sat, Sun.* **Map** *p308 E7.*
Free walk-in emergency clinic.

Western General Hospital

Crewe Road South, Stockbridge, EH4 (537 1338). Bus 28, 29, 80. **Open** *7-9pm Mon-fri; 10am-noon, 7-9pm Sat, Sun.*
Free walk-in emergency clinic, for Lothian residents only.

Doctors

If you're a British citizen or working in the city, you can go to any GP for diagnosis and treatment. People who are ordinarily resident in the UK, such as overseas students, can also register with an NHS doctor. For a list of names of GPs in your area, contact the Primary Care Department (*see above*).

If you are not eligible to see an NHS doctor, you will be charged cost price for medicines prescribed by a private doctor.

Directory

Opticians

For dispensing opticians, *see page 184.*

Princess Alexandra Eye Pavilion

Chalmers Street, South Edinburgh, EH3 (536 3753). Bus 23, 28, 45. **Map p309 E7.**
For emergency eye complaints, the Eye Pavilion operates a free walk-in service.

STDs/HIV/AIDS

The Genito-Urinary Medicine (GUM) clinic (listed below) is affiliated to the Royal Infirmary of Edinburgh. It provides free, confidential advice and treatment of STDs and non-sex related problems, such as thrush (yeast infections) and cystitis (urinary tract infections). It also offers information and counselling on HIV and STDs, and can conduct a confidential blood test to determine HIV status. Government and Health Education pamphlets – *AIDS: The Facts, Safer Sex and the Condom* and *AIDS: The Test* – are available from the GUM clinic and by post from: Health Education Board for Scotland, Woodburn House, Canaan Lane, EH10.

Solas

2-4 Abbeymount, Calton Hill, EH8 (661 0982/www.waverleycare.com). Bus 35, 35A. **Open** *Drop-in & Café* 11am-8pm Tue, Thur; 11am-4pm Wed, Fri; closed Sat-Mon. *Telephone enquiries* 9am-5pm Mon-Fri; closed Sat, Sun. **No credit cards.** **Map p307 J4.**
The city's HIV/AIDS information and support centre. A wide range of therapies is on offer (including counselling and complementary therapies, arts classes, support for children and young people), which can be booked in advance, plus a good café with a keenly priced menu. See the freebies for details of other gay health agencies.

Genito-Urinary Medicine Clinic

Lauriston Building, Lauriston Place, South Edinburgh, EH3 (men 536 2103/women 536 2104). Bus 23, 28, 45. **Open** 8.30am-4.30pm Mon-Wed,

Fri; 8.30am-6.30pm Thur; closed Tue, Sat, Sun. *Walk-in clinic* (emergencies only) 9-10am daily; otherwise by appointment. **Map p309 E7.**
Free and confidential service offering counselling for people who are HIV positive.

Helplines & information

Advice Shop

South Bridge, Royal Mile, EH1 (2251255). **Open** *phone lines* 8.30am-4.40pm Mon-Thur; 8.30am-3.50pm Fri; closed Sat, Sun. *Drop-in service* 9.30am-4pm Mon-Thur; 9.30am-3pm Fri; closed Sat, Sun.
Advice on consumer problems and welfare benefits.

AIDS Helpline

0800 567123. **Open** 24hrs daily.
A free and confidential info service.

Alcoholics Anonymous

225 2727. **Open** 24hrs daily.
Confidential, round-the-clock help and advice.

Childline

0800 1111. **Open** 24hrs daily.
Free and confidential national helpline for children and young people in trouble or danger.

Citizens' Advice Scotland

Dundas St, New Town, EH3 (557 1500/fax 557 3543). Bus 23, 27. **Open** 9am-5pm Mon-Fri; closed Sat, Sun. **Map p306E3.**
Citizens' Advice Bureaux are independent, offering free advice on legal, financial and personal matters. The only city-centre branch is at the above address. Check the phone book for other branches.

Drinkline

0800 9178282. **Open** 9am-11pm Mon-Fri; 6-11pm Sat, Sun.
For help with drink problems.

Edinburgh Bisexual Group

58A Broughton Street, Broughton, EH1 (557 3620). **Open** phone for details.
Information and support for bisexual people.

Edinburgh Rape Crisis Centre

556 9437. **Open** 1-3pm Mon, Thur; 6-8pm Fri; closed Tue, Wed, Sat, Sun.
Free, confidential rape counselling. If you phone out of hours, leave a message and someone will call you back as soon as possible.

Edinburgh Women's Aid

97-101 Morrison Street, West Edinburgh, EH3 (229 1419). Bus 2, 28. **Open** *Walk-in* 10am-3pm Mon, Wed, Fri; 2-7pm Thur; 10am-12.30pm Sat; closed Tue, Sun. *Telephone enquiries* 1.30-3.30pm Tue; 10am-2pm Thur; closed Mon, Wed, Fri-Sun.
Refuge referral for women experiencing domestic violence. An after-hours answerphone gives numbers for immediate help.

Gamblers Anonymous

020 7384 3040. **Open** 9am-8pm daily.
Advice is offered by members of the fellowship. Referrals to meetings.

Gay Switchboard

556 4049. **Open** 7.30am-10pm daily.

Health Information Service

0800 224488. **Open** 10am-5pm Mon-Fri; closed Sat, Sun.
A free telephone information service giving details about local NHS services, waiting times, common diseases, conditions and treatments.

Lesbian Line

557 0751. **Open** 7.30-10pm Mon, Thur; closed Tue, Wed, Fri-Sun.

Lothian Gay & Lesbian Switchboard

556 4049. **Open** 7.30-10.30pm daily.

The Rights Office

Southside Community Centre, Nicholson Street, South Edinburgh, EH8 (667 6339). Bus 7, 8, 31, 80. **Open** 10am-12.30pm Mon, Wed; closed Tue, Thur-Sun. **Map p310 G6.**
Walk-in centre giving free, confidential advice and advocacy.

The Samaritans

0345 909 090/221 9999. **Open** 24hrs daily.
The Samaritans will listen to anyone with an emotional problem.

Victim Support

2 Nicholson Square, South Edinburgh, EH8 (Edinburgh helpline 0845 603 9213/ national helpline 0845 303 0900). Bus 7, 8, 31, 80. **Open** *Edinburgh helpline* 9am-4.30pm Mon-Fri; closed Sat, Sun. *National helpline* 9am-9pm Mon-Fri; 9am-7pm Sat, Sun. **Map p310 G6.**
Victims of crime who phone Victim Support are put in touch with a volunteer who provides emotional and practical support, including information on legal procedures and advice on compensation. Interpreters can be arranged.

prestigious, fee-paying schools. The days when only former pupils could play for the likes of Edinburgh Accies, Heriot's, Stewart's-Melville and Watsonians are long gone, but the school-based rivalries remain. Edinburgh also has a flourishing summer touch rugby scene, administered by *Scottish Rugby* magazine (0141 242 1400).

Murrayfield Stadium
7 Roseburn Street, West Edinburgh (346 5000/ tickets 0870 900 9933/shop 346 5044/www.sru.org.uk). Bus 3, 3A, 21, 25, 25A. **Credit** MC, V.
Tours of the stadium, lasting an hour, are conducted between 10am and 3pm on a Tuesday, Wednesday and Thursday. Details and booking forms can be obtained from the marketing department of the SRU (Scottish Rugby Union).

Skiing

Midlothian Ski Centre
Biggar Road, Hillend, EH10 (445 4433). Bus 4. **Open** 9.30am-9pm Mon-Sat; 9.30am-7pm Sun. **Cost** *main slope* £6 first hour (£4 concessions); £2.50 each additional hour (£1.60 concessions); *nursery slopes* £3.70; £2.40 concessions. **Credit** MC, V.
Situated to the south of Edinburgh, the Midlothian Ski Centre has the longest artificial ski slope in the whole of Europe, at 400m. Prices include the hire of boots, skis and poles and use of the chairlift. There's an additional charge of £1.50 for the first hour, and 50p per additional hour, for snowboards or specialist skis.

Snooker

The Angle Club
3 Jordan Lane, Morningside, South Edinburgh, EH10 (447 8814). Bus 11, 16, 17, 23. **Open** 11am-midnight, Mon-Thur, Sun; 11am-1am Fri, Sat. **Cost** *snooker* £3.84-£4.08 per hour; *pool* £4.75-£5 per hour. **Credit** AmEx, MC, V.
Ten snooker tables, seven pool tables and a bar/café are the attractions at the Angle Club.

Marco's Snooker Halls
55 Grove Street, West Edinburgh, EH3 (228 2141). Bus 1, 28, 34, 35. **Open** 8am-11pm daily. **Cost** *snooker* £3.90 per hour; *pool* £4.50. **Credit** MC, V. **Map** p308 C7.
Facilities include 15 snooker and 18 pool tables as well as a bar/café. Also gyms, sunbeds, squash courts and classes.
Branch 146 Slateford Road, West Edinburgh, EH14 (443 2211).

Tennis

Craiglockhart Tennis & Sports Centre
177 Colinton Road, South Edinburgh, EH14 (general sport 443 0101/tennis 444 1969). Bus 10, 10A, 27, 45, 47. **Open** 9am-10pm daily. **Cost** phone for details. **No credit cards.**
The sports centre has a fitness room, badminton and squash courts and a crèche. It also runs step and aerobics classes. The tennis centre has six indoor and eight outdoor courts.

Is it the Alps? No, it's the **Midlothian Ski Centre**.

Theatre & Dance

August might be the best time to see theatre and dance in Edinburgh, but the Festival means that the city's theatres just strive harder all year round.

Theatre

While the politicians and the Scottish Arts Council are debating the merits of a National Scottish Theatre, Edinburgh is getting on with providing the goods. Local theatres produce everything from world premieres of new plays to strong revivals, student productions, amateur musicals, fringe and community-based work. On the touring side, productions from all levels visit the city, be they subsidised theatre or London's big West End musicals.

Of the city's two main producing houses, the world-famous **Traverse Theatre** (*see page 221*) specialises in new writing. Aside from its own productions, its little'n'large twin spaces are programmed with a selection of touring drama, dance and comedy. The **Royal Lyceum** (*see page 221*) fulfils the capital's mainstream rep brief, producing between six and eight productions over its autumn and spring subscription seasons, as well as shows at Christmas and in summer.

Of the two council-owned venues, after a bumpy financial ride over its first few years of operation, the **Edinburgh Festival Theatre** (*see page 204*) was brought into a co-management deal with the **King's Theatre** (*see page 221*). Both are now achieving financial and production targets. Today the Festival operates as a lyric theatre, taking opera, music and ballet, while the King's is Edinburgh's major receiving house, getting the best in large touring theatrical and musical productions.

The commercially run **Edinburgh Playhouse** (*see page 221*) has been making vast sums as the city's receiving house for large-scale touring musicals. A recent change in ownership looks set to enhance its artistic credibility with the addition of occasional touring ballet, opera and rock events.

Occupying a radically different – but widely respected – position on the theatrical spectrum, **Theatre Workshop** (*see page 221*) specialises in high-quality community-based work – both education- and performance-based – and books a lively mix of touring drama and dance. The **Netherbow Arts Centre** (*see page 221*) and **St Bride's Centre** (*see page 222*) both periodically stage new and experimental work. Meanwhile the **Brunton Theatre** in Musselburgh (*see page 221*) acts mostly as a receiving house for small-scale touring Scottish theatre, with an accent on dance.

In addition to venue-based work, Edinburgh is also home to several of Scotland's top touring companies, including the adventurously hard-hitting Boilerhouse and the female-led Stellar Quines.

There is also a strong student presence on the boards in Edinburgh. The drama department of Queen Margaret University College recently took over the **Gateway Theatre** (Elm Row, Leith Walk; 317 3939) and puts on student productions there.

There are some 35 amateur theatrical and musical companies in Edinburgh. The best of these take on week-long runs in the **King's Theatre** and the **Churchill Theatre** (for both, *see page 221*). Details of the different groups are available from the **Scottish Community Drama Association** (557 5552). **Showstoppers** (25 Blackfriars Street, EH1, 558 9800), the theatrical gift shop just off the Royal Mile, is a good place to contact them as well as buy tickets for their productions.

BUYING TICKETS

Tickets for many major venues can be booked through the **Ticketline** network (220 4349; 10am-8pm Mon-Sat; 11am-6pm Sun); otherwise contact individual box offices listed under the relevant venues.

Venues

Bedlam Theatre

11b Bristo Place, South Edinburgh, EH1 (225 9893/ www.eusa.ed.ac.uk/societies/bedlam). Bus 23, 28, 45. **Open** only for performances and during Fringe; phone for details. **Tickets** £3.50-£6.50. **No credit cards. Map** p309 F6.

Run by the Edinburgh University Students Association, which puts on a good number of small productions and hosts the Festival of New Theatre every spring.

Brunton Theatre

Bridge Street, Musselburgh, EH21 (665 2240). Bus 15, 44. **Open** 10am-8pm Mon-Sat (10am-6pm if no performance); closed Sun. **Tickets** *drama* £4-£8; *dance* £3.50-£7.50; *variety* £6-£9. **Credit** MC, V.

Besides the strong programme of touring drama,

Insurance

You should arrange insurance to cover personal belongings before travelling to Edinburgh, as it is difficult to organise once you have arrived. Non-UK citizens should ensure that medical insurance is included in their travel insurance. If your country has a reciprocal medical treatment arrangement with the UK you will have limited cover, but you should make sure you have the necessary documentation before you arrive. If you cannot access the information in your own country, contact the Primary Care Department in Edinburgh (536 9000).

Internet

Scotland

www.holiday.scotland.net

Official site of the Scottish Tourist Board, with information on accommodation, restaurants, arts events, nightlife and more in your choice of format, from data-only to fully plugged in. There's lots of accommodation of all kinds, with a disabled option, but the search could be better constructed and there's no booking facility. There are some very useful links, though.

www.scotland.net

Scotland Online: a mainstream magazine for such Scottish essentials as a tartan guide and a searchable golf database. Also carries news and features and a travel site produced in conjunction with the Scottish Tourist Board.

www.historic-scotland.gov.uk

Home pages for the government body in charge of Scotland's historic monuments. There are strong databases on listed buildings, tourist attractions, literature and calendar events. Updated every three months.

www.nts.org.uk

The National Trust for Scotland's site provides the opening times,

prices and details of all its properties. It also includes up-to-date news and an online mail order catalogue.

http://scotch.com

The ultimate whisky lover's guide: beautifully illustrated musings on all aspects and varieties of the noble drink.

Edinburgh

www.ebs.hw.ac.uk

The best place to start when planning a visit to Edinburgh, this site has everything from the official guide to Edinburgh to a history of cheese-making in Scotland. On the way, it includes an Edinburgh-based search engine, history, film sites, business pages, directories of what's on, when and where, as well as a very useful selection of links.

www.edinburgh.org

The home base of the Edinburgh Tourist Board is long on looks but short on solid info. An improved accommodation database is planned.

www.edinburgh.gov.uk

The City of Edinburgh Council's website isn't particularly pretty but it does have useful up-to-date information and maps.

Entertainment

www.timeout.com

Click on the Edinburgh or Glasgow button for *the List*'s and *Time Out*'s directional pick of local arts and entertainment. Updated frequently.

www.eae.co.uk

Edinburgh's main publicity distribution company, responsible for distributing most of the posters and leaflets you'll see around the city also runs this 'virtual leaflet rack', giving details of forthcoming arts and entertainment fixtures. Coverage is patchy: on one visit there were four (albeit useful) folk listings but, improbably, 'no events' under cinema.

www.go-edinburgh.co.uk

Full details of Edinburgh's annual festivals. Thorough background and good information (including a page for would-be performers), and a text-only option. Links to the fringe and festival programmes online.

www.spidacom.co.uk/EDG

This guide to Edinburgh's restaurants had a sparse start, but is

constantly being updated and does offer online booking, which can be handy.

www.edinburgh-galleries.co.uk

This site will tell you what's showing where at the main Edinburgh galleries and a virtual trip round one or two of them.

www.electrum.co.uk/pubs

Provides a virtual jaunt through Edinburgh's watering holes in the company of a wasted youth, a history geek or an architecture appreciator. Slow and scanty, but fun and pretty frank, with useful maps.

Media

www.scotsman.com

News, sport and arts from Edinburgh-based newspaper the *Scotsman*. Good for tuning into local opinion and issues (especially the archive), but doesn't include any city guides or what's on elements.

www.theherald.co.uk

Daily news and sport from the electronic version of Glasgow's *Herald*. It's bright, fast and simple but again doesn't go beyond the usual newspaper content.

www.record-mail.co.uk/rm

In-yer-face tabloid take on news and sport from the *Daily Record* and *Sunday Mail*. Includes *Discover Scotland*, the paper's professionally engineered visitor site, with split screen, good searches (accommodation and so on) and maps for each entry (we liked the 'locate nearest pub' option). Also contains useful what's on and gig and pub guides.

Politics & business

www.scottish.parliament.uk

Devolution is here to stay, and the Scottish Parliament's website is a user-friendly guide to how it operates, what it's up to at the moment, what it has done already and how to visit it.

www.edinburgh-in.com/chamber.htm

If you want to start a company in Edinburgh or find out about businesses in the city the Chamber of Commerce's website should be able to tell you what you need to know.

www.ebs.hw.ac.uk/ EFL/english
A guide to the city's major language schools.

www.scotweb.co.uk
This is primarily an online sales forum for Scottish goods and services, but there's a lot more interesting stuff, too: consult the Tartan (yellow) Pages or the white (email) pages, read Piping World or Scottish Life and browse Whisky Web or the Scotweb history site.

Legal aid & immigration advice

If a legal problem arises, contact your embassy, consulate or high commission, go to a branch of **Citizens' Advice Scotland** or **The Rights Office** (for both, *see page 280*) or contact one of the organisations listed below. Ask about Legal Aid eligibility. For leaflets explaining how the system works, write to the **Scottish Legal Aid Board**. If you need a lawyer contact the **Law Society of Scotland**, which will direct you to solicitors specialising in immigration advice. Otherwise **Edinburgh & Lothians Race Equality Council** and the **Immigration Advisory Service** in Glasgow both provide information on problems relating to visas and immigration.

Edinburgh & Lothians Race Equality Council
14 Forth St, Broughton, EH1 (556 0441). Bus 8. **Open** 9.30am-1pm, 2-5pm Mon-Fri; closed Sat, Sun. Phone for surgery times. **Map** p307 G3.

Immigration Advisory Service
115 Bath St, Glasgow, G2 (0141 248 2956). **Open** 10am-4pm Mon-Fri; closed Sat, Sun. **Map** p302 C2.

Law Society of Scotland
26 Drumsheugh Gardens, New Town, EH3 (226 7411). Bus 13,
19, 55, 82. **Open** 9am-5pm Mon-Fri; closed Sat, Sun. **Map** p308 C5.

Scottish Legal Aid Board
44 Drumsheugh Gardens, New Town, EH3 (226 7061). Bus 13, 19, 55, 82. **Open** 9am-5pm Mon-Fri; closed Sat, Sun. *Switchboard* 8.30am-5pm Mon-Fri; closed Sat, Sun. **Map** p308 C5. Publishes information leaflets on criminal and civil Legal Aid; can advise on how to make a complaint against the Scottish Legal Advice Board.

Libraries

Central Library
George IV Bridge, Royal Mile, EH1 (242 8000). Bus 23, 28, 45. **Open** 10am-8pm Mon-Thur; 10am-5pm Fri, 9am-1pm Sat; closed Sun. **Map** p314 C3.
The library stocks a selection of American and European publications including *Le Monde*, *Repubblica*, *El País* and *Frankfurter Allgemeine Zeitung*, and also has a large reference section (242 8060). Proof of identity is required to join the lending library (242 8020). The Edinburgh Room (242 8030) and the Scottish Room (242 8070) are dedicated to local and Scottish material.

National Library of Scotland
George IV Bridge, Royal Mile, EH1 (226 4531/www.nls.uk). Bus 23, 28, 45. **Open** 9.30am-8.30pm Mon, Tue, Thur, Fri; 10am-8.30pm Wed; 9.30am-1pm Sat; closed Sun. **Map** p314 C3.
The National Library of Scotland is a deposit library and is entitled to a copy of all works published in the UK and Ireland. It receives as many as 350,000 items annually, including books, pamphlets, periodicals, maps and music. The Reading Rooms are open for reference and research; admission is by ticket to approved applicants. There's also a varied programme of exhibitions on Scottish subjects.

University of Edinburgh Main Library
George Square, South Edinburgh, EH8 (650 3384). Bus 40, 41, 42. **Open** *term-time* 9am-10pm Mon, Tue, Thur; 10.15am-10pm Wed; 9am-5pm Fri, Sat; noon-5pm Sun; *holiday time* 9am-5pm Mon, Tue, Thur, Fri; 9am-9pm Wed; closed Sat, Sun. **Map** p310 G7.

With a valid matriculation card or ISIC, international students who aren't studying at the University may use the library for reference purposes only. Alternatively, full membership is available at £30/£60 for 3 months, £55/£100 for 6 months or £110/£160 for 12 months. Lower rates quoted are for reference only and higher rates for reference and borrowing.

Media

Most of Scotland's newspapers – and much of its TV output – operate on a quasi-national basis pitched somewhere between the regional media and London's self-styled 'national' press.

The attitudes and arguments on display both reflect and illuminate the current state of that nebulous beast known as Scottish identity. From the time-honoured east/west rivalry for the title of Scotland's national daily broadsheet – perpetuated in the battle between the *Scotsman*, published in Edinburgh, and the Glasgow-based *Herald* – to the thorny question of the tabloid *Daily Record*'s Rangers affiliations; from Radio Scotland's Sony award-winning output to the famously surreal couthiness of the *Sunday Post* letters page, the cultural divergences that impelled the long campaign for devolution continue to pervade the Scottish media.

The battle rages on at the BBC as to whether Scotland should have its own separate six o'clock news slot. Where the actuality of devolution has had a more pronounced effect is in the virtual removal of what little Scottish coverage there was in the UK-based press. Scotland's media continues to fight its own battles and England continues to ignore them – *plus ça change, plus c'est la même chose.*

Newspapers

The Scotsman

www.scotsman.com
Edinburgh-based broadsheet.
Somewhat more establishment
in tone than its Glasgow rival,
the editorial line tends towards
the mid-market, while the arts
and features tend to have an east-
coast bias.

The Herald

www.theherald.co.uk
Glasgow-based broadsheet. Has
the edge in terms of news coverage
(though many argue the opposite,
and the balance shifts back and
forth in any case). Any Glasgow
bias in its arts and features coverage
complements the *Scotsman*'s east-
coast orientation.

Daily Record

www.record-mail.co.uk
Glasgow-based tabloid. Scotland's
best selling daily is published by the
Mirror Group. Lots of froth but some
good campaigning journalism.

Evening News

www.edinburghnews.com
Edinburgh's evening daily tabloid.
The latest headlines from around the
world are combined with a strong
local Edinburgh flavour. The
Saturday *Pink* section carries all
the sports results.

Evening Times

www.eveningtimes.co.uk
Glasgow's daily evening tabloid.

Scotland on Sunday

www.scotlandonsunday.com
The *Scotsman*'s sister publication is
a bit more frothy, but has good
analysis of Scottish issues.

The Sunday Herald

www.sundayherald.com
Sister paper to the *Herald*, the
Sunday Herald combines good news
reporting and analysis with lively
and intelligent arts coverage.

Sunday Mail

www.record-mail.co.uk
Sunday sister to the *Daily Record*,
with which it shares strong
sports coverage and a
campaigning instinct.

Sunday Post

This Dundee-published Sunday
treat that was once a by-word
for couthy tittle tattle and
reactionary opinion has become
increasingly – and blandly – like
the other Sunday tabloids. At
least it's still the home of the Oor
Wullie comic strip.

Sunday Times

London-based pioneer of the
'supermarket' approach to Sunday
newspapers. Its ever-expanding
multi-section format includes a
reasonable Scottish supplement,
Ecosse, comprising features, reviews
and listings.

Magazines

Chapman

Established for more than a quarter
of a century and currently appearing
four times annually, *Chapman* is a
highly regarded platform for new
writing (fiction and poetry) as well as
reviews and general debate on
contemporary Scottish culture.

Cencrastus

Subtitled 'Scottish and International
Literature, Arts and Affairs', this
thrice-yearly publication has moved
in a more satirical direction, and is
not afraid to take the odd broadswipe
at the Scottish Parliament.

Edinburgh Book Collector

www.scotbooksmag.demon.co.uk
Covering Scottish books in their
widest interpretation, the content
of this quarterly magazine ranges
from interviews with writers to
new writing, reviews and
publishing matters.

Edinburgh Review

By far the oldest of Edinburgh's
literary magazines, founded in 1802,
the *Review* now appears twice a year
and features fiction, poetry, criticism
and literary/cultural argument.

Scotsgay

www.scotsgay.co.uk
This Edinburgh-based magazine
appears monthly and is distributed
free in gay venues. It covers
events related to the lesbian, gay
and bisexual community, and
includes comprehensive
entertainment listings.

Listings

The List

Fortnightly listings magazine for
Edinburgh and Glasgow (published
Thursdays). Visitors to either city
will find that a copy will provide
many a valuable shortcut when
planning their time. It gives details of
everything from mainstream cinema
releases to readings by local writers
and concerts of all sizes and genres.
On the whole it's both reliable and
comprehensive, though it's always
worth phoning ahead to double-check

before setting off to an event.
It switches to weekly issues for
the Festival, when its time-banded
sections and extensive preview
coverage offer a useful –
though fallible – guide through
the bewildering plethora of
attractions on offer.

Television

On the broadcasting front,
both the BBC and ITV in
Scotland opt in and out of the
UK-wide output. BBC Scotland
and the independent Scottish
Television (STV) also
contribute regularly to their
respective networks. Since
devolution, the ongoing debate
has been as to whether or not
BBC Scotland should have a 6
o'clock news slot of its own –
with London saying that
there's not enough Scottish
news to fit the slot and
Scotland disagreeing
vehemently. The debate
continues.

BBC Scotland's TV drama
has been on something of a
winning streak, with both one-
off and serial dramas and
comedies – Rab C Nesbitt
being only the best-known –
while also venturing
successfully into the film
business with the critically
acclaimed *Small Faces* and
Mrs Brown. On the factual
side, its arts documentary
strand, Ex-S, has also picked
up a good many plaudits. STV,
meanwhile, produces a diverse
range of home-grown special-
interest programmes such as
Get It On (fashion), *Don't Look
Down* (arts) and *Scottish
Passport* (holidays), in
addition to mainstream
popular drama. Both stations
also broadcast much of their
own, Scottish-centred sports
coverage – especially in the
football season.

Radio

BBC Radio Scotland

(92.4-94.7 FM & 810 MW)
Enjoying particularly widespread
popularity and respect for its mix of

talk- and music-based programming, Radio Scotland's news coverage offers an illuminating alternative to the reports from London, while its arts, documentary, sports and short-story strands are all worth listening to. The nightly rotation of music shows ranges from the *Brand New Opry's* country selection, to folk and traditional-based sounds in *Celtic Connections* and *Travelling Folk.*

Beat FM

(105.7FM & 106.1FM).
www.beat106.com
Scotland's new and liveliest addition to the music scene. Beat FM bills itself as Scotland's radio revolution and plays a wide-ranging selection of dance music, with well-respected club DJs taking over on Friday and Saturday nights.

Radio Forth

(97.3 FM & 1548 MW)
Edinburgh-based music-oriented commercial station. Wins awards for both its frequencies. FM and MW cater for the younger and more mature ends of the mainstream/chart audience respectively. Features local and Scottish acts and is a must for travel news.

Scot FM

(101.1 FM)
Country-wide, fairly downmarket approach to talk radio. Its early attempts to introduce Scotland to the shock-jock formula had mixed results, to say the least.

Alternative

The fringe media scene in Edinburgh has been expanding steadily in recent years, having been boosted both by Scotland's lively cultural/political mood and the impact of the IT revolution. Probably the best-known publication in this context is *Rebel Inc*, famously the first to publish the work of one Irvine Welsh back in the early 1990s, and now generally recognised as a landmark force in new Scottish writing.

These days the magazine lends its name to an imprint of Edinburgh independent publishers Canongate, championing the same ilk of authors in book form. The 'small magazine' sector features three main

Edinburgh-based titles – *Chapman, Cencrastus* and *New Edinburgh Review*, each mixing its own combination of fiction, poetry, reviews, interviews, features and essays. The Scottish version of *Hello!, Hiya!*, had a mercifully brief life before meeting its timely demise. 'Zines and fanzines come and go periodically – though they can be hard to find – catering for tastes from Riot Grrls to football supporters.

Britain's currency is the pound sterling (£). One pound equals 100 pence (p). 1p and 2p coins are copper; 5p, 10p, 20p and 50p coins are silver; the £1 coin is yellowy-gold; the £2 coin is silver with a yellowy-gold surround. There are three Scottish clearing banks, all of which issue their own paper notes: the Bank of Scotland, the Royal Bank of Scotland and the Clydesdale Bank. The colour of paper notes varies slightly between the three, but an approximation is as follows: green £1 (Scotland only; England and Wales have done away with the £1 note); blue £5; brown £10, purple/pink £20, red or green £50 and, unique to Scotland, a bold red £100. You can exchange foreign currency at banks or bureaux de change.

It's a good idea to try to use up all your Scottish currency before leaving the country: the further south you go, the more wary people will be of accepting it although it is legal tender.

Banks

Banks have variable opening hours, depending on the day of the week. Minimum opening hours are 9am-4pm, but some are open until 5.30pm. Cashpoint machines (ATMs), usually situated outside a bank

or building society (most building societies operate as banks), give access to cash 24 hours a day though many are now charging for the privilege.

Banks generally offer the best exchange rates, although they can vary considerably from place to place and it pays to shop around. Commission is sometimes charged for cashing travellers' cheques in foreign currencies, but not for sterling travellers' cheques, provided you cash them at a bank affiliated to the issuing bank (get a list when you buy your cheques). Commission is charged if you change cash into another currency. You always need identification, such as a passport, when cashing travellers' cheques.

There are branches of the three Scottish clearing banks and cash machines throughout the city. There are, however, few branches of the English clearing banks. These are situated at:

Barclays Bank

1 St Andrew Square, New Town, EH2 (0845 6000180). Bus 8, 12, 16, 16, 25, 25A. **Open** 9.30am-4.30pm Mon, Tue, Thur, Fri; 10am-4.30pm Wed; closed Sat, Sun. **Map** p314 D1.

HSBC Bank

76 Hanover Street, New Town, EH2 (456 3200). Bus 13, 19, 55, 82. **Open** 9.30am-4.30pm Mon-Fri; closed Sat, Sun. **Map** p314 C1.

Lloyds TSB Bank

28 Hanover St, New Town, EH2 (0845 3003398). Bus 13, 19, 55, 82. **Open** 9am-5pm Mon, Tue, Fri; 9.30am-5pm Wed; 9am-6pm Thur; 9am-12.30pm Sat; closed Sun. **Map** p314 B1.

National Westminster Bank

80 George Street, New Town, EH2 (0845 6090000). Bus 13, 19, 55, 82. **Open** 9am-5.30pm Mon, Tue, Thur, Fri; 9.30am-5pm Wed; closed Sat, Sun. **Map** p314 B1.

Bureaux de change

You will be charged for cashing travellers' cheques or buying and selling foreign

A right barrel of laughs – the witches of *Macbeth* get heavy at the **Royal Lyceum**.

dance and musicals, the Brunton Theatre Company puts on about three new productions every year. Under the control of artistic director David Mark Thomson, these have recently been receiving exceptionally good notices.

Churchill Theatre

Morningside Road, South Edinburgh, EH10 (447 7597). Bus 11, 16, 17, 23. **Open** only for performances; phone for times. **Tickets** £3-£10. **No credit cards**.

A council-run venue on the south side of town, which is regularly used by local amateur theatrical and musical companies.

Edinburgh Playhouse

18-22 Greenside Place, Calton Hill, EH1 (Tickets Direct 0870 606 3424/www.tickets-direct.co.uk). Bus 7, 12, 16. **Open** *box office* performance days 10am-8pm Mon-Sat; closed Sun; non-performance days 10am-6pm Mon-Sat; closed Sun; *phone* 8.30am-10pm Mon-Fri; 8.30am-9.30pm Sat; 10am-8pm Sun. **Tickets** £7.50-£35. **Credit** AmEx, MC, V. **Map** p307 G3.

A wide stage and huge capacity make this the perfect venue for touring West End musicals.

King's Theatre

2 Leven Street, Tollcross, South Edinburgh, EH3 (529 6000/www.eft.co.uk). Bus 11, 16, 17, 23. **Open** *box office* 1-6pm Mon-Sat (1pm-curtain up performance days); closed Sun. **Tickets** £4-£16. **Credit** AmEx, DC, MC, V. **Map** p309 D7.

The lavish interior of this grand old Edwardian theatre to the south of the city centre makes it the perfect setting for the best touring theatre. It is also favoured by top local amateur companies.

Netherbow Arts Centre

43 High Street, Royal Mile, EH1 (556 9579). Bus 35, 35A. **Open** *box office* 9.30am-8pm performance days. **Tickets** £3-£10. **Credit** MC, V. **Map** p310 G5.

Situated beneath John Knox House Museum (*see p50*), this tiny space is the venue for some excellent children's theatre as well as its own and touring productions. It also has an excellent café.

Royal Lyceum

Grindlay Street, South Edinburgh, EH3 (248 4848/ www.infoser.com/infotheatre/lyceum). Bus 11, 15, 24. **Open** *box office* 10am-6pm Mon; 10am-7pm Tue-Sat; closed Sun. **Tickets** £1-£16. **Credit** AmEx, MC, V. **Map** p314 A3.

The theatre manages to juggle populist appeal with the natural inclination of artistic director Kenny Ireland towards adventure by integrating a mixture of classics and adaptations with new works and new writing. Production values are never less than solid, though the shows themselves can tend towards the workmanlike.

Theatre Workshop

34 Hamilton Place, Stockbridge, EH3 (226 5425/ jsimpson@twe.org.uk). Bus 35. **Open** *box office* 9.30am-5.30pm Mon-Fri; closed Sat, Sun. **Tickets** £3-£6.50. **Credit** MC, V. **Map** p306 D3.

The talents of this Stockbridge theatre lie in its community work, often putting on professional productions built around local issues. Its in-house company combines the talents of able-bodied and disabled actors under the direction of Robert Rae.

Traverse Theatre

10 Cambridge Street, South Edinburgh, EH1 (228 1404/www.traverse.co.uk). Bus 11, 15, 24. **Open** *performance days* 10am-6pm Mon, 10am-

8pm Tue-Sun; *non-performance days* 10am-6pm Mon-Sat; closed Sun. **Tickets** £4-£8. **Credit** MC, V. **Map** p314 A3.

Even if you don't like what you see, a visit to the Traverse will not be a waste of time. Artistic director Philip Howard continues the tradition of nurturing home-grown Scottish and Edinburgh-based writing talent, a policy that has brought its own rewards with the likes of Liz Lochhead's *Perfect Days* going on to a national tour and the launch of the careers of David Greig and David Harrower. As you'd expect, the Traverse tends to attract the younger, more adventurous end of the theatre-going population, its post-show numbers swollen by the arts and media types who frequent its hip café-bar.

Dance

Edinburgh's dance enthusiasts are well-served. The major touring classical ballet companies make frequent use of the **Edinburgh Festival Theatre**'s (*see page 204*) and the **Edinburgh Playhouse**'s (*see page 221*) large stages. The Festival Theatre also plays host to the big modern dance companies such as Rambert and V-Tol. **Scottish Ballet**, although based in Glasgow, has made the Festival Theatre its second home. The company, under the recently appointed artistic director Robert North, appears to be in good shape for some innovative and popular seasons to come.

The **Traverse Theatre** (*see page 221*) and, to a lesser extent, the **Brunton Theatre** (*see page 220*), play host to smaller touring dance companies. **Dance Base** (*see below*) is the umbrella association for independent dance organisations and companies and home to X-Factor, Curve Foundation and Tabula Rasa.

Venues

Dance Base

The Assembly Rooms, 54 George Street, New Town, EH2 (225 5525/www.dancebase.co.uk). Bus 13, 19, 55, 82. **Open** 10am-4pm Mon-Fri; closed Sat, Sun. **Tickets** vary. **No credit cards. Map** p314 B1.

Currently based at The Assembly Rooms, this umbrella association expects to move to a purpose-built studio and office complex on the Grassmarket in spring 2001. It has the UK's largest participatory programme of dance, with classes, workshops and residencies across town.

St Bride's Centre

10 Orwell Terrace, South Edinburgh, EH11 (346 1405). Bus 3, 21, 25. **Open** box office 9am-5pm Mon-Fri; closed Sat, Sun. **Tickets** 50p-£10. **Credit** MC, V. **Map** p308 B7.

A community venue in an old church that is often used by touring dance companies and for ceilidhs. Smaller touring theatre productions also come here.

Scottish Ballet performing *Prince Rama and the Demons*.

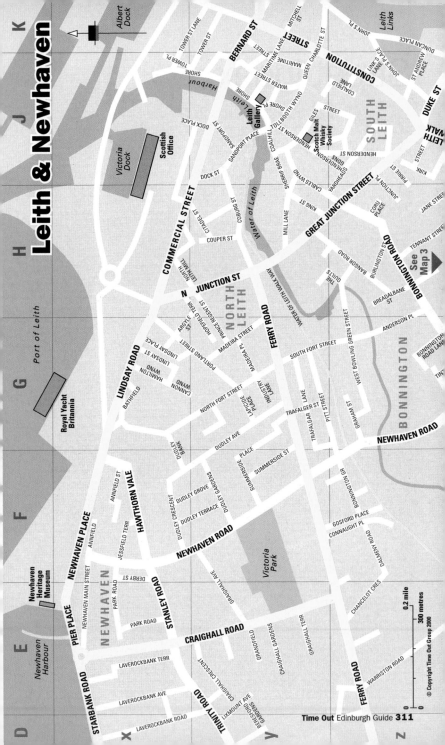

Leith & Newhaven

Albert Dock

Victoria Dock

Scottish Office

Port of Leith

Royal Yacht Britannia

Newhaven Heritage Museum

Newhaven Harbour

TOWER STREET LANE
TOWER ST
TOWER PL
SHORE
Harbour
Leith
DOCK PLACE
DOCK ST
SANDPORT ST
SANDPORT PLACE
Leith Gallery
SHORE
BROAD WYND
WATER STREET
MARITIME LANE
MARITIME STREET
BERNARD ST
MITCHELL ST
STREET
QUEEN CHARLOTTE ST
Leith Links
JOHN S PL
DUNCAN PLACE
JOHN S PLACE
LINK S PLACE
JOHN S LANE
ST ANDREW PLACE
CONSTITUTION
SOUTH LEITH
DUKE ST
LEITH WALK
KIRK STREET
STREET

CITADEL ST
COMMERCIAL STREET
COUPER ST
COBURG ST
DOCK ST
Water of Leith
SHERRIF BRAE
GILES STREET
COALHILL
CABLES WYND
TOLLBOOTH WYND
HENDERSON GDNS
COATFIELD LANE
Scotch Malt Whisky Society
HENDERSON STREET
KING ST
MILL LANE
YARDHEADS
JUNCTION PL
CORU PLACE
GREAT JUNCTION STREET
JANE STREET
PIRRIE ST

NORTH JUNCTION ST
NORTH LEITH
NORTH JUNCTION ST
HOPEFIELD TERR
ARGYLE ST
PRINCE REGENT ST
MADEIRA STREET
MADEIRA PL
INDUSTRY LANE
FERRY ROAD
WATER OF LEITH WALKWAY
THE QUILTS
BANGOR ROAD
BURLINGTON STREET
See Map 3
BONNINGTON ROAD
BREADALBANE ST
TENNANT STREET
ANDERSON PL
BONNINGTON
BONNINGTON ROAD LANE

LINDSAY ROAD
BATHFIELD
LINDSAY ST
LINDSAY PLACE
HAMILTON WYND
CANNON WYND
PORTLAND STREET
NORTH FORT STREET
LAPICIDE PLACE
SOUTH FORT STREET
WEST BOWLING GREEN STREET
GRAHAM ST
PITT STREET
TRAFALGAR ST
TRAFALGAR LANE
BONNINGTON GR
GOSFORD PLACE
CONNAUGHT PL
DALMENY ROAD
NEWHAVEN ROAD

NEWHAVEN PLACE
HAWTHORN VALE
ANNFIELD ST
ANNFIELD
JESSFIELD TERR
DUDLEY BANK
DUDLEY AVE
DUDLEY CRESCENT
DUDLEY GROVE
DUDLEY TERRACE
DUDLEY GARDENS
SUMMERSIDE PLACE
SUMMERSIDE ST
NEWHAVEN ROAD
Victoria Park
GRAHAM AVE
BONNINGTON

PIER PLACE
NEWHAVEN MAIN STREET
NEWHAVEN
PARK ROAD
DERBY ST
PARK ROAD
STANLEY ROAD
CRAIGHALL ROAD
GRANFIELD
CRAIGHALL GARDENS
GRAIGHALL TERR
CHANCELOT CRES
GOSFORD PLACE
CONNAUGHT PL
FERRY ROAD
WARRISTON ROAD

STARBANK ROAD
LAVEROCKBANK TERR
LAVEROCKBANK AVE
LAVEROCKBANK ROAD
TRINITY ROAD
LIXMOUNT AVE
CRAIGHALL CRESCENT
PEFFERBANK GARDENS

0.2 mile
0
300 metres
0
© Copyright Time Out Group 2000

Time Out Edinburgh Guide **311**

Street Index

Edinburgh

Glasgow

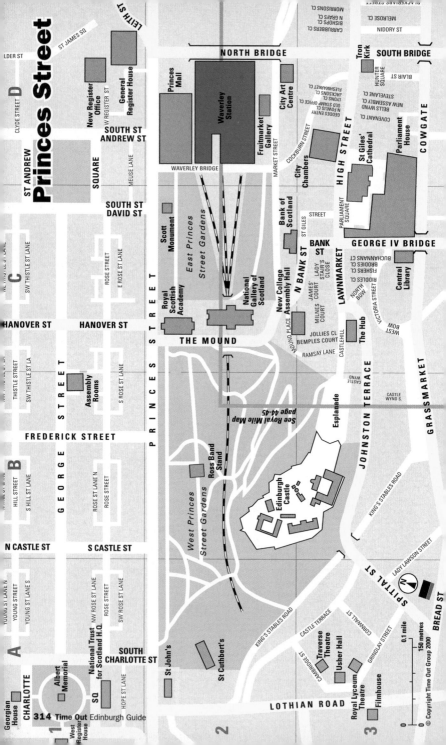

Princes Street

LEITH ST
ST JAMES SQ
LDER ST
W REGISTER ST
CLYDE STREET

NORTH BRIDGE
SOUTH BRIDGE

New Register Office
General Register House

ST ANDREW
SQUARE

SOUTH ST
ANDREW ST

MEUSE LANE

SOUTH ST
DAVID ST

Princes Mall
Waverley Station
City Art Centre
Fruitmarket Gallery

Tron Kirk
HUNTER SQUARE
BLAIR ST
HUNTER SQUARE

MORRISON'S CL
BISHOPS CL
CARRUBBERS CL
MELROSE CL
NIDDRY ST
BLACKFRIARS STREET

CARRUBBERS CL
BISHOPS CL
N GRAYS CL
FLESHMARKET CL
GEDDES ENTRY
OLD FISHMARKET CL
LYON CL
JACKSONS CL
NEW ASSEMBLY CL
BELLS WYND
STEVENLANE
OLD STAMP OFFICE CL
N FOULIS CL
COVENANT CL

COWGATE

WAVERLEY BRIDGE

MARKET STREET

COCKBURN STREET

HIGH STREET

St Giles' Cathedral
Parliament House

Scott Monument

East Princes Street Gardens

Bank of Scotland
St Giles
STREET
City Chambers

BANK ST
PARLIAMENT SQUARE

GEORGE IV BRIDGE

Royal Scottish Academy
National Gallery of Scotland

New College
Assembly Hall
N BANK ST
LADY STAIR'S CLOSE
JAMES COURT
MILNES COURT
LAWNMARKET

BUCHANAN CT
BRODIES CT
FISHERS CL
RIDDLES CL
NORTH BOW

Central Library

HANOVER ST
HANOVER ST

THE MOUND

YOUNG PLACE
JOLLIES CL
BEMPLES COURT
CASTLEHILL
RAMSAY LANE

The Hub

VICTORIA STREET

WEST BOW

THISTLE STREET
SW THISTLE ST LA
N THISTLE ST LANE
SW THISTLE ST LANE

ROSE STREET
E ROSE ST LANE

Assembly Rooms

P R I N C E S   S T R E E T

See Royal Mile Map page 44-45

Esplanade

JOHNSTON TERRACE
CASTLE WYND S.
CASTLE WYND

GRASSMARKET

GEORGE   STREET

FREDERICK STREET

S ROSE ST LANE
ROSE STREET

Ross Band Stand

West Princes Street Gardens

Edinburgh Castle

HILL STREET
S HILL ST LANE

B

ROSE STREET
ROSE ST LANE N

KING'S STABLES ROAD

YOUNG STREET
YOUNG ST LANE N
YOUNG STREET
YOUNG ST LANES

N CASTLE ST
S CASTLE ST

NW ROSE ST LANE
ROSE STREET
SW ROSE ST LANE

KING'S STABLES ROAD

SPITTAL ST

LADY LAWSON STREET

BREAD ST

A

Georgian House
Albert Memorial

CHARLOTTE

West Register House

SQ

National Trust for Scotland H.Q.

HOPE ST LANE

SOUTH
CHARLOTTE ST

St John's

St Cuthbert's

CASTLE TERRACE

CAMBRIDGE ST
GRINDLAY STREET
CORNWALL STREET

Traverse Theatre
Usher Hall

Royal Lyceum Theatre
Filmhouse

LOTHIAN ROAD

0   0.1 mile
0   150 metres

N

© Copyright Time Out Group 2000

314 Time Out Edinburgh Guide

TimeOut Edinburgh — Please let us know what you think

About this guide...

1. How useful did you find the following sections?

	Very	Fairly	Not very
In Context	□	□	□
Sightseeing	□	□	□
Accommodation	□	□	□
Consumer	□	□	□
Arts & Entertainment	□	□	□
Trips Out of Town	□	□	□
Directory	□	□	□
Maps	□	□	□

2. Did you travel to Edinburgh...?

Alone □   With children □
As part of a group □   On vacation □
On business □   To study □
With a partner □   I live here. □

3. How long was your trip Edinburgh? (write in)

_____ days

4. Where did you book your trip?

Time Out Classifieds □
On the Internet □
With a travel agent □
Other (write in) □
_____

5. Where did you first hear about this guide?

Advertising in *Time Out* magazine □
On the Internet □
From a travel agent □
Other (write in) □
_____

6. Is there anything you'd like us to cover in greater depth?

_____
_____
_____

7. Are there any places that should/ should not* be included in the guide? (*delete as necessary)

_____
_____
_____
_____
_____
_____

8. How many other people have used this guide?

none □ 1 □ 2 □ 3 □ 4 □ 5+ □

9. What city or country would you like to visit next? (write in)

_____

About other *Time Out* publications...

10. Have you ever bought/used *Time Out* magazine?

Yes □   No □

11. Have you ever bought/used any other *Time Out* City Guides?

Yes □   No □

If yes, which ones?
_____

12. Have you ever bought/used other *Time Out* publications?

Yes □   No □

If yes, which ones?
_____

About you...

13. Title (Mr, Ms etc):

First name:
Surname:
Address:

Postcode:
Email:
Nationality:

14. Date of birth □□/□□/□□

15. Sex: male □   female □

16. Are you...?
Single
Married/Living with partner

17. What is your occupation?

18. At the moment do you earn...?

under £15,000 □
over £15,000 and up to £19,999 □
over £20,000 and up to £24,999 □
over £25,000 and up to £39,999 □
over £40,000 and up to £49,999 □
over £50,000 □

□ Please tick here if you'd like to hear about offers and discounts from *Time Out* products and relevant companies.

Time Out Guides

FREEPOST 20 (WC3187)
LONDON
W1E 0DQ

Time Out

City Guides are available from all good bookshops or through Penguin Direct.

Simply call 020 8757 4036 (9am–5pm) or fill out the form below, affix a stamp and return.

ISBN	title	retail price	quantity	total
0140289445	Time Out Guide to **Amsterdam**	£9.99		
0140289410	Time Out Guide to **Barcelona**	£10.99		
0140289399	Time Out Guide to **Berlin**	£10.99		
0140284052	Time Out Guide to **Boston**	£10.99		
0140289429	Time Out Guide to **Brussels**	£9.99		
0140286330	Time Out Guide to **Budapest**	£10.99		
0140290778	Time Out Guide to **Chicago**	£10.99		
0140281738	Time Out Guide to **Dublin**	£10.99		
0140289453	Time Out Guide to **Edinburgh**	£9.99		
0140293930	Time Out Guide to **Florence & Tuscany**	£10.99		
0140289402	Time Out Guide to **Las Vegas**	£10.99		
0140273158	Time Out Guide to **Lisbon**	£9.99		
0140289372	Time Out Guide to **London**	£10.99		
0140274456	Time Out Guide to **Los Angeles**	£9.99		
014027443X	Time Out Guide to **Madrid**	£9.99		
0140266852	Time Out Guide to **Miami**	£9.99		
014027314X	Time Out Guide to **Moscow**	£9.99		
0140274480	Time Out Guide to **New Orleans**	£9.99		
0140274529	Time Out Guide to **New York**	£9.99		
0140289380	Time Out Guide to **Paris**	£10.99		
0140274448	Time Out Guide to **Prague**	£9.99		
0140287558	Time Out Guide to **Rome**	£10.99		
0140289364	Time Out Guide to **San Francisco**	£10.99		
014029077X	Time Out Guide to **The South of France**	£10.99		
0140274642	Time Out Guide to **Sydney**	£10.99		
0140284605	Time Out Guide to **Tokyo**	£10.99		
0140284060	Time Out Guide to **Venice**	£10.99		
0140280677	Time Out Guide to **Vienna**	£10.99		
0140284591	Time Out Guide to **Washington**	£10.99		
		+ postage & packing		£1.50
		Total Payment		

(Please use block capitals)

Cardholder's Name

Address

Town _____ Postcode

Daytime Telephone Number

Method of Payment (UK Credit cards only)

Barclaycard/Visa

Access Card/Mastercard

Signature (if paying by credit card) _____

Expiry date

Cheque
I enclose a cheque £ _____ made payable to 'Penguin Direct'

Delivery will normally be within 28 working days. The availability and published prices quoted are correct at time of going to press but are subject to alteration without prior notice. Order form valid until May 2001. **Please note that this service is only available in the UK.** Please note your order may be delayed if payment details are incorrect.

Penguin Direct
Penguin Books Ltd
Bath Road
Harmondsworth
West Drayton
Middlesex
UB7 0DA

currency at a bureau de change. Commission rates, which should be clearly displayed, vary.

Banks, travel companies and the major rail stations have bureaux de change, and there are many in tourist areas. Most are open standard business hours (9am-5.30pm Mon-Fri), but one that is open longer is FEXCO Ltd, situated inside the **Edinburgh & Scotland Information Centre** (*see page 289*).

Lost/stolen credit cards

Report lost or stolen credit cards immediately to both the police and the 24-hour services listed below. Inform your bank by phone and in writing.

American Express (*personal card 01273 696933/corporate card 01273 689955).*
Diners Club/Diners Club International (*general enquiries & emergencies 01252 513500/0800 460800).*
Eurocard (*00 49 697 933 1910).* This German number will accept reversed charges in an emergency.
MasterCard (*0800 964767).*
Visa (*0800 895082).*

Money transfers

The information centre above the Princes Mall (formerly Waverley Shopping Centre) can advise on **Western Union** money transfer, or call Western Union direct on 0800 833833. Alternatively contact your own bank to find out which British banks it is affiliated with; you can then nominate an Edinburgh branch to have the money sent to.

Police & security

The police are a good source of information about the locality and are used to helping visitors find their way around. If you have been robbed, assaulted or the victim of any

crime, look under 'Police' in the phone directory for the nearest police station, or call directory enquiries (free from public payphones) on 192.
Dial 999 only in an emergency.
If you have a complaint to make about the police, be sure to take the offending officer's ID number, which should be prominently displayed on his or her epaulette.

You can then register a complaint at any police station, visit a solicitor or Citizens' Advice Bureau or contact The Complaints Department, Police Headquarters, Lothian and Borders Police, Fettes Avenue, Edinburgh, EH4 1RB (311 3377; Map p305 A3).

Violent crime is relatively rare in Edinburgh, but, as in any major city, it is unwise to take any risks. Thieves and pickpockets specifically target unwary tourists. Use common sense and follow these basic rules:

● Keep your wallet and purse out of sight. Don't wear a wrist wallet (they are easily snatched). Keep your handbag securely closed.
●Don't leave a handbag, briefcase, bag or coat unattended, especially in pubs, cinemas, department stores or fast food shops, on public transport, at railway stations and airports, or in crowds.
● Don't leave your bag or coat beside, under or on the back of your chair.
● Don't wear expensive jewellery or watches that can be easily snatched.
● Don't put your purse down on the table in a restaurant or on a shop counter while you scrutinise the bill.
● Don't carry a wallet in your back pocket.
● Don't flash your money or credit cards around.
● Avoid parks after dark. Late at night, try to travel in groups of three or more.

Postal services

Compared to some other countries, the UK has a reliable postal service. If you have a query on any aspect of Royal Mail services contact

Customer Services on 0345 740740/fax 550 8360 (Edinburgh) or 0345 740740/fax 0141 242 4120 (Glasgow). For business enquiries contact the **Royal Mail Business Centre for Scotland** on 0345 950 950/ fax 0141 242 4652. You can ask for a Royal Mail Fact File and any post office leaflets to be sent to you.

Post office opening hours are usually 9am-5.30pm Mon-Fri; 9am-12.30pm Sat, with the exception of **St James Post Office**. Listed below are two other main central offices. Consult the phone book for other offices within Edinburgh:
Frederick Street Post Office *40 Frederick Street, New Town, EH2 (0345 223344). Bus 13, 19, 55, 82.* **Map** p314 B1.
Hope Street Post Office *7 Hope Street, New Town, EH2 4EN (226 6823). Princes St buses.* **Map** p314 A1.
St James Post Office *8-10 Kings Mall, St James Centre, New Town, EH1 (556 0478). Princes St buses.* **Open** 9am-5.30pm Mon; 8.30am-5.30pm Tue-Fri; 8.30am-6pm Sat; closed Sun. **Map** p307 G4

Stamps

You can buy stamps at post offices and at any newsagents that display the appropriate red sign. Stamps can be bought individually (at post offices only) or, in the case of first class (for next-day delivery within mainland Britain) or second class (two-to three-day delivery in mainland Britain), in books of four or ten, at post offices, supermarkets and some shops. At the time of writing (April 2000), prices were 19p for second-class letters (inland only) and 27p for first-class inland letters and letters weighing up to 20g to EU countries. Postcards cost 34p to send abroad. Rates for other letters and parcels vary according to weight and destination.

Poste restante

If you intend to travel around Britain, friends from home can write to you care of a post office, where mail will be kept at the enquiry desk for up to one month. The envelope should be marked 'Poste Restante' in the top left-hand corner, with your name displayed above the address of the post office where you want to collect your mail. Take ID when you collect your post. The **Hope Street** post office (*see above*) offers this service.

If you are keeping in touch with home by email there are various internet cafés, such as **Cyberia** (*see page 139*) or **Web 13** (*see page 146*), where you can pick up your mail.

Express delivery services

All companies can arrange pick-up.

DHL
Unit 15/4-15/5 South Gyle Crescent, South Gyle Industrial Estate, WEs Edinburgh, EH12 (0345 100300). South Gyle rail. **Open** *Phone line* 24hrs daily. *Office* 8.30am-6.45pm Mon-Fri; 9am-noon Sat; closed Sun. **Credit** AmEx, DC, MC, V. Worldwide express delivery service. Next-day deliveries can be made within the EU (not guaranteed), and the USA if booked before 2pm.

Federal Express
c/o Securicor, 23 South Gyle Crescent, South Gyle Industrial Estate, West Edinburgh, EH12 (0800 123800). South Gyle rail. **Open** 7.30am-7.30pm daily. **Credit** AmEx, MC, V. FedEx can deliver next day by 8am to certain destinations across the USA (mainly New York and other major cities). More than 210 countries are served.

UPS
30 South Gyle Crescent, South Gyle Industrial Estate, West Edinburgh, EH12 (0345 877 877/fax 314 6820). South Gyle rail. **Open** 8am-8pm Mon-Fri; 9am-2pm Sat; closed Sun. **Credit** AmEx, MC, V. UPS offers express delivery to more than 200 countries; cheaper, slower services are also available. Deliveries

to some destinations can be guaranteed to arrive by 8.30am or 10.30am the next day.

Public holidays

See page 95.

Public toilets

Hunters Square
By the Tron, Royal Mile, EH1. **Open** 8am-10pm daily. **Map** p314 D3.

The Mound
Princes Street, New Town, EH2. **Open** 8am-10pm daily. **Map** p314 C2. Disabled access 24hrs using National Key Scheme.

Princes Mall
Waverley Bridge, New Town, EH1. **Open** 8.30am-6pm daily. **Map** p314 D2.

West Princes St Gardens
Princes St, New Town, EH2. **Open** 8am-10pm daily. Disabled access from Princes Street Gardens only. **Map** p314 B2.

Religion

Baptist
Charlotte Baptist Chapel *West Rose Street, New Town, EH2 (225 4812). Bus 3, 3A, 12, 16, 17.* **Open** *office* 9am-4pm Mon-Fri; closed Sat, Sun. **Services** 10am (prayer meeting), 11am, 5.45pm (prayer meeting), 6.30pm, Sun; 8pm (prayer meeting) Tue. **Map** p314 A1.

Buddhist
There is no central meeting place for Edinburgh's diverse Buddhist groups, which tend to share space with other faiths or organisations. Phone 332 7987 for information.

Catholic
St Mary's Cathedral *61 York Place, Broughton, EH1 (556 1798). Bus 8.* **Open** 7am-6pm Mon-Fri, Sun; 7am-7pm Sat. **Services** 7.30am, 9.30am, 11.30am, 6pm feast days or holidays of obligation; 7.30am, 12.45pm Mon-Fri; 10am, 12.45pm, 6pm (vigil mass) Sat; 7.30am, 9.30am, 11.30am, 7.30pm Sun. **Confessions** heard 10.30-11.30am, 1.15-2pm, 5-5.45pm Sat. **Map** p307 G4.

Church of Scotland
St Giles' Cathedral *Royal Mile, EH1 (225 4363). Bus 35, 35A.* **Open** *Easter-Sept* 9am-7pm Mon-Fri, 9am-5pm Sat, 1-5pm Sun; *Sept-Easter* 9am-5pm Mon-Sat, 1-5pm Sun.

Services 8am, noon Mon-Fri; noon, 6pm (Holy Communion) Sat; 8am (Holy Communion), 10am (Holy Communion), 11.30am, 8pm Sun. **Map** p314 D3.

Episcopalian
Cathedral Church of St Mary *Palmerston Place, New Town, EH12 (225 6293). Bus 3, 3A, 12, 25.* **Open** 7.15am-6pm Mon-Sat; 7.30am-6pm Sun (till 9pm in summer). **Services** 7.30am (Eucharist), 1.05pm, 5.30pm (choral evensong) Mon, Tue, Wed, Fri; 7.30am (Eucharist), 11.30am (Eucharist), 1.05pm, 5.30pm (Eucharist), Thur; 7.30am Sat; 8am (Eucharist), 10.30am (choral Eucharist), 3.30pm (choral evensong) Sun. **Map** p308 B6.

Hindu
Edinburgh Hindu Mandir & Cultural Centre (Temple & Community Centre) *St Andrew Place (former St Andrew's Church), Leith, EH6 (667 6064/440 0084). Bus 16, 22, 34.* **Open/services** 4-6pm every 2nd Sun of the month; noon-2pm every 4th Sun of the month. **Map** p311 Jz.

Islamic
Mosque & Islamic Centre *50 Potterow, South Edinburgh, EH8 (667 1777). Bus 40, 41, 42.* **Open** dawn-dusk daily. **Services** phone for details. **Map** p310 G6.

Jewish
Synagogue Chambers *4 Salisbury Road, South Edinburgh, EH16 (667 3144). Bus 7, 8, 31, 80.* **Open/services** phone for details. **Map** p310 J8.

Methodist
Nicolson Square Methodist Church *Nicolson Square, South Edinburgh, EH8 (662 0417). Bus 7, 8, 31, 80.* **Open** *basement chapel & café* 8.30am-3.30pm Mon-Fri; closed Sat, Sun; church open to tourists at lunchtime in summer. **Services** 11am, 6.30pm Sun. **Map** p310 G6.

Quaker
Quaker Meeting House *7 Victoria Terrace, Victoria Street, Royal Mile, EH1 (225 4825). Bus 35, 35A.* **Open** 9am-10pm daily. **Services** 12.30pm Wed; 11am Sun. **Map** p314 C3.

Sikh
Sikh Temple *7 Mill Lane, Leith, EH6 (553 7207). Bus 7, 10, 34.* **Open** phone in advance. **Services** 11.30am, 3pm Sun. **Map** p311 Hy.

Students

Edinburgh University is renowned worldwide and has an unbeatable reputation for medicine and scientific research; its degrees carry hefty academic kudos. Founded in 1583, and with 15,600 full-time students, the University boasts an impressive roll-call of former pupils, including Sir Walter Scott, Robert Louis Stevenson and Charles Darwin.

There are eight faculties, with departments scattered across town, and the Old College boasts some stunning architecture. With this impressive historical baggage, Edinburgh University also has an – arguably justifiable – reputation for a disproportionate number of yahs (snobs of predominantly southern English origin). On the flip side, Edinburgh is also home to a number of newer colleges and former polytechnics.

For academic books, **James Thin** (*see page 165*) is unbeatable.

Universities/colleges

Edinburgh College of Art

Lauriston Place, South Edinburgh, EH3 Bus 23, 28, 45. (221 6000/ www.eca.ac.uk). **Map** p309 E6.
One of the most prestigious art colleges in the UK: competition for places here is stiff. Studies on offer range from film to textiles and sculpture.

Heriot-Watt University

Riccarton Campus, Currie, EH14 (449 5111/www.hw.ac.uk). Bus 25.
A vocational university specialising in business, finance, languages, science and engineering subjects.

Napier University

Craiglockhart Campus, 219 Colinton Road, South Edinburgh, EH14 (444 2266/www.napier@ac.uk). Bus 23.
Founded in 1964 and named after mathematical whizz-kid John Napier, this former polytechnic with a reputation for a more eclectic (and down-to-earth) student body than Edinburgh University was granted university status in 1992. Offering predominantly vocational courses, its employment record for graduates is second to none.

Queen Margaret University Campus

Clerwood Terrace, West Edinburgh, EH12 (317 3000/www.qmuc.ac.uk). Bus 12, 23, 26.
An assortment of predominantly degree courses – everything from nursing, nutrition and tourism to management, business and drama.

University of Edinburgh

Old College, South Bridge, South Edinburgh, EH8 (650 1000/ www.ed.ac.uk). Bus 7, 8, 31, 80. **Map** p310 G6.
One of the UK's oldest and most reputable universities offers a staggering range of academic degree courses. There's also a good selection of part-time special-interest courses in the day-time and evening. Its international office is at 57 George Square EH8 (650 4300).

Language courses

A full list of the vast number of schools offering English language courses can be found

---

Tongue twisters

Scottish is a whole language to itself and its regional variations are legendary. The Edinburgh vernacular is constantly being transformed by incomers from all over Scotland. Here are a few pointers.

Barry – good, excellent, attractive. A general term of acclaim.

Bampot – a nutter.

Ben – the back room of the house.

Chum – to accompany.

Couthy – plain or homely (of a person); agreeable, snug, comfortable (of a place).

Dod – a small amount, a dab. Often used in conjunction with 'wee'.

Douce – kind, gentle, soothing (pejoratively – sedate).

Dreich – wet, dull, tedious, dreary – of the weather or a person. The 'ch' is pronounced as in the German composer Bach.

Eijit – a fool, idiot.

Gallus – cheeky, self-confident or daring. In Glasgow: stylish or impressive.

Get – to go with (as in the phrase 'shall I get you down the road?')

Haar – sea mist, especially from the North Sea.

Hen – a female (informal).

Ken – know, understand – also interpolated (seemingly at random) into speech.

Laldy – as in the folk music phrase 'to give it laldy' – to play vigorously.

Loch – a lake. There are only two lakes in Scotland.

Lugs – ears.

Messages – shopping, groceries.

Nash – to leave precipitously (as in 'I better nash, the pub's about to close').

Oxter – armpit.

Pished – drunk.

Radge – barmy, mad, a bit too extrovert for comfort.

Scran – food.

See – take, for example (as in 'see that wee jimmy, he's well radge).

See you! – 'Hey!', 'Oi you!' or 'I say, old chap!'

Slater – woodlouse.

Stay – live (as in 'where do you stay?')

Stushie – a fight or altercation.

Teuchter – someone from the Highlands (pejorative).

Wee – small, a small quantity.

Weejie – a Glaswegian (highly derogatory).

---

in the *Yellow Pages*. The following is a small selection of some of the best and most well known. Some offer TEFL courses; phone for rates.

Berlitz
26 Frederick Street, New Town, EH2 (226 7198/fax 225 2918/ www.edinburgh@berlitz.co.uk). Bus 13, 19, 55, 82. Map p314 B1.

Edinburgh Language Centre
10B Oxford Terrace, New Town, EH4 (tel/fax 343 6596/ language@mcmail.com). Bus 13, 19, 55, 82. Map p305 B4.

Institute for Applied Language Studies
21 Hill Place, South Edinburgh, EH8 (650 6200/fax 667 5927/ www.ials.ed.ac.uk). Bus 7, 8, 31, 80. Map p310 G6.

Regent Edinburgh
29 Chester Street, New Town, EH3 (225 9888/fax 225 2133/ www.regent.org.uk). Bus 13. Map p308 B5.

Stevenson College
Sighthill Campus, Bankhead Avenue, Sighthill, EH11 (535 4600/fax 535 4666/ www.stevenson.ac.uk). Bus 22.

Student travel

Edinburgh Travel Centre
92 South Clerk Street, South Edinburgh, EH8 (667 9488). Bus 7, 8, 31, 80. **Open** 9am-5.30pm Mon-Fri; 10am-1pm Sat; closed Sun. Map p310 H8. **Branch:** 3 Bristo Square, South Edinburgh, EH8 (668 2221).

USIT Campus
53 Forrest Road, South Edinburgh, EH3 (668 3303/ www.usitcampus.co.uk). Bus 23, 28, 40, 45. **Open** 9am-5.30pm Mon, Tue, Thur, Fri; 10am-5.30pm Wed; 10am-5pm Sat; closed Sun. Map p309 F6.

Telephones

The telephone code for Edinburgh is 0131. If you're calling from outside the UK, dial the international code, followed by 44 (code for Britain), then the ten-digit number starting with 131

(omitting the first 0). The code for Glasgow and its environs is 0141.

International dialling codes

Australia 00 61; **Belgium** 00 32; **Canada** 00 1; **France** 00 33; **Germany** 00 49; **Ireland** 00 353; **Italy** 00 39; **Japan** 00 81; **Netherlands** 00 31; **New Zealand** 00 64; **Spain** 00 34; **USA** 00 1.

Operator services

Operator
Call 100 for the operator in the following circumstances: when you have difficulty in dialling; for an early-morning alarm call; to make a credit card call; for information about the cost of a call; and for international person-to-person calls. Dial 155 if you need to reverse the charges (call collect) or if you can't dial direct. Be warned, though – this service is very expensive.

Directory enquiries
Dial 192 for any number in Britain, or 153 for international numbers. Phoning directory enquiries from a private phone is expensive, and only two enquiries are allowed per call. If you phone from a public call box, directory enquiries calls are free.

International telemessages/ telegrams
Call 0800 190190 to phone in your message and it will be delivered by post the next day (£8.99 for up to 50 words, an additional £1 for a greetings card). There is no longer a domestic telegram service, but you can still send telegrams abroad. Call the same number.

Public phones

Public payphones take coins, credit cards or prepaid phonecards (and sometimes all three). The minimum cost is 10p, although some payphones (such as the counter-top ones found in many pubs) require a minimum of 20p. British Telecom phonecards are available from post offices

and many newsagents in denominations of £2, £5, £10 and £20.

Call boxes with the green Phonecard symbol take prepaid cards. A notice in the box tells you where to find the nearest stockist. A digital display shows how many units you have remaining on your card.

Telephone directories

There is one alphabetical phone directory for Edinburgh; it lists business and commercial numbers as well as private phone numbers and is available at post offices and libraries. Hotels will also have a copy and it is issued free to all residents with telephones, as is the *Yellow Pages* directory, which lists businesses and services.

Tipping

In Britain it is accepted that you tip in taxis, minicabs, restaurants (some waiting staff are forced to rely heavily on gratuities), hairdressers', hotels and some bars (not pubs) – ten to 15 per cent is normal. Be careful to check whether service has been added automatically to your bill – some restaurants include service and then also leave the space for a gratuity on your credit card slip.

Tourist information

The Edinburgh & Lothians Tourist Board operates the information centres listed below. There are also 24-hour electronic information units at the Edinburgh and Scotland Information Centre and in Rutland Place at the west end of Princes Street. The tourist board website at www.edinburgh.org has further information. For more websites, *see page 281*.

Edinburgh & Scotland Information Centre

*above Princes Mall, 3 Princes Street New Town, EH1 (473 3800).
Princes St buses.* **Open** *May, June, Sept* 9am-7pm Mon-Sat; 10am-7pm Sun; *July-Aug* 9am-8pm Mon-Sat; 10am-8pm Sun; *Oct-Apr* 9am-6pm Mon-Sat; 10am-6pm Sun. **Map** p314 D2.

Edinburgh Airport Tourist Information Desk

Edinburgh Airport, EH12 (473 3800). **Open** *Apr-Oct* 6.30am-10pm daily; *Nov-Mar* 7.30am-9.30pm daily.

Visas

Citizens of EU countries do not require a visa to visit the UK; citizens of other countries, including the USA, Canada and New Zealand, require only a valid passport for a visit of up to six months.

To apply for a visa, and to check your visa status before you travel, contact the British Embassy, High Commission or Consulate in your own country.

A visa allows you entry for a maximum of six months. For information about work permits *see below*.

Home Office

Immigration & Nationality Department, Block C, Whitgraft Centre, Croydon CR9 1AT (08706 067766/ www.homeoffice.gov.uk/rnd/hpg.htm). **Open** *telephone enquiries* 9am-4.45pm Mon-Wed; 10am-4.45pm Thur; 9am-4.30pm Fri; closed Sat, Sun.
The immigration department of the Home Office deals with all queries about immigration matters, visas and work permits for citizens from the Commonwealth and a few other countries.

Women

Security

Despite the still-popular stereotype of the red-blooded Scottish male, and that of the country's macho drinking culture, Edinburgh (central-ish Edinburgh at least) is a pretty safe and civilised place for women. The worst hassle you're likely to encounter is from passing groups of lagered-up lads.

There's generally a reasonable safety-in-numbers feel on the streets throughout Edinburgh's main drag and its immediate hinterland, even into the wee small hours (the lively entertainment scene means the streets are rarely deserted).

The main areas best avoided by women on their own at night are the Cowgate (mad and quite threatening when the clubs and pubs spill out across the streets), Lothian Road (a preponderance of decidedly laddish pubs and a history of violence at chucking-out time), the dockside and backstreet areas of Leith – particularly Coburgh Street – one of Edinburgh's main red-light districts – and the Meadows. The latter's paths look safe and brightly lit, but prove deceptively long and tree-screened once you actually set off down them; it has been the scene of several assaults in the past. The Royal Mile, too, perhaps more unexpectedly, has seen its share of such incidents, mainly because of the cover provided by the innumerable narrow alleys, or wynds, leading off it: it's highly picturesque by day, but can be spookily dark and shadowy at night.

Further afield, if you go to one of the city's big peripheral housing schemes, take local advice, and get your directions firmly sorted. The geographical layout of these areas is frequently bewildering, to say the least, and the levels of social deprivation to be found in some of them present a starkly different face of Edinburgh to the economic and architectural wealth of the centre.

Eating & drinking

Eating-, drinking- and accommodation-wise, Edinburgh these days caters for enough visitors of every variety to be pretty easy-going and flexible about different travellers' circumstances. For a relaxed solo meal, though, cafés can often be a better (and cheaper) bet for women than restaurants, with several good city-centre ones opening late into the evening.

Try **Bann's** *(see page 136)*, or **Susie's Wholefood Diner** *(see page 137)* for a tasty array of vegetarian snacks and meals, cakes and pastries, or the **Blue Moon Café** *(see page 143)*, a gay-run but straight-friendly establishment.

Accommodation

Edinburgh is sorely lacking in women-only or specifically designated women-friendly establishments. What you will find, though, is a sufficient quantity and diversity of places to lay your hat so that finding something secure and suitable should pose no real problem.

The bigger chain hotels, of which Edinburgh boasts several, tend to be well geared up to the needs of lone female guests, while many of the abundant B&Bs and guest-houses offer single rooms along with the kind of welcome that has made Scottish hospitality famous. Some B&Bs take a decidedly starchier or stingier approach: do sound out your prospective landlady (its generally a she) with some care.

One hostel that offers accommodation to women and married couples only is the **Kinnaird Christian Hostel** (13-14 Coates Crescent, EH3; (225 3608), which accepts women whatever their circumstances. Two other recommended women-run guesthouses are the **Amaryllis** (21 Upper Gilmore Place, EH3; 229 3293) and the **Armadillo** (12 Gilmore Place, EH3; 229 6457).

Getting around

There's a pretty comprehensive (and safe) bus network covering Edinburgh and its environs (*see page 273*). Many of the city's (black) taxi firms have now signed up to a policy of giving priority to lone women, whether they're phoning up or flagging down. Bear in mind, though, that taxis are often like gold dust between midnight and 3am at weekends, when the post-pub and club traffic is at its peak; book in advance or be prepared to wait or walk.

Activities

For those curious about women's often-overlooked place in Edinburgh's long and colourful history, the **Central Library** on George IV Bridge (*see page 282*) has a good booklet describing a Herstory Walk of the Royal Mile, starting at the Castle with St Margaret's Chapel, the oldest building in use in Edinburgh, and ending at Holyrood Palace, home to Mary Queen of Scots, taking in nearly 40 different sites en route.

Health & advice

For more contraception and sexual health agencies *see page 279*; for more women's crisis support services *see page 280*.

Finding a summer job in Edinburgh, or temporary employment if you are on a working holiday, can be a long, drawn-out process. If you can speak English and at least one other language well, and are an EU citizen or have a work permit, you should probably be able to find something in either catering, bar/restaurant or shop work.

Graduates with an English or a foreign-language degree could try teaching. If your English is not too good, you could try distributing free leaflets. Ideas can be found in *Summer Jobs in Britain*, published by Vacation Work, 9 Park End Street, Oxford (£8.99 plus £1.50 p&p). The Central Bureau for Educational Visits & Exchanges (3-4 Bruntsfield Crescent, EH10, 447 8024/ www.britishcouncil.org) has other publications.

To find work, look in the *Scotsman*, local and national papers and newsagents' windows, or write to, phone or visit employers. Some advertise vacancies on Jobcentre noticeboards; there is often temporary and unskilled work available; look in the *Yellow Pages* under 'Employment Agencies'.

For office work, sign on with temp agencies. If you have shorthand, typing or wordprocessing skills, such agencies may be able to find you well-paid assignments.

Work for foreign visitors

With few exceptions, citizens of non-European Economic Area (EEA) countries need a work permit before they are legally able to work in the UK. One of the advantages of working here is the opportunity to meet people, but for any employment it is essential that you speak reasonable English. For office work you need a high standard of English and relevant skills.

Work permits

EEA citizens, residents of Gibraltar and certain categories of other overseas nationals do not require a work permit. However, others who wish to come to the UK to work must obtain a permit before setting out.

Prospective employers who have a vacancy that they are unable to fill with a resident or EEA national must apply for a permit to the **Department for Education & Employment** (Level 5, Moorfoot, Sheffield, S1 4PQ (0114 259 4074). Permits are only issued for jobs that require a high level of skill and experience. The employer must be able to demonstrate to the DfEE that there is no resident/EEA labour available.

There is a Training & Work Experience Scheme that enables non-EEA nationals to come to the UK for training towards a professional or specialist qualification, or to undertake a short period of managerial level work experience. Again, this should be applied for before coming to the UK. Listed below are other possibilities.

Voluntary work

Voluntary work in youth hostels provides board, lodging and some pocket money. For advice on voluntary work with charities contact the Home Office (*see page 289*).

Working holidaymakers

Citizens of Commonwealth countries, aged 17-27, may apply to come to the UK as a working holidaymaker. This allows them to take part-time work without a DfEE permit. They must contact their nearest British Diplomatic Post to obtain the necessary entry clearance before travelling to the UK.

Further Reading

Whole tomes have been filled with quotations from transfixed visitors describing Edinburgh as the 'windy city', 'Auld Reekie' and the 'Athens of The North'. But for a taste of the real Edinburgh, the one that you won't really get to know until you've stayed here a while, start with the many modern works of popular fiction set in the city.

Classic fiction

Hogg, James *Confessions of a Justified Sinner*
An ironic jibe against religious bigotry in the 17th and 18th centuries. Set in the turmoil of the Edinburgh of that time, it has a peculiarly haunting description of Arthur's Seat in the haar (sea mist). The *Canongate Classics* edition contains a particularly useful introduction.
Scott, Walter *The Heart of Midlothian*
Contains, amongst other things, an account of the Porteous lynching of 1736.
Spark, Muriel *The Prime of Miss Jean Brodie*
Practically the official Edinburgh novel. Edinburgh-born Spark has created an enduring icon in Jean Brodie, who makes a stand against the city's moral intransigence.
Stevenson, Robert Louis *Edinburgh Picturesque Notes*
What it says on the cover – perceptive, witty and the source of many subsequent opinions about Edinburgh.

Modern fiction

Banks, Iain *Complicity*
A visceral, body-littered thriller, with spot-on characterisation of both city and protagonists.
Boyd, William *New Confessions*
A fine portrait of late 19th-century Edinburgh, as seen by a young boy growing up in an austere household.
Butlin, Ron *Night Visits*
Set in 'an Edinburgh at its grandest, coldest and hardest... as if nothing less than such a stony grip and iron inflexibility were needed to prevent unimaginable pain', as the *TLS* so eloquently put it.
Hird, Laura *Born Free*
Family life on a modern Edinburgh housing estate. Hird's debut novel is so well observed and humourously put that it almost hurts to read it.

Jardine, Quentin *Skinner novels*
Jardine's detective, Skinner, is too perfect for comfort, but reflects the morally aloof side of the Edinburgh psyche. *Skinner's Festival* is the best.
Johnston, Paul *Body Politic, The Bone Yard, Water of Death*
Future detective fiction with a nightmare vision of Edinburgh as a city state with a year-round Festival where the impoverished populace lives to serve the needs of its tourists. Fanciful and erudite, at times it seems a bit too possible for comfort.
Meek, James *MacFarlane Boils The Sea*
This poetic, merciless description of late 1980s Edinburgh in winter gets into every cranny of the city.
Rankin, Ian *Inspector Rebus novels*
Quality genre detective fiction. Hard-bitten Rebus inhabits an Edinburgh that is the reality for most of its residents. All the novels carry their weight, but the earliest reveal Edinburgh at its most gritty and latest have the best sense of place.
Warner, Alan *The Sopranos*
A wry, cheeky and brilliantly observed story of reprobate choirgirls down from Oban.
Welsh, Irvine *Trainspotting*
The first and best of Welsh's novels about the culture of drugs, clubs and unemployed youth that Edinburgh's more genteel residents do their best to ignore. His later work is more self-indulgent but his observation of the language is spot on.
Williamson, Kevin Ed *Children of Albion Rovers*
Short stories that grip grimly to the Edinburgh underbelly – from where there are surprisingly revealing views. Williamson's Rebel Inc imprint gives vent to the radge generation's splenetic prose.

History & politics

Daitches, David *Edinburgh*
A highly readable and academically sound history.
Prebble, John *The King's Jaunt*
Everything you could want to know (and more) about George IV's agenda-setting visit of 1822.
Smout, TC *A History of the Scottish People 1560-1830*
The definitive social history of Scotland.
Youngson AJ *The Making of Classical Edinburgh*
An exhaustive account, with superb photographs and plans, of the building of the New Town, from its conception right down to the details of its realisation.

Culture

Bold, Alan *Scotland – A Literary Guide*
About as complete a guide as you will need.
Bruce, George *Festival of the North*
The story of the Edinburgh International Festival, from its conception to its birth in 1947 and its subsequent growth until 1975.
Daitches, David *The New Companion to Scottish Culture*
A useful encyclopedia which, if rather wordy and not as well indexed as it should be, serves its job well.
Dale, Michael *Sore Throats and Overdrafts*
The Fringe, as told by its administrator from 1978 to 1985.
Dudley Edwards & Richardson (Eds) *Edinburgh*
One of the better literary anthologies on the city.
Hardy, Forsyth *Slightly Mad and Full of Danger*
The history of the Film Festival by one of its founders.
Lamond & Tucek *The Malt Whisky File*
All the distilleries and nearly every malt that is sold is reviewed, with useful tasting notes giving marks for sweetness, peatiness and availability.
Mackie, Albert *Speak Scotch or Whistle*
'A braw wee book, ken, wie yu fair smatterin' o wureds yous can yuze'.
Moffat, Alistair *The Edinburgh Fringe*
A history of the Fringe from its arrival in 1947 through to 1977.

Glasgow

Burgess, Moira *Imagine a City – Glasgow in Fiction.*
An informed and entertaining examination of the books and writing that reflect the city.
Daitches, David *Glasgow*
As readable and academically sound as his Edinburgh history.
Gray, Alasdair *Lanark*
A surreal description of Glasgow in the 1940s and '50s – and a fascinating examination of the Scottish psyche.
Scott, Walter *Rob Roy*
Contains several obvertions of the Merchant City in the early 18th century.
Torrington, Jeff *Swing Hammer, Swing*
Set in the slums of the Gorbals as they were demolished in the 1960s.

Index

Advertisers' Index

Maps

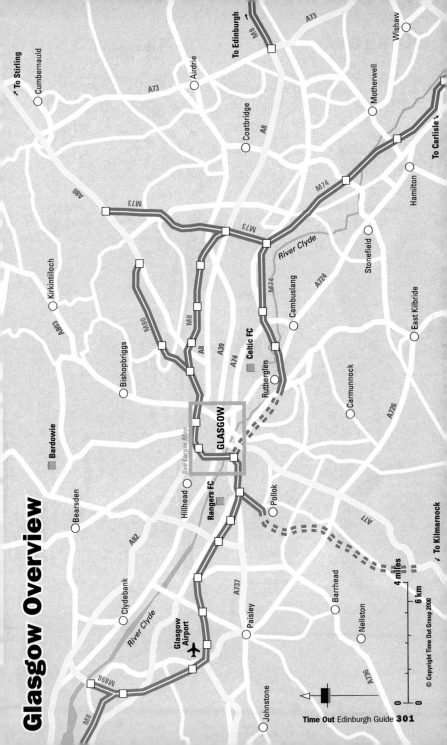

Glasgow Overview

© Copyright Time Out Group 2000

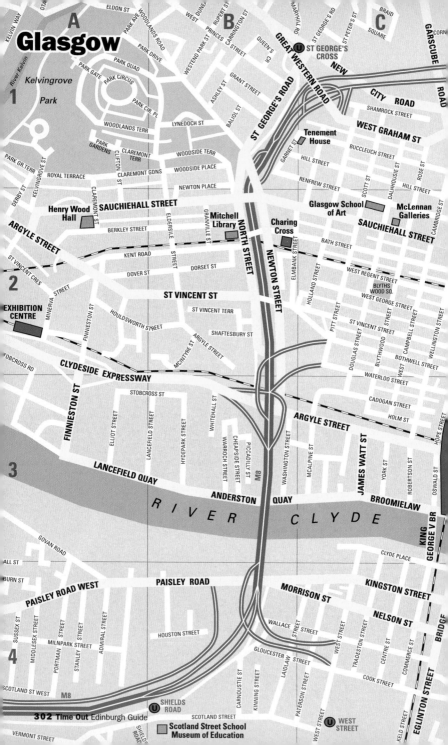

Glasgow

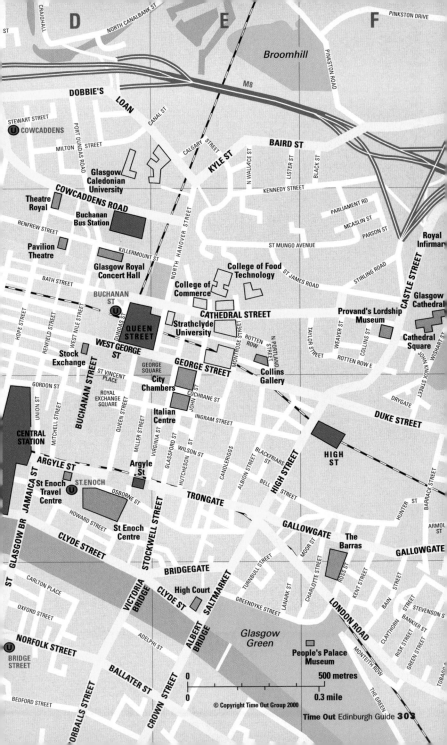

Edinburgh Overview

Firth of Forth

Inchkeith

Inchcolm

Inchmickery

Cramond Island

Gullane

Aberlady

Longniddry

To Berwick on Tweed

A1

Pencaitland

Glenkinchie Distillery

Cockenzie

Tranent

Oxenford

Pathhead

A68

To Galashiels →

Prestonpans

Preston Grange Mining Museum

Musselburgh Racecourse

A1

Musselburgh

Dalkeith

Scottish Mining Museum Newtongrange

Gorebridge

A7

A720

Portobello

Duddingston

Craigmillar Castle

CITY BYPASS

Bonnyrigg & Lasswade

Meadowbank

Leith

Holyrood Park

Royal Observatory Visitor Centre

Loanhead

L O T H I A N

Newhaven

See Larger Maps

EDINBURGH

Rosslyn Chapel

Roslin

Rosyth

Inverkeithing

North Queensferry

Deep Sea World

Forth Road Bridge

South Queensferry

Cramond

Lauriston Castle

Zoo

Murrayfield Stadium

A720

Hillend

Midlothian Ski Centre

Glencorse Reservoir

Penicuik

← To Biggar

A702

CITY BYPASS

Currie

Balerno

A70

Threipmuir Reservoir

Pentland Hills

Edinburgh Airport

Royal Highland Showground Ingliston

M8

M9

Ratho

To Glasgow →

4 miles

6 km

0

0

© Copyright Time Out Group 2000

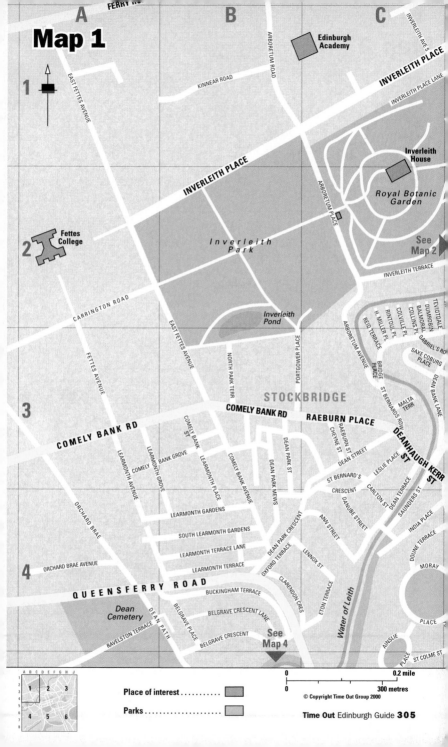

Map 1

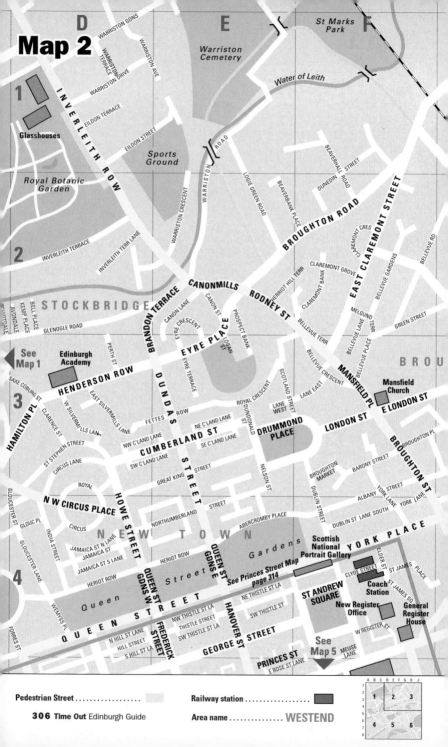

Map 2

D **E** **F**

St Marks Park

WARRISTON GDNS

Warriston Cemetery

1

WARRISTON TERRACE

WARRISTON DRIVE

WARRISTON AVE

Water of Leith

EILDON TERRACE

Glasshouses

EILDON STREET

Sports Ground

WARRISTON ROAD

LOGIE GREEN ROAD

BEAVERHALL STREET

DUNEDIN STREET

BEAVERBANK PLACE

Royal Botanic Garden

WARRISTON CRESCENT

BROUGHTON ROAD

EAST CLAREMONT STREET

CLAREMONT CRES

BELLEVUE RD

2

INVERLEITH ROW

INVERLEITH TERRACE

INVERLEITH TERR LANE

HERIOT HILL TERR

CLAREMONT GROVE

CLAREMONT BANK

BELLEVUE GARDENS

MELGUND TERR

GREEN STREET

BELL PLACE

KEMP PLACE

AVONDALE

PORTMORE

STOCKBRIDGE

BRANDON TERRACE

CANONMILLS

RODNEY ST

BELLEVUE TERR

BELLEVUE LANE

GLENOGLE ROAD

CANON LANE

EYRE CRESCENT

CANON ST

PROSPECT BANK

MANSFIELD PL

BELLEVUE PLACE

BELLEVUE CRESCENT

See Map 1

Edinburgh Academy

PERTH ST

EYRE PLACE

LOGAN ST

SCOTLAND STREET

Mansfield Church

E LONDON ST

BROU

SAXE COBURG ST

HENDERSON ROW

DUNDAS STREET

EYRE TERRACE

ROYAL CRESCENT

LANE EAST

MANSFIELD PL

LONDON ST

BROUGHTON PL

3

HAMILTON PL

CLARENCE ST

W SILVERMILLS LANE

EAST SILVERMILLS LANE

FETTES ROW

NE C'LAND LANE

DUNDONALD STREET

LANE WEST

BROUGHTON ST

ST STEPHEN STREET

NW C'LAND LANE

CUMBERLAND ST

SE C'LAND LANE

DRUMMOND PLACE

BARONY STREET

CIRCUS LANE

SW C'LAND LANE

NELSON ST

BROUGHTON MARKET

YORK STREET

ALBANY ST

YORK LANE

ROYAL

GREAT KING STREET

DUBLIN STREET

YORK LANE

GLOUCESTER ST

N W CIRCUS PLACE

HOWE STREET

STREET

ABERCROMBY PLACE

DUBLIN ST LANE SOUTH

BROUGHTON ST

GLOUC PL

CIRCUS

NORTHUMBERLAND

N E W   T O W N

YORK PLACE

INDIA STREET

Gardens

Scottish National Portrait Gallery

ELDER ST

ST JAMES

4

GLOUCESTER LANE

JAMAICA ST LANE

HERIOT ROW

QUEEN ST GDNS E

See Princes Street Map page 314

CLYDE STREET

ST JAMES SQ

JAMAICA ST

JAMAICA ST S LANE

QUEEN ST GDNS W

Coach Station

ST JAMES PLACE

FORRES ST

WEMYSS PL

HERIOT ROW

Queen

FREDERICK STREET

HANOVER STREET

NE THISTLE ST LA

ST ANDREW SQUARE

New Register Office

General Register House

N HILL ST LANE

NW THISTLE ST LA

THISTLE STREET

QUEEN STREET

SW THISTLE ST LA

GEORGE STREET

W REGISTER ST

HILL STREET

S HILL ST LA

See Map 5

MEUSE LANE

PRINCES ST

E ROSE ST LANE

Pedestrian Street . . . .

Railway station . . . .

306 Time Out Edinburgh Guide

Area name . . . . WESTEND

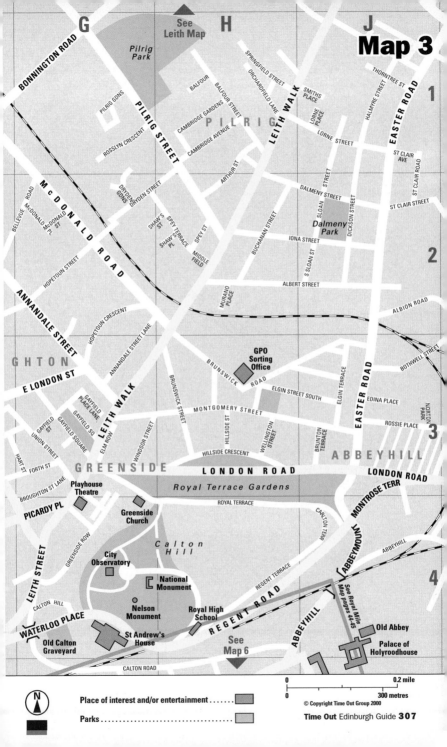

See
Leith Map

Pilrig
Park

BONNINGTON ROAD

SPRINGFIELD STREET
ORCHARDFIELD LANE
SMITHS PLACE
LEITH WALK
THORNTREE ST
HALMYRE STREET
EASTER ROAD

PILRIG GDNS
PILRIG STREET
BALFOUR
BALFOUR STREET
CAMBRIDGE GARDENS
LORNE PLACE
LORNE STREET
ST CLAIR AVE

ROSSLYN CRESCENT
CAMBRIDGE AVENUE
PILRIG
ST CLAIR STREET

BELLEVUE
McDONALD PL
McDONALD
McDONALD ROAD
DRYDEN GDNS
DRYDEN STREET
ARTHUR ST
STREET
DALMENY STREET
SLOAN STREET
DICKSON STREET
ST CLAIR STREET

SHAW'S ST
SHAW'S TERRACE
SPEY ST
SPEY ST
**Dalmeny
Park**

HOPETOUN STREET
MIDDLE FIELD
BUCHANAN STREET
IONA STREET
S SLOAN ST
ALBERT STREET

ANNANDALE STREET
HOPETOUN CRESCENT
MURANO PLACE
ALBION ROAD

BOTHWELL STREET

GHTON

E LONDON ST
ANNANDALE STREET LANE
LEITH WALK
BRUNSWICK STREET
BRUNSWICK ROAD
**GPO
Sorting
Office**
ELGIN TERRACE
EASTER ROAD
NORTON PARK

GAYFIELD PLACE LANE
ELGIN STREET SOUTH
EDINA PLACE

GAYFIELD ST
GAYFIELD STREET
GAYFIELD SQ
ELM ROW
MONTGOMERY STREET
HILLSIDE ST
WELLINGTON STREET
BRUNTON TERRACE
ROSSIE PLACE

UNION STREET
GAYFIELD SQUARE
WINDSOR STREET
3

HART ST
FORTH ST
HILLSIDE CRESCENT
ABBEYHILL

GREENSIDE
LONDON ROAD
LONDON ROAD

BROUGHTON ST LANE
Royal Terrace Gardens
MONTROSE TERR

**Playhouse
Theatre**
ROYAL TERRACE

PICARDY PL
**Greenside
Church**
CARLTON TERR
ABBEYMOUNT
ABBEYHILL

GREENSIDE ROW
*Calton
Hill*
ABBEYHILL

**City
Observatory**

LEITH STREET
**National
Monument**
REGENT TERRACE

CALTON HILL
**Nelson
Monument**
**Royal High
School**
REGENT ROAD
See Royal Mile
Map on pages 44-45
Old Abbey

WATERLOO PLACE
**St Andrew's
House**
4

**Old Calton
Graveyard**
**Palace of
Holyroodhouse**

CALTON ROAD
See
Map 6
ABBEYHILL

0   0.2 mile

0   300 metres

© Copyright Time Out Group 2000

N

Place of interest and/or entertainment . . . .

Parks . . . .

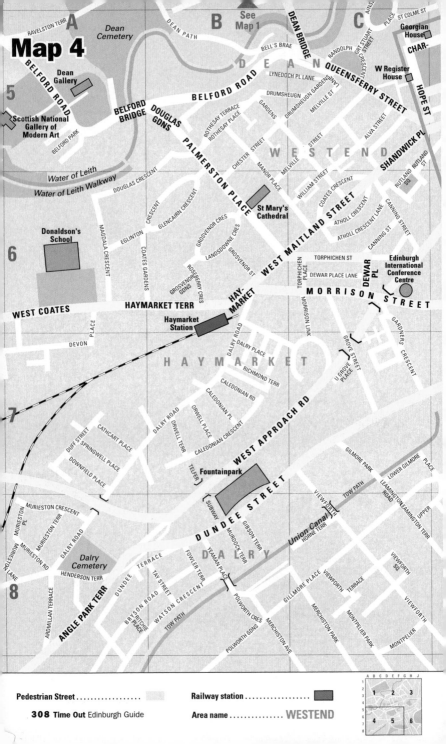

Map 4

A B See Map 1 C

Ravelston Terr

Dean Cemetery

Dean Path

DEAN PATH

DEAN BRIDGE

BELL'S BRAE

ST COLME ST

Georgian House

W Register House

CHAR-

BELFORD ROAD

Dean Gallery

BELFORD BRIDGE

DOUGLAS GDNS

DEAN

QUEENSFERRY STREET

RANDOLPH

GT STUART STREET

CRESCENT

PLACE

AINSLIE

HOPE ST

5

Scottish National Gallery of Modern Art

BELFORD ROAD

LYNEDOCH PL LANE

DRUMSHEUGH

GARDENS

DRUMSHEUGH GARDENS

MELVILLE ST

ALVA STREET

W E S T E N D

SHANDWICK PL

Belford Park

ROTHESAY TERRACE

ROTHESAY PLACE

PALMERSTON PLACE

CHESTER STREET

MANOR PLACE

GARDENS

MELVILLE STREET

WILLIAM STREET

COATES CRESCENT

RUTLAND ST

RUTLAND SQ

Water of Leith

Water of Leith Walkway

DOUGLAS CRESCENT

CRESCENT

GLENCAIRN CRESCENT

St Mary's Cathedral

WEST MAITLAND STREET

ATHOLL CRESCENT

CANNING STREET

Edinburgh International Conference Centre

6

Donaldson's School

MAGDALA CRESCENT

EGLINTON

COATES GARDENS

GROSVENOR CRES

LANDSDOWNE CRES

GROSVENOR ST

ATHOLL CRESCENT LANE

ATHOLL CRESCENT

CANNING ST

TORPHICHEN ST

TORPHICHEN PLACE

DEWAR PLACE LANE

DEWAR PL

WEST COATES

HAYMARKET TERR

HAY-MARKET

GROSVENOR GDNS

ROSEBERRY CRES

MORRISON LINK

MORRISON STREET

PLACE

DEVON

Haymarket Station

DALRY ROAD

DALRY PLACE

GROVE STREET

U GROVE PLACE

GARDNERS

CRESCENT

7

H A Y M A R K E T

RICHMOND TERR

CALEDONIAN RD

CALEDONIAN PL

ORWELL PLACE

CALEDONIAN CRESCENT

WEST APPROACH RD

GILMORE PARK

LOWER GILMORE PLACE

DUFF STREET

CATHCART PLACE

SPRINGWELL PLACE

DALRY ROAD

ORWELL TERR

TELFER

GILMORE

LEAMINGTON ROAD

LEAMINGTON TERR

UPPER

DOWNFIELD PLACE

Fountainpark

SUBWAY

DUNDEE STREET

VIEWFORTH

TOW PATH

MURIESTON CRESCENT

MURIESTON PL

MURIESTON TERR

MURIESTON RD

DALRY ROAD

GIBSON TERR

HORNE TERR

Union Canal

VIEWFORTH

LOUISON

LANE

Dalry Cemetery

HENDERSON TERR

DUNDEE TERRACE

TAY STREET

MURDOCK TERR

FOWLER TERR

YEAMAN PLACE

D A L R Y

GILLMORE PLACE

VIEWFORTH TERRACE

VIEWFORTH SQ

8

ANGLE PARK TERR

ARDMILLAN TERRACE

BRYSON ROAD

RITCHIE PLACE

WATSON CRESCENT

TOW PATH

POLWORTH CRES

POLWORTH GDNS

MERCHISTON AVE

MERCHISTON PARK

MONTPELIER PARK

MONTPELIER

VIEWFORTH

Pedestrian Street . . . .

Railway station . . . .

Area name . . . . WESTEND